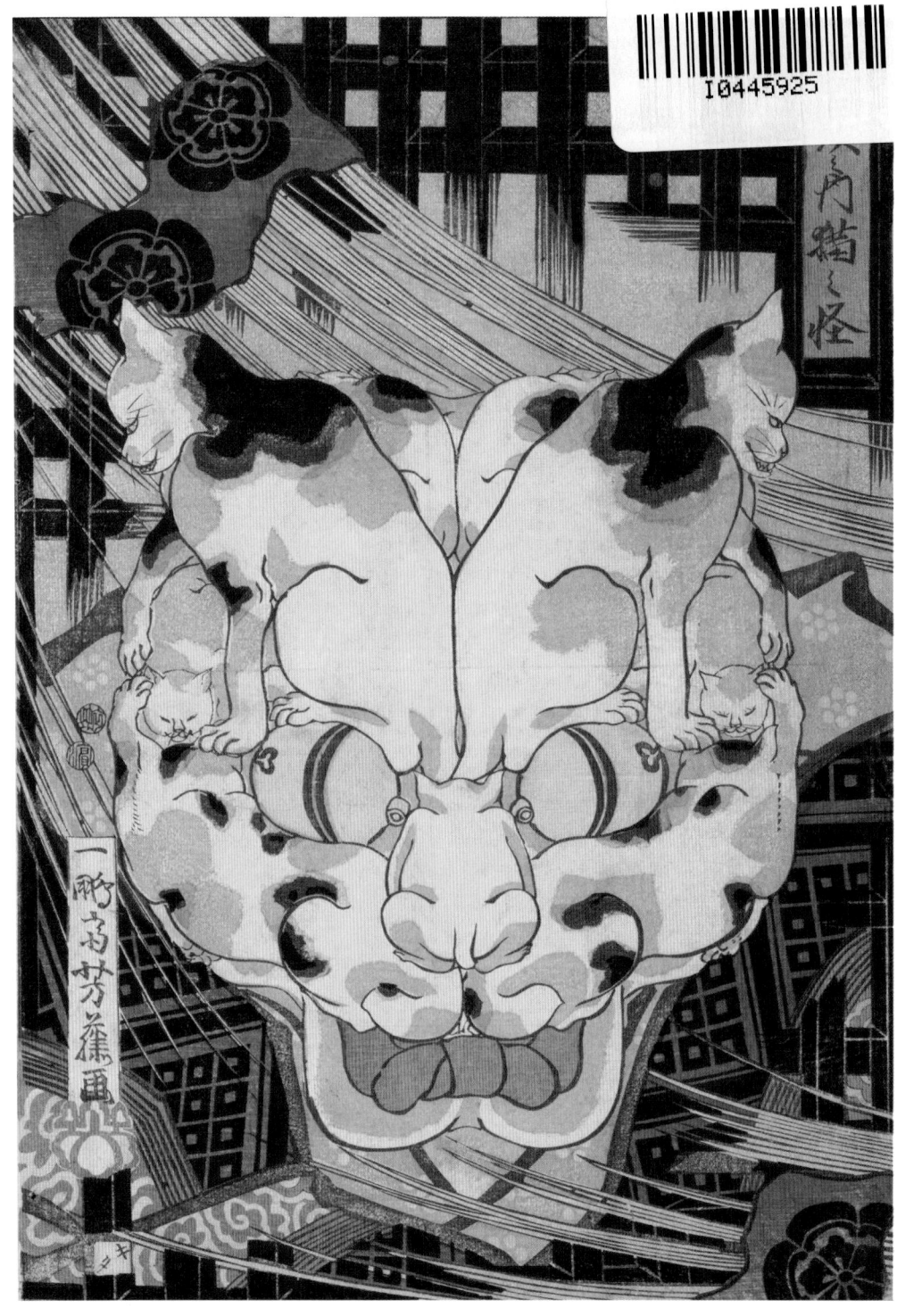

Something Wicked from Japan

Ghosts, Demons & *Yōkai* in *Ukiyo-e* Masterpieces

【浮世絵でみる！お化け図鑑】

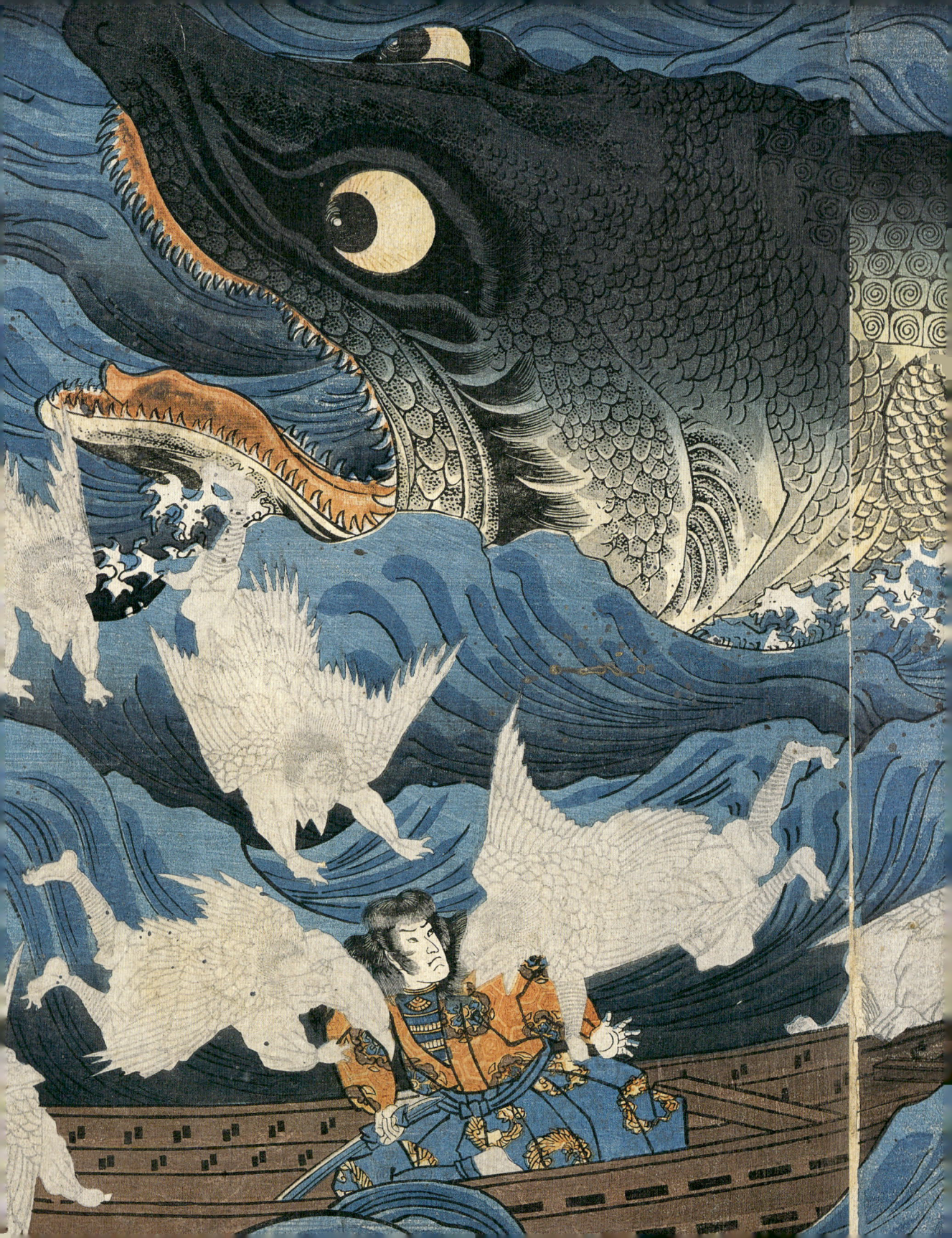

目次　Contents

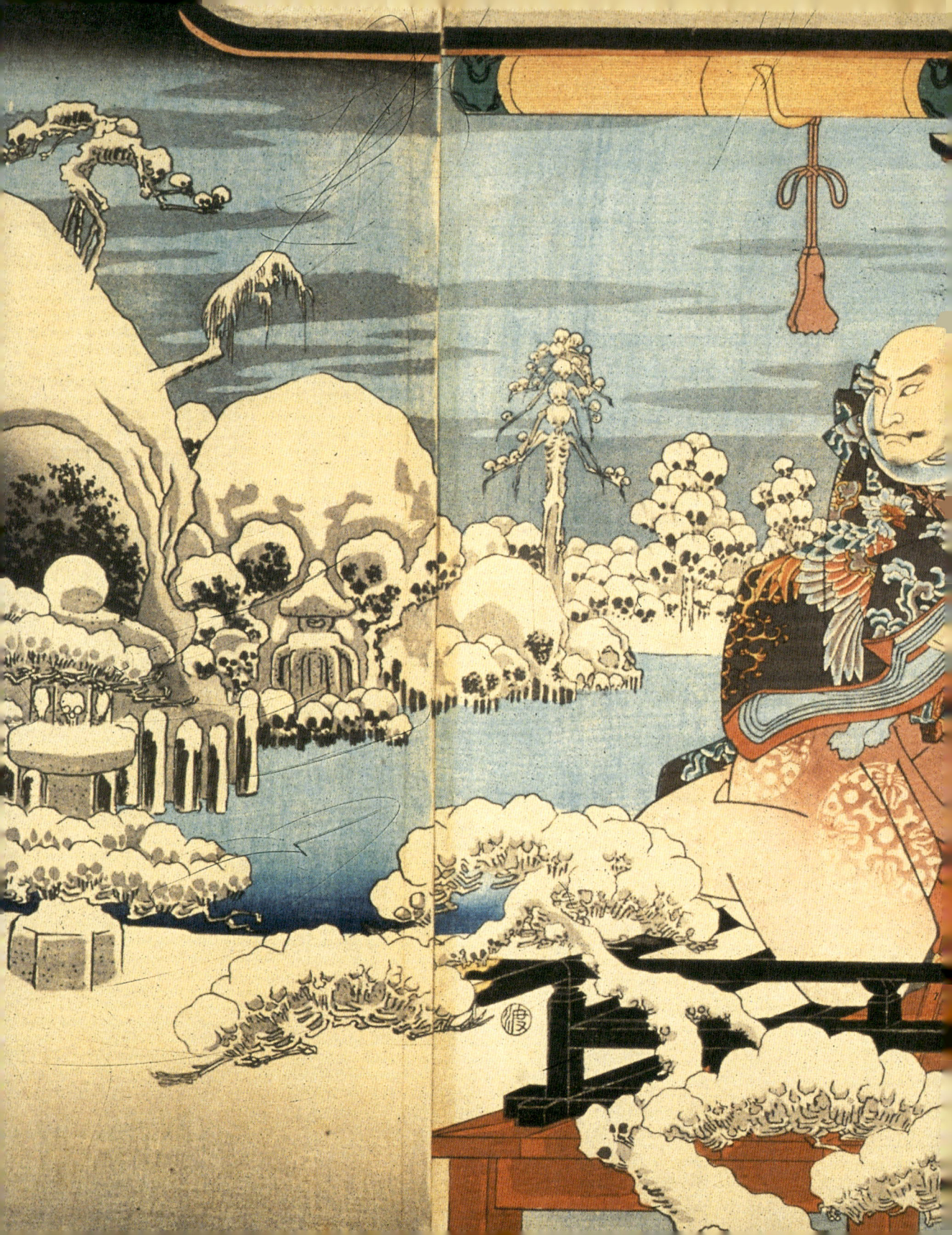

Something Wicked from Japan

Ghosts, Demons & *Yōkai* in *Ukiyo-e* Masterpieces

【浮世絵でみる！お化け図鑑】

いま、お化け浮世絵が面白い

中右 瑛（国際浮世絵学会常任理事）

ゴジラやジョーズもどきの、一見、ユーモラスで可笑しな江戸のモンスターたち。挽歌を奏でる哀しくも恐ろしいお岩やお菊の亡霊。江戸時代よりいまも徘徊する政界の百鬼夜行。いつの時代も「お化け」はいっぱいだ。

天神縁起や大江山酒呑童子退治、百鬼夜行等の絵巻物は古くから伝承されてきたが、幽霊や妖怪など一般に「お化け」と呼ばれる輩が浮世絵に頻繁に登場し始めたのは、文化・文政期以降～幕末の頃（1804-1868）である。

幕末期は、庶民文化が爛熟を極めたが、一方、幕財政破綻、過激な「天保改革」、大地震、事件が多発し、人心は乱れ、幕府腐敗、犯罪多発、世も末とまで言われるほどにエロ、グロ、ナンセンスの体たらくを示し、暗い不安な騒擾世相がお化け浮世絵に反映されている。

劇界では、四世鶴屋南北狂言「東海道四谷怪談」などの幽霊芝居がぞくぞくと上演され大人気となる。一方、読本界では奇っ怪な妖怪が登場する曲亭馬琴の『椿説弓張月』や『南総里見八犬伝』などの不思議な魔界小説がベストセラーとなり、肝試しの怪談夜噺「百物語」がブームになる。

お芝居や小説、怪談話に登場する幽霊や妖怪が浮世絵にも登場。絵師たちの斬新、奇想なる表現力が妖怪ロマンを掻き立てたのだ。

「百物語」をいち早く浮世絵に取り入れたのは北斎。幽霊を視覚化した豊国一派。剣豪武蔵、豪傑為朝らヒーローたちや妖術師滝夜叉姫らを巨大モンスターと対峙させた冒険ロマンを劇画化した国芳とそのスクール絵師。『平家物語』の怨霊をシュール手法で雪景色に溶け込ませトリックアートにした広重。

化け猫、三国を股にかける九尾の悪狐、大鯉、妖術の大蝦蟇など。また、人間の貪欲を諧謔したドラマチックな化け物「鶖」。他に政治、時局を諷刺したパロディもある。スリリング、ショッキング、ミステリアス、ブラックユーモア、奇想天外なキャラクターがいっぱい登場する。

テレビや映画、グラビア誌がなかった時代の娯楽の一つで、奇想天外なお化け劇画を江戸人たちは血沸き肉踊る思いで見ていたに違いない。

いま、浮世絵のお化けが面白いのである。

Foreword

Today, ghost *ukiyo-e* are intriguing

Ei Nakau (Permanent Board Member of the International Ukiyo-e Society)

The monsters of Edo: at first glance, cute and comical shadows of Godzilla and Jaws. The sad yet spine-chilling wraiths Oiwa and Okiku sound their elegies. The Night Parade of One Hundred Demons of politics has wandered all the way from the Edo period to the present day. All eras have their ghosts by the dozen.

The *Tenjin Engi*, the defeat of Shuten-dōji of Mount Ōe, the *Night Parade of One Hundred Demons* and other scroll paintings have been passed down from ancient times, but the generation of apparitions (*yūrei*) and demonic creatures (*yōkai*) under the general heading of *obake* first appeared frequently in *ukiyo-e* from the Bunka-Bunsei era onward, in the latter days of the Tokugawa shogunate (1804-1868).

At the end of the Edo period, popular culture flourished, but on the other side of the coin, the Tokugawa financial collapse, the drastic Tenpō Reforms (1830-1843), severe earthquakes, endless attacks, civil unrest, government corruption and rampant crime verging on the end of days are shown in degenerate extremes of erotica, grotesquerie and nonsense, casting the reflection of a dark and insecure rioting society into ghost *ukiyo-e*.

In the world of the theatre, Nanboku Tsuruya IV's play *Tōkaidō Yotsuya Kaidan (The Ghost Story of Tōkaidō Yotsuya)* and other ghostly dramas thrilled audiences and gained wild popularity. Meanwhile, in the world of books, grotesque monsters appeared in wondrous novels of devildom, becoming bestsellers such as Kyokutei Bakin's *Chinsetsu Yumeharizuki (The Crescent Moon)* and *Nansō Satomi Hakkenden (The Chronicles of Eight Dog Heroes of the Satomi Clan of Nansō)*, and the test of courage known as the *Hyakumonogatari (One Hundred Tales)* was all the rage.

The ghosts and demons of plays, books and scary stories also appeared in *ukiyo-e*. Novel and whimsical artistic expressions were fueled by fantastic monsters.

The first to integrate the *Hyakumonogatari (One Hundred Tales)* into *ukiyo-e* was Hokusai. The Toyokuni school made ghosts visible. Kuniyoshi and his school of artists dramatized the adventures of heroes like great swordsman Miyamoto Musashi from the 17th century and the 12th–century daring warrior Minamotono Tametomo, or wielders of sorcery like Princess Takiyasha, who faced down gigantic monsters. Hiroshige used trick art to surreally blend the vengeful spirits of the *Heike Monogatari (The Tale of the Heike clan)* into a snowy landscape.

Monster cats (*bakeneko*), the nine-tailed fox which spanned three countries, giant carp and huge sorcerous toads are among those represented here. Also, the Nue, the freakish monster who made a mockery of human greed. In addition, there are parodies satirizing the government and current issues of the day. Fantastic characters throng these pages, full of thrills, shocks, mysteries, and black humor.

As the sole amusement in an era which lacked television, movies or magazines, the outrageous images of ghostly dramas would have definitely stirred up the blood of an Edo period audience.

Today, ghost *ukiyo-e* are intriguing.

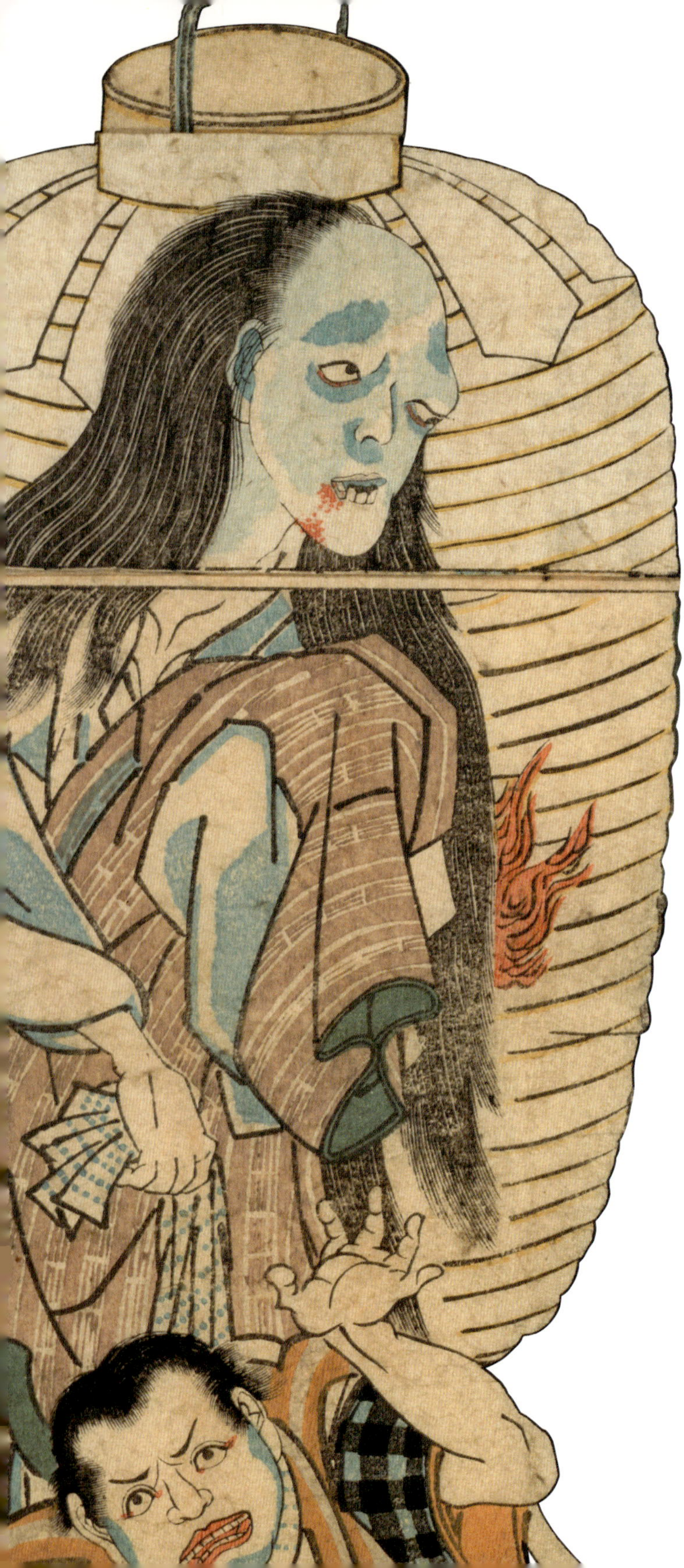

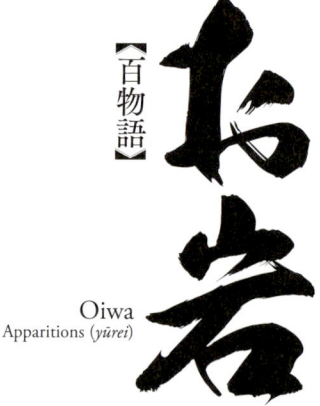

【東海道四谷怪談】
歌川国貞（三代豊国）天保2年（1831）
お岩の亡霊に悩まされる伊右衛門は、蛇山の庵室に
籠っていました。提灯から現れたお岩の亡霊が、伊右
衛門の悪事に加担した秋山長兵衛を絞殺します。

Tōkaidō Yotsuya Kaidan
(The Ghost Story of Tōkaidō Yotsuya)
by Utagawa Kunisada
(also known as Utagawa Toyokuni III)

Tormented by the ghost of Oiwa, Iemon has taken refuge in a hermitage at Hebiyama (lit. "Snake Mountain"). Emerging from the burning lantern, Oiwa's ghost is strangling Akiyama Chōbē, Iemon's accomplice.

【百物語】

お岩

Oiwa
Apparitions (*yūrei*)

歌舞伎「東海道四谷怪談」等の主人公・お岩は、夫
の民谷伊右衛門に虐げられる日々をすごしていました。
ある日、毒でお岩のまぶたは腫れあがり、髪の毛もごっ
そり抜け落ちてしまいます。夫の裏切りを知ったお岩は
恨みながら、もだえ死にます。さらに伊右衛門は、自分
が雇っていた浪人・小仏小平が、家宝の薬を盗んだ
ことに腹を立て殺し、お岩と小平の死体を戸板の表と
裏に釘づけにし、川へ流してしまいます。その後、伊右
衛門は二人の亡霊に祟られ、破滅していきました。

Oiwa, the main character from kabuki play *Tōkaidō Yotsuya Kaidan*, is constantly picked on by her husband, Tamiya Iemon. One day, Oiwa's eyelids swell, and her hair falls out in clumps; she has been poisoned. Oiwa dies writhing in bitter agony. Angered by the stealing of his family's traditional medicine by his hired *rōnin* Kobotoke Kohei, Iemon commits a further murder, nails the corpses of Kohei and Oiwa to opposite sides of a door, and casts them into the river. Subsequently, Iemon is haunted by their two ghosts, and brought to his ruin.

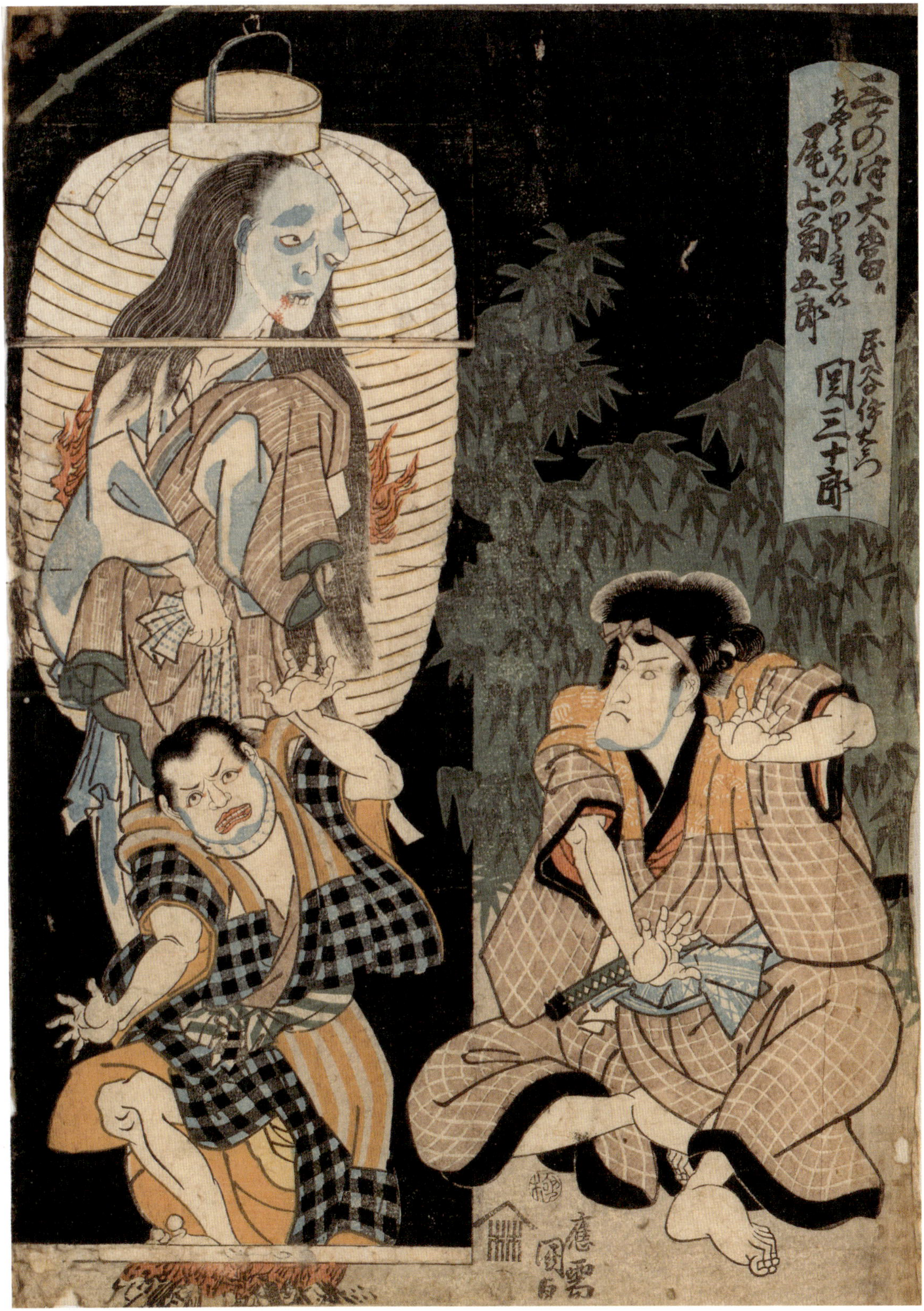

四ツ谷怪談大喜利

ちやうちんのぬけきられ

尾上菊五郎

民谷伊右ヱ門

関三十郎

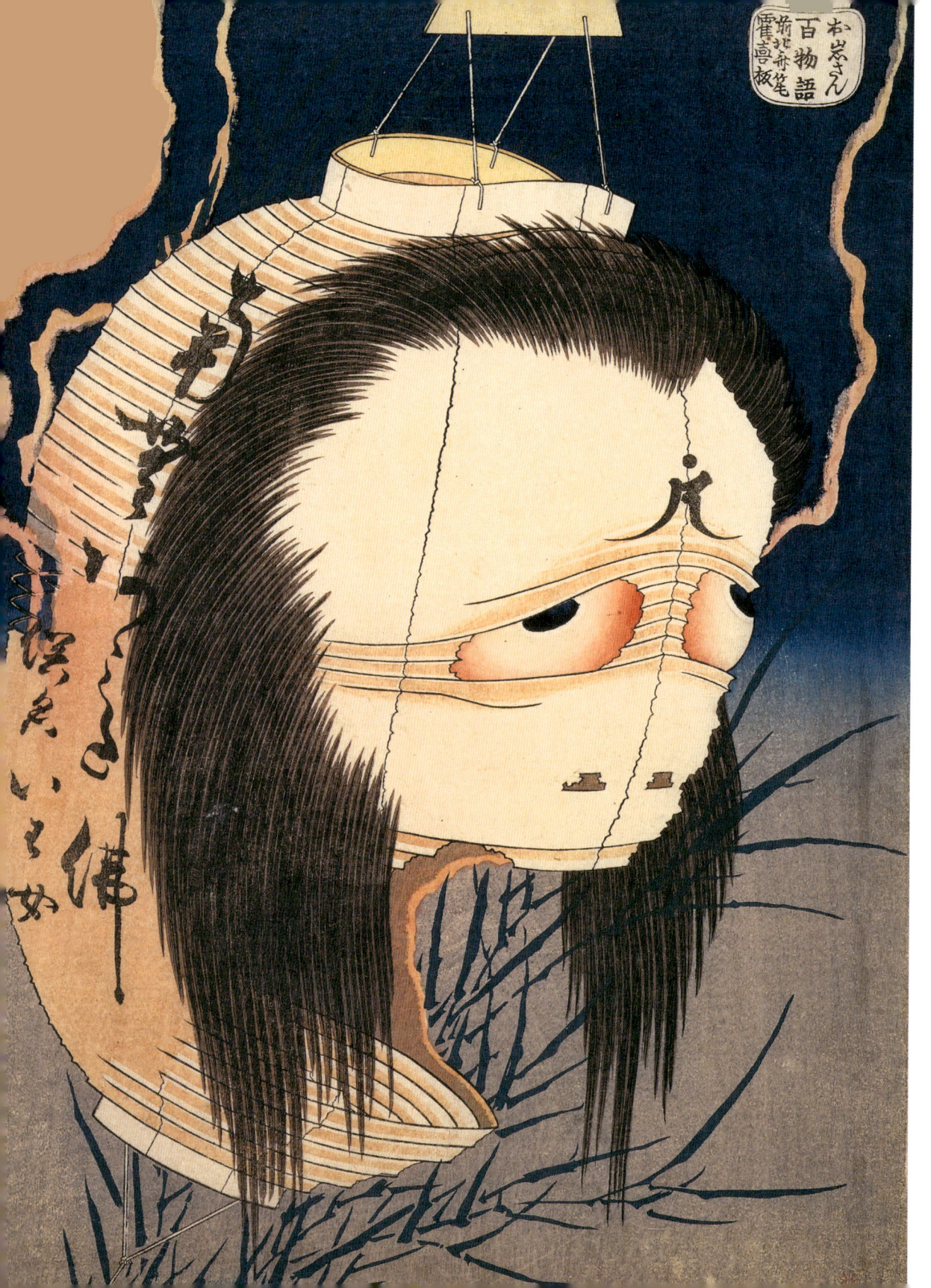

← 【百物語 お岩さん】葛飾北斎 天保2年(1831)頃

提灯に乗り移ったお岩の亡霊。毒薬を飲まされてまぶたは垂れ下がり、髪の毛はごっそり抜け落ちました。

Oiwa-san from the *Hyakumonogatari (One Hundred Tales)* by Katsushika Hokusai

Oiwa's ghost is possessing the lantern. Her eyelids have swollen and sagged, and her hair has fallen out in clumps from the poison she took.

【百物語 お岩 見立 民谷伊右衛門 嵐璃寛】
春江斎北英 天保3-4年(1832-33)

提灯に乗り移ったお岩の霊が不義の夫・民谷伊右衛門を襲います。伊右衛門に扮するのは、上方で活躍した役者二代目嵐璃寛。

Oiwa (Parody featuring actor Arashi Rikan as Tamiya Iemon)
from the *Hyakumonogatari (One Hundred Tales)* by Shunkōsai Hokuei

The Hebiyama hermitage scene from kabuki play *Tōkaidō Yotsuya Kaidan*. Iemon is played by Arashi Rikan II, an actor who was active in the Kyoto and Osaka area.

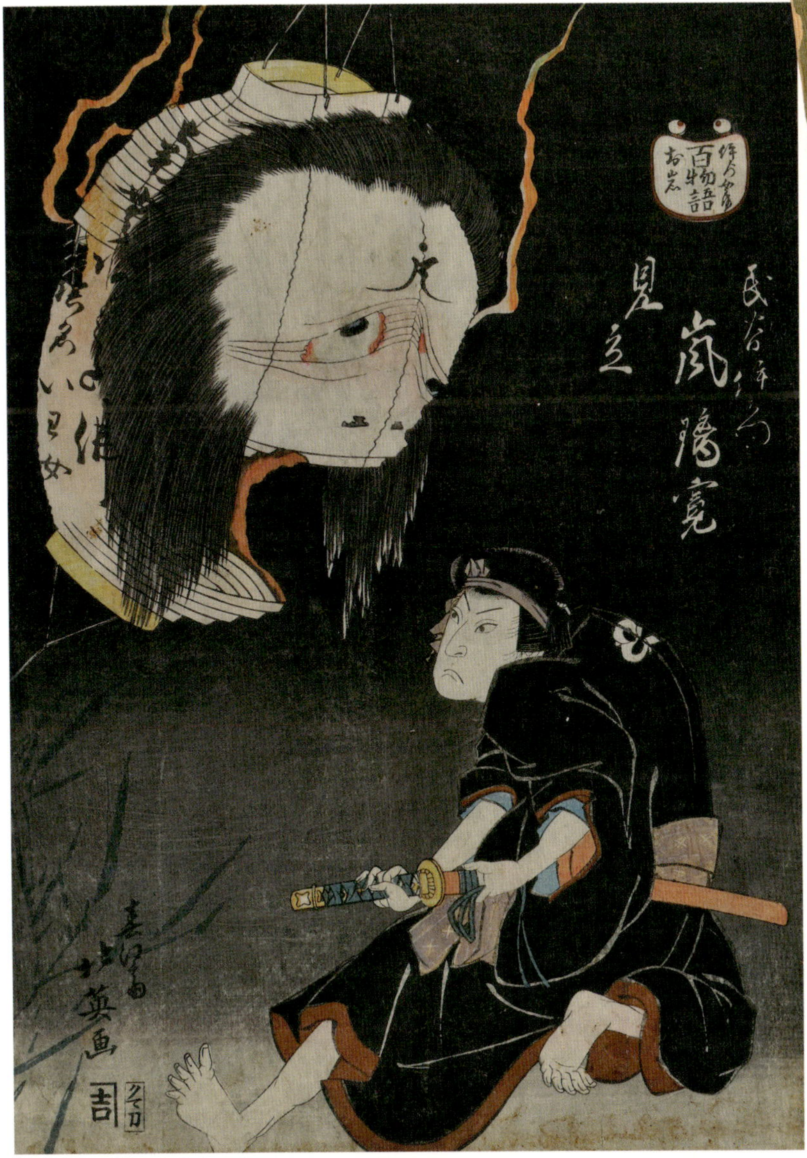

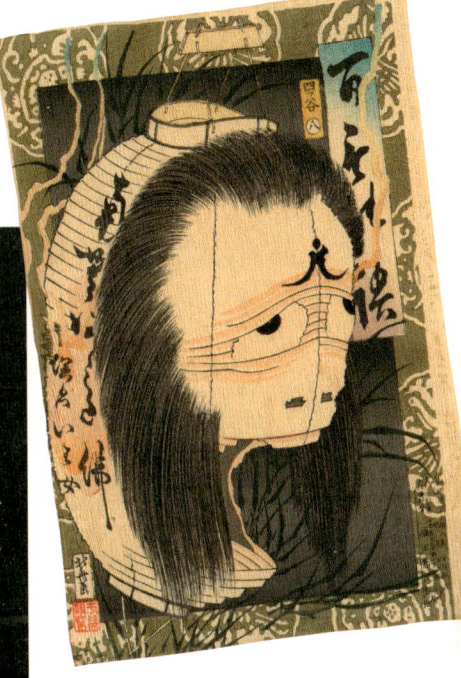

【百物語 四ツ谷】
落合芳幾 明治23年(1890)

芳幾描く「百物語」は、版画を押し揉んで皺をつけた「縮緬絵」という手法で作られています。「北斎画」の署名の下に、「芳幾模写」の朱印が押されています。

Yotsuya from
the *Hyakumonogatari
(One Hundred Tales)*
by Ochiai Yoshiiku

Yoshiiku's One Hundred Tales were made with the technique called *chirimen-e* ("crêped" print), where woodblock prints are rolled and rubbed to create crinkles. The red seal 'Copy by Yoshiiku' is imprinted under Hokusai's signature, 'Hokusai-ga'.

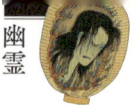

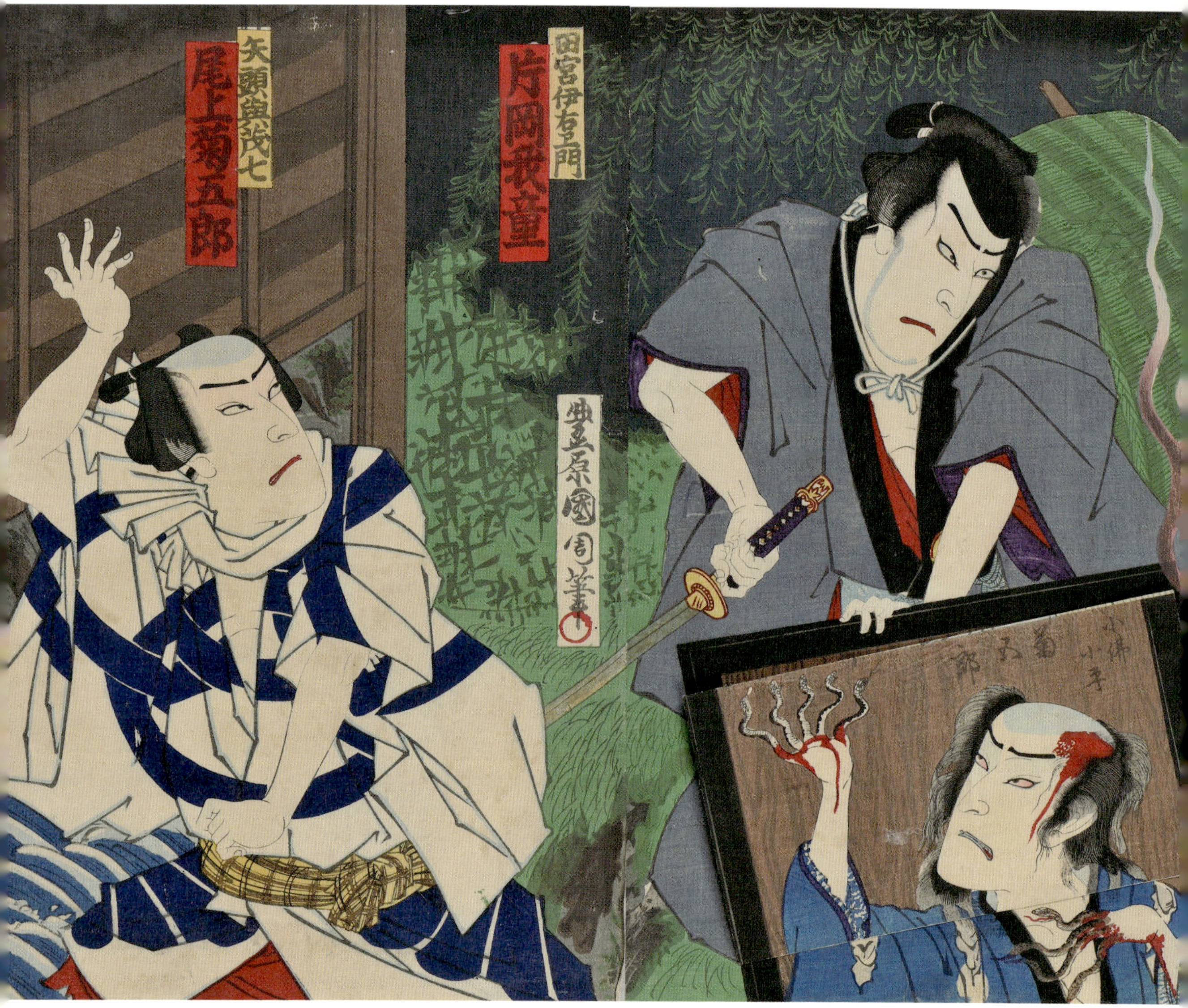

幽霊

【「形見草四谷怪談」お岩・小佛小平早替りの図】豊原国周　明治17年（1884）

釣りに出た伊右衛門が、流れてきた戸板を引き寄せると、そこには毒で醜くなったお岩の死骸と、裏面には指が蛇と化した小平の死骸が張りつけられていました。

The Hayagawari (quick change of costume) of Oiwa/Kobotoke Kohei from *Katamigusa Yotsuya Kaidan*
by Toyohara Kunichika

While fishing, Iemon pulls in a door panel drifting by, and on the door is the corpse of Oiwa deformed by poison, and on the underside, the corpse of Kohei, whose fingers have turned into snakes.

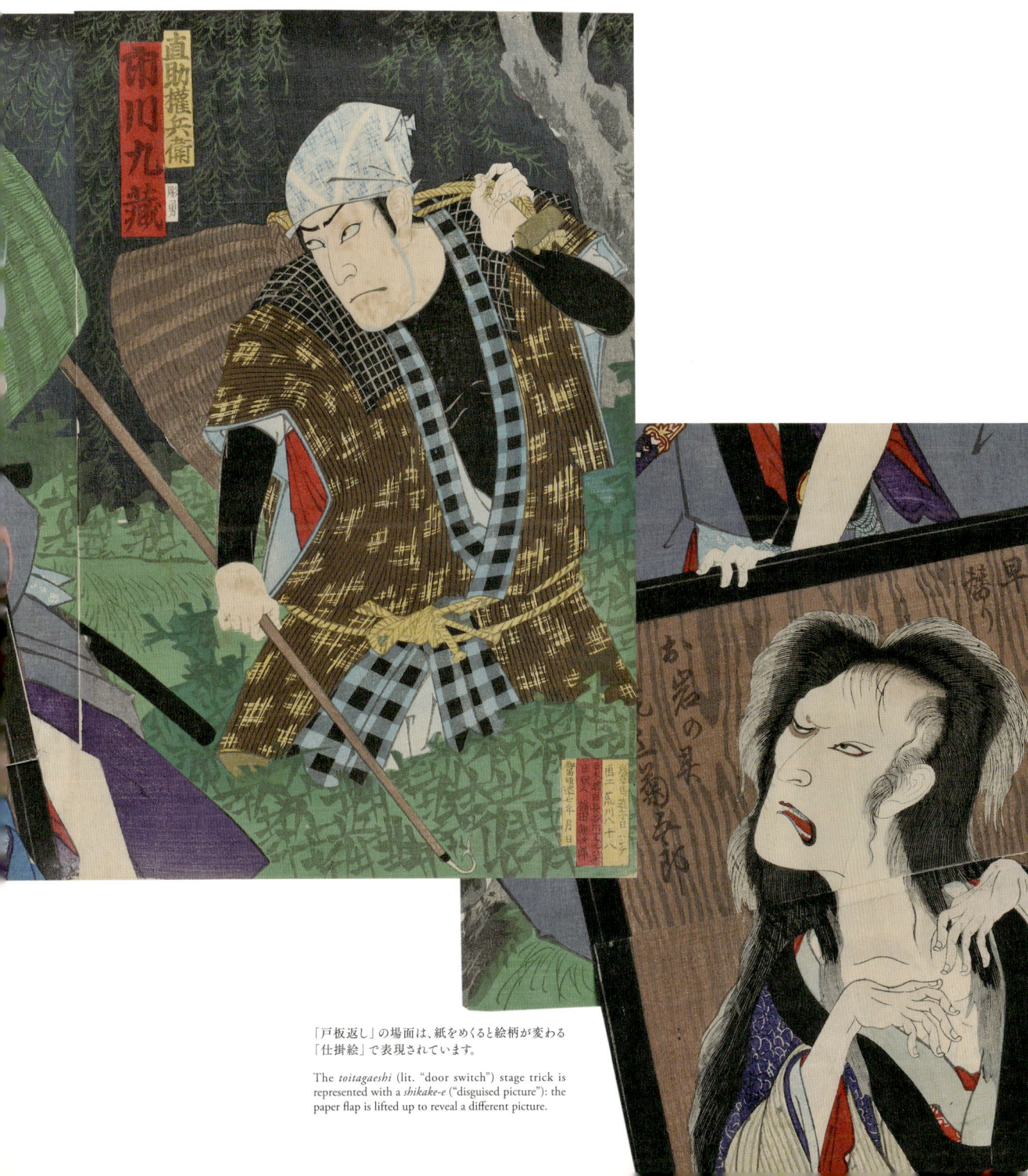

「戸板返し」の場面は、紙をめくると絵柄が変わる
「仕掛絵」で表現されています。

The *toitagaeshi* (lit. "door switch") stage trick is
represented with a *shikake-e* ("disguised picture"): the
paper flap is lifted up to reveal a different picture.

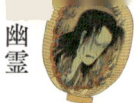

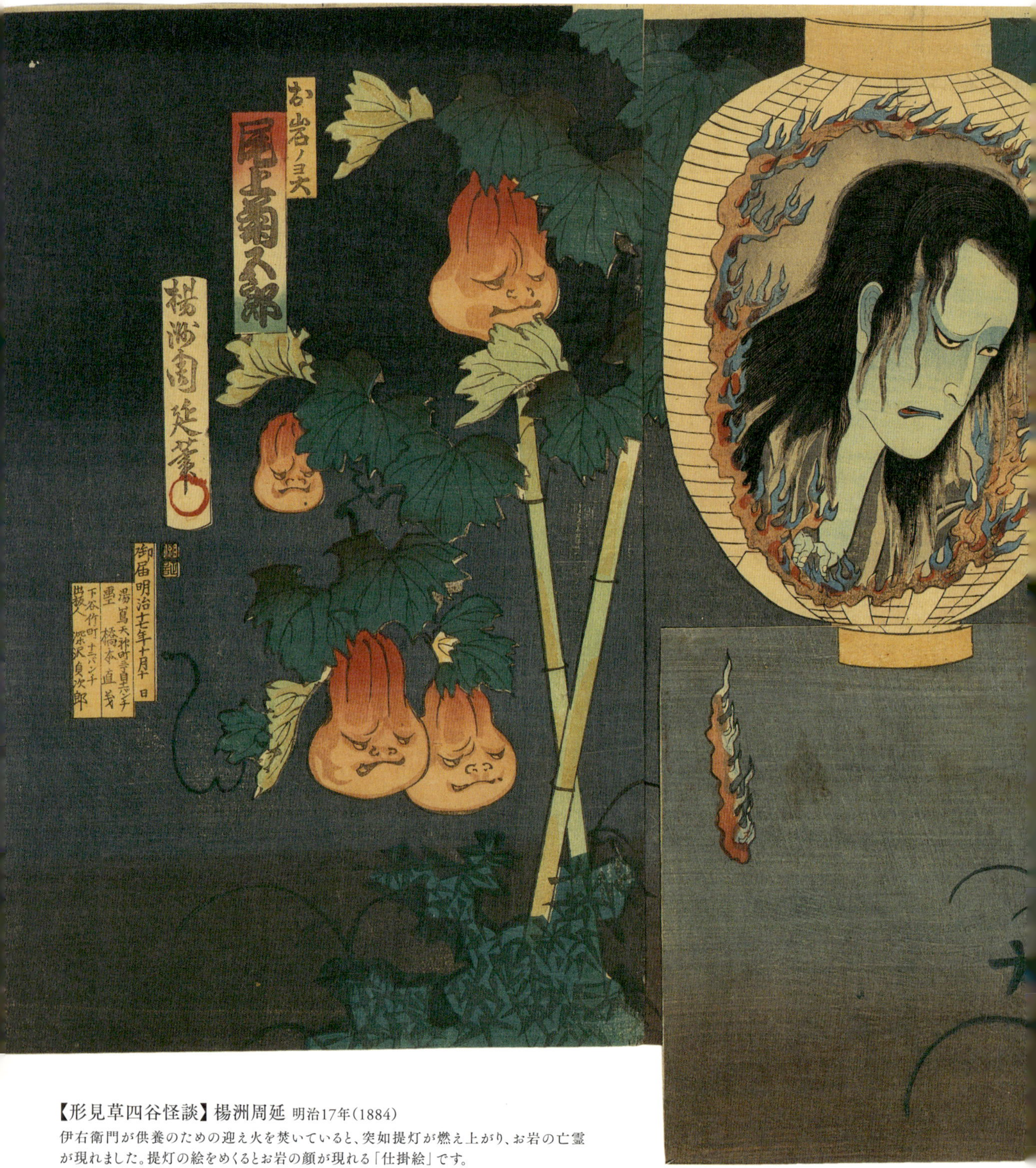

【形見草四谷怪談】楊洲周延 明治17年（1884）

伊右衛門が供養のための迎え火を焚いていると、突如提灯が燃え上がり、お岩の亡霊
が現れました。提灯の絵をめくるとお岩の顔が現れる「仕掛絵」です。

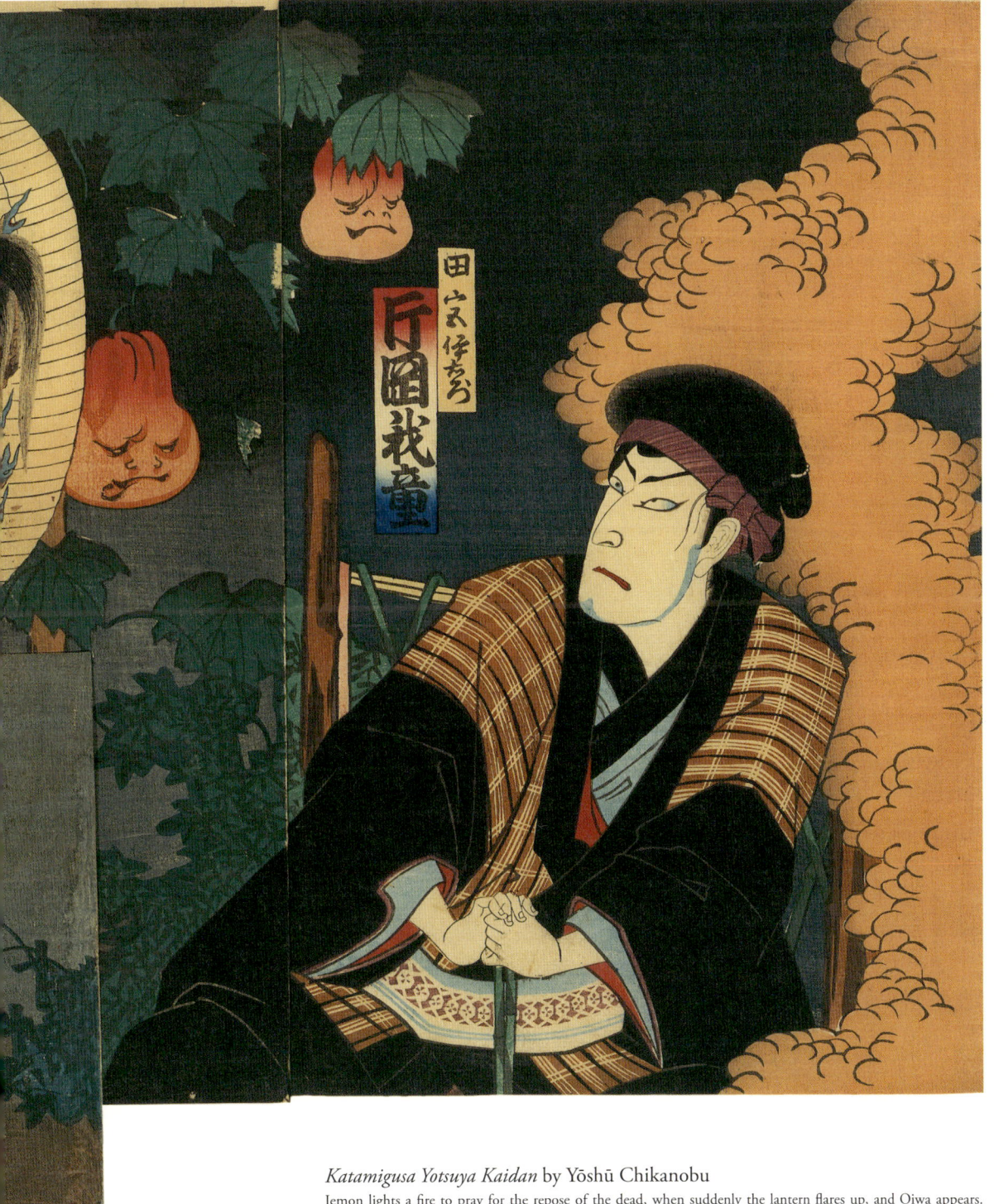

Katamigusa Yotsuya Kaidan by Yōshū Chikanobu
Iemon lights a fire to pray for the repose of the dead, when suddenly the lantern flares up, and Oiwa appears.
This is a *shikake-e* ("disguised picture"): the viewer flips the lantern down to reveal Oiwa's face.

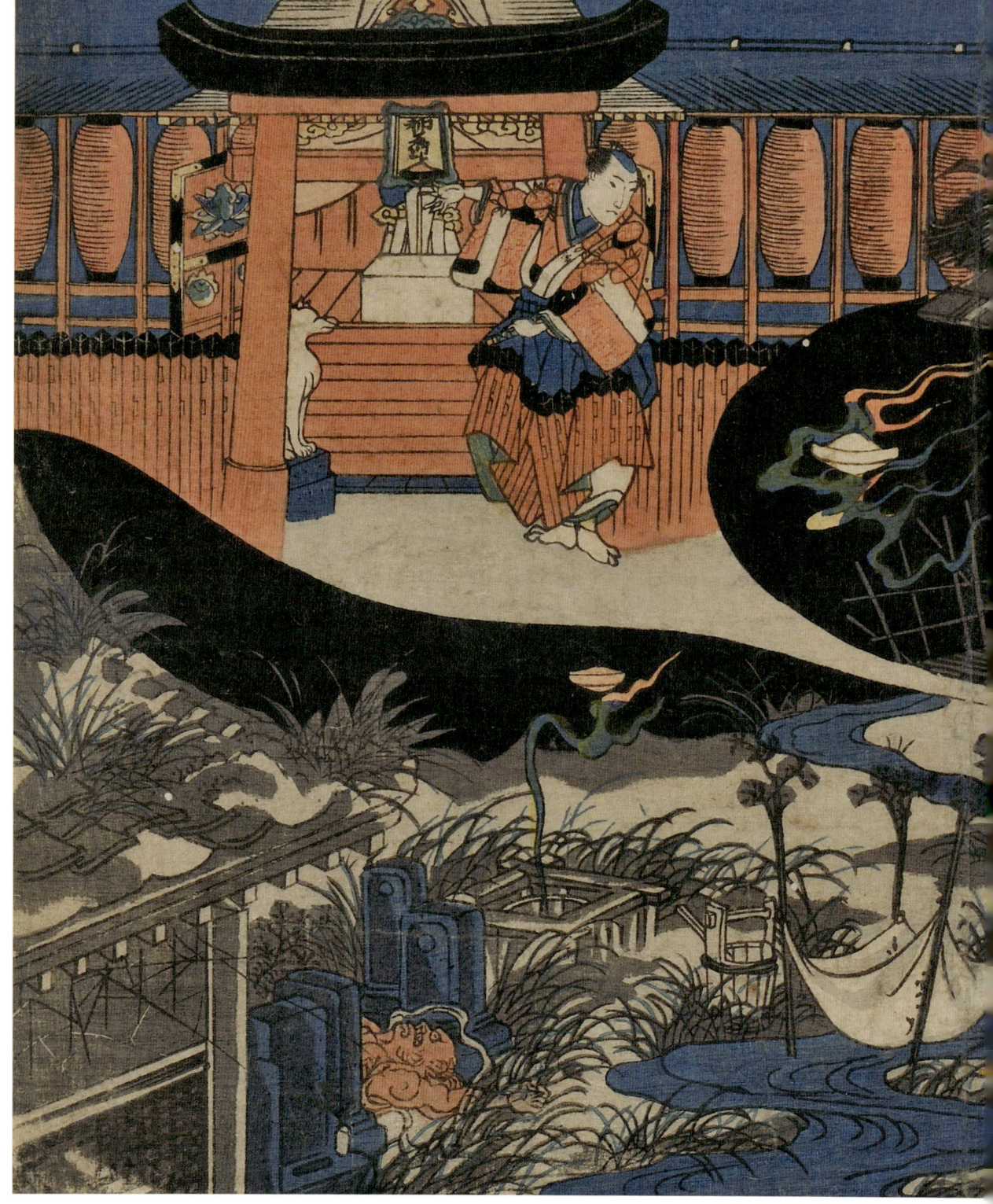

【見世物興行 竹沢藤次 曲独楽師】歌川国芳 弘化元年(1844)
竹沢藤次は幕末の曲独楽師で、両国広小路にて見世物興行を行いました。図は「於岩稲荷怪談廻」という演目で、指や羽子板に独楽をのせて回しています。提灯から炎とともに独楽が飛び出すと、お岩の大きな顔が現れるというゼンマイからくりの演出もあったようです。

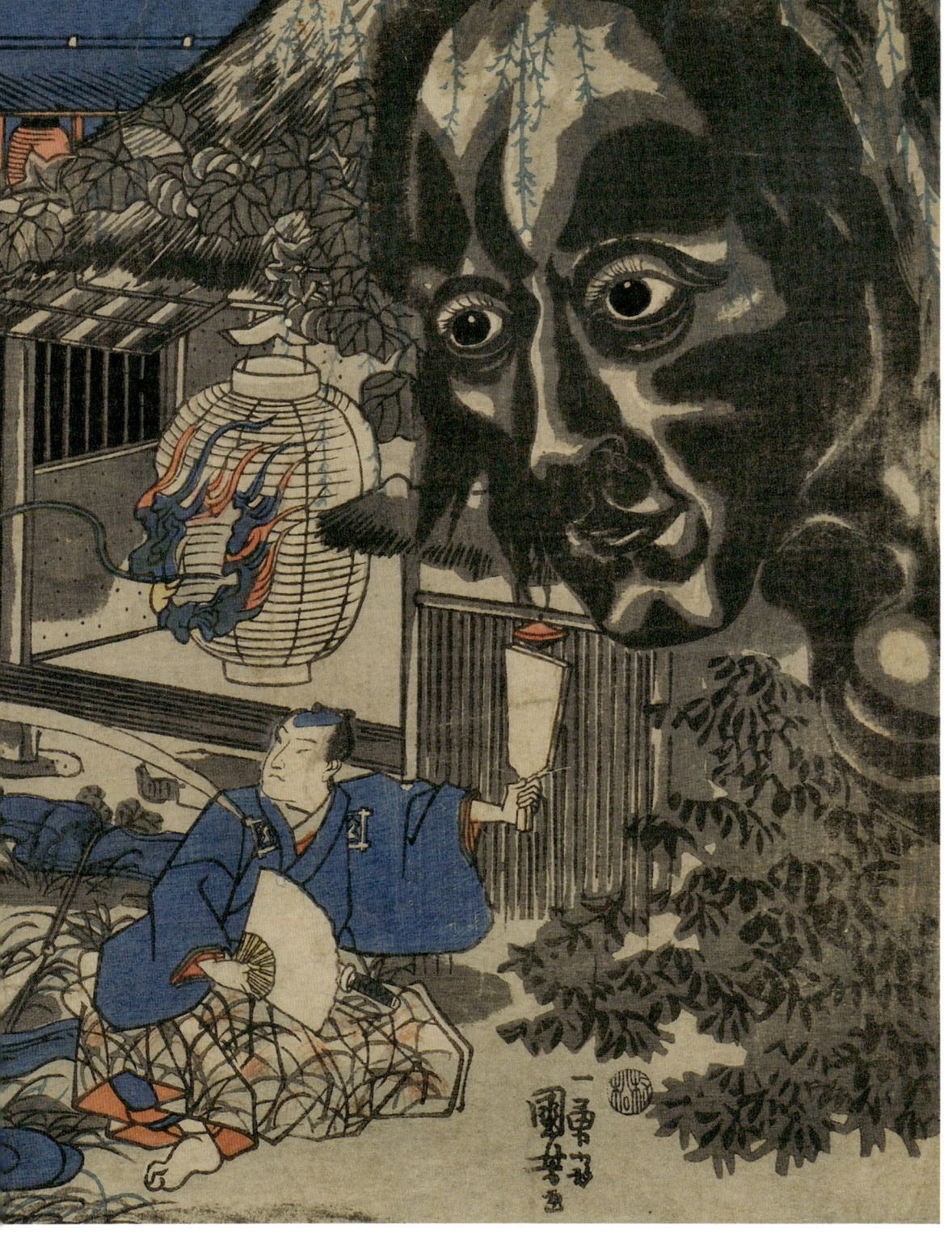

Oiwa Inari Kaidan Mawashi, a Spinning-top Performance by Takezawa Tōji by Utagawa Kuniyoshi

Takezawa Tōji, spinning top master of the late Edo, gave performances at Ryōgoku Hirokōji. The performance shown features tops spinning on fingers and wooden rackets. As a top spins out of the flaming lantern, a spring-loaded magician's trick reveals the huge face of Oiwa.

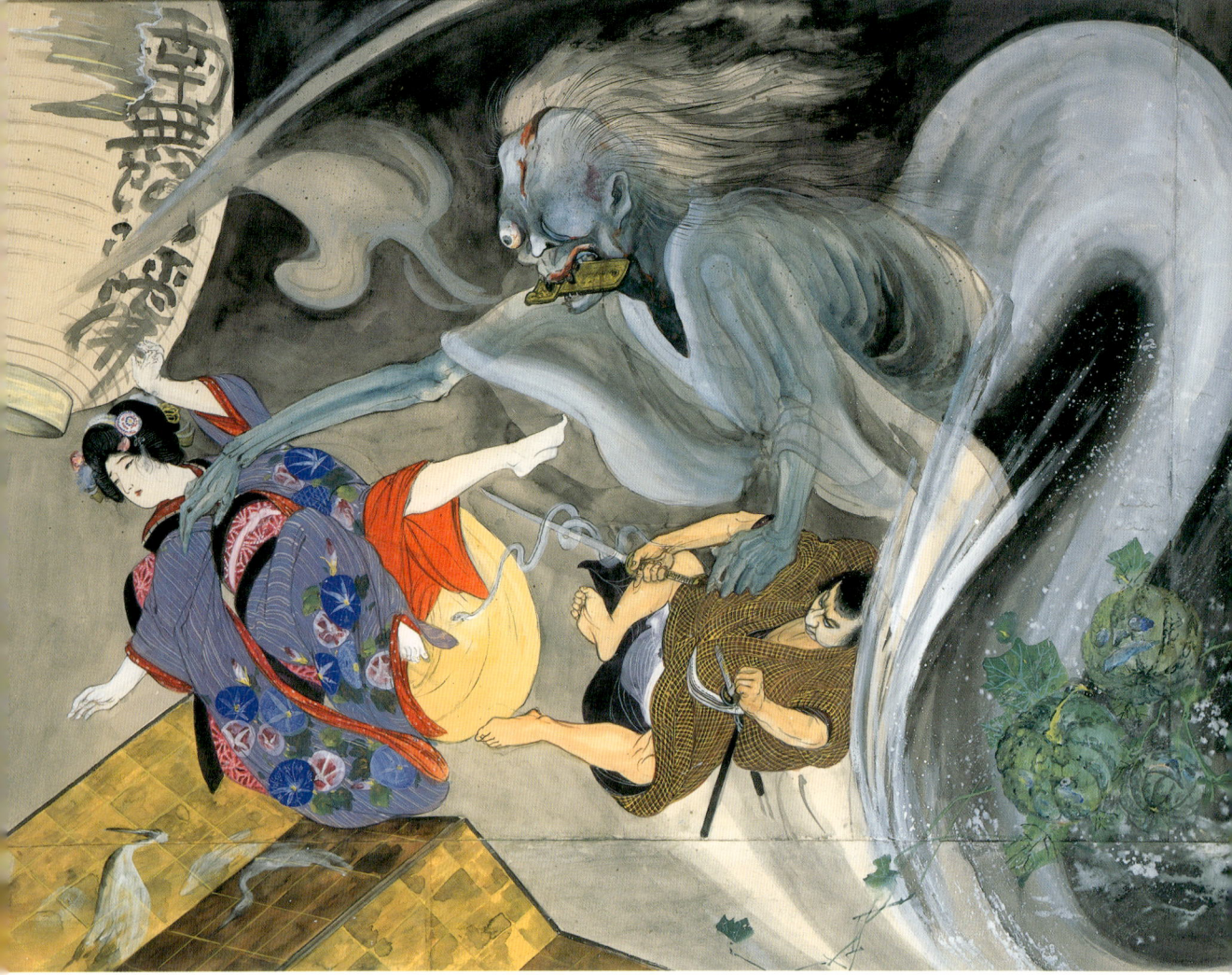

【東海道四谷怪談】伊藤晴雨

お岩の霊に悩む伊右衛門が庵室に籠っていると、夢の中で
美しい娘に出会いました。娘は若かりし頃のお岩にそっくり
でしたが、突如恐ろしい幽霊になり伊右衛門を襲います。

Tōkaidō Yotsuya Kaidan
(The Ghost Story of Tōkaidō Yotsuya) by Itō Seiu

Troubled by spirits of the dead, Iemon has secluded himself in the
hermitage. In a dream, he meets a beautiful maiden. The maiden
looks just like Oiwa did in the days of her youth, but suddenly
changes into a horrific ghost and attacks him.

【木曾街道六十九次之内 追分 おいわ宅悦】　　　　　→
歌川国芳 嘉永5年（1852）

宿駅名の「追分」が、「お岩」の「毛」と語呂合わせになっていま
す。毒で醜い姿となったお岩が櫛で髪を梳くと、髪の毛がごっそり
と抜け落ちました。

Oiwake: Oiwa and Takuetsu from the series
Sixty-nine Stations of the Kiso Highway
by Utagawa Kuniyoshi

The post station named Oiwake (which means "where two roads
split") is used as a play on words with *Oiwa ke* (lit. "Oiwa's hair").
This is the *kamisuki* ("haircombing") scene, in which Oiwa, who has
been hideously disfigured by poison, runs a comb through her hair,
and the hair comes out in clumps.

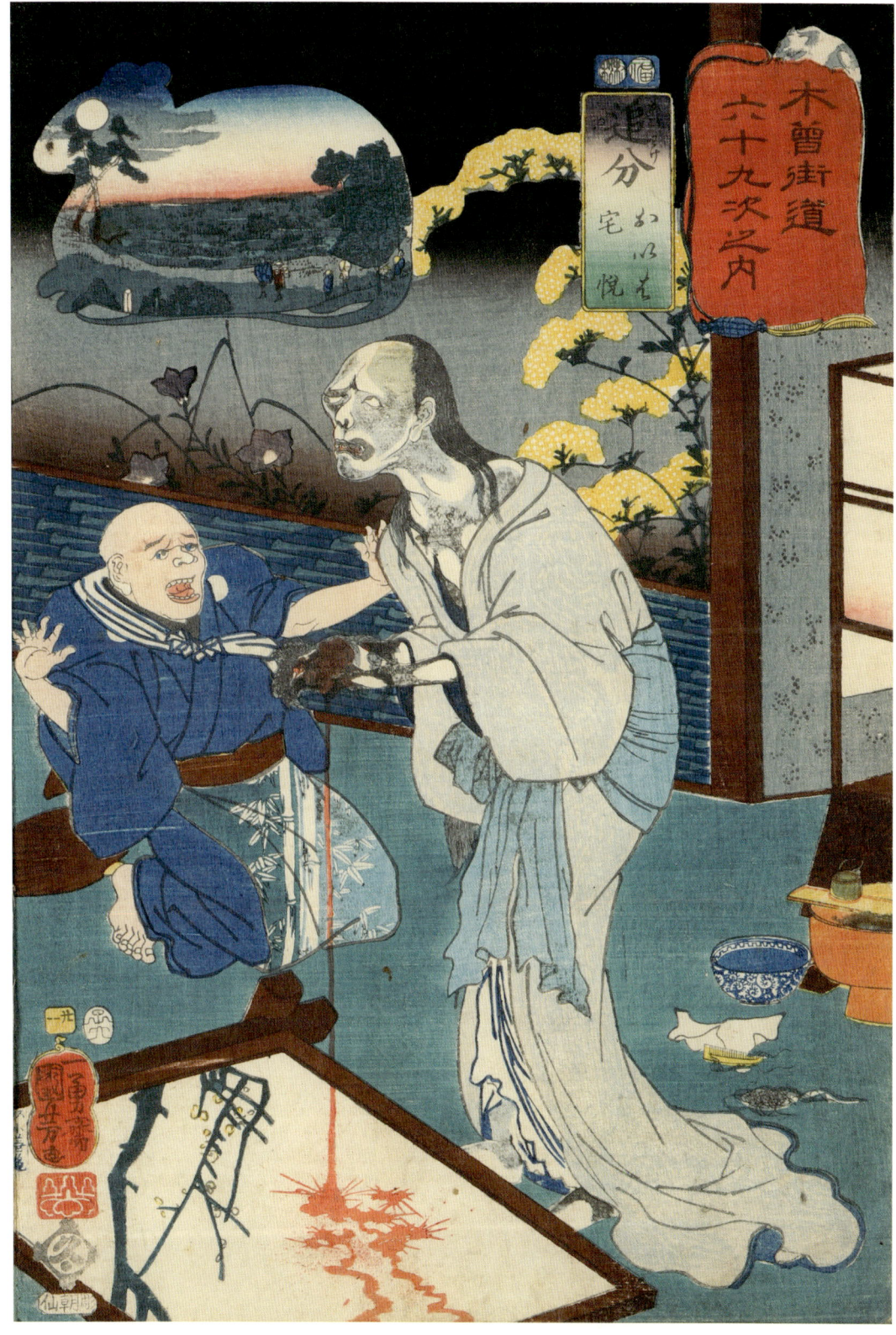

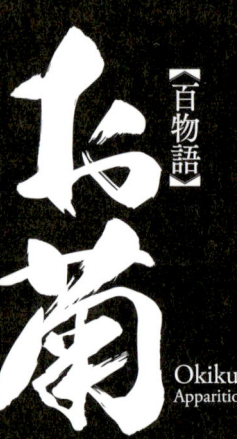

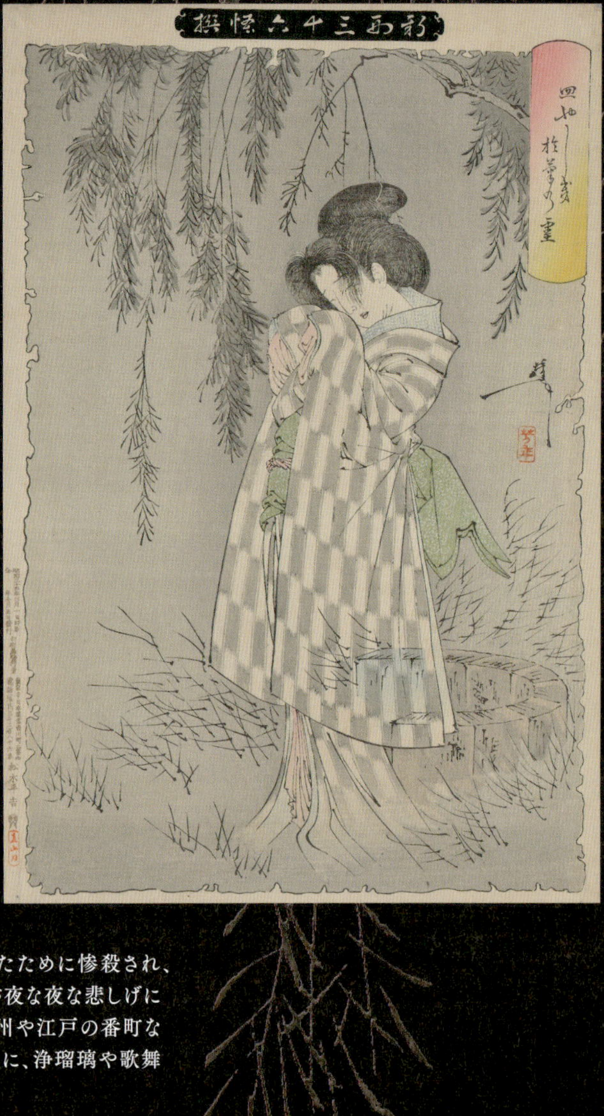

お菊

Okiku
Apparitions (*yūrei*)

主人の秘蔵の皿を一枚割ってしまったために惨殺され、井戸へ投げ込まれたお菊。その亡霊が夜な夜な悲しげに皿を数えるという、怪談「皿屋敷」。播州や江戸の番町などを舞台とし、各地に広まりました。のちに、浄瑠璃や歌舞伎などに脚色されます。

As punishment for breaking one of her master's treasured plates, Okiku was brutally killed and thrown into the well. In the ghost story *Sara-yashiki*, night after night her ghost mournfully counts the plates. Set in Banshū and Banchō, Edo, the tale spread far and wide. Later it was adapted for *jōruri* and kabuki plays.

【新形三十六怪撰 皿やしき於菊の霊】月岡芳年 明治23年(1890)

Okiku's Ghost in the Mansion of Plates
from the series *Shinkei sanjūrokkaisen (New Forms of Thirty-Six Ghosts)*

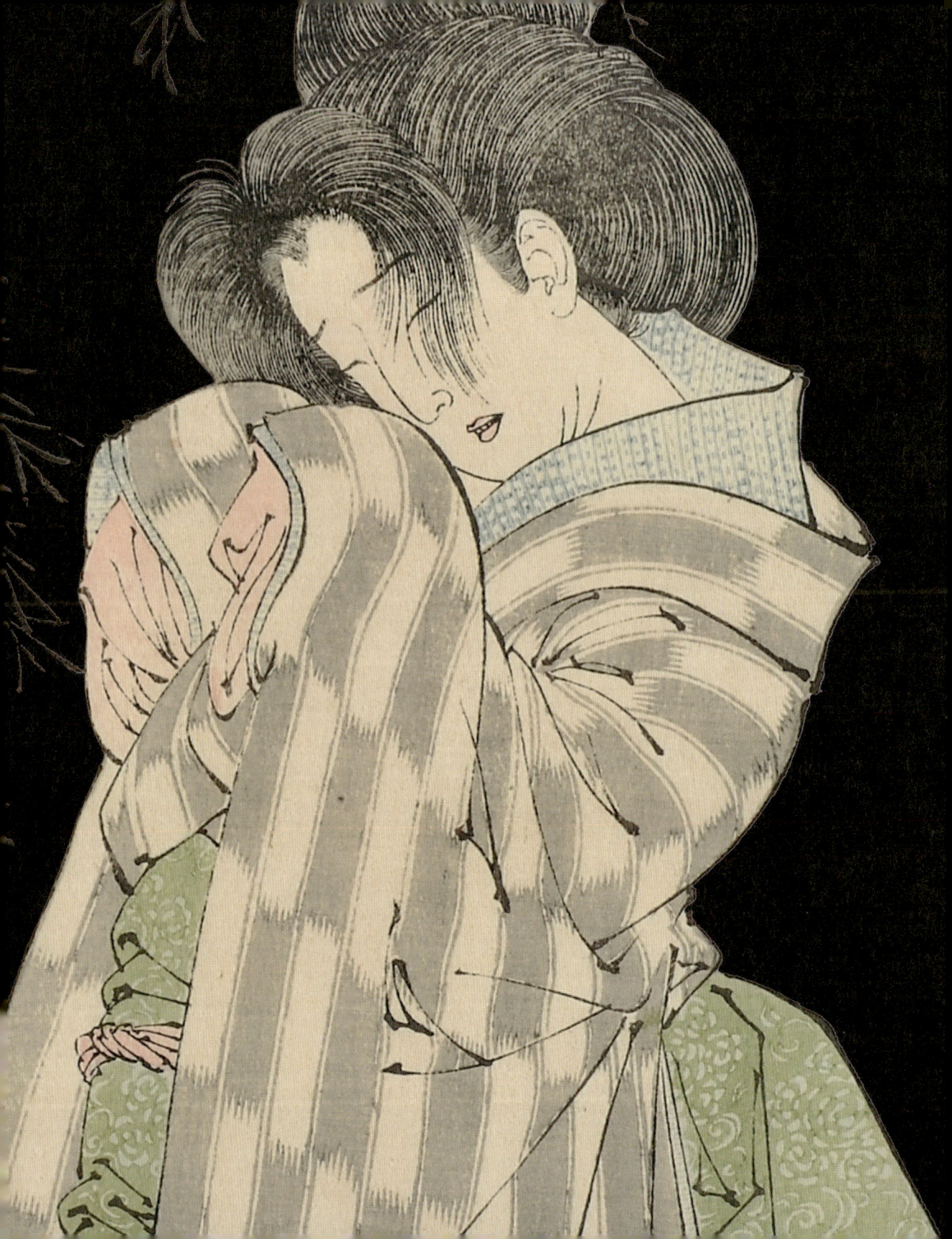

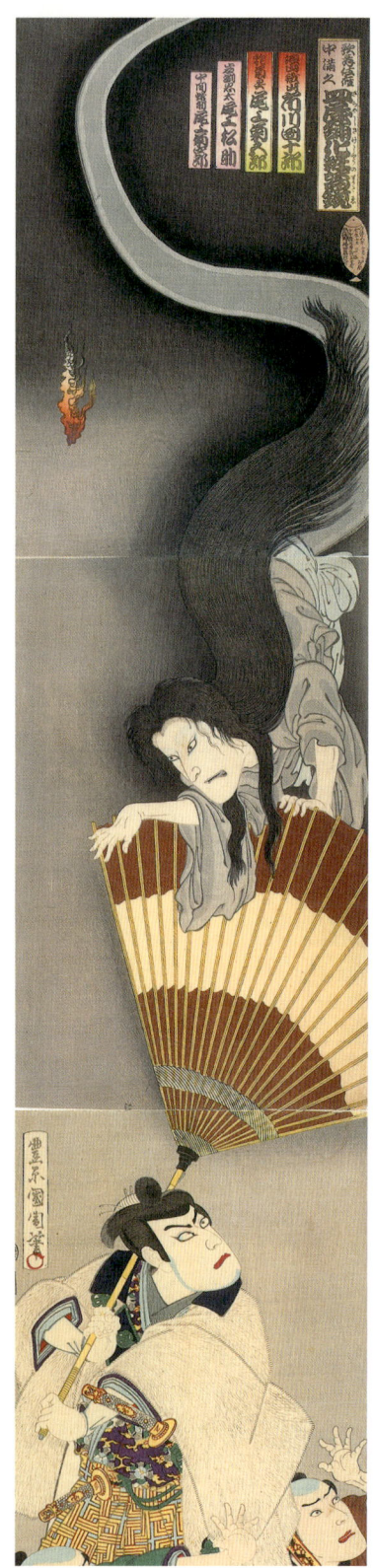

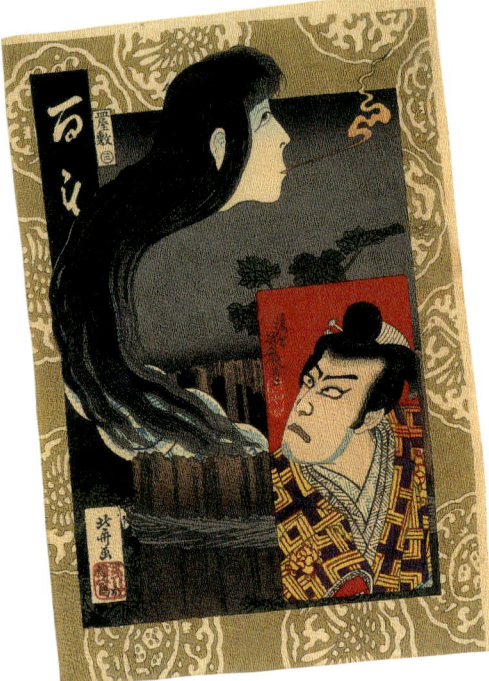

【百物語 皿屋敷】落合芳幾 明治23年（1890）
北斎版を模写した芳幾の「皿屋敷」。コマ絵は、九代目市川団十郎が扮する浅山鉄山です。

Sara-yashiki from the *Hyakumonogatari*
(One Hundred Tales) by Ochiai Yoshiiku
Yoshiiku's *Sara-yashiki* is a reproduction of a Hokusai print. The *koma-e* (an illustration within a larger picture) depicts Ichikawa Danjūrō IX, playing Asayama Tetsuzan.

【百物語 さらやしき】葛飾北斎 天保2年（1831）頃 →
ろくろ首のように伸びた首は皿でできており、「一枚…」「二枚…」と数えながら徐々に這い出る様子が表現されています。

Sara-yashiki (The Mansion of the Plates)
from the *Hyakumonogatari (One Hundred Tales)*
by Katsushika Hokusai
Okiku creeps out inch by inch, counting "one plate... two plates...", her neck made of plates and elongated like a *rokurokubi* (a type of demonic creature whose necks stretch to amazing lengths).

【皿屋鋪化粧姿鏡】豊原国周 明治25年（1892）
歌舞伎「皿屋敷化粧姿視」より。お菊の霊が、城主暗殺を企てる浅山鉄山を襲います。お菊が霊力で鉄山を引き寄せると、蛇の目傘が裏返りました。

Sara-yashiki Keshō no Sugatami (The Makeup Mirror of the Mansion of Plates)
by Toyohara Kunichika
From kabuki play *Sara-yarashiki Keshō no Sugatami*. Okiku's ghost is attacking Asayama Tetsuzan who schemed to assassinate the lord of the castle. Okiku pulls at Tetsuzan with supernatural strength, turning his *janome* (lit. snake's eye) umbrella inside out.

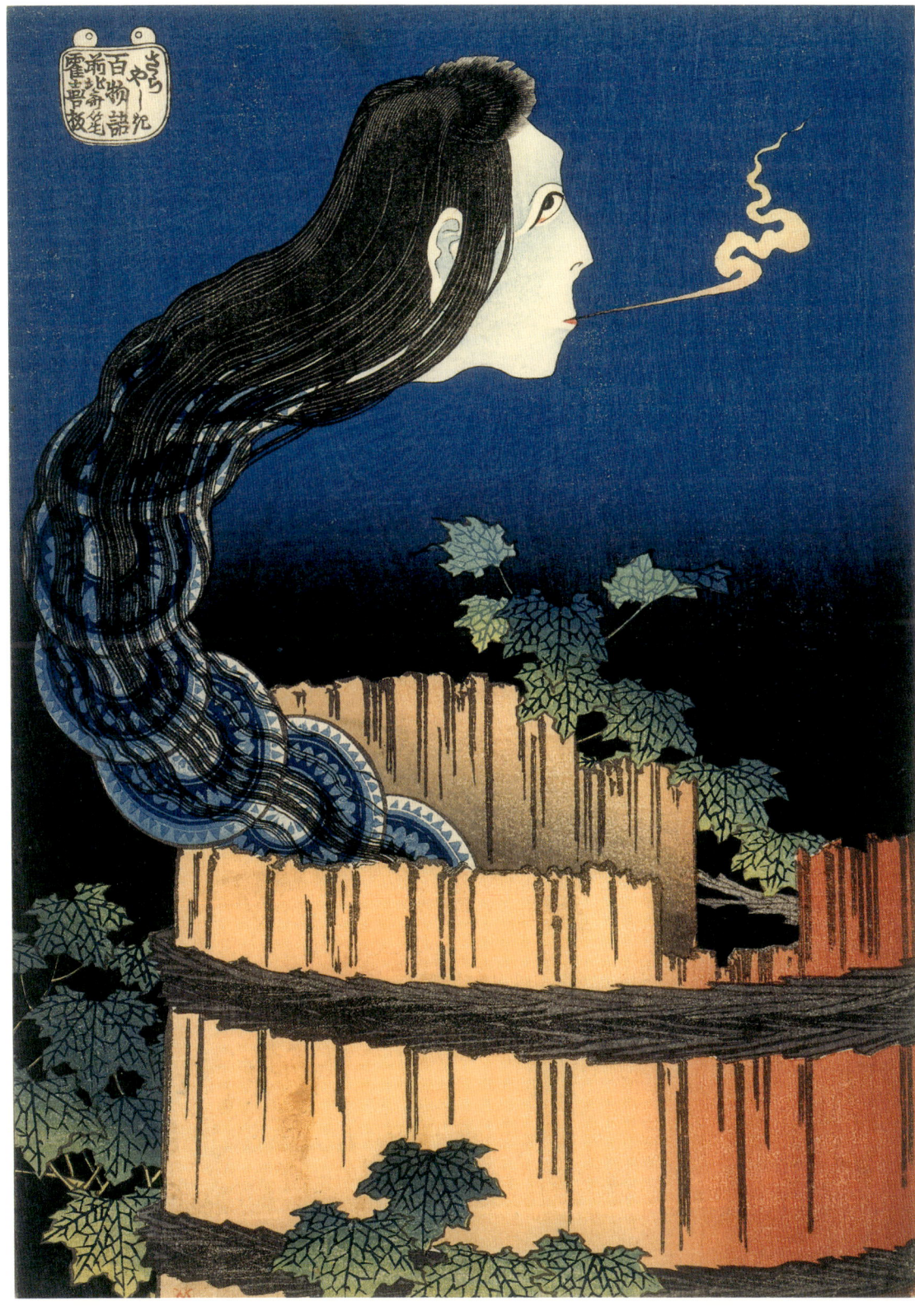

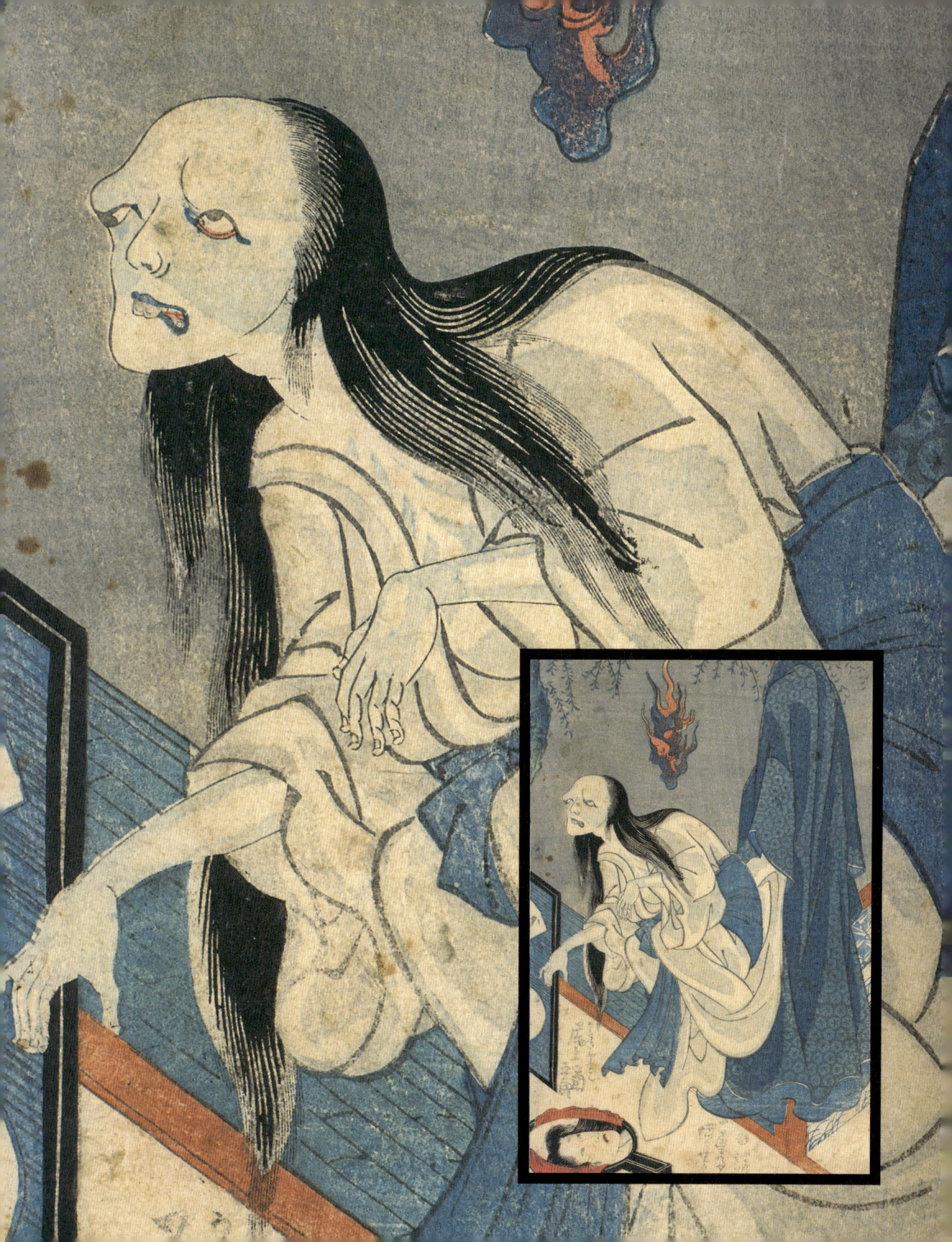

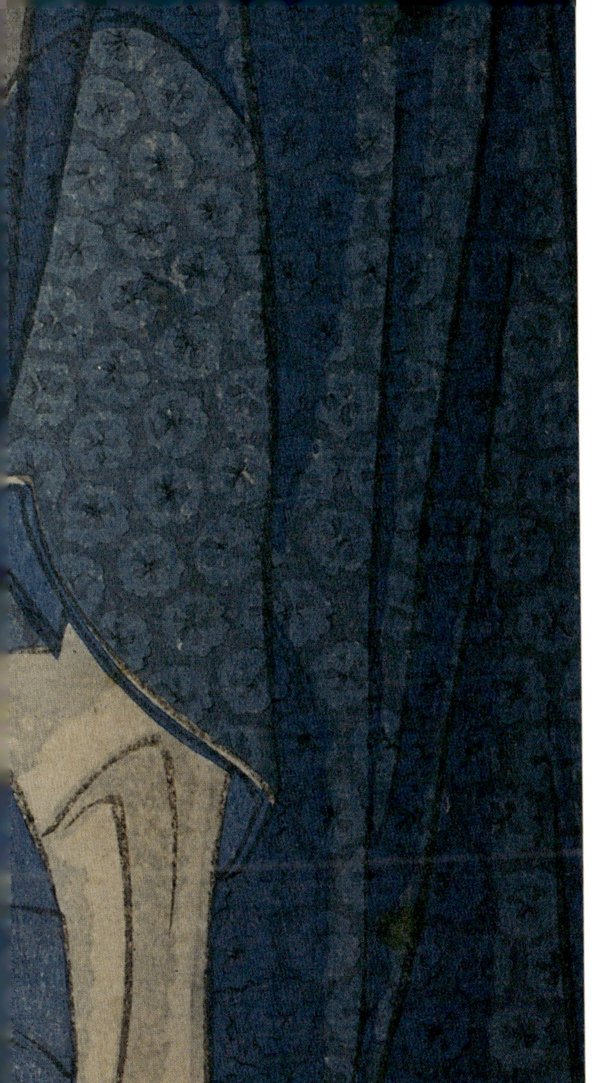

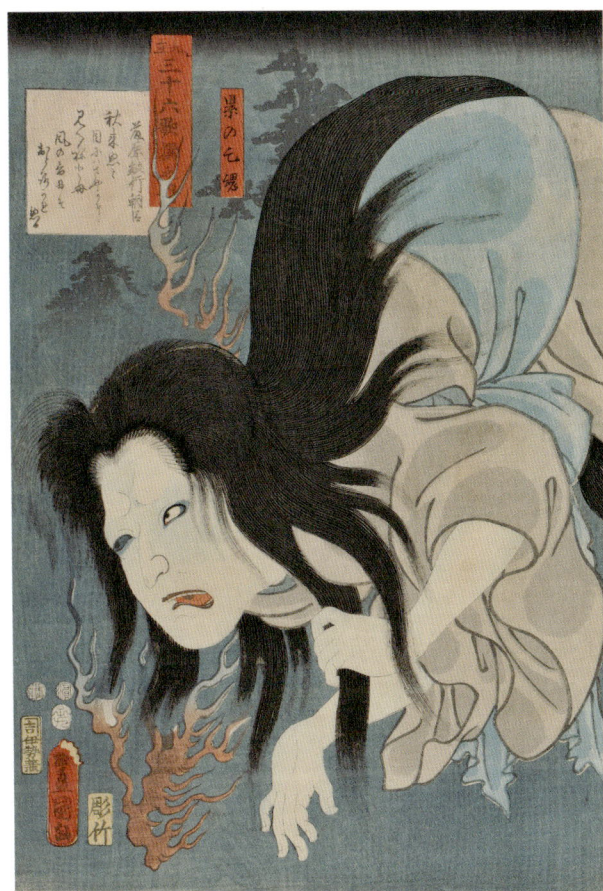

累
Kasane
Apparitions (*yūrei*)

農婦の累は、顔が醜い上に嫉妬深かったので、夫の与右衛門に鬼怒川で殺されてしまいます。その怨念により与右衛門の一族は祟られますが、祐天上人の祈りによって累の怨霊は成仏します。

The peasant Kasane has a hideously ugly face and a jealous streak, which lead her husband Yoemon to his decision to murder her by the Kinu River. Yoemon's entire family are then haunted by the supernatural grudge he has brought on himself, but through the prayers of priest Yūten Shōnin, Kasane's vengeful spirit is laid to rest.

【見立三十六歌撰之内 累の亡魂】
歌川国貞（三代豊国）嘉永5年（1852）
怪しげな炎とともに累の霊が現れました。四代目市川小団次の役者似顔になっています。画中には、藤原敏行の和歌「秋来ぬと目にはさやかに見えねども 風の音にぞおどろかれぬる」が添えられ、累の出現の様子を秋の到来になぞらえています。

The Departed Soul of Kasane
from the series *Mitate sanjurokkasen no uchi*
(Ghostly Parallels with the Thirty-Six Poets)
by Utagawa Kunisada (also known as Utagawa Toyokuni III)
Kasane's ghost manifests with eerie flames. This is a portrait of actor Ichikawa Kodanji IV. The picture illustrates a *waka* poem by Fujiwara no Toshiyuki, which likens the coming of autumn to a the feeling of a visitation from Kasane: "Nothing can be seen to show that autumn has come, yet suddenly I am struck by the sound of the wind."

← 【かさねぼうこん 尾上菊五郎】
歌川国芳 天保4年（1833）
歌舞伎「かさね菊絹川染」より。おとろおとろしい炎とともに、柱に吊るした着物から累の亡霊が現れます。演じるのは、三代目尾上菊五郎です。

The Departed Soul of Kasane featuring Onoe Kikugorō III
by Utagawa Kuniyoshi
From kabuki play *Kasane-giku Kinugawa-zome*. With ominous flames, Kasane's ghost emerges from a kimono hung on a pillar. In the kabuki performance, Kasane's ghost was played by Onoe Kikugorō III.

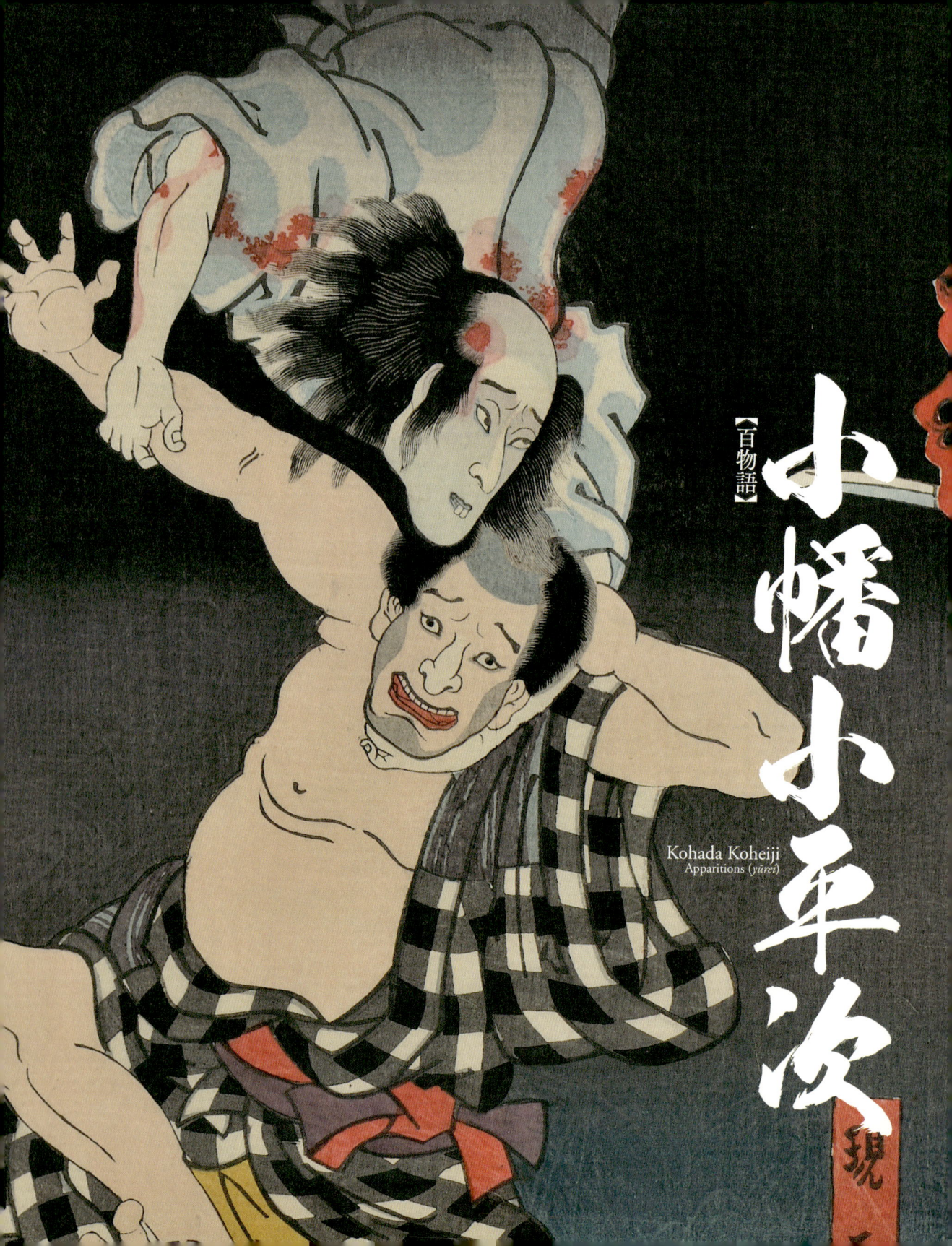

【百物語】

小幡小平次

Kohada Koheiji
Apparitions (*yūrei*)

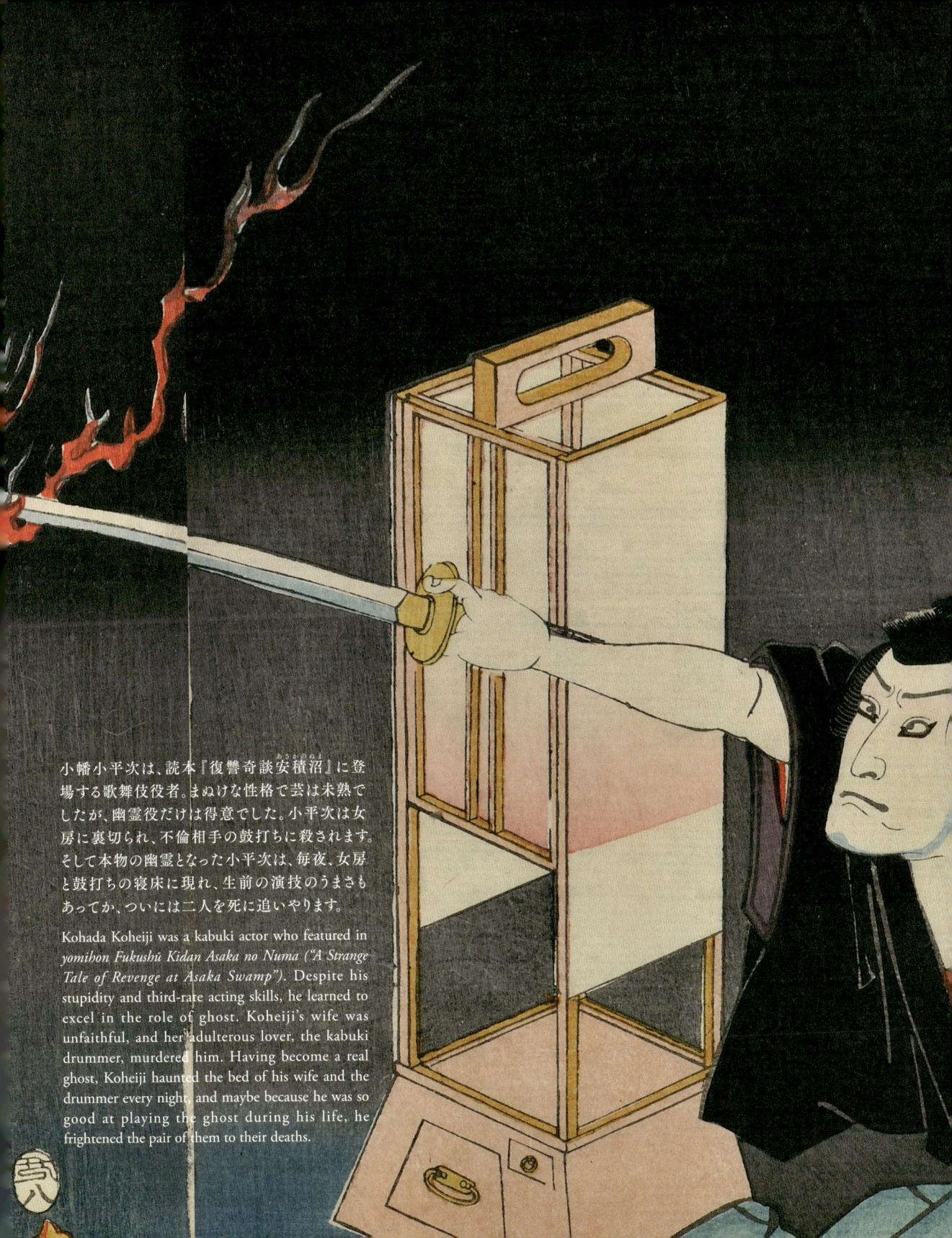

小幡小平次は、読本『復讐奇談安積沼』に登
場する歌舞伎役者。まぬけな性格で芸は未熟で
したが、幽霊役だけは得意でした。小平次は女
房に裏切られ、不倫相手の鼓打ちに殺されます。
そして本物の幽霊となった小平次は、毎夜、女房
と鼓打ちの寝床に現れ、生前の演技のうまさも
あってか、ついには二人を死に追いやります。

Kohada Koheiji was a kabuki actor who featured in
*yomihon Fukushū Kidan Asaka no Numa ("A Strange
Tale of Revenge at Asaka Swamp")*. Despite his
stupidity and third-rate acting skills, he learned to
excel in the role of ghost. Koheiji's wife was
unfaithful, and her adulterous lover, the kabuki
drummer, murdered him. Having become a real
ghost, Koheiji haunted the bed of his wife and the
drummer every night, and maybe because he was so
good at playing the ghost during his life, he
frightened the pair of them to their deaths.

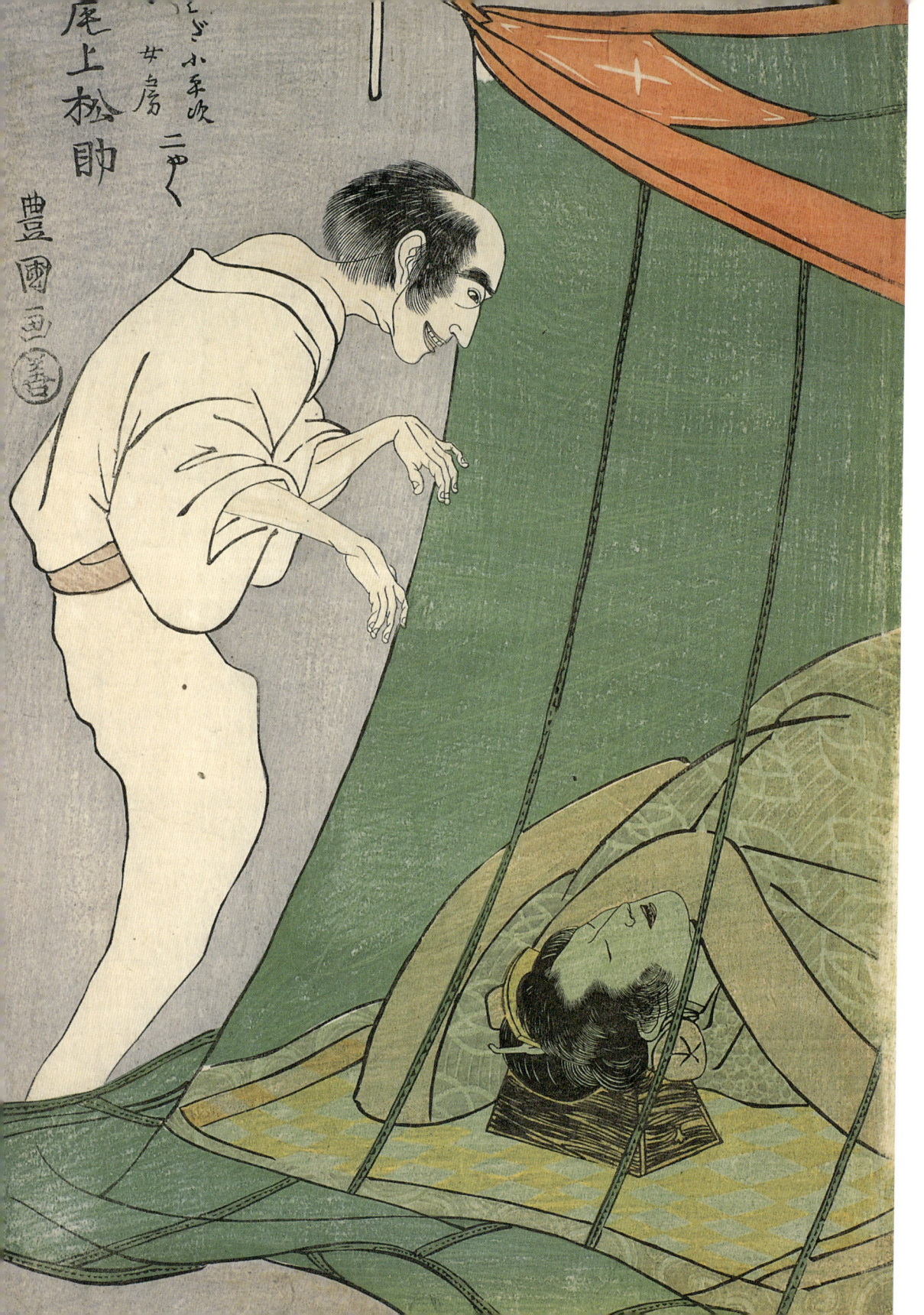

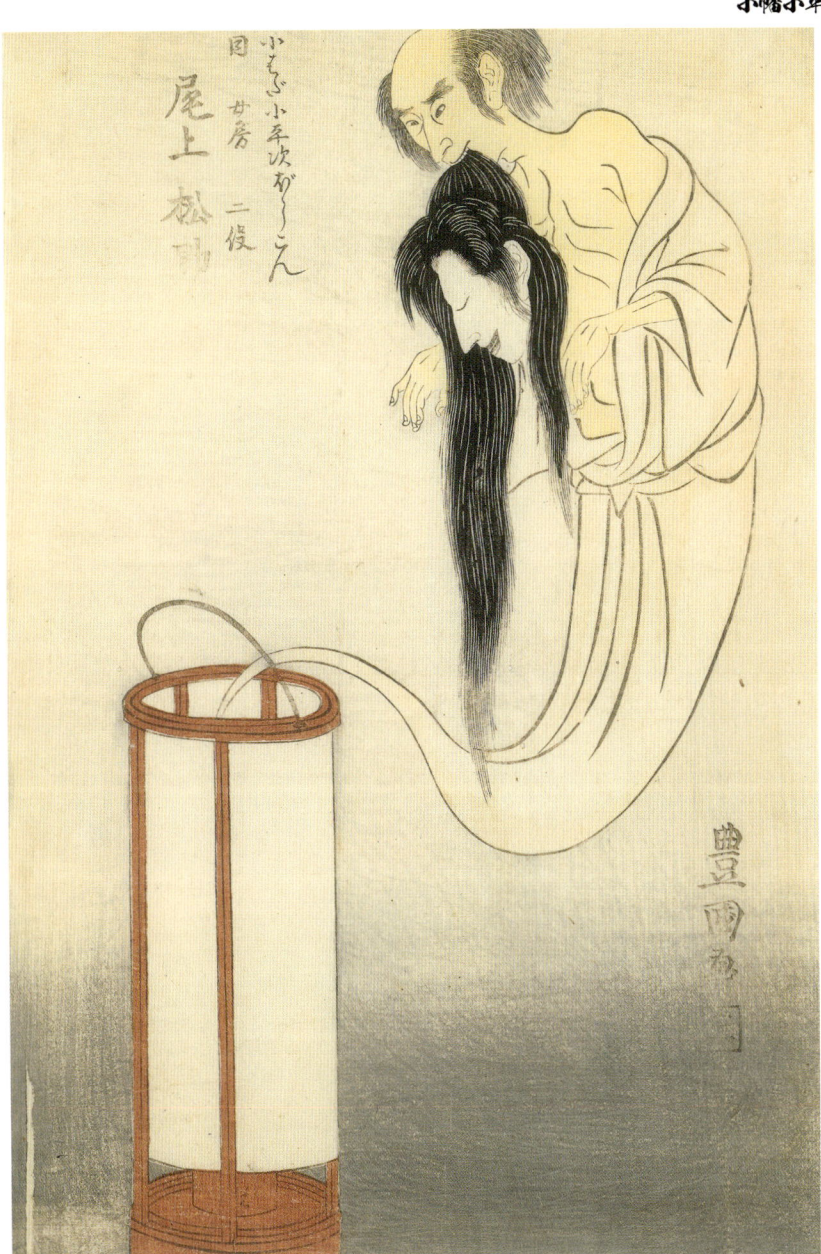

← 【小幡小平次、同女房・尾上松助】
初代歌川豊国 文化5年（1808）
歌舞伎「彩入御伽艸」の一場面。搔巻（袖付の布団）に
くるまって眠るおとわの枕元に、殺害され幽霊となった夫・
小平次の霊が現れます。

*Actor Onoe Matsusuke as Kohada Koheiji
and His Wife* by Utagawa Toyokuni I
One scene of kabuki play *Iroe-iri Otogizōshi (A Colorful
Companion Tale)*. The ghost of murdered Koheiji appears by the
bedside of his wife Otowa, who is sleeping rolled up in a *kaimaki*
(a type of futon with sleeves like a kimono).

【「彩入御伽艸」小平次の亡魂】初代歌川豊国 文化5年（1808）
歌舞伎「彩入御伽艸」より、不義の妻・おとわの首を咥えた小平次の霊。小平次
役の初代尾上松助は、おとわ役もこなし、同場面で姿を素早く変える「早替り」で
話題を呼びました。

*The Departed Soul of Koheiji in Iroe-iri Otogizōshi
(A Colorful Companion Tale)* by Utagawa Toyokuni I
From a scene of kabuki play *Iroe-iri Otogizōshi (A Colorful
Companion Tale)* , the ghost of Koheiji is depicted emerging from the
lantern with the bitten-off head of his wife Otowa in his mouth. The
actor Onoe Matsusuke I who played the role of Koheiji took on
multiple roles, including Koheiji's wife Otowa, and popularized the
hayagawari (quick-change) in which he changed costume on stage in
the blink of an eye.

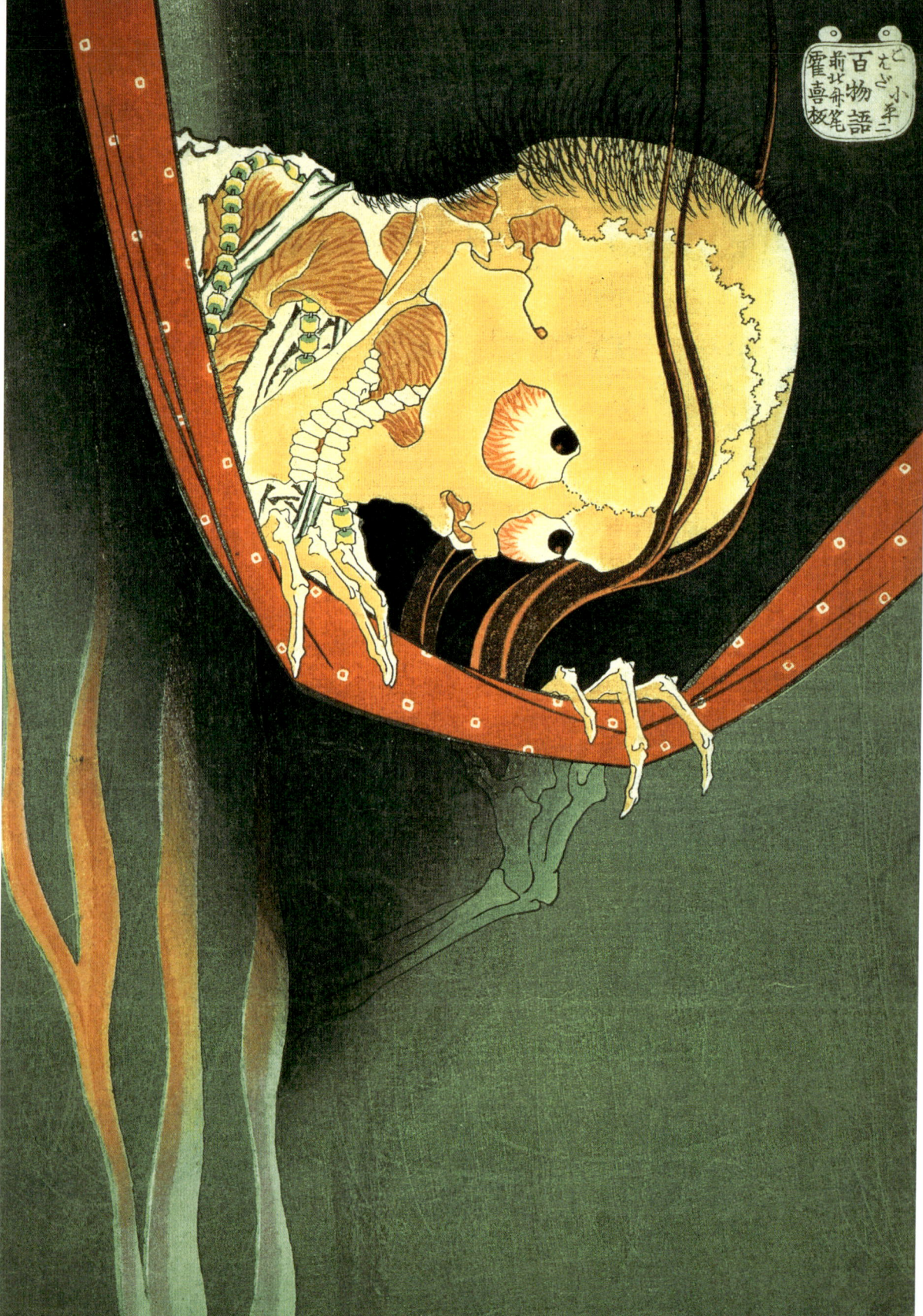

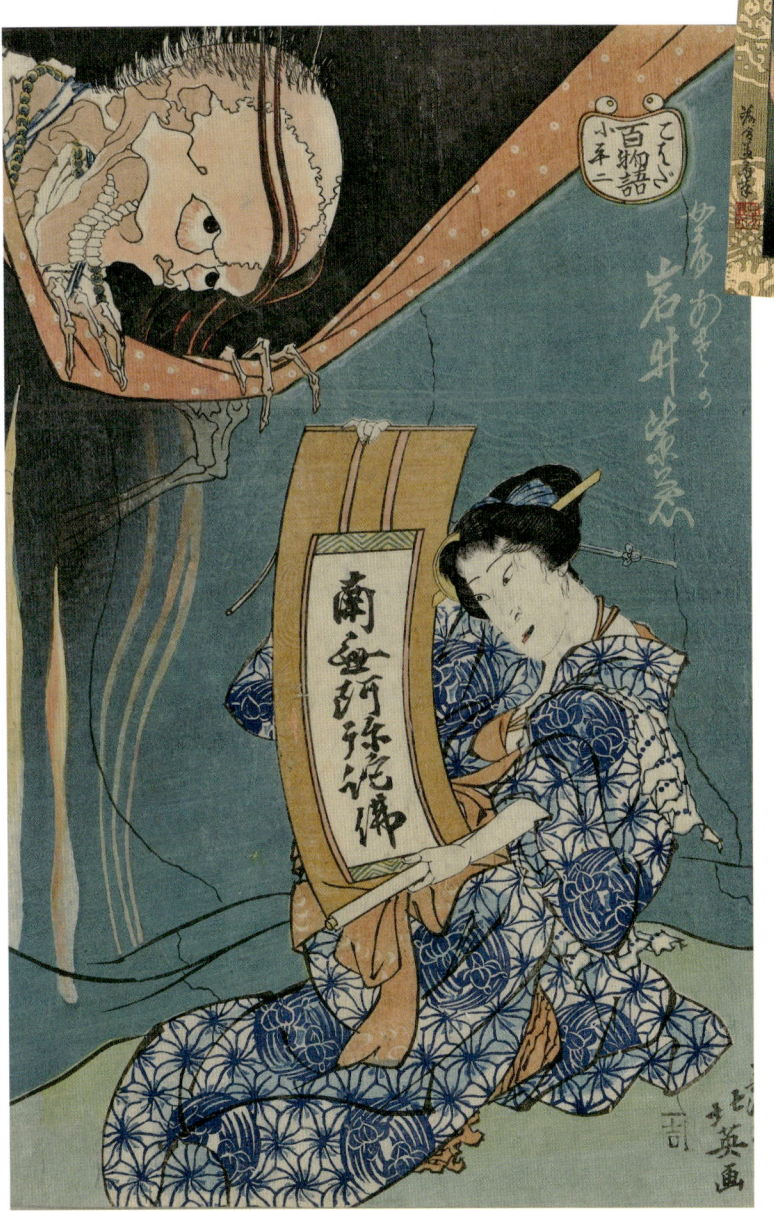

【百物語 小幡小平次】葛飾北斎 天保2年（1831）頃
妻に裏切られ、その不倫相手に惨殺された小平次の亡霊が、復讐のため妻の枕元に現れます。

Kohada Koheiji from the *Hyakumonogatari*
(One Hundred Tales) by Katsushika Hokusai
Betrayed by his wife, and killed by her lover, the ghost of Koheiji appears at his wife's bedside for revenge.

【百物語 小幡小平次】
落合芳幾 明治23年（1890）
芳幾版では、小平次とともに、蚊帳の中の悪女房も描かれています。画面右上の「北斎画」の署名の下に、「芳幾模写」の朱印が押されています。

Kohada Koheiji from the
Hyakumonogatari (One Hundred Tales)
by Ochiai Yoshiiku
In Hokusai's original picture, only Koheiji is depicted, but Yoshiiku has added the unfaithful wife in the middle of the mosquito net. In the upper right, along with the title, is the signature 'Hokusai-ga' from the original print, and under that is the red seal 'Copy by Yoshiiku'.

【百物語 小幡小平次 見立
女房あさか 岩井紫若】
春江斎北英 天保3-4年（1832-33）頃
北英版「百物語」。小平次の女房・おとわは、実は悪人・浅山鉄山の妹・浅香でした。初代岩井紫若の役者似顔絵になっています。

Kohada Koheiji (parody featuring Iwai Shijaku I as the wife Asaka)
from the *Hyakumonogatari*
(One Hundred Tales)
by Shunkōsai Hokuei
A Hokuei print of the *Hyakumonogatari (One Hundred Tales)*. Koheiji's wife Otowa is portrayed as being actually Asaka, the younger sister of the evil Asayama Tetsuzan, probably a play on words with the Asaka Swamp where Koheiji was murdered in the original book. This is a portrait of actor Iwai Shijaku I.

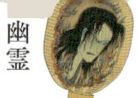

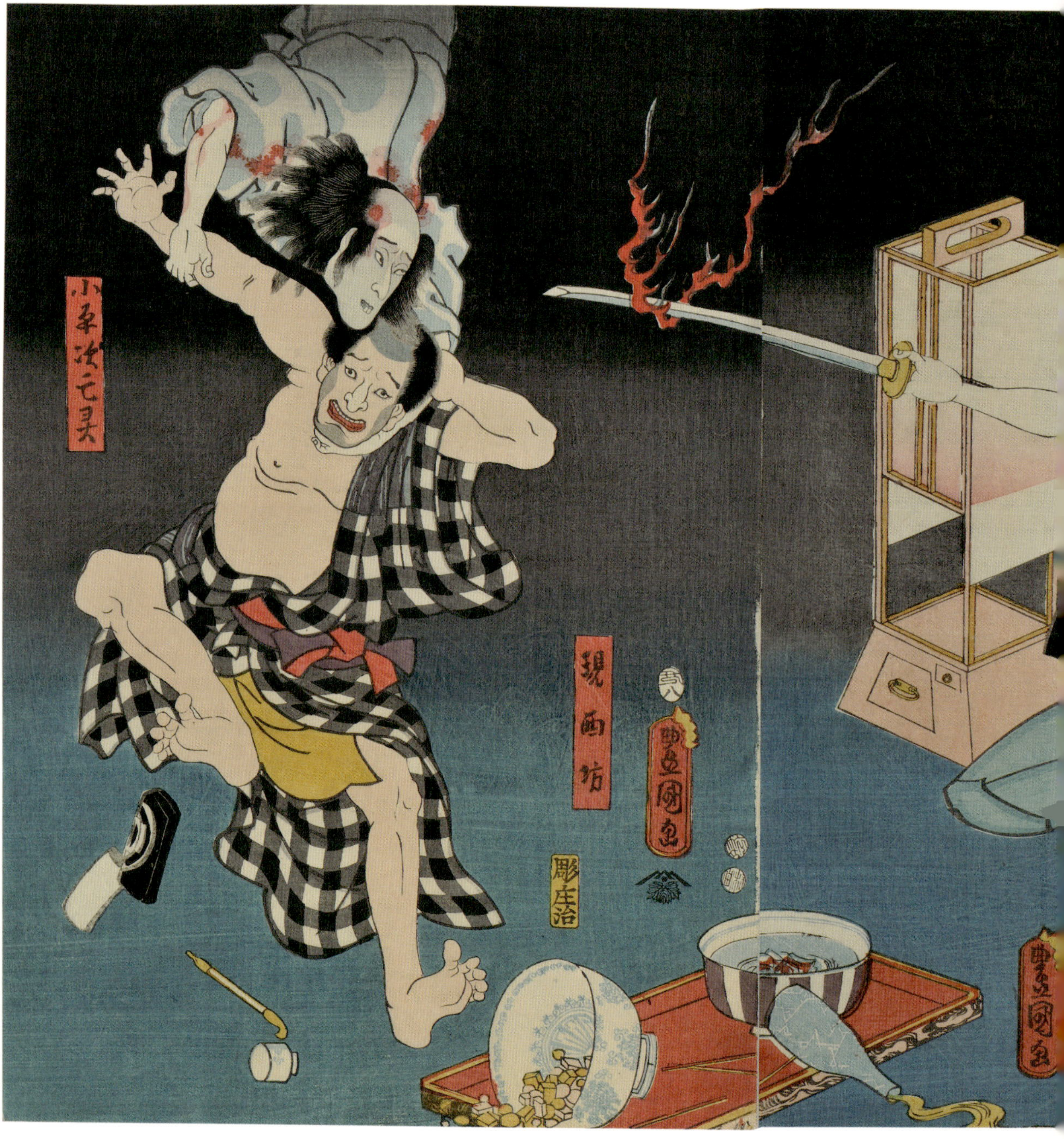

幽
霊

32

【小幡小平次の霊】歌川国貞（三代豊国）嘉永6年（1853）
歌舞伎「怪談小幡小平次」より。小平次の霊が天井から現れ、現西坊を襲います。
小平次の妻・お塚の不倫相手・安達左九郎が、刀で斬りつけます。

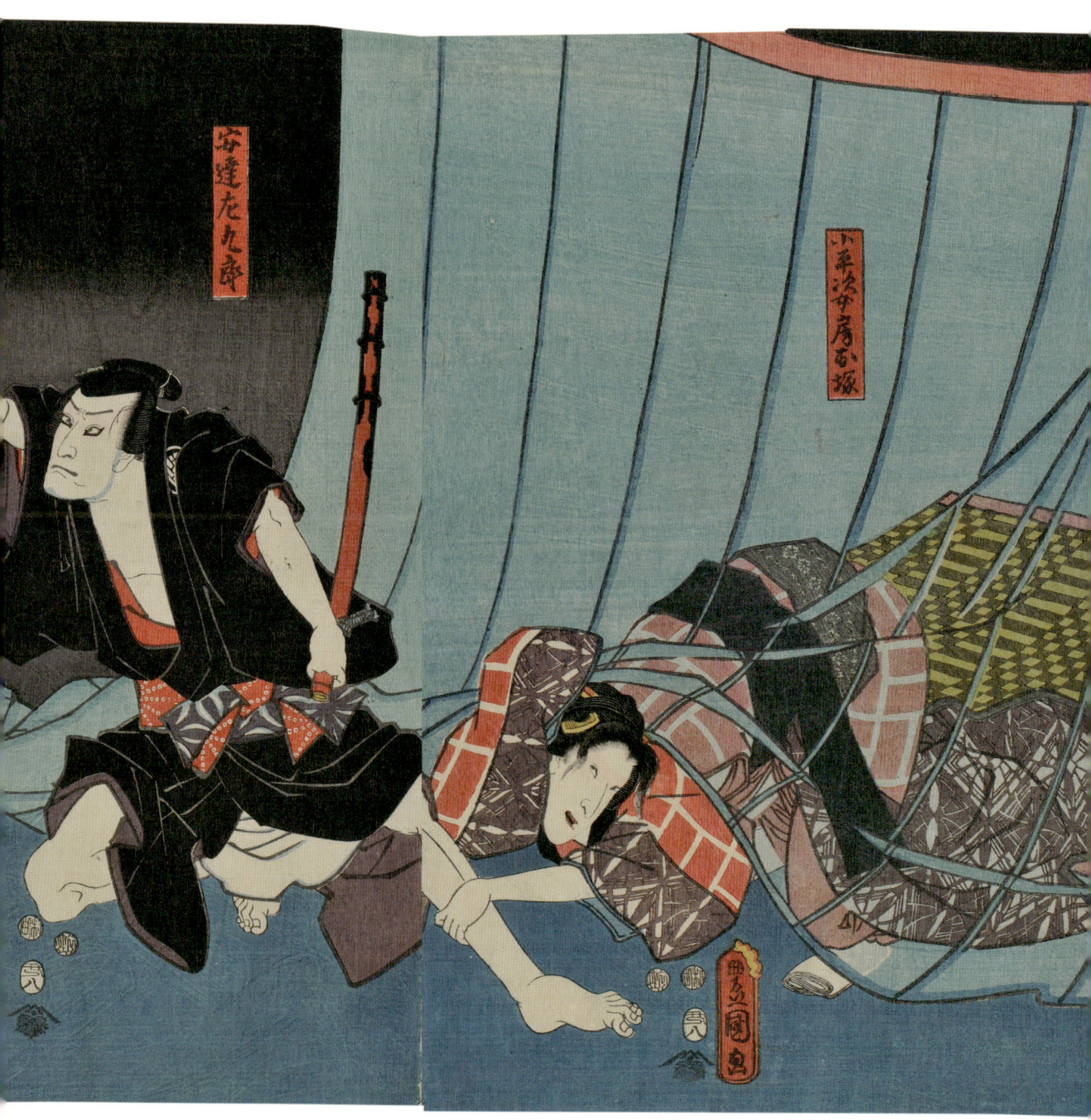

The Ghost of Kohada Koheiji by Utagawa Kunisada (also known as Utagawa Toyokuni III)
From kabuki play *Kaidan Kohada Koheiji (The Ghost Story of Kohada Koheiji)*. Koheiji's ghost appears from overhead, and attacks
Gensaibō. Adachi Sakurō, Koheiji's wife Otsuka's adulterous lover, slashes at him with a sword.

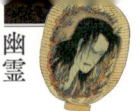

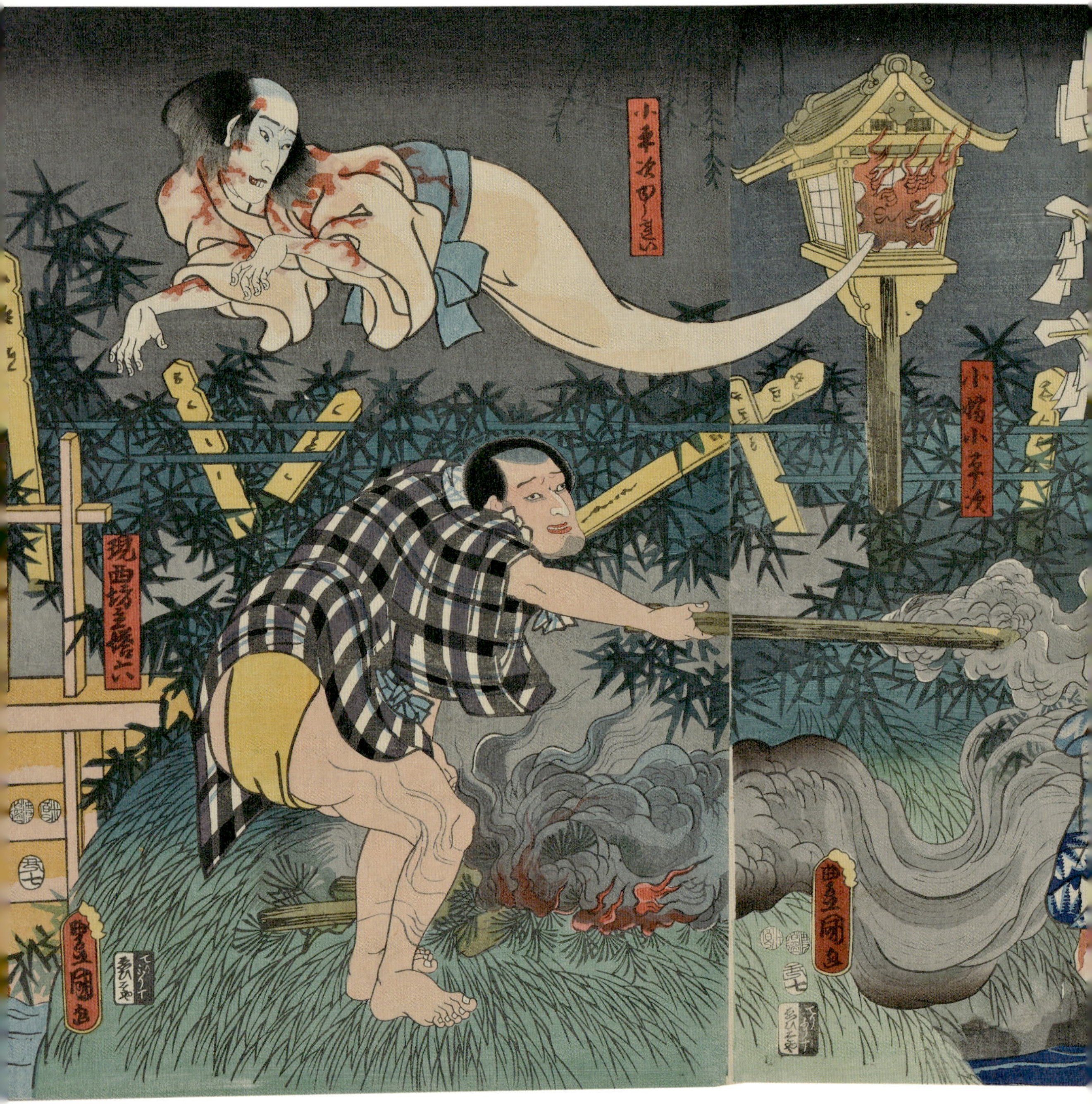

幽霊

【小幡小平次の霊】歌川国貞（三代豊国）嘉永6年（1853）
歌舞伎「怪談小幡小平次」より。柱に縛りつけられた小平次を、安達左九郎が斬り
つけ、現西坊が焚火で熱した棒切れを小平次に押しつけます。

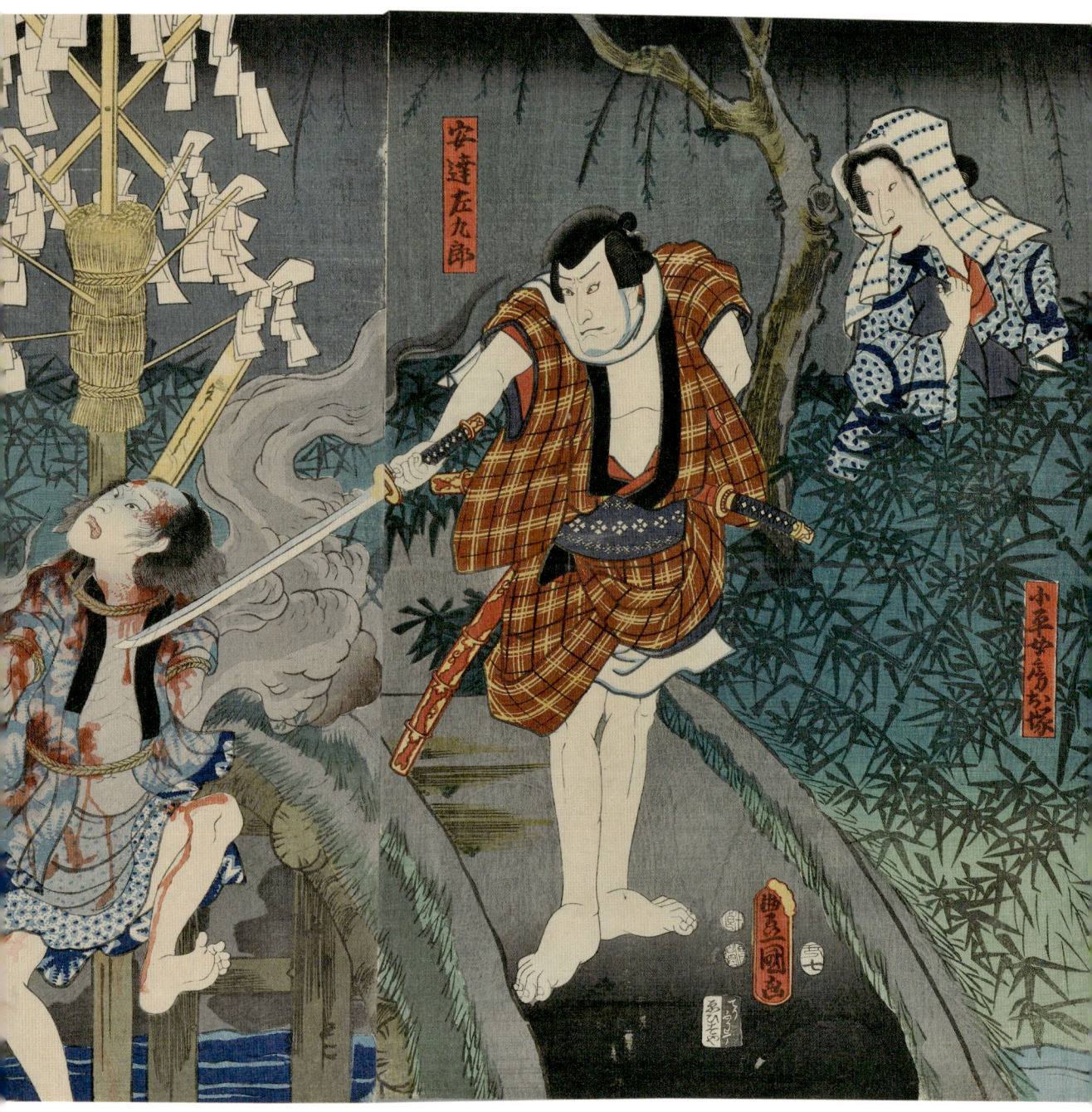

The Ghost of Kohada Koheiji by Utagawa Kunisada (also known as Utagawa Toyokuni III)
From *Kaidan Kohada Koheiji (The Ghost Story of Kohada Koheiji)*. This is the scene of Koheiji's savage killing. Tied to a post, Koheiji is slashed with a sword by his wife Otsuka's lover Adachi Sakurō, and poked with a burning branch by Gensaibō.

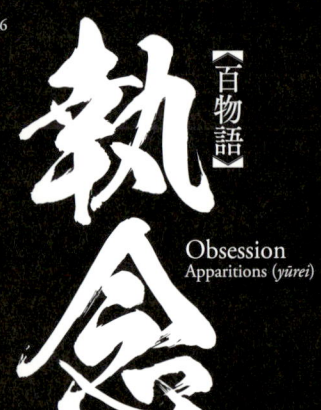

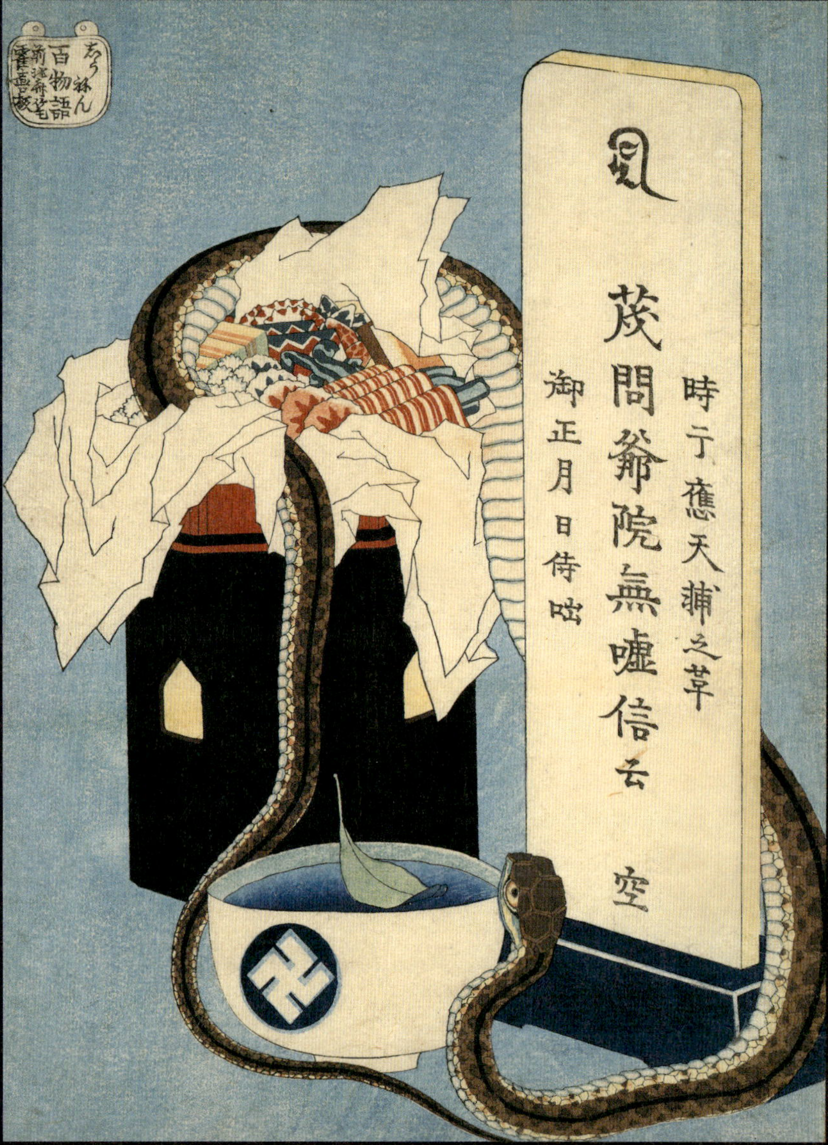

執念【百物語】

Obsession
Apparitions (*yūrei*)

古来、蛇は執念の象徴とされてきました。一匹の蛇が位牌とお供えに絡みつき、天を仰ぎます。位牌の主は蛇となり、なおも現世への執着を断ち切れないのでしょう。

The Japanese word *shiunen* is used here to mean obsession. A snake, gazing heavenward, is coiled around a Buddhist mortuary tablet and a table on which offerings are heaped. The snake is a metaphor for depth of obsession, which means that even though the person whose mortuary tablet it is has died, their obsession with the mortal world remains.

【百物語 しうねん】葛飾北斎　天保2年（1831）頃

「しうねん」とは「執念」のこと。戒名の「茂間爺院無噓信士」は、妖怪「ももんじい」のシャレ。湯呑みの「卍」印は北斎を示します。

Shiunen (Obsession) from the *Hyakumonogatari (One Hundred Tales)* by Katsushika Hokusai

The posthumous Buddhist name Momonjii-in Mukyoshinji written on the tablet is a pun on the *yōkai* monster called Momonjii, and the Buddhist *manji* symbol (卍) on the cup represents Hokusai, who had begun to use the pseudonym Gakyō Rōjin Manji (The Old Man Mad About Art).

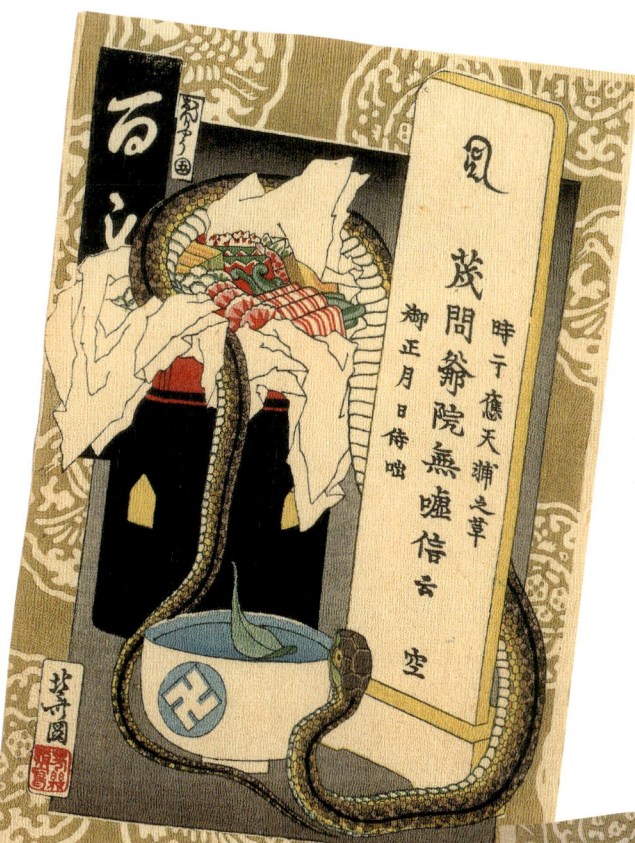

【百物語 おんりやう】落合芳幾 明治23年(1890)
芳幾版の題名は、「おんりやう（怨霊）」となっています。

Onriyau (Vengeful Spirit)
from the *Hyakumonogatari (One Hundred Tales)*
by Ochiai Yoshiiku

The title of the print by Hokusai is *Shiunen (Obsession)*, but this print by Yoshiiku is entitled *Onriyau (Vengeful Spirit)*.

【百物語 執念】落合芳幾 明治23年(1890)
こちらは、幽霊画で有名な円山応挙の画を模写したもの。

Obsession from the *Hyakumonogatari*
(One Hundred Tales) by Ochiai Yoshiiku

This is a copy of Maruyama Ōkyo's famous work, as a *yūrei-ga* (lit. "ghost picture").

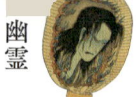

幽霊

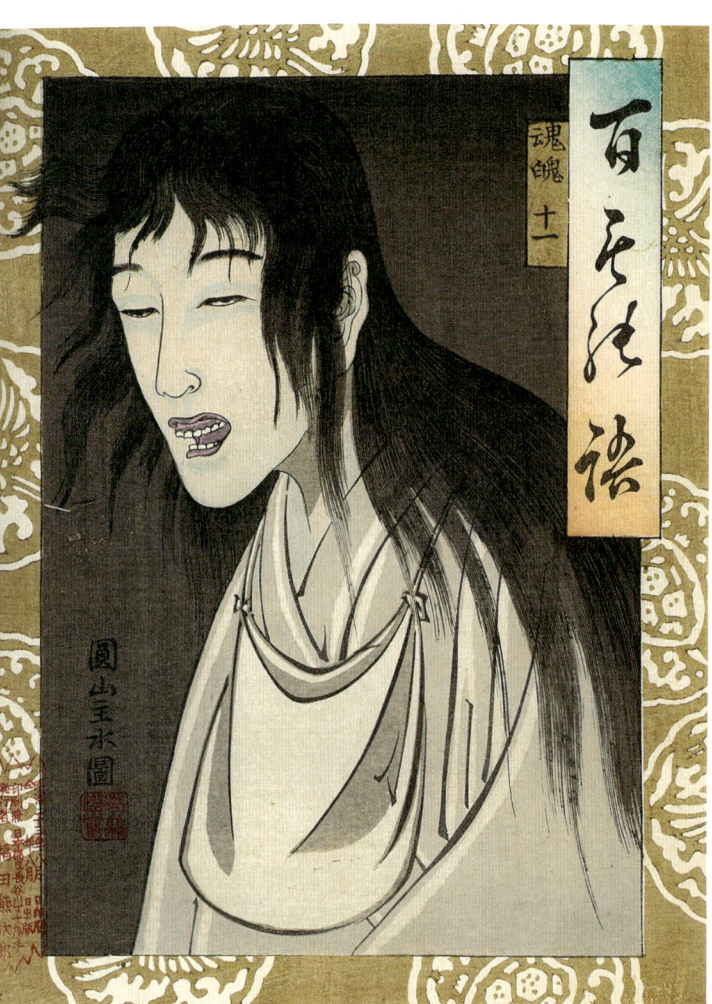

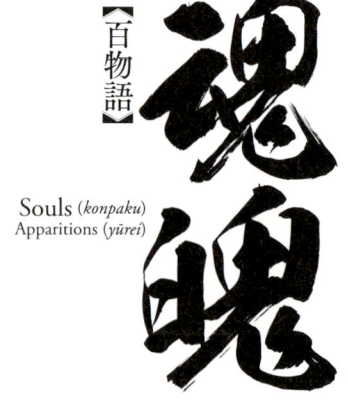

【百物語】

魂魄

Souls (*konpaku*)
Apparitions (*yūrei*)

「魂魄」とは死者の霊魂のこと。白の死装束で現れた女の幽霊。応挙画の模写で、応挙の通称である「圓山主水」の署名があります。

Konpaku are souls: the spirits of the dead. The ghost of a woman appears dressed for death in a white shroud and a bag hung around her neck (*zudabukuro*). Her eyes, slitted eerily open, give the impression that even now her dead flesh might return to life. As this is a copy of a work by Maruyama Ōkyo, on the lower left of the picture is the signature Maruyama Mondo, one of Ōkyo's pseudonyms.

【百物語 魂魄】落合芳幾 明治23年（1890）
Konpaku (Soul) from the *Hyakumonogatari (One Hundred Tales)* by Ochiai Yoshiiku

38

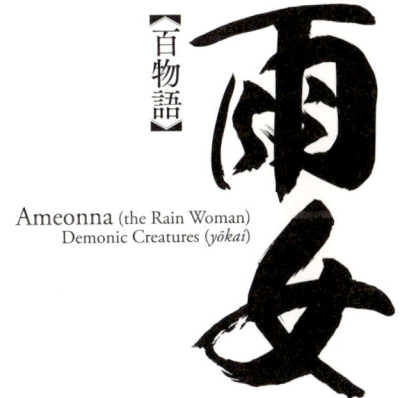

【百物語】

Ameonna (the Rain Woman)
Demonic Creatures (*yōkai*)

朝には雲となり夕方には雨となって、愛しい男に会いに来るという雨女。図は絵画と漆芸で活躍した柴田是真の模写です。

Ameonna comes to meet the man she loves as clouds in the morning and as rain in the evening. This work is a copy of a piece by Shibata Zeshin, a painter and lacquerer active in the 19th century.

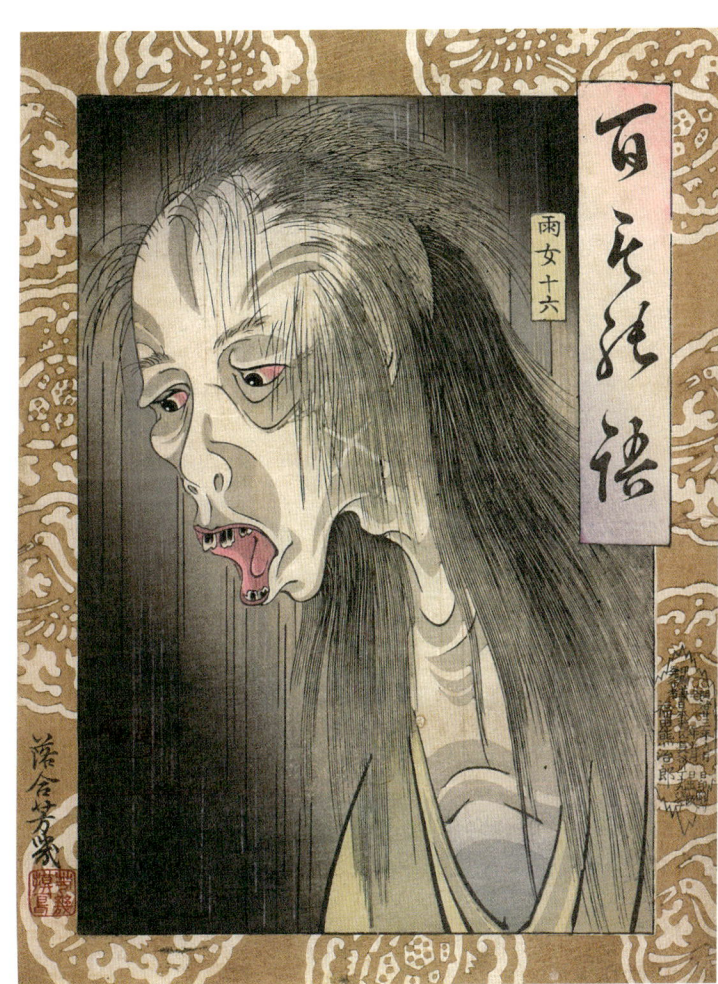

【百物語 雨女】落合芳幾 明治23年（1890）

The Rain Woman from the *Hyakumonogatari (One Hundred Tales)* by Ochiai Yoshiiku

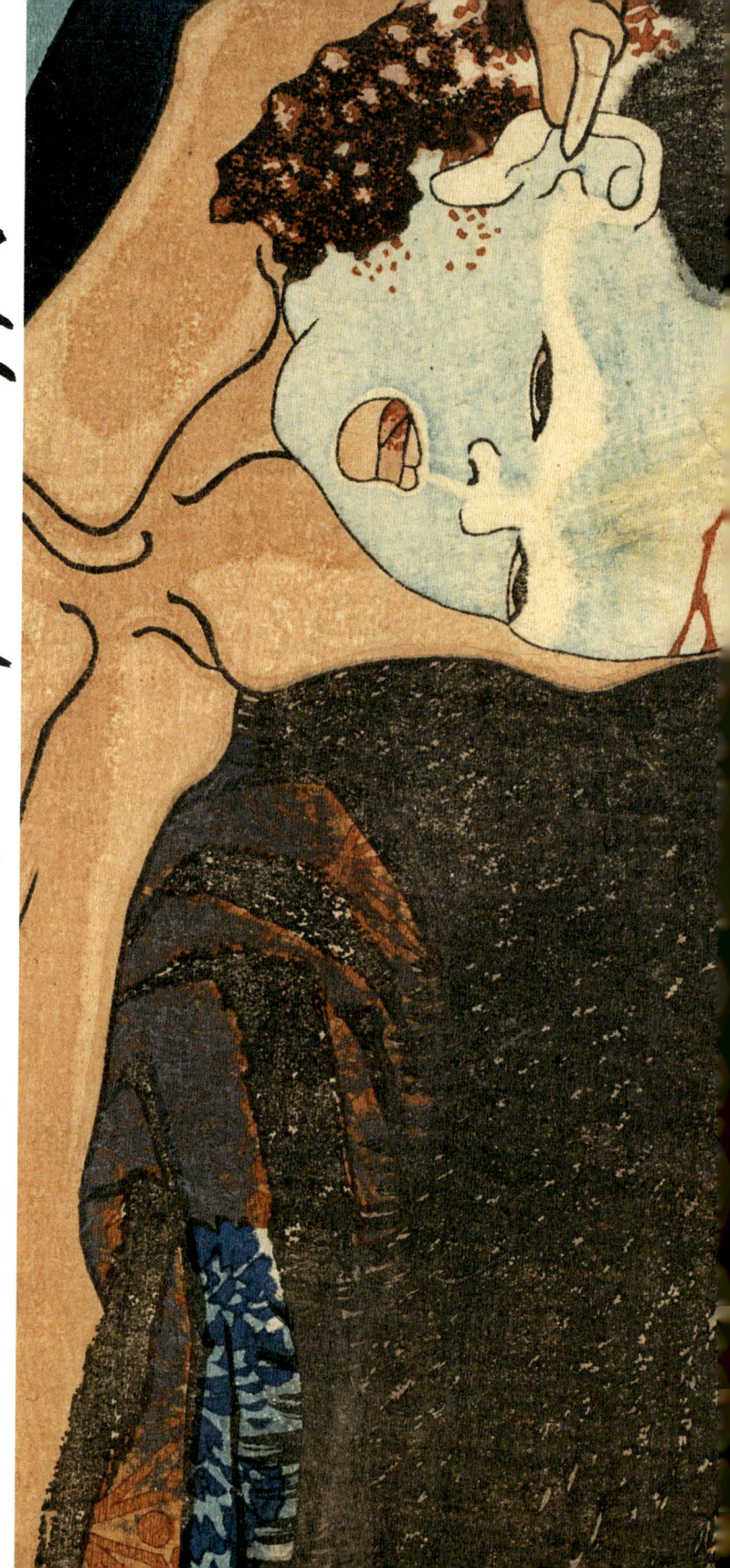

【百物語】

笑いはんにや

Warai han'nya (Laughing Demoness)
Demonic Creatures (*yōkai*)

「はんにや」とは「般若」のこと。嫉妬に狂い鬼に化けた女を意味します。長く尖った爪で赤ちゃんの生首をつかみ、まるで柘榴を食べるかのように喰らいつきます。赤ちゃんのちぎれた傷口と半開きの目が生々しい。目尻をゆがませ、にたりと笑う表情からは、この女の狂気がうかがえます。

The word *han'nya* means a female demon. Warped by envy, this woman has been twisted into a monster. She clutches the severed head of a baby with long pointy claws, as if about to bite into it like a pomegranate. The baby's half-open eyes and torn wound are graphic. The woman's feral nature is evident in her deranged eyes and wildly laughing grimace.

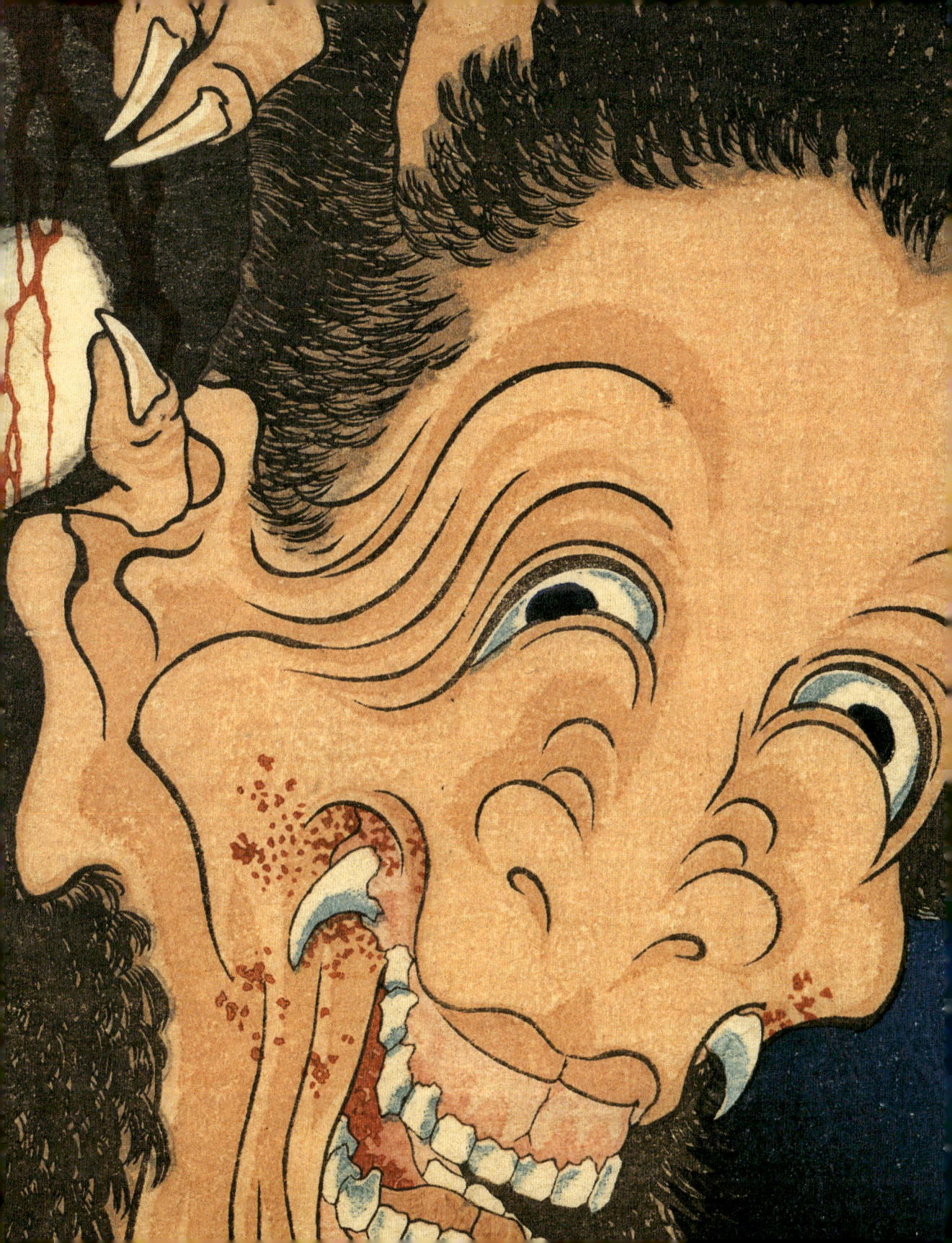

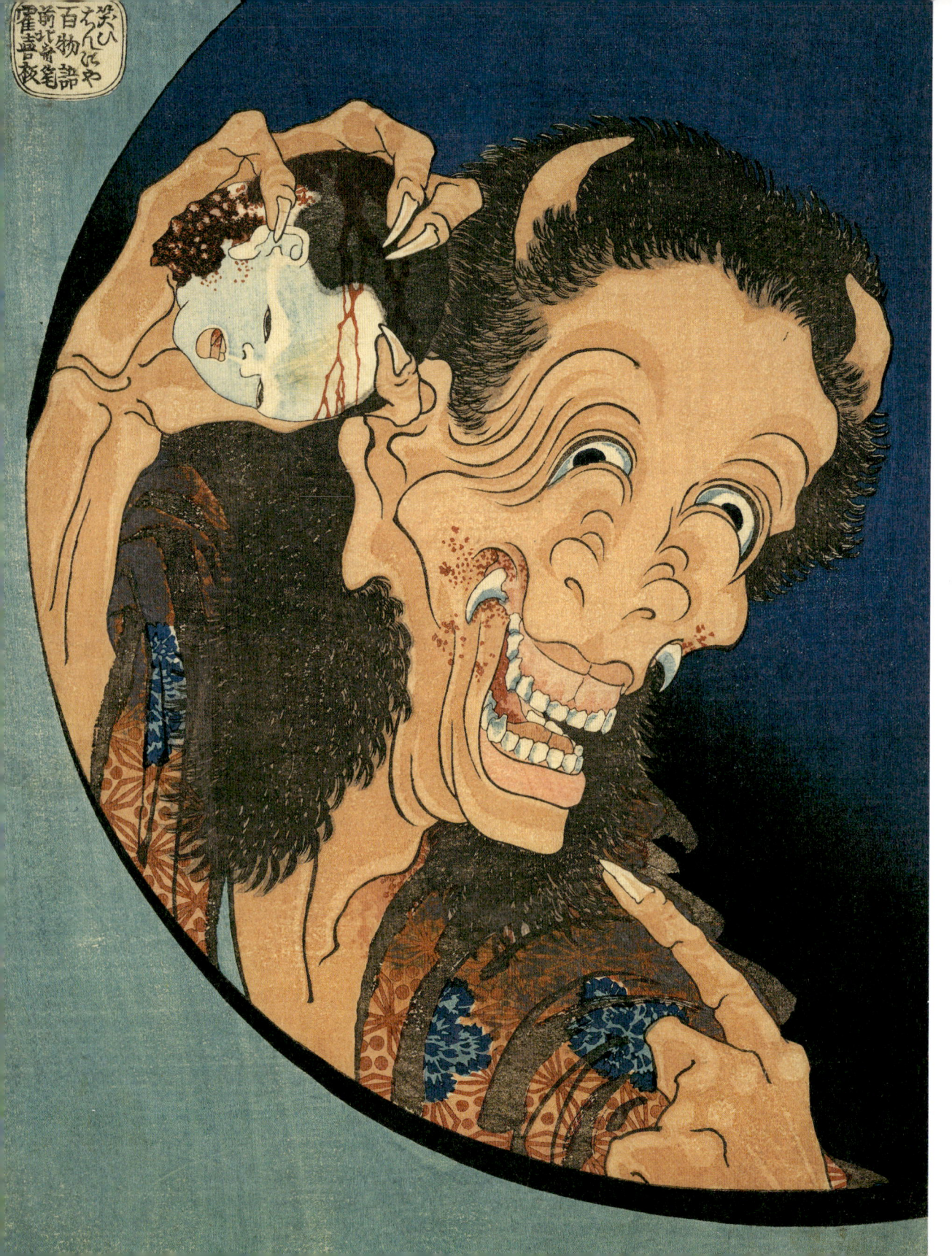

←【百物語 笑ひはんにや】葛飾北斎 天保2年(1831)頃

Warai han'nya (Laughing Demoness) from the *Hyakumonogatari (One Hundred Tales)*
by Katsushika Hokusai

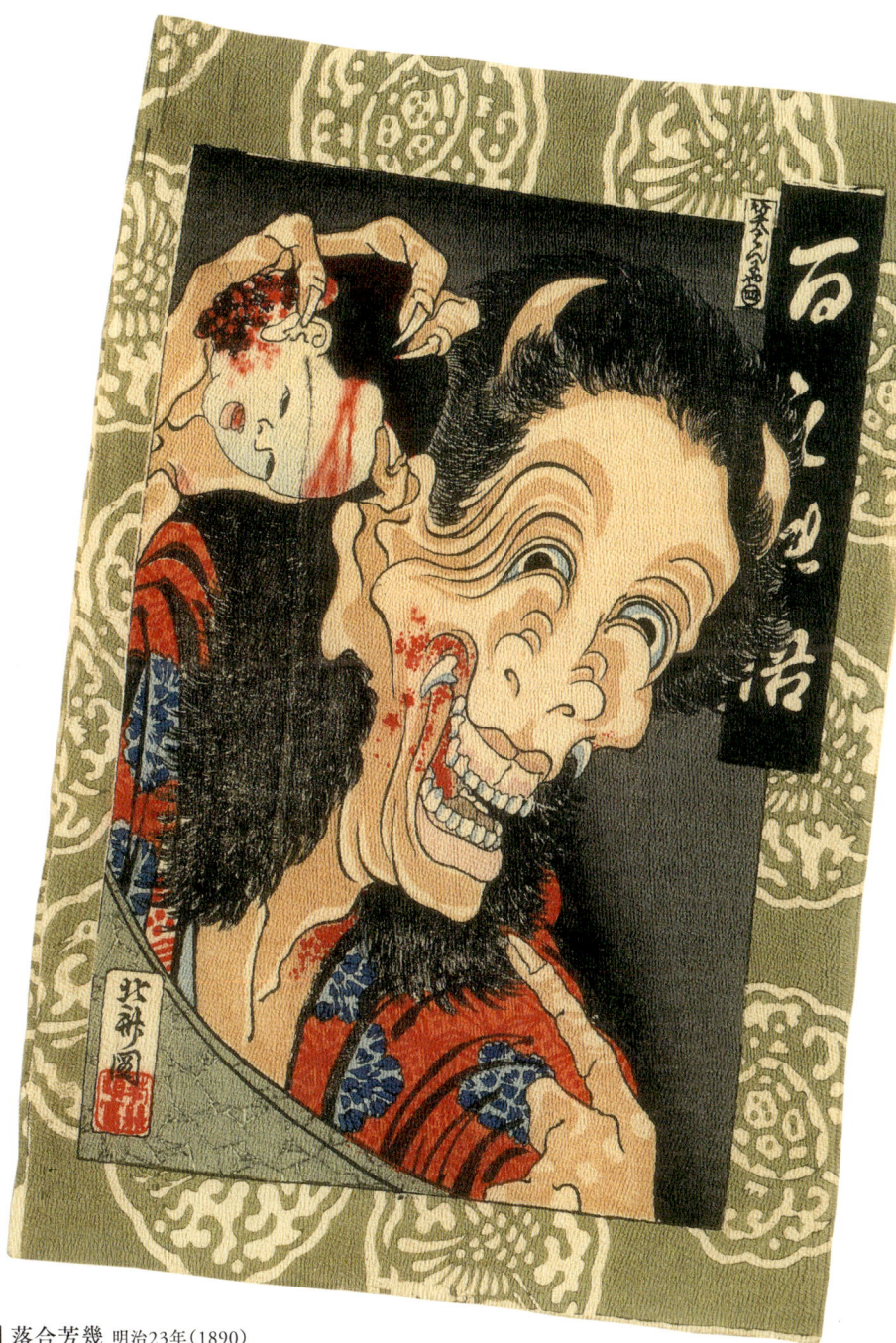

【百物語 笑はんにや】落合芳幾 明治23年(1890)
芳幾版「笑い般若」。「北斎図」の下には「芳幾模写」の朱印が押されています。

Warai han'nya (Laughing Demoness) from the *Hyakumonogatari (One Hundred Tales)*
by Ochiai Yoshiiku

Laughing Demoness, stamped by Yoshiiku. Under the signature 'Hokusai-ga' is imprinted the red seal, 'Copy by Yoshiiku'.

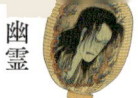

佐倉宗吾は江戸時代前期に実在したとされる、下総国（千葉県）佐倉藩の村役人です。領主のひどい政治に苦しむ村民のために、江戸の将軍に直訴しましたが捕えられ、妻子とともに磔にされました。死後、怨霊となった宗吾が領主を呪うという物語は、歌舞伎などに脚色されました。

In the early Edo period, a man named Sakura Sōgo, who was a village headman in the Sakura Domain of Shimousa Province (present-day northern Chiba), sacrificed himself for justice. He made an unlawful direct appeal to the Edo Shōgun Tokugawa Ietsuna on behalf of the villagers suffering under the diabolical rule of feudal lord Hotta Masanobu, but was captured and crucified along with his wife and children. After his death, Sōgo rose again as a vengeful spirit to plague Hotta Masanobu. This story was dramatized in kabuki play *Higashiyama Sakura Sōshi (A Tale of Higashiyama Cherry Blossoms)*.

【浅倉当吾の亡霊と織越大領】
歌川国貞（三代豊国）嘉永4年（1851）

歌舞伎「東山桜荘子」より、毎夜、怪異に悩まされる領主の織越大領。香炉から一筋の煙が立ちのぼり、浅倉当吾（佐倉宗吾）の霊が現れました。磔姿の当吾が手にするのは「上」と記された直訴状です。

Lord Orikoshi and the Ghost of Asakura Tōgo
by Utagawa Kunisada
(also known as Utagawa Toyokuni III)

From kabuki play *Higashiyama Sakura Sōshi*. When the play was first performed, Sakura Sōgo and Hotta Masanobu went under the pseudonyms Asakura Tōgo and Lord Orikoshi Masatomo. Every night, Lord Orikoshi (center) is tormented by mysterious phenomena. A stream of smoke rises from the incense burner, and Tōgo's ghost (right) appears. In the crucified Tōgo's hand is his direct appeal, with the character "上" written on it.

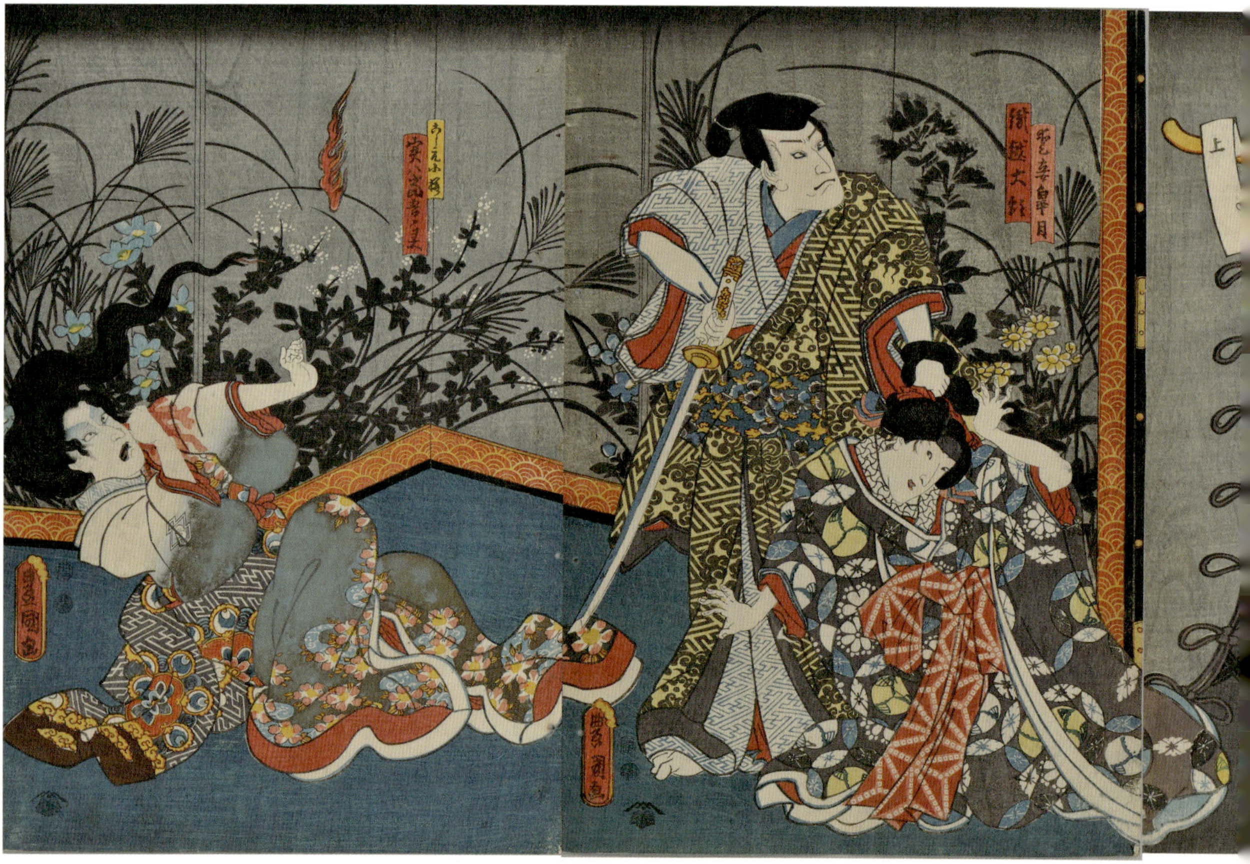

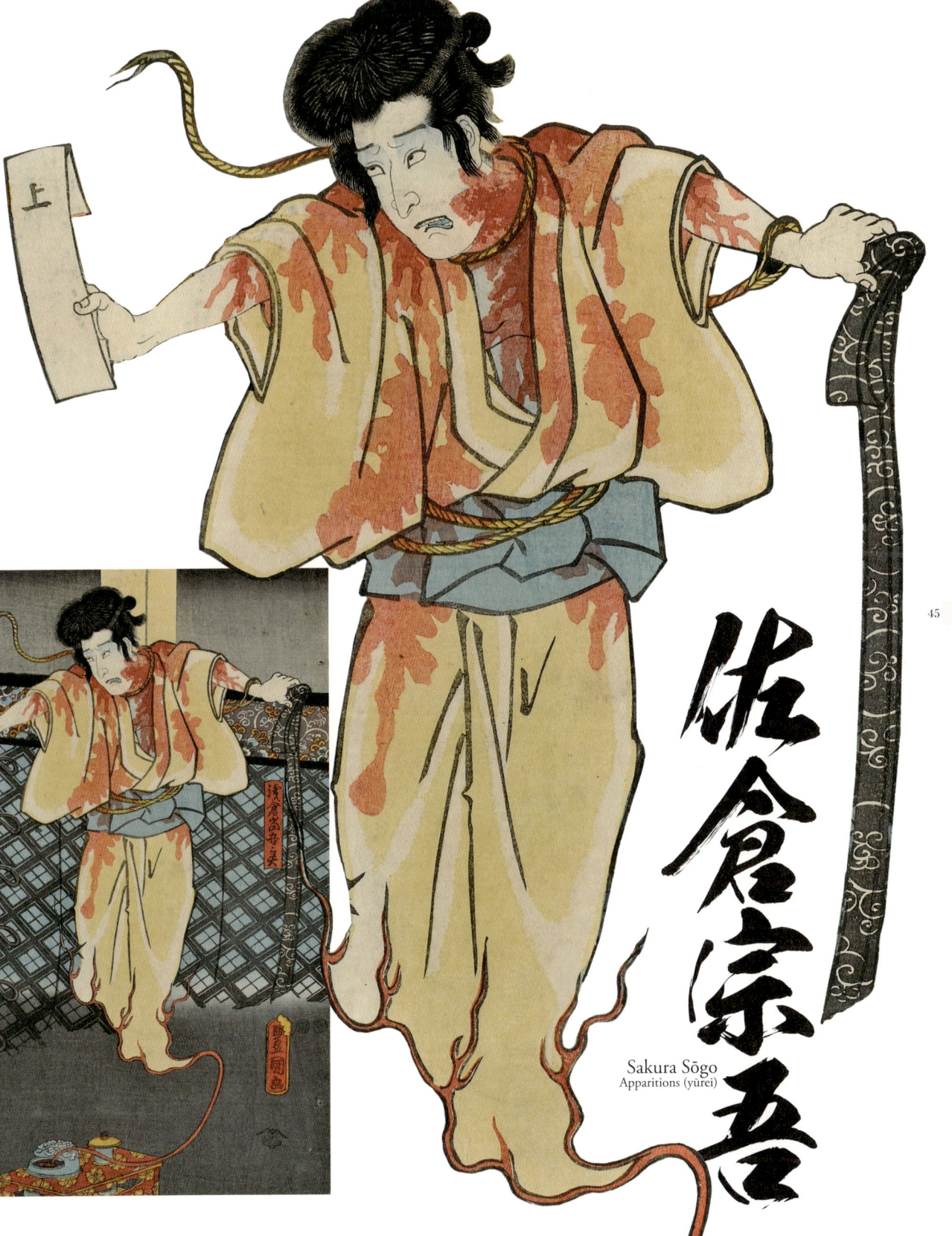

佐倉宗吾

Sakura Sōgo
Apparitions (yūrei)

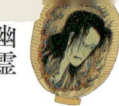

佐倉宗吾の妻

The Wife of Sakura Sōgo
Apparitions (*yūrei*)

46

歌舞伎「佐倉惣吾伝」より、宗吾とともに磔にされた妻の霊。つかみあげられているのは領主堀田家の家臣・山住五平太で、宗吾事件に便乗し、お家乗っ取りを企てる悪臣です。

The ghost of Sōgo's wife, who was crucified along with him, from kabuki play *Sakura Sōgo Den (The Tale of Sakura Sōgo)*. The man she is clutching is Yamazumi Goheida, an evil retainer of the Hotta family, who tried to use the Sōgo incident to seize power.

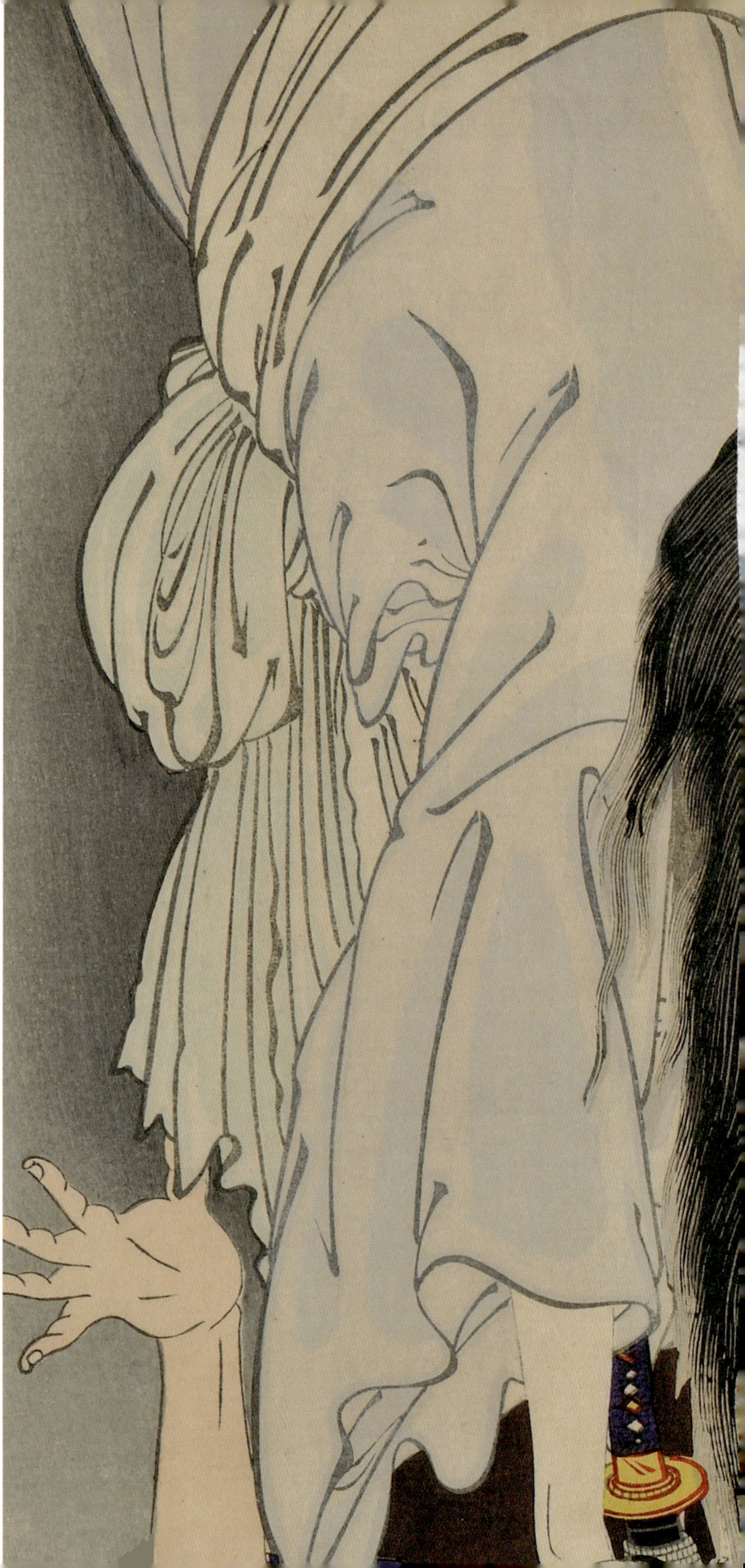

【宗吾妻】豊原国周 明治26年（1893）
Sōgo's Wife by Toyohara Kunichika

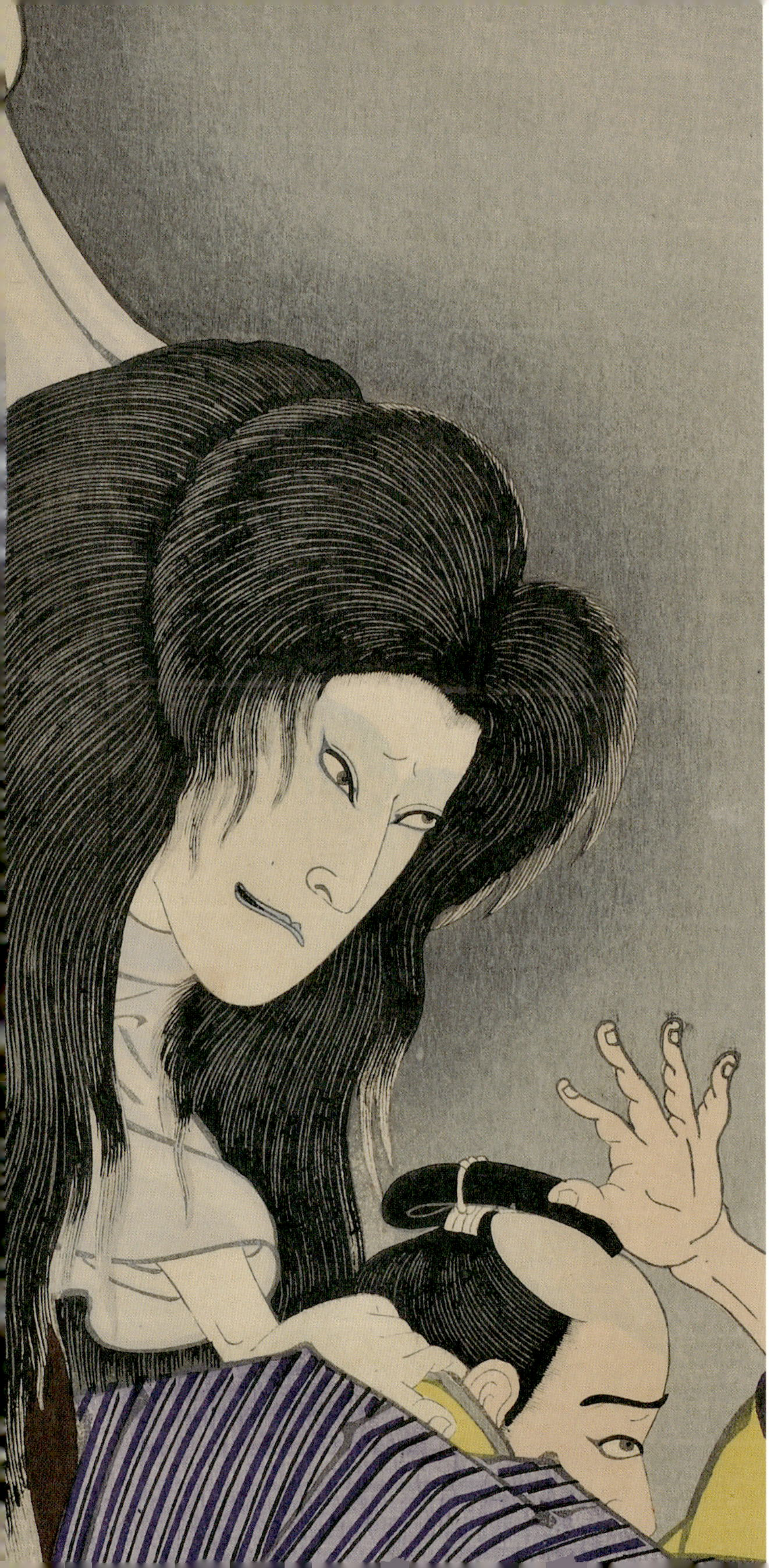

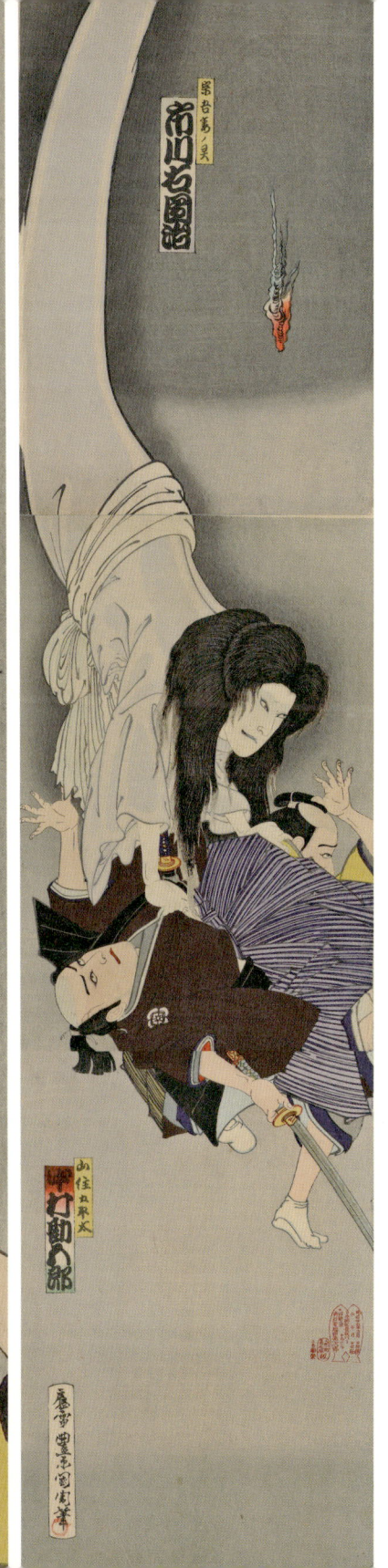

清玄

Seigen
Apparitions (*yūrei*)

清水寺の僧・清玄は、仏教の掟を破って桜姫に恋をしてしまい、寺を追い出されます。ついには桜姫の家来に殺されますが、幽霊になってもなおお姫にしつこくつきまといます。

Kiyomizu temple priest Seigen violates the precepts of Buddhism by falling in love with Princess Sakura, and is expelled from the temple. He is eventually killed by the retainers of Princess Sakura, but even after death continues to stalk her relentlessly as a ghost.

【見立三十六歌撰之内 清玄】
歌川国貞（三代豊国）嘉永5年（1852）
桜を散らす雨風の中、清玄の亡霊が現れました。八代目市川団十郎の役者似顔絵となっています。在原業平の歌「世の中にたえて桜のなかりせば 春の心はのどけからまし」は、もしこの世に桜姫がいなかったら、心穏やかに春を過ごせるだろう、という清玄の心情を表しています。

Seigen from the series *Mitate sanjurokkasen no uchi
(Ghostly Parallels with the Thirty-Six Poets)*
by Utagawa Kunisada (also known as Utagawa Toyokuni III)

A portrait of actor Ichikawa Danjūrō VIII, one of a series of *nise-e* (portrayals of actors), with inspiration from *waka* poems of thirty-six poets selected by Fujiwara no Kintō to represent the essence of Japanese poetry in the Heian period. The poem by Ariwara no Narihira, "If there were no sakura (cherry blossoms) in this world, my heart in spring would be calmer", expresses Seigen's feelings as he muses that if Princess Sakura did not exist, he might be at peace in the springtime.

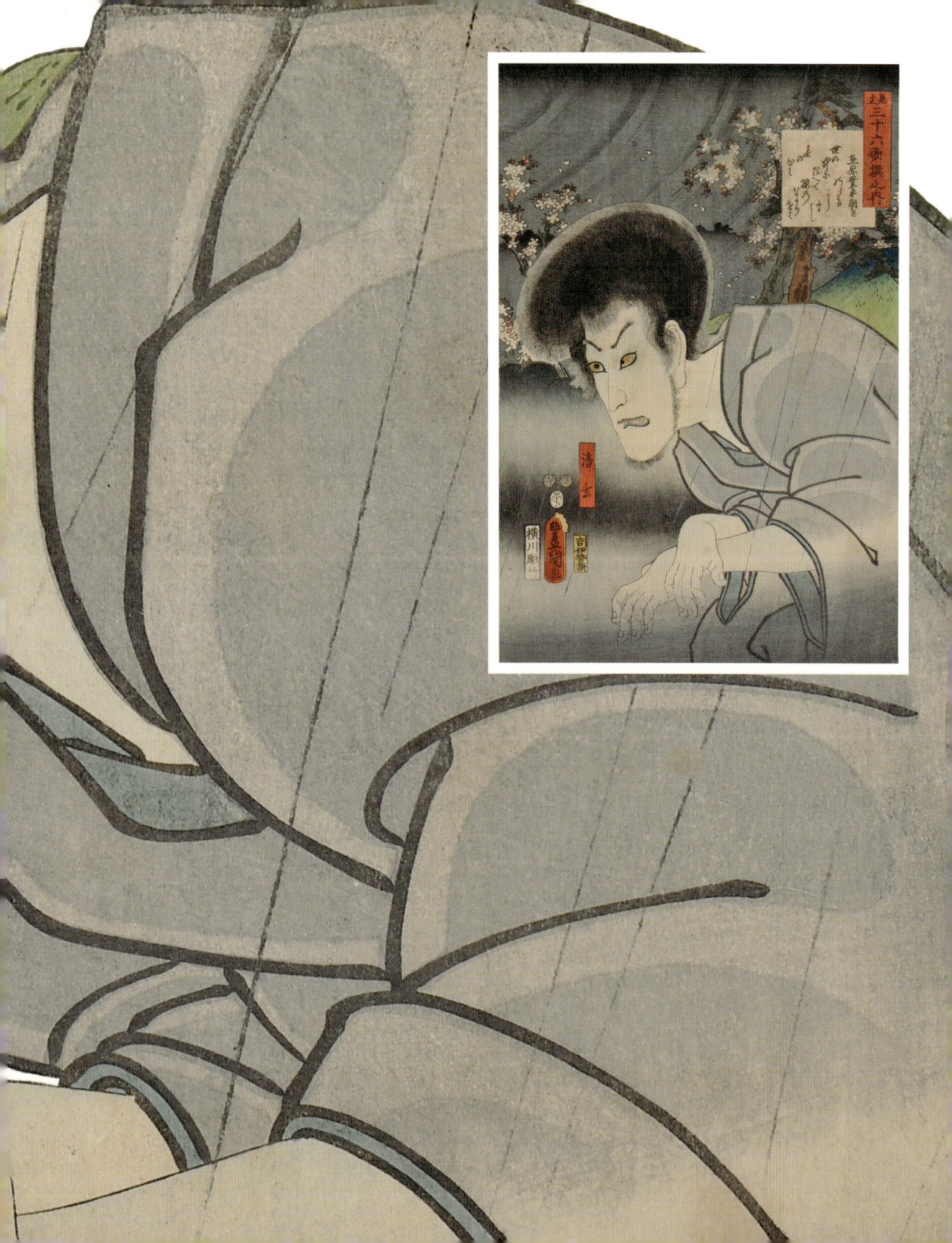

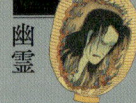

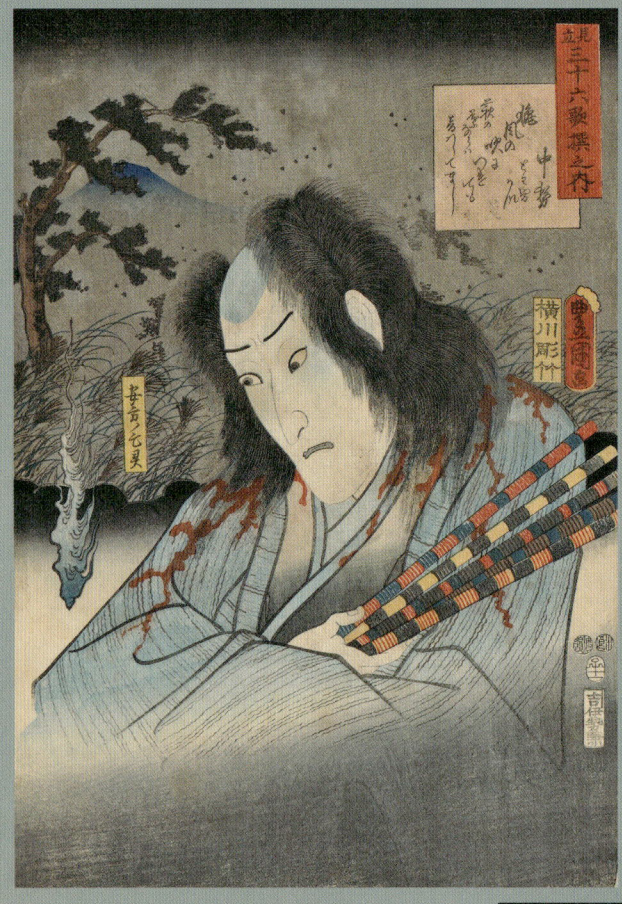

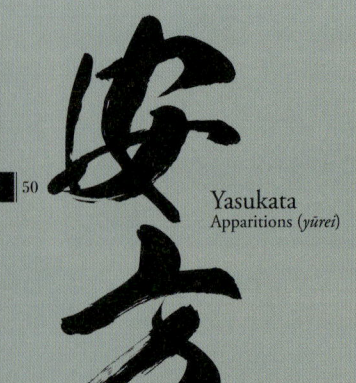

Yasukata
Apparitions (*yūrei*)

読本「善知鳥安方忠義伝」で知られる安方は、平安中期の武将・平将門の忠臣で、死後なお亡霊となって、蜂起を企てる将門の遺児・良門のもとに現れ、やめさせようとします。図は、初代大川橋蔵の役者似顔絵となっています。中務の和歌「秋風の吹につけてもとはぬかな　荻の葉ならば音はしてまし」が添えられます。

Well known through the eponymous *yomihon Utō Yasukata Chūgiden* (*The Loyalty of Utō Yasukata*), Yasukata was a military commander and loyal subject of Taira no Masakado in the mid-Heian period who became a ghost after death, and appeared to Yoshikado, the son of the late Masakado, in an effort to dissuade him from attempting an uprising. This is a portrait of actor Ōkawa Hashizō I. A *waka* poem by Nakatsukasa accompanies the image: "The autumn wind is blowing and still you do not visit, if you were silver-grass at least you would rustle at me."

【見立三十六歌撰之内 安方の亡霊】
歌川国貞（三代豊国）嘉永5年（1852）

The Shade of Yasukata from the series *Mitate sanjurokkasen no uchi* (*Ghostly Parallels with the Thirty-Six Poets*) by Utagawa Kunisada (also known as Utagawa Toyokuni III)

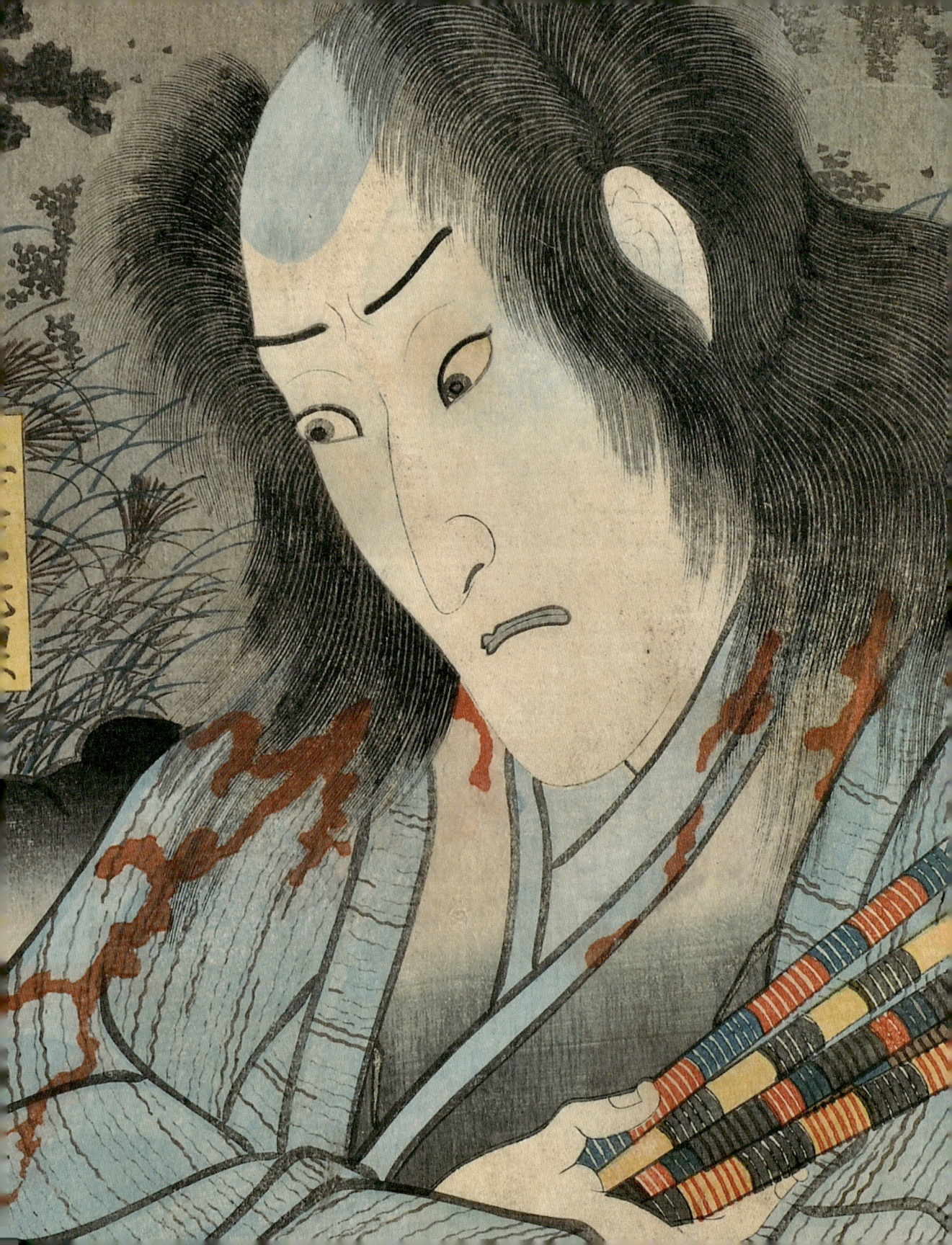

鎌田又八と菊野

Kamada Matahachi and Kikuno
Apparitions (*yūrei*)

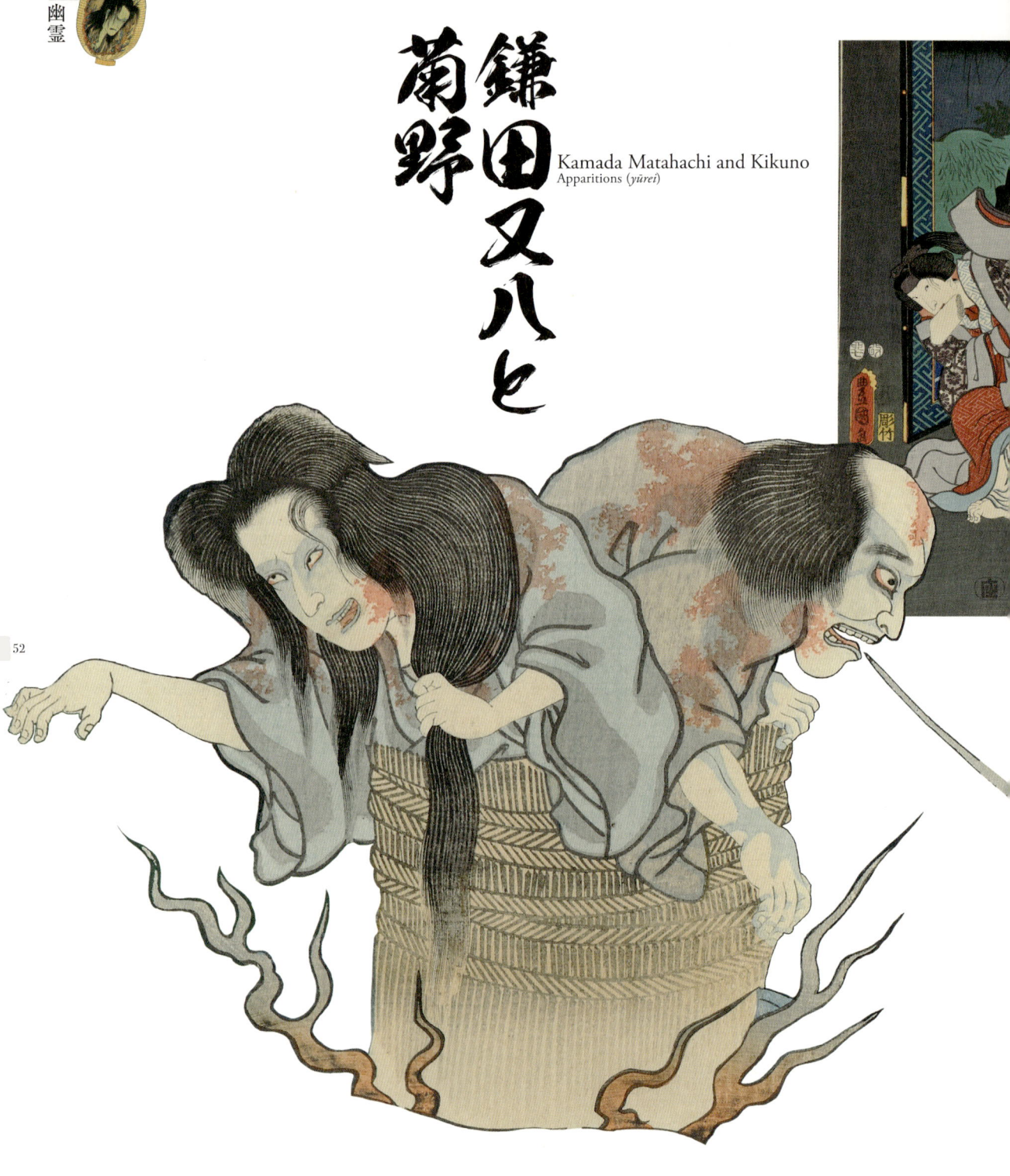

52

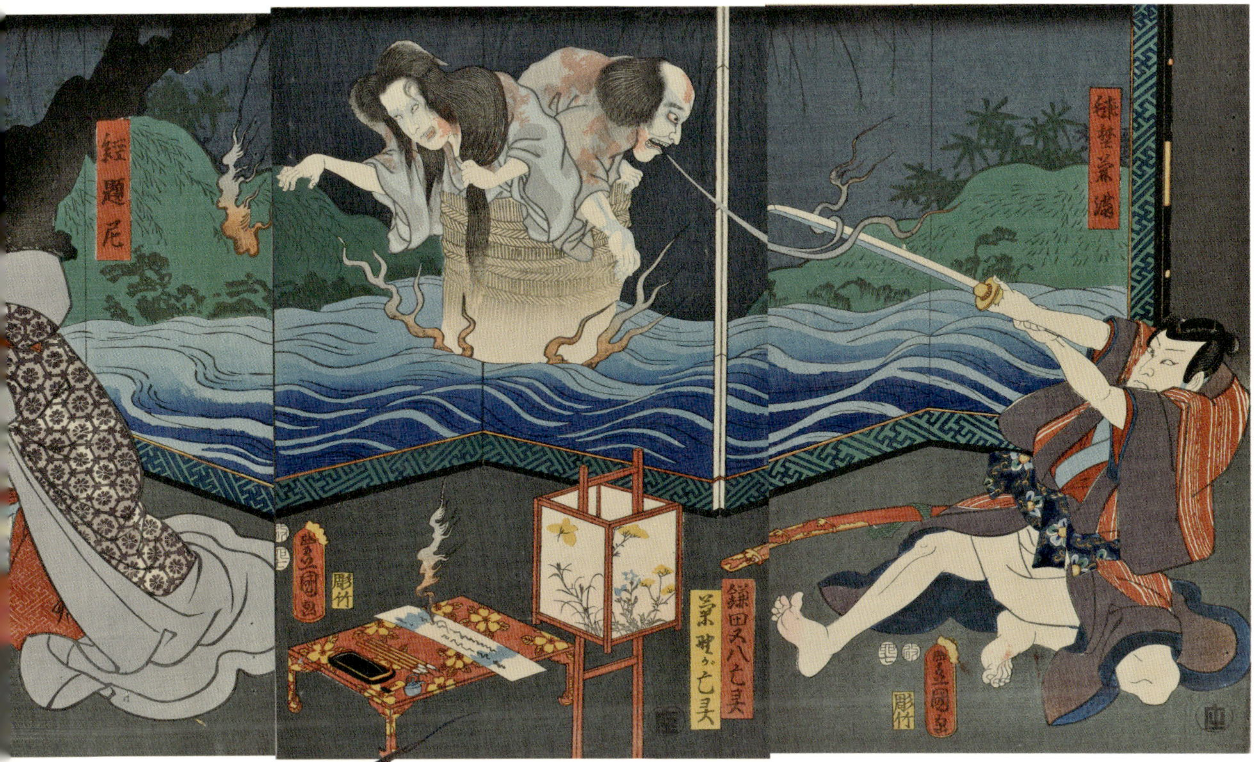

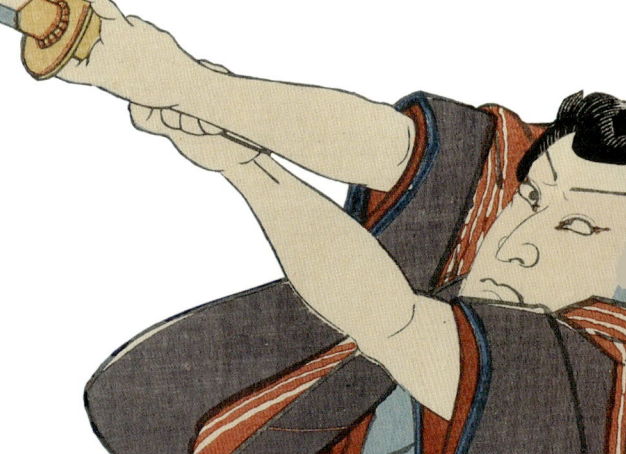

【鎌田又八亡霊と菊野亡霊】
歌川国貞（三代豊国） 安政2年（1855）

The Ghosts of Kamada Matahachi and Kikuno
by Utagawa Kunisada
(also known as Utagawa Toyokuni III)

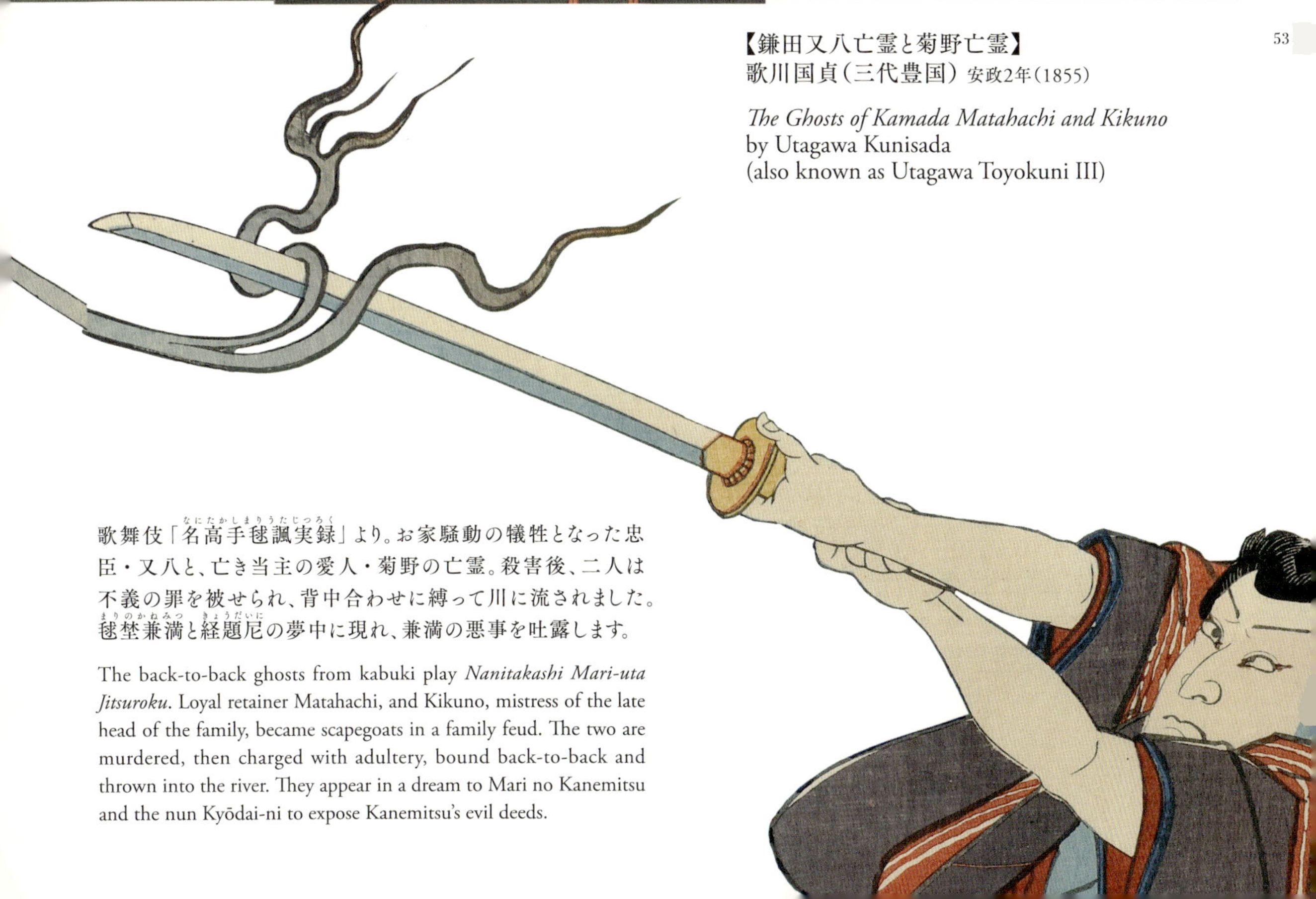

歌舞伎「名高手毬諷実録」より。お家騒動の犠牲となった忠
臣・又八と、亡き当主の愛人・菊野の亡霊。殺害後、二人は
不義の罪を被せられ、背中合わせに縛って川に流されました。
毬埓兼満と経題尼の夢中に現れ、兼満の悪事を吐露します。

The back-to-back ghosts from kabuki play *Nanitakashi Mari-uta
Jitsuroku*. Loyal retainer Matahachi, and Kikuno, mistress of the late
head of the family, became scapegoats in a family feud. The two are
murdered, then charged with adultery, bound back-to-back and
thrown into the river. They appear in a dream to Mari no Kanemitsu
and the nun Kyōdai-ni to expose Kanemitsu's evil deeds.

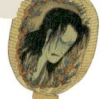

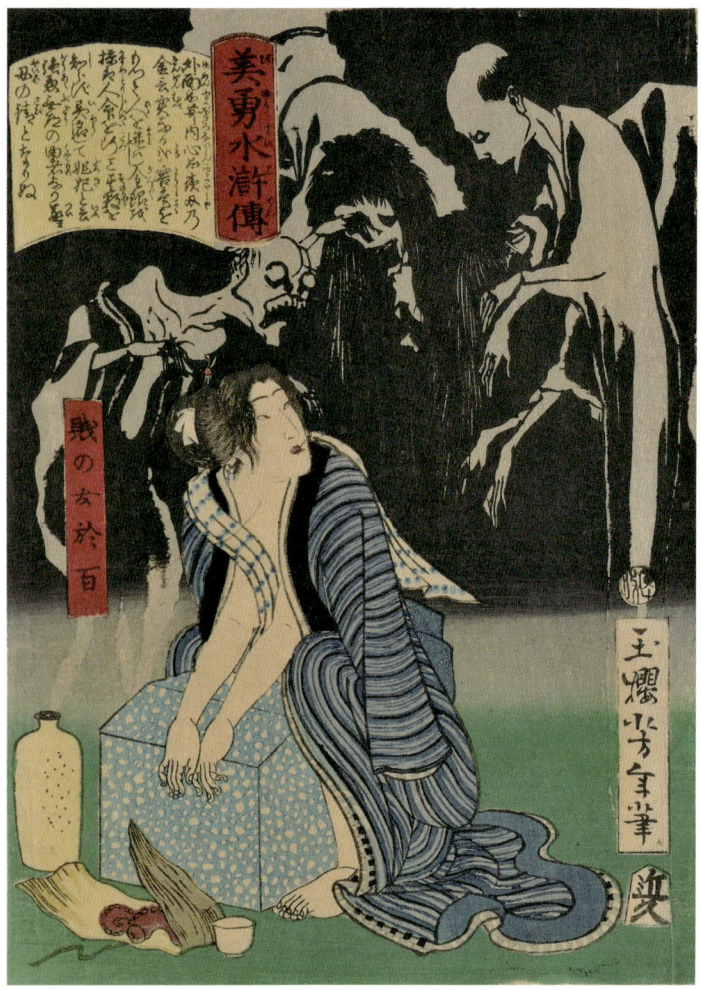

於百は京都祇園の遊女で、鴻池の愛人となったのち、度々
主人や旦那を変えました。やがて秋田藩の悪臣・中川
采女の愛人となり、悪女ぶりを発揮します。背後には於百の
犠牲になった男たちの亡霊がうごめいています。

Ohyaku is a courtesan in Gion, Kyoto, who after becoming the
lover of Kōnoike, uses her feminine wiles to social climb
through a string of increasingly higher-ranked husbands and
lovers. The story goes that when she eventually becomes the
lover of Nakagawa Uneme, evil retainer of the Akita Domain,
her cruelty is given full rein. In the background, the ghosts of
the men who became Ohyaku's victims are writhing.

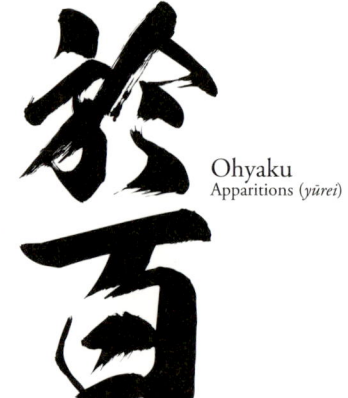

Ohyaku
Apparitions (*yūrei*)

【美勇水滸傳・賤の女於百】月岡芳年 慶応2年（1866）

Shizunome Ohyaku from the series *Biyū Suikoden (Sagas of Beauty and Bravery)*
by Tsukioka Yoshitoshi

54

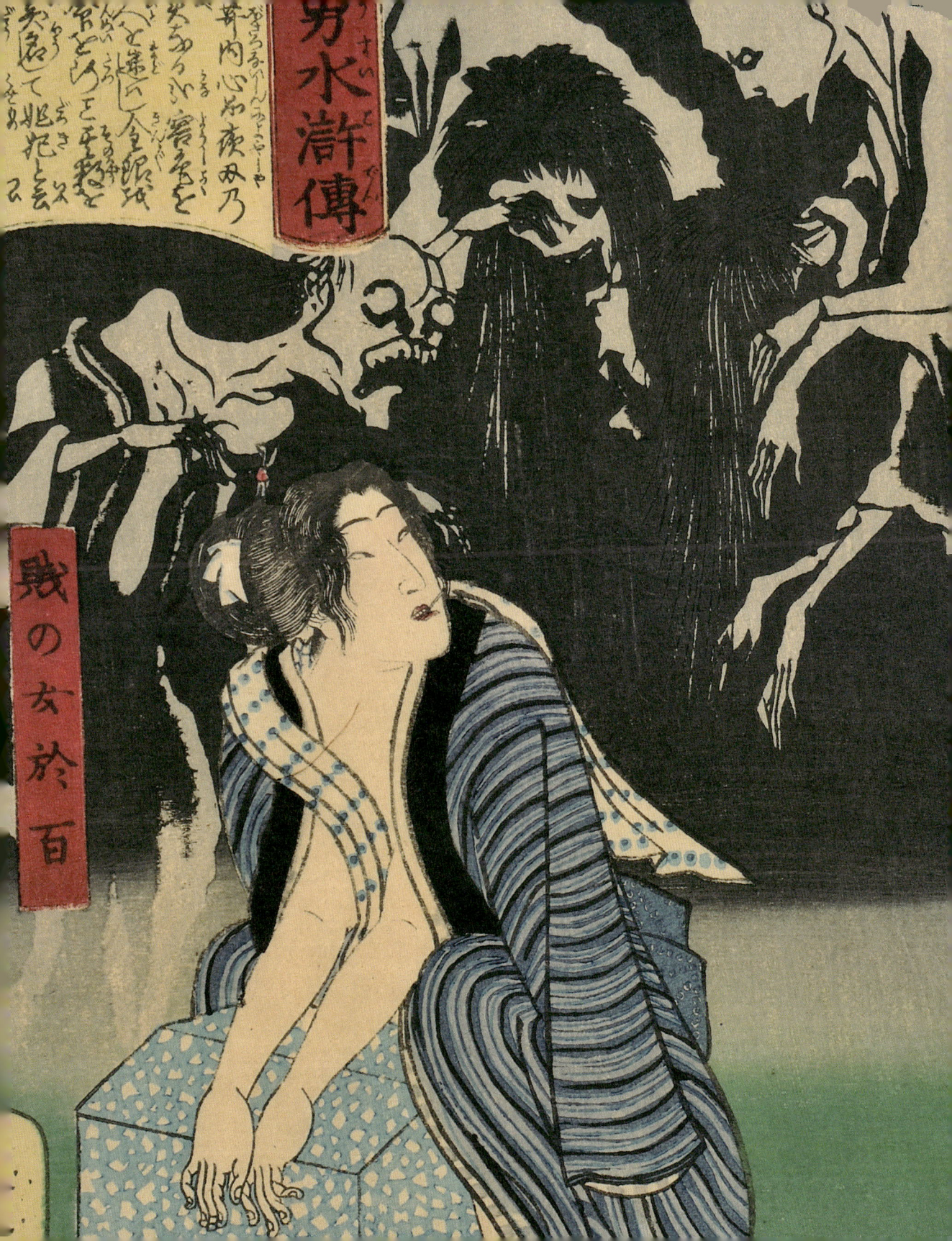

賊
の
女
於
百

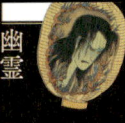

幽
霊

幽霊

Yūrei
Apparitions (*yūrei*)

この世に恨みを残した死者が、霊となって再び現れ出る姿を幽霊といいます。その幽霊も江戸時代になると、歌舞伎や落語に登場し、幽霊をテーマにした浮世絵も競って制作されました。。

Yūrei are apparitions of the dead who still hold a grudge against the living world, and become ghosts to rise again. In the Edo period, these apparitions featured in plays and *rakugo* (comedy), and there was a competitive market for *yūrei*-themed *ukiyo-e*.

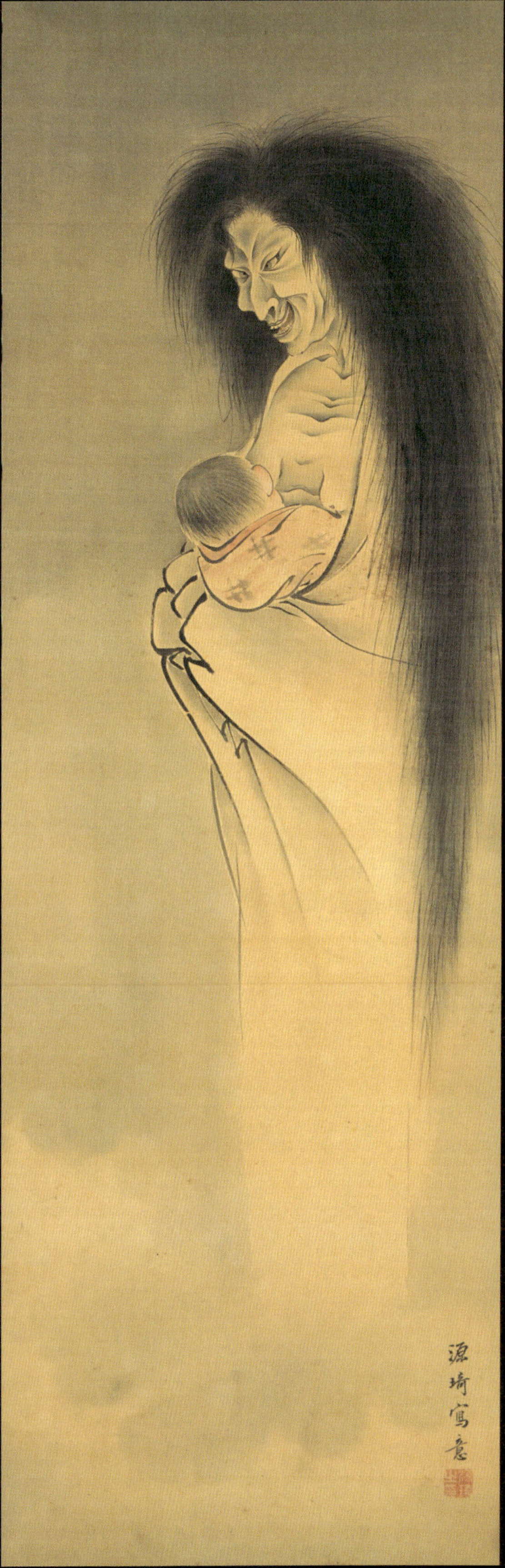

【子持ち幽霊】駒井源琦 江戸時代後期

口が裂けそうなほど、にたりと笑う女の幽霊。その吊り上がった目尻、曲がった鼻筋、角張った頬骨、乱れた髪は、子供を取って喰う鬼婆のように見えます。あるいは、お乳を吸わせるように赤ん坊を抱いていることから、「産女」と呼ばれる難産で亡くなった幽霊でしょうか。

Apparition with Child
by Komai Genki (late 18th century)

A ghost who grins so widely, it looks like her mouth could rip apart. With fierce eyes, a crooked nose, angular cheekbones, and wild hair, she could be a hag who steals children to eat. Alternatively, judging by the way she cradles a baby as if to breastfeed, she could be the ghost of a woman who died in childbirth, known as the Ubume.

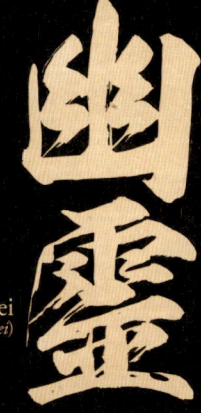

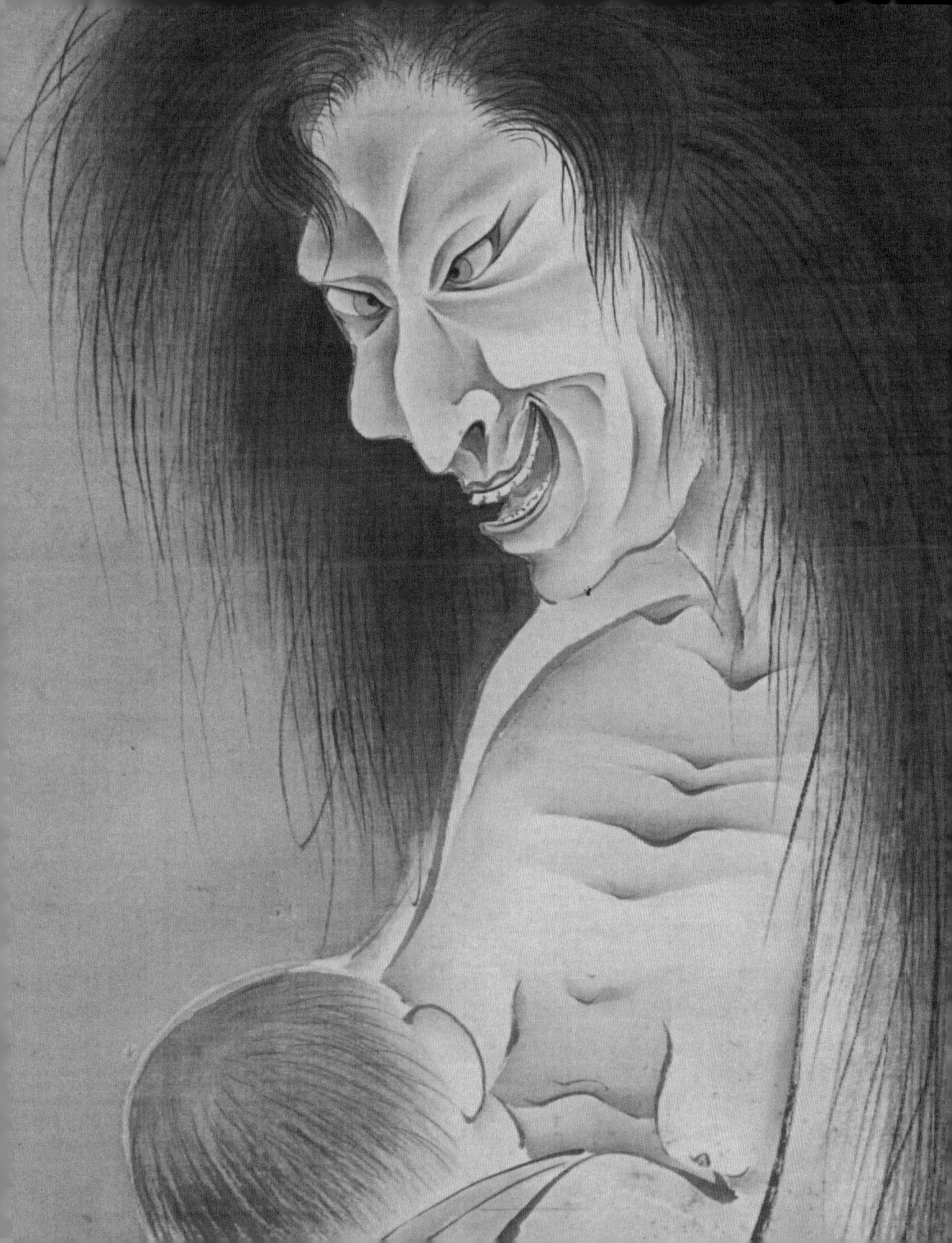

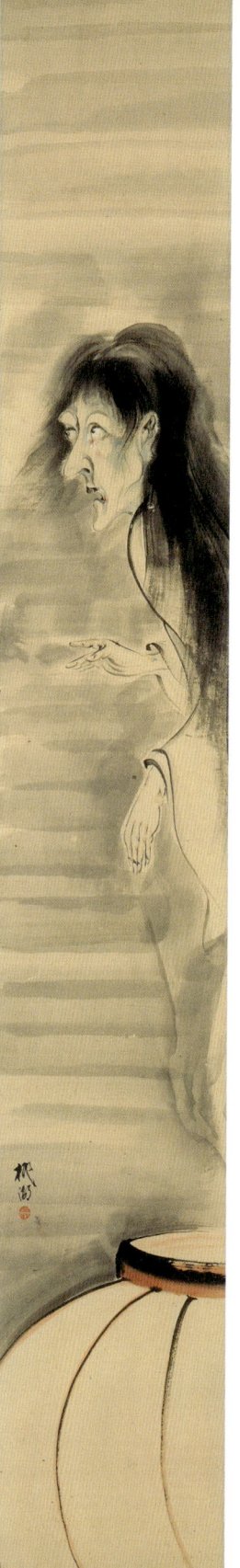

【あんどんに幽霊】桃湖 明治時代

あんどんに照らし出され、ぼんやりと闇夜に浮かぶ
女の幽霊。目と口から血を垂れ流し、驚いたような
表情を見せています。その視線の先には、恨めしい
相手がいるのでしょうか。

Ghost in the Lamp by Tōko
(late 19th century – early 20th century)

Lit by the lamp, the ghost of a woman hovers hazily in
the dark night. Her face shows her surprise, as the
blood drains from her eyes and mouth. Her eyes are
fixed on the object of her undying hatred.

【男の幽霊】無款 明治時代
Male Ghost by Anonymous
(late 19th century – early 20th century)

【女の幽霊】無款 明治時代
Female Ghost by Anonymous
(late 19th century – early 20th century)

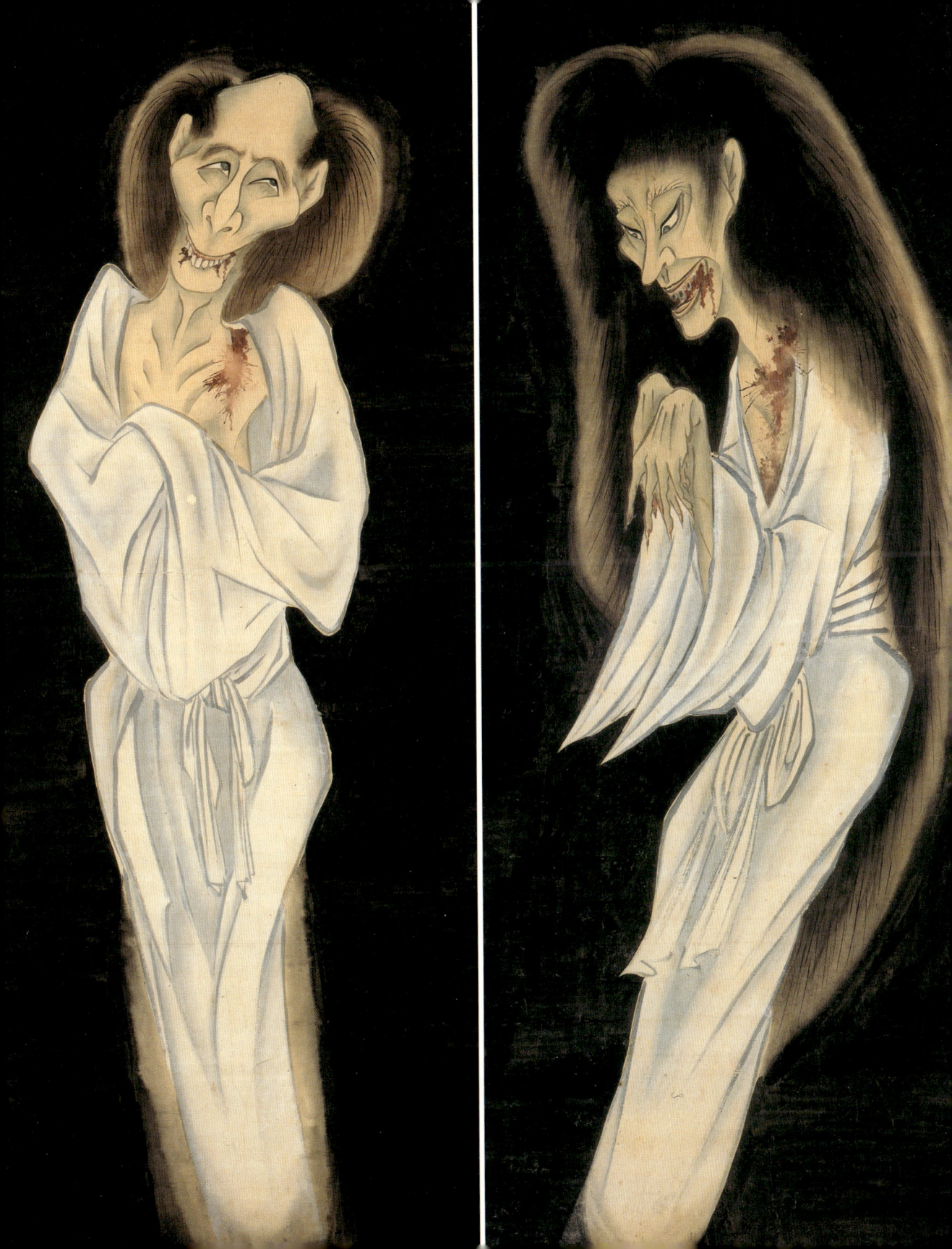

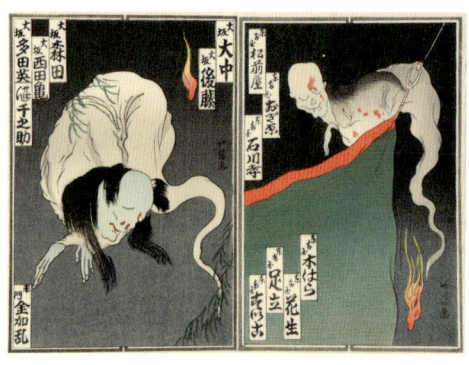

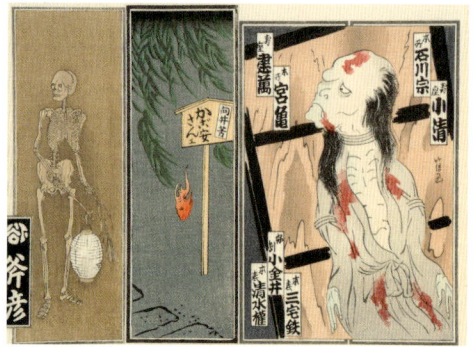

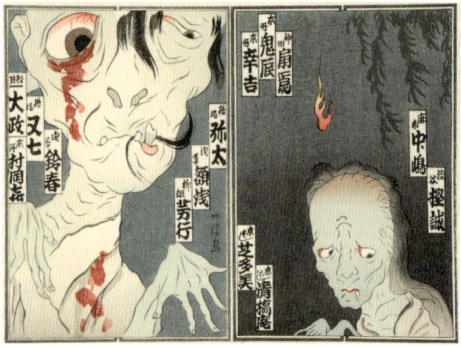

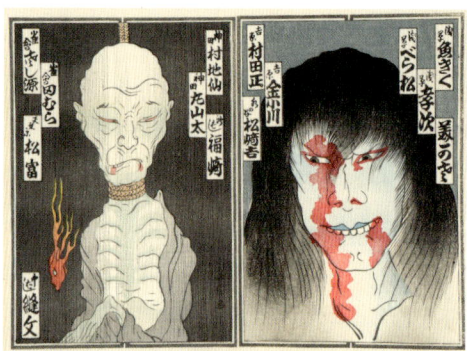

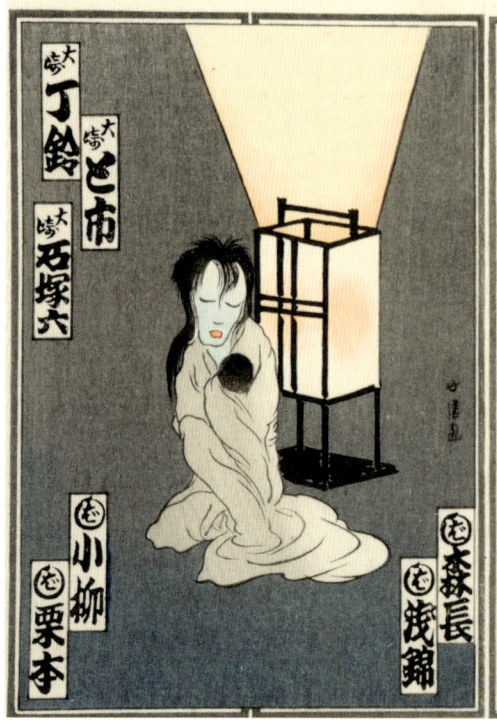

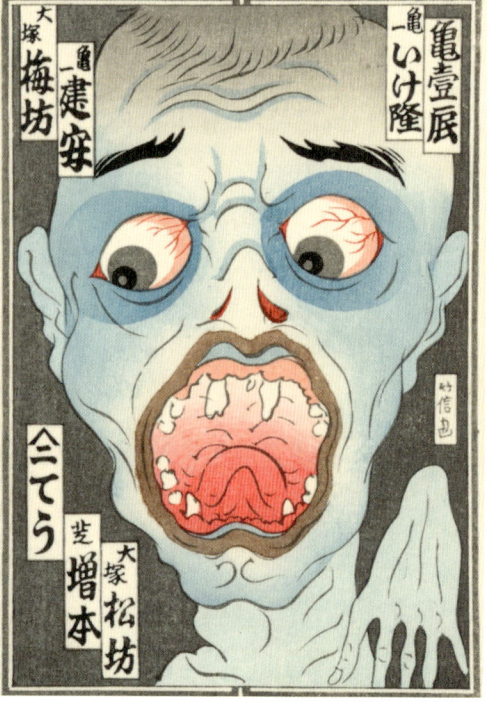

【納札會幽霊集】竹信 大正11年（1922）7月4日 　版元：美登里連

社寺に参詣した際に記念として収める納札は、次第に美的工夫が凝らされるようになり、趣味を共有する者同士での交換が
流行しました。本作品は、幽霊尽くしの納札画帖で、画中には「連」と呼ばれる同好仲間の名前が札形に記されています。

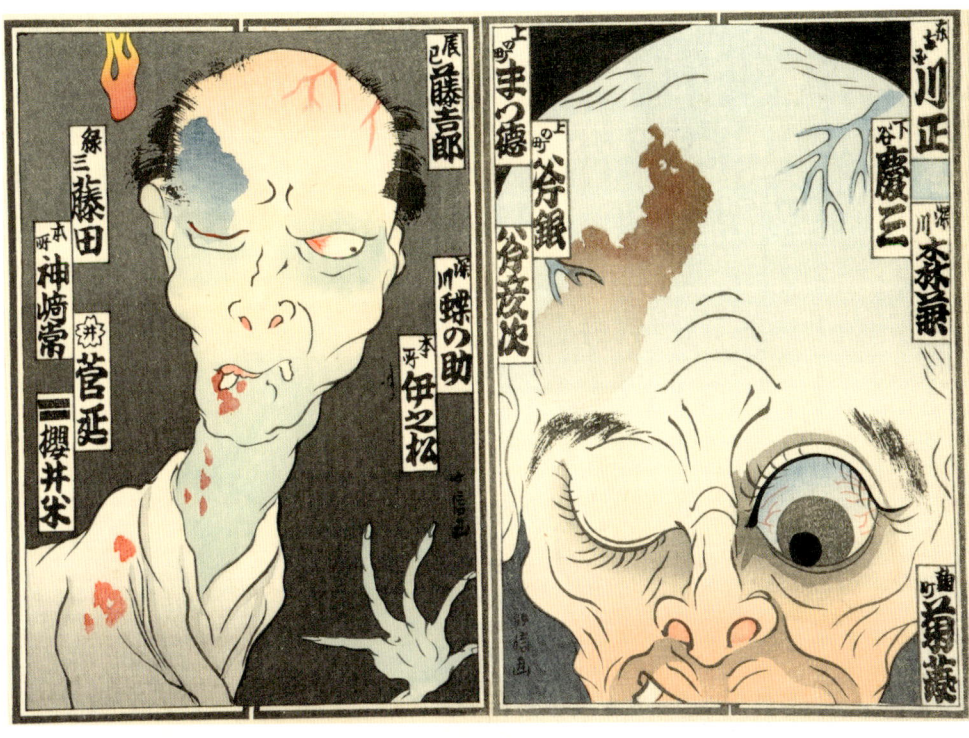

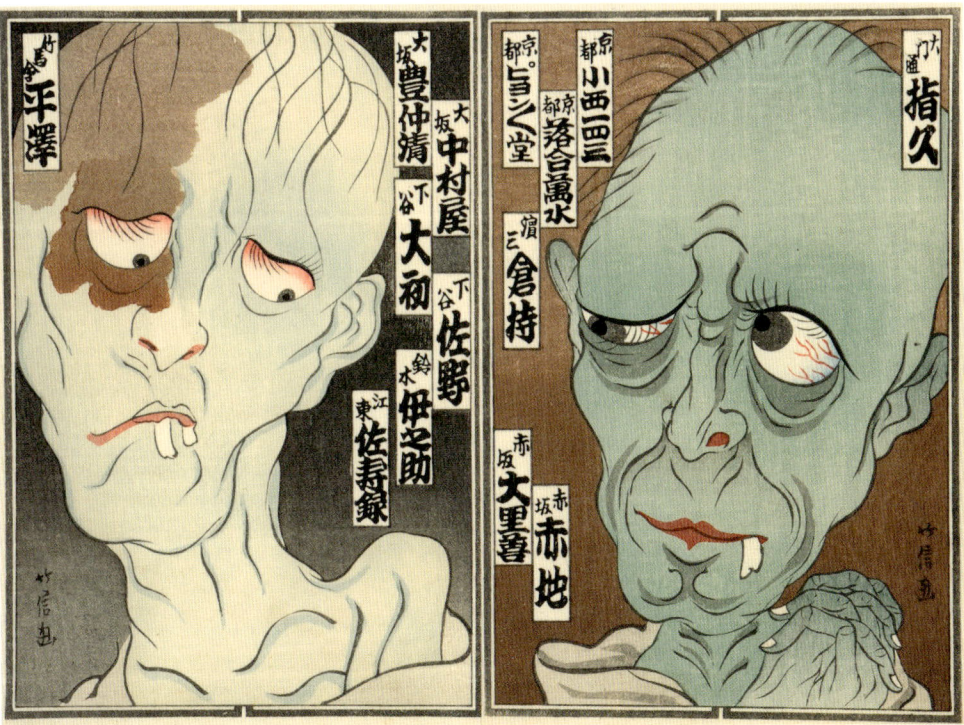

Ghostly Collection of Votive Cards by Takenobu

Votive cards (*nōsatsu*) were kept as remembrances of visits to shrines or temples, gradually becoming more attractively designed, and trading cards became popular with collectors. This work is a book of cards dedicated to apparitions (*yūrei*), and the names of groups of collectors (*ren*) are written in the pictures on the cards.

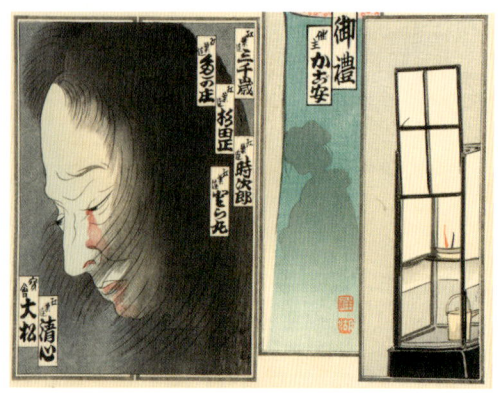

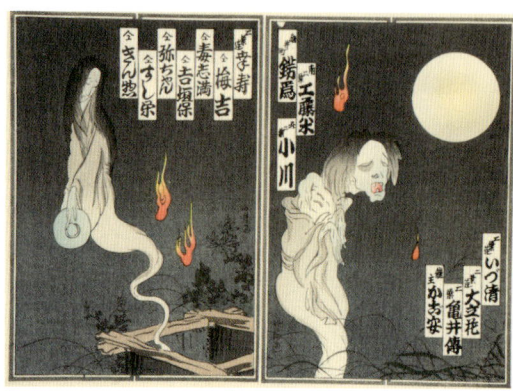

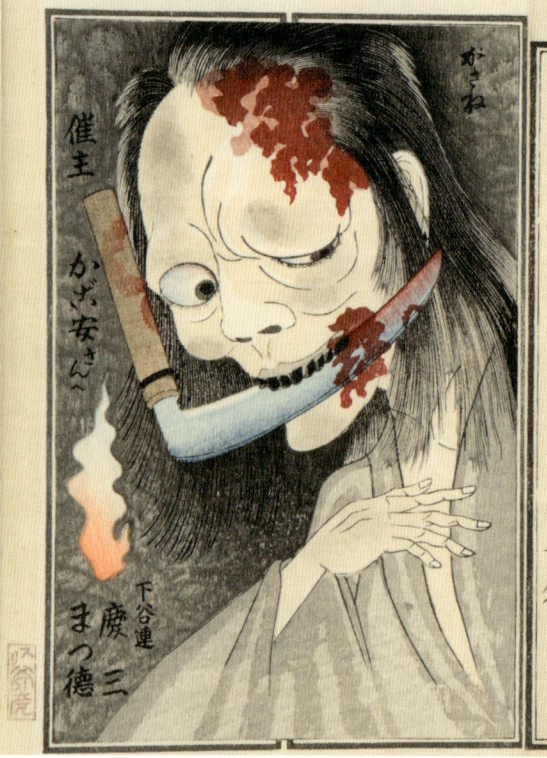

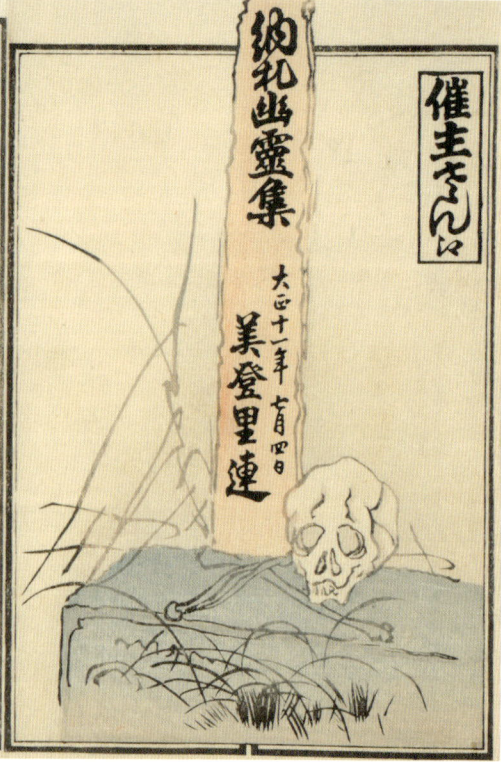

62

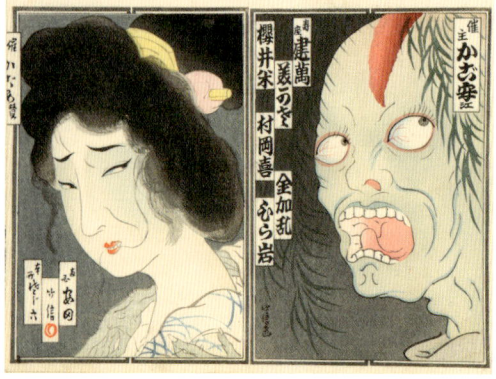

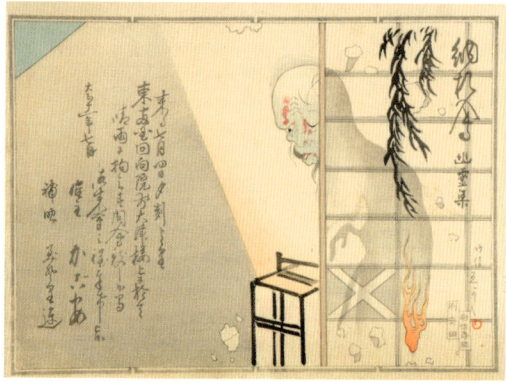

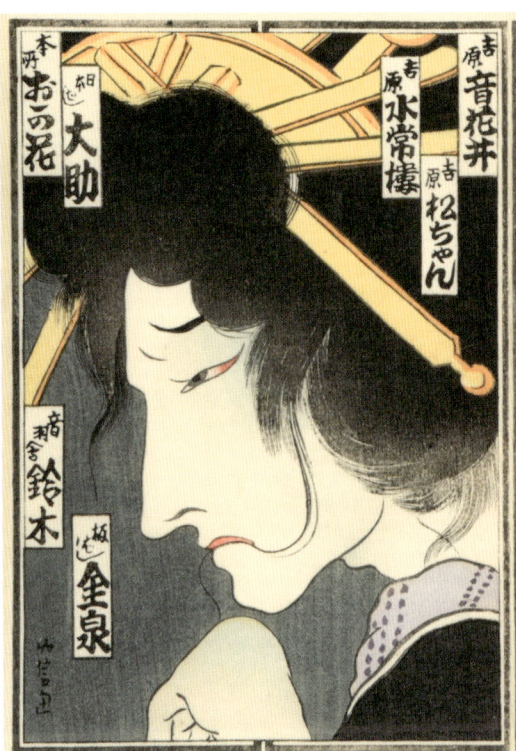

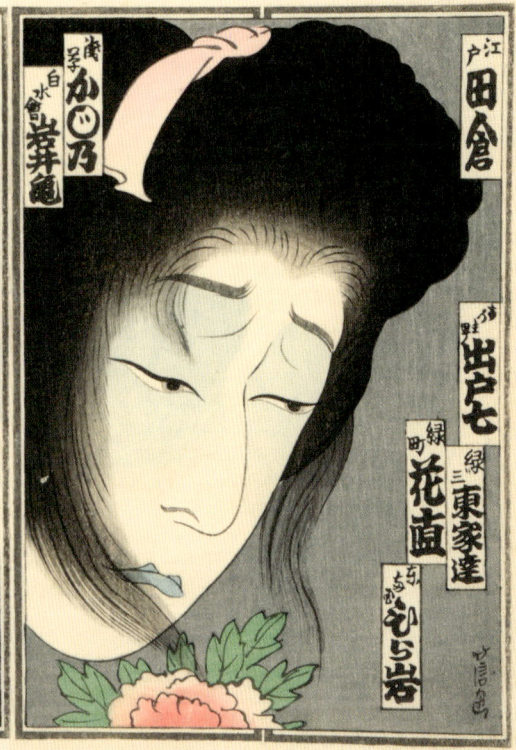

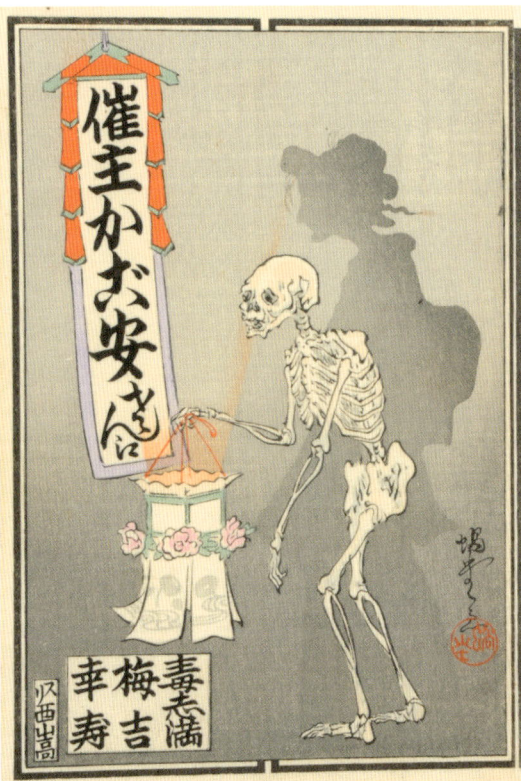

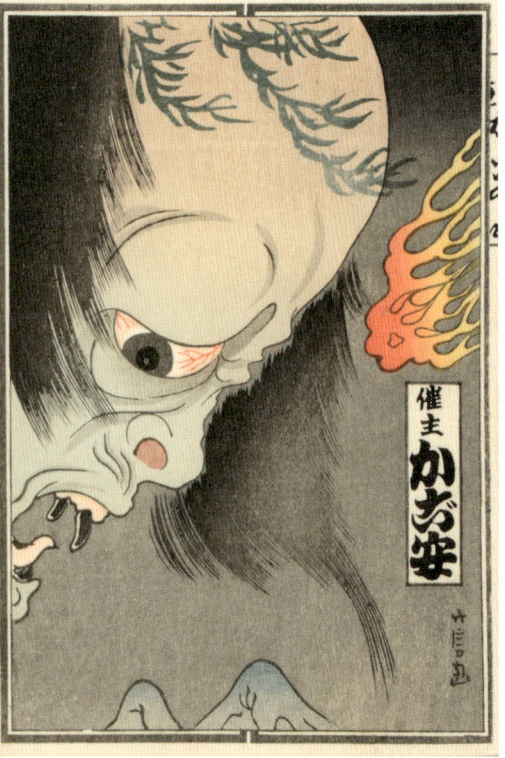

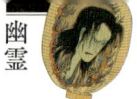
地獄太夫

Jigoku Dayū
Apparitions (*yūrei*)

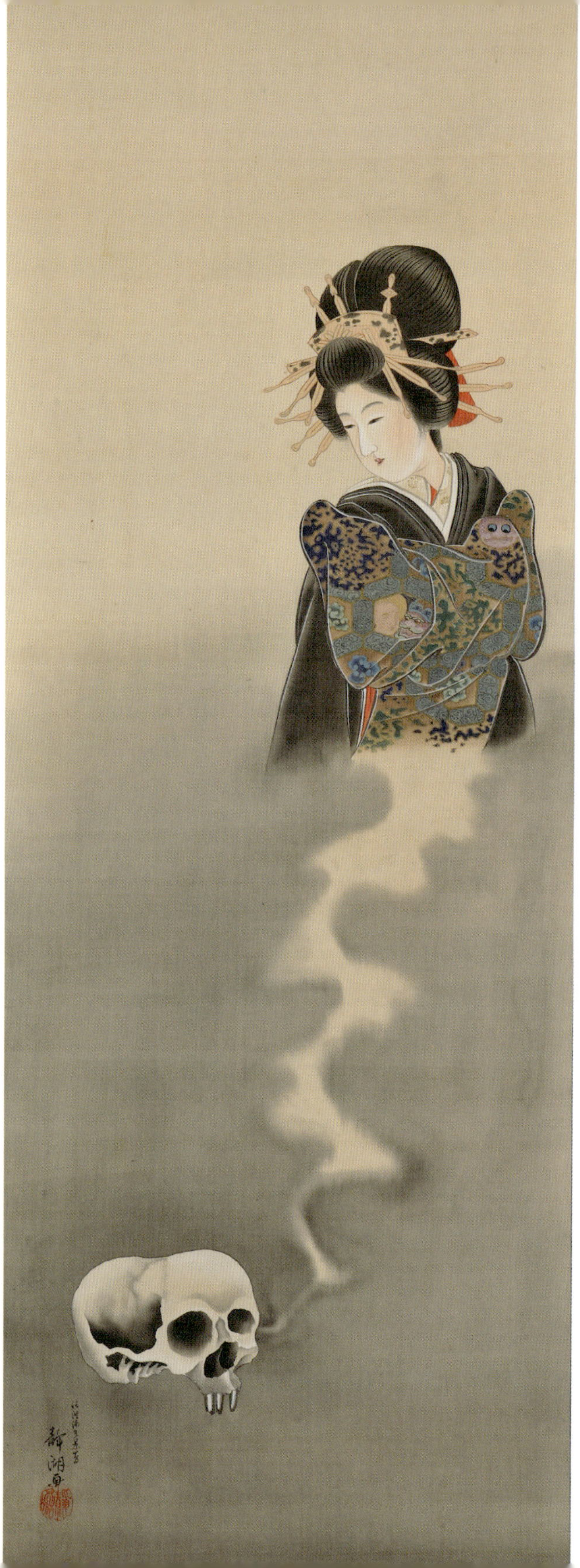

髑髏から一筋の煙とともに現れた美人。室町時代、和泉国堺の高須遊郭にいた遊女、地獄太夫である。一休禅師が訪れた際に、「聞きしより見て恐ろしき地獄かな」と詠んだところ、「しにくる人の落ちざるは無し」と返したという。太夫の帯には地蔵菩薩と閻魔大王の模様が施される。

A beautiful woman who materializes out of a waft of smoke from a skull. Jigoku Dayū was a courtesan in the Takasu pleasure quarters of Sakai, Izumi Province, in the Muromachi period. When Zen monk Ikkyū visited her, he composed the following verse, "A more terrifyingly enticing vision of hell than rumor tells", and she replied, "No souls who come to me escape damnation." Jizō Bosatsu (Ksitigarbha, the bodhisattva of hell-beings and deceased children) and the King of Hell are printed on the *obi* sash of the *tayū* (the highest rank of courtesan).

【地獄太夫図】静湖 明治時代中期
Jigoku Dayū by Seiko (End of 19th century)

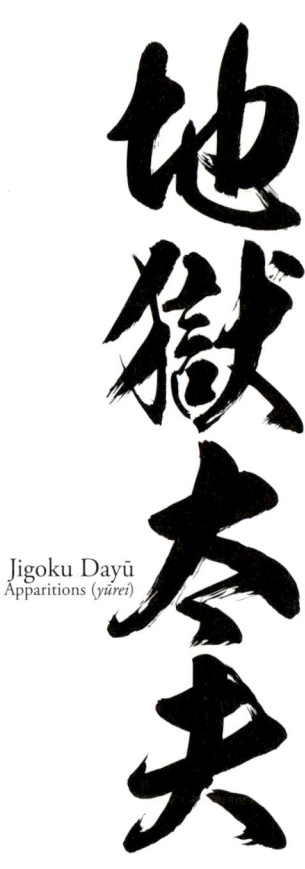

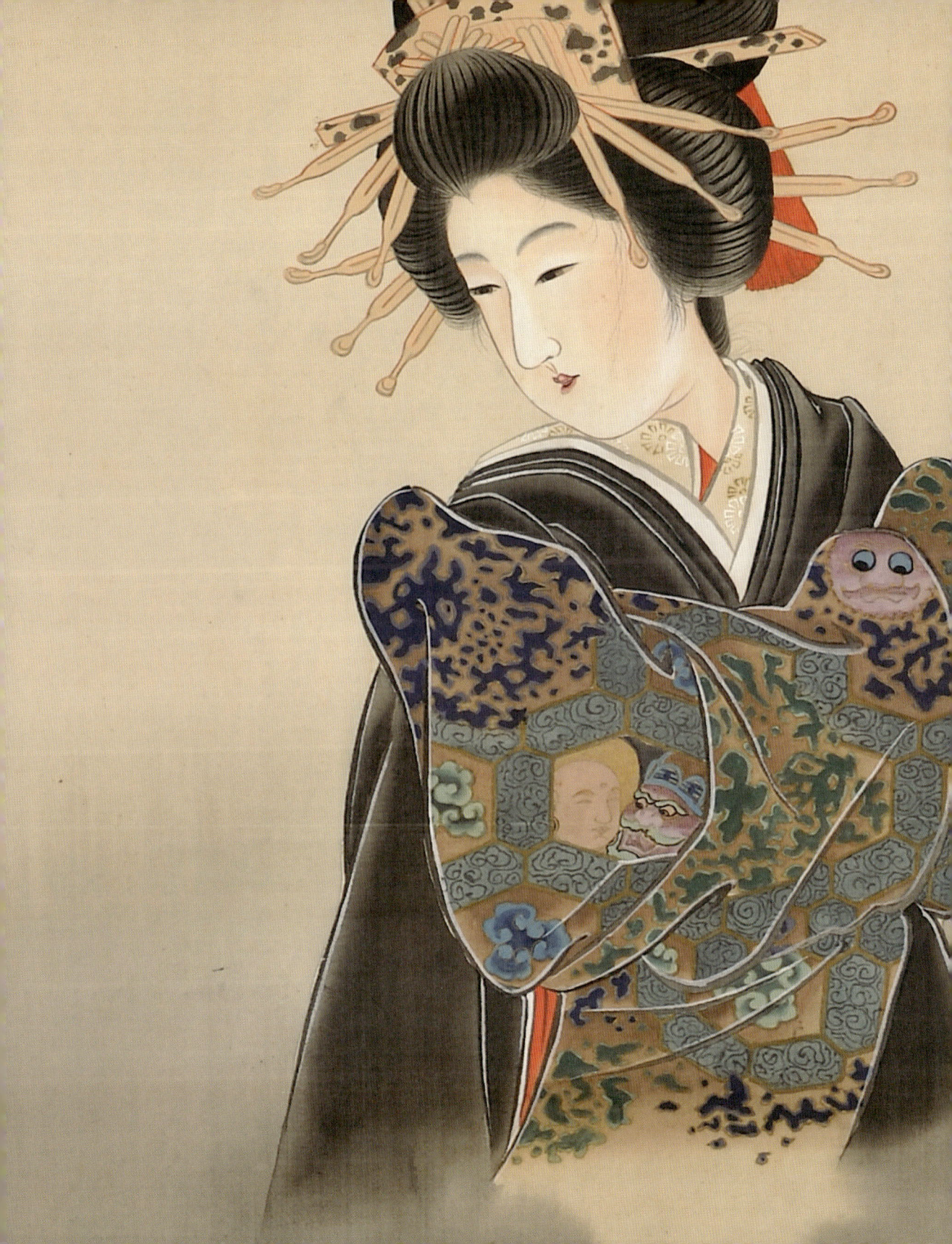

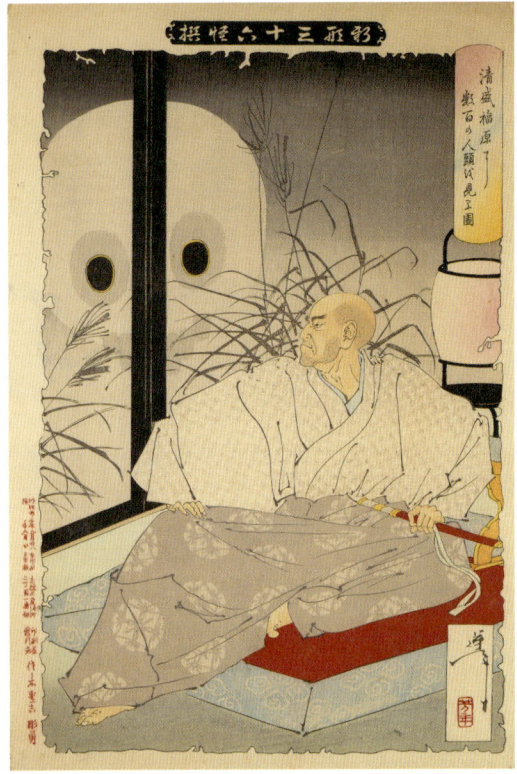

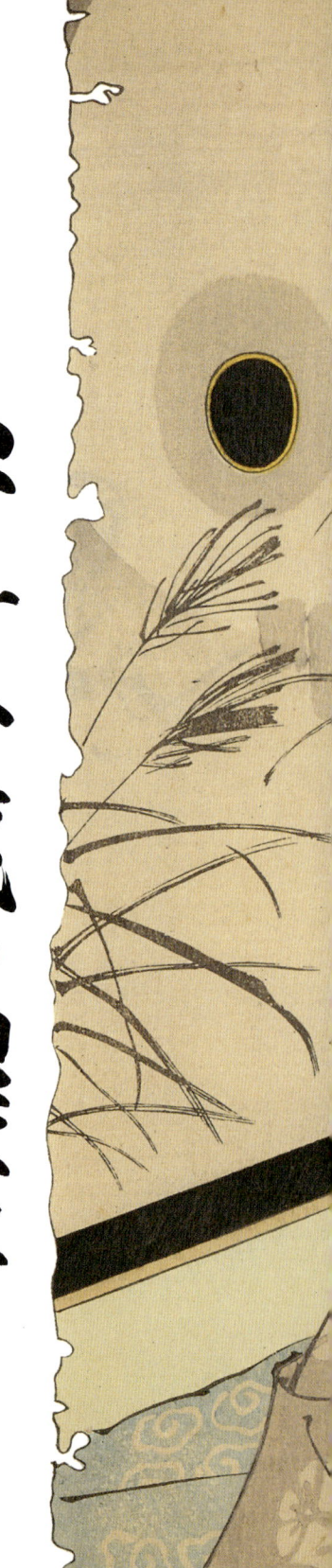

Vengeful Spirits of the Genpei War
Onryō (Vengeful Spirits)

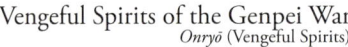

今から約830年前の平安時代の終わりに、平氏と源氏が政権をめぐって争った「源平合戦」にまつわる怪奇伝説の数々を紹介します。平清盛を恨む源氏の怨念が祟ったのか、清盛は熱病に倒れました。やがて、栄華を誇った平氏も力を失い、ついには源氏に滅ぼされてしまいました。そして次は、その平氏の怨霊たちが源氏を襲いました。

More than 830 years ago at the end of the Heian period, the Taira (also known as Heike, lit. House of Taira) and Minamoto (Genji) clans battled for power in the Genpei War, a conflict around which many grotesque legends arose. Taira no Kiyomori was felled by a fever, which was attributed to a Minamoto curse from beyond the grave. At the height of their prosperity the Taira lost their power, and were crushed by the Minamoto. Finally, the vengeful spirits of the dead Taira warriors attacked the Minamoto.

【新形三十六怪撰 清盛福原に数百の人頭を見る】
月岡芳年 明治23年(1890)
平清盛が福原に遷都した際、不思議な現象が次々と起こります。清盛が寝ていると、襖に髑髏の顔がぼんやりと現れました。

Kiyomori Sees Hundreds of Skulls at Fukuhara from the series
Shinkei sanjūrokkaisen (New Forms of Thirty-Six Ghosts) by Tsukioka Yoshitoshi
After Taira no Kiyomori relocates the capital to Fukuhara, mysterious phenomena begin to occur in quick succession. Kiyomori is sleeping when a skull appears mistily on the sliding door.

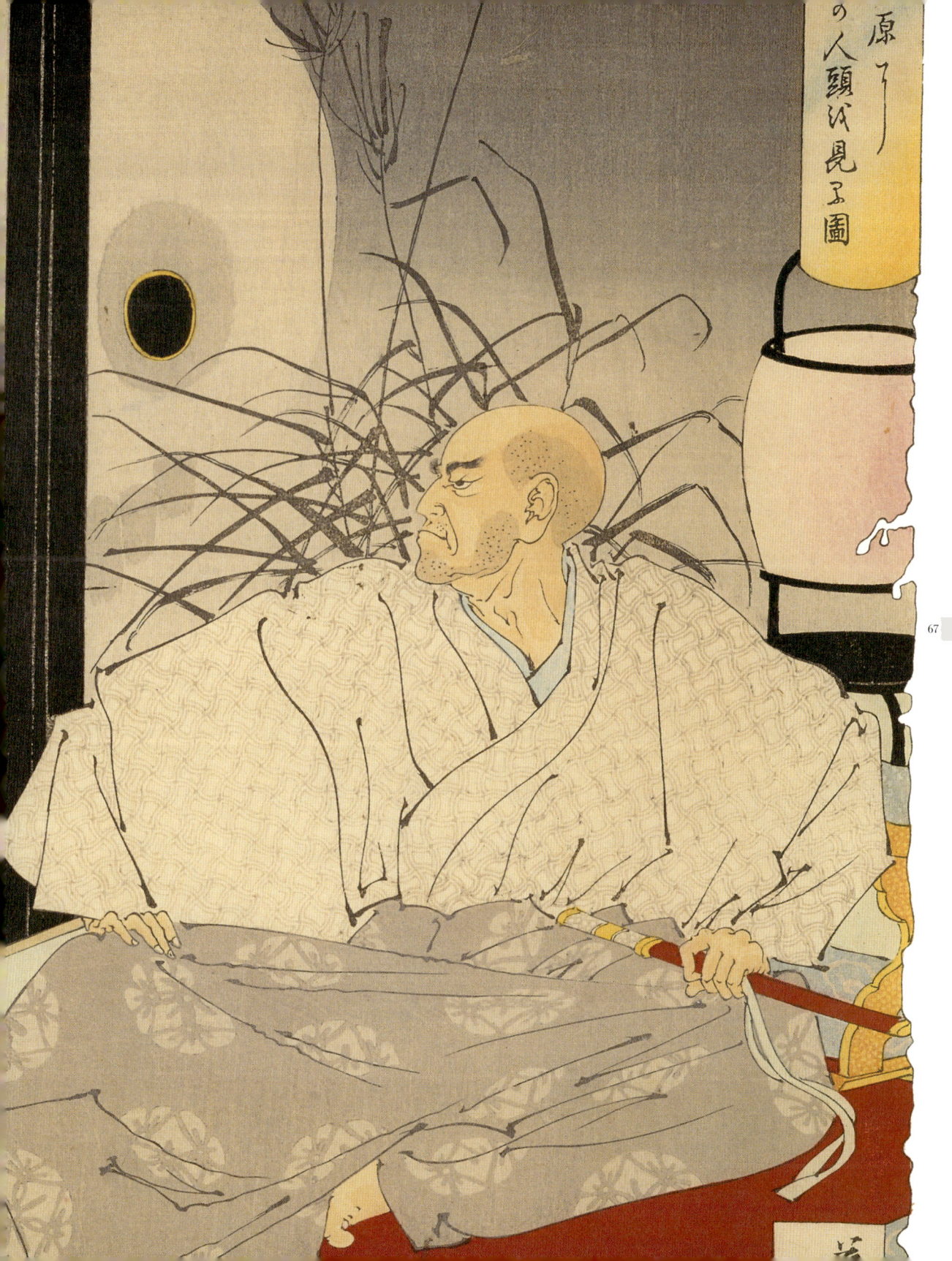

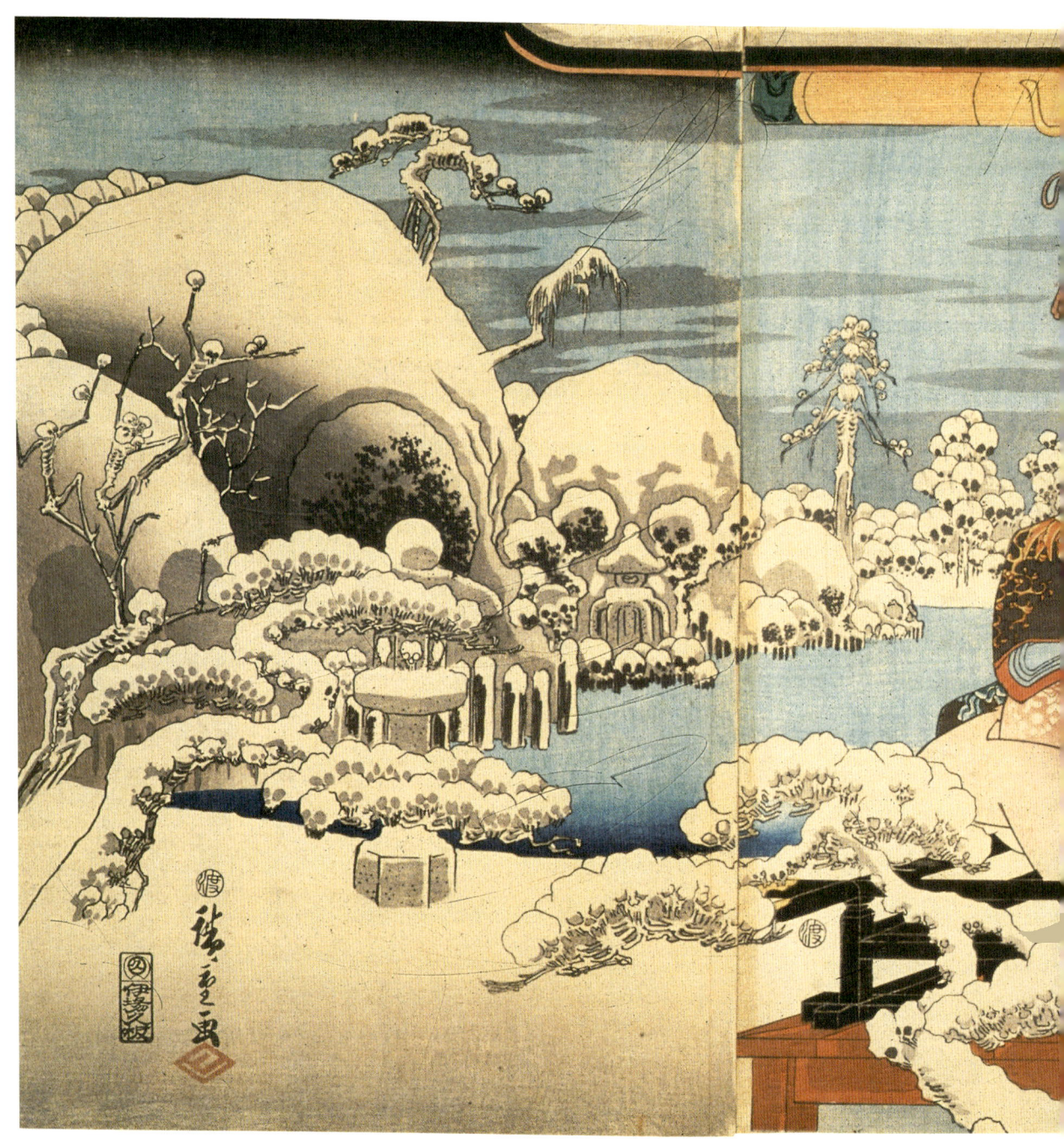

【平清盛怪異を見る図】歌川広重　天保14年〜弘化4年（1843-47）
雪の庭のあちこちから骸骨が現れ、清盛をじっと見つめます。清盛が睨み返すと、ゆっくり消えていったそうです。

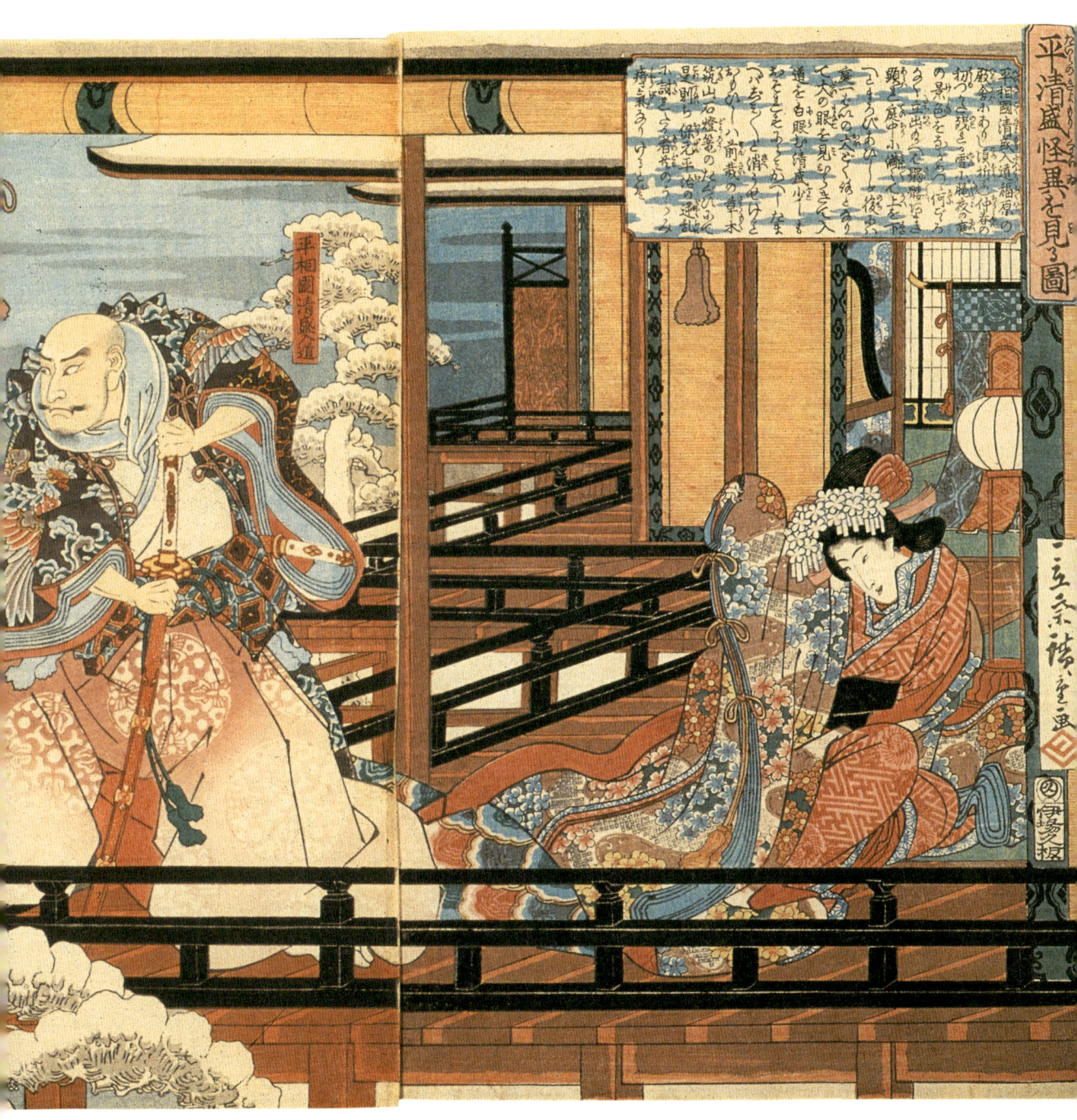

Taira no Kiyomori Haunted by Strange Sights by Utagawa Hiroshige
Skeletons appear all over the snowy garden, staring at Kiyomori. As he returns their gaze, they slowly fade away.

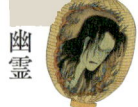

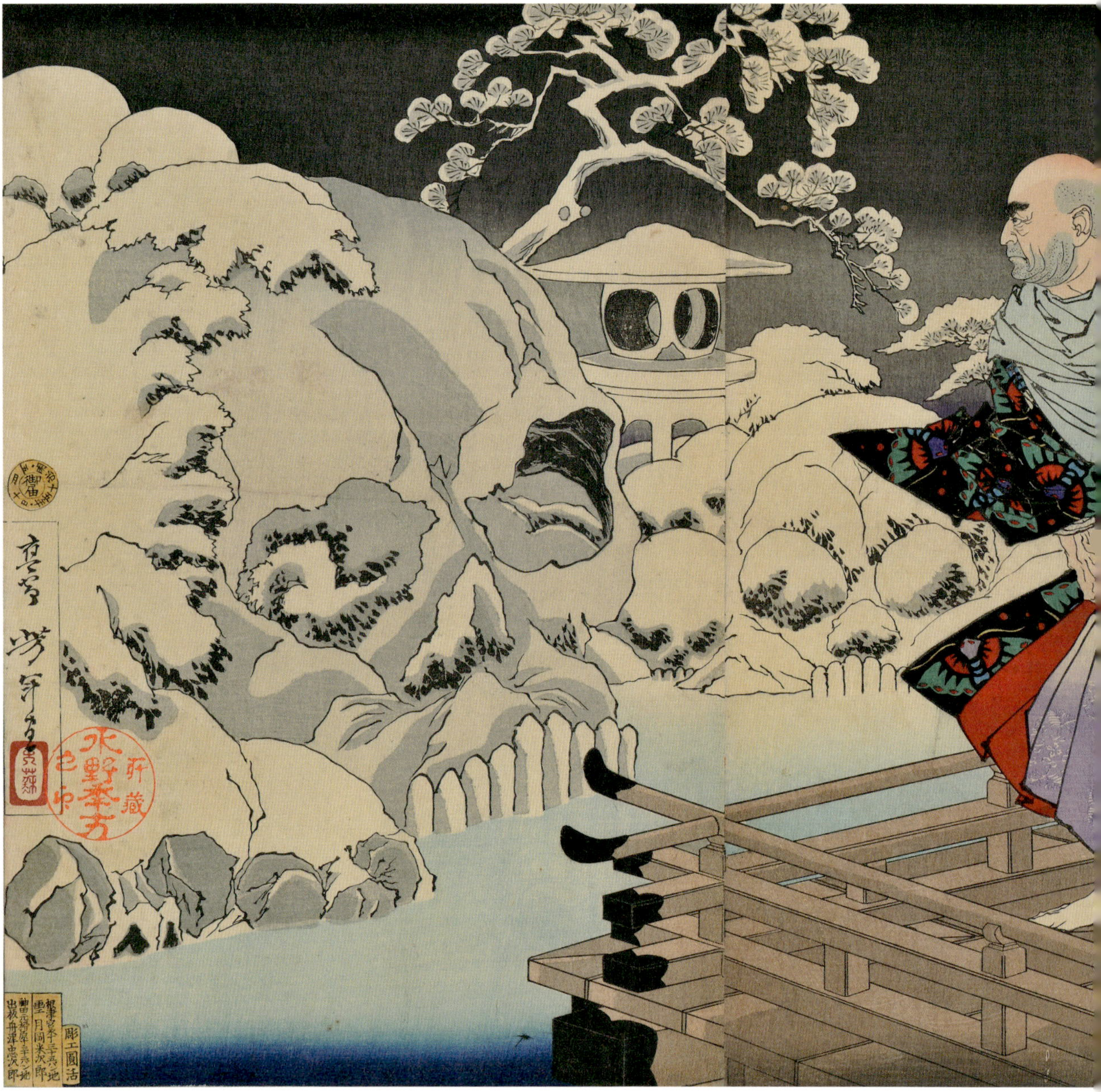

70

【新容六怪撰】月岡芳年 明治15年（1882）

広重の「平清盛怪異を見る図」を参考に、芳年がのちに描いた作品。積もった雪や池の岩肌に浮かび上がる髑髏の顔を、清盛はキッと睨みつけます。
不気味な風に御簾はめくり上がり、女御たちは慄いています。

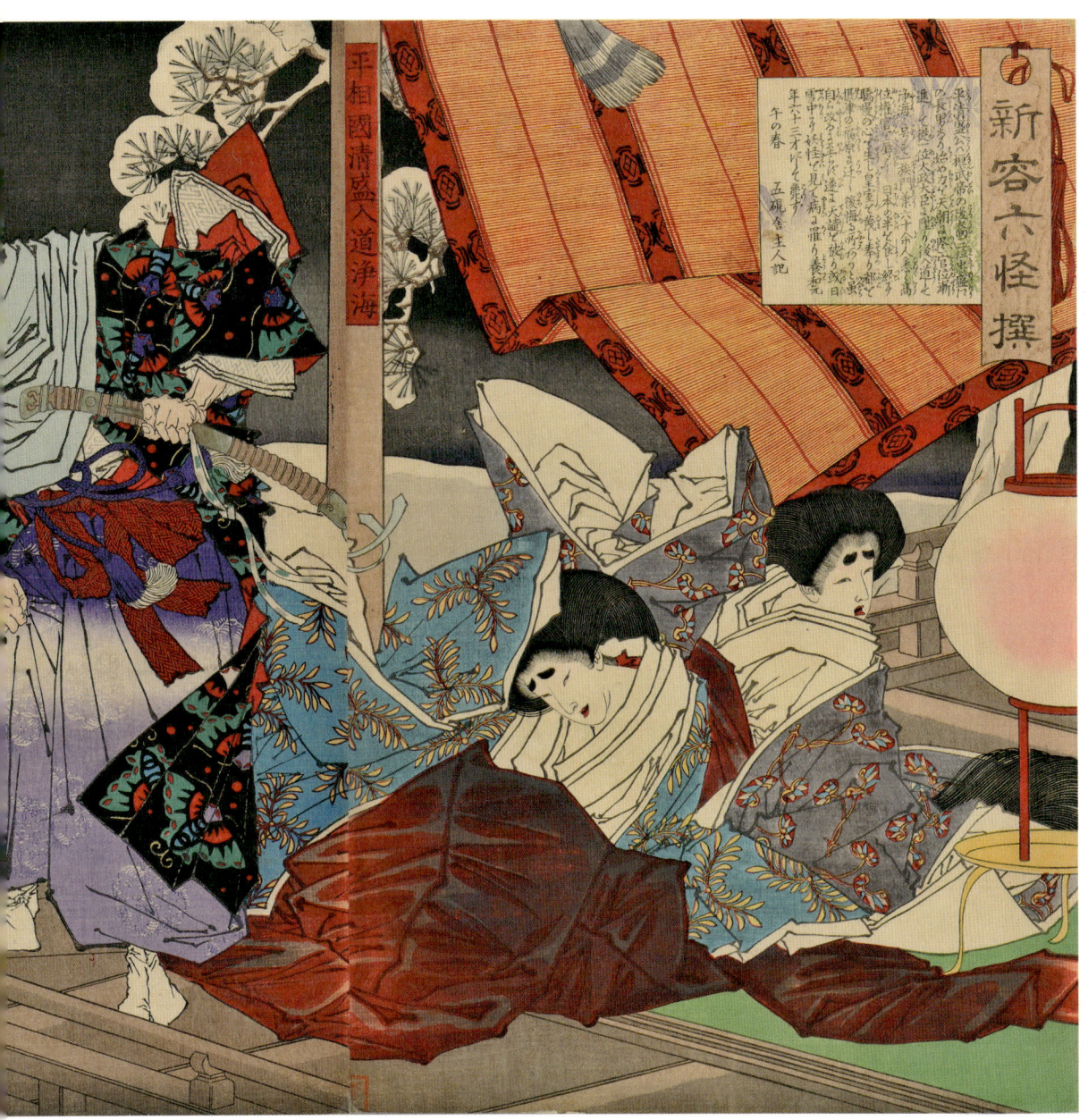

Shinyō rokkaisen (Six New Monsters) by Tsukioka Yoshitoshi

A work by Yoshitoshi inspired by Hiroshige's *Taira no Kiyomori Haunted by Strange Sights*, the only known print of this series so far. Startled, Kiyomori glares at the skulls emerging from the snow and the rocks of the pond. The court ladies shudder as an eerie wind flicks up the bamboo blind.

【清盛入道布引滝遊覧悪源太義平霊討難波次郎】

月岡芳年 明治元年(1868)

悪源太義平は平安時代末期の源氏の武将です。平清盛暗殺に失敗し、難波次郎(二郎)によって斬首されるとき、「終には必ず雷となって蹴殺さんずるぞ」と言い残しました。のち、次郎は清盛に従って訪れた布引の滝で、雷にうたれて死んでしまいます。滝の上には、雷となった悪源太。真っ逆さまに落ちていく難波次郎。下から清盛が睨みつけます。

Kiyomori and the Sight-seeing Trip to Nunobiki Waterfall: The Spirit of Akugenta Yoshihira Strikes Nanba Jirō
by Tsukioka Yoshitoshi

Akugenta Yoshihira was a military commander of the Minamoto clan (Genji) at the end of the Heian period. After a failed attempt to assassinate Taira no Kiyomori, Akugenta was executed by Nanba Jirō, and just before he died, he vowed that he would turn into lightning and strike Jirō down. Later on, when visiting Nunobiki Waterfall with Kiyomori, Jirō was struck by lightning and killed. Akugenta, who has transformed into lightning, is above the waterfall. Nanba Jirō is falling head over heels. Kiyomori glares from below.

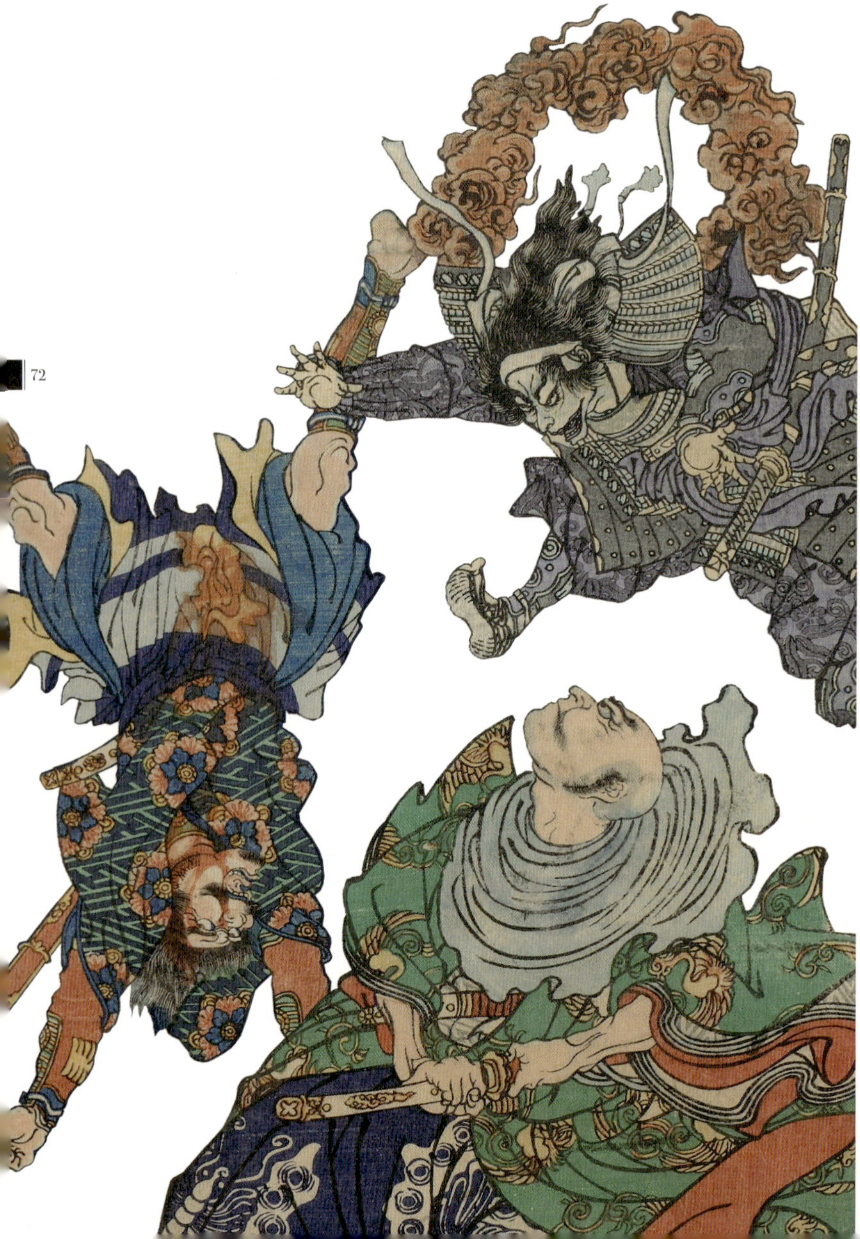

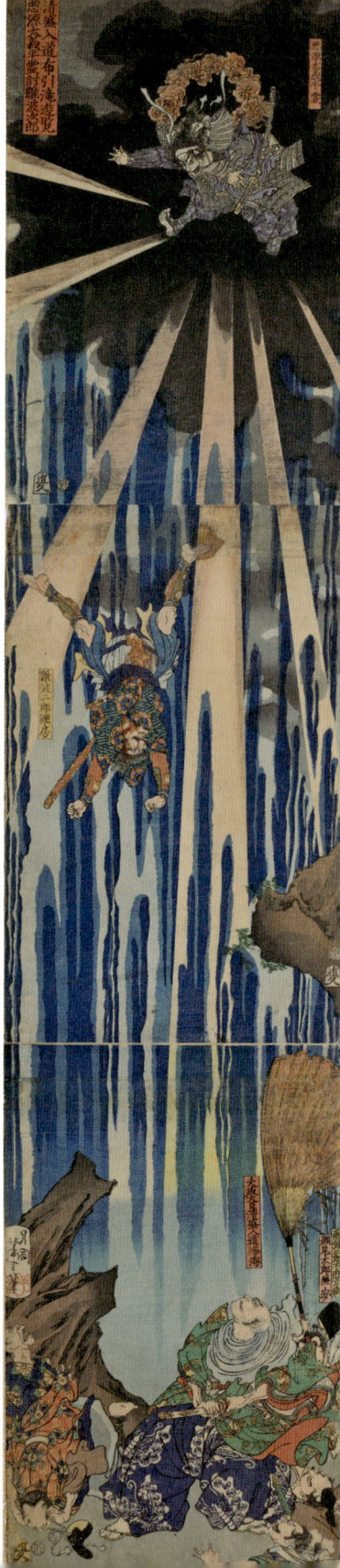

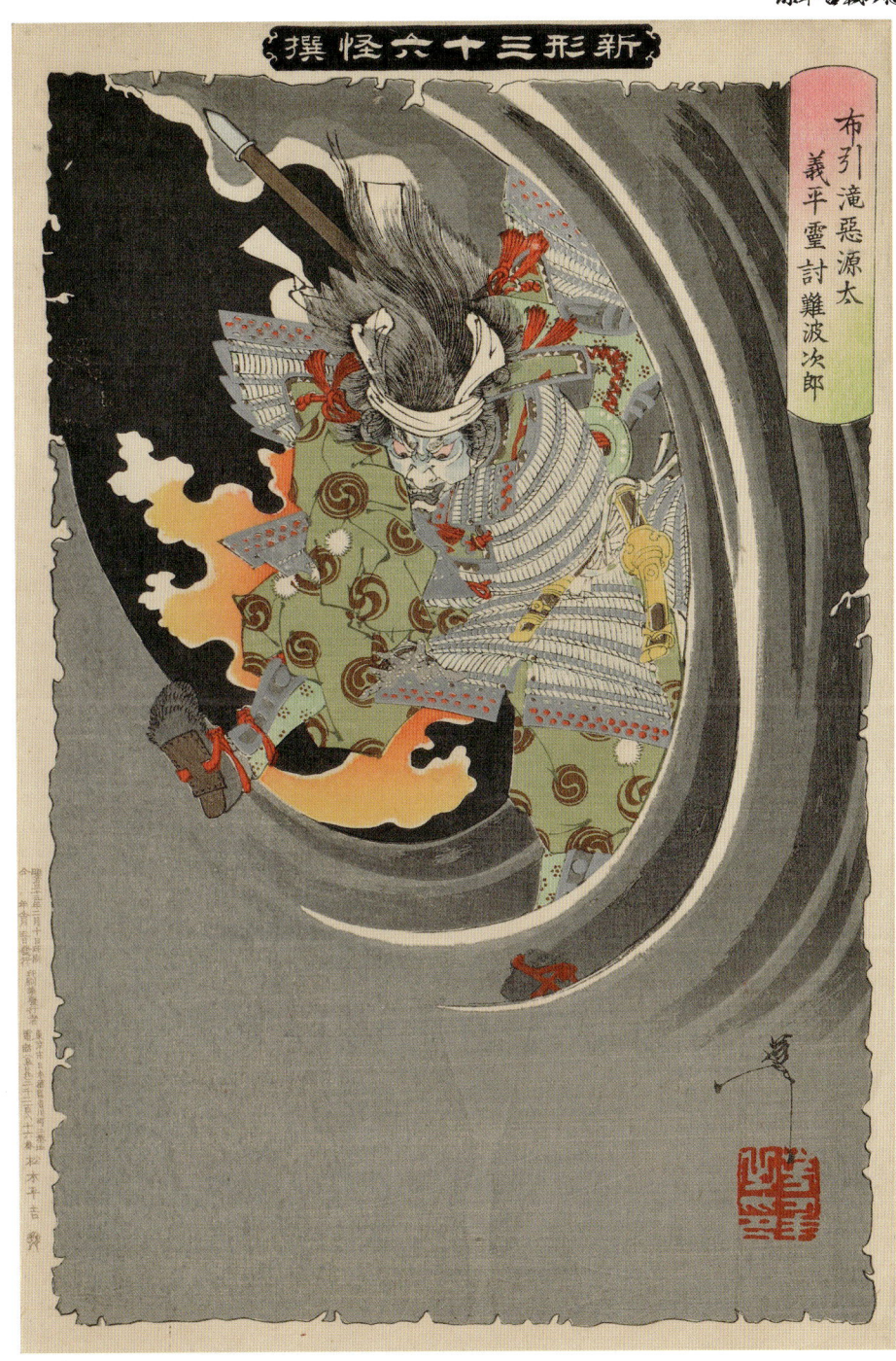

【新形三十六怪撰 布引滝悪源太義平霊討難波次郎】月岡芳年 明治22年（1889）
雷となった悪源太の怨霊。目を大きく見開き、掌を地上へ向けて雷を放つ瞬間を見事に捉えています。

The Ghost of Akugenta Yoshihira Attacking Nanba Jirō at Nunobiki Waterfall
from the series *Shinkei sanjūrokkaisen (New Forms of Thirty-Six Ghosts)* by Tsukioka Yoshitoshi

The vengeful spirit of Akugenta has transformed into thunder and lightning. The moment in which he thrusts his palm earthward to unleash the lightning, eyes blazing, is beautifully captured.

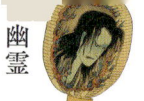
幽霊

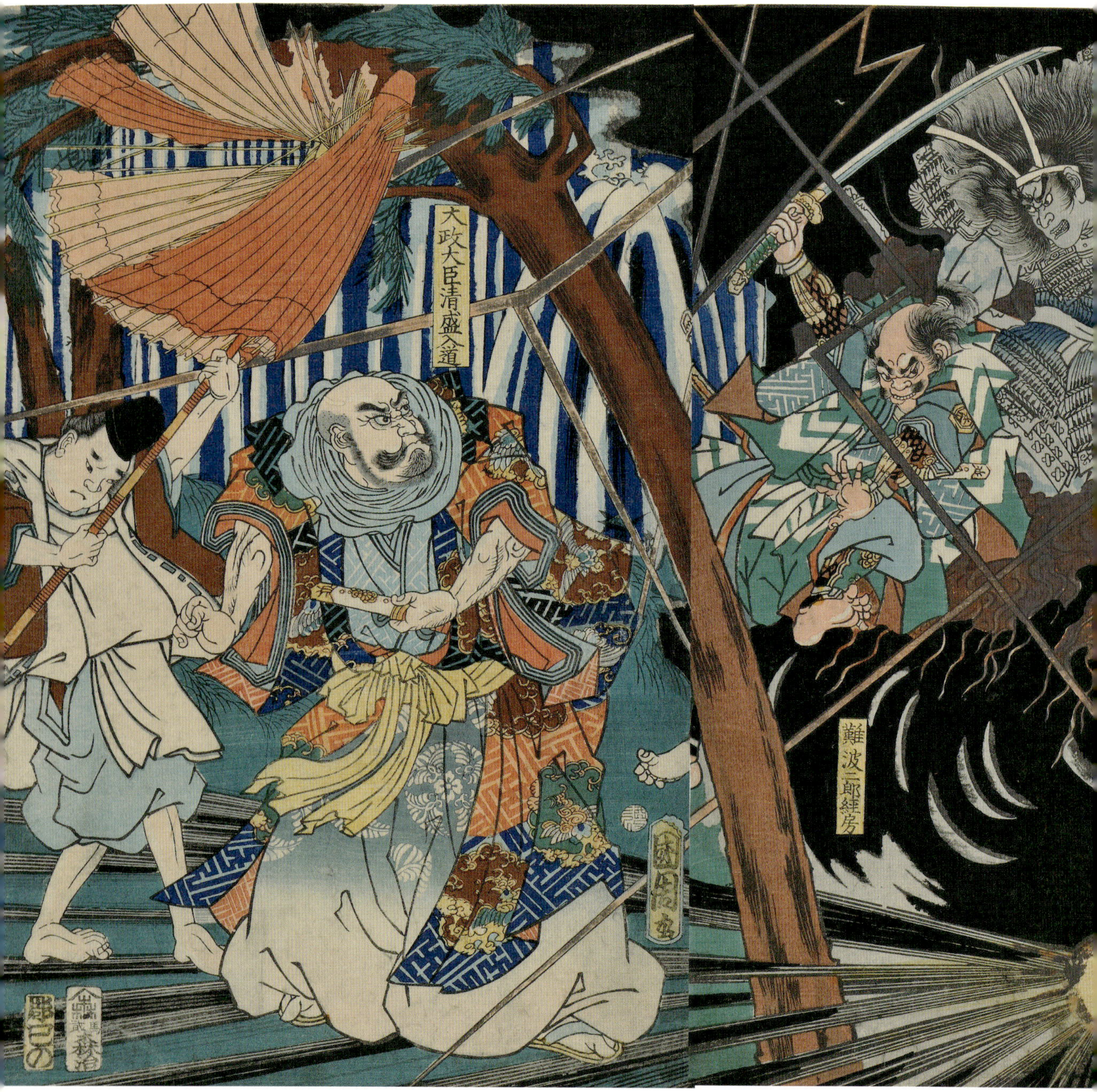

大政大臣清盛入道

難波二郎経房

【清盛入道布引の滝遊覧の図】豊原国周 文久元年(1861)
稲光を放ちながら現れた悪源太が、難波次郎の首根っこをつかみます。清盛は悪源太をキッと睨みつけ、
家臣の主馬判官守国は斬りかかります。

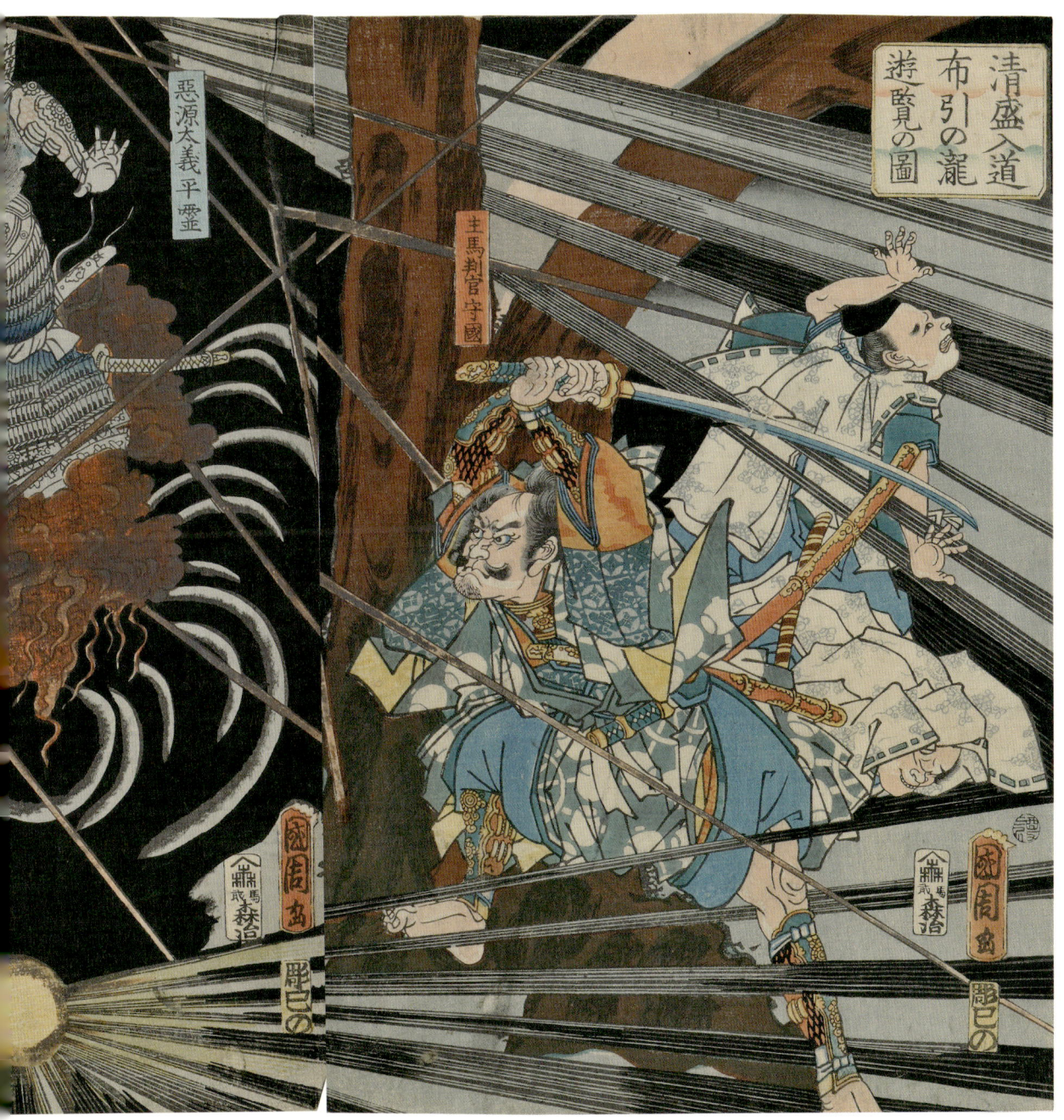

Kiyomori's Sightseeing Trip to Nunobiki Waterfall by Toyohara Kunichika

Appearing with a volley of lightning, Akugenta grabs Nanba Jirō by the scruff of the neck. Kiyomori glares enraged at Akugenta, and his retainer Morikuni attacks.

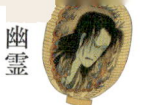

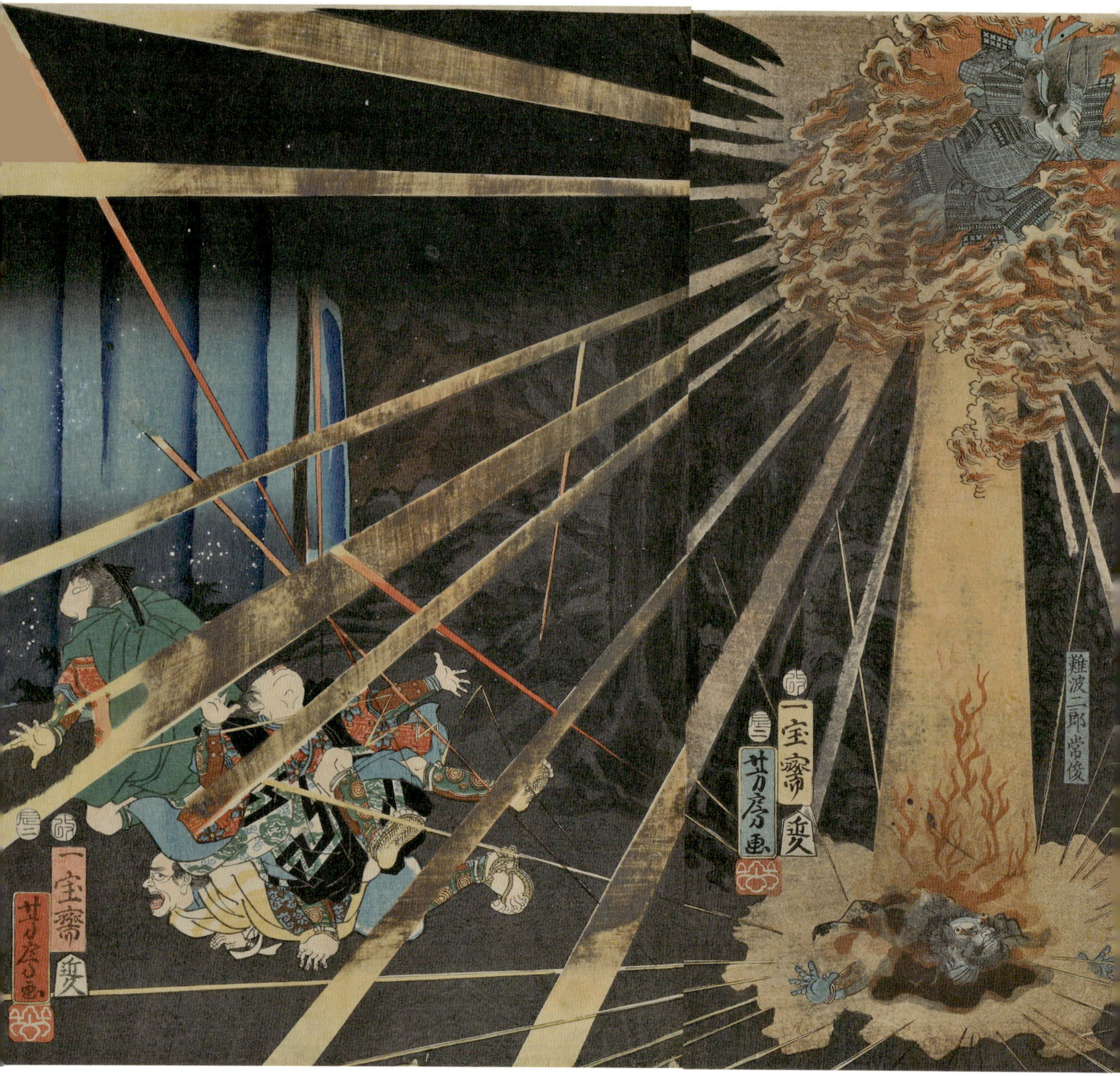

【清盛布引滝遊覧義平霊難波討図】歌川芳房 安政3年（1856）

燃え盛る炎に包まれて現れたのは、雷となった悪源太の怨霊。仇の難波次郎（二郎）めがけて稲妻を落とします。
次郎はひとたまりもなく黒こげになってしまいました。次に狙うのは平清盛です。

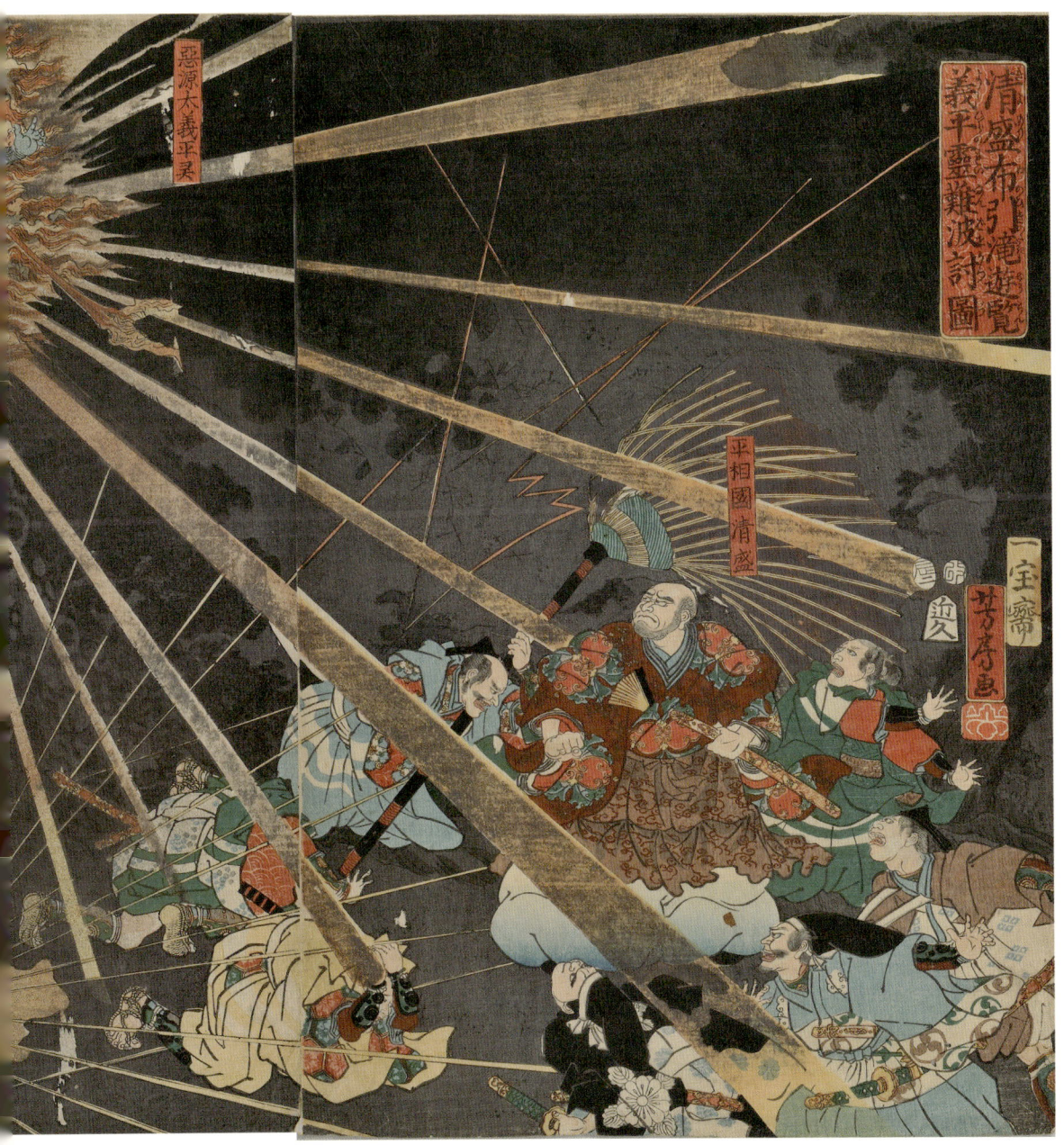

The Ghost of Akugenta Taking Revenge on Nanba at Nunobiki Waterfall by Utagawa Yoshifusa

Wreathed in a raging blaze is the vengeful spirit of Akugenta, who has transformed into lightning. He shoots a bolt of lightning down on his enemy Nanba Jirō. Jirō is burned black in an instant. Akugenta's next target is Taira no Kiyomori.

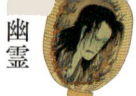

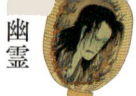

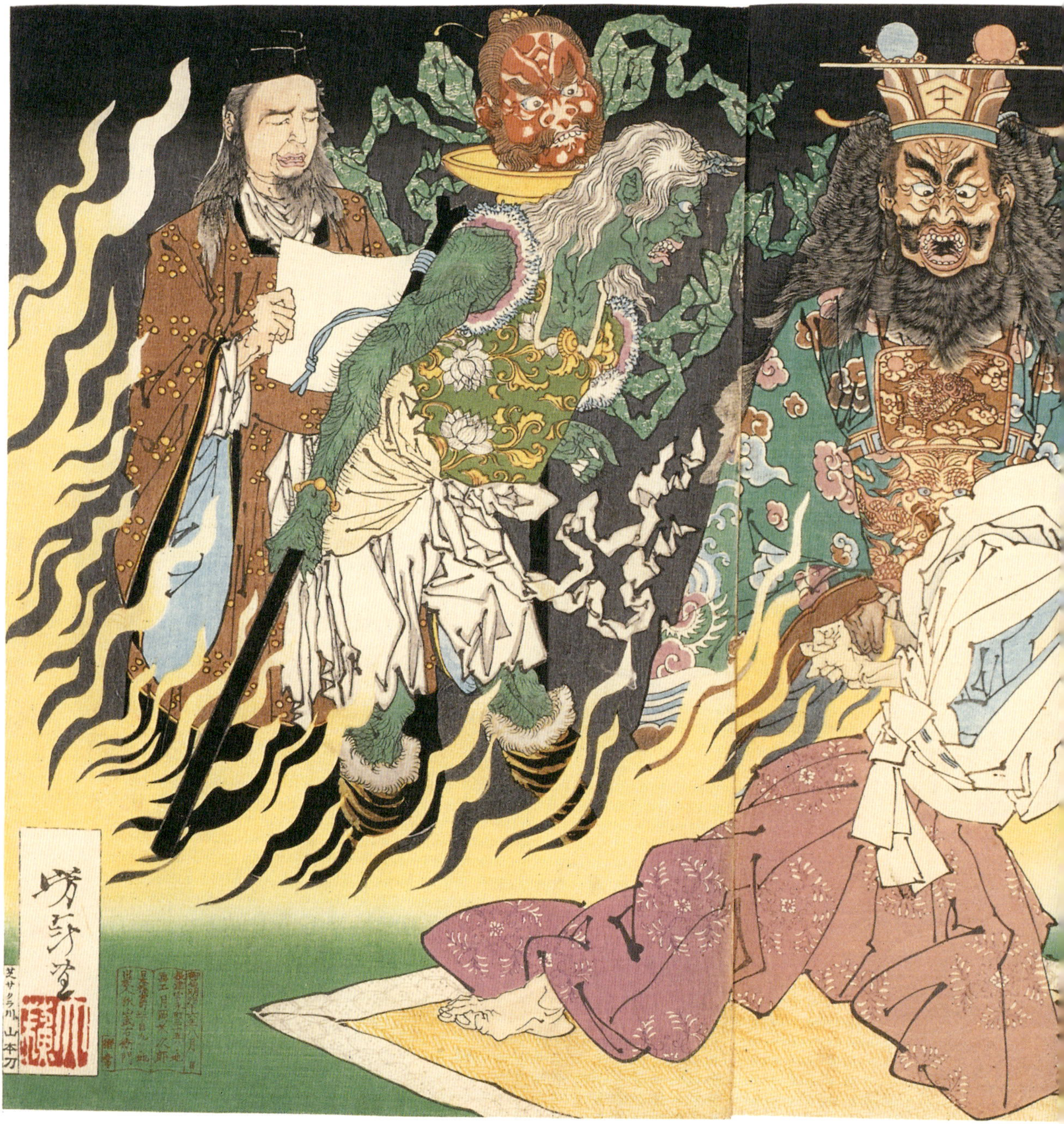

【平清盛炎焼病之図】月岡芳年 明治16年(1883)

熱病でもだえ苦しむ平清盛の最期。体は火のように熱く、水風呂に入れれば水は沸騰し、水をかけても熱さで飛び散り、さらには炎となったそうです。
かたわらの妻時子と三男宗盛は、もはや祈るしかないといった表情です。背景には閻魔大王とその眷属たち。

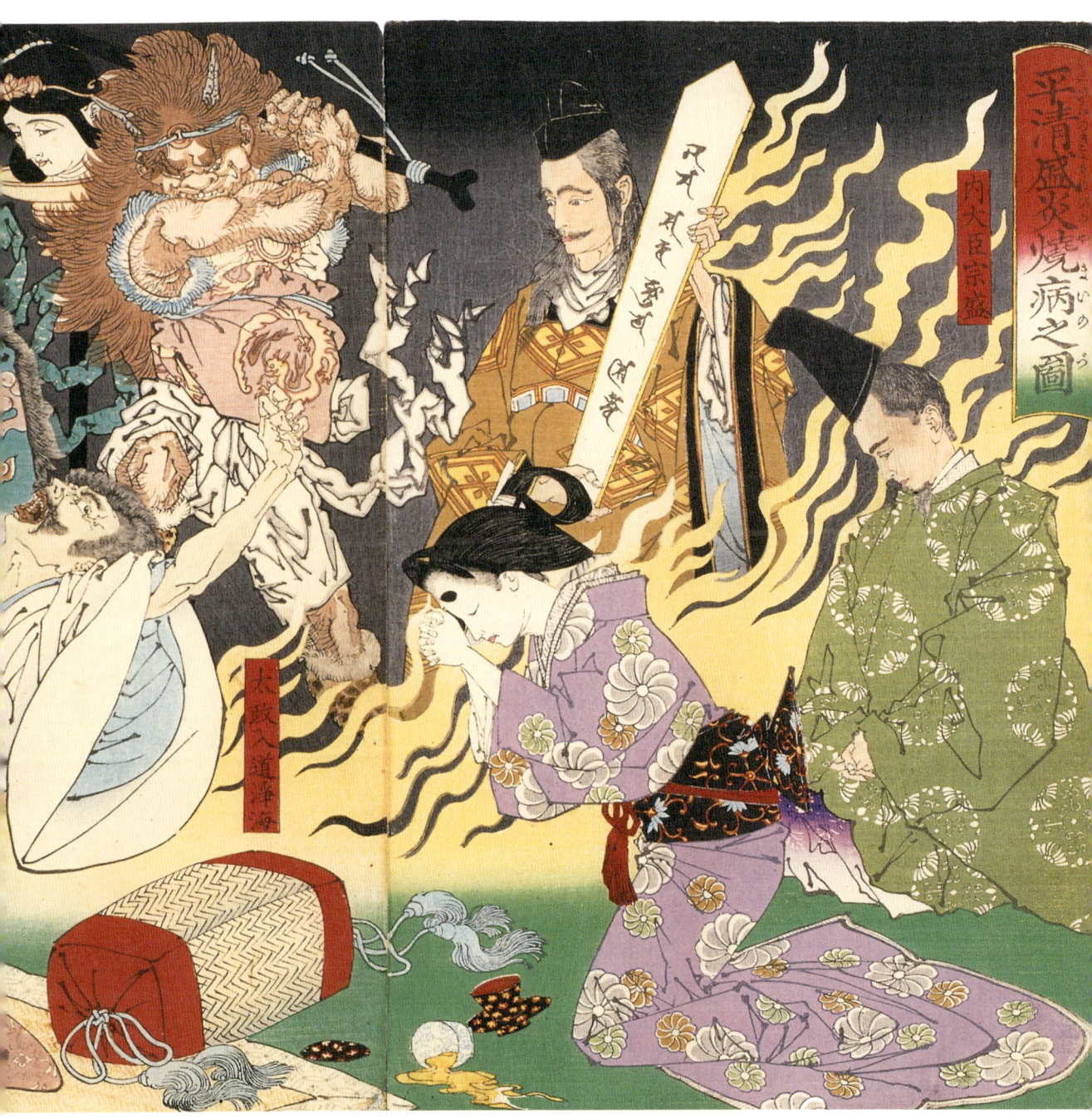

平清盛炎焼病之図

内大臣宗盛

太政入道浄海

The Fever of Taira no Kiyomori by Tsukioka Yoshitoshi

Taira no Kiyomori's final moments, spent writhing in an agony of delirium. His body burned like fire, so that the water boiled when he got into the bath, and water on his skin evaporated with the heat, which blazed up even higher than before. Beside him, the resigned expressions of his wife Tokiko and third son Munemori show that there is nothing more they can do for him except pray. In the background are the King of Hell and his followers. His oldest son Shigemori, who died before him, is also present.

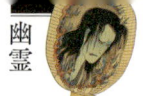
【文治元年平家の一門亡海中落入る図】月岡芳年 嘉永6年（1853）

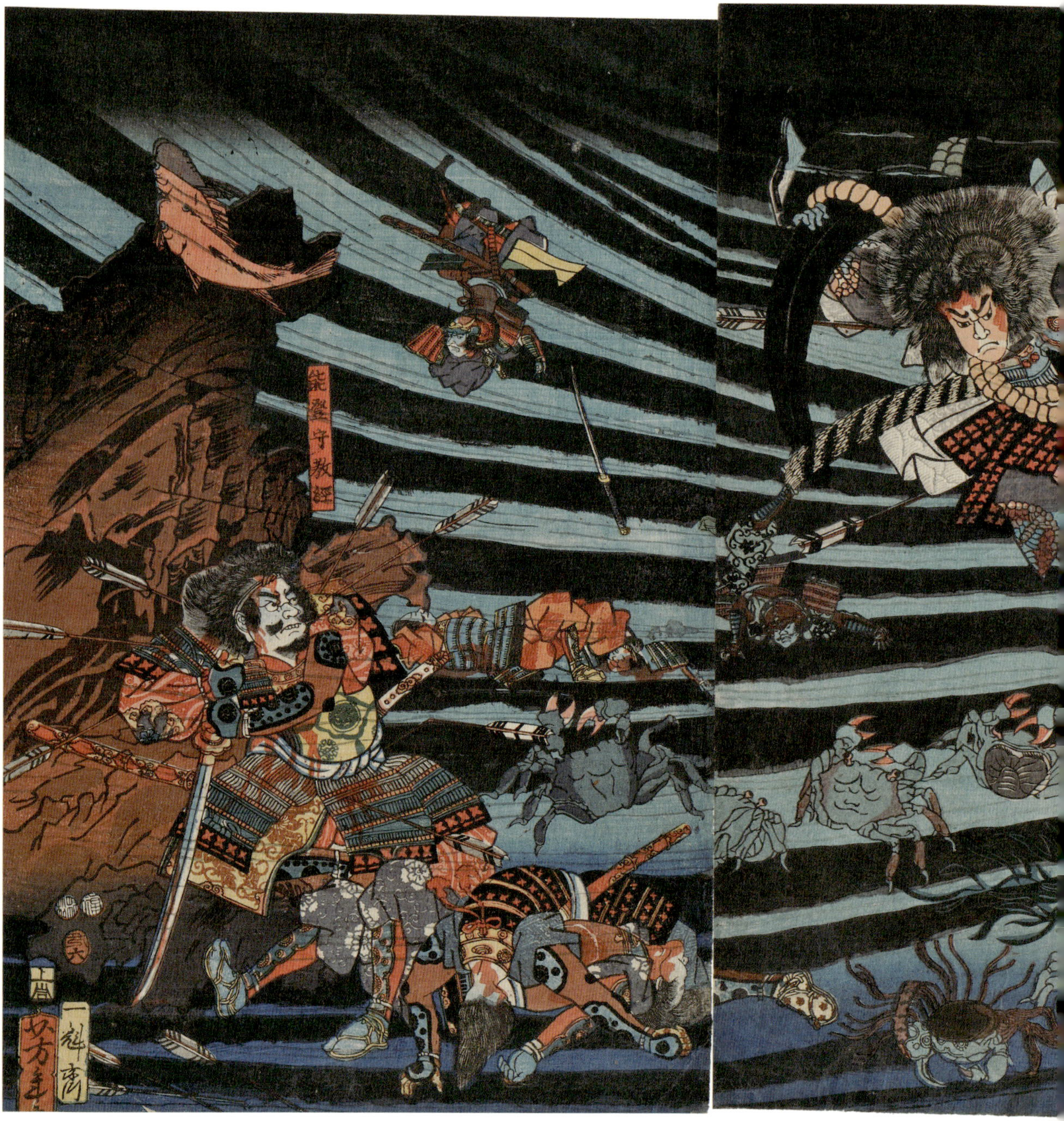

大碇を体に巻きつけ海に沈む平知盛。壇ノ浦で平家の敗戦を見届け、入水しました。不気味な平家蟹がうごめ
く海底では、安徳天皇、家臣の能登守教経（のとのかみのりつね）、伊賀平内（いがのへいない）など、先に入水した平家一門の霊が待っていました。

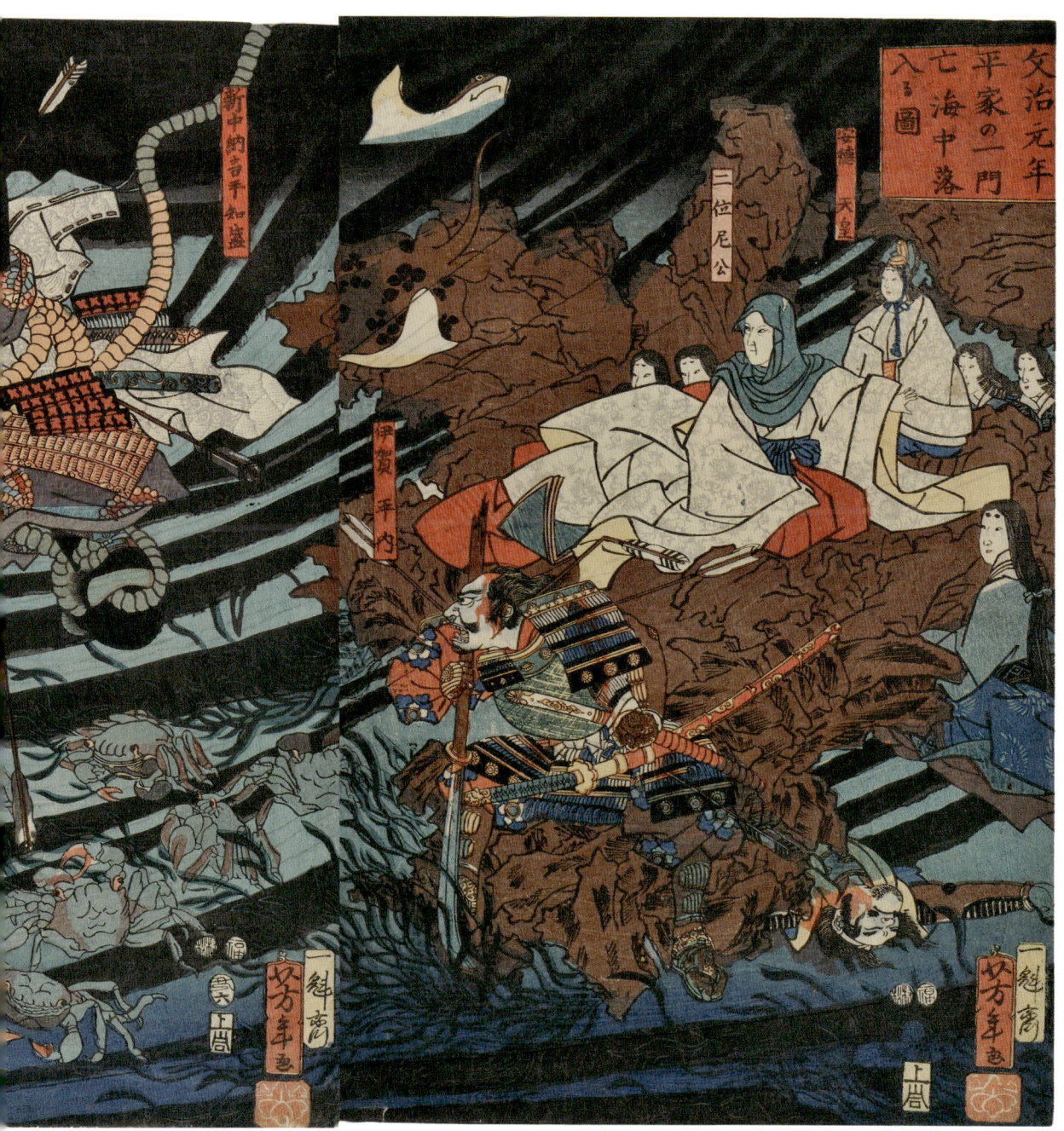

In 1185 the Heike Clan Sank into the Sea and Perished by Tsukioka Yoshitoshi

Taira no Tomomori sinks into the sea on a huge anchor. Seeing his clan defeated at Dan-no-ura, he drowned himself. On the sea floor, writhing with sinister Heike crabs, the ghosts of the Taira who went before him are waiting, with Emperor Antoku and Notonokami Noritsune among them.

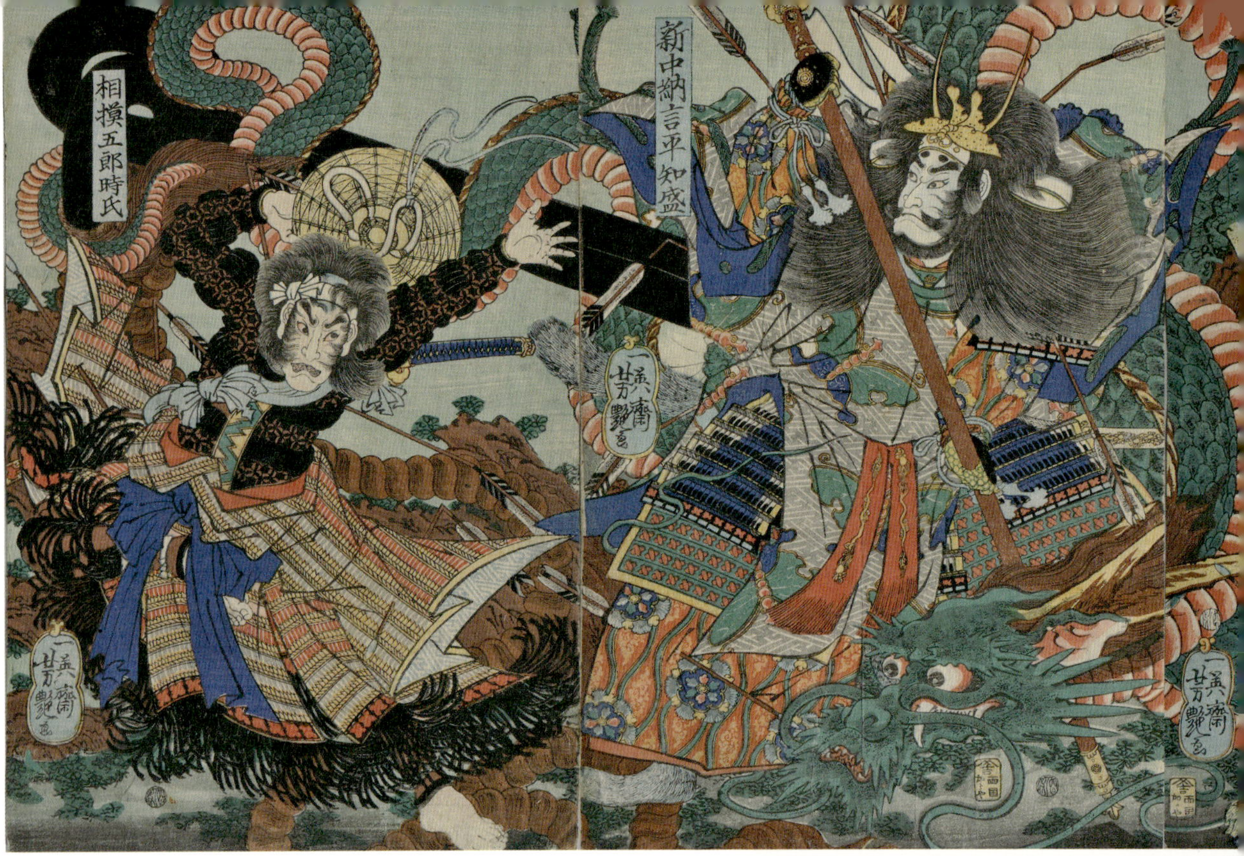

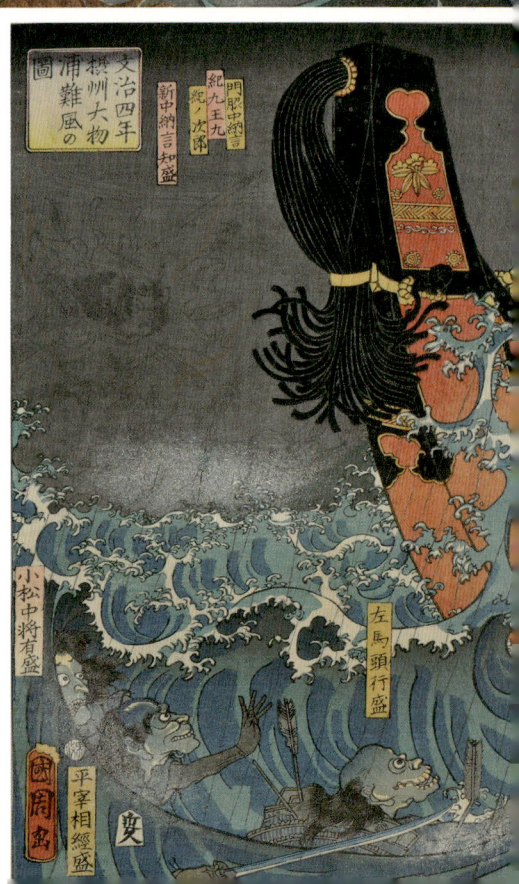

【文治四年摂州大物浦難風の図】
豊原国周 万延元年（1860）
平家の亡霊が次々と波間から現れ、源義経一行を乗せた船を襲います。亡霊の顔は半ば骸骨と化し、ゾンビのようでもあります。背景の墨で摺られた暗闇の部分をよく見ると、武者の組む騎馬に乗った平知盛が描かれています。

In 1188, Minamoto no Yoshitsune Encounters a Typhoon in Daimotsu Bay in Settsu Province
by Toyohara Kunichika

Ghosts of the Taira emerge from the waves one after another, launching attacks on the ship of Yoshitsune and his men. Like zombies, the flesh of their faces has been partially eaten away. Taira no Tomomori on the shoulders of his men can be seen in the murk of the background ink.

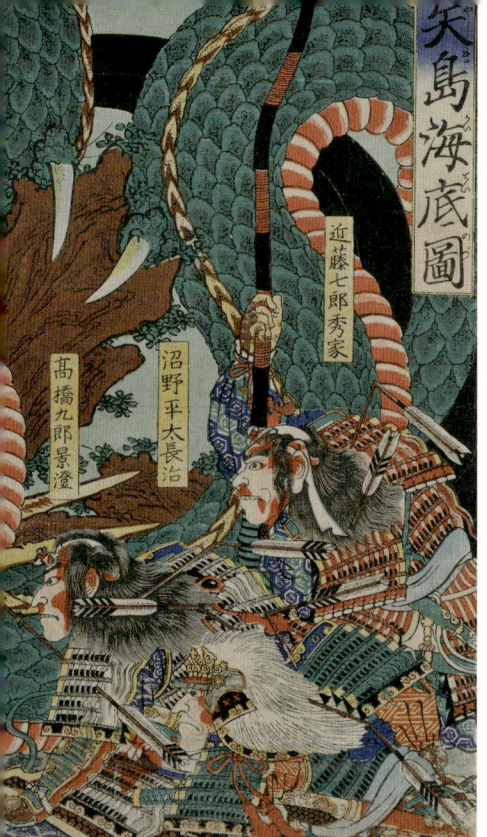

【矢島海底図】一英斎芳艶 文久元年（1861）

壇ノ浦で敗れた平知盛は大碇とともに入水しましたが、その亡霊はなお
も源氏への復讐を狙っています。海に沈んだ平家一門は竜宮城にいた
とも言われ、身をうねらせた竜が知盛に従います。源義経の動向を知ら
せるため、郎党の相模五郎が駆けつけてきました。

Yashima kaitei no zu (The Bottom of the Sea at Yashima)
by Ichieisai Yoshitsuya

Defeated at Dan-no-ura, Taira no Tomomori threw himself into the sea with
an anchor, but his ghost still seeks revenge. Some say the drowned Taira were
at Ryūgū-jō, undersea palace of the coiling dragon who followed Tomomori.
Sagami Gorō (left) rushes to report Yoshitsune's movements.

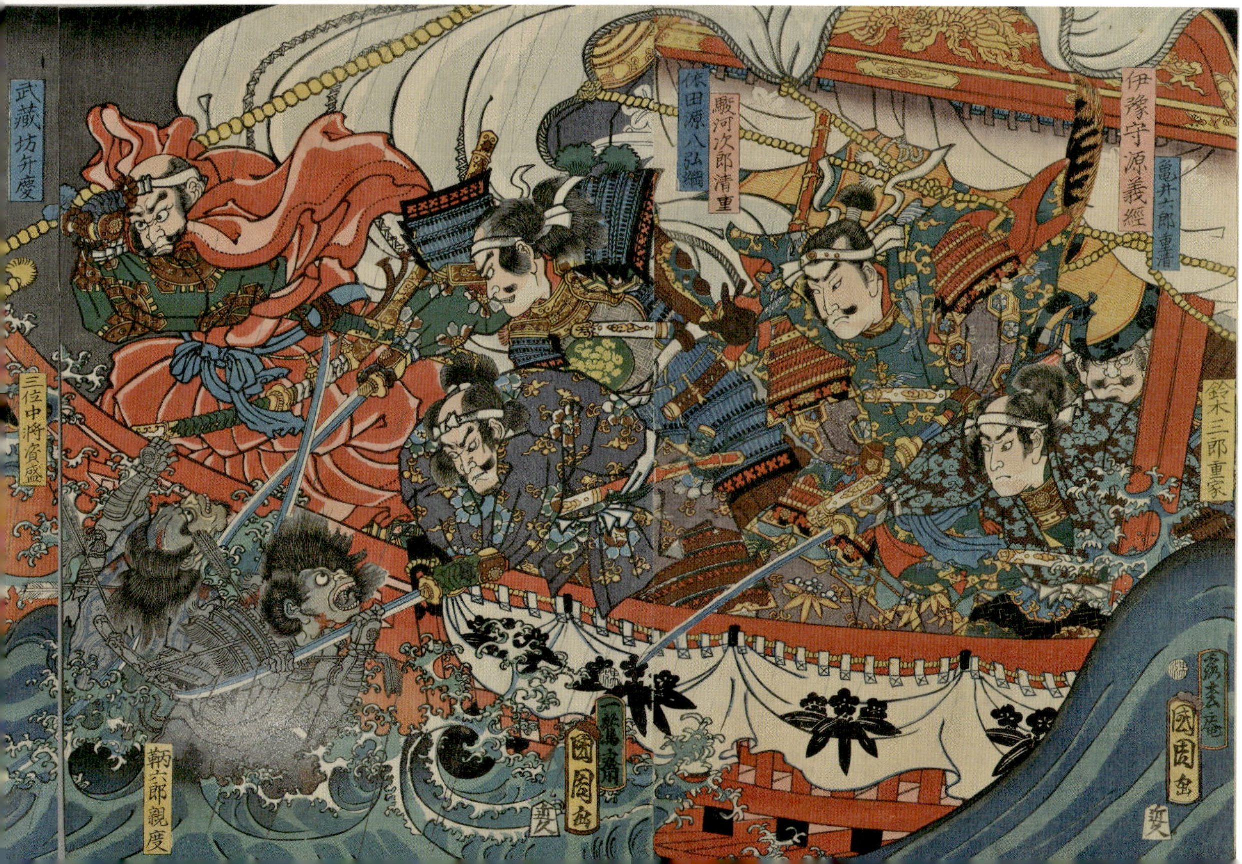

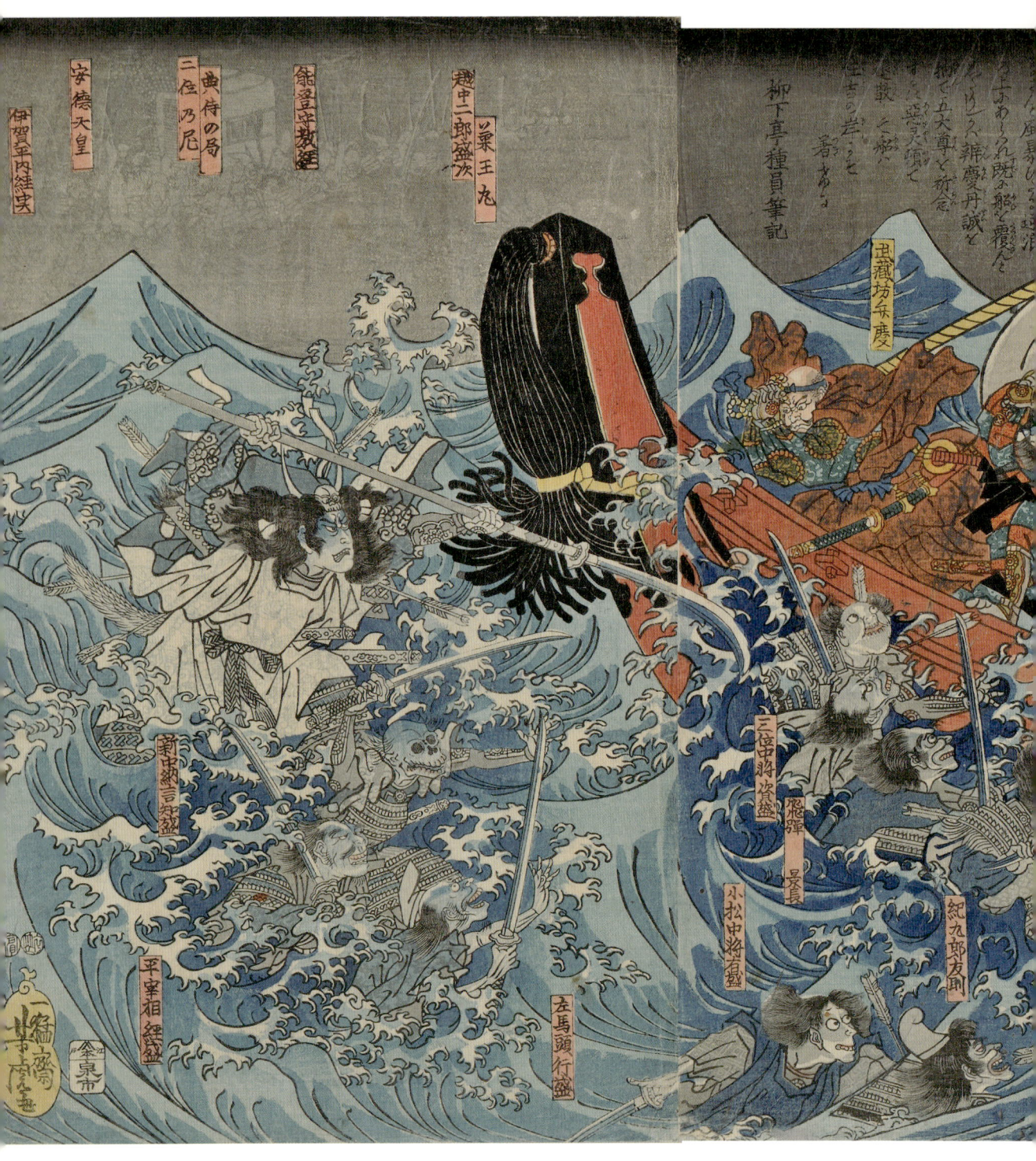

【文治四年源義経 摂州大物浦難風之図】歌川芳虎 弘化4年～嘉永元年（1847-48）頃
大物浦の大嵐は、壇ノ浦の戦いで敗れ、海に沈んだ平家の怨霊の仕業でした。平知盛など、平家の亡霊が波間から現れ、義経に襲いかかります。舳先では弁慶が悪霊退散を念じています。

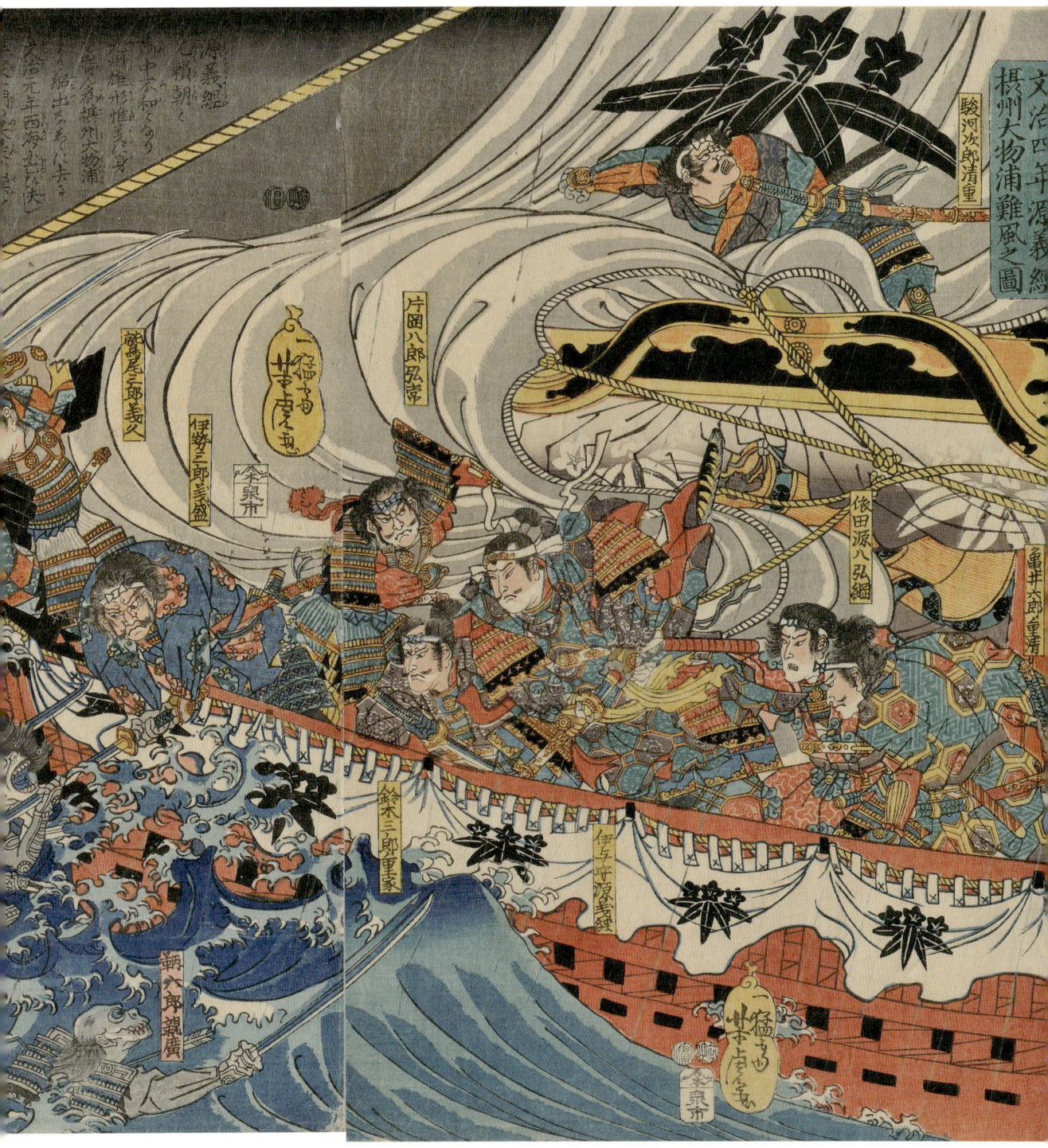

In 1188, Minamoto no Yoshitsune Encounters a Typhoon in Daimotsu Bay in Settsu Province by Utagawa Yoshitora

The tempest in Daimotsu Bay is the work of vengeful spirits of the Taira clan, who were defeated and drowned at the Battle of Dan-no-ura. Taira no Tomomori and his fellow ghosts emerge from the waves to attack Yoshitsune. On the bow, Benkei is chanting to drive away evil spirits.

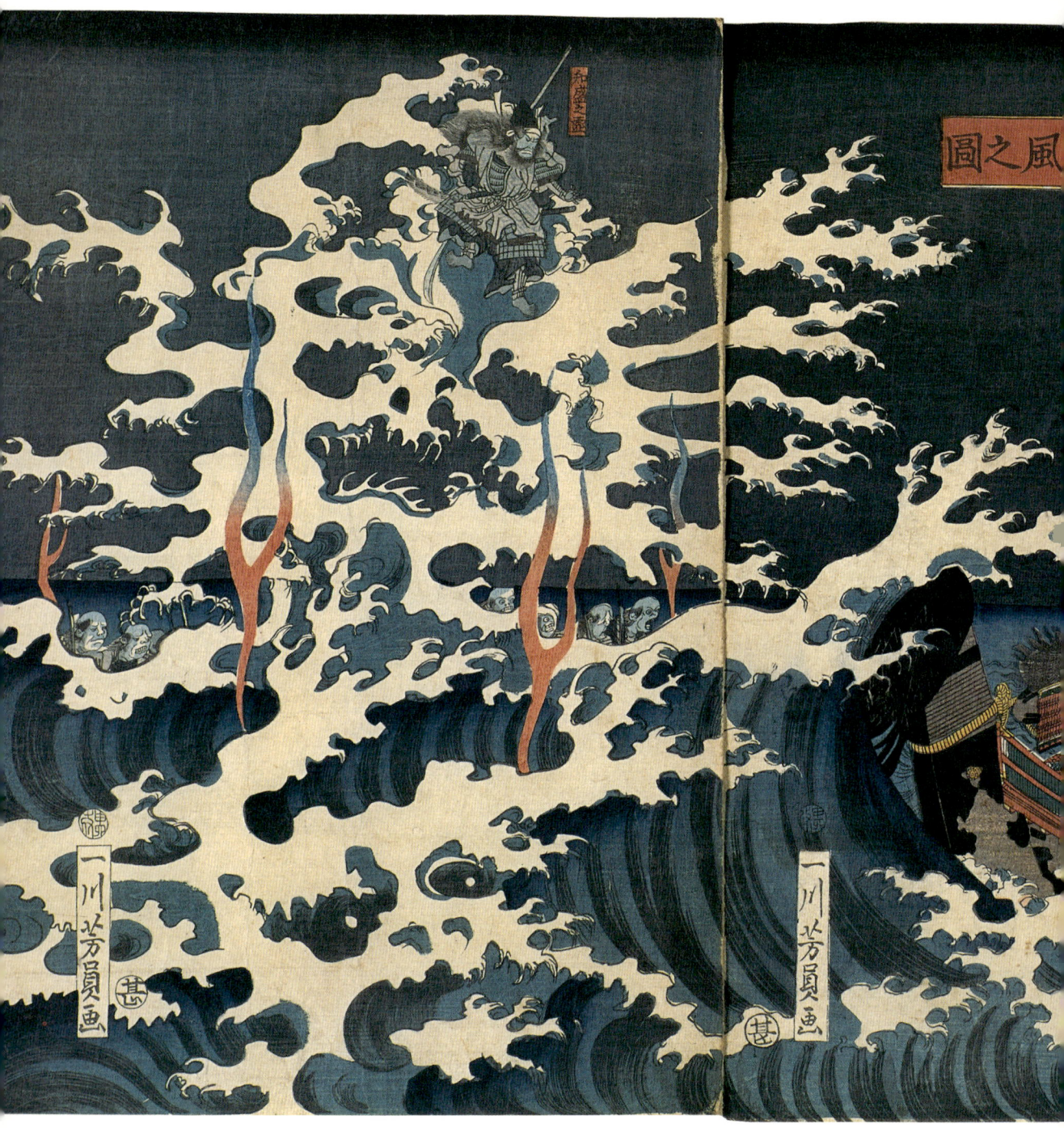

【大物浦難風之図】歌川芳員　万延元年（1860）
大物浦で大嵐に遭遇する源義経一行。そそり立つ大波の上に、壇ノ浦の戦いで敗れて入水した平知盛の亡霊が現れました。
よく見ると、波しぶきの形がお化けの顔になっています。波の裏側にも、平氏の亡霊たちが、小さく描き込まれています。

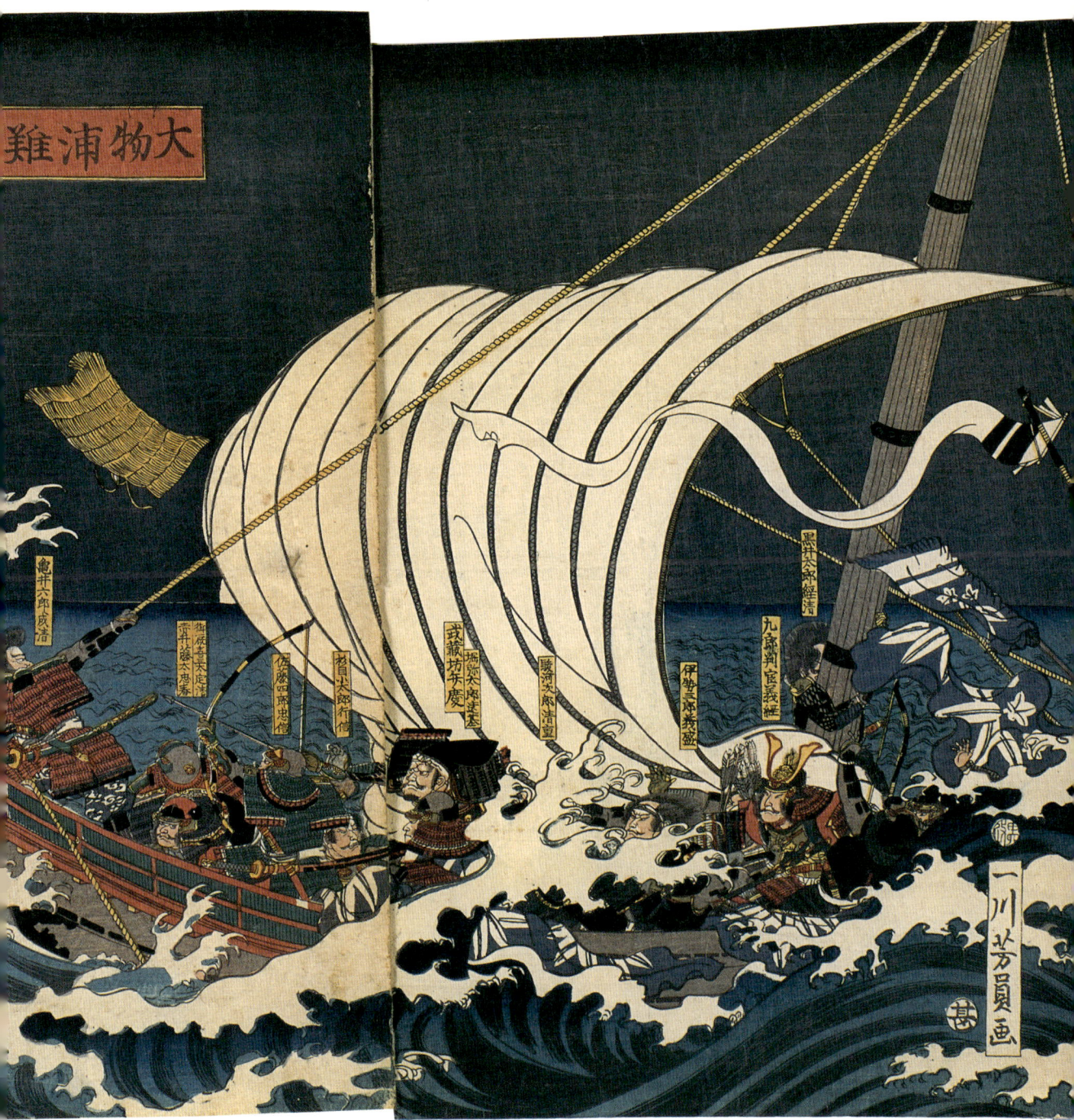

Adverse Wind on Daimotsu Bay by Utagawa Yoshikazu

Minamoto no Yoshitsune and his company are caught in a tempest in Daimotsu Bay. Towering above on the top of the wave is the ghost of Taira no Tomomori, who should have sunk to the bottom of the ocean with his anchor, the flying crest of foam is forming into monsters, and ghostly flames rise among the waves. A close examination reveals the ghosts of Taira clan warriors just visible behind the wave.

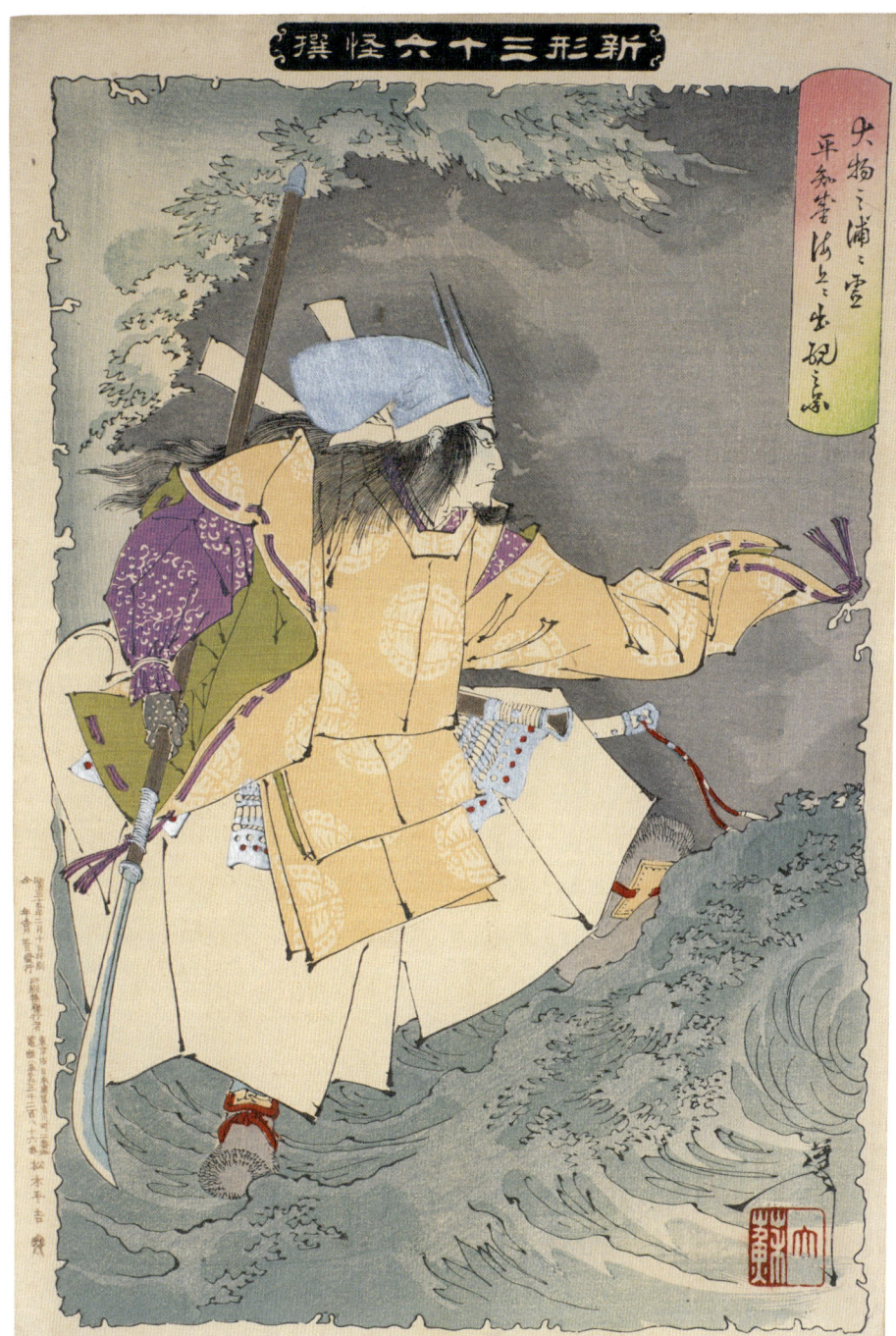

【新形三十六怪撰 大物之浦ニ霊平知盛海上ニ出現之図】月岡芳年 明治24年 (1891)

壇ノ浦で入水した平知盛の亡霊が、大嵐の大物浦海上に現れました。キッと見据える先には、源義経一行を乗せた船。その表情には源氏への激しい怨念と、復讐への決意が見られます。

The Ghost of Taira no Tomomori Appearing at Daimotsu Bay from *Shinkei sanjūrokkaisen (New Forms of Thirty-Six Ghosts* by Tsukioka Yoshitoshi

The ghost of Taira no Tomomori, who drowned himself at Dan-no-ura, has appeared in the storm on the sea at Daimotsu Bay. His eyes are locked on the ship of Minamoto no Yoshitsune and his men. His fierce hatred for the Minamoto and determination for revenge can be seen on his face.

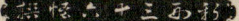

【新形三十六怪撰 ぼたんとうろう】月岡芳年 明治24年（1891）

Botan Dōrō (The Peony Lantern) from the series
Shinkei sanjūrokkaisen (New Forms of Thirty-Six Ghosts)
by Tsukioka Yoshitoshi

89

Otsuyu (*Botan Dōrō, the Peony Lantern*)
Apparitions (*yūrei*)

お露

旗本の娘お露は浪人・萩原新三郎に恋
し焦がれ死に、乳母のお米は後追い自殺
しました。亡霊となったお露とお米は、牡
丹灯籠を灯して夜な夜な新三郎のもとに
通い、新三郎はついに取り殺されました。

Otsuyu, the daughter of a *hatamoto* (a high-ranking samurai),
dies of her desperate longing for masterless samurai Hagiwara
Shinzaburō, and her nursemaid Oyone commits suicide to follow
her into death. The ghosts of Otsuyu and Oyone light the peony
lantern and visit Shinzaburō every night, until finally he is killed.

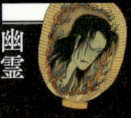
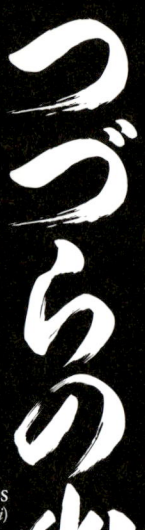

つづらの幽霊

Ghosts in Boxes
Apparitions (*yūrei*)

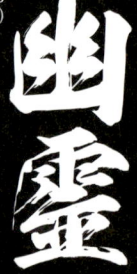

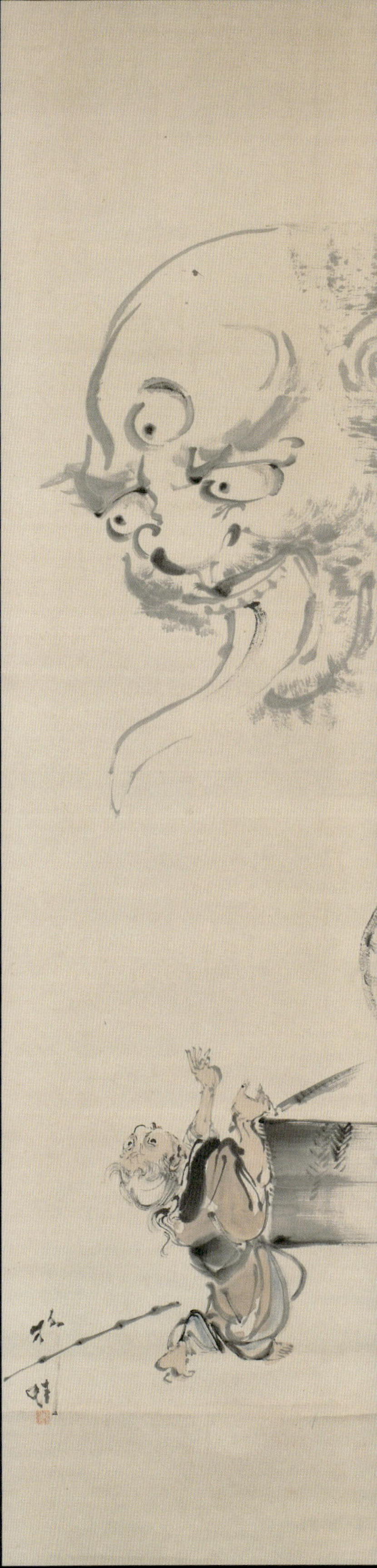

昔話「舌切り雀」。糊をなめた雀の舌をはさみで切ってしまう残酷なおばあさん。一方、おじいさんは雀に親切をしたお礼に、宝のつづらをもらいました。おじいさんを羨んで、おばあさんは雀の宿を訪ねます。欲張って大きいつづらを選ぶと、中から三つ目小僧などの妖怪や幽霊が飛び出しました。そして、驚いたおばあさんは死んでしまいます。

A scene from folk tale *The Tongue-Cut Sparrow (Shitakiri-suzume)*. The cruel old woman cut out the sparrow's tongue with scissors, angry that it had eaten her starch. Meanwhile, the old man got a basket full of treasure, as a thank-you gift for his kindness to the sparrow. Envious of the old man, the old woman visited the sparrow's inn and greedily chose a big basket, only to find three-eyed goblins, apparitions, and other monsters inside. Taken by surprise, the old woman died.

【舌切雀奇譚・つづらから三ツ目坊主】
竹内柳蛙（五代歌川国政）明治時代後期〜大正時代

The Tale of the Tongue-cut Sparrow:
Three-eyed Goblins out of the Basket
by Takeuchi Ryu-a (also known as Utagawa Kunimasa V)
(End of 19th century – early 20th century)

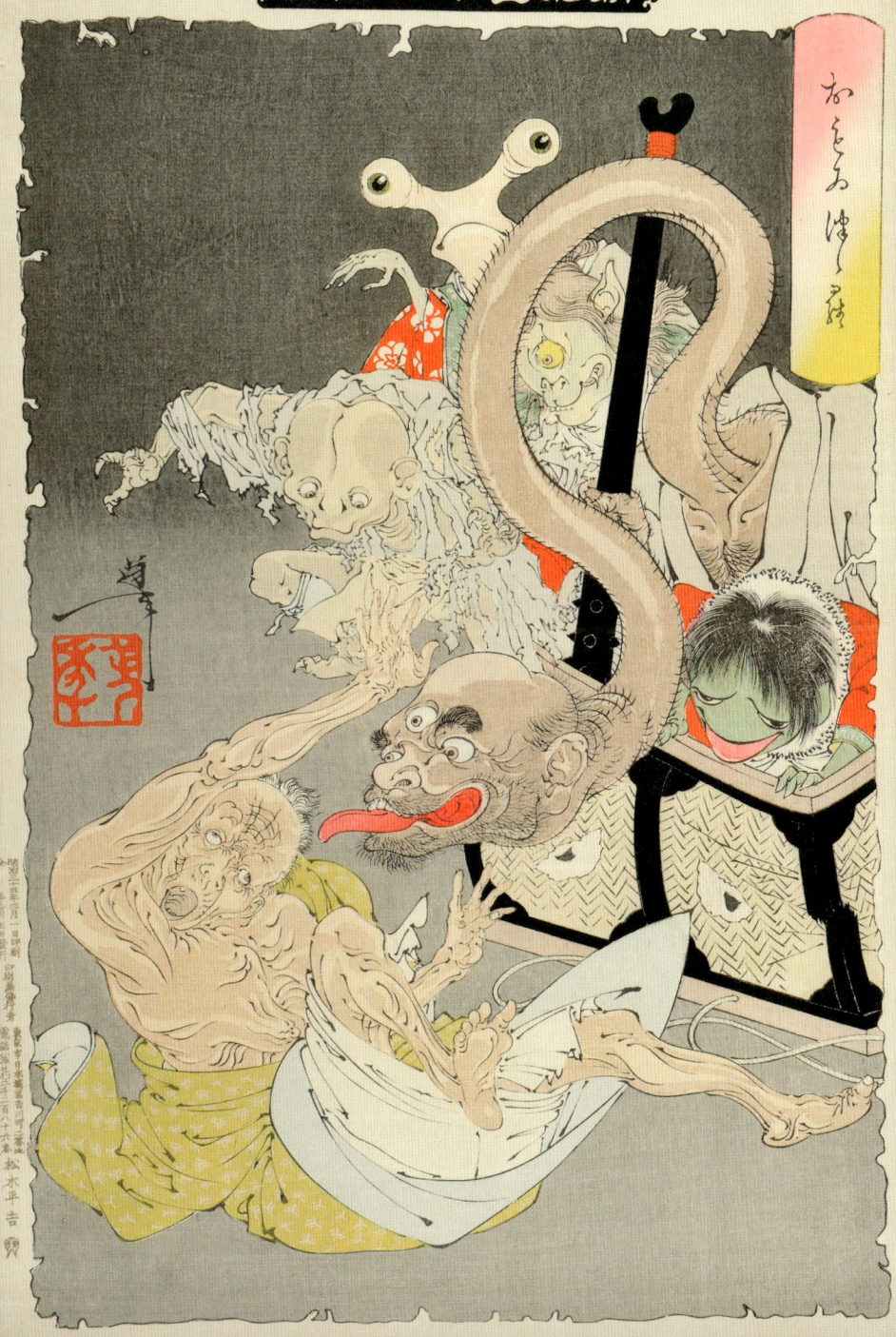

【新形三十六怪撰 おもゐつづら】月岡芳年 明治25年（1892）

Omoi tsuzura (Pandora's Box) from the series *Shinkei sanjūrokkaisen (New Forms of Thirty-Six Ghosts)*
by Tsukioka Yoshitoshi

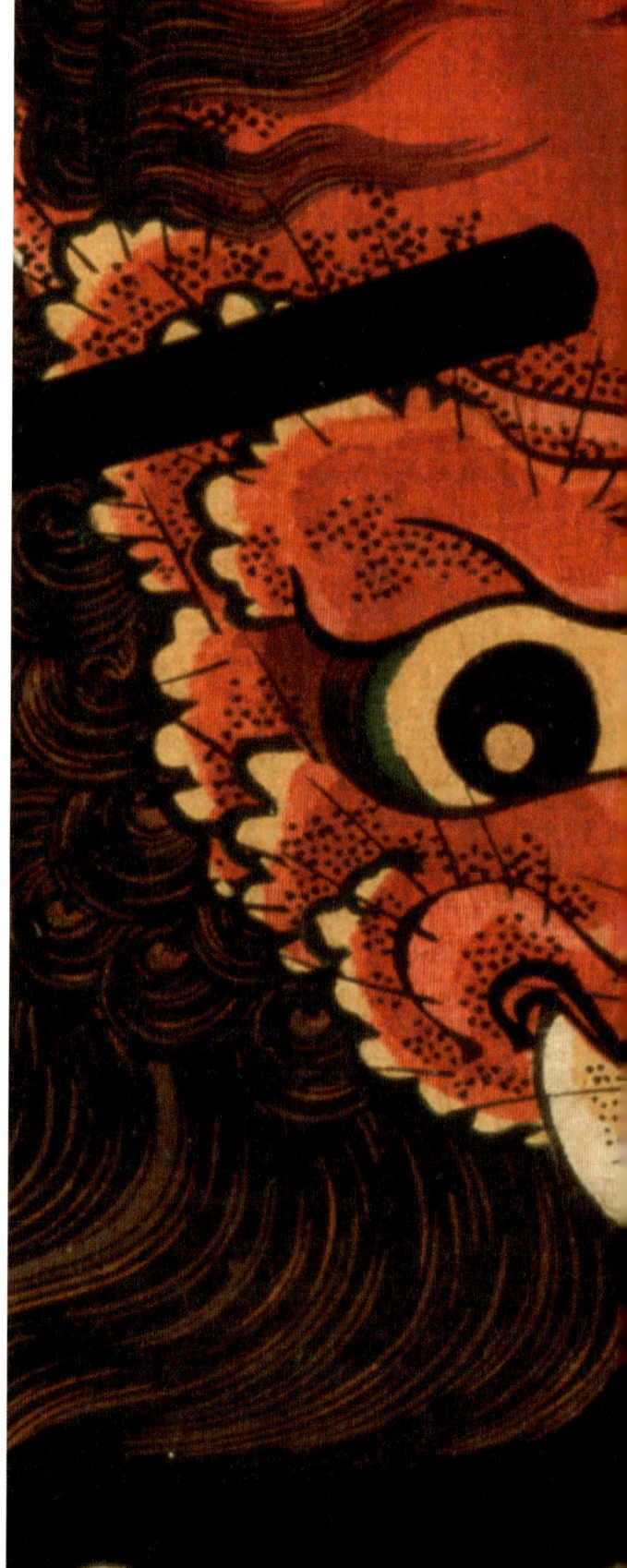

酒呑童子

Shuten-dōji
Ogres (*oni*)

酒呑童子は大江山に住む鬼で、都に出没しては財物や婦女子の略奪を繰り返していました。源頼光は神から授かった毒酒で童子を泥酔させ、その首を斬り落としますが、童子の首は怒り狂いながら襲ってきました。頼光とともに戦う家来、渡辺綱、坂田金時、碓井貞光、卜部季武は「頼光四天王」と呼ばれ、数々の武勇伝を残しました。

Shuten-dōji, an ogre who lived in Mount Ōe, was making a habit of frequenting the town and pillaging women and property. With the help of poisoned liquor from a god, Minamoto no Yorimitsu got Shuten-dōji blind drunk and decapitated him, but was then attacked by his enraged severed head. Many heroic tales also remain of the exploits of the Raikō Shitennō, the four loyal retainers who fought alongside Yorimitsu (Raikō); Watanabe no Tsuna, Sakata no Kintoki, Usui Sadamitsu, and Urabe no Suetake.

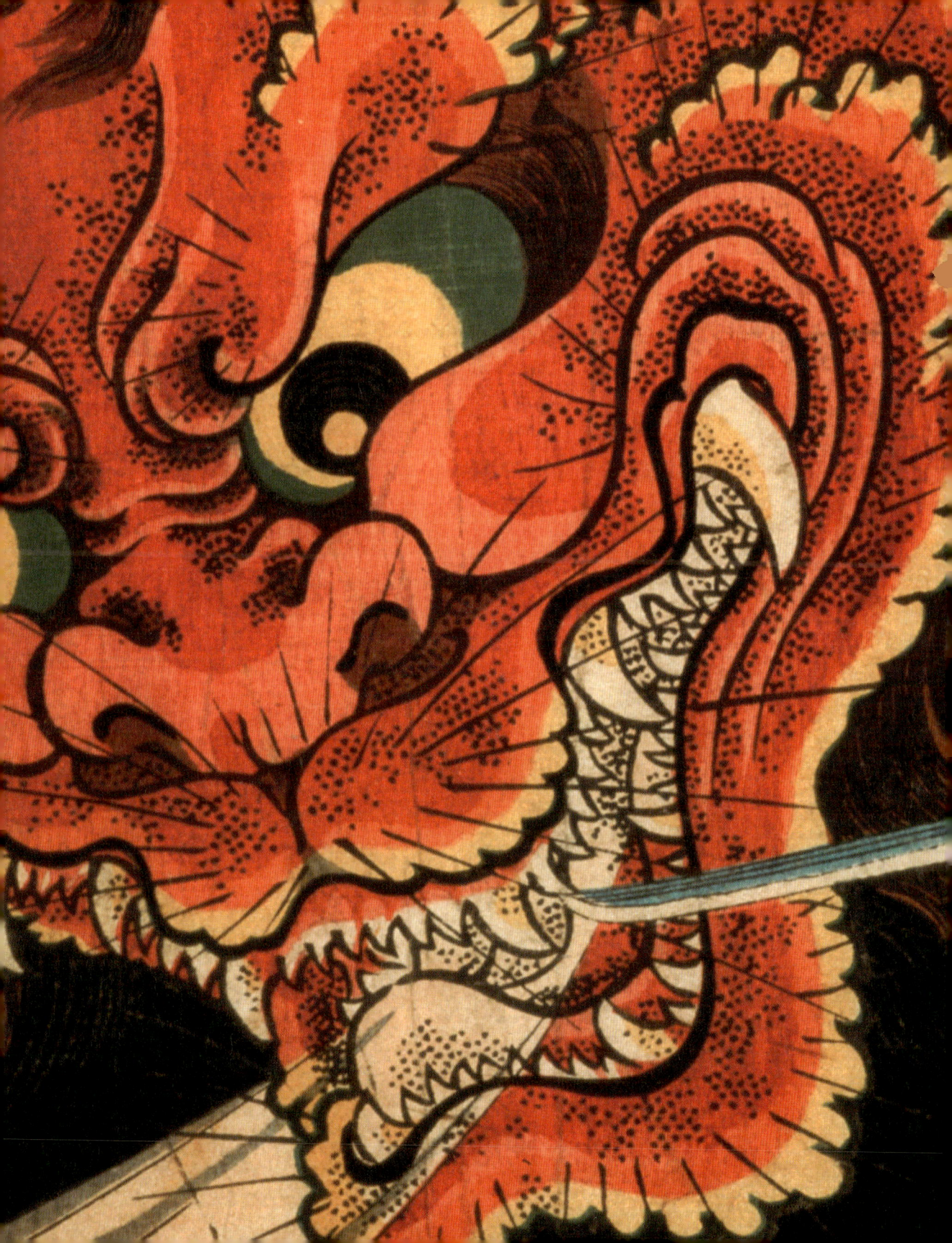

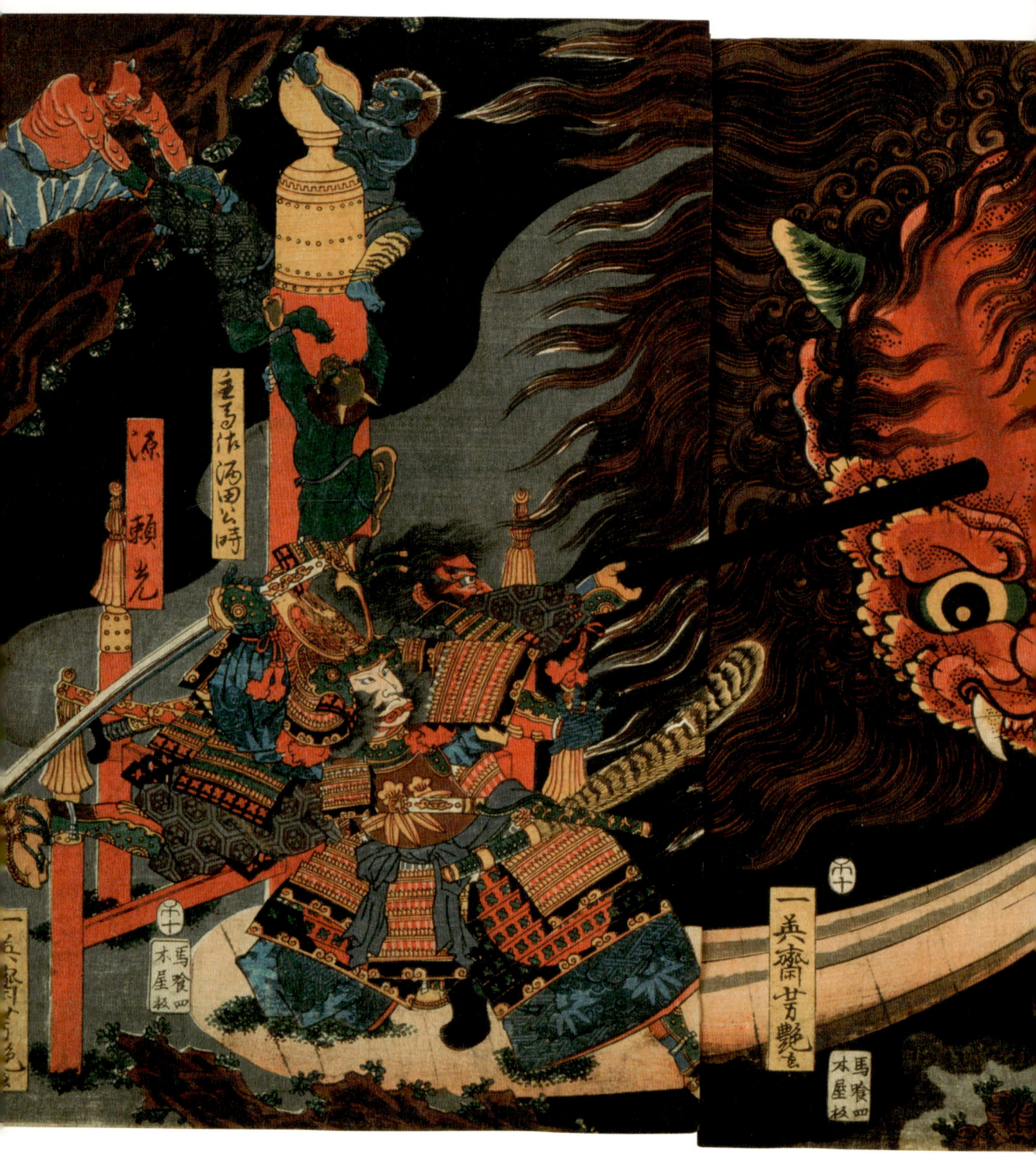

【大江山酒呑退治】歌川芳艶 安政5年（1858）

毒酒を飲まされ寝首を掻かれた酒呑童子。目と歯をむき出したどう猛な顔つきは、怒りに燃えて真っ赤です。左手前の人物が源頼光、その後ろが坂田金時。右手前から、渡辺綱、碓井（図では「碓氷」）貞光、卜部季武。左上には退散する手下の鬼どもが描かれています。

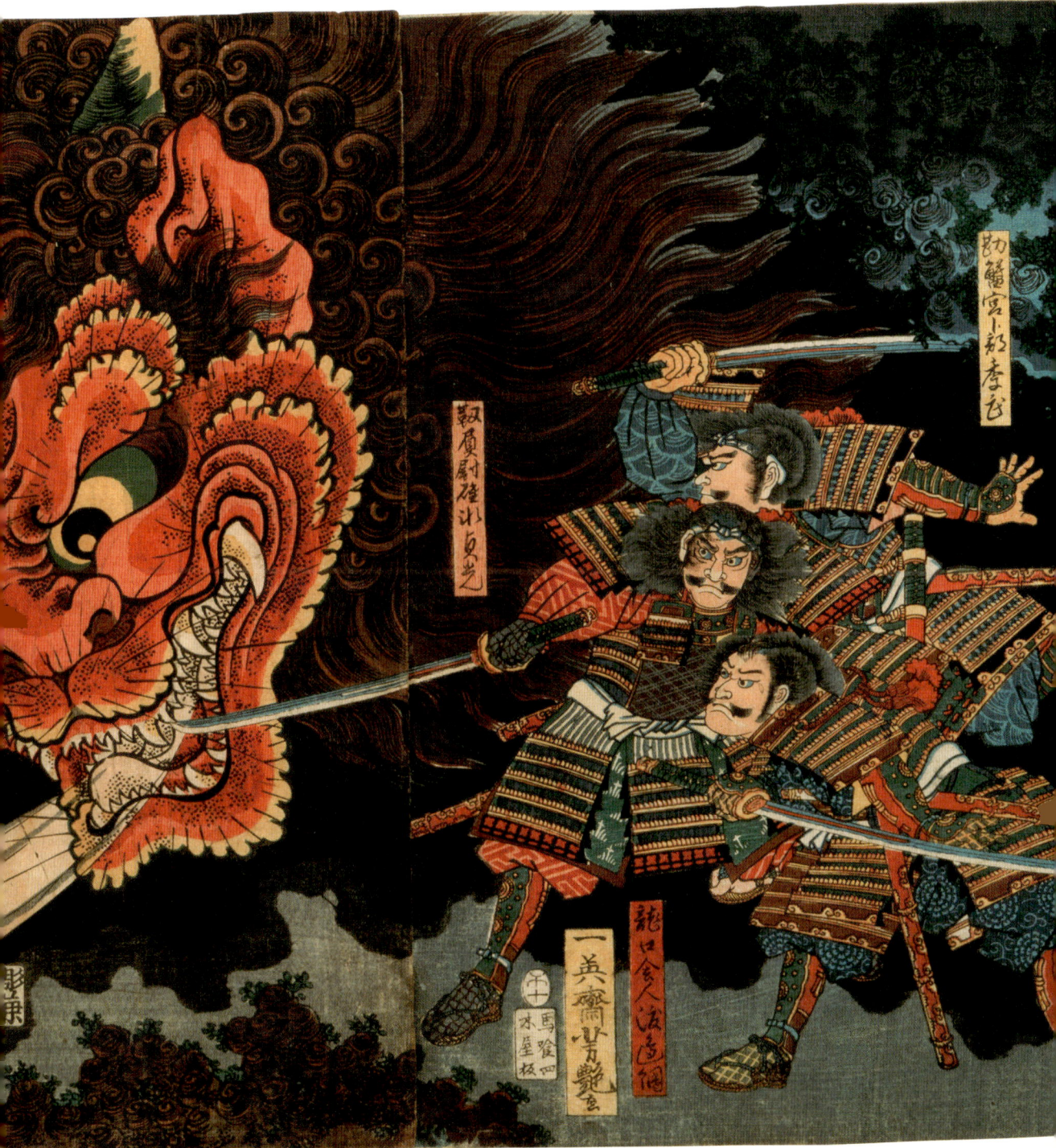

The Downfall of Shuten-dōji of Mount Ōe by Utagawa Yoshitsuya

Shuten-dōji has had his sleeping head cut off, after being slipped poisoned liquor. Eyes popping and teeth bared, his furious face is bright red with burning rage. The person nearest on the left is Minamoto no Yorimitsu, and behind him is Sakata no Kintoki. From the right foreground, Watanabe no Tsuna, Usui Sadamitsu (with a non-standard kanji spelling used for 'Usui' in the picture), and Urabe no Suetake. On the upper left, the ogre followers are shown in retreat.

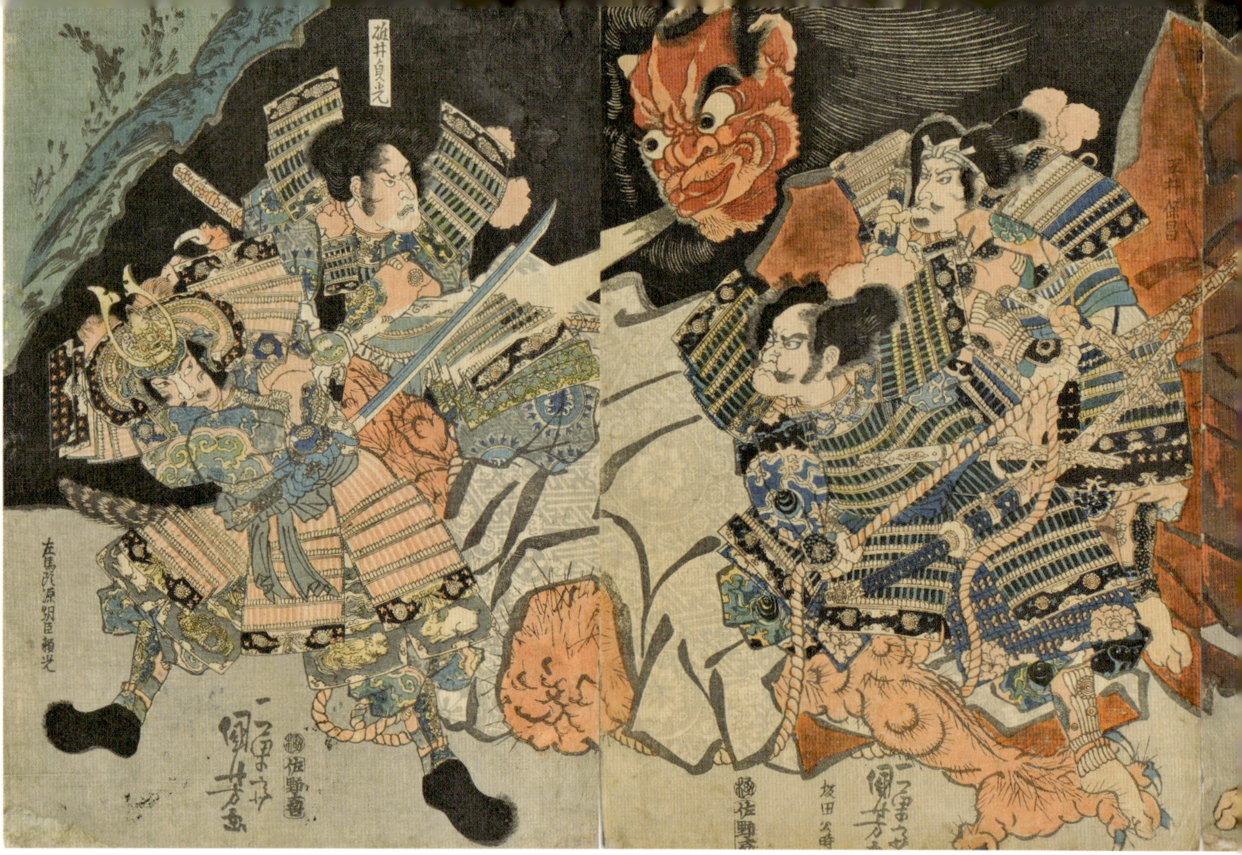

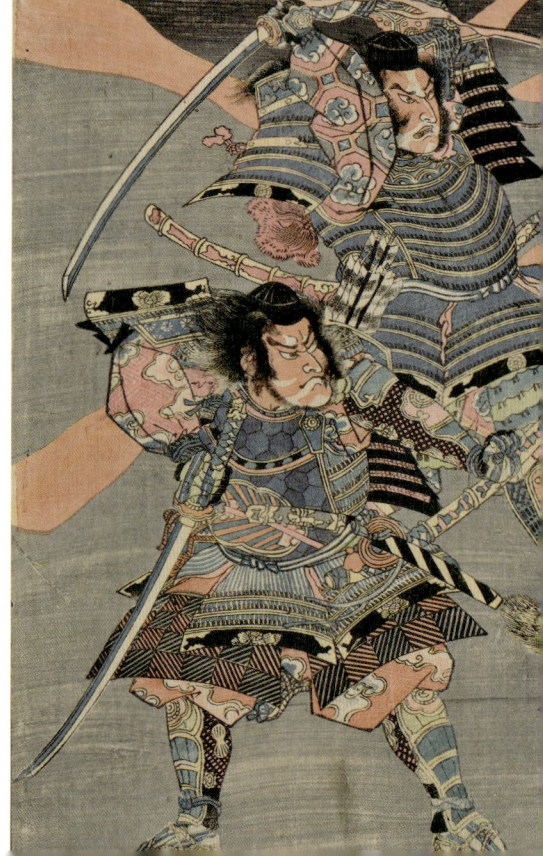

【大江山酒呑退治】勝川春亭 文化年間（1804-18）頃
斬り落とされた酒呑童子の首が、宙を飛びながら火を噴いて源頼光に襲いかかります。童子は頼光の頭に喰らいつきますが、頼光が神から授かった星兜を被っていたので、その威力にはかないませんでした。

The Downfall of Shuten-dōji of Mount Ōe
by Katsukawa Shuntei

This is the scene in which Shuten-dōji's decapitated head attacks Minamoto no Yorimitsu, flying mid-air and breathing fire. Shuten-dōji bites onto Yorimitsu's head, but Yorimitsu is wearing the *hoshi-kabuto* helmet given to him by a god, and Shuten-dōji can not prevail against its power.

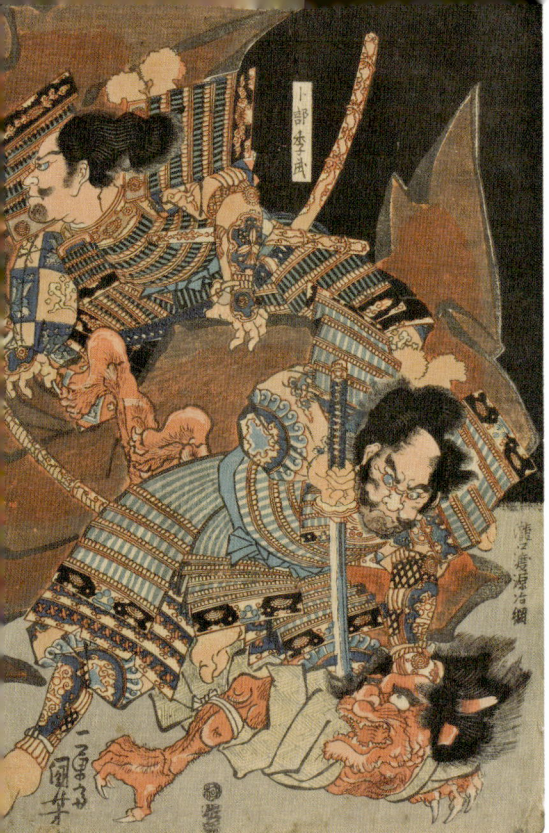

【大江山酒呑退治】歌川国芳　天保年間（1830-44）頃

源頼光の酒呑童子退治。本図では、源頼光の家来は四人ではなく、五人描かれています。もう一人は、頼光四天王とともに大江山に向かった藤原（平井）保昌で、酒呑童子の右側に描かれた人物がその人です。

The Downfall of Shuten-dōji of Mount Ōe
by Utagawa Kuniyoshi

Minamoto no Yorimitsu's defeat of Shuten-dōji. In this picture, Minamoto no Yorimitsu's retainers number not four, but five. The additional warrior is Fujiwara no (Hirai) Yasumasa, on the right-hand side of Shuten-dōji.

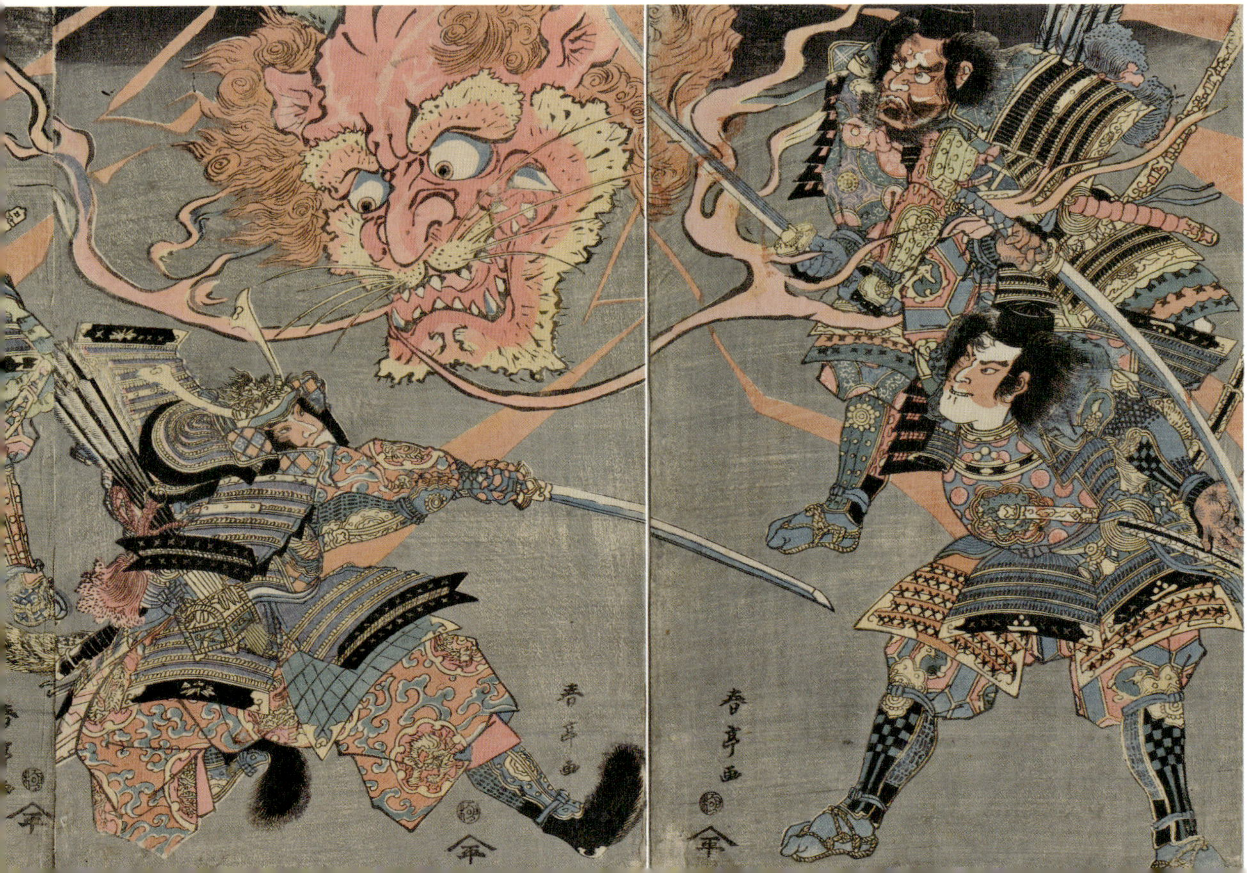

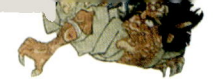

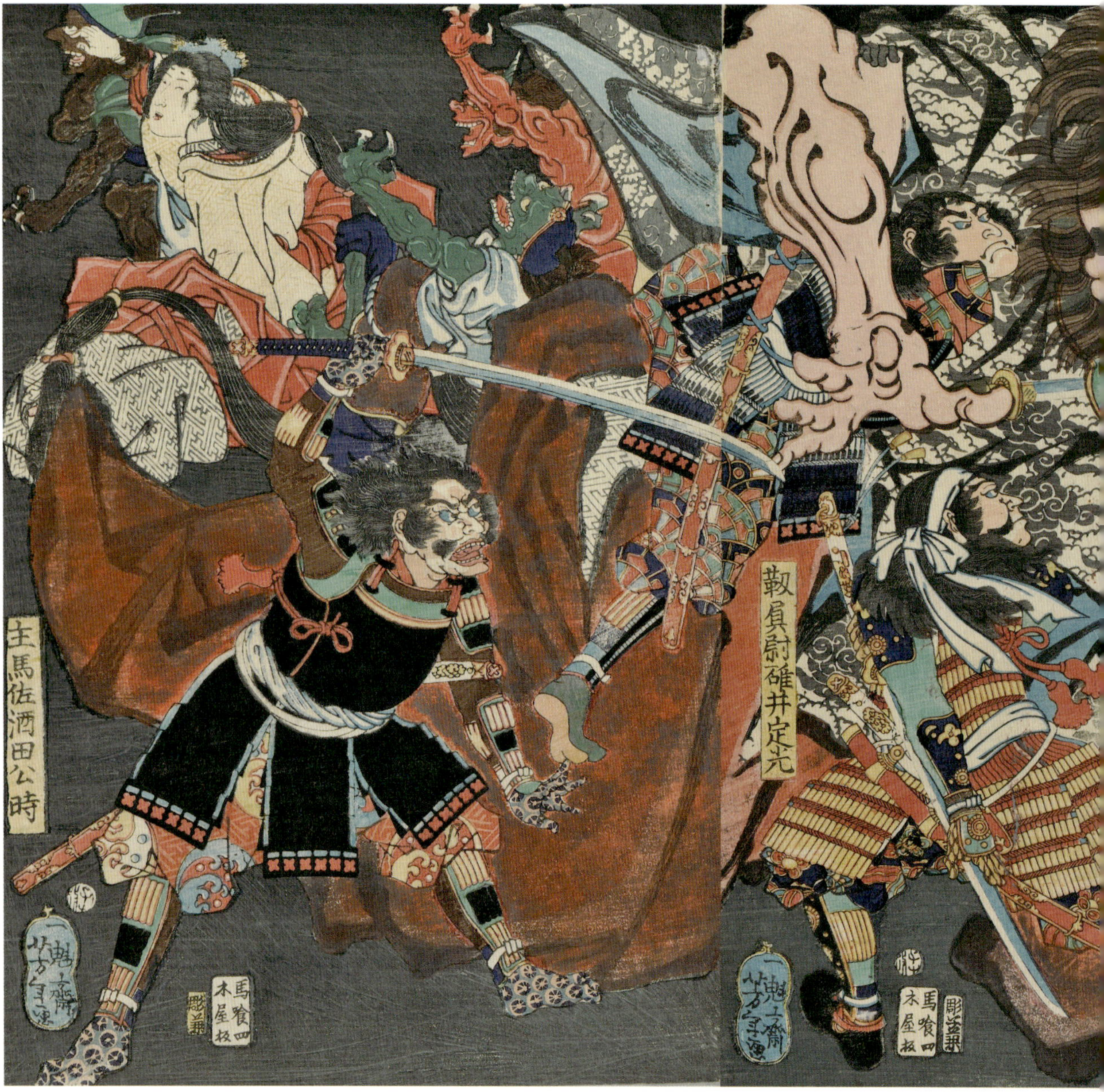

鬼

98

主馬佐坂田公時

鞍員尉碓井定光

【頼光四天王大江山鬼神退治之図】月岡芳年　元治元年(1864)
寝込みを襲われ慌てふためく酒呑童子に、源頼光一党が斬りかかります。本図も、藤原保昌が加わっています。
左上の女性は、都からさらわれてきた貴族の娘です。手下の鬼が乱暴に腕をつかみ、連れ出そうとしています。

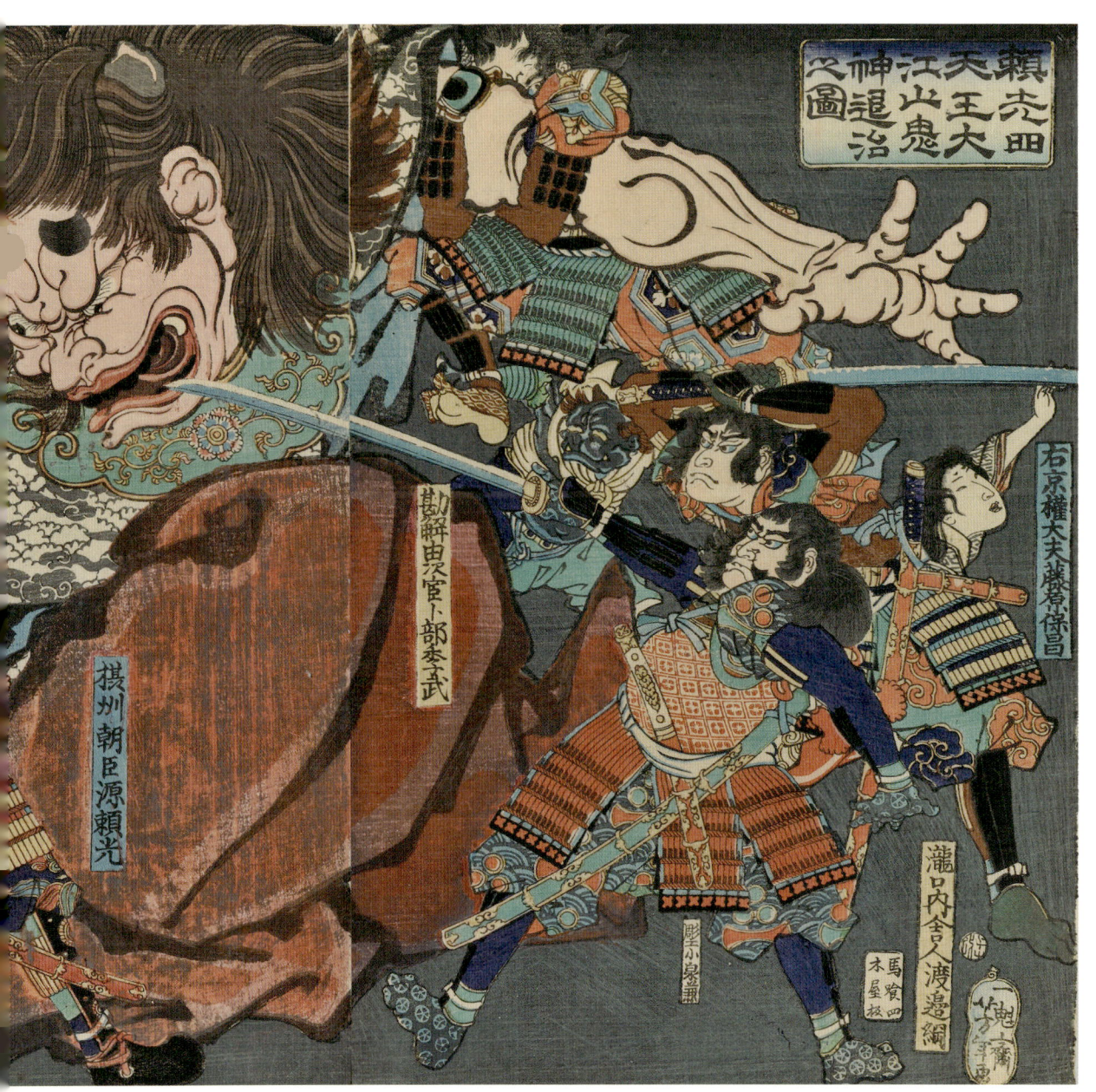

The Four Loyal Retainers of Yorimitsu Defeat the Ogre Gods at Mount Ōe by Tsukioka Yoshitoshi

The scene in which Minamoto no Yorimitsu's party are attacking Shuten-dōji, who is flustered at having been caught sleeping. The girl on the right-hand edge is alarmed by the sudden melee and tries to flee. Clinging to her arm as if to pull her away is an ogre follower (on the upper left).

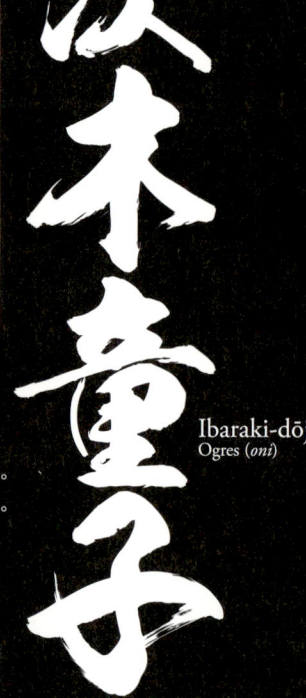

「イッヒッヒ」と笑いながら飛び去る白髪の老婆。実は、羅生門にすむ鬼の茨木童子が化けた姿なのです。酒呑童子の手下で、羅生門（または一条戻橋）にて頼光四天王の一人、渡辺綱に片腕を斬り落とされ奪われました。綱の伯母に化けた茨木童子は綱のもとを訪ね、まんまと腕を奪い返しました。

茨木童子
Ibaraki-dōji
Ogres (*oni*)

A white-haired old woman flies away, cackling "Eee-hee-hee!" This is actually a shape taken by the ogre Ibaraki-dōji, who lives in the ruined Kyoto city gatehouse, Rashōmon. As Shuten-dōji's henchman, his arm was chopped off and taken by Watanabe no Tsuna, one of the Raikō Shitennō, at Rashōmon (or the Ichijō Modori-bashi Bridge). Ibaraki-dōji changes into the shape of Tsuna's aunt to visit him, and succeeds in getting his arm back.

【新形三十六怪撰 老婆鬼腕を持去る図】月岡芳年 明治22年（1889）

The Old Devil Woman Retrieving Her Arm from the series *Shinkei sanjūrokkaisen (New Forms of Thirty-Six Ghosts)* by Tsukioka Yoshitoshi

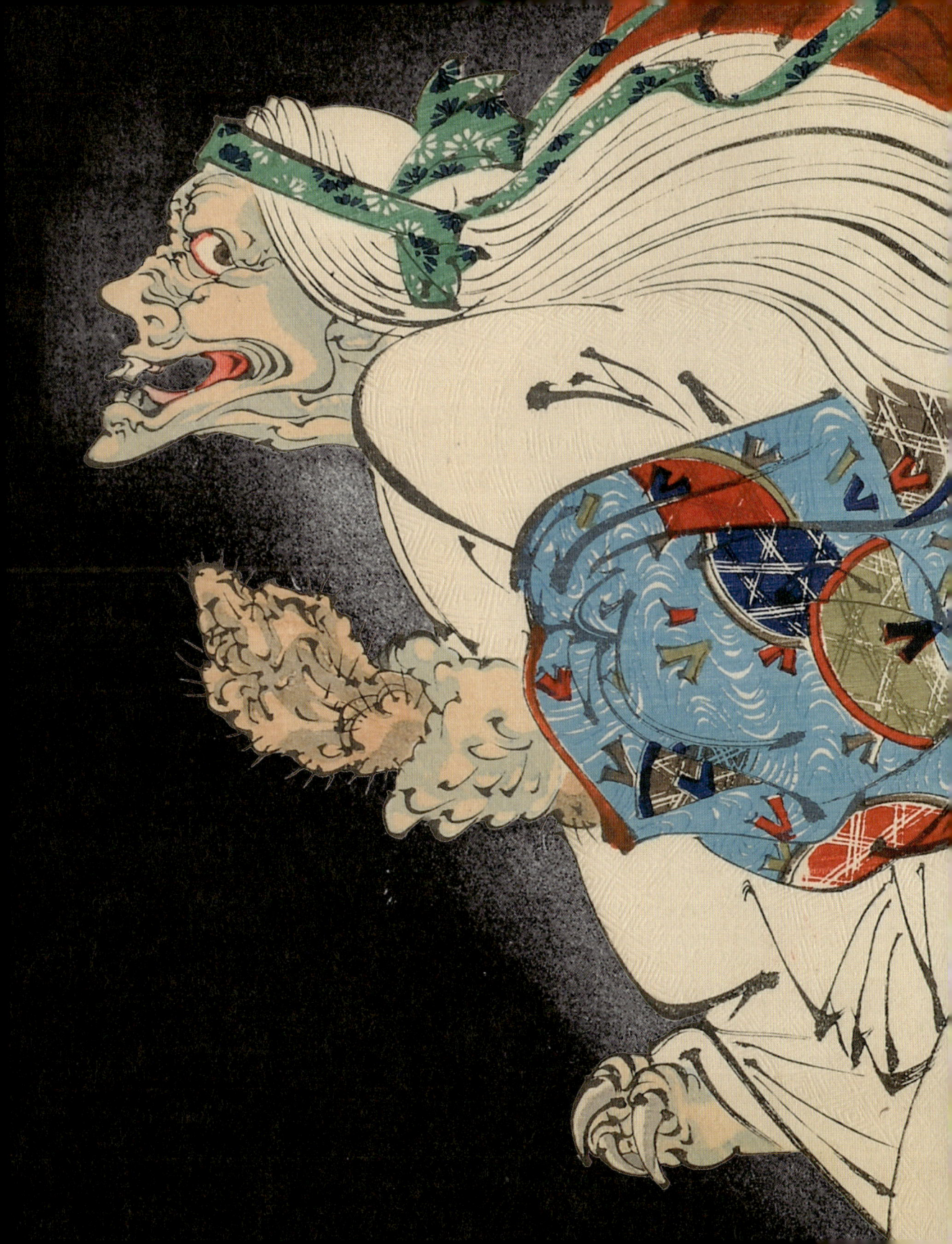

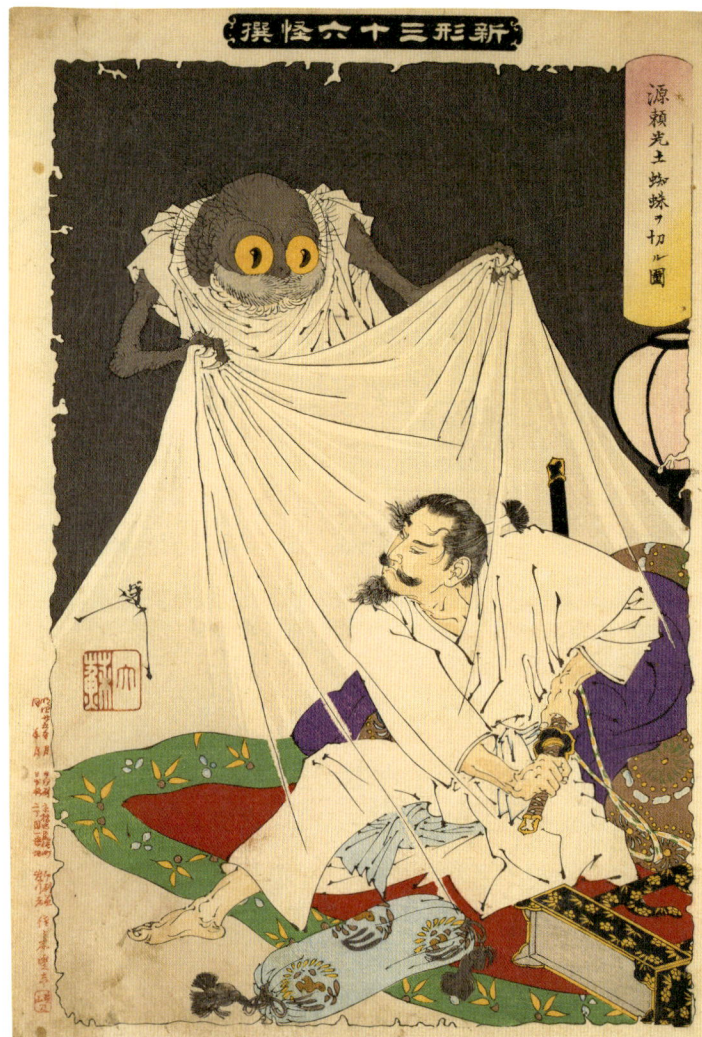

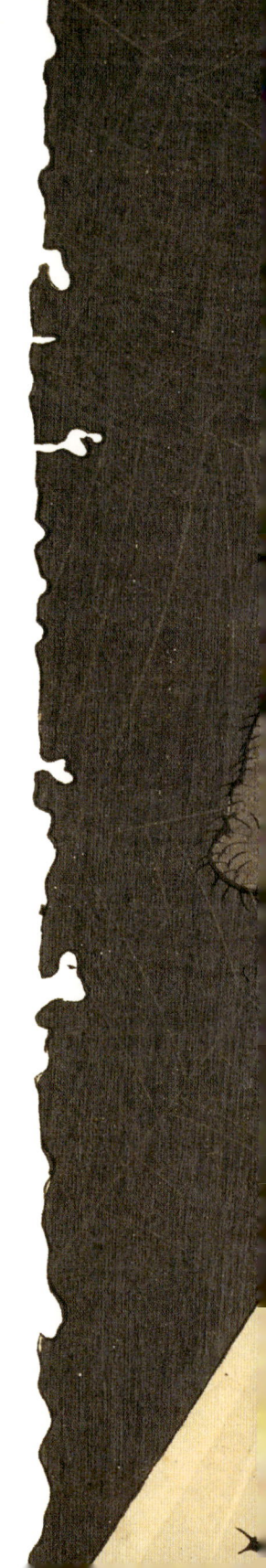

源頼光のもうひとつの伝説、土蜘蛛退治。病床の頼光の枕元に、白衣を着て僧に
化けた土蜘蛛の妖怪が現れました。土蜘蛛は膜状に張った蜘蛛の巣で、頼光を
捕らえようとしています。これに気づいた頼光は、刀に手をかけ蜘蛛に向かいます。

The defeat of the Earth Spider is another heroic tale of Minamoto no Yorimitsu.
Monsters appearing by the sickbed of Yorimitsu are the work of the demonic
Tsuchigumo, the Earth Spider. In the form of a monk wearing white, Tsuchigumo is
trying to capture Yorimitsu by covering him with sheets of spider web. Having realized
what is happening, Yorimitsu rounds on the spider, hand on his sword.

【新形三十六怪撰 源頼光土蜘蛛ヲ切ル図】月岡芳年 明治25年 (1892)
Minamoto no Yorimitsu Preparing to Kill the Earth Spider
from the series *Shinkei sanjūrokkaisen (New Forms of Thirty-Six Ghosts)* by Tsukioka Yoshitoshi

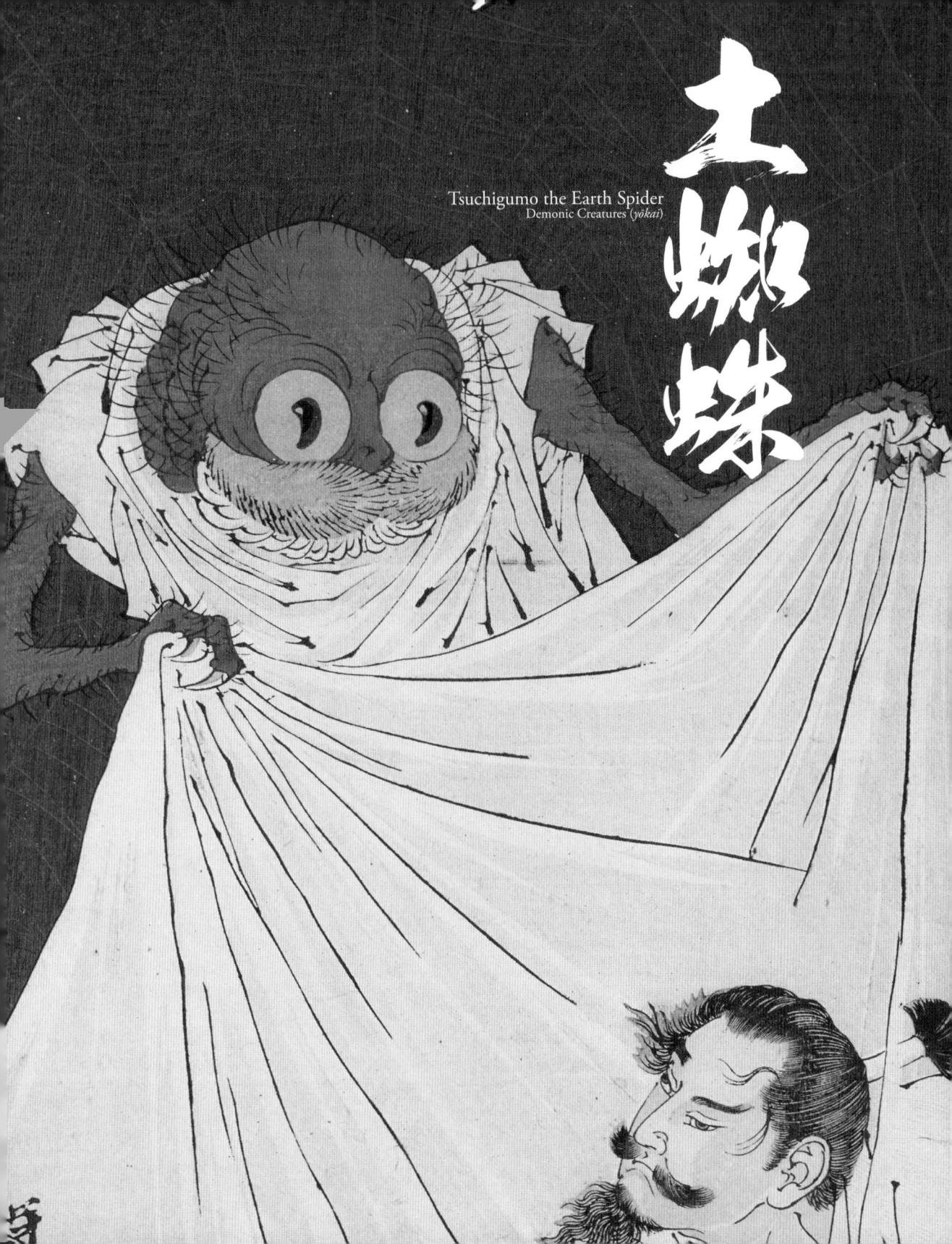

Tsuchigumo the Earth Spider
Demonic Creatures (*yōkai*)

土蜘蛛

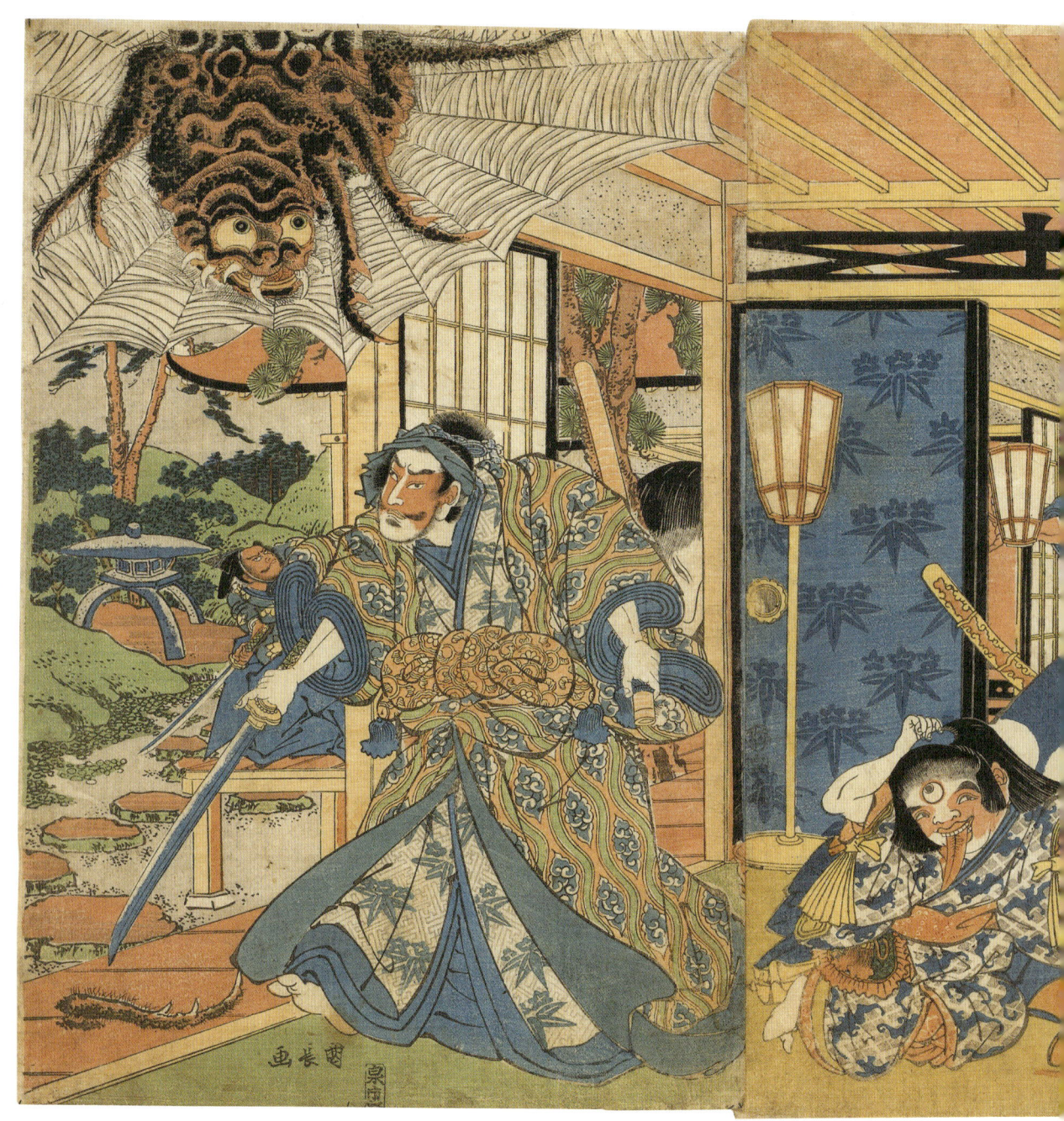

104

【源頼光屋舗に妖怪現る】 歌川国長 文政年間（1818-30）

頼光の屋敷に現れた妖怪たち。天井の左側では、土蜘蛛がにたりと笑います。右側には、長い首の見越し入道。その他、
三つ目の茶汲み小僧、舌を出す一つ目小僧、大首女など、妖怪たちが大暴れ。すべて土蜘蛛が操っています。

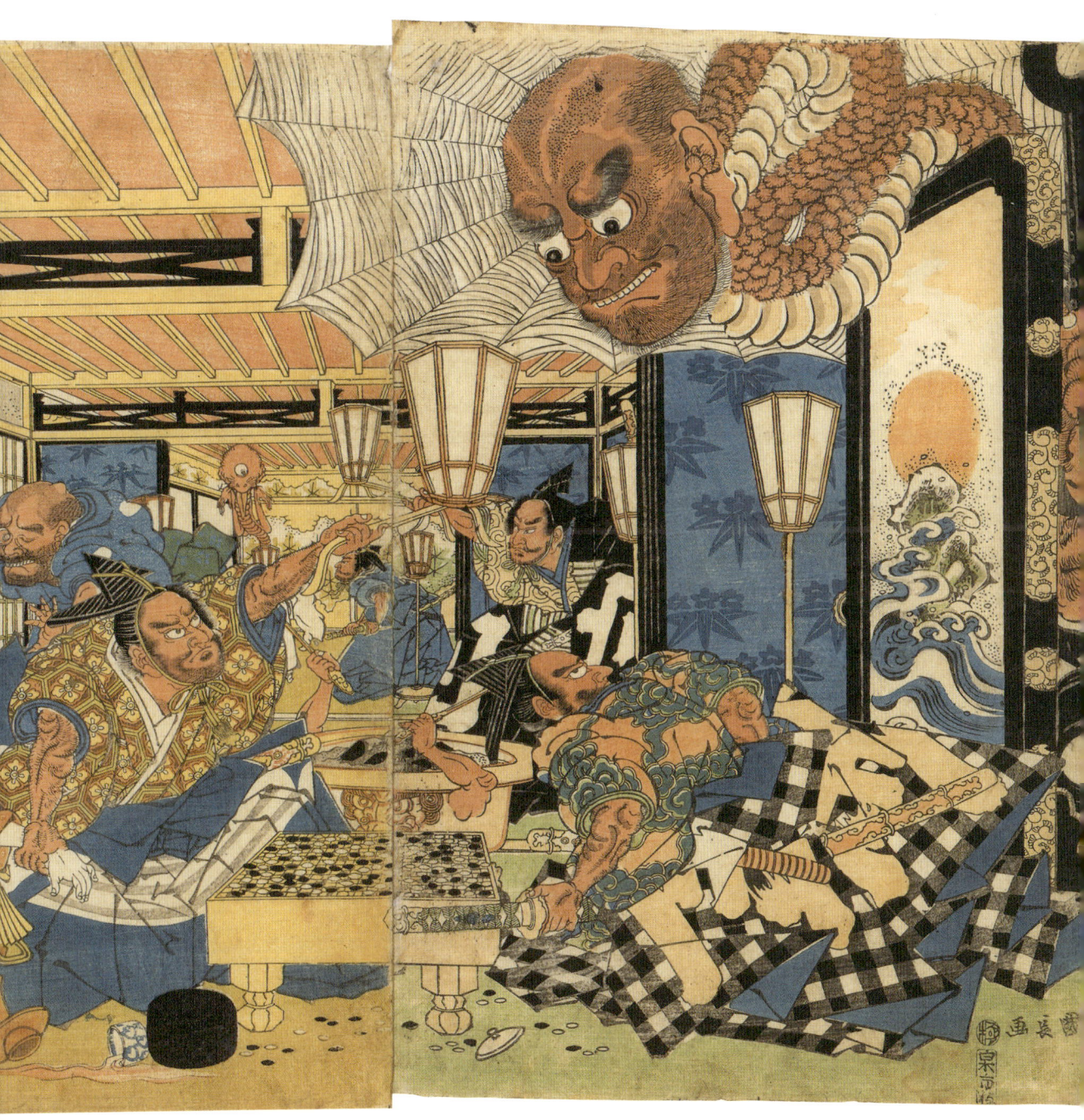

Monsters Appear in the Mansion of Minamoto no Yorimitsu by Utagawa Kuninaga

A pack of *yōkai* (monsters) have appeared in Yorimitsu's mansion. On the left side of the ceiling, Tsuchigumo the Earth Spider is grinning. On the right, a long-necked *mikoshi nyūdō* goblin leers. Among the *yōkai* wrecking havoc are a three-eyed tea-serving goblin, a one-eyed goblin with his tongue poking out, and a large-headed female. All are controlled by the Earth Spider.

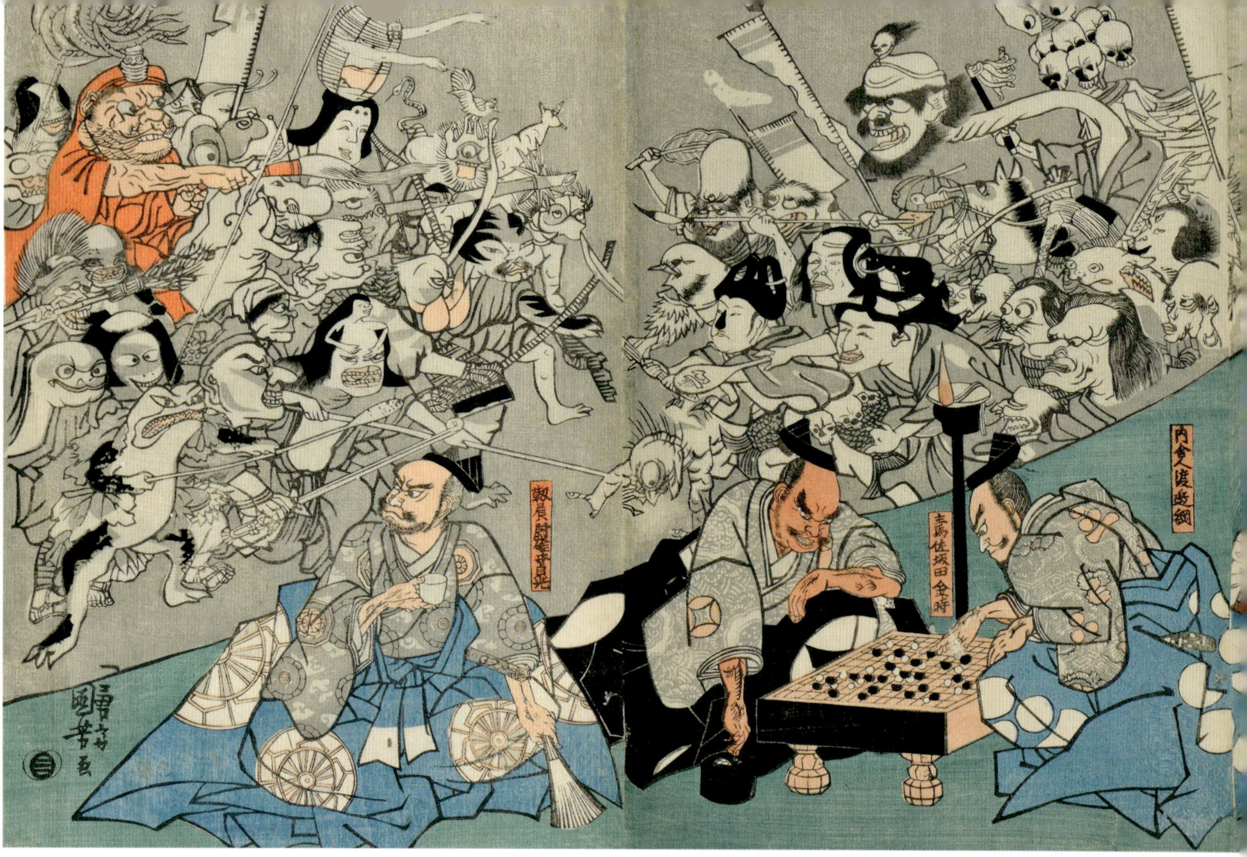

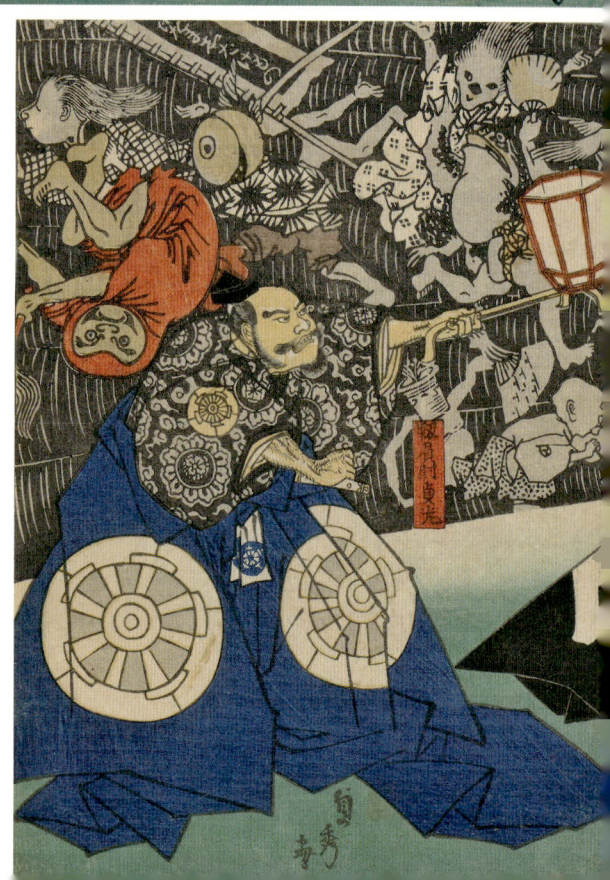

【源頼光朝臣と四天王・土蜘蛛の図】

歌川貞秀 天保14年（1843）

前図の国芳描く土蜘蛛図の評判を受け、今度は久太郎という版元が、
貞秀に同様の図を描かせました。化け物の部分をなくして検閲を通し、
店頭に並べ、化け物入りの図は奥に隠して尋ねてきた人だけに売りまし
たが、評判になってしまったため久太郎と貞秀は罰せられました。

*Tsuchigumo the Earth Spider, Minamoto no Yorimitsu and
his Four Loyal Retainers* by Utagawa Sadahide

The Kuniyoshi print of the Earth Spider by Kuniyoshi gained a reputation,
which led publisher Kyūtarō to commission Sadahide to create a similar
print. To get past the censors, the monsters were redacted, and this version
was sold over-the-counter. The version with the monsters included was
hidden out the back, and only sold to customers who asked for it, but caused
a sensation, which resulted in the punishment of Kyutarō and Sadahide.

【源頼光公舘土蜘作妖怪図】

歌川国芳　天保13-14年（1842-43）

当時、この図は天保改革を諷刺した判じ物であると評判になりました。頼光は将軍徳川家慶、卜部季武は老中水野忠邦、妖怪は改革で損をした者たちを暗示するといわれています。抵触を恐れた版元はこの図を回収し、版木は処分したため筆禍を免れました。

The Earth Spider Conjures Up Demons at the Mansion of Minamoto no Yorimitsu by Utagawa Kuniyoshi

Back in the day, this print gained notoriety as an allusion to the Tenpō Reforms. Yorimitsu (sleeping) was interpreted as representing Shōgun Tokugawa Ieyoshi, Urabe no Suetake as senior councillor Mizuno Tadakuni, and the monsters as the people suffering under the reforms. Fearing reprisals, the publisher recalled the print and disposed of the printing block, and so avoided penalties.

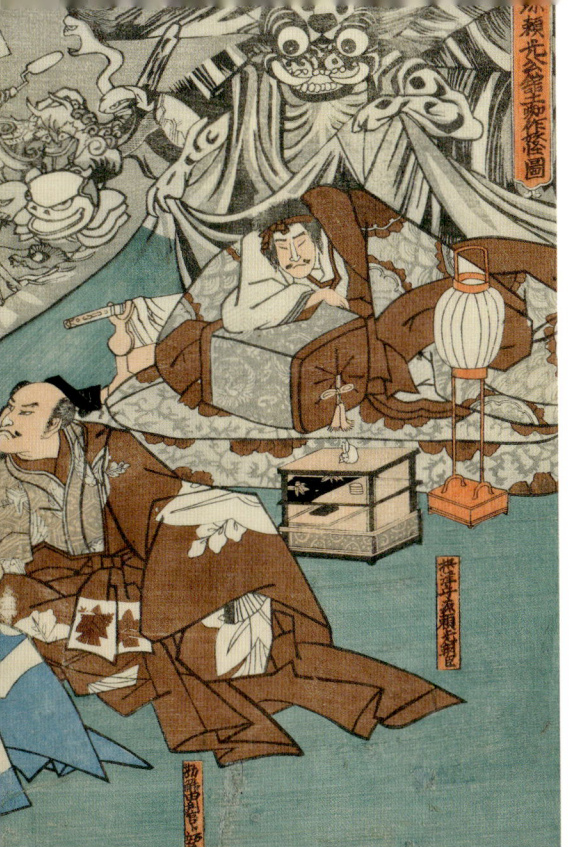

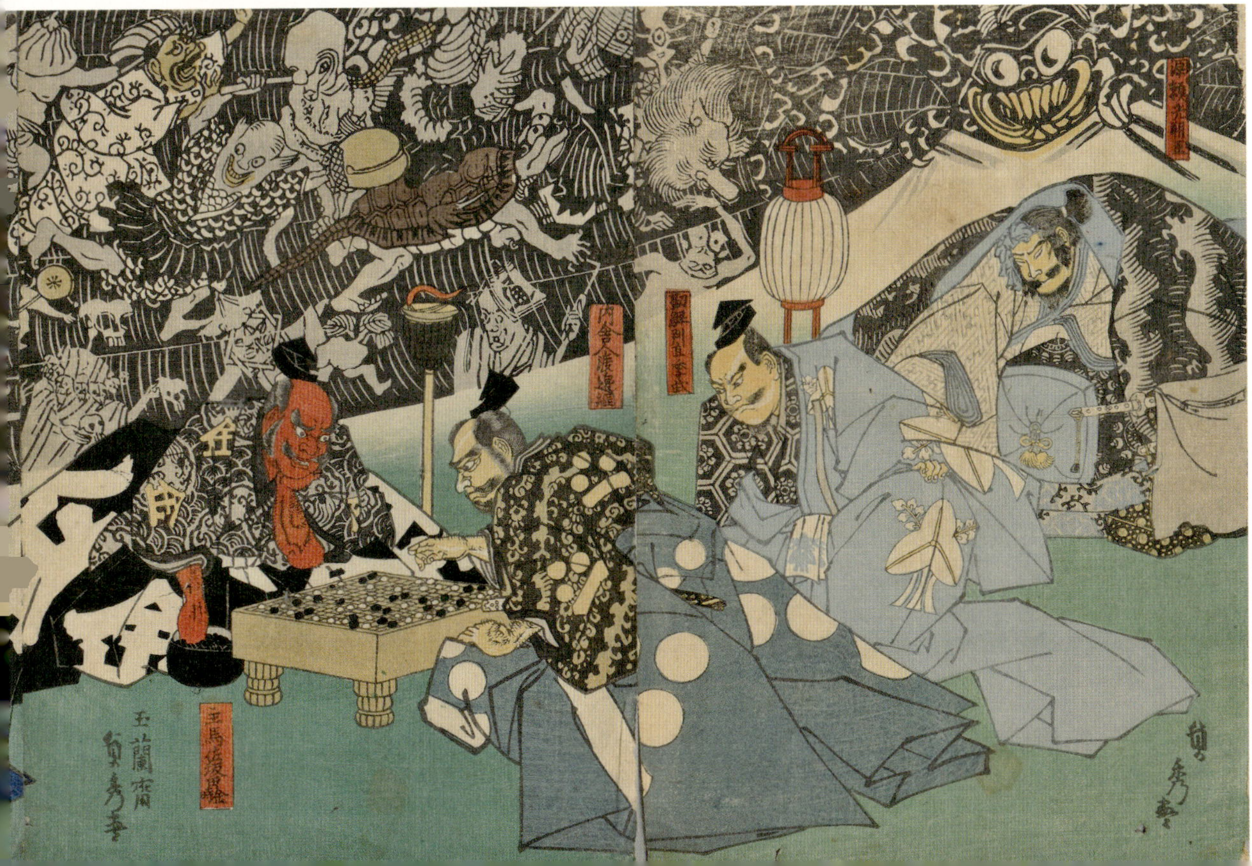

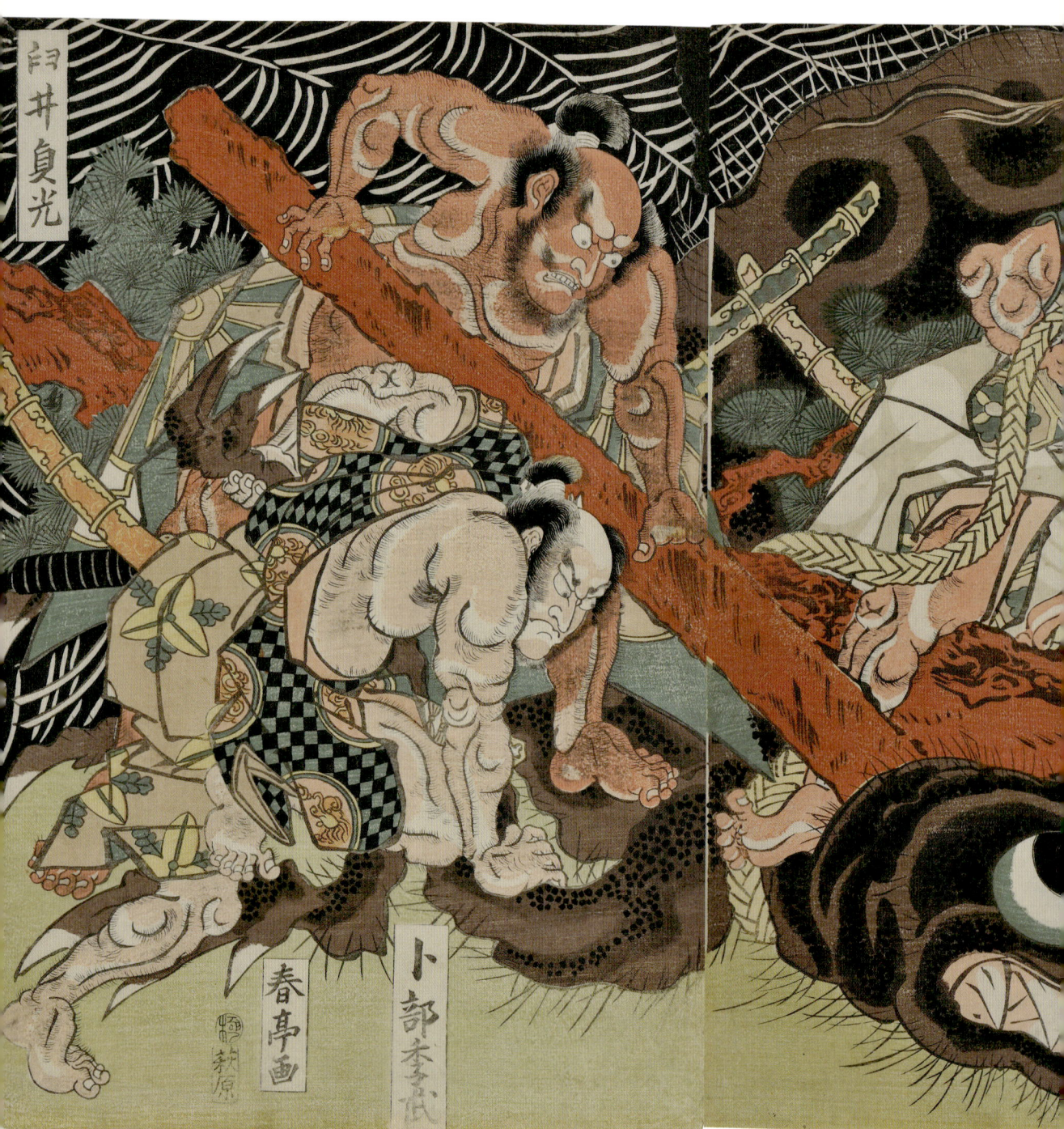

【土蜘蛛退治の図】 勝川春亭　文化（1804-18）末期～文政（1818-30）初期

暴れ狂う土蜘蛛の妖怪を、剛腕の頼光四天王が押さえつけ、縄で縛って捕獲します。

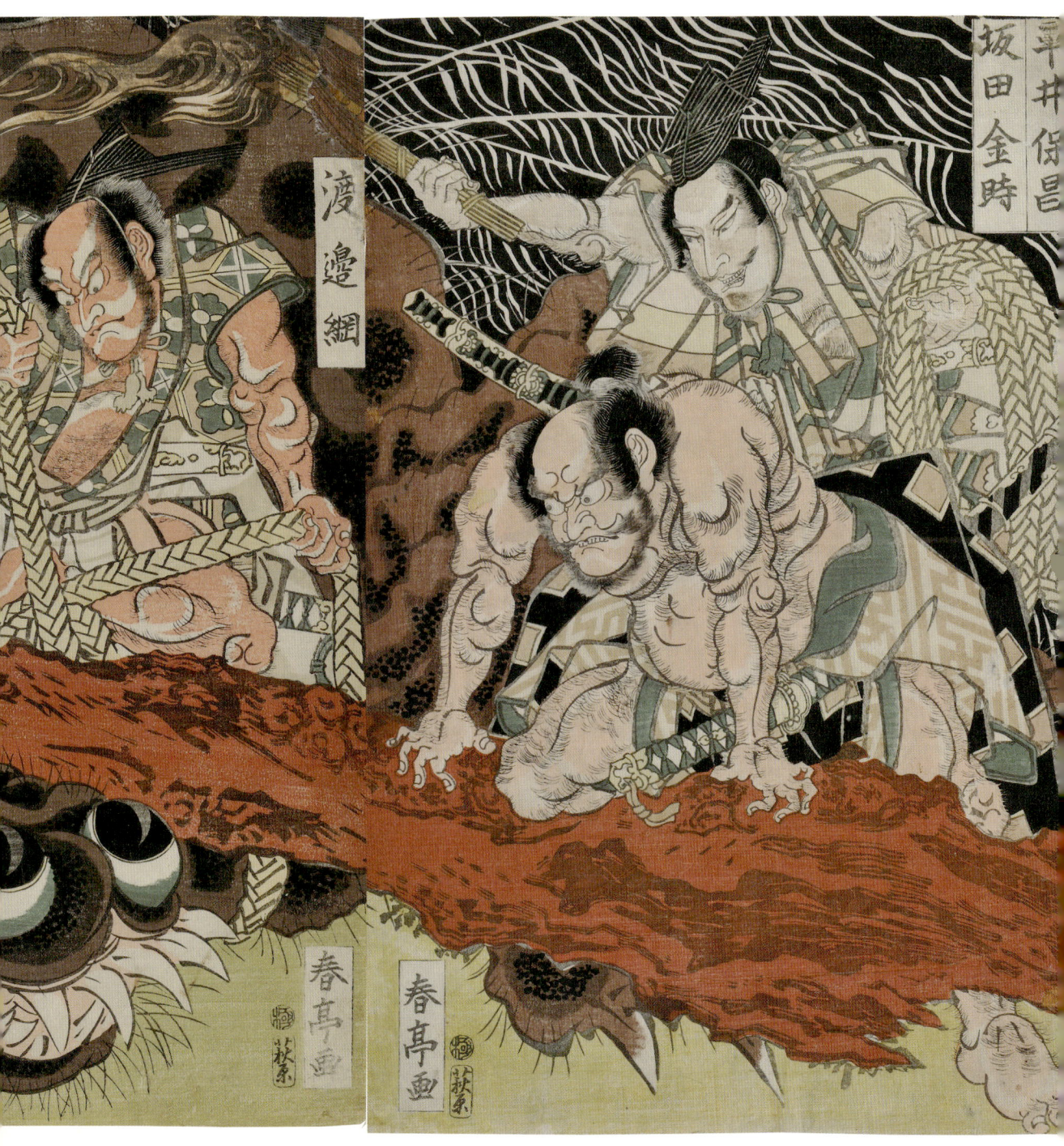

The Defeat of the Earth Spider by Katsukawa Shuntei

The powerful Raikō Shitennō are holding down the rampaging monster Tsuchigumo, binding it with rope to capture it.

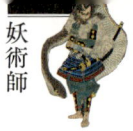

妖術師

【妖術師】
天竺徳兵衛

Tenjiku Tokubē
Wielders of Magic (*yōjutsushi*)

妖術で大蝦蟇を操る徳兵衛は、実は木曽義仲の遺児・大日丸で、父の遺志を継いで日本転覆を企てます。

Tokubē, who charms a giant toad with sorcery, is actually Dainichimaru, the son of the late Kiso Yoshinaka, and to fulfil his father's dying wish, he attempts the overthrow of Japan.

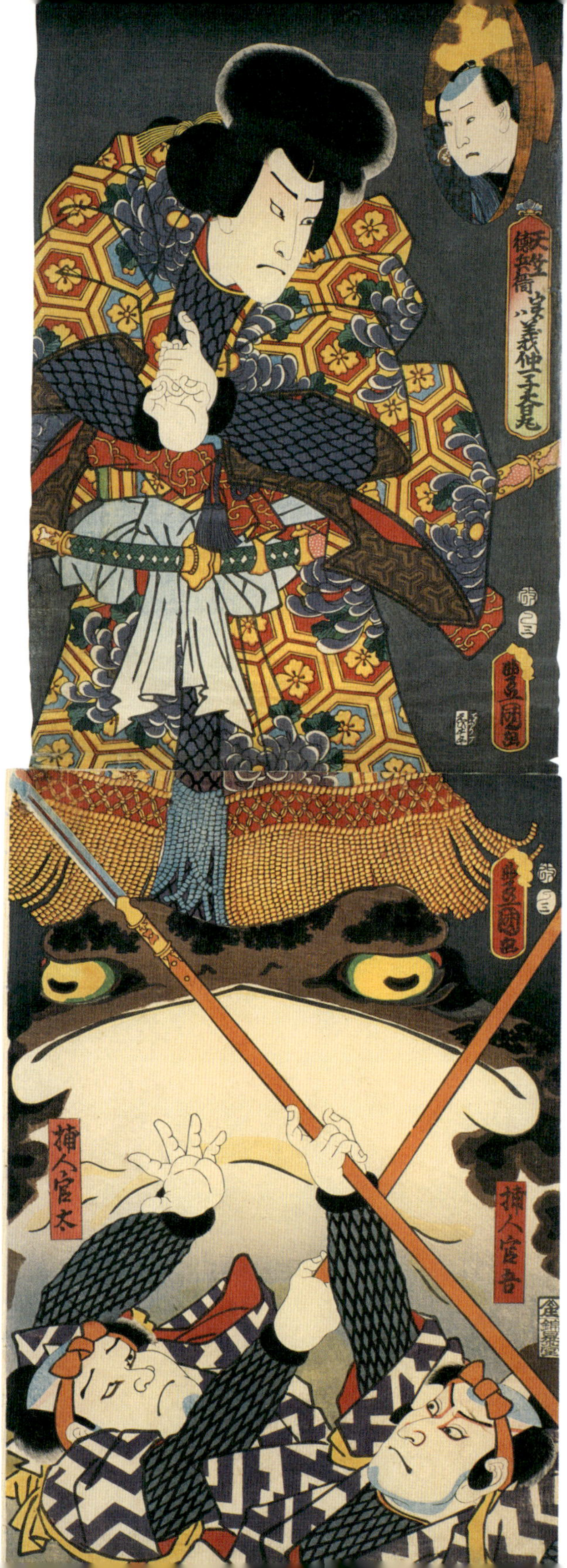

【天竺徳兵衛 実ハ義仲一子大日丸】
歌川国貞（三代豊国）安政4年（1857）
Tenjiku Tokubē: Actually Yoshinaka's son Dainichimaru
by Utagawa Kunisada
(also known as Utagawa Toyokuni III)

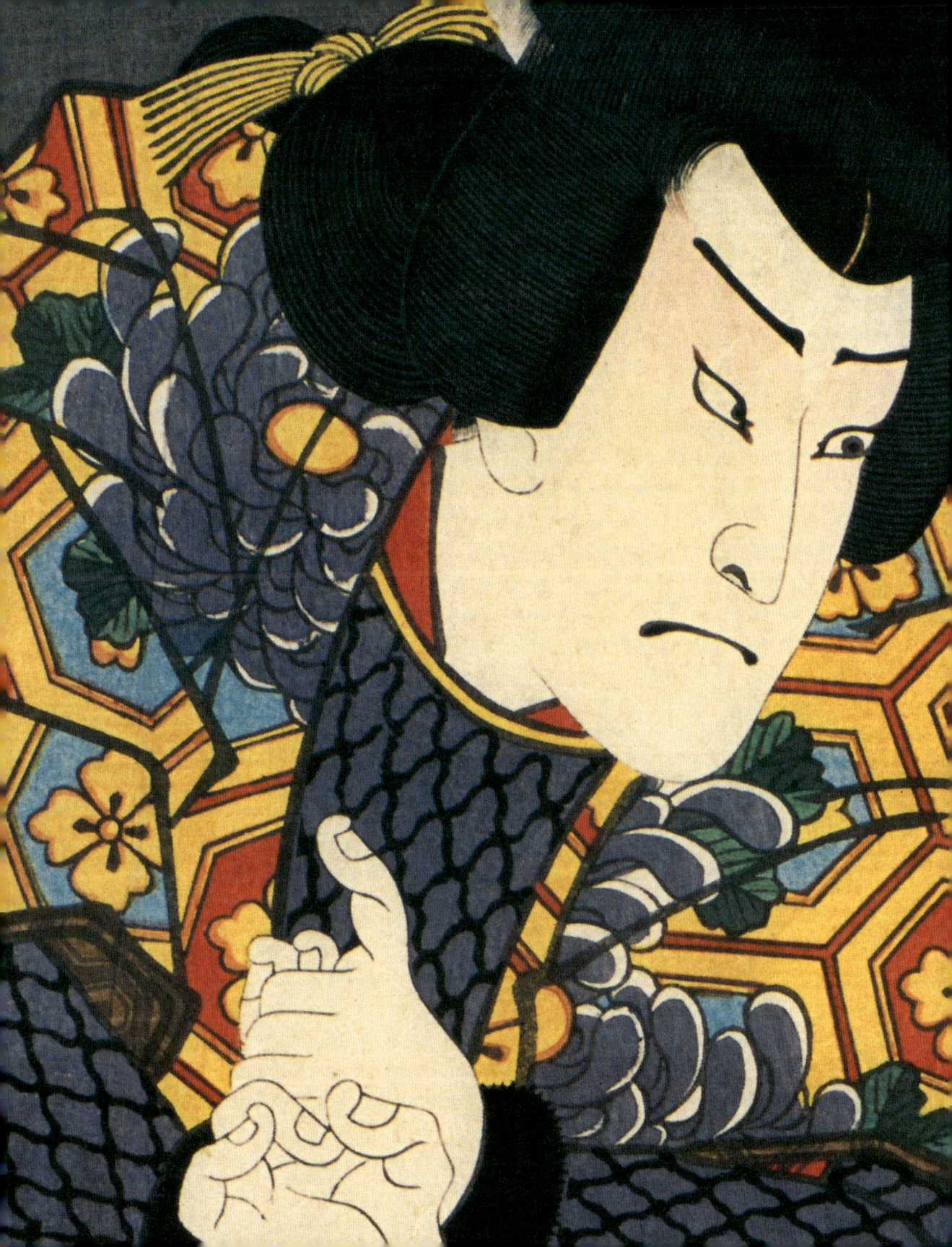

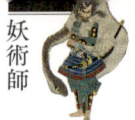

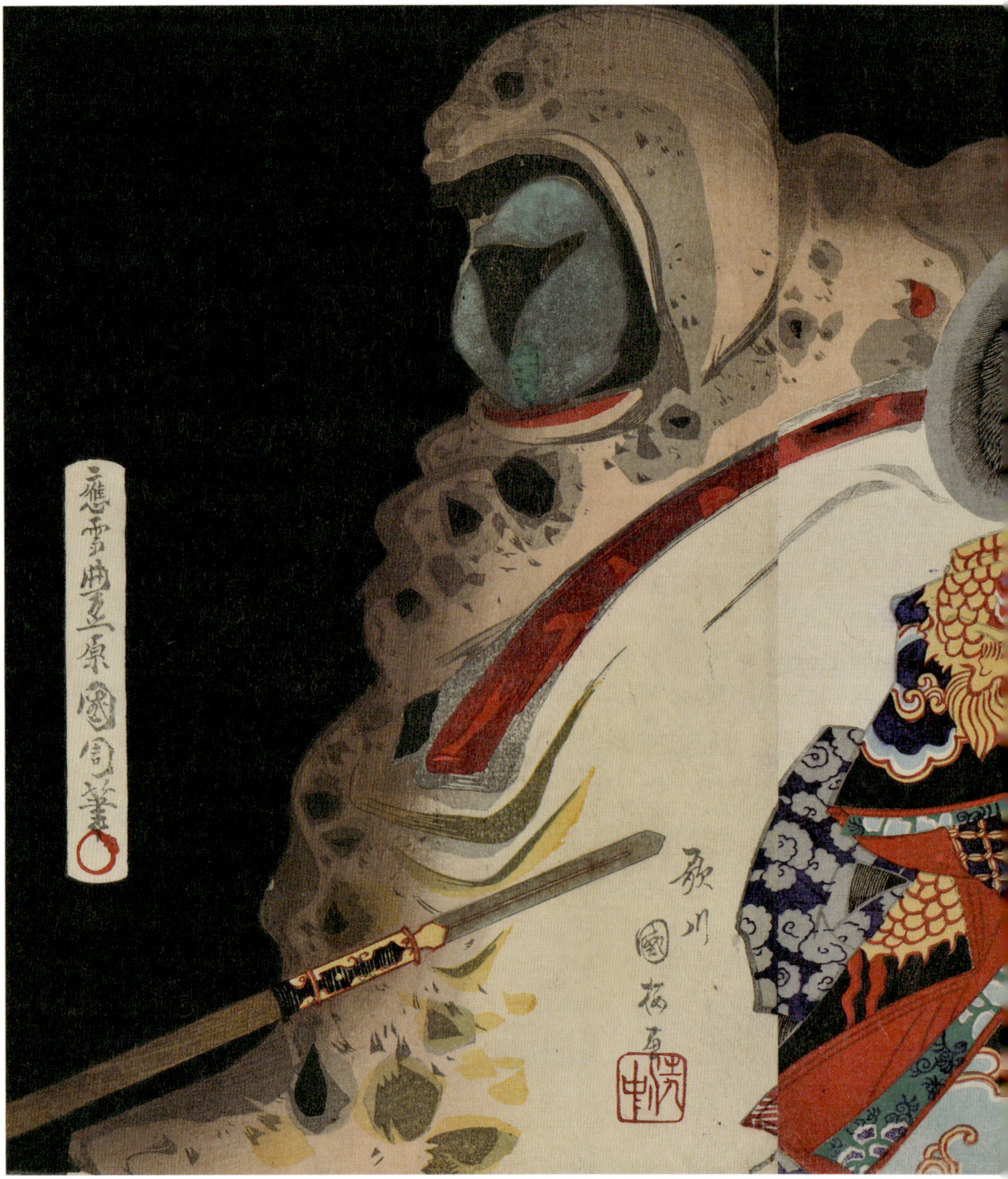

【天竺徳兵衛・尾上菊五郎】豊原国周・歌川国梅 明治16年（1883）

歌舞伎「増補天竺徳兵衛」より。徳兵衛が巨大な蝦蟇とともに登場。五代目尾上菊五郎扮する天竺徳
兵衛を国周が描き、背後の蝦蟇を国梅が描きました。

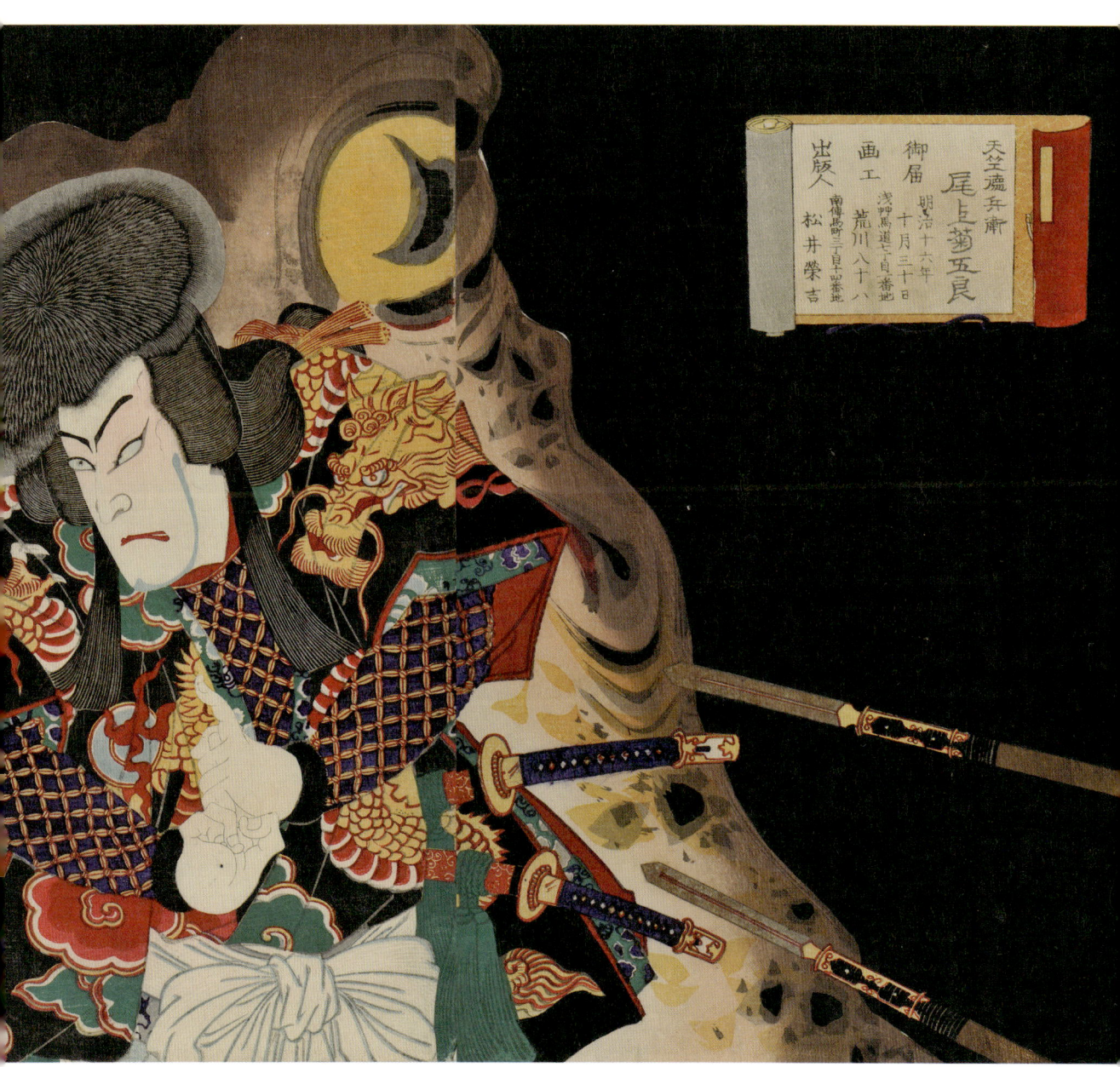

Onoe Kikugorō V as Tenjiku Tokubē by Toyohara Kunichika and Utagawa Kuniume

A scene from the kabuki play *Zōho Tenjiku Tokubē*, in which Tokubē takes the stage accompanied by a huge toad. Tenjiku Tokubē, played by Onoe Kikugorō V, was drawn by Kunichika, and the toad in the background was drawn by Kuniume. This is a unique combined work which carries a feeling of tension.

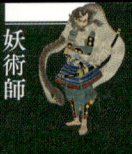

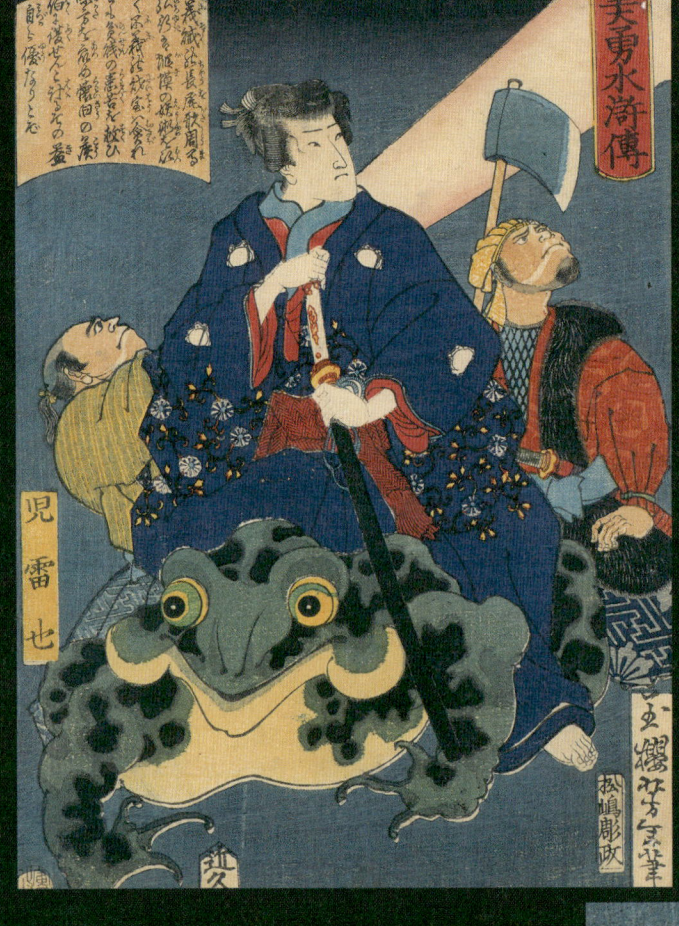

児雷也

Jiraiya
Wielders of Magic (*yōjutsushi*)

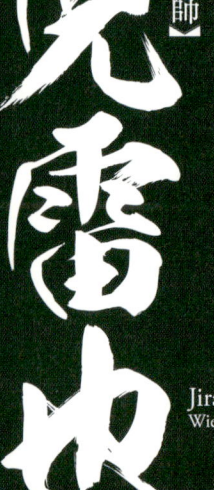

児雷也は仙素道人に蝦蟇の妖術を学び、蛞蝓使いの綱手姫とともに、親の仇・大蛇丸に立ち向かいます。また、お金持ちから盗んで貧民に分け与えるヒーローとしても有名です。

Jiraiya learnt toad magic from Senso-dōjin, and joined forces with the slug sorceress Princess Tsunade to confront their archenemy Orochimaru. He is known as a hero who stole from the rich to give to the poor.

【美勇水滸傳・児雷也】月岡芳年 慶応2年（1866）
Jiraiya from the series *Biyū Suikoden (Sagas of Beauty and Bravery)* by Tsukioka Yoshitoshi

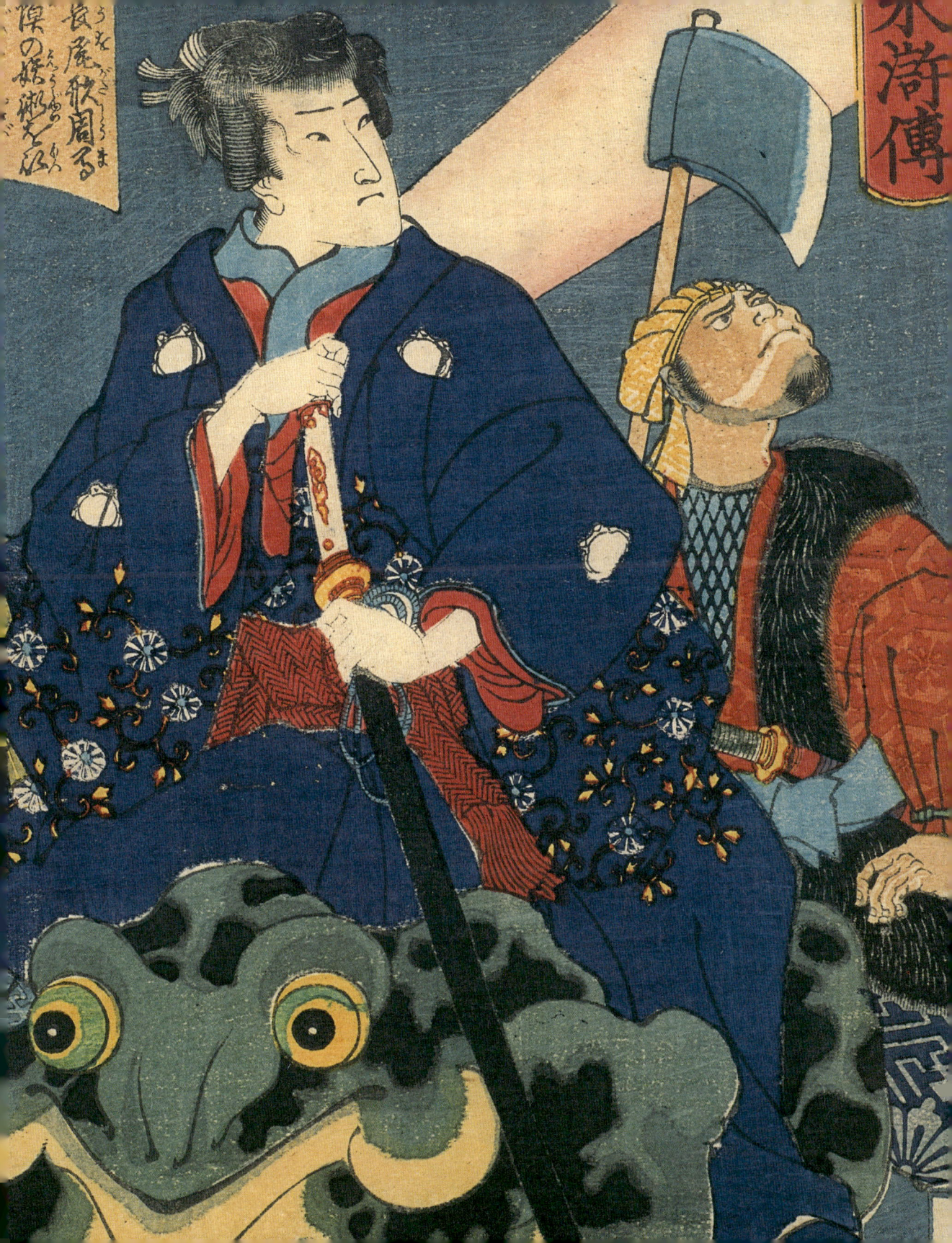

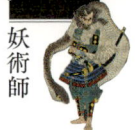

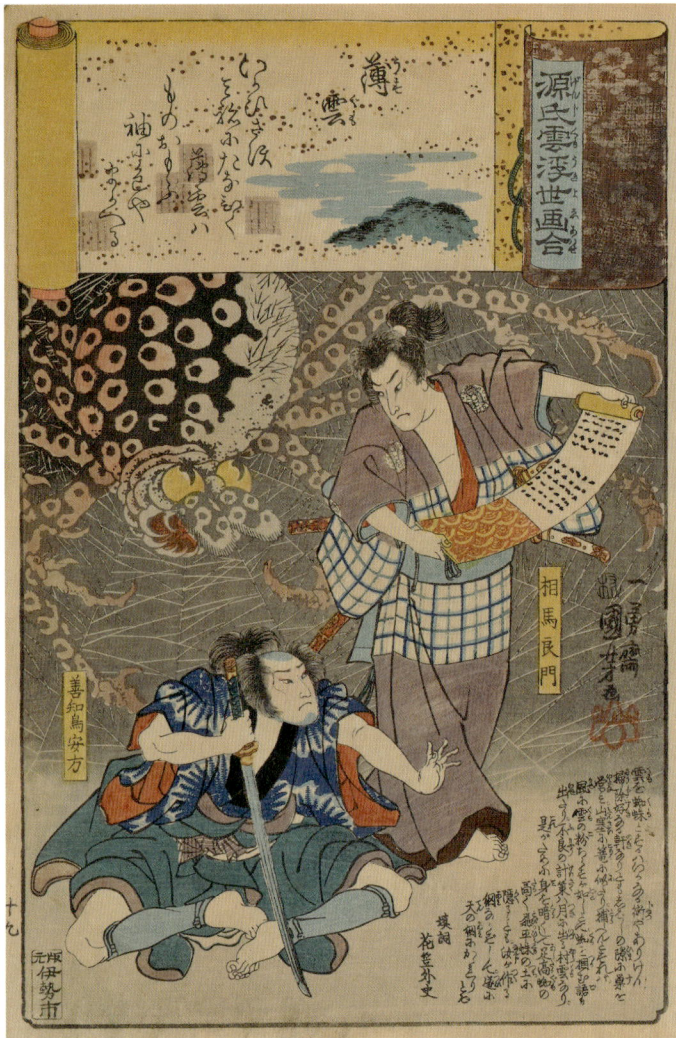

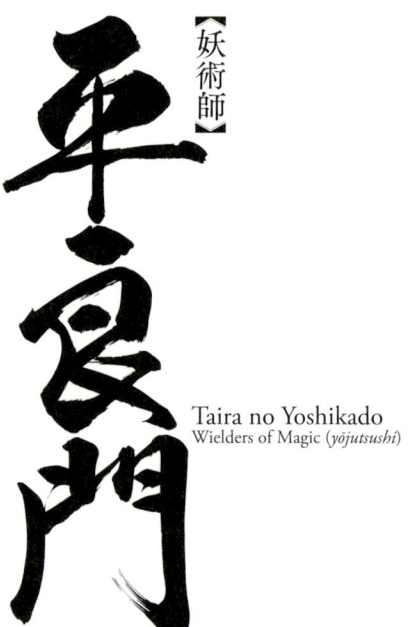

【妖術師】

Taira no Yoshikado
Wielders of Magic (*yōjutsushi*)

平（相馬）良門は肉芝仙人より妖術を授かり、父の遺志を継いで謀反を企て ます。父の家臣であった善知鳥安方は、良門の企てを止めようとしますが、聞き 入れられなかったため、自害し亡霊となって忠告し続けようとします。

This print is based on *yomihon Utō Yasukata Chūgiden (The Loyalty of Utō Yasukata)*. Summoned by magic, the frogs divide into enemies and allies to do battle. Their puppeteer sits in the center making arcane gestures and muttering mystic words. Taira no Yoshikado (right) and Igaju no Tarō (left) are planning a rebellion to fulfill their father and lord's last wishes.

【源氏雲浮世画合・相馬良門と大蜘蛛】歌川国芳 天保14年〜弘化3年（1843-46）

Sōma Yoshikado and the Big Spider from the series *Genji kumo ukiyo-e awase (Genji Clouds Matched with Ukiyo-e Pictures)* by Utagawa Kuniyoshi

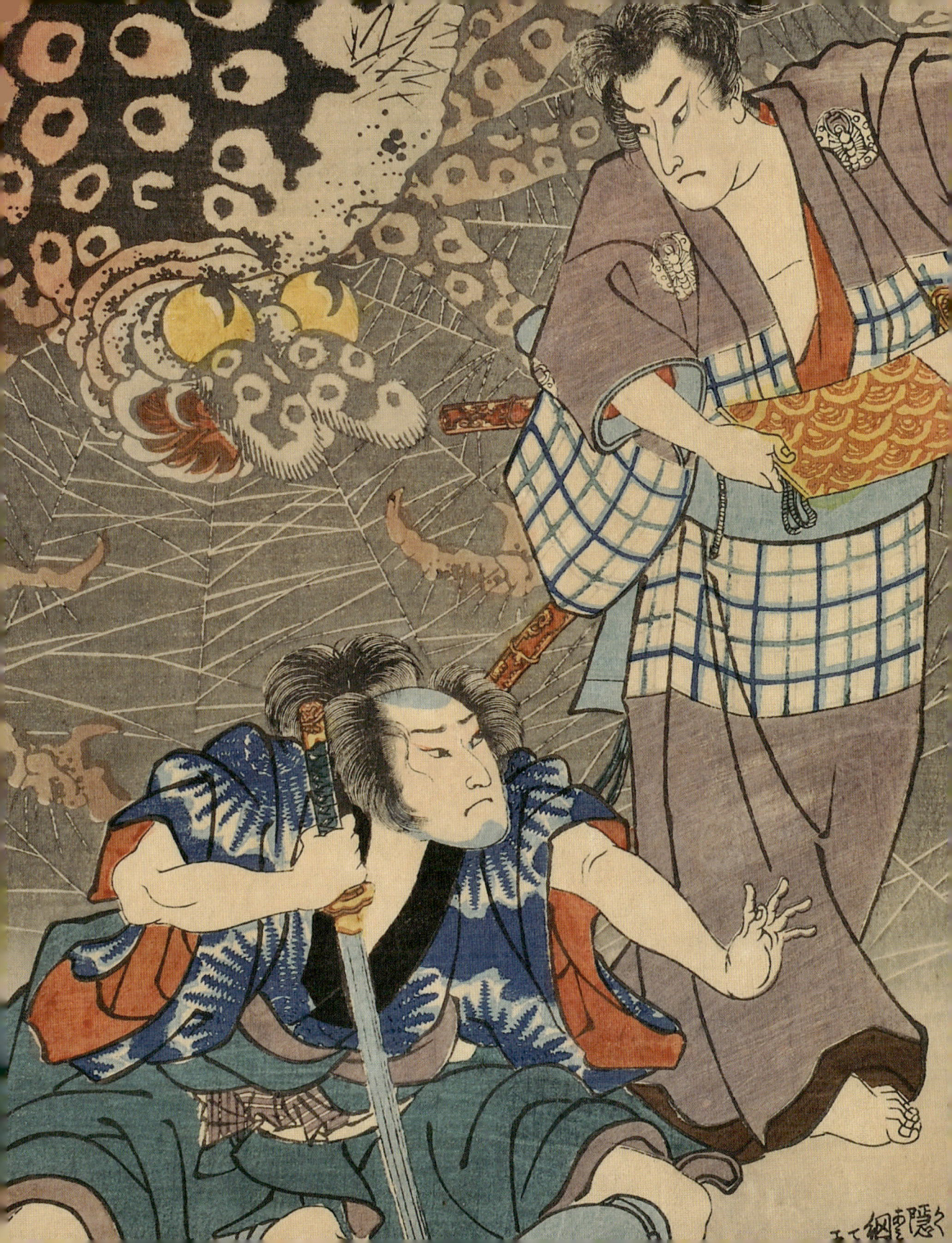

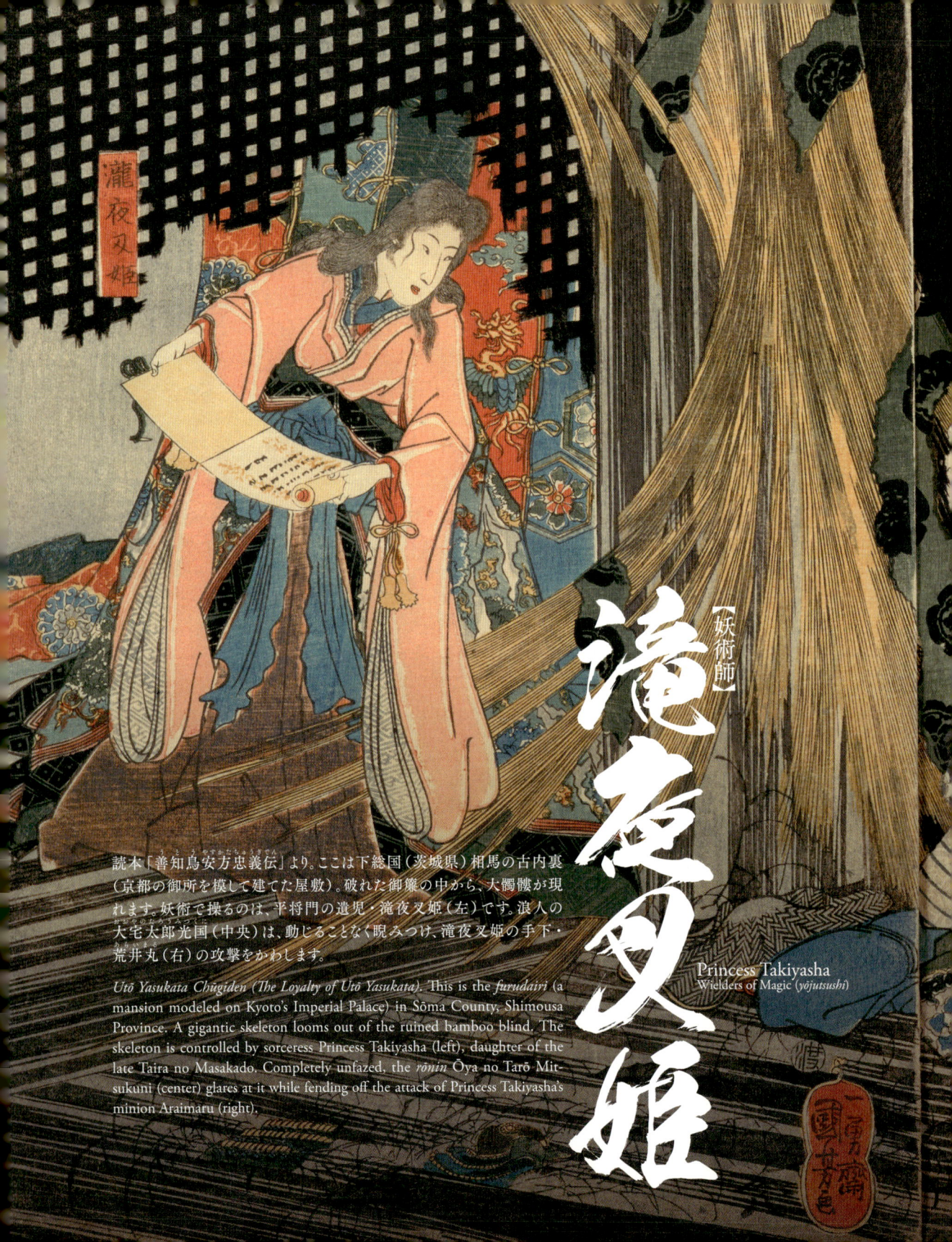

妖術師

滝夜叉姫

瀧夜叉姫

読本「善知鳥安方忠義伝」より。ここは下総国（茨城県）相馬の古内裏（京都の御所を模して建てた屋敷）。破れた御簾の中から、大髑髏が現れます。妖術で操るのは、平将門の遺児・滝夜叉姫（左）です。浪人の大宅太郎光国（中央）は、動じることなく睨みつけ、滝夜叉姫の手下・荒井丸（右）の攻撃をかわします。

Utō Yasukata Chūgiden (The Loyalty of Utō Yasukata). This is the *furudairi* (a mansion modeled on Kyoto's Imperial Palace) in Sōma County, Shimousa Province. A gigantic skeleton looms out of the ruined bamboo blind. The skeleton is controlled by sorceress Princess Takiyasha (left), daughter of the late Taira no Masakado. Completely unfazed, the *rōnin* Ōya no Tarō Mitsukuni (center) glares at it while fending off the attack of Princess Takiyasha's minion Araimaru (right).

Princess Takiyasha
Wielders of Magic (*yōjutsushi*)

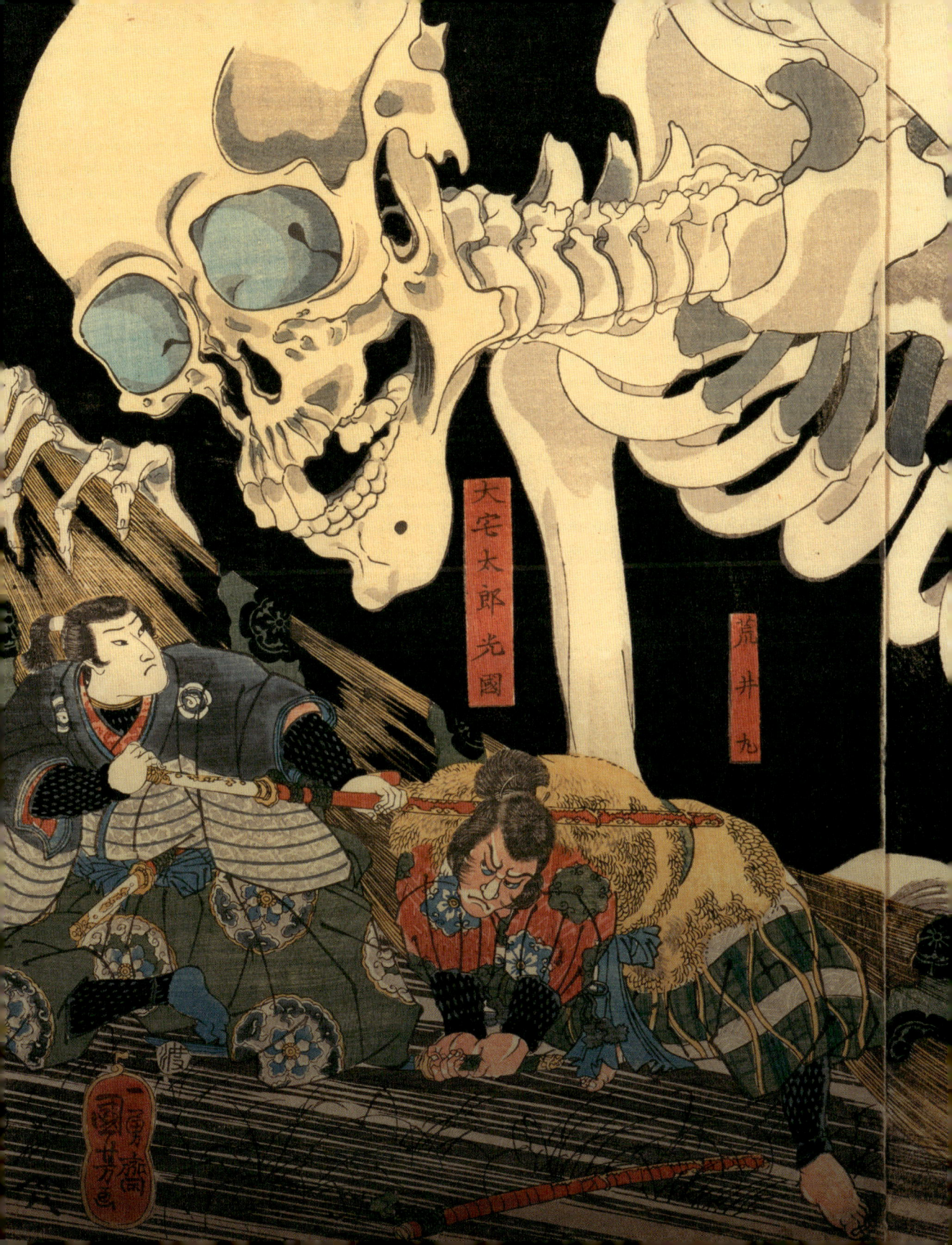

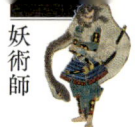

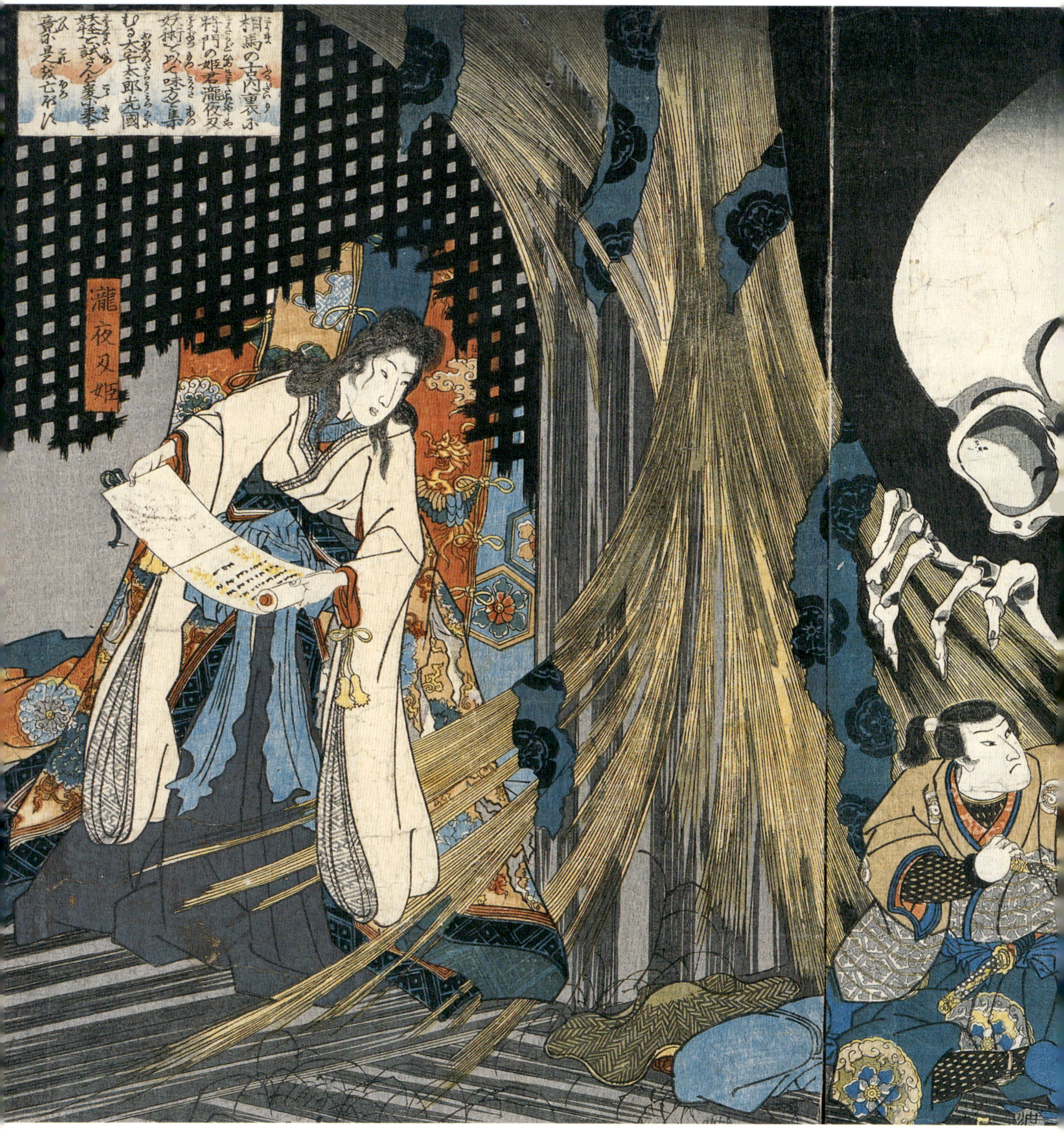

瀧夜叉姫

相馬の古内裏ニ
将門の姫君瀧夜叉
妖術をもて味方を
あつむ大宅太郎光國
妖怪にたぶらかされ
しかど是を討亡し
かの古内裏
意恐是妖亡ぼせ

【相馬の古内裏・滝夜叉姫と大骸骨】歌川国芳 弘化2-3年（1845-46）頃

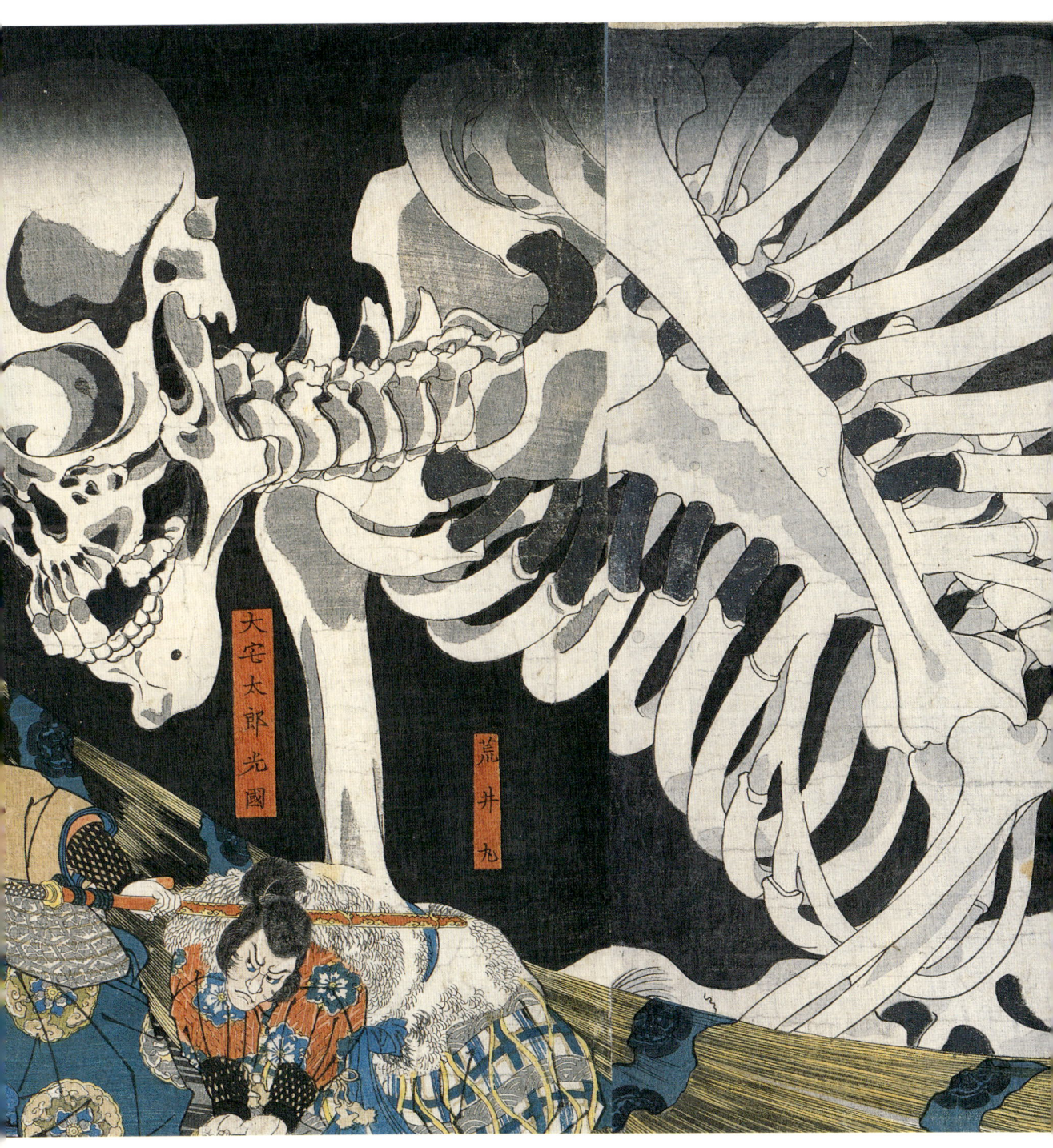

Sōma no furudairi: Princess Takiyasha and the Huge Skeleton by Utagawa Kuniyoshi

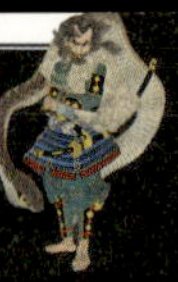

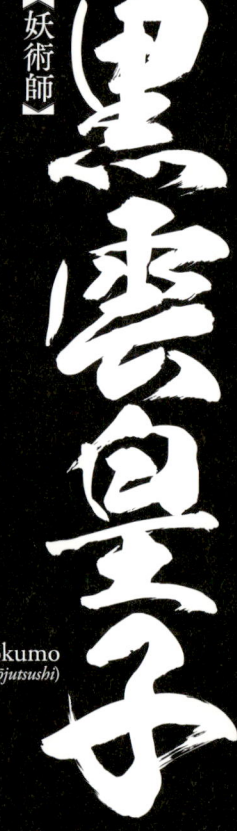

【妖術師】黒雲皇子

Prince Kurokumo
Wielders of Magic (*yōjutsushi*)

謀反を企てる黒雲皇子。背後には、皇子に妖術を授けた土蜘蛛の妖怪。
同じく、謀反を企てる平良門が旅の途中で出会い、妖術競べをすること
になりました。黒雲皇子の妖術で現れた官女姿の女郎蜘蛛が、良門に
斬りかかります。こののち二人は結託します。

Prince Kurokumo (Black Cloud) plots rebellion. Tsuchigumo the Earth Spider,
who has given sorcery to the prince, lurks in the background. Taira no
Yoshikado, who likewise plots rebellion, has encountered him on his travels,
and they are striving to best each other in a contest of sorcery. Summoned by
Prince Kurokumo's sorcery, female spiders who manifest in the form of court
ladies are attacking Yoshikado. Later on, the two rivals join forces.

【美勇水滸傳 黒雲皇子 将軍太郎平良門】
月岡芳年 慶応3年（1867）

Prince Kurokumo and Shōgun Tarō Taira no Yoshikado
from the series *Biyū Suikoden (Sagas of Beauty and Bravery)*
by Tsukioka Yoshitoshi

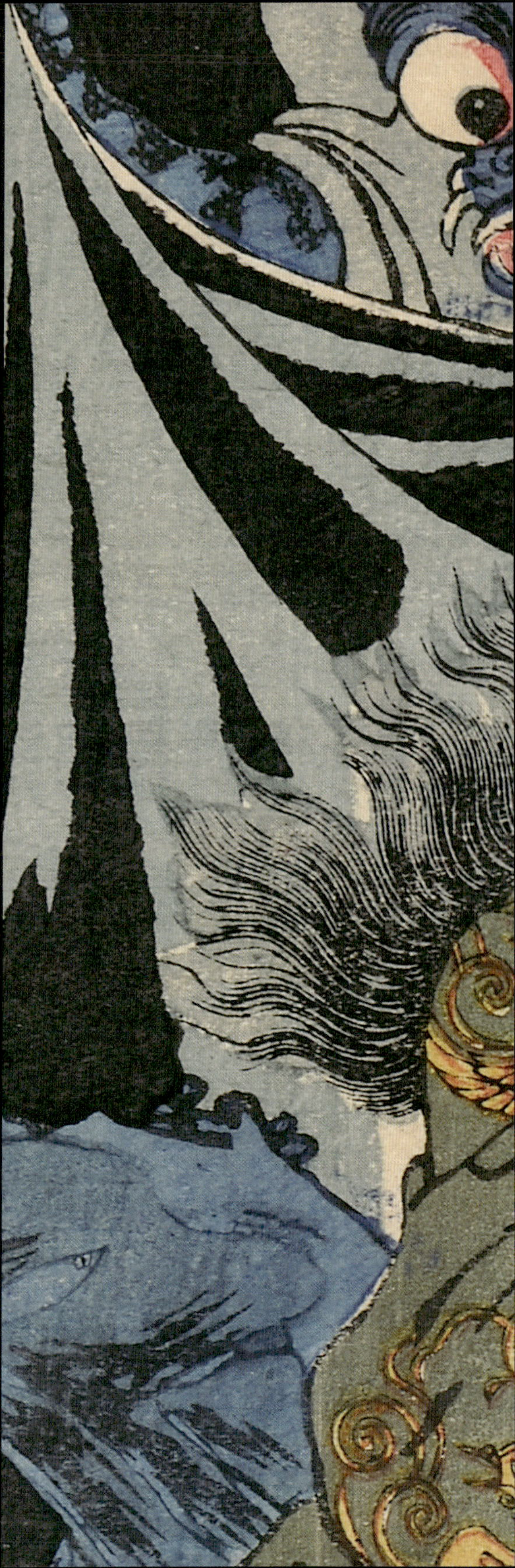

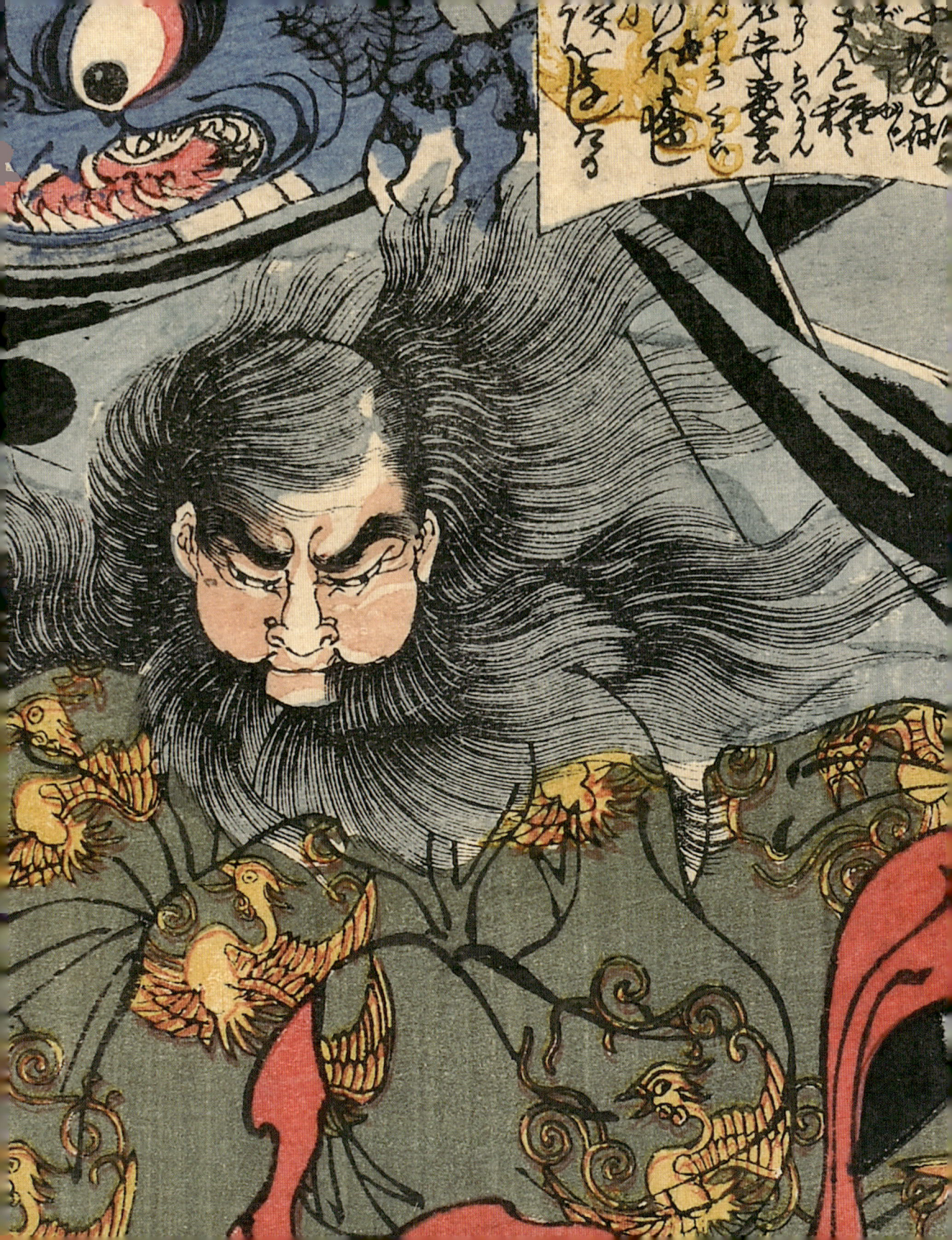

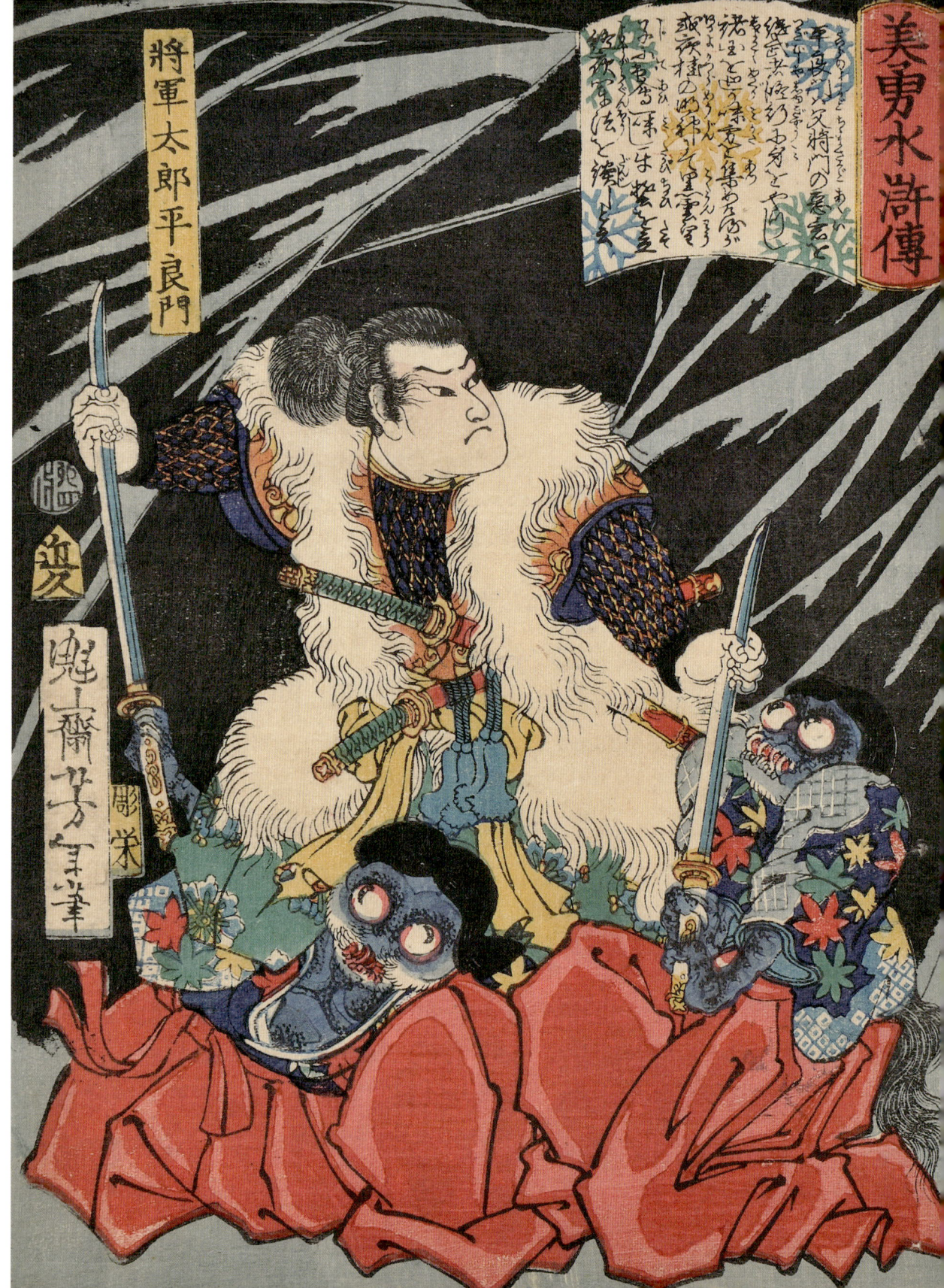

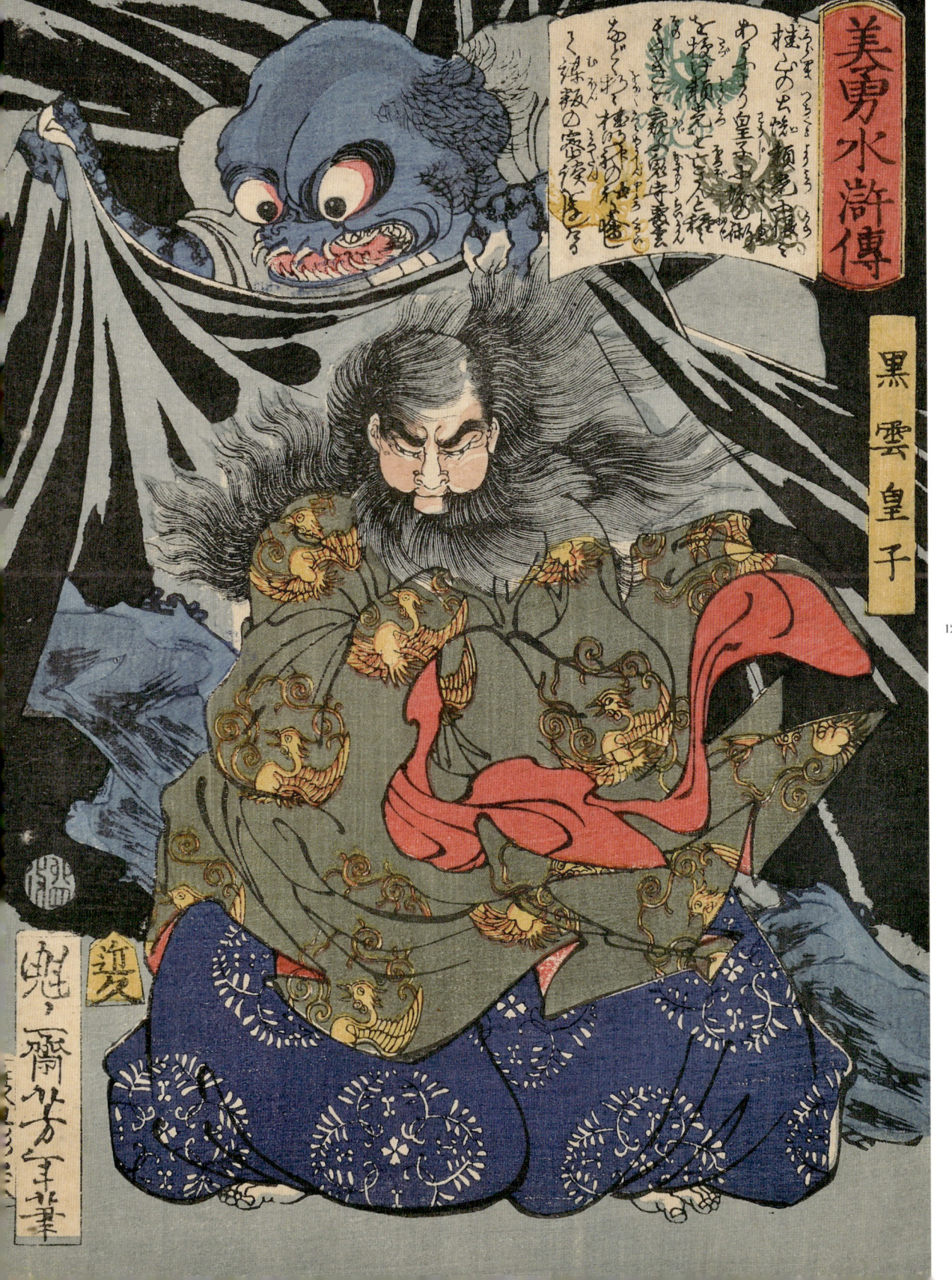

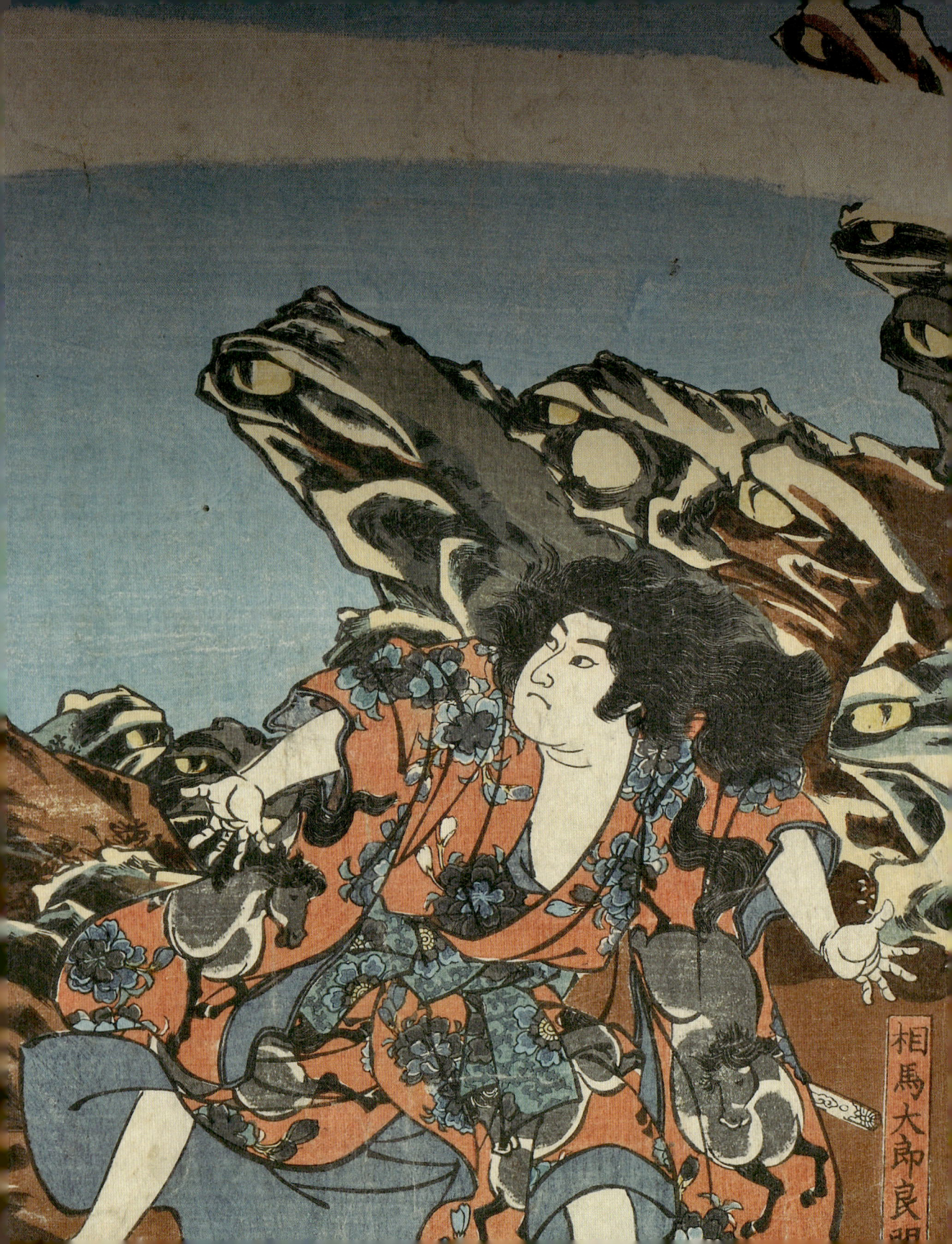

相馬太郎良明

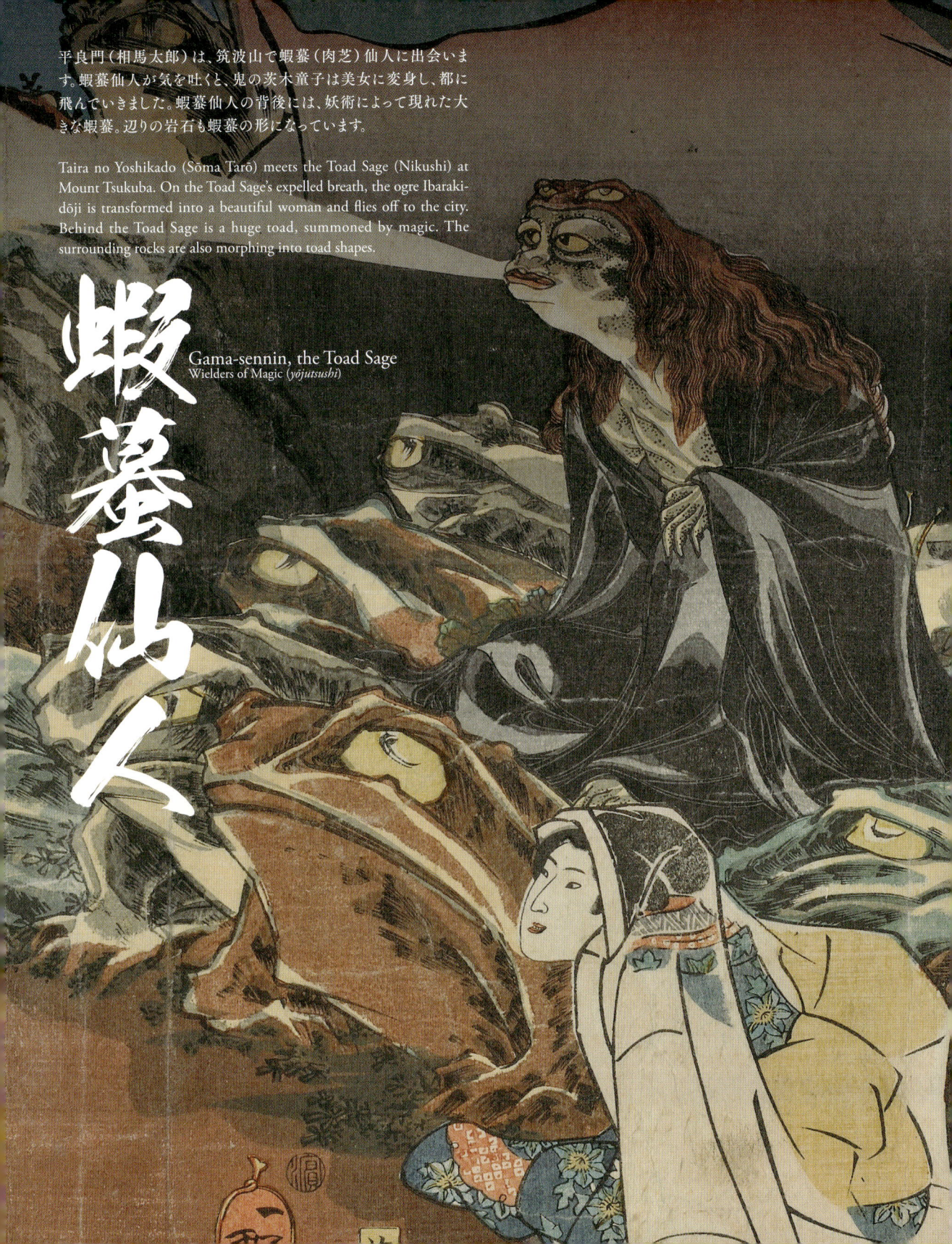

平良門（相馬太郎）は、筑波山で蝦蟇（肉芝）仙人に出会います。蝦蟇仙人が気を吐くと、鬼の茨木童子は美女に変身し、都に飛んでいきました。蝦蟇仙人の背後には、妖術によって現れた大きな蝦蟇。辺りの岩石も蝦蟇の形になっています。

Taira no Yoshikado (Sōma Tarō) meets the Toad Sage (Nikushi) at Mount Tsukuba. On the Toad Sage's expelled breath, the ogre Ibaraki-dōji is transformed into a beautiful woman and flies off to the city. Behind the Toad Sage is a huge toad, summoned by magic. The surrounding rocks are also morphing into toad shapes.

蝦蟇仙人

Gama-sennin, the Toad Sage
Wielders of Magic (*yōjutsushi*)

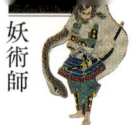

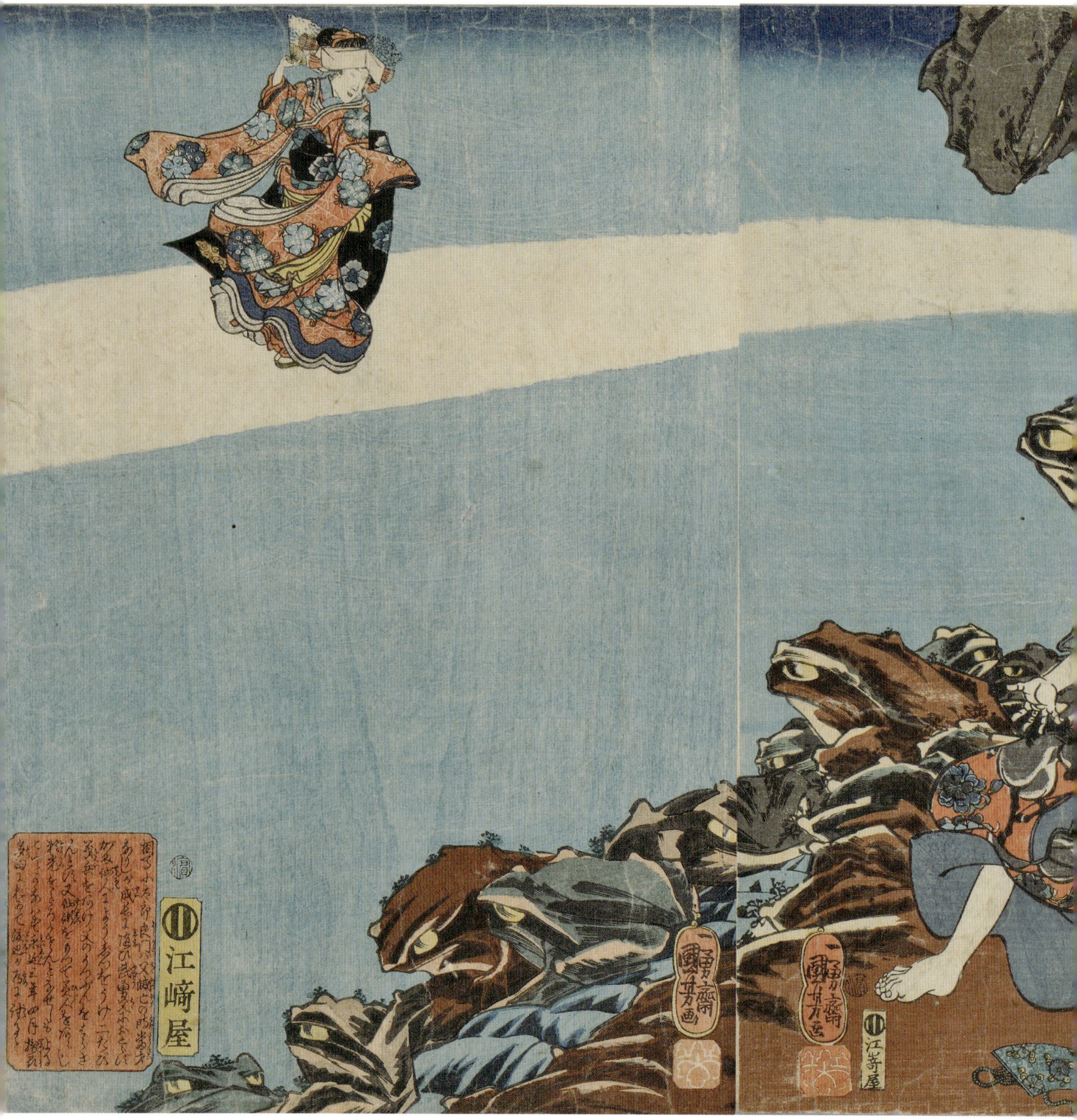

【蝦蟇仙人と相馬太郎良門】歌川国芳 弘化元～3年（1844-46）

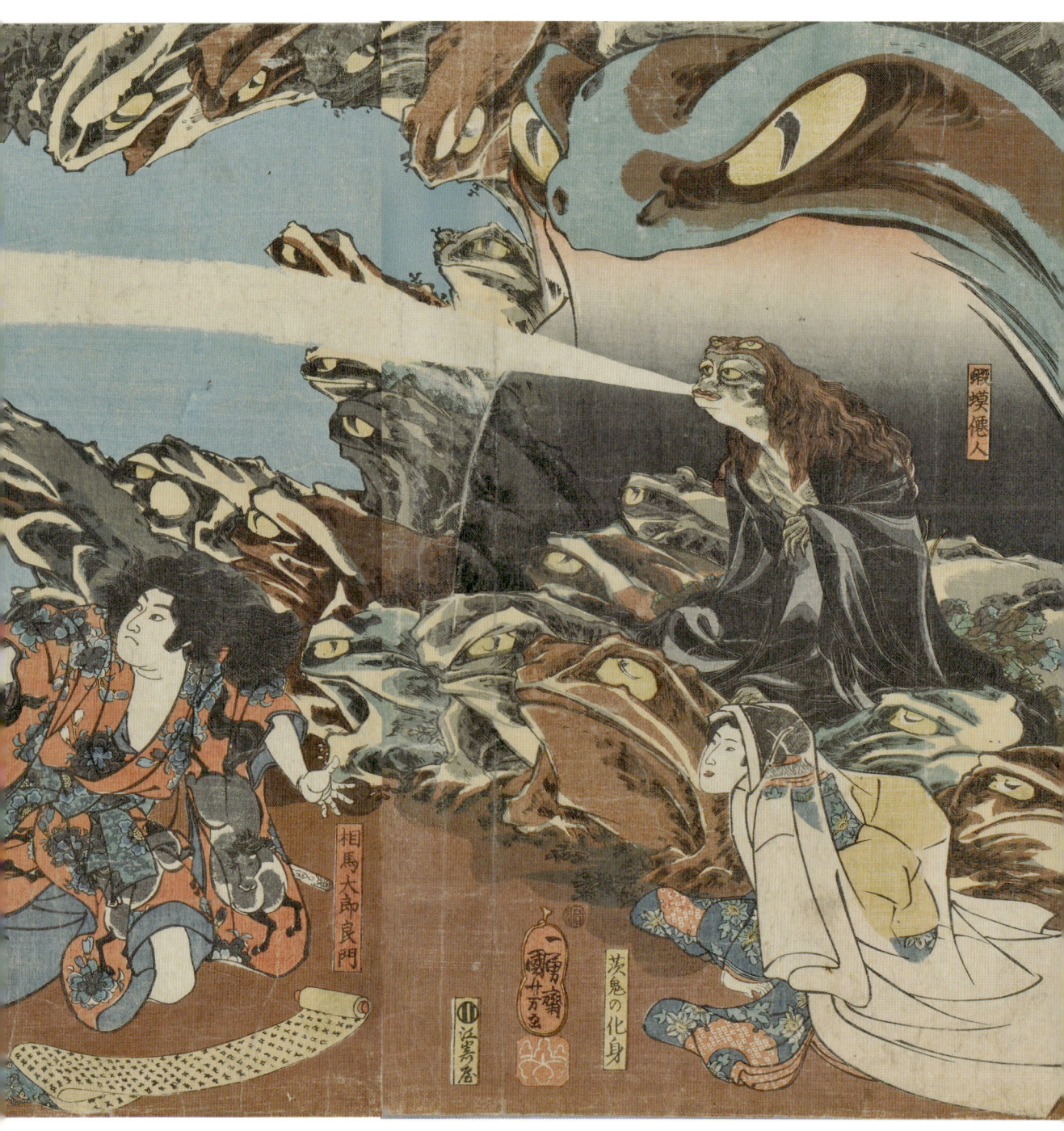

Gama-sennin and Sōma Tarō Yoshikado by Utagawa Kuniyoshi

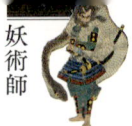

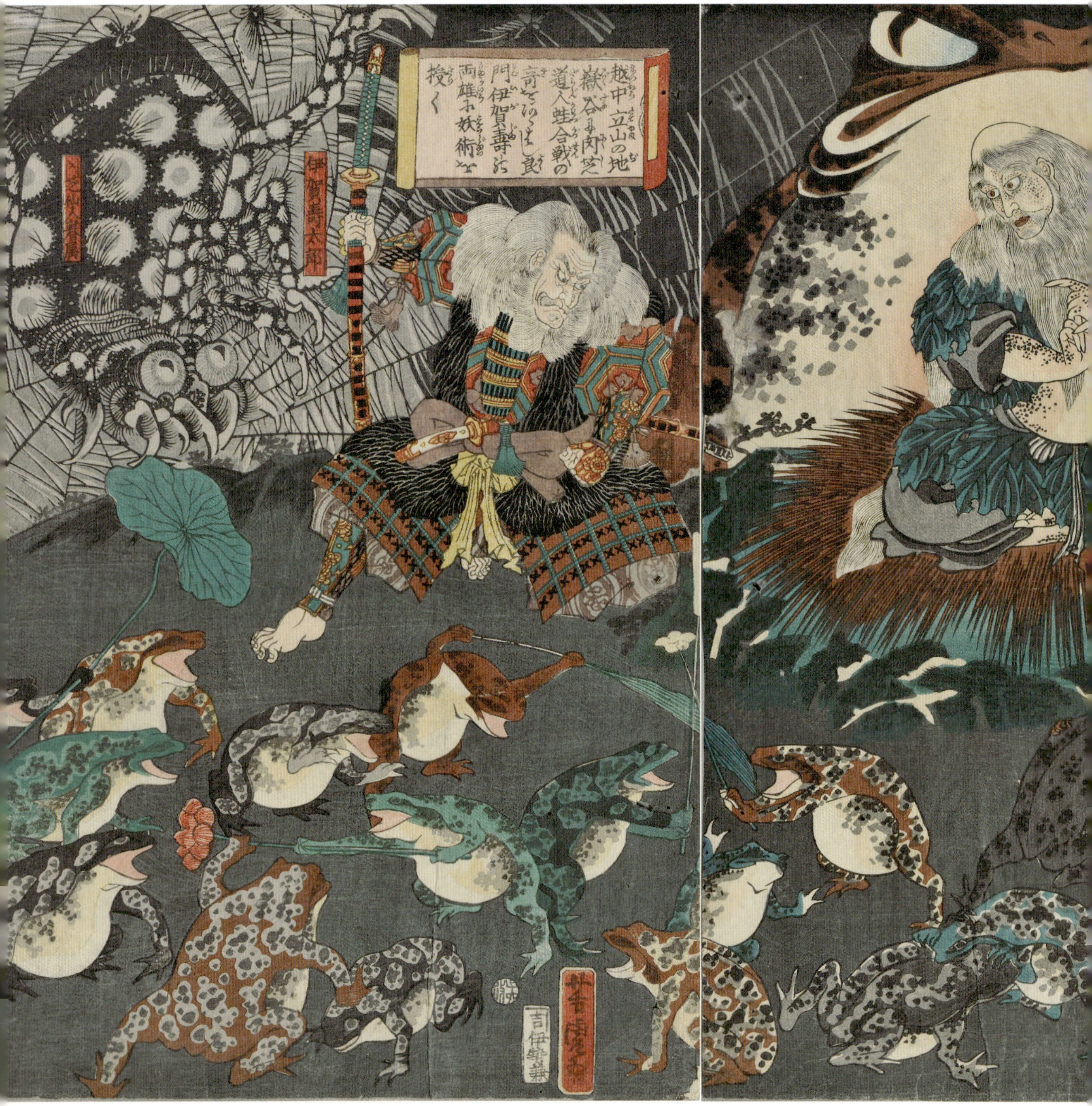

【越中立山の地獄谷に肉芝道人蛙合戦の奇をあらはし 良門伊賀寿の両雄に妖術を授く】

歌川芳虎 元治元年(1864)

読本「善知鳥安方忠義伝」より。妖術で現れた蛙たちが、敵味方に分かれて戦いを繰り広げます。蛙たちを操るのは、中央に座した肉芝(蝦蟇)仙人。
指で印を結び怪しい呪文を唱えます。右の将軍太郎平良門と左の伊賀寿太郎は、父や主君の遺志を継ぎ謀反を企てます。

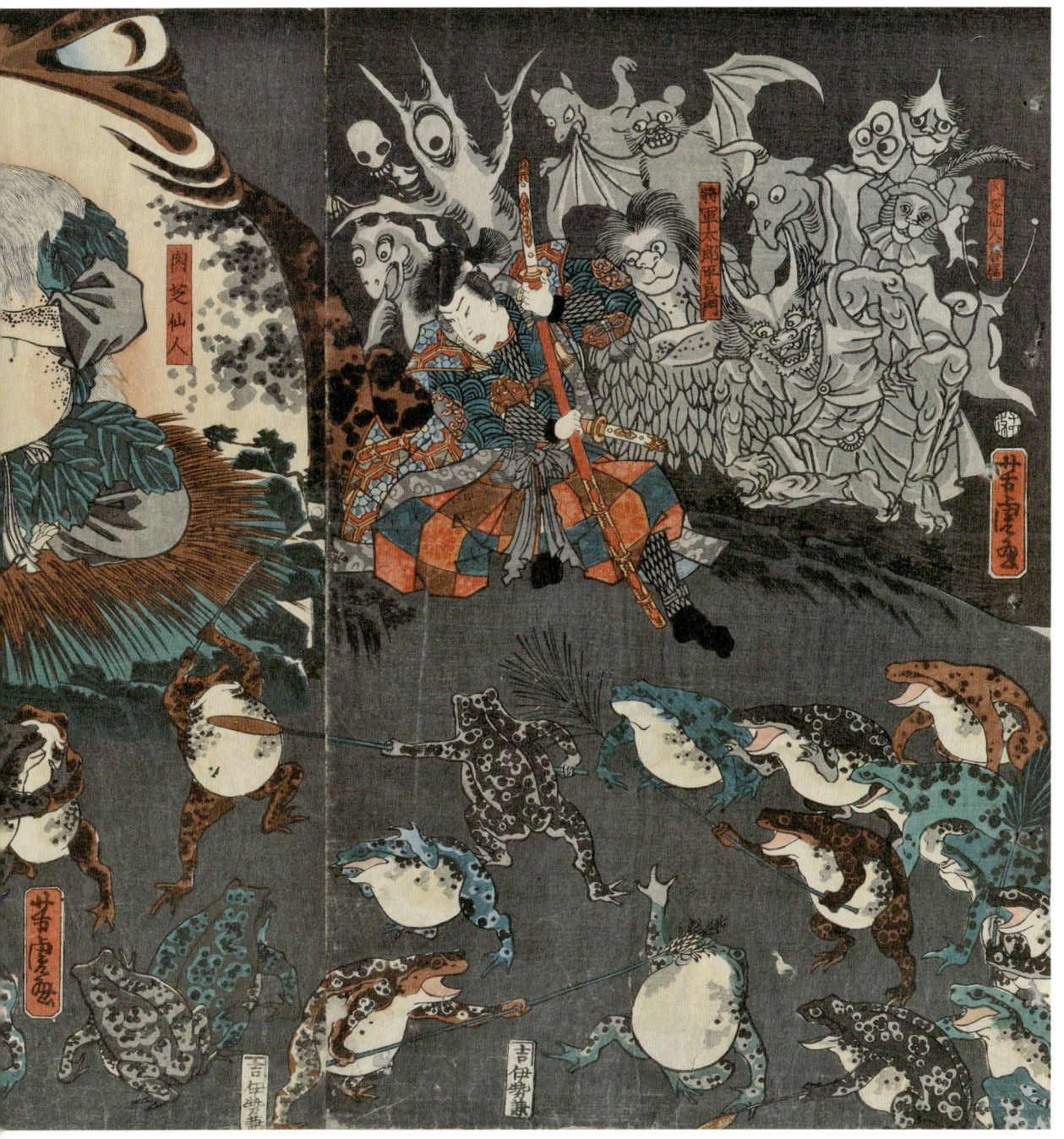

The Sage Nikushi Conjures Up a Frog Battle to Teach the Two Heroes Igaju and Yoshikado Sorcery in Jigoku Valley, Tateyama, Ecchū Province by Utagawa Yoshitora

From *yomihon Utō Yasukata Chūgiden (The Loyalty of Utō Yasukata)*. Summoned by magic, frogs divide into enemies and allies to do battle. Sitting in the center and controlling the frogs is the sage Nikushi. He gestures and mutters with mystic meaning. Taira no Yoshikado (right) and Igaju no Tarō (left) are planning a rebellion to fulfil the last wishes of their father and lord.

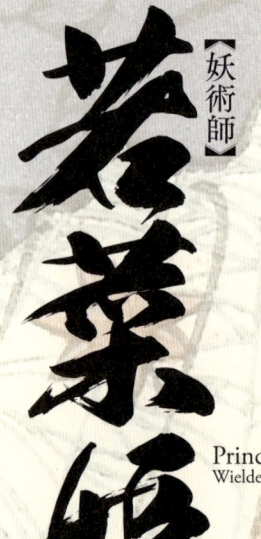

【妖術師】

若菜姫

Princess Wakana
Wielders of Magic (*yōjutsushi*)

132

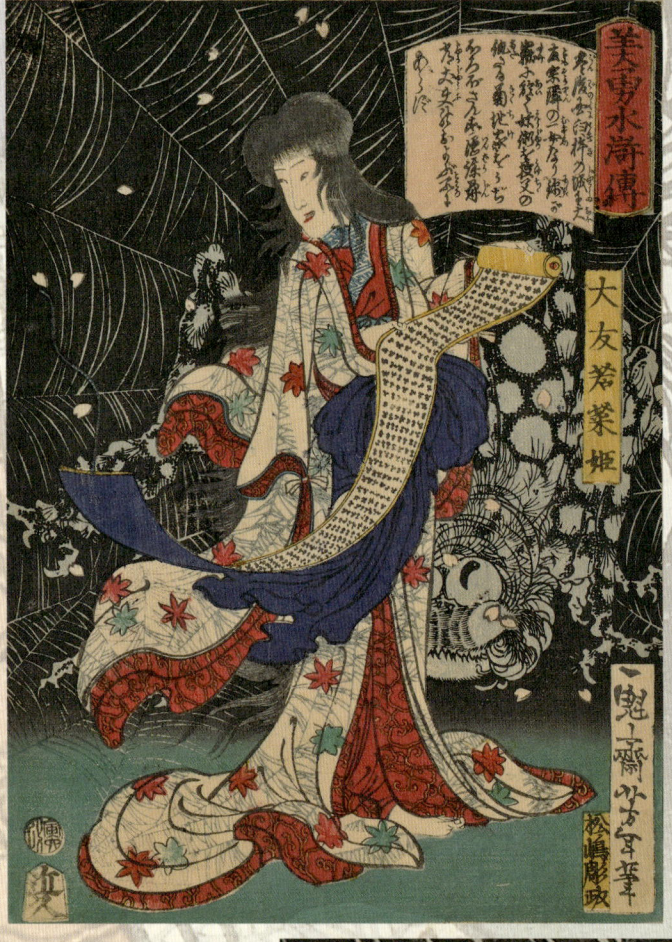

伝記小説『白縫譚』の主人公、大友宗麟の遺児・若菜姫は、蜘蛛の精に授かった妖術を使い、男装して白縫大尽と名乗り、仇敵の菊池家を亡ぼそうと暗躍します。

Main character from fictionalized biography *Shiranui Monogatari*. Using sorcery from a spider spirit, Princess Wakana (daughter of the late Ōtomo Sōrin) disguises herself as a man and takes the name Shiranui Daijin in order to secretly engineer the destruction of her mortal enemies, the Kikuchi family.

【美勇水滸伝 大友若菜姫】月岡芳年 慶応2年（1866）
大友若菜姫が、蜘蛛の精霊より授かった巻物を読んでいるところ。

Ōtomono Wakana-hime from the series *Biyū Suikoden (Sagas of Beauty and Bravery)* by Tsukioka Yoshitoshi
The princess Ōtomono Wakana-hime is reading a scroll given to her by the spider spirit.

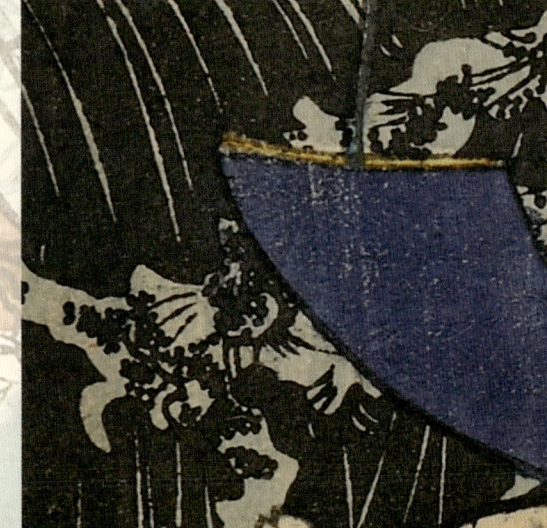

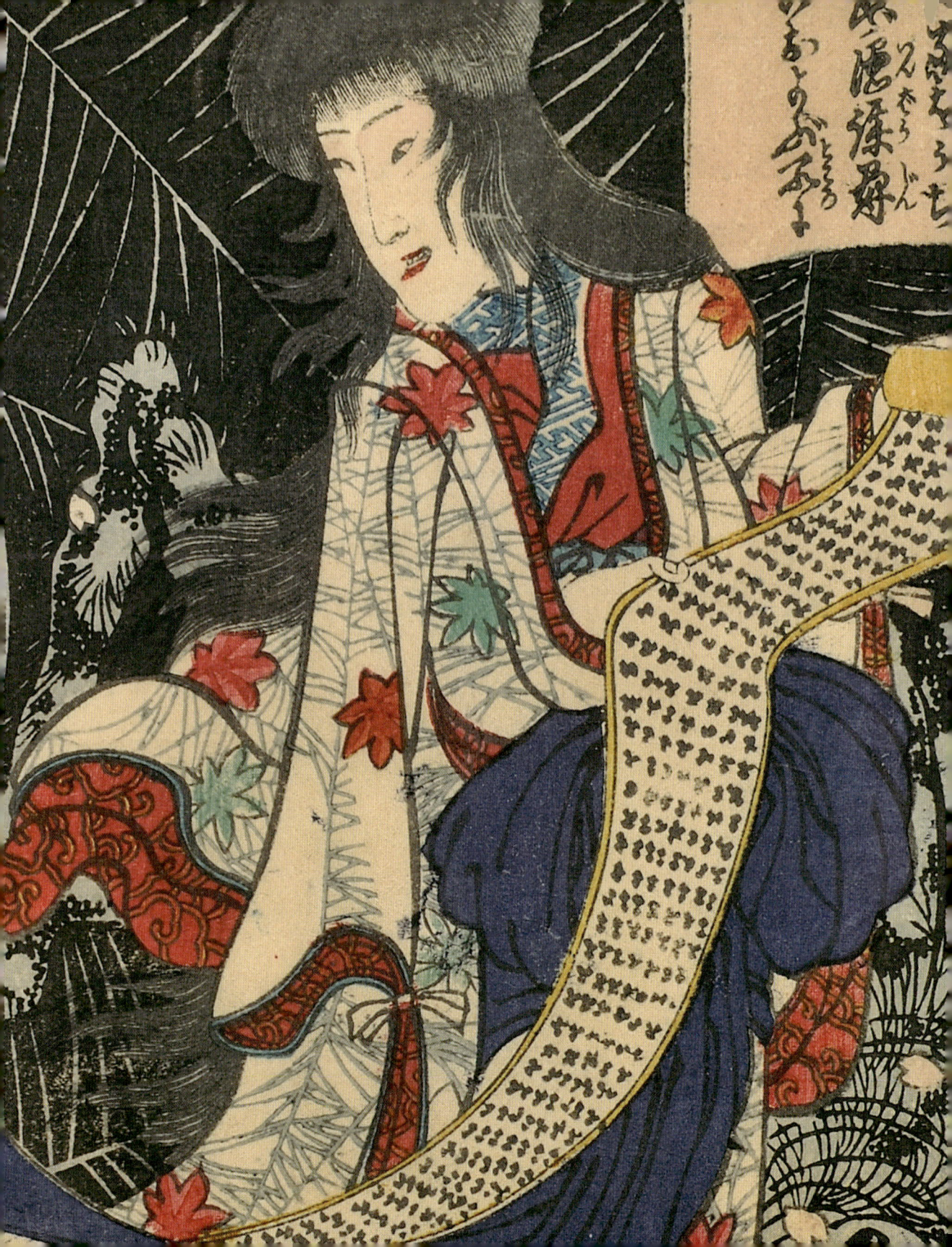

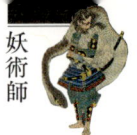
妖術師

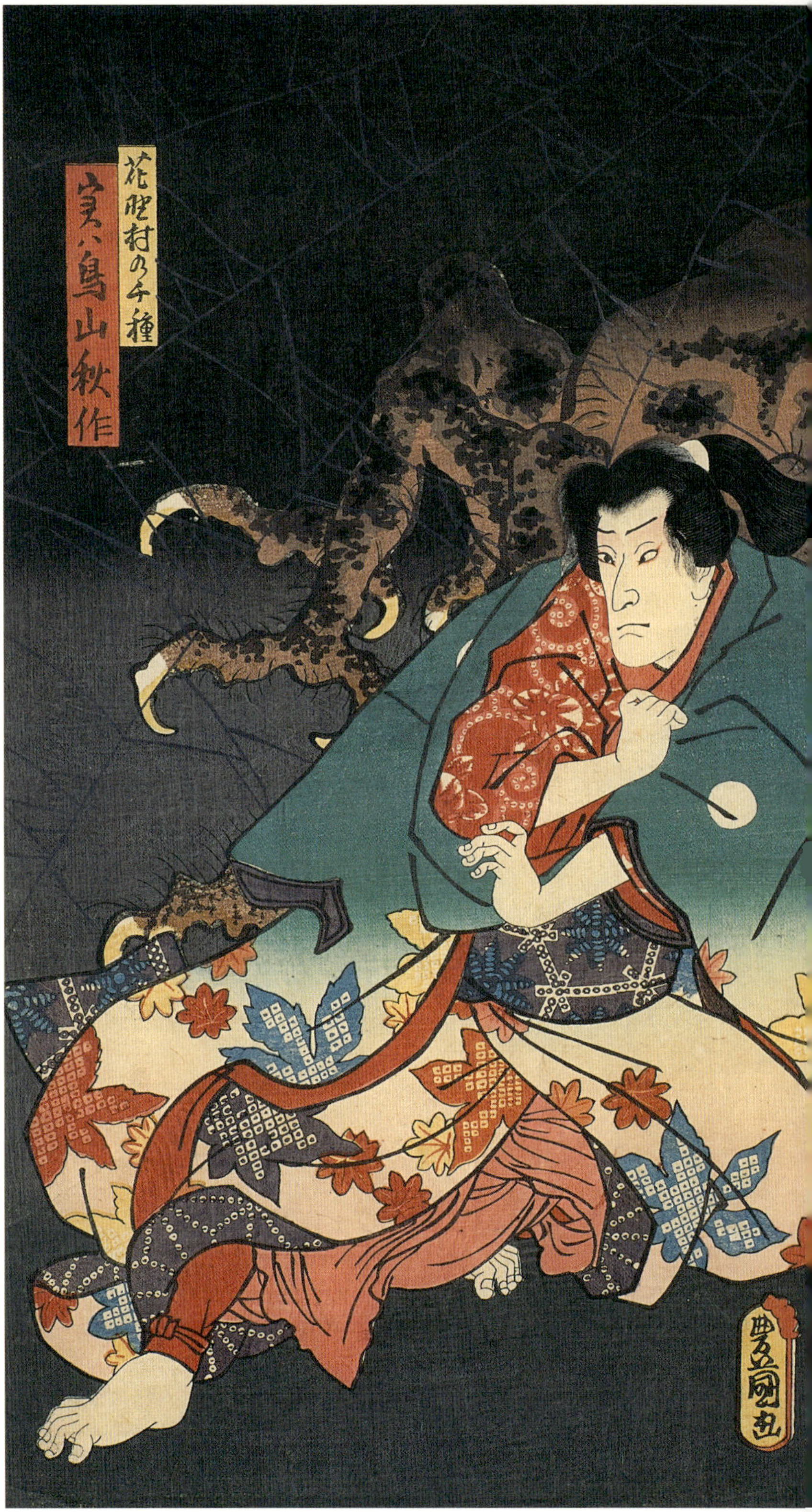

134

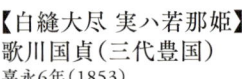

【白縫大尽 実ハ若那姫】
歌川国貞（三代豊国）
嘉永6年（1853）
歌舞伎「しらぬひ譚」より。蜘蛛の妖術使いの
大友若那姫（右）に、菊池家忠臣の鳥山秋作
（左）が立ちはだかります。

Shiranui Daijin, Actually Princess
Wakana by Utagawa Kunisada
(also known as Utagawa Toyokuni III)
The scene where Toriyama Akisaku (left) confronts
Princess Ōtomo no Wakana (right), the spider
sorceress. Akisaku, a loyal retainer of the Kikuchi
family, is portrayed as a handsome young man.

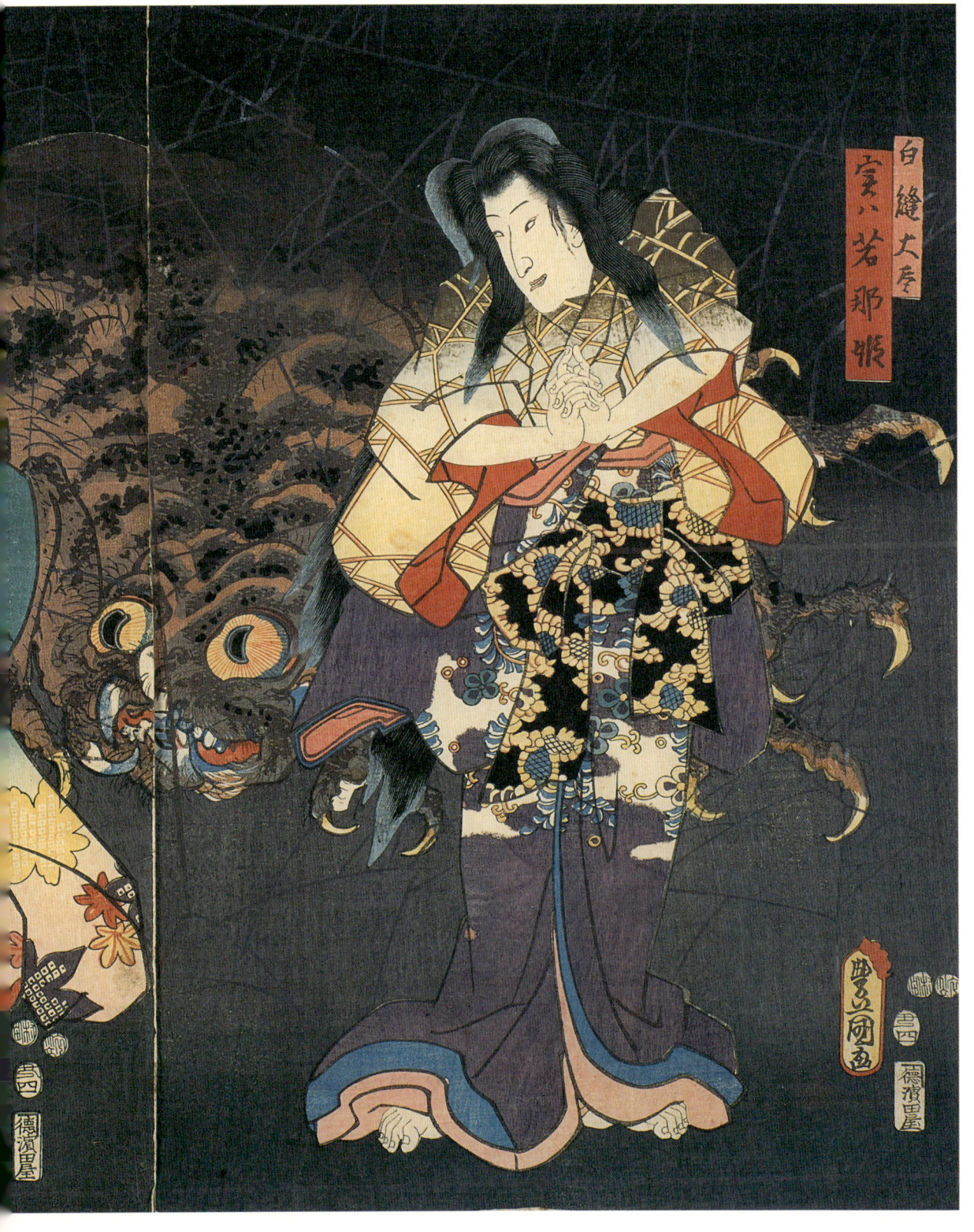

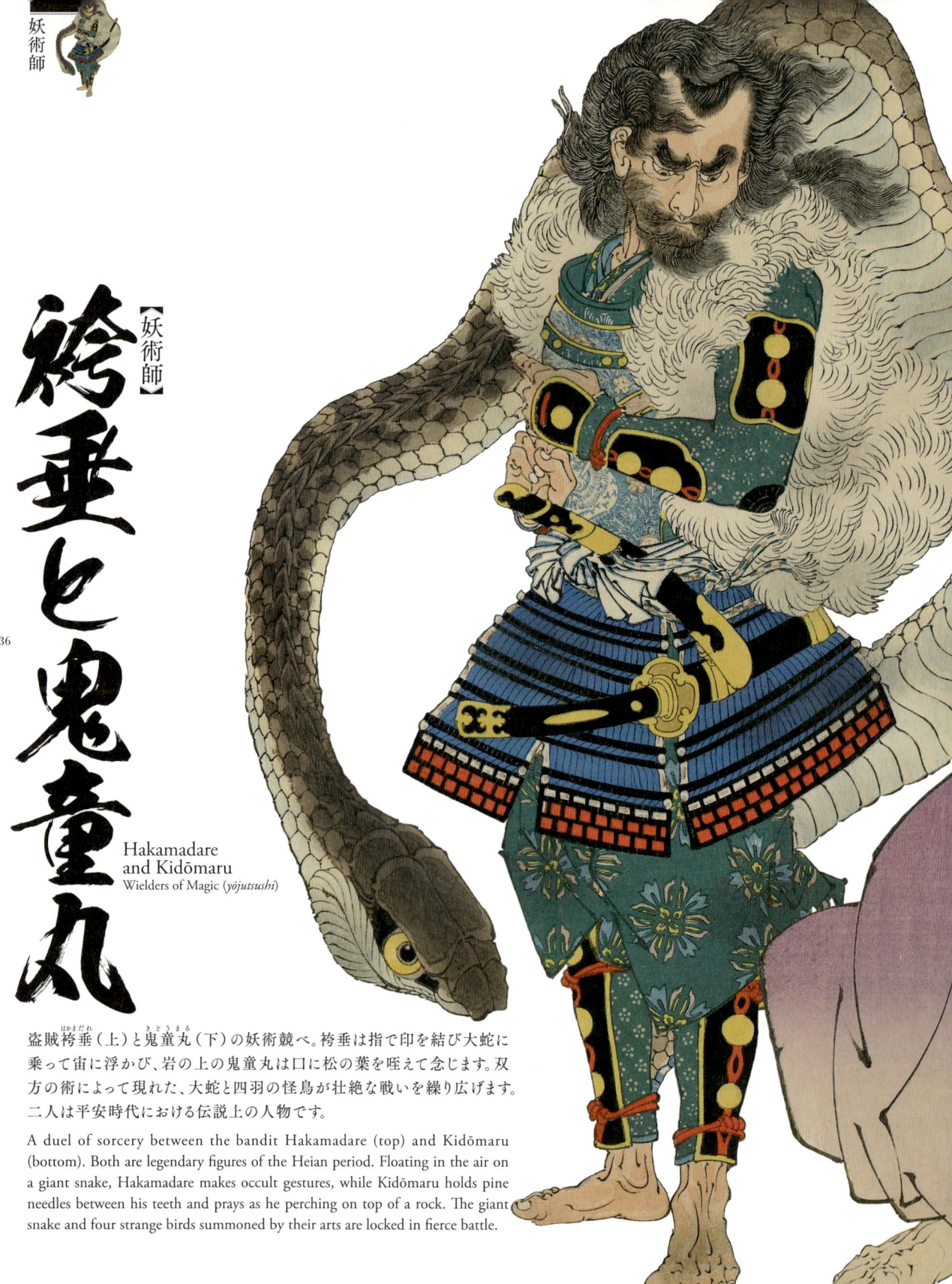

【妖術師】袴垂と鬼童丸

Hakamadare
and Kidōmaru
Wielders of Magic (*yōjutsushi*)

盗賊袴垂（上）と鬼童丸（下）の妖術競べ。袴垂は指で印を結び大蛇に乗って宙に浮かび、岩の上の鬼童丸は口に松の葉を咥えて念じます。双方の術によって現れた、大蛇と四羽の怪鳥が壮絶な戦いを繰り広げます。二人は平安時代における伝説上の人物です。

A duel of sorcery between the bandit Hakamadare (top) and Kidōmaru (bottom). Both are legendary figures of the Heian period. Floating in the air on a giant snake, Hakamadare makes occult gestures, while Kidōmaru holds pine needles between his teeth and prays as he perching on top of a rock. The giant snake and four strange birds summoned by their arts are locked in fierce battle.

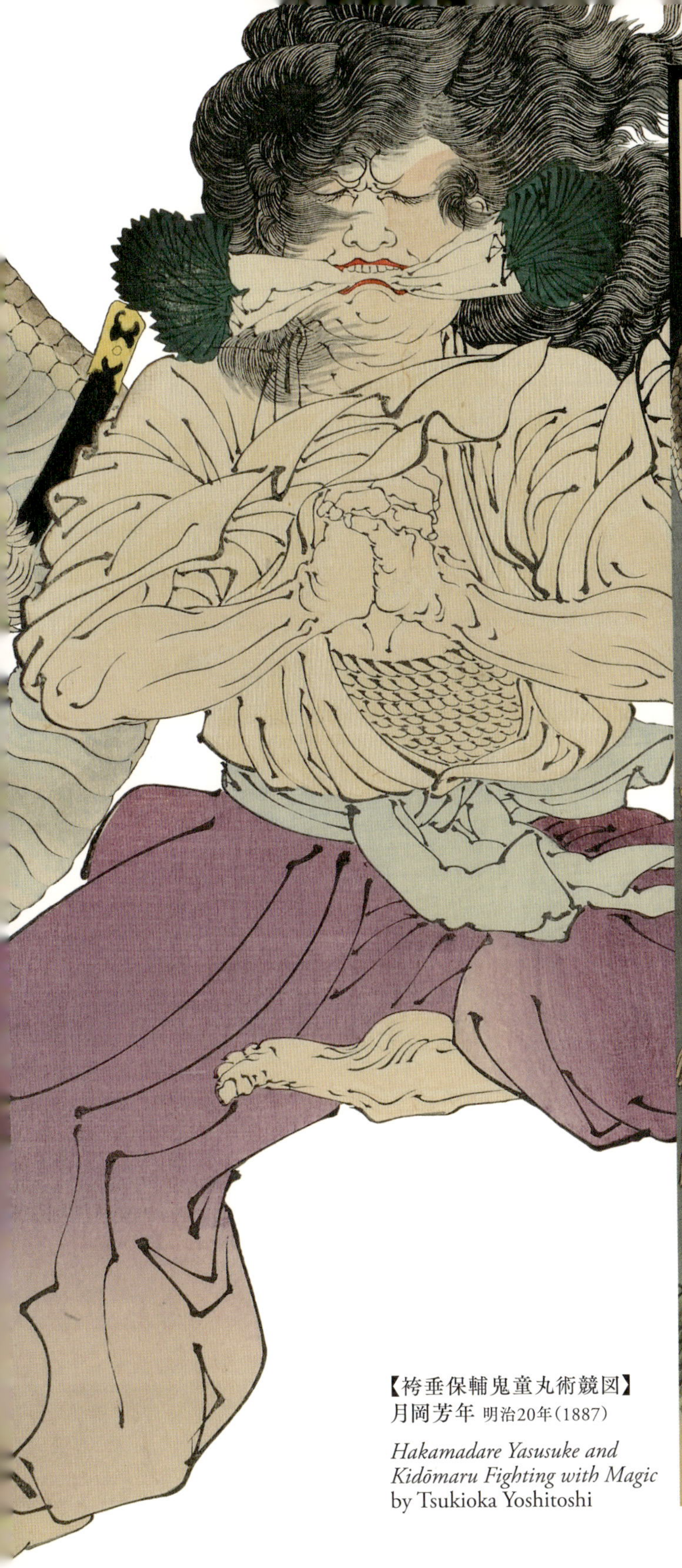

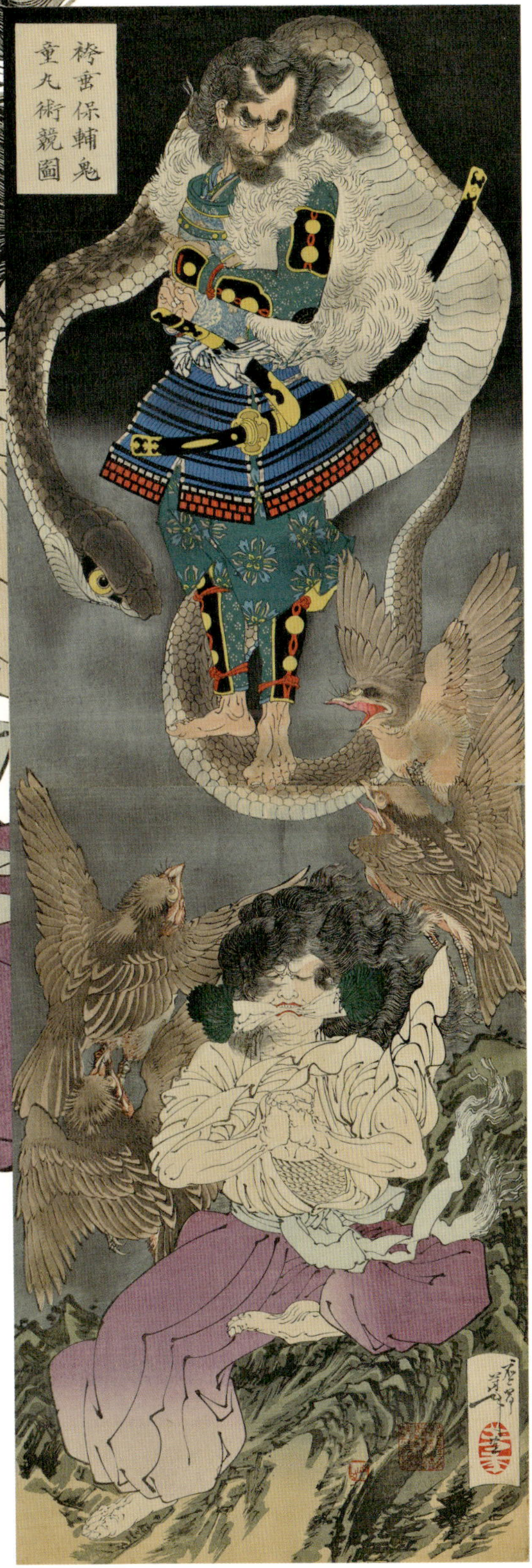

【袴垂保輔鬼童丸術競図】
月岡芳年 明治20年（1887）

Hakamadare Yasusuke and
Kidōmaru Fighting with Magic
by Tsukioka Yoshitoshi

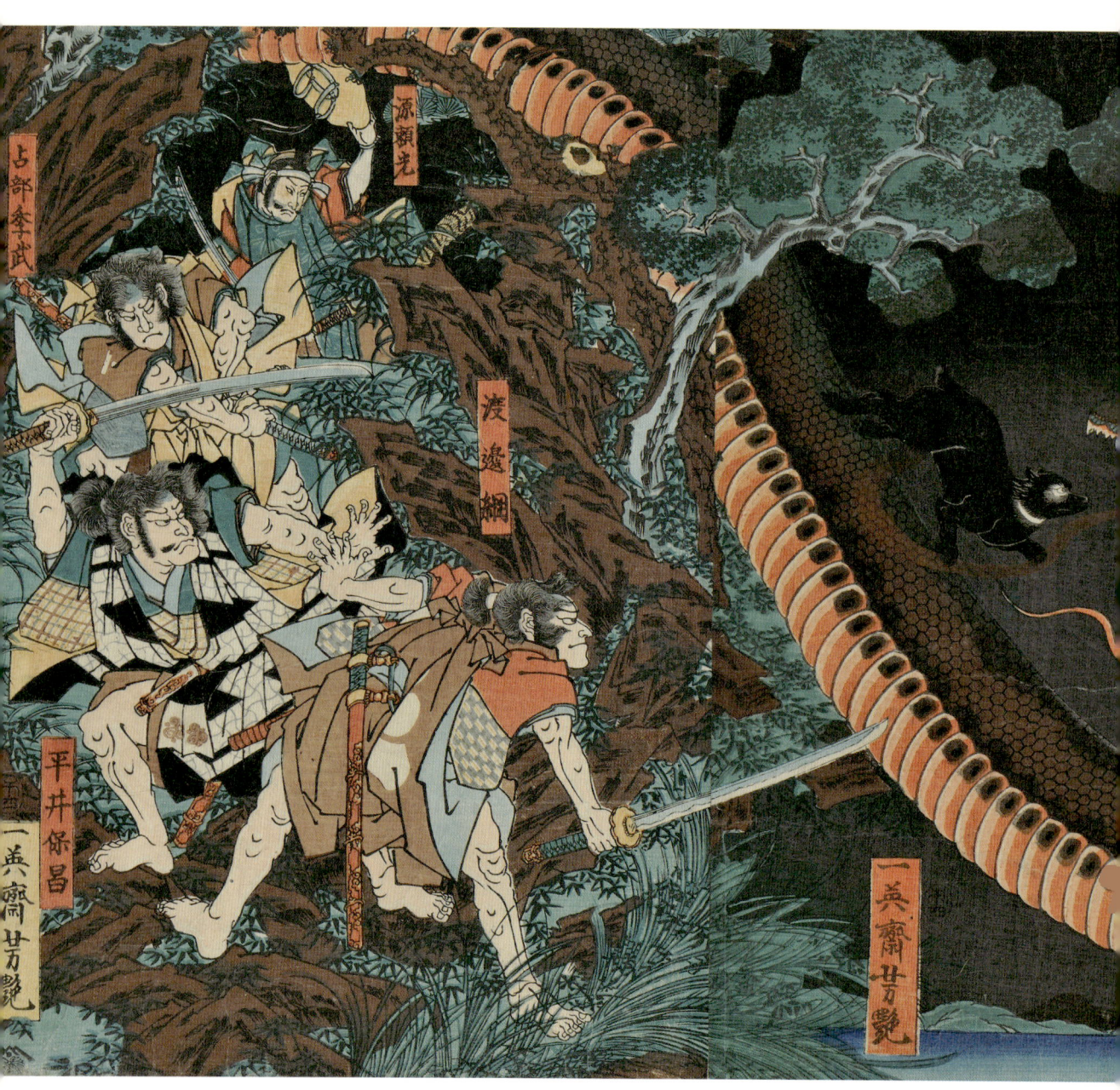

【破奇術頼光袴垂為掇】歌川芳艶 安政5年(1858)

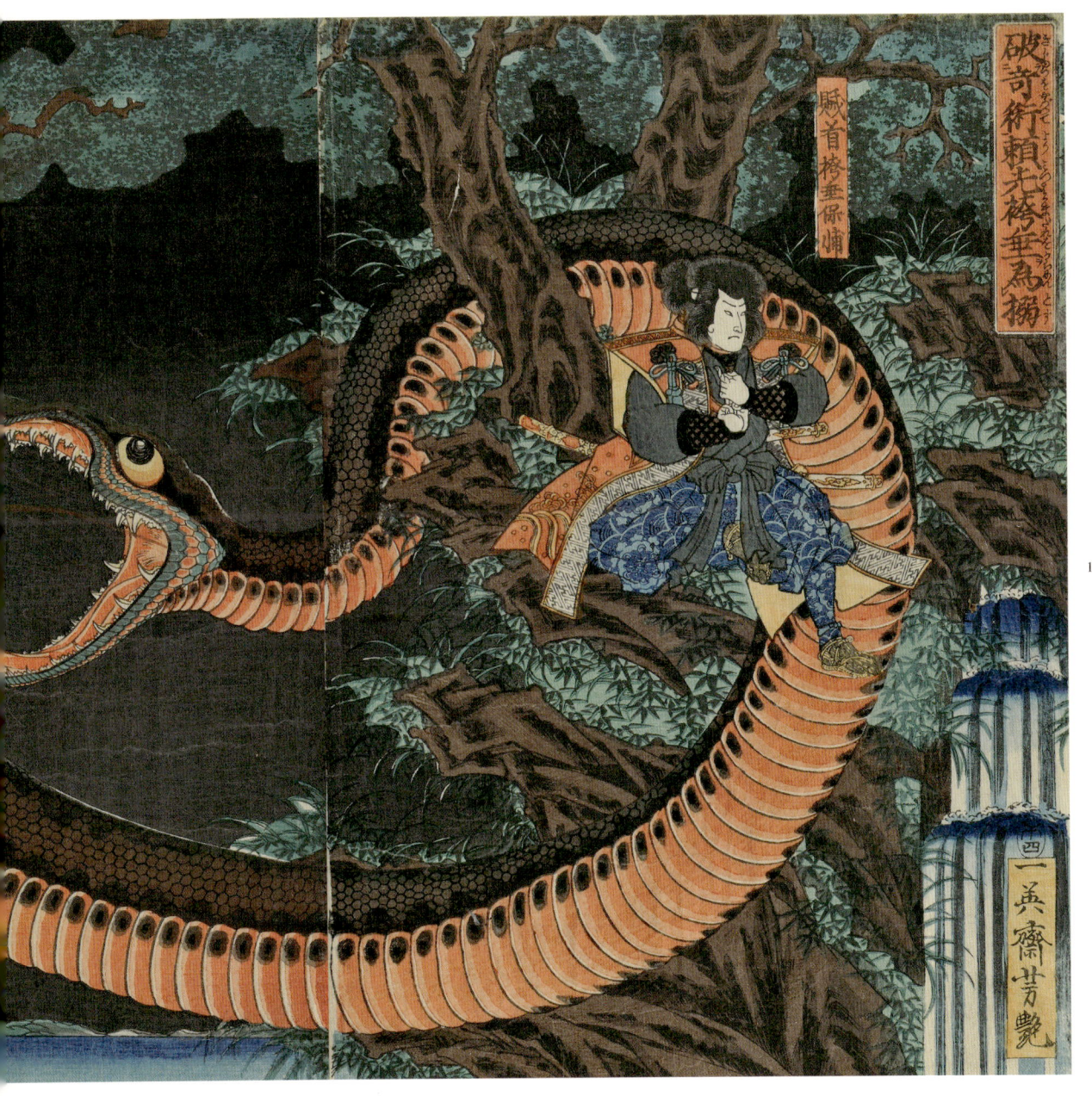

Yorimitsu Tries to Capture Hakamadare by Destroying His Magic by Utagawa Yoshitsuya

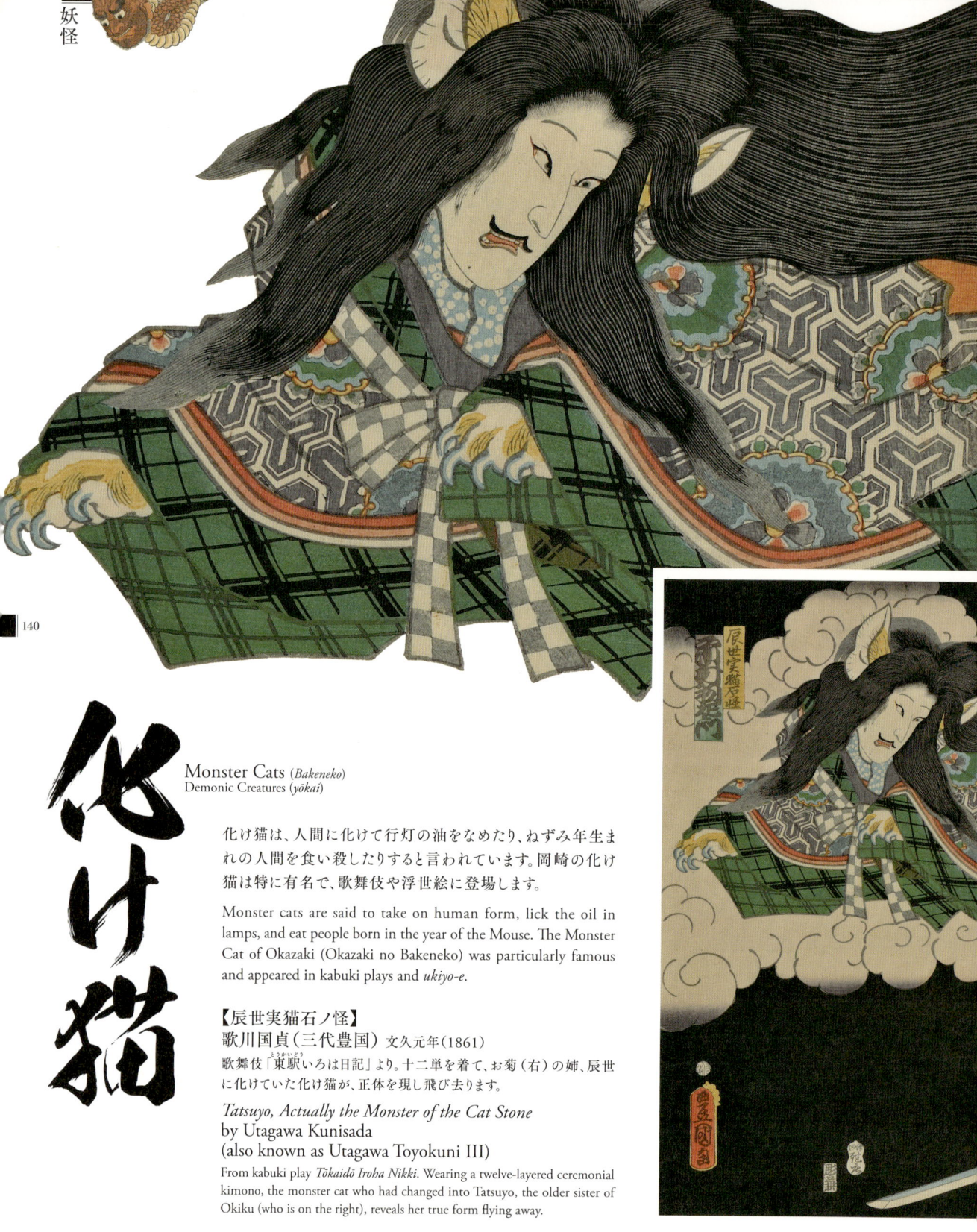

140

化け猫

Monster Cats (*Bakeneko*)
Demonic Creatures (*yōkai*)

化け猫は、人間に化けて行灯の油をなめたり、ねずみ年生まれの人間を食い殺したりすると言われています。岡崎の化け猫は特に有名で、歌舞伎や浮世絵に登場します。

Monster cats are said to take on human form, lick the oil in lamps, and eat people born in the year of the Mouse. The Monster Cat of Okazaki (Okazaki no Bakeneko) was particularly famous and appeared in kabuki plays and *ukiyo-e*.

【辰世実猫石ノ怪】
歌川国貞（三代豊国） 文久元年（1861）
歌舞伎「東駅いろは日記」より。十二単を着て、お菊（右）の姉、辰世に化けていた化け猫が、正体を現し飛び去ります。

Tatsuyo, Actually the Monster of the Cat Stone
by Utagawa Kunisada
(also known as Utagawa Toyokuni III)

From kabuki play *Tōkaidō Iroha Nikki*. Wearing a twelve-layered ceremonial kimono, the monster cat who had changed into Tatsuyo, the older sister of Okiku (who is on the right), reveals her true form flying away.

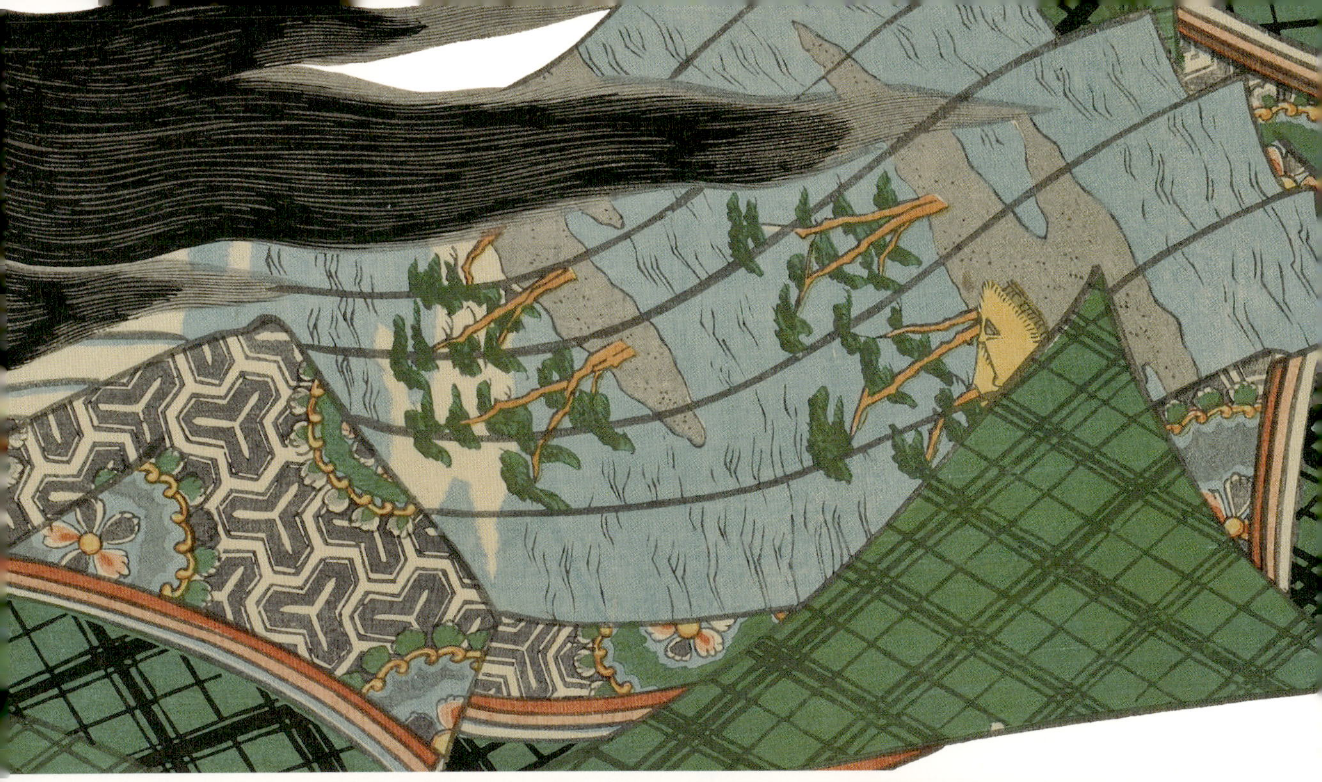

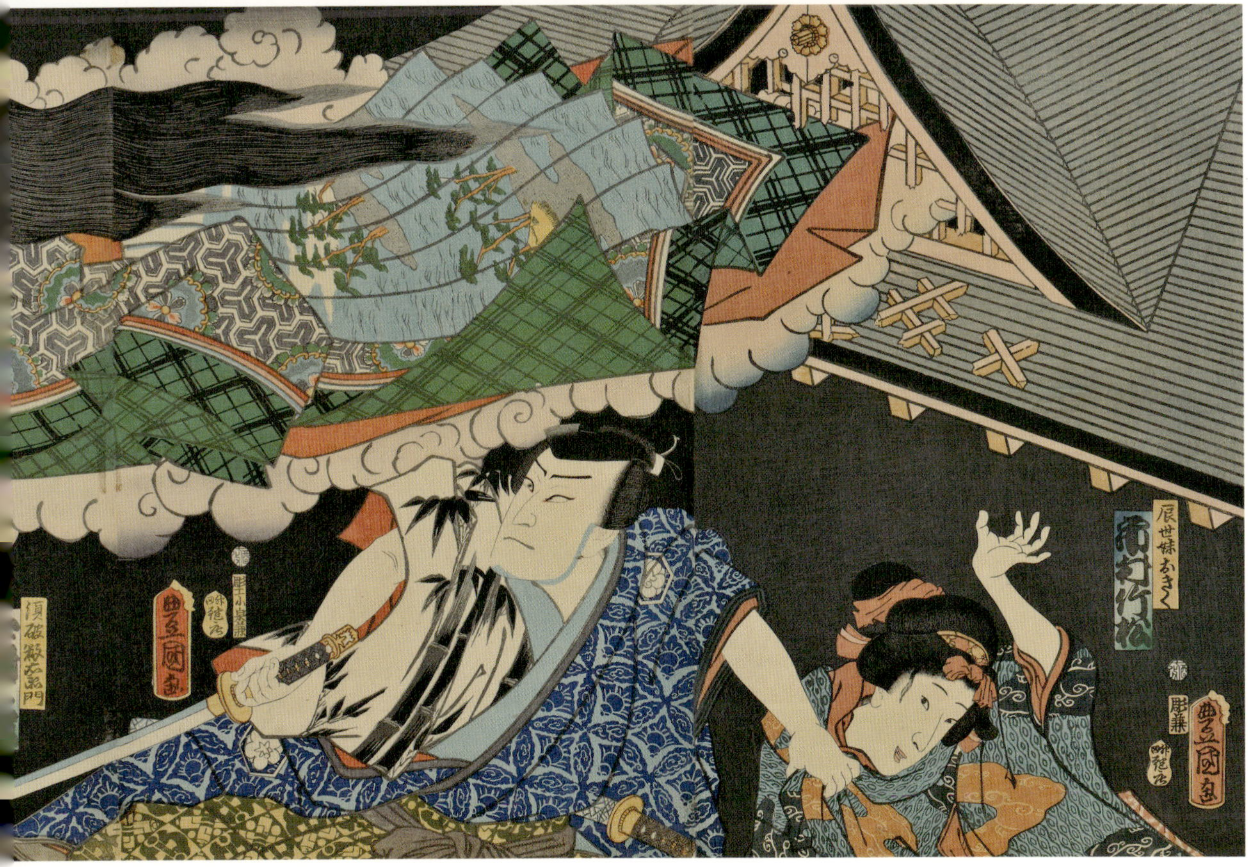

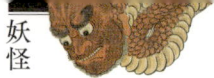

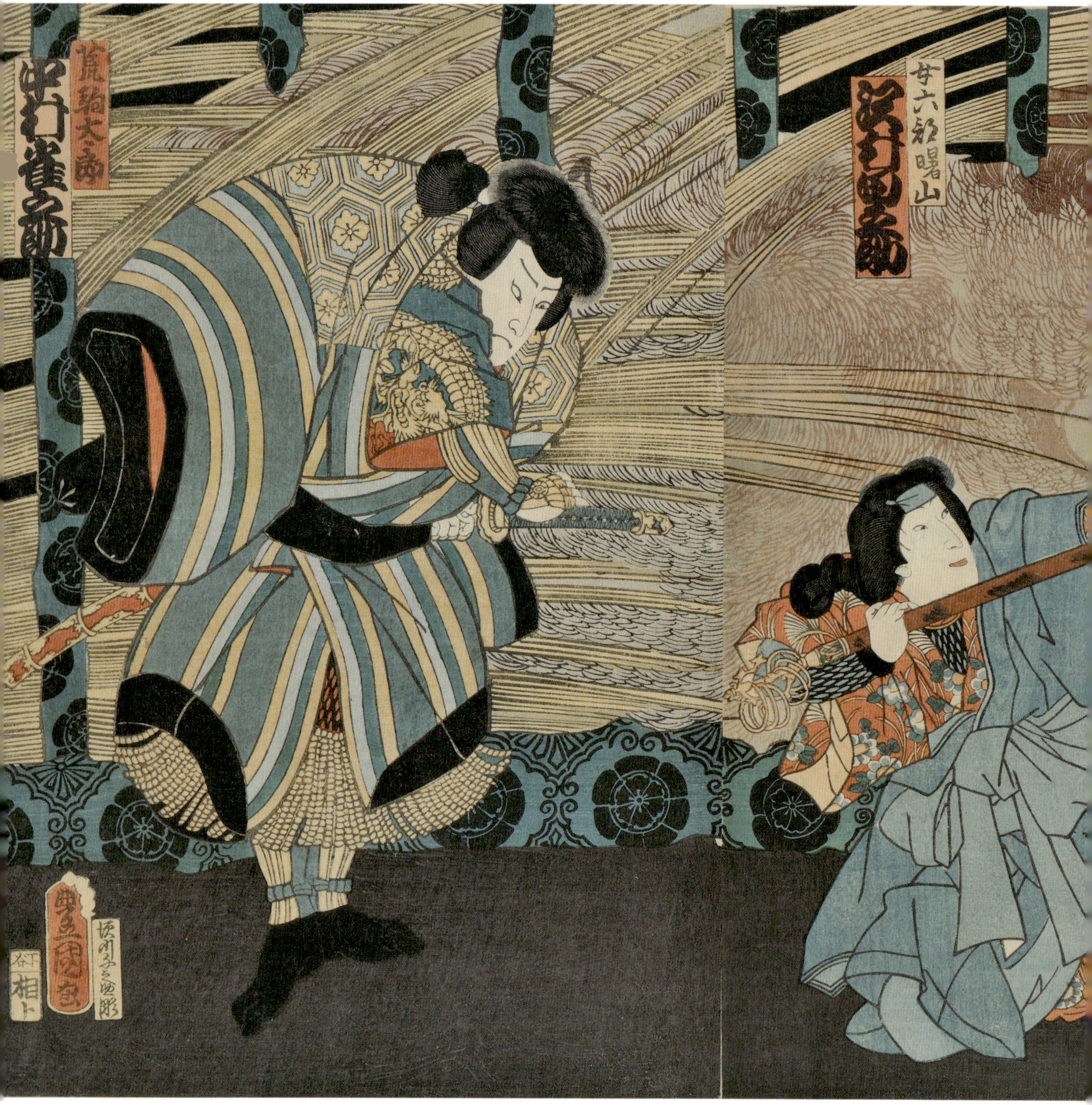

妖怪

【東駅いろは日記】歌川国貞（三代豊国）文久元年（1861）
女巡礼の曙山が、錫杖を武器に敵と戦う場面。よく見ると背後の破れた御簾の中から、
巨大な化け猫の顔が不気味に浮びあがり、目をぎょろりと光らせています。

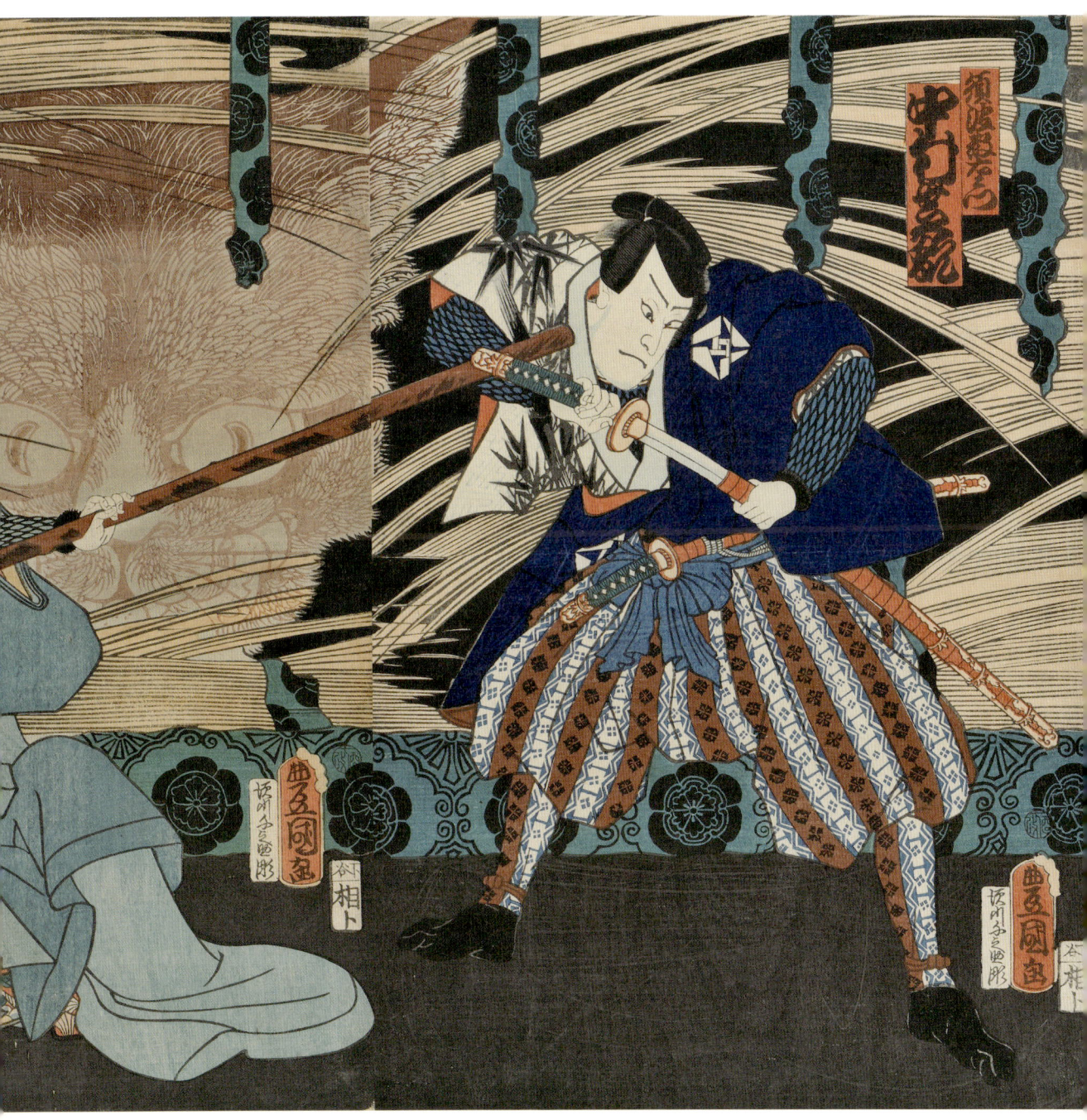

Tōkaidō Iroha Nikki (A to Z Journal of the Tōkaidō Highway) by Utagawa Kunisada (also known as Utagawa Toyokuni III)

The scene where Shozan the pilgrim takes on an enemy using her staff as a weapon. Behind the tattered bamboo blind in the background, the eerie silhouette of a monster cat's massive head can be seen, staring eyes watchful.

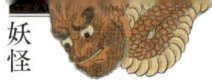

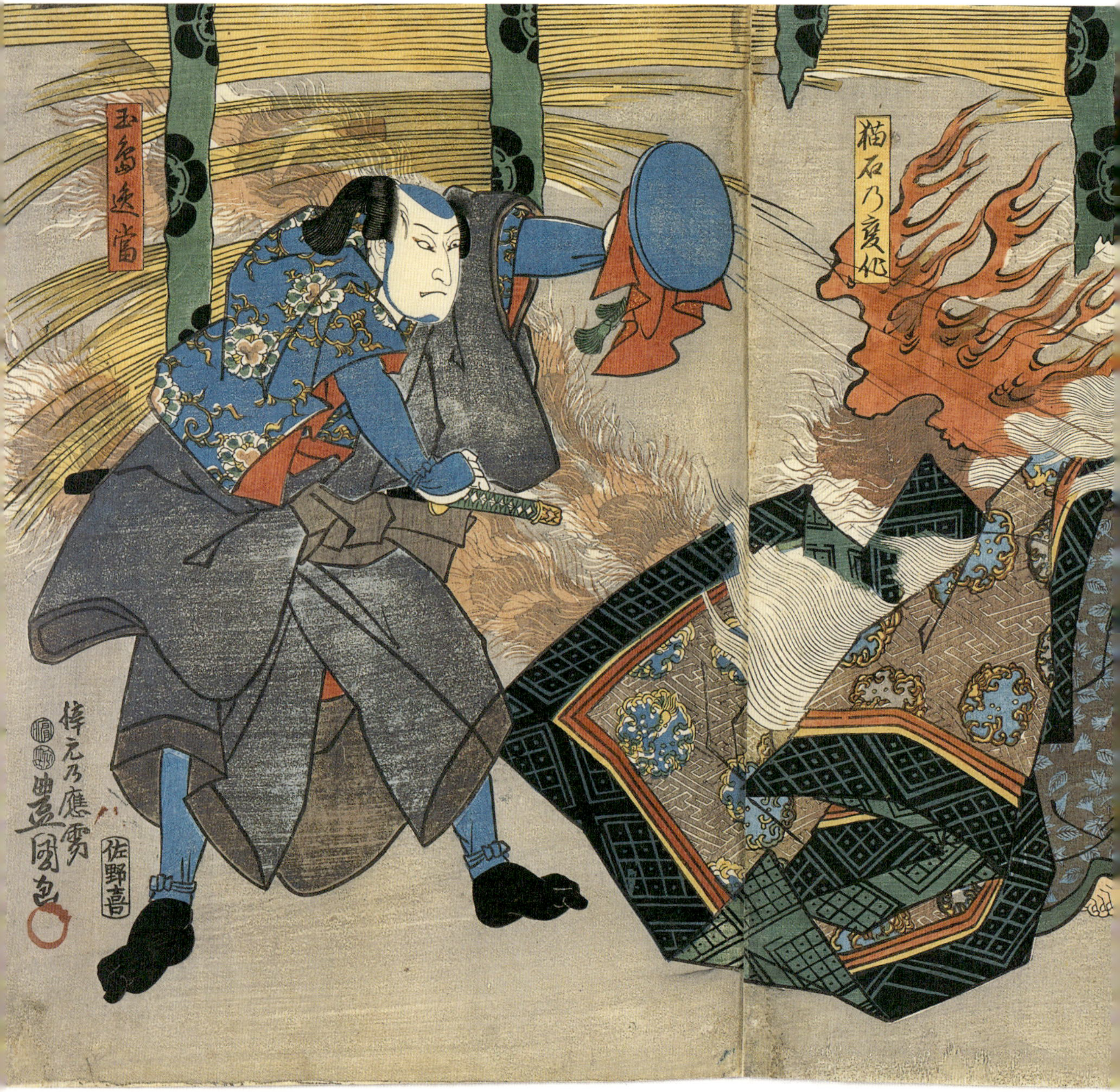

妖怪

【昔語岡崎猫石妖怪】歌川国貞（三代豊国）弘化4年（1847）
歌舞伎「尾上梅寿一代噺」より。古寺にすむ老女に宝鏡を向けると、その威力で本性を現しました。実は猫石が化けたもので、破れた御簾の中から化け猫が火を噴きながら顔をのぞかせています。

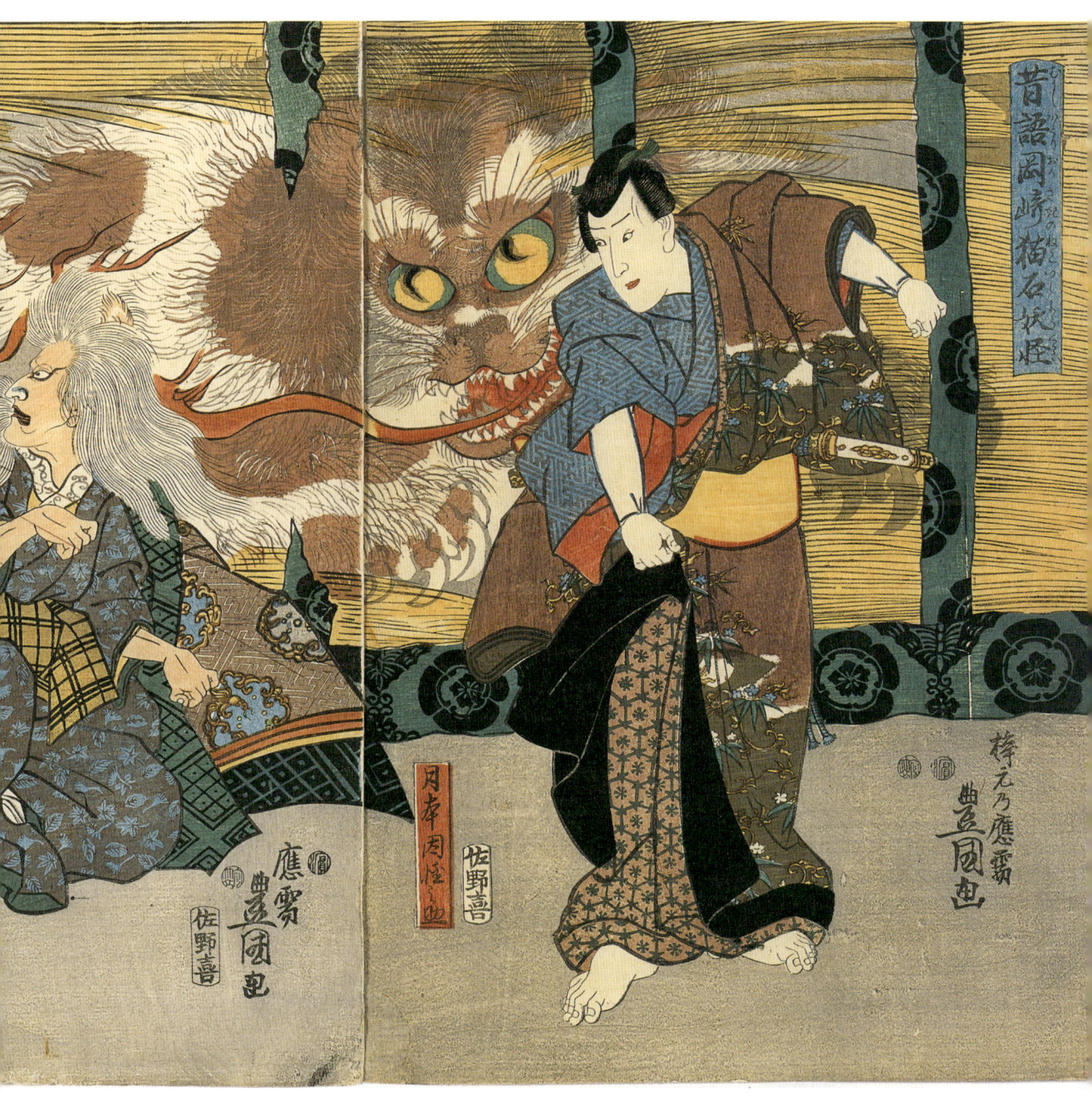

The Old Tale of the Monster of the Okazaki Cat Stone by Utagawa Kunisada (also known as Utagawa Toyokuni III)

From kabuki play *Onoe Kikugorō Ichidai Banashi*. The old woman of the ancient temple faces the precious mirror, and by its power her true nature is revealed. She is really a shape taken by the Cat Stone, and the defeated monster cat shows its face, spitting fire, from the bamboo blind.

妖怪

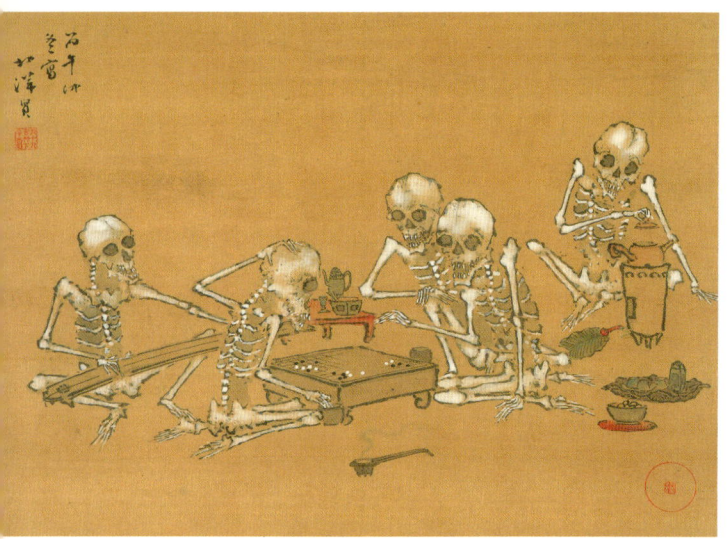

【骸骨囲碁遊び】葛飾北洋 江戸時代後期

Skeletons Playing Igo
by Katsushika Hokuyō (Late 18th century)

146

月夜の晩、ダンスを楽しむ骸骨たち。酒宴の席でしょうか、笑い踊るにぎやかな様子が、軽やかなタッチで繊細に描かれています。

Skeletons who love to dance on moonlit nights. Drawn delicately with a light touch, this could be a drinking party, lively with laughter and dancing. The consummate skill of the artist is shown in the accuracy of anatomical proportions and the intricacy of fine details, right down to the small bones of fingers and joints.

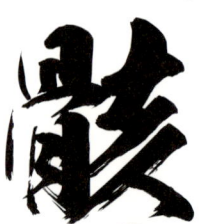

Skeletons
Demonic Creatures (*yōkai*)

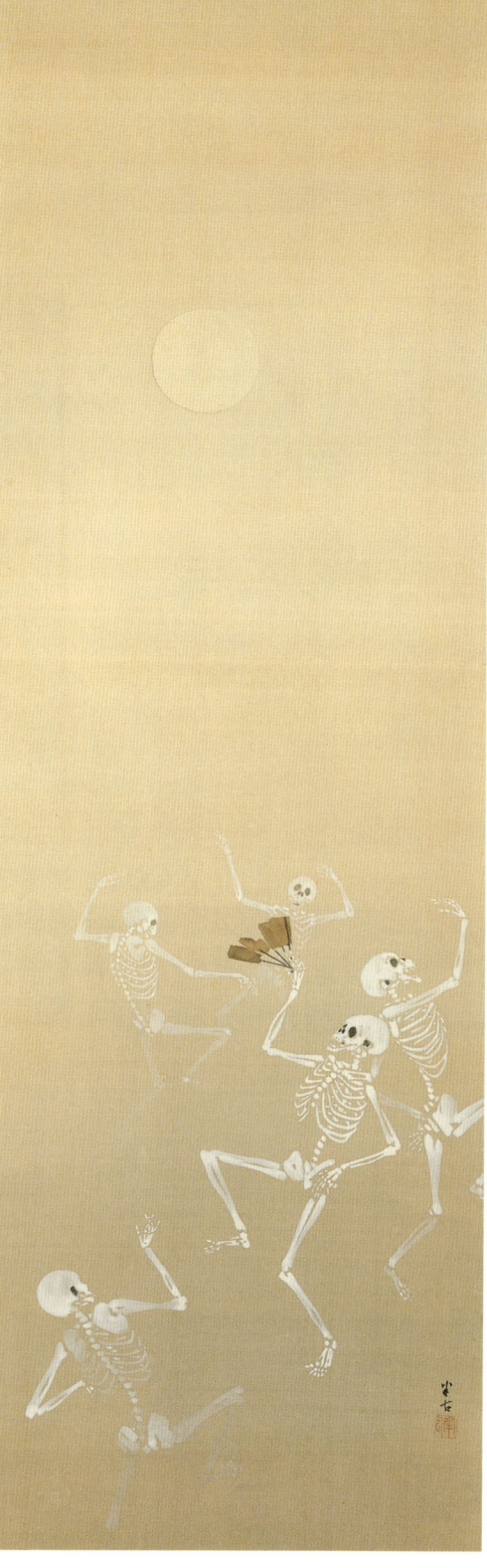

【月下骸骨踊り】梶田半古 明治時代

Skeletons Dance in the Moonlight
by Kajita Hanko
(End of 19th century – early 20th century)

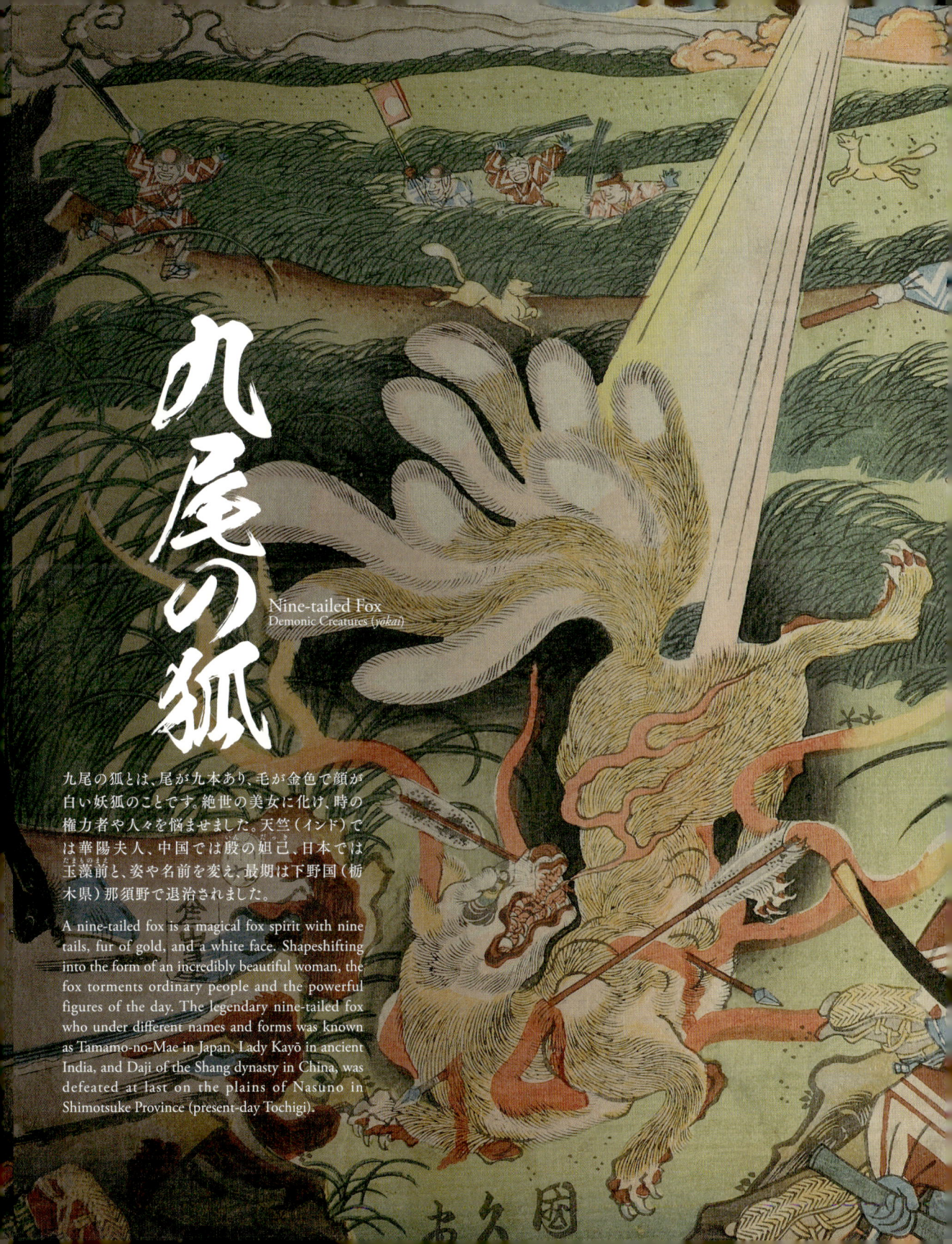

九尾の狐

Nine-tailed Fox
Demonic Creatures (*yōkai*)

九尾の狐とは、尾が九本あり、毛が金色で顔が白い妖狐のことです。絶世の美女に化け、時の権力者や人々を悩ませました。天竺（インド）では華陽夫人、中国では殷の妲己、日本では玉藻前と、姿や名前を変え、最期は下野国（栃木県）那須野で退治されました。

A nine-tailed fox is a magical fox spirit with nine tails, fur of gold, and a white face. Shapeshifting into the form of an incredibly beautiful woman, the fox torments ordinary people and the powerful figures of the day. The legendary nine-tailed fox who under different names and forms was known as Tamamo-no-Mae in Japan, Lady Kayō in ancient India, and Daji of the Shang dynasty in China, was defeated at last on the plains of Nasuno in Shimotsuke Province (present-day Tochigi).

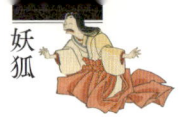

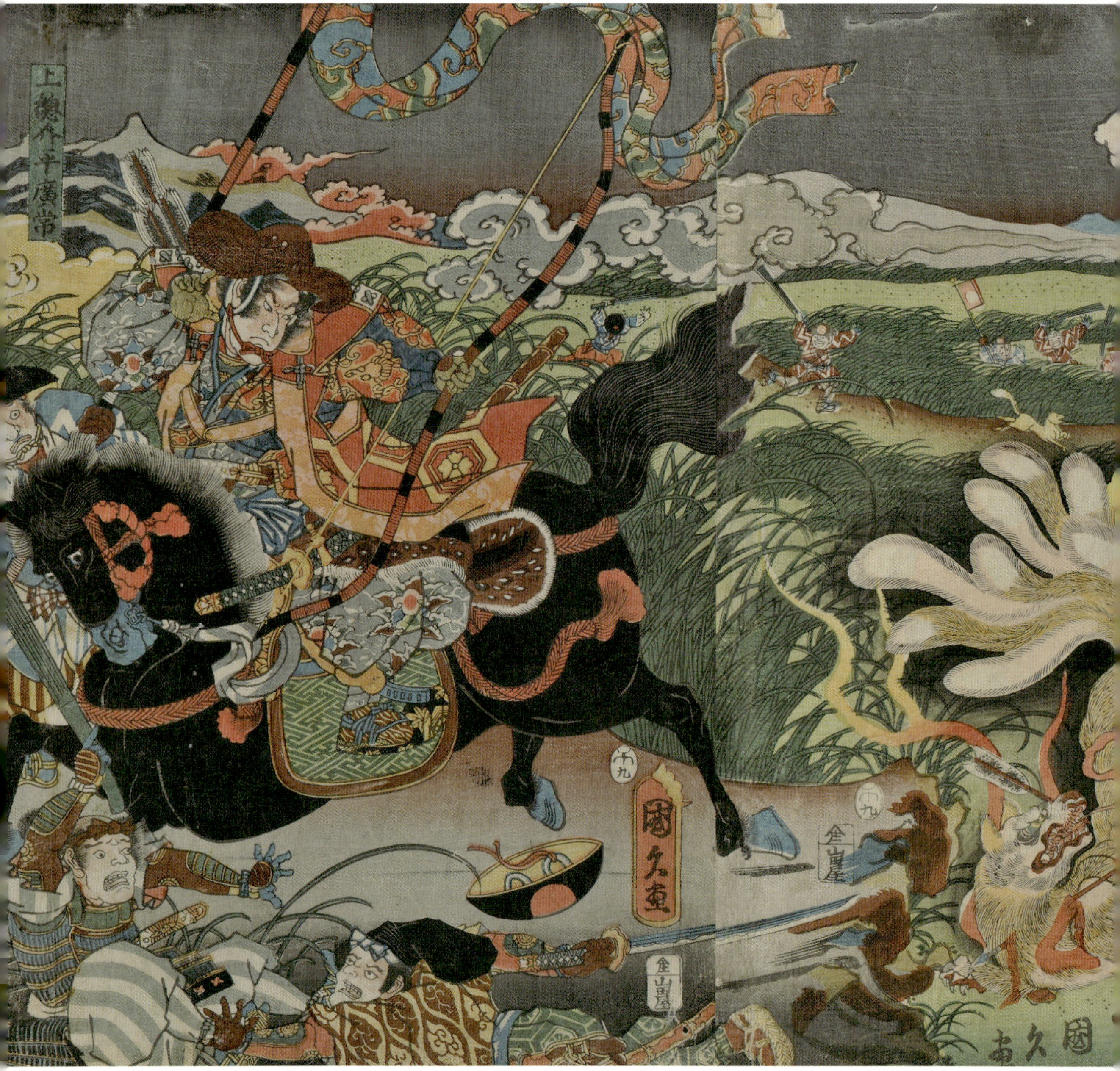

妖狐

【三浦上総両介那須野九尾狐討取】歌川国久　安政5年（1858）

平安後期、鳥羽上皇の寵愛を受けた玉藻前は、実は九尾の狐の化身でした。陰陽師の安倍氏に見破られ、那須野に飛び去ります。朝命を受けた三浦介平義明と上総介平広常が、矢で射ち殺しました。

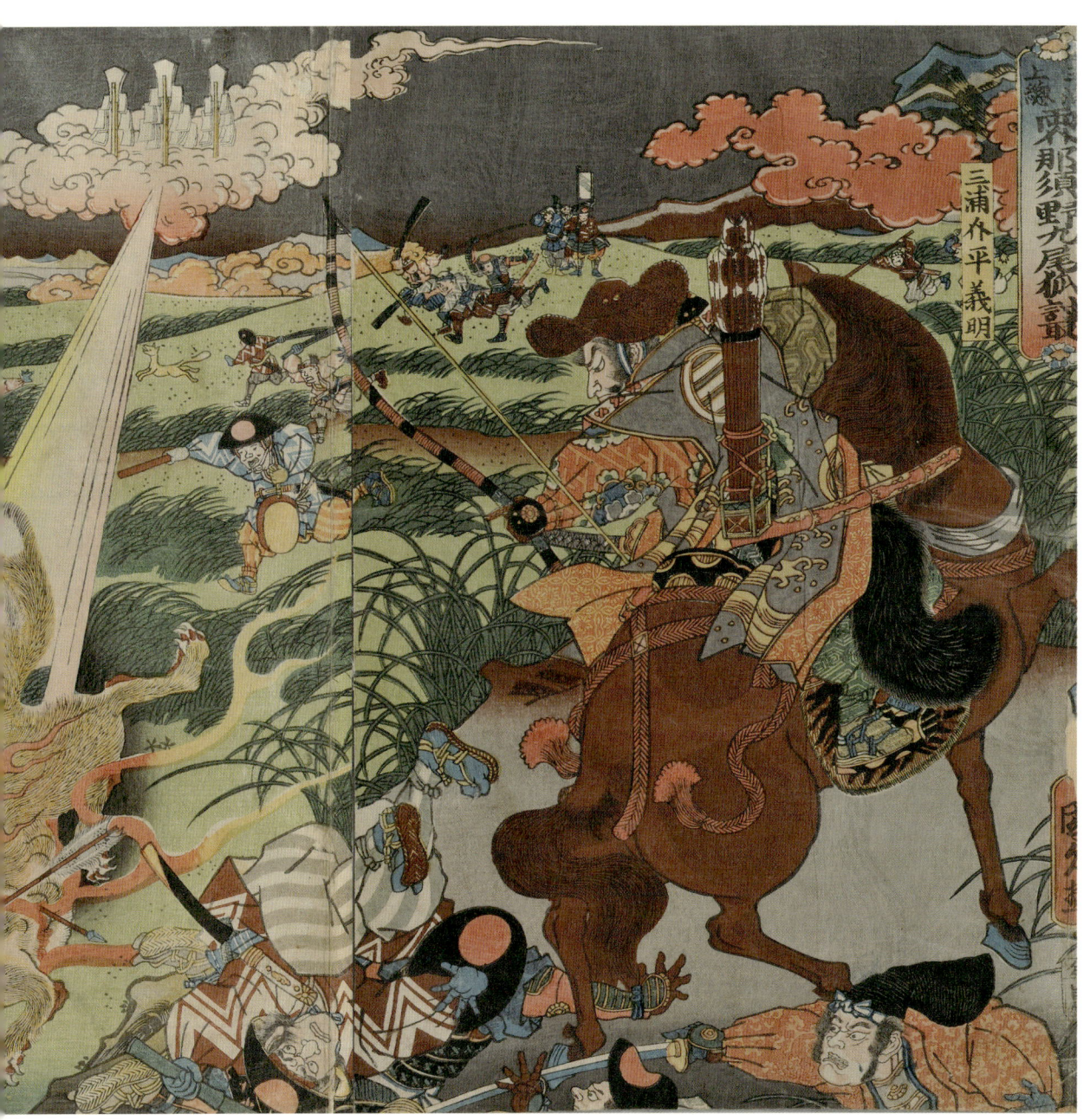

Miura-no-suke and Kazusa-no-suke Defeat the Nine-tailed Fox on Nasuno Moor by Utagawa Kunihisa

Tamamo-no-Mae, who became the most favoured courtesan of Emperor Toba in the late Heian period, was actually the shapeshifting nine-tailed fox. Unmasked by a yin-yang master of Abe no Seimei, the fox fled to the plains of Nasuno. By Imperial order, Miura-no-suke Tairano Yoshiaki and Kazusa-no-suke Tairano Hirotsune slew it with arrows.

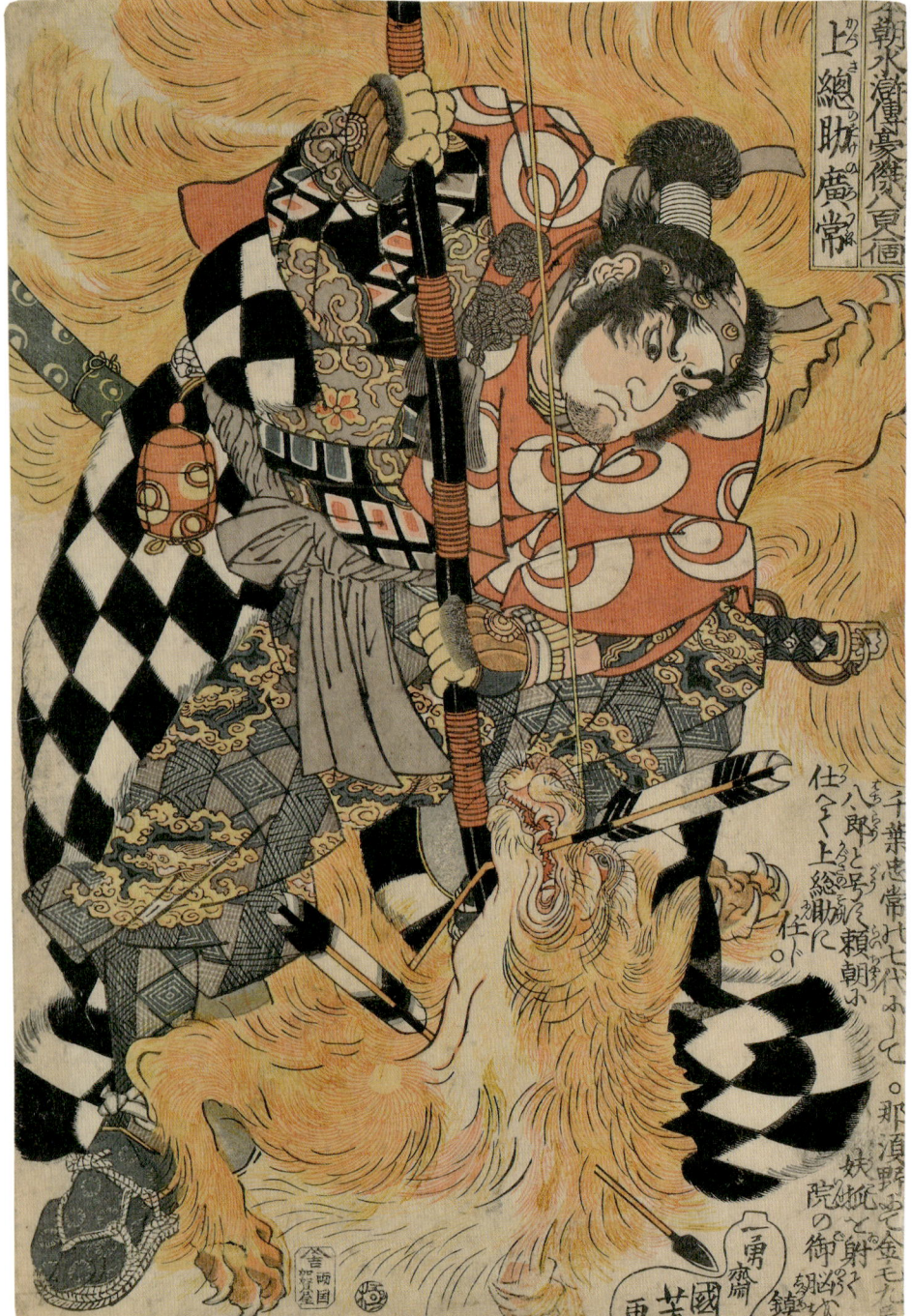

150

【本朝水滸傳豪傑八百人ノ一個 上総助廣常】歌川国芳 天保元〜2年（1803-31）
上総介（助）広常は勅命を受けて、三浦介義明とともに那須野にて九尾の狐を射止めました。

Kazusa-no-suke Hirotsune, One of the Eight Hundred Heroes of the Japanese Water Margin
by Utagawa Kuniyoshi
By Imperial order, Kazusa-no-suke Hirotsune (and Miura-no-suke Yoshiaki) felled the nine-tailed fox at Nasuno.

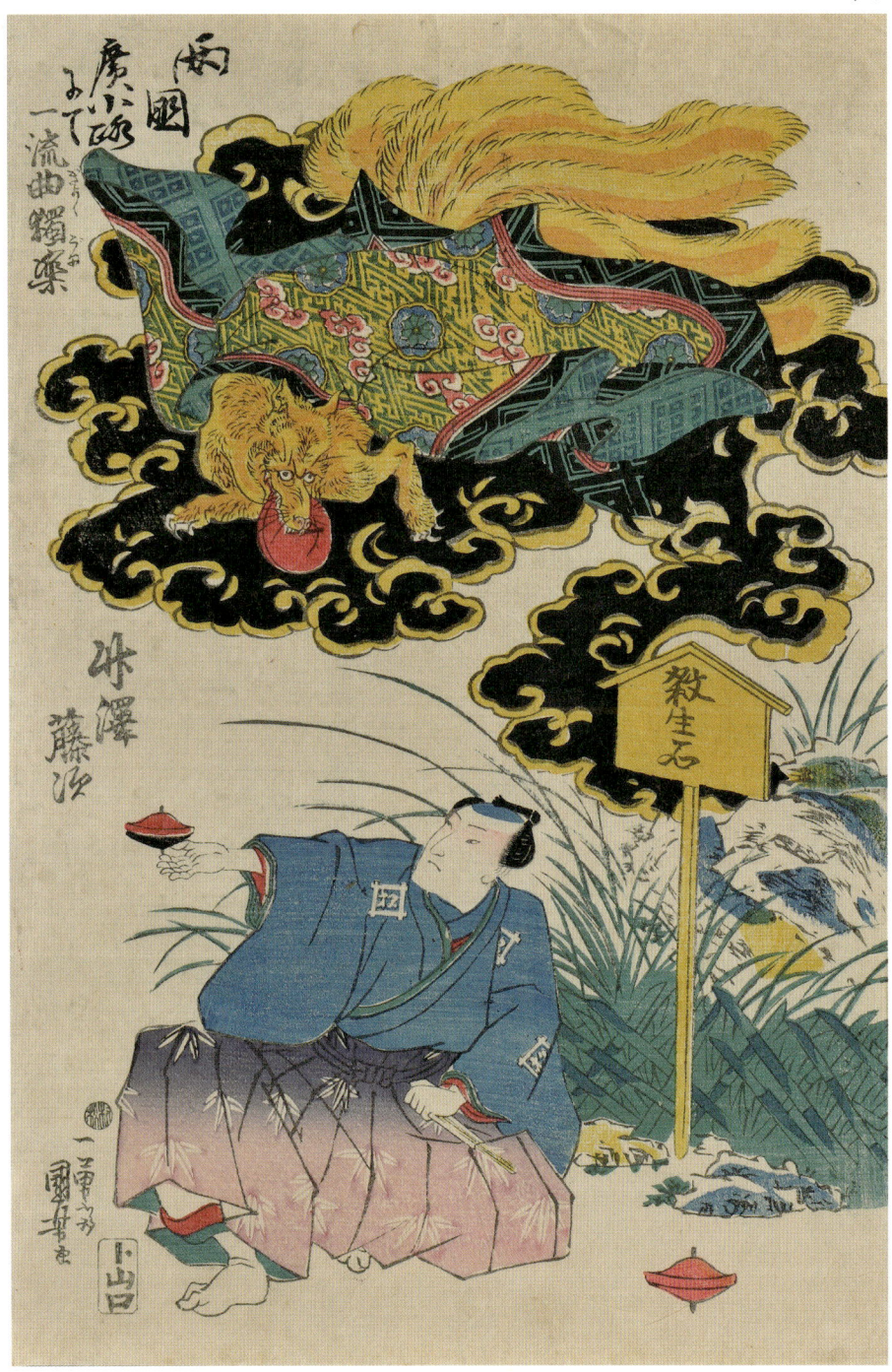

【両国広小路にて一流曲独楽 竹沢藤次 殺生石】歌川国芳 弘化元年（1844）

退治された妖狐の屍は石となり、道行く人に毒を吐いたため、「殺生石」と呼ばれました。幕末の曲独楽師・竹沢藤次は、この九尾の狐をテーマにした「金毛九尾三国渡」という見世物興行を行い、人気を博しました。

Sesshō-seki (the Murder Stone): Exceptional Spinning-top Performance by Takezawa Tōji at Ryōgoku Hirokōji by Utagawa Kuniyoshi
The corpse of the slain fox spirit turned into a stone, and became known as the Murder Stone (Sesshō-seki) for its habit of poisoning passersby. Late Edo spinning top master Takezawa Tōji used the theme of the nine-tailed fox for his popular show *Golden Fur, Nine Tails, Spanning Three Countries.*

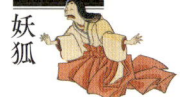
妖狐

【三国妖狐伝 第一斑足王御てんのだん】
葛飾北斎 文化4年（1807）

天竺で生まれ、長い年月を経て妖狐となった九尾の狐。仏
教を破滅させ、この世を魔界にするため、華（花）陽夫人に
化け、時の権力者・斑足王をたぶらかします。諸侯・普明長
者の宝剣「獅子王」の威力で、東の空へ逃げていきました。

Act I, The Palace of King Hanzoku
from the series *Sangoku yōko-den*
(The Tale of the Magical Fox in Three Countries)
by Katsushika Hokusai

Born in ancient India, it took many long years for the nine-tailed
fox to become a fox spirit. To doom Buddhism and turn the
world into a hell on earth, the fox transformed into Lady Kayō
and bewitched the powerful King Hanzoku. Banished by the
power of the Lord Fumei-chōja's precious sword Shishiō, she
flees into the eastern sky.

154-155ページ
【三国妖狐伝 唐土紂王館の段】
葛飾北斎 文化4年（1807）

ここは中国、殷の紂王の御殿。九尾の狐は妲己に化けて紂
王をたぶらかし、淫楽に耽り、残虐を極めていました。良臣
の西伯文王は謀反の疑いで捕えられ、命乞いに来た幼子
の錦舎を目の前で斬殺されてしまいます。

The Palace of Chinese King Zhou
from the series *Sangoku yōko-den*
(The Tale of the Magical Fox in Three Countries)
by Katsushika Hokusai

This is Shang dynasty King Zhou's palace in China. Transformed
into the concubine Daji to entrap King Zhou, the nine-tailed
fox wallows in carnal pleasures and cruel atrocities. Ji Chang (the
"Duke of the West") has been seized on suspicion of treachery,
and his young son, who came to plead for his life to be spared, is
put to the sword before his eyes.

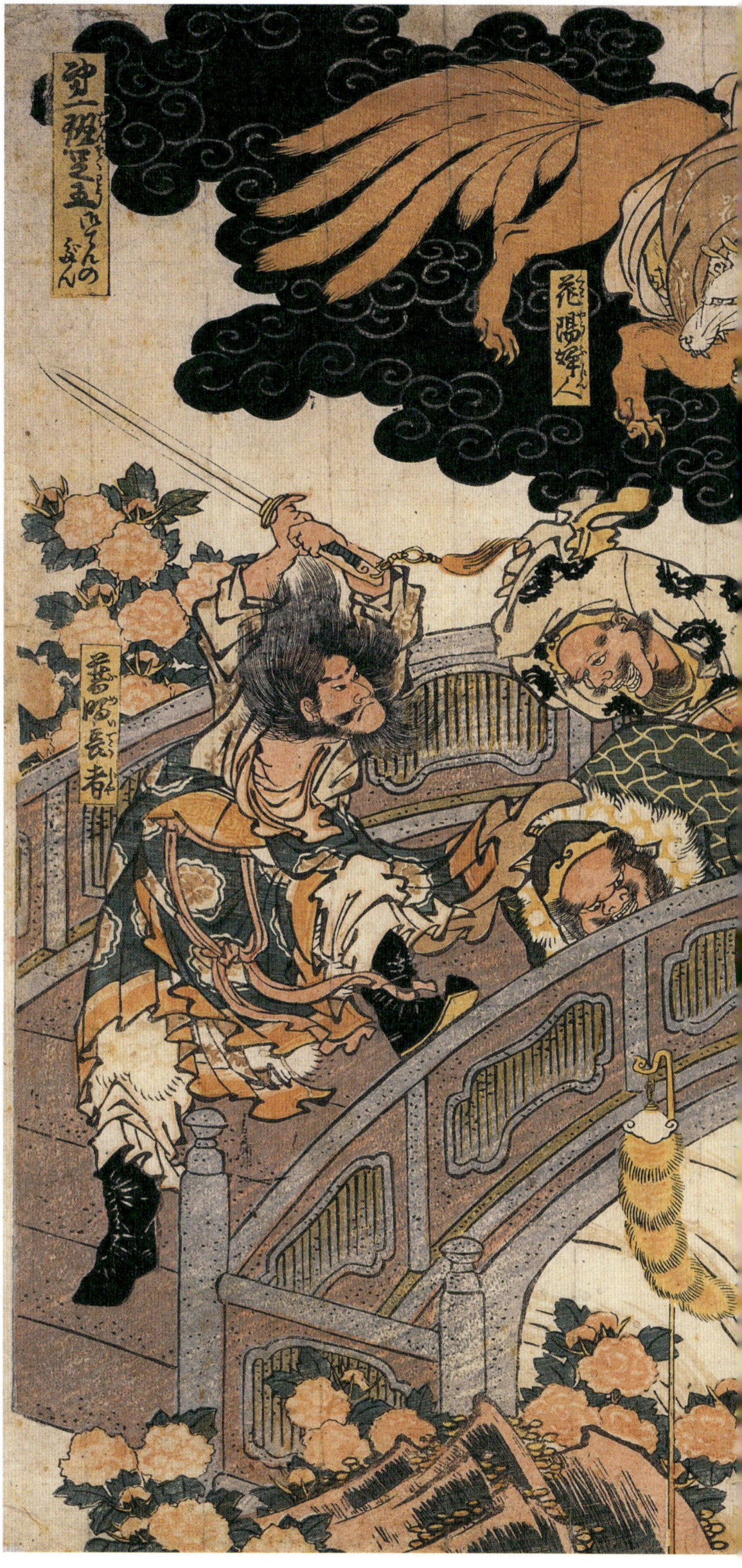

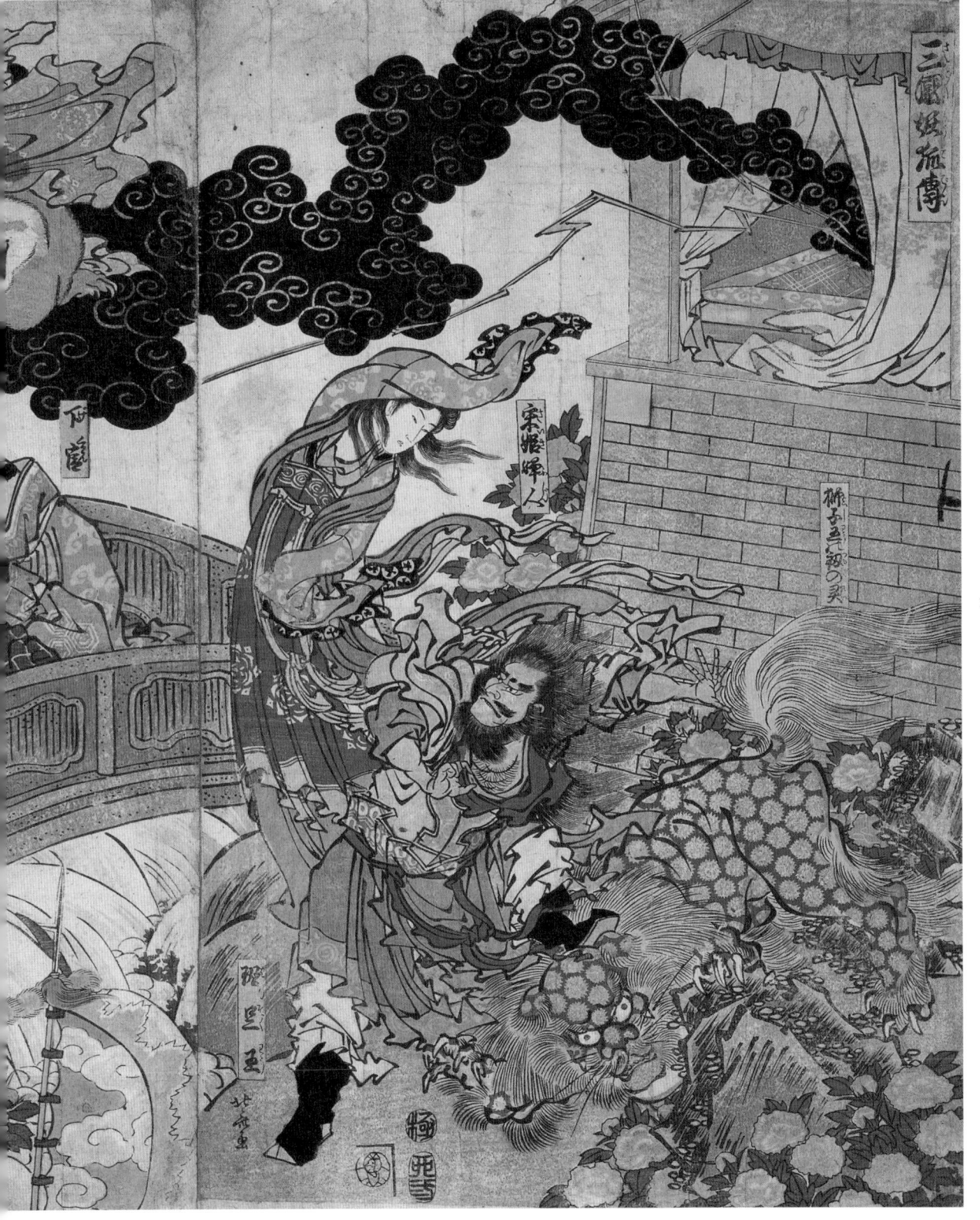

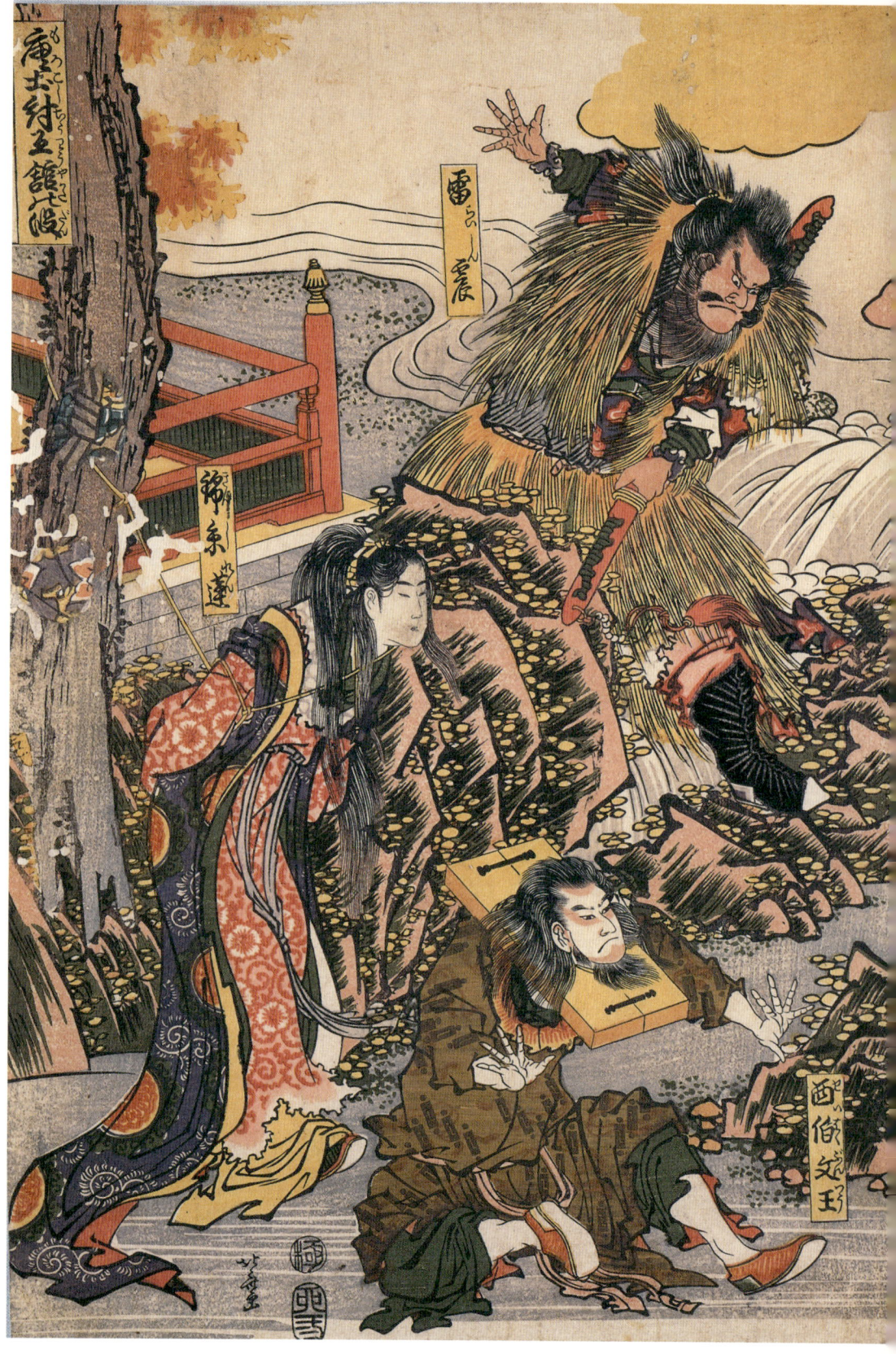

154

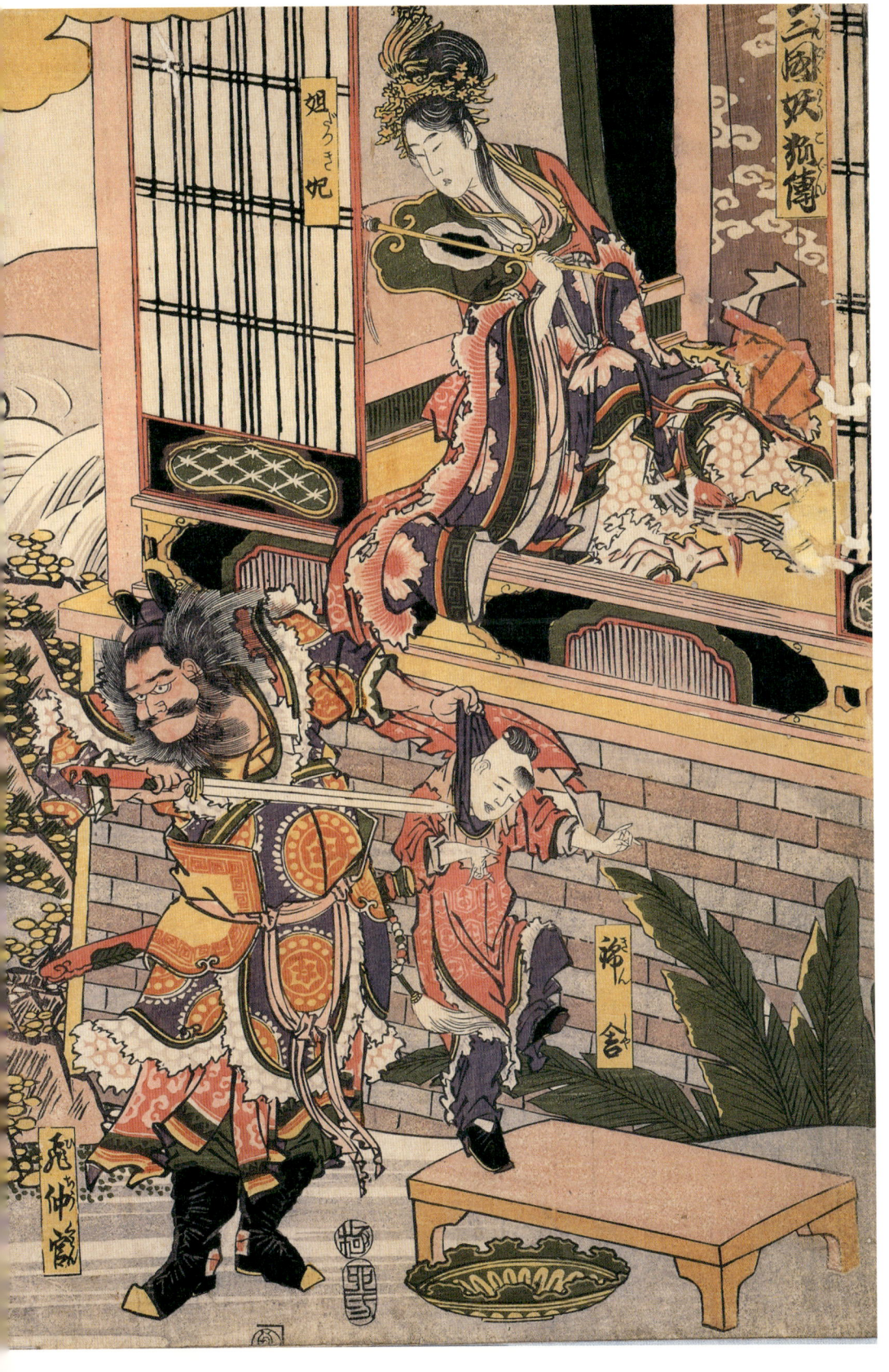

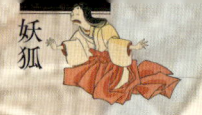

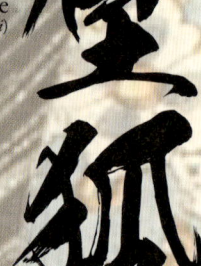

於佐壁狐

The Fox of Osakabe
Demonic Creatures (*yōkai*)

156

於佐壁狐は、姫路城の守護神である刑部大明神
の正体として知られていますが、一方では、天守閣
にすむ妖狐とも言われ、宮本武蔵によって退治され
たことが伝わっています。

The Fox of Osakabe is known as the true form of
Osakabe Daimyojin, the guardian deity of Himeji
Castle, but conflictingly is also said to be a mischievous
fox spirit living in the castle tower who was defeated by
Miyamoto Musashi.

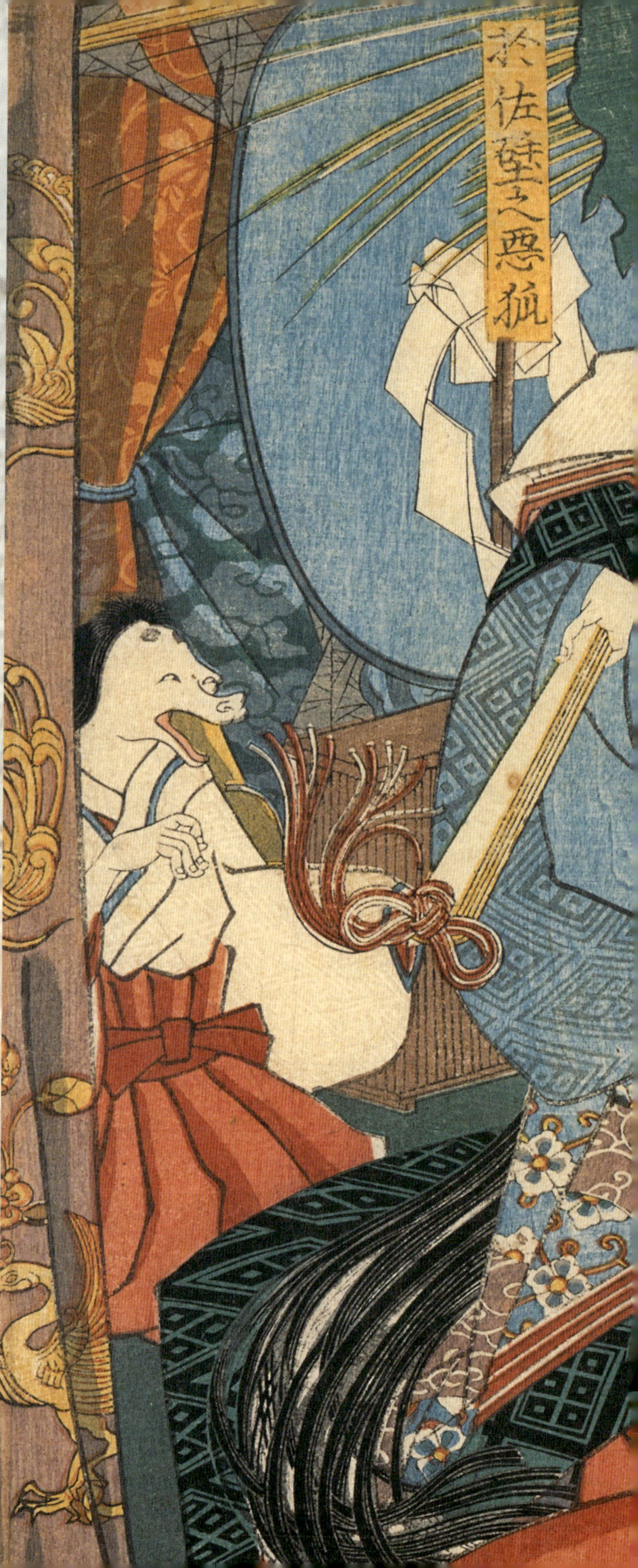

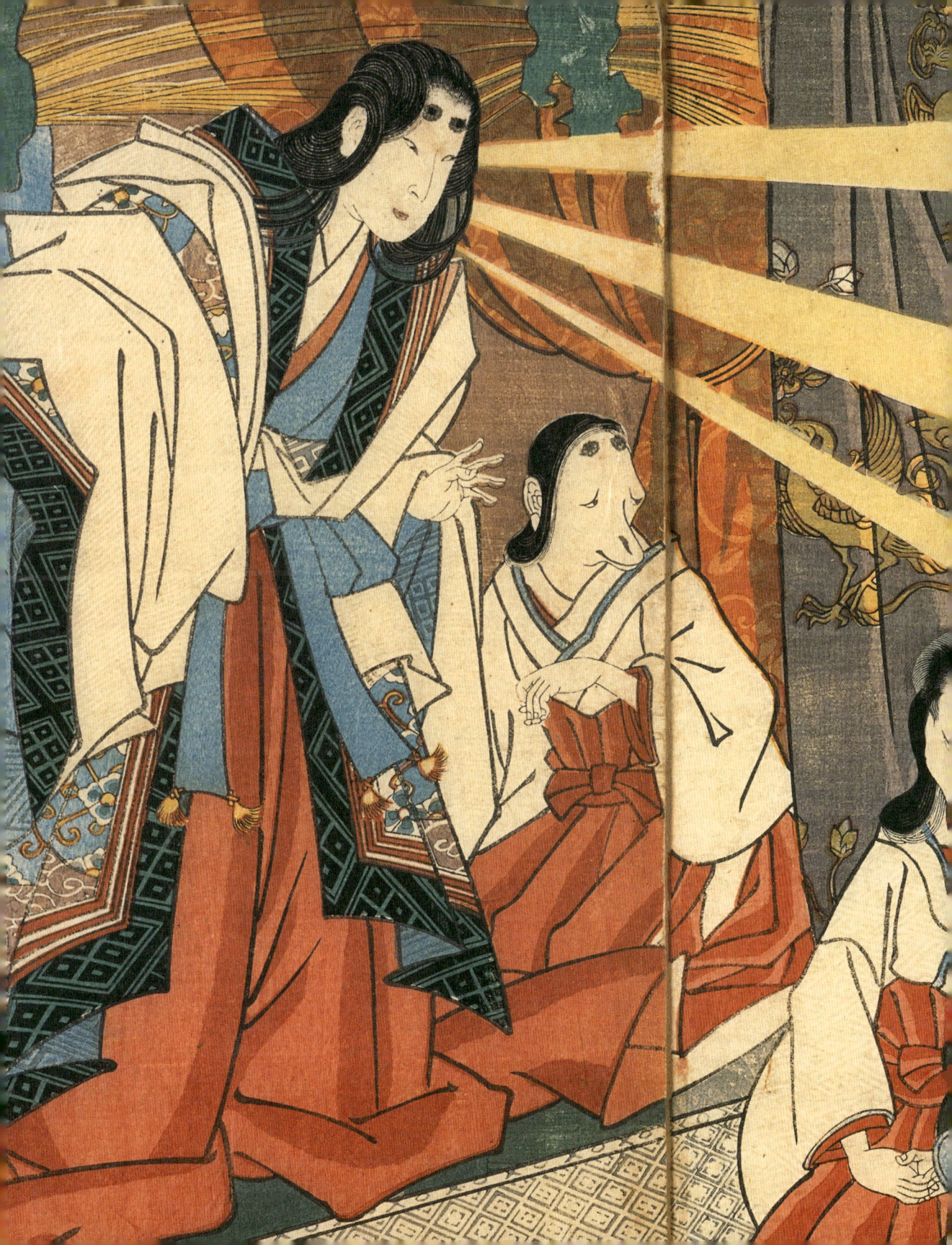

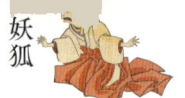

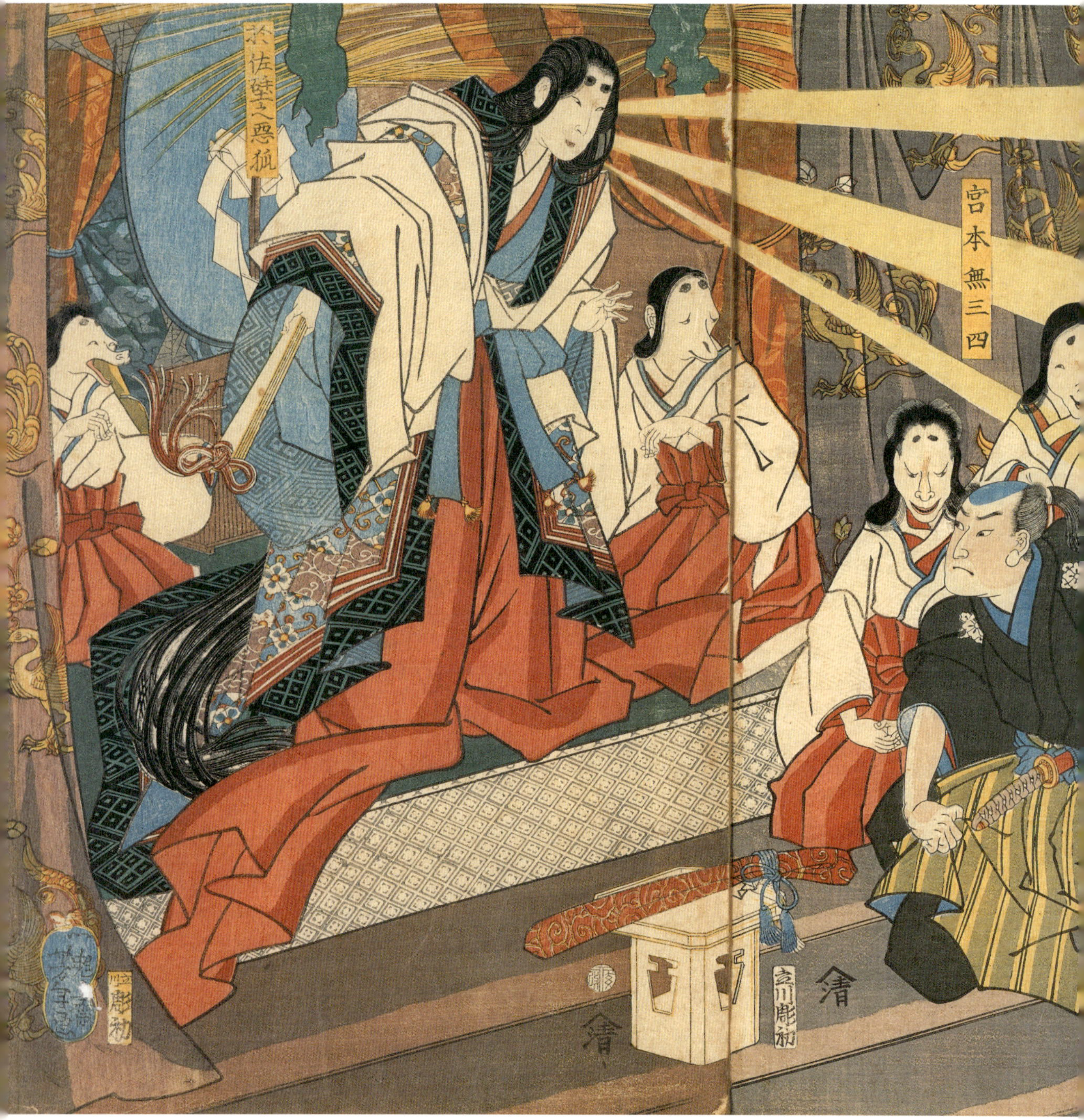

【播州姫路於佐壁狐を宮本無三四が退治せん】月岡芳年　文久3年（1863）

姫路城の天守から、夜な夜な発せられる怪しげな光。宮本武蔵（無三四）が確かめに行くと、巫女に化けた於佐壁狐たちの仕業でした。

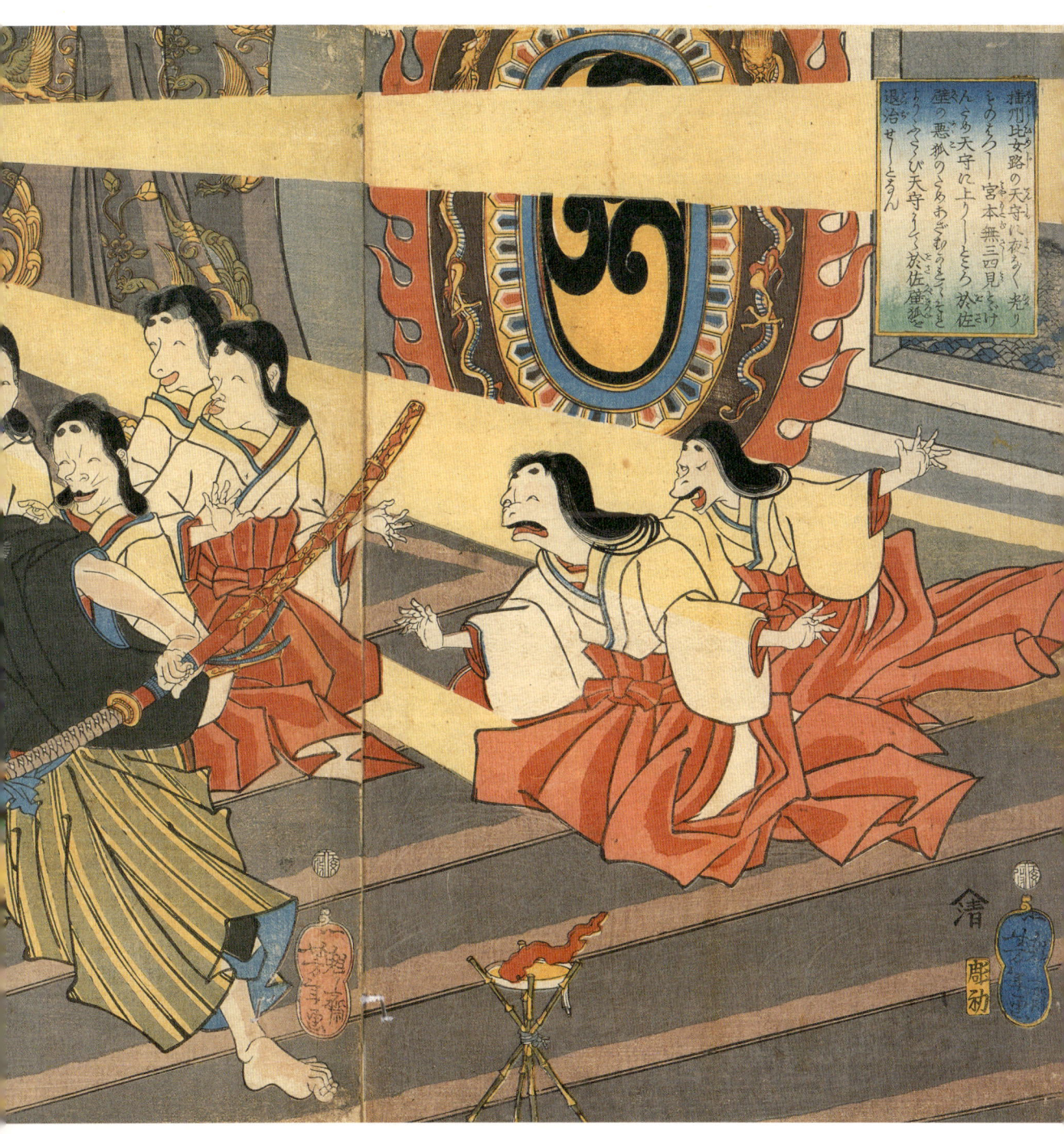

Miyamoto Musashi Banishes the Foxes of Osakabe in Himeji, Banshū by Tsukioka Yoshitoshi

Night after night, a strange light shone from the central tower of Himeji Castle. Miyamoto Musashi goes to investigate, and discovers that it is the work of the Osakabe foxes, who have changed into priestesses.

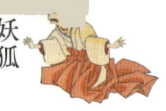

狐の嫁入り

The Wedding of Foxes
Demonic Creatures (*yōkai*)

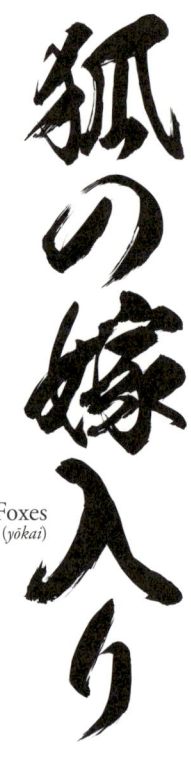

真夜中に丑の刻参りの女が偶然目撃したのは、豪勢な狐の嫁入り行列。実はこの図は、本書監修の中右氏の説によると、幕末に行われた公武合体策の一つ、皇女和宮の将軍家への降嫁を諷刺したものであるとのこと。降嫁が実行される前年の出版ですが、その噂は既に江戸市中にも出回っていたのでしょう。反幕勢力の目をくらますこの政略結婚は、「狐の嫁入りのごとくまやかしである」という諧謔が込められています。丑の刻参りの女は、突如として湧いた縁談に困惑するしかない和宮でしょうか。

In the dead of night, a woman visiting the shrine to place a curse in the witching hour happens upon a lavish wedding procession of foxes. According to the theory of supervising editor Mr. Nakau, this print may actually be a caricature of the politically expedient marriage of Imperial Princess Kazunomiya into the nonroyal Shōgun's family, one of the measures taken towards the union of the Imperial Court and the shogunate in the latter days of the Tokugawa. The print was published the year before the marriage took place, but rumors of it must have already been circulating in the city of Edo. This strategic marriage to dazzle the eyes of the anti-shogunate elements was mocked as "a foxes' wedding, all smoke and mirrors". The shrine visitor could be Kazunomiya, perplexed by a sudden proposal of marriage appearing out of nowhere.

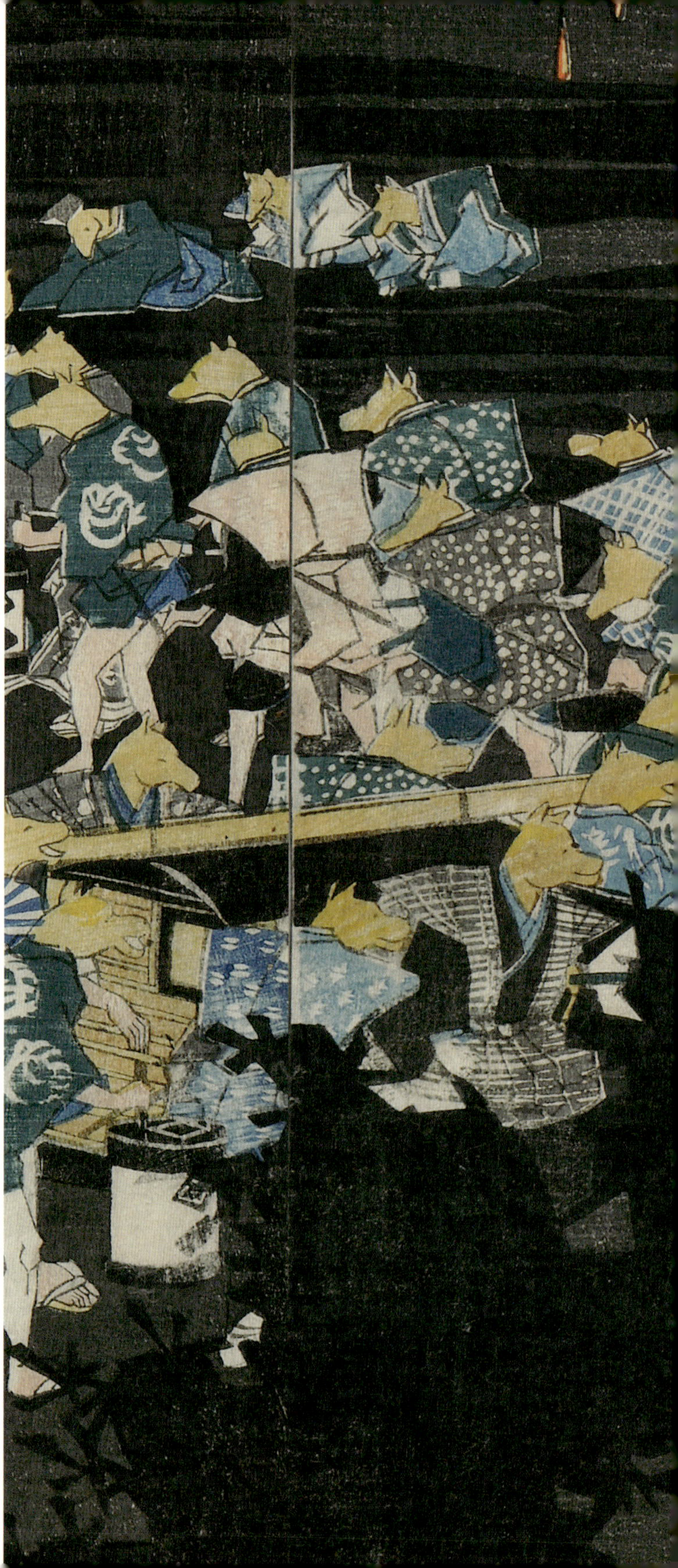

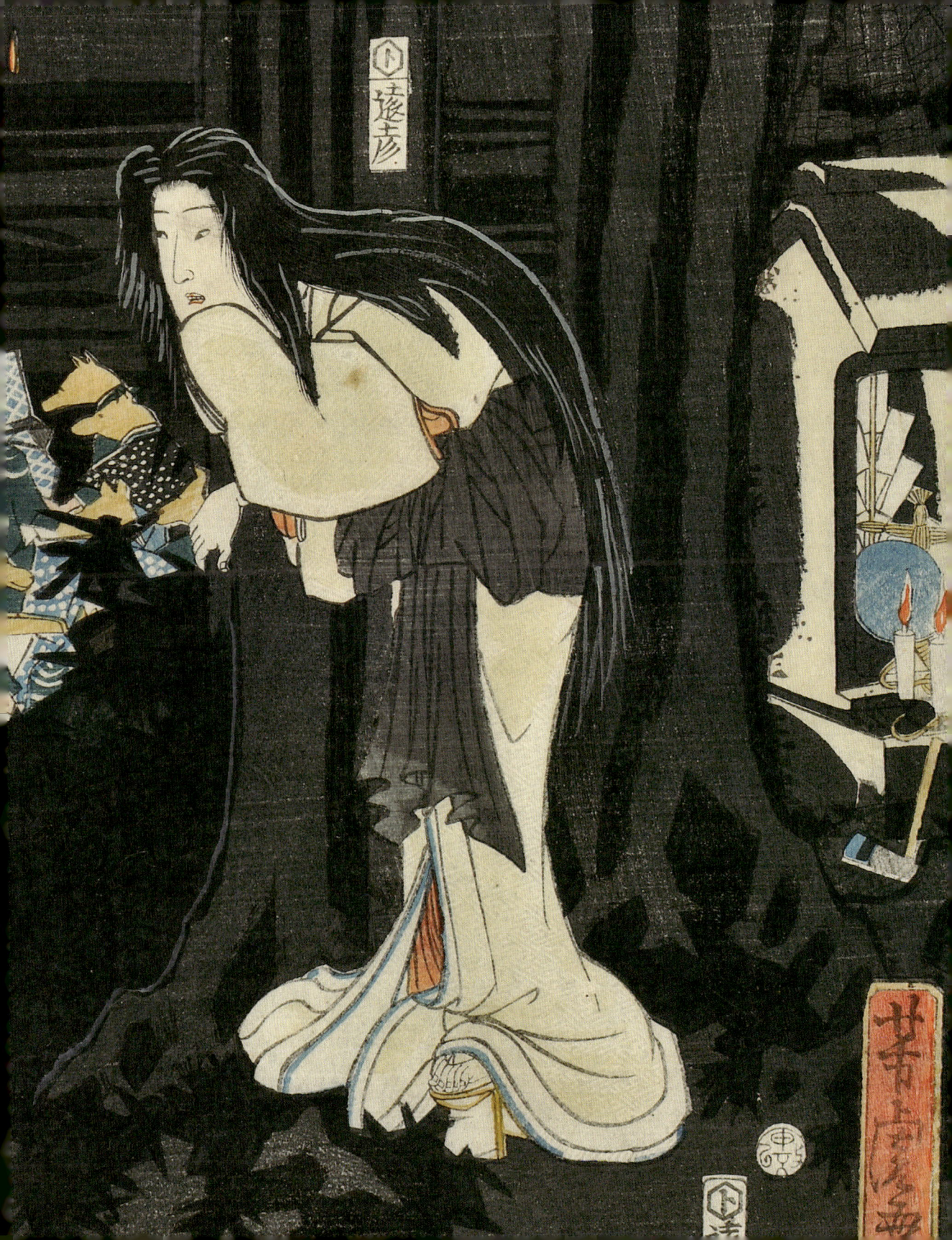

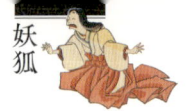

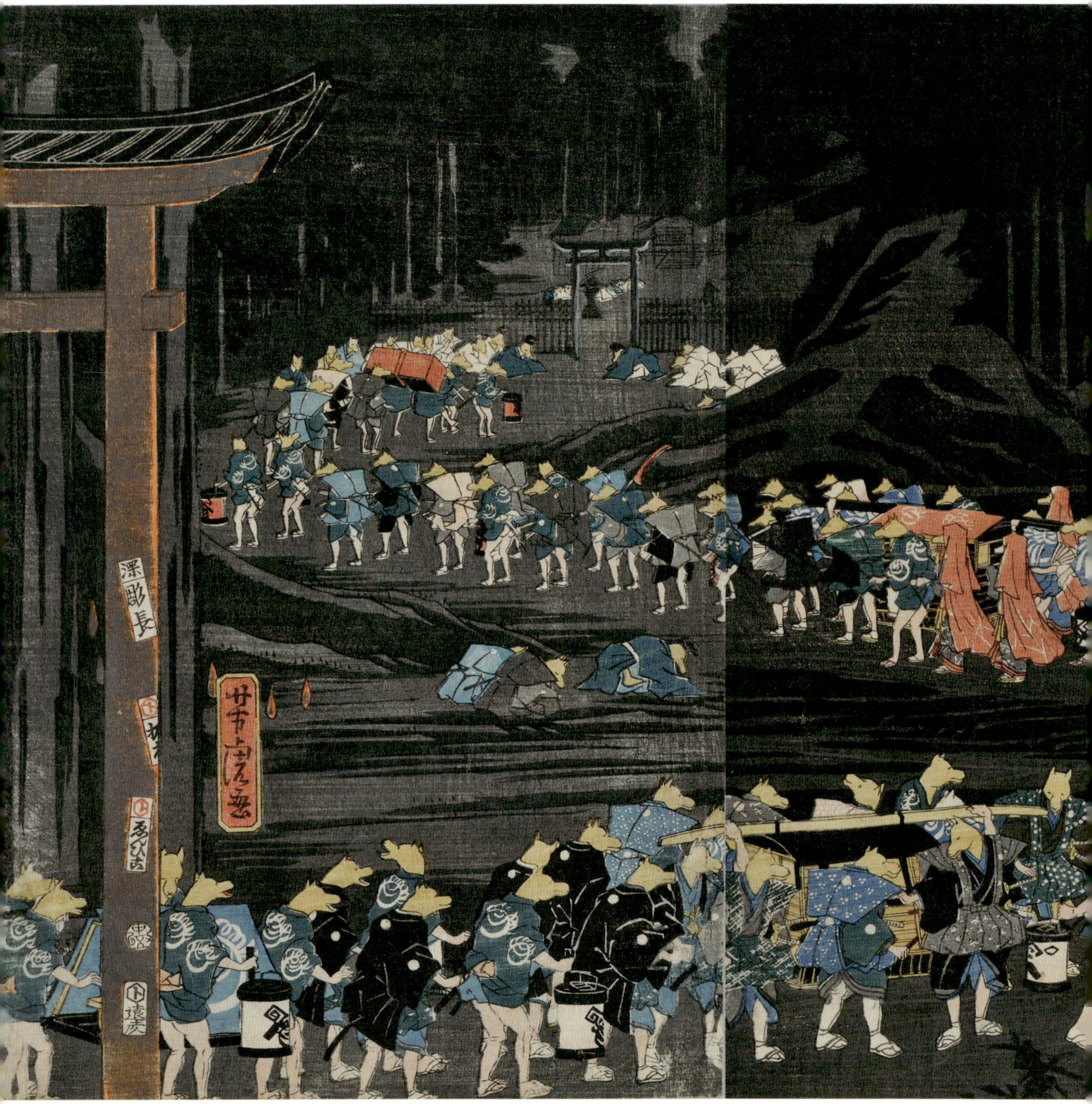

妖狐

【時参不計狐嫁入見図】歌川芳虎 万延元年（1860）

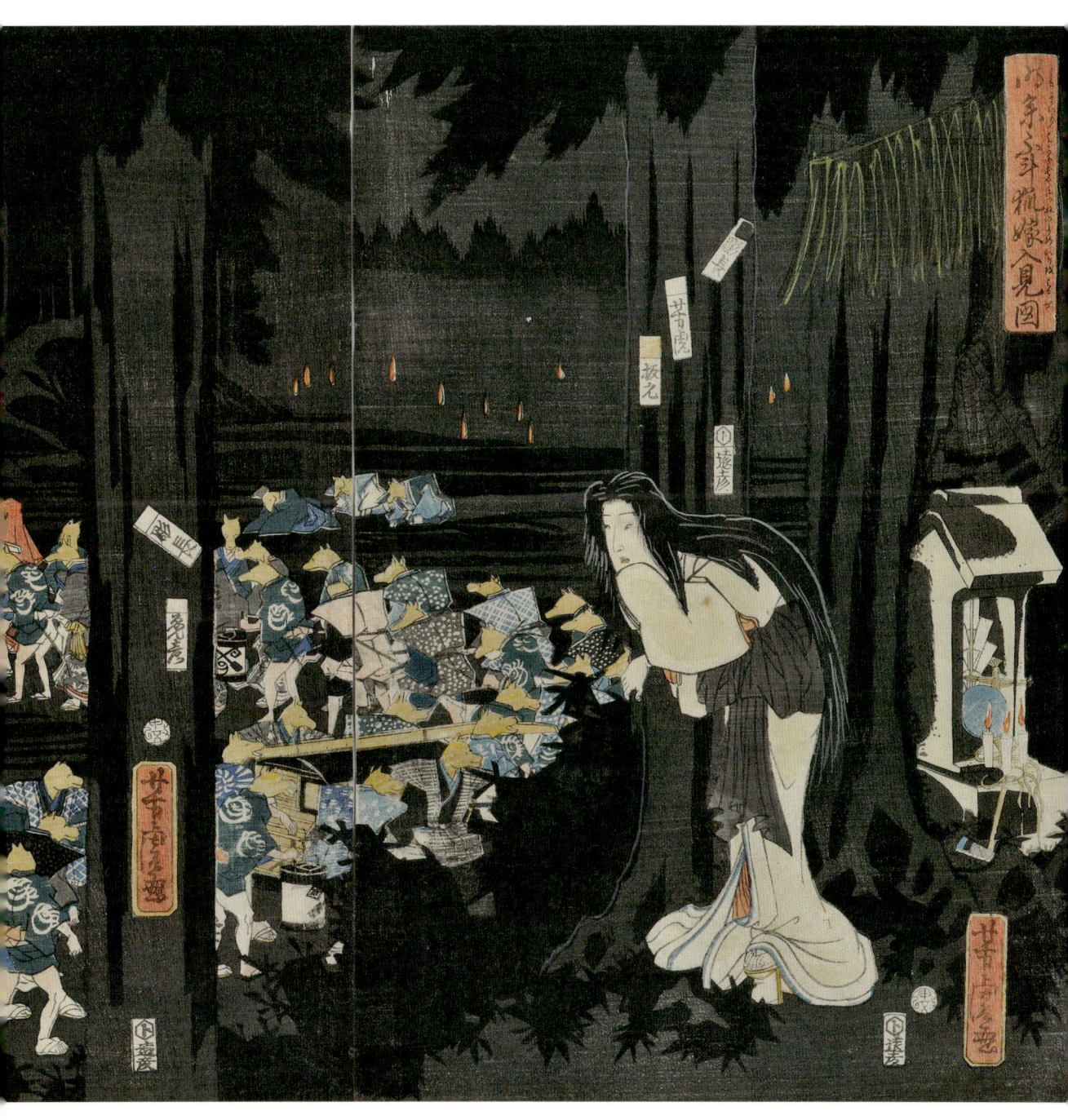

The Fox Wedding Procession: Stumbling Across a Foxes' Wedding on a Shrine Visit by Utagawa Yoshitora

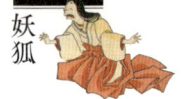

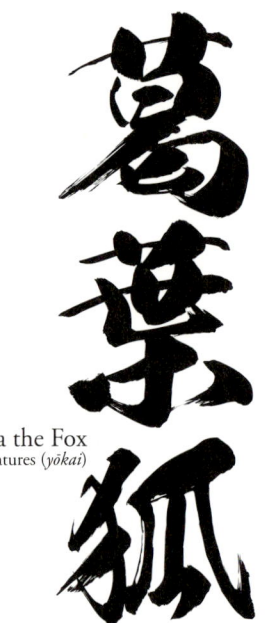

Kuzunoha the Fox
Demonic Creatures (*yōkai*)

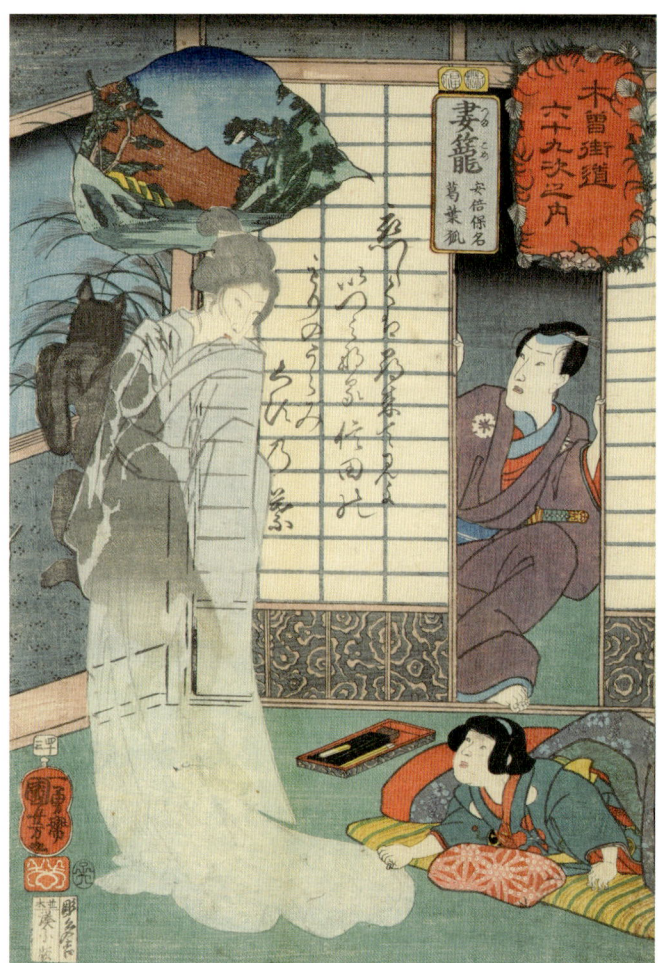

葛葉狐は和泉国（大阪府）信太森にすむ伝説の白狐。女に化け安部保名の妻となり、安倍晴明を生んだと言われています。ある時、正体が保名にばれてしまい、愛児に別れを告げ、泣く泣く信太森に帰っていきました。

Kuzunoha the Fox is the legend of a white fox who lived in Shinodanomori Forest in Izumi Province (present-day Osaka). It is said that the fox changed into a woman, became the wife of Abe no Yasuna, and gave birth to a son, Abe no Seimei, who later became a famous yin-yang master (the Merlin of Japan). One day, her true form is discovered by Yasuna, and without saying goodbye to her beloved child, she returns weeping to Shinodanomori Forest.

【木曽街道六十九次之内 妻籠 安倍保名 葛葉狐】歌川国芳 嘉永5年（1852）
「恋しくば尋ね来て見よいづみ（和泉）なる 信田（太）のもりのうらみくずの葉」と障子に書き残す葛葉。本性の狐のシルエットが、悲しげに泣いています。

Tsumagome: Abe no Yasuna and the Fox Kuzunoha from the series *Sixty-nine Stations of the Kiso Highway* by Utagawa Kuniyoshi

Kuzunoha leaves this message behind on the sliding door: "If you miss me, come to Shinodanomori Forest in Izumi Province to see regretful Kuzunoha (lit. arrowroot leaves)". The silhouette of her true form as a fox is crying pitifully.

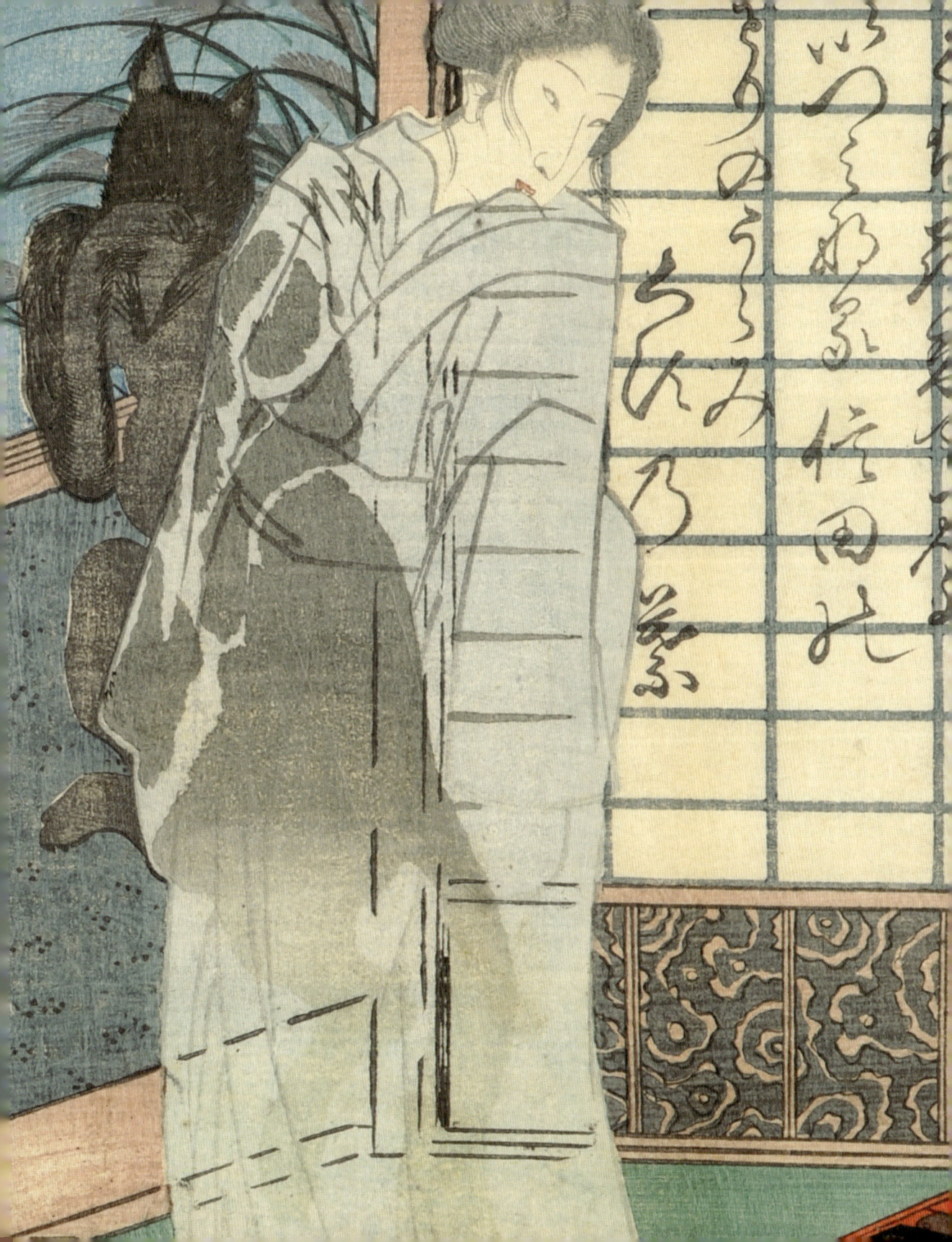

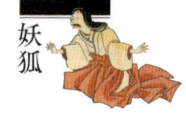

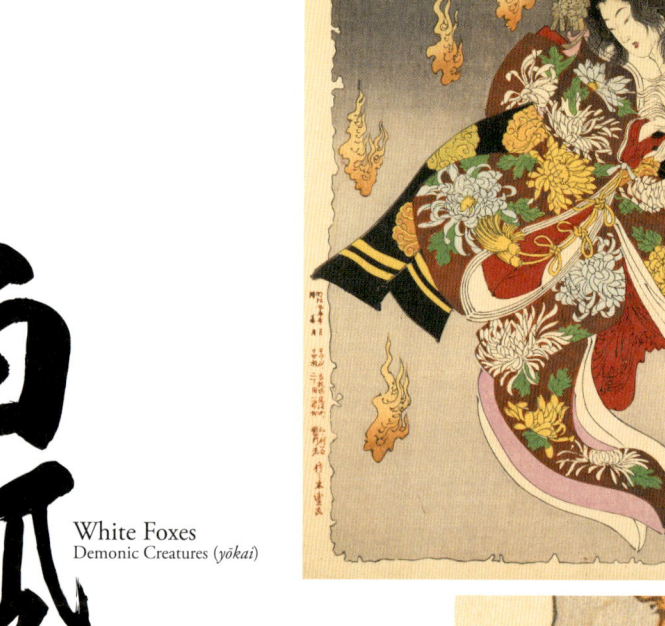

白狐

White Foxes
Demonic Creatures (*yōkai*)

166

浄瑠璃や歌舞伎の「本朝廿四孝」に登場する八重垣姫。
婚約者の武田勝頼に危険を知らせるため、武田家の家宝
の兜に込められた諏訪神社の神の使い白狐の霊力を借
りて、凍った諏訪湖を飛んで渡ります。

Princess Yaegaki in kabuki play *Honchō Nijūshikō (Japan's Twenty-Four Examples of Filial Piety)*. Alerted to the danger her betrothed Takeda Katsuyori is in, she uses the magical helmet of the Takeda family to enlist the help of the miraculous powers of the white fox spirit of Suwa Shrine, and flies across frozen Lake Suwa.

【新形三十六怪撰 二十四孝狐火之図】
月岡芳年 明治25年（1892）
勝頼を一途に恋い慕う姫が手にしているのは、武田家の家宝の兜。

Foxfire of Twenty-Four Examples of Filial Piety
from the series *Shinkei sanjūrokkaisen (New Forms of Thirty-Six Ghosts)*
by Tsukioka Yoshitoshi

The princess, who loves Katsuyori with all her heart, has the Takeda family's heirloom helmet in her hand. The opulently-patterned red *uchikake* (formal outer garment) is a classic princess style. Her pure beauty is striking.

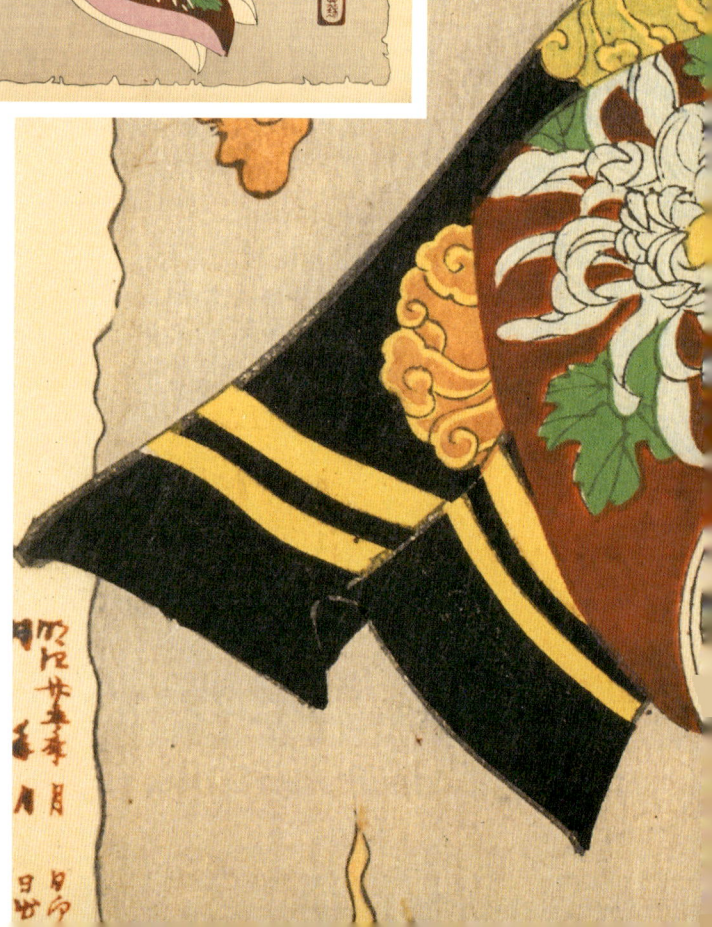

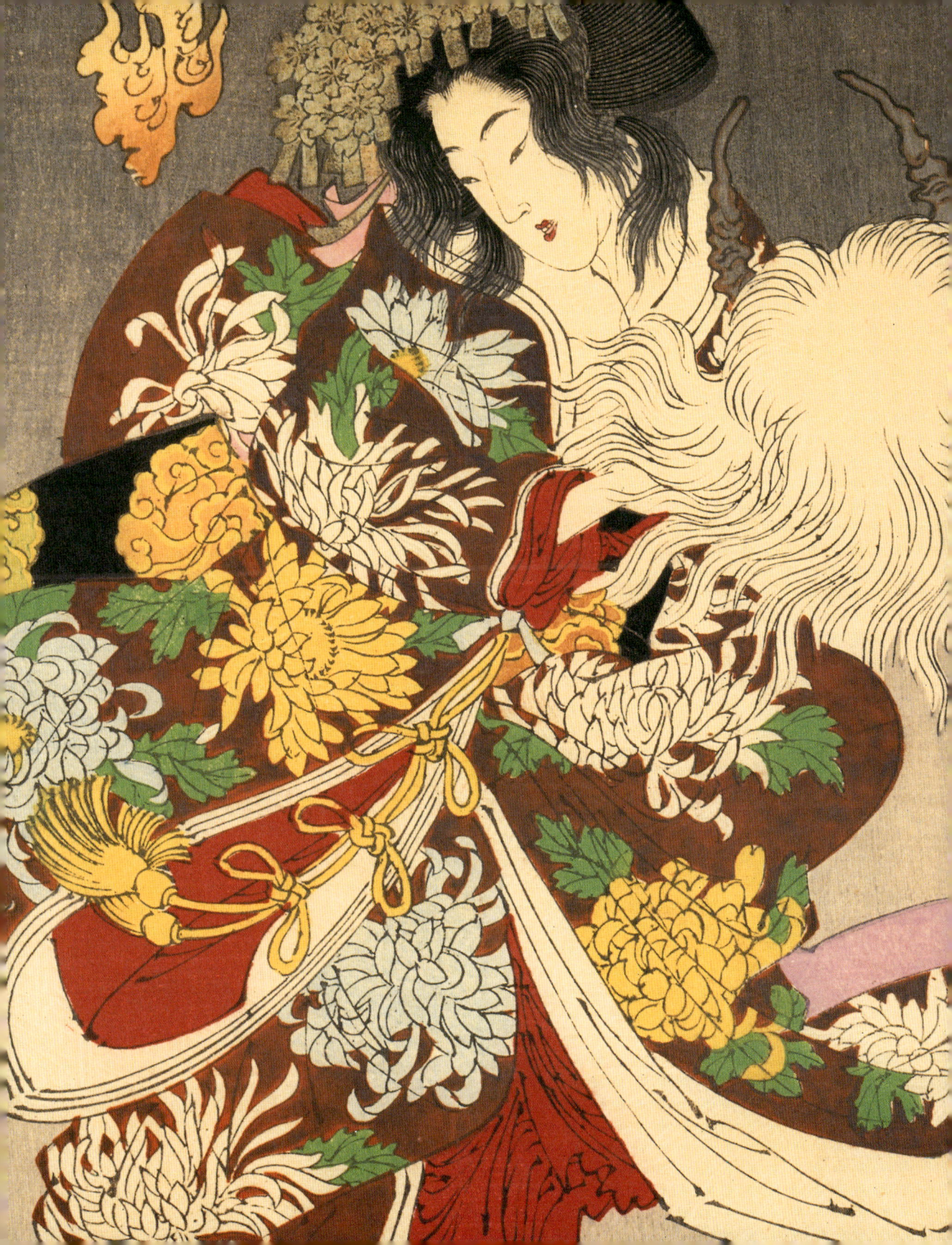

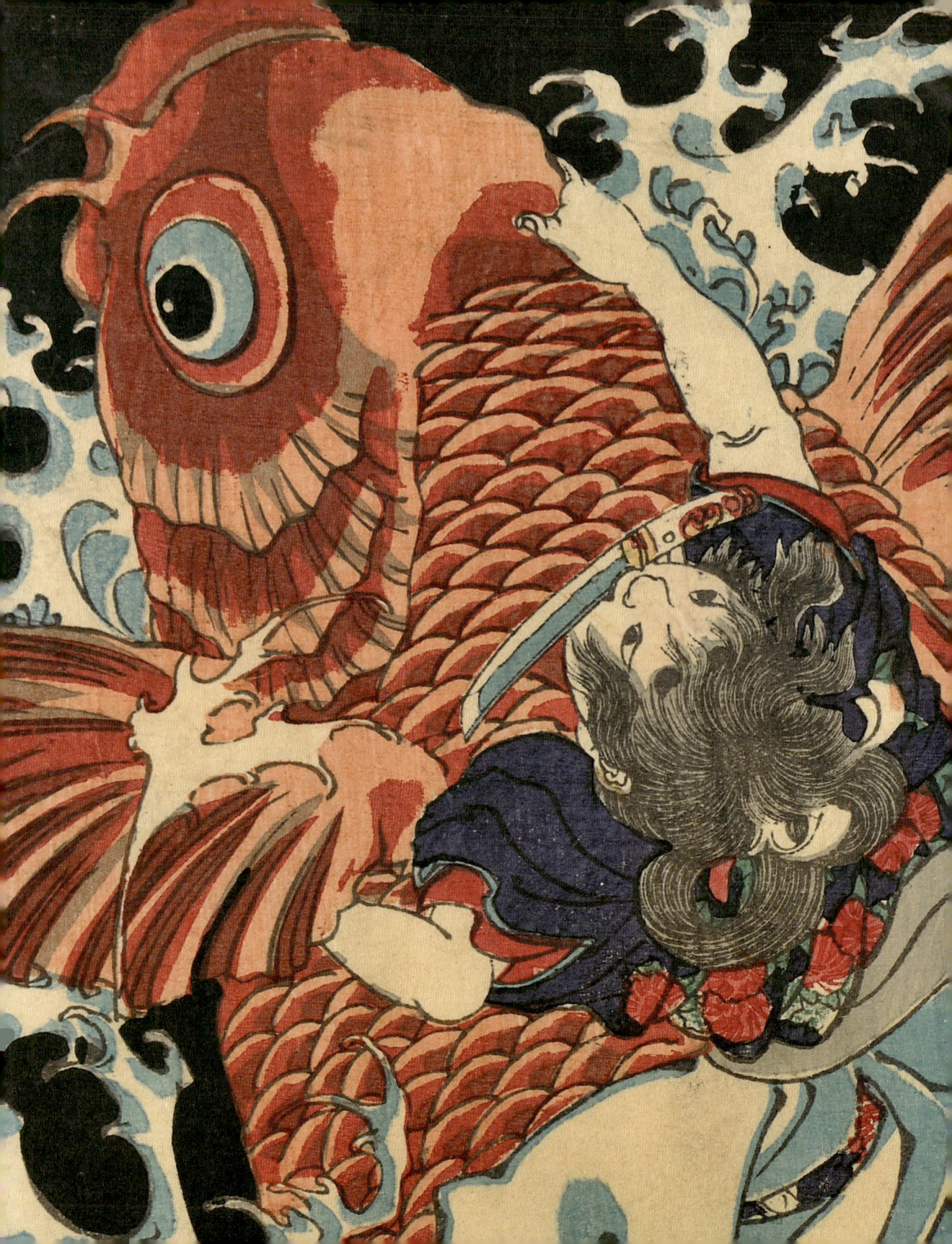

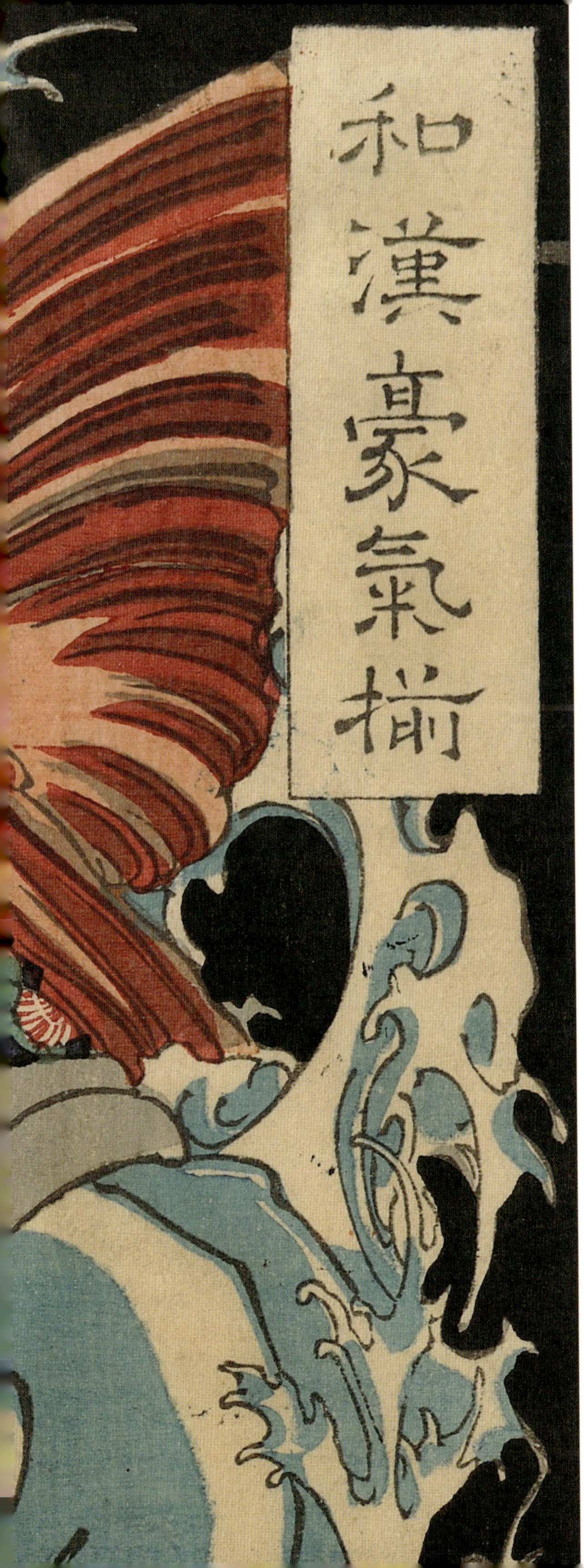

和漢豪氣揃

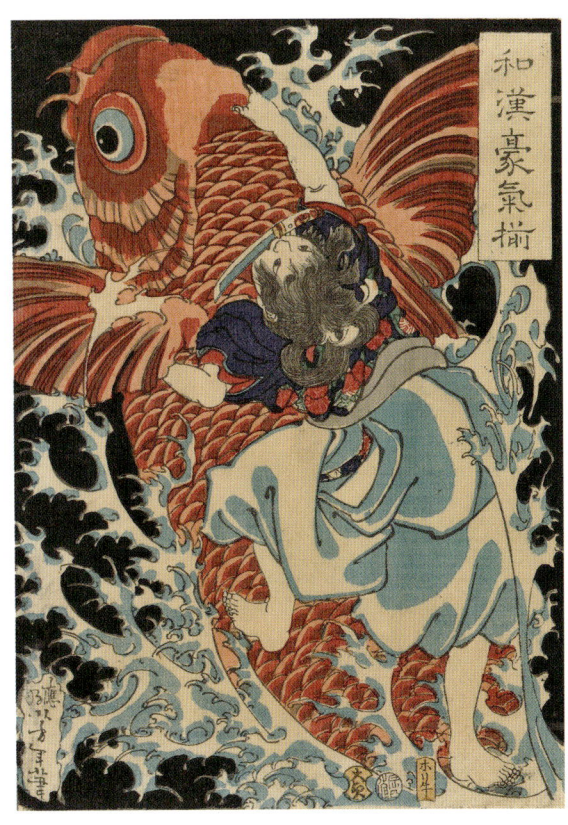

Monster Carp
Demonic Creatures (*yōkai*)

鬼若丸の鯉退治。鬼若丸とは武蔵坊
弁慶の幼名。比叡山で学んでいた幼
少の頃、お化け鯉を退治したという伝
説があります。

Oniwakamaru's defeat of the carp.
Oniwakamaru ("Ogre Child") was the
childhood name of Musashibō Benkei.
There is a legend that he defeated the
monster carp as a youth when he was
studying Buddhism at Mount Hiei.

【和漢豪気揃 鬼若丸鯉魚を捕う】
月岡芳年 明治元年（1868）
Oniwakamaru Seizes the Carp
from the series *Wakan gōki zoroi (Valor in China and Japan)*
by Tsukioka Yoshitoshi

お化け鯉

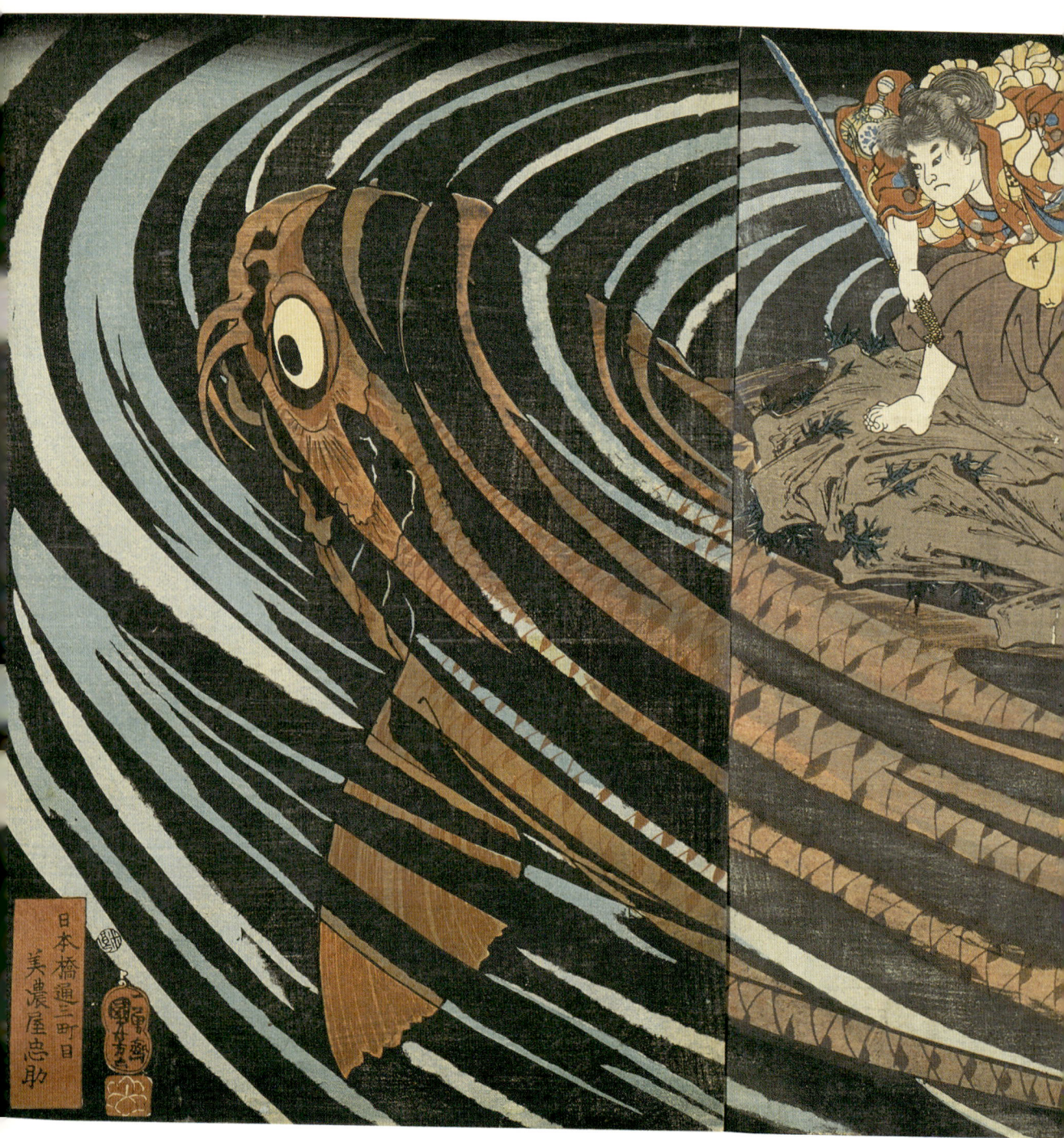

妖怪

【鬼若丸大鯉退治の図】歌川国芳 弘化2年（1845）頃

三枚続の大画面に、水中を徘徊する巨大な鯉が描かれています。鬼若丸はじっと見据え、斬りかかるチャンスをうかがっています。

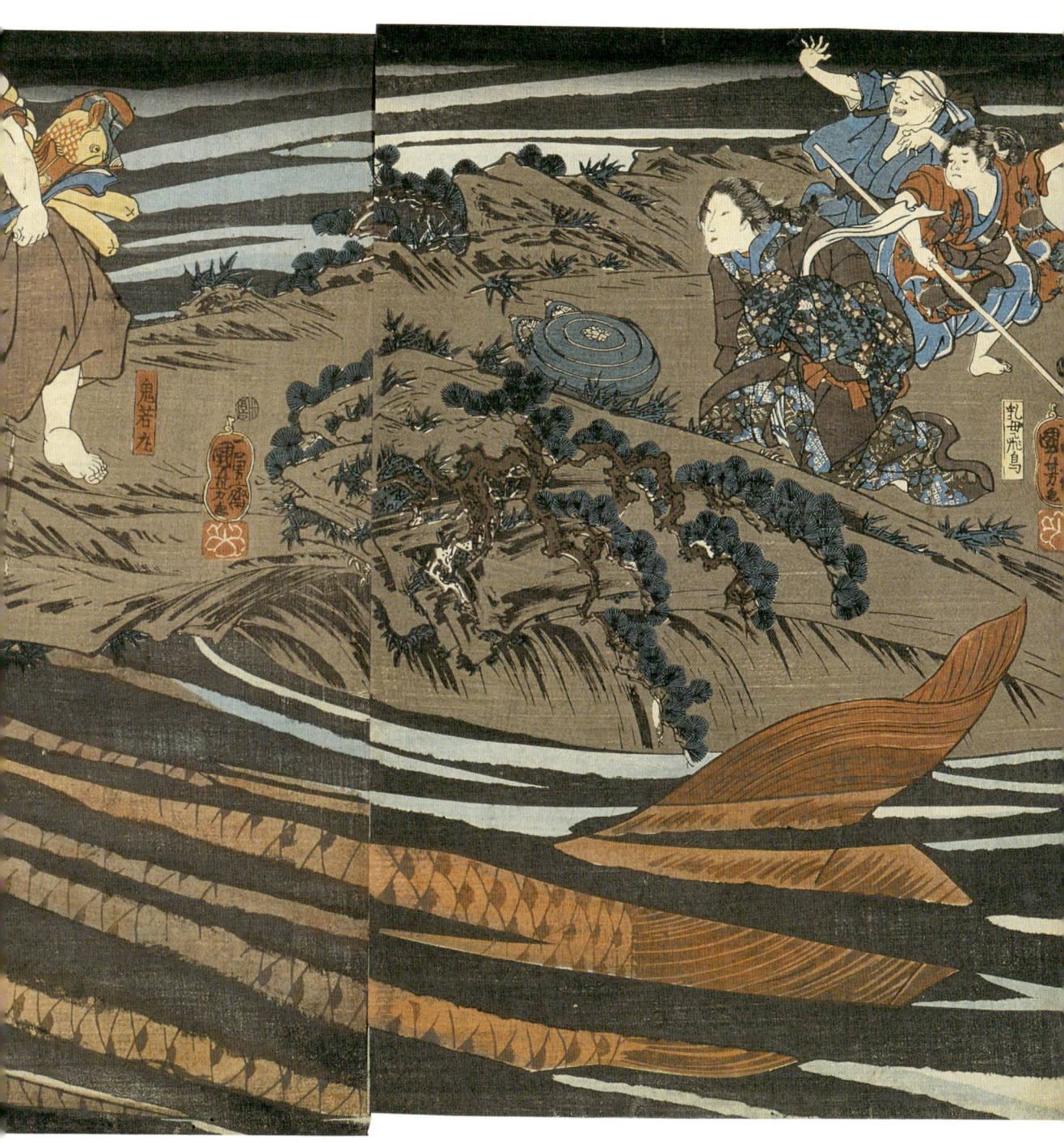

Oniwakamaru Preparing to Kill the Giant Carp by Utagawa Kuniyoshi

In this large triptych, under the water a gigantic carp is roaming about. Oniwakamaru keeps his eyes on it, waiting for the chance to strike.

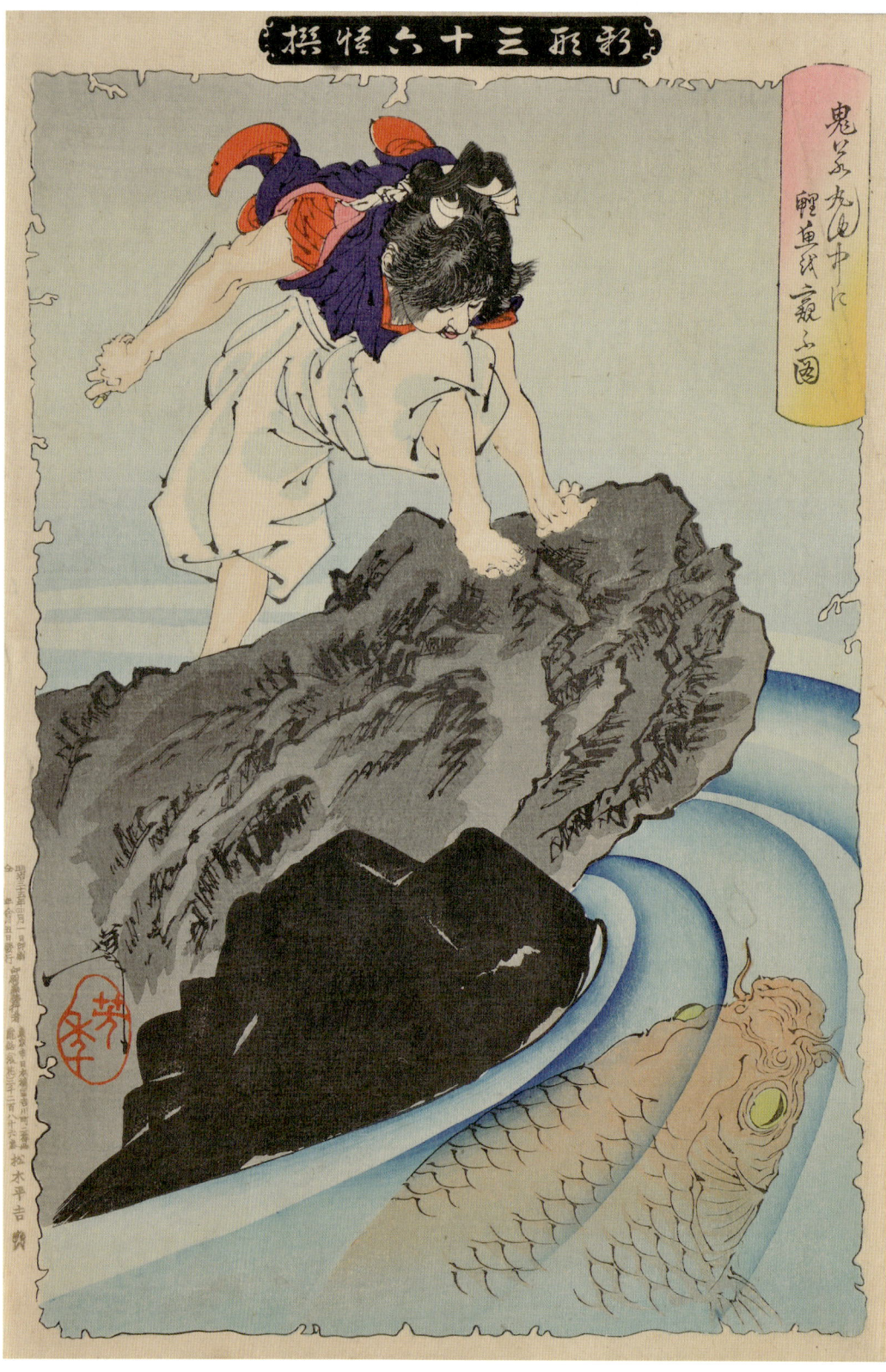

鬼若丸池中に
鯉魚を窺ふ図

172

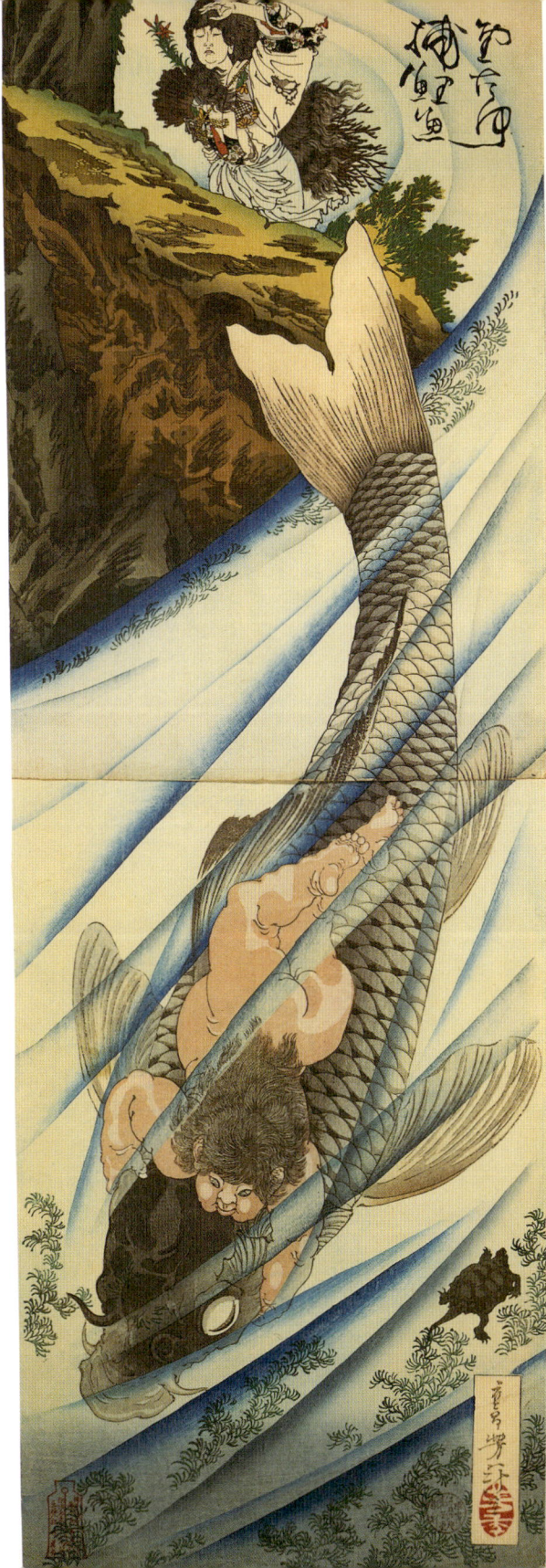

← **【新形三十六怪撰 鬼若丸池中に鯉魚を窺ふ図】**
月岡芳年 明治22年(1889)
岩の上に乗った鬼若丸が短刀を構えて、不気味なお化け鯉を
狙います。

Oniwakamaru Watches the Great Carp in the Pond
from the series *Shinkei sanjūrokkaisen*
(New Forms of Thirty-Six Ghosts)
by Tsukioka Yoshitoshi
On top of a rock, Oniwakamaru readies his dagger, aiming at the
nightmarish monster carp.

【金太郎捕鯉魚】月岡芳年 明治18年(1885)
金太郎は頼光四天王の一人、坂田金時の幼名。熊などの野獣
と仲良く育ち、怪力の持ち主と言われています。数ある伝説のひ
とつが、お化け鯉退治です。崖の上から見下ろしているのは、
母・足柄山の山姥。

Kintarō Captures the Carp by Tsukioka Yoshitoshi
Kintarō is the childhood name of Sakata no Kintoki, one of the
Four Loyal Retainers (Raikō Shitennō). The child of the mountain
witch of Mount Ashigara, he possessed superhuman strength and
grew up with bears and other wild beasts as his friends. Many
legends surround him, but only one of these is depicted here: the
defeat of the monster carp. Watching from above on the cliff is his
mother, the mountain witch.

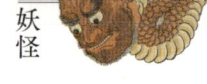

妖怪

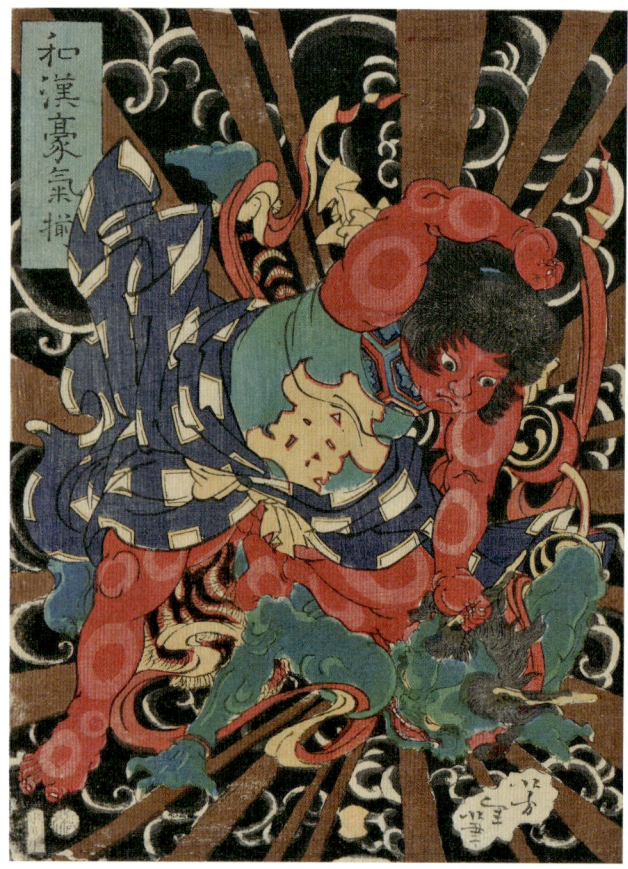

Thunder and Lightning
Demonic Creatures (*yōkai*)

雷

雷は雲の上にいて、虎皮の褌を締め、太鼓を打ち鳴らし、へそを取ると
言われています。金太郎は、へそを取られると思ったのでしょうか。雷に
またがり、角をつかんで殴りかかります。

Thunder is rumored to live on top of the clouds, wearing a tiger-skin
loincloth, beating on drums, and stealing people's belly buttons. Did Kintarō
think his bellybutton would be nabbed? Kneeling on the thunder god, he
lays hold of one horn, the better to strike at it.

【和漢豪気揃 金太郎雷を捕う】月岡芳年 明治元年(1868)

Kintarō Seizes Thunder from the series *Wakan gōki zoroi* (*Valor in China and Japan*)
by Tsukioka Yoshitoshi

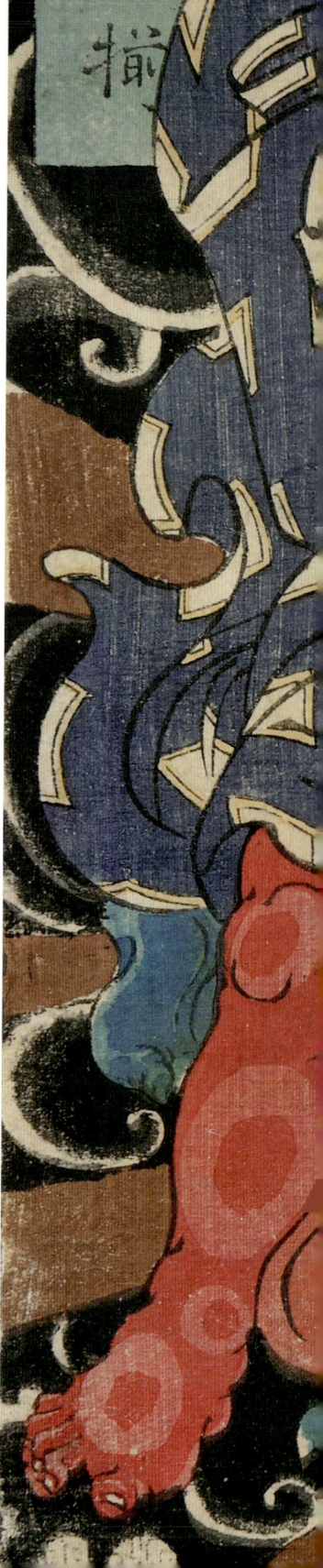

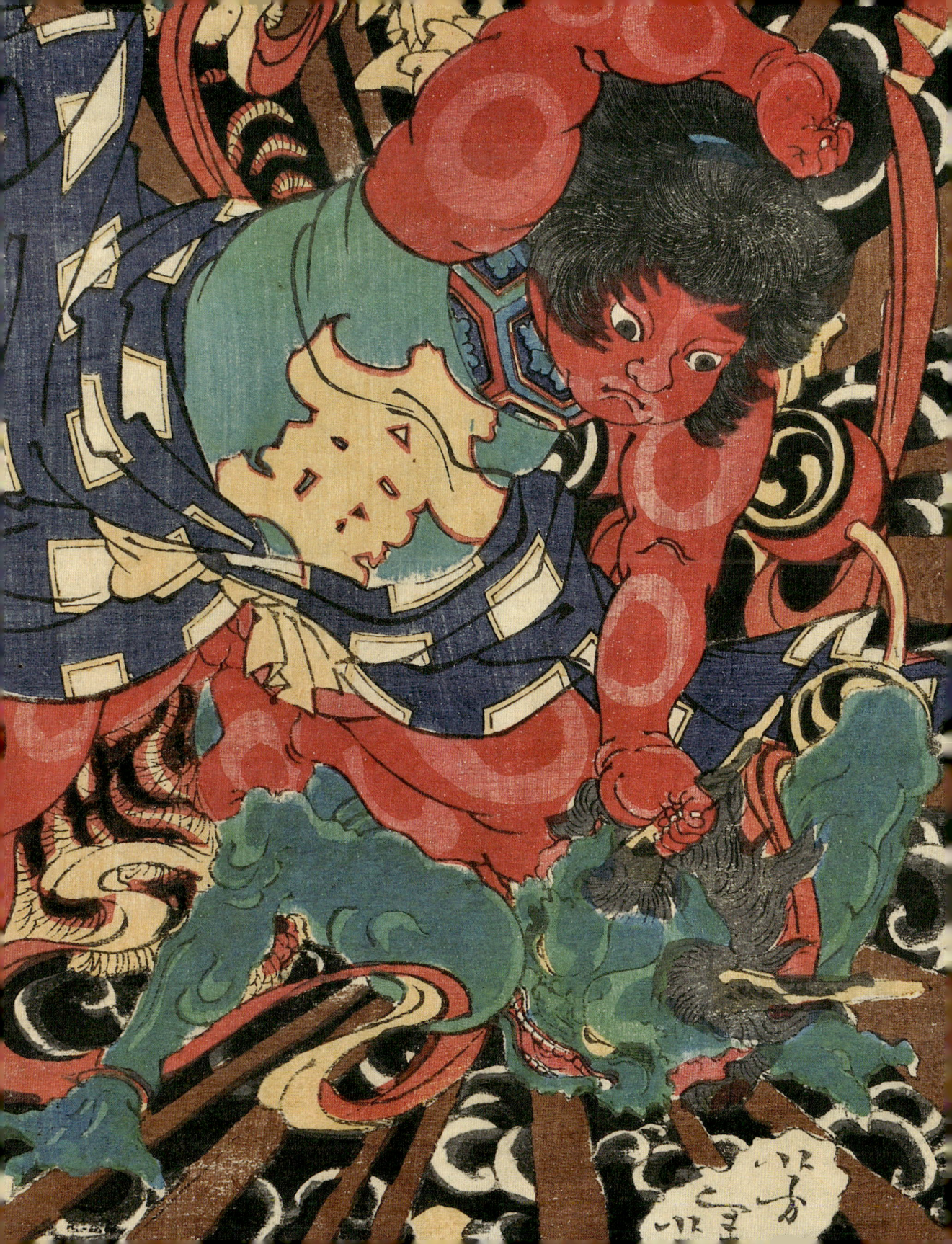

一つ目小僧

One-eyed Goblins
Demonic Creatures (*yōkai*)

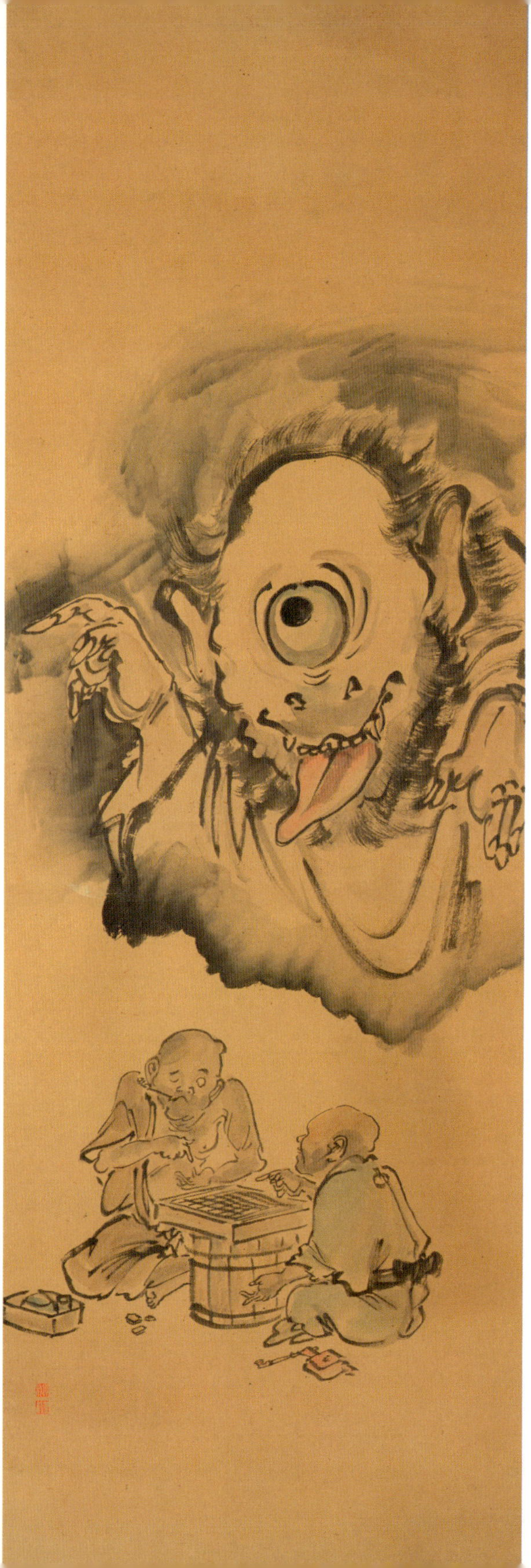

顔の真ん中に大きな目玉がある妖怪、一つ目小僧。
人を驚かすのが好きで、長い舌で顔をなめたりします。
部屋の中に突如現れた一つ目小僧ですが、将棋を
指す二人の男は気づいていないようです。

One-eyed goblins are demonic creatures with a single
large eye in the middle of their faces. They love to shock
people by licking their faces with long tongues. A one-
eyed goblin suddenly appears in the middle of the room,
and just stares without any further mischief, but the two
absorbed in a game of *shōgi* (Japanese chess) do not seem
to notice.

【一つ目小僧】
竹内柳蛙（五代歌川国政）明治時代後期～大正時代

One-eyed Goblin
by Takeuchi Ryu-a (also known as Utagawa Kunimasa V)
(Early 20th century)

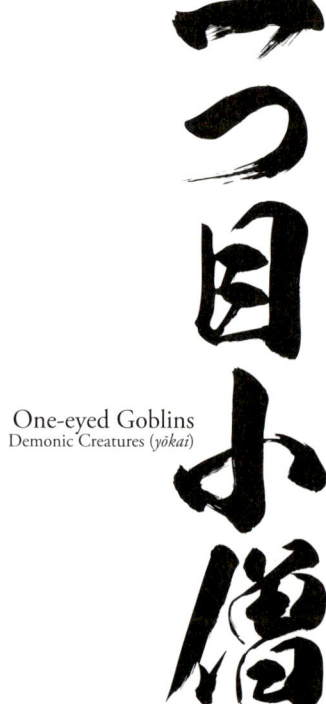

もののけ

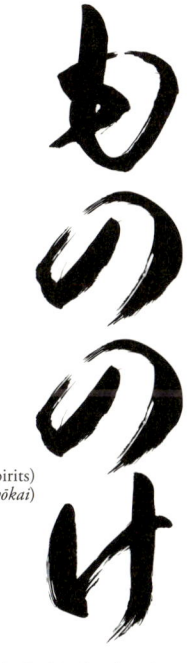

Mononoke (Malevolent Spirits)
Demonic Creatures (*yōkai*)

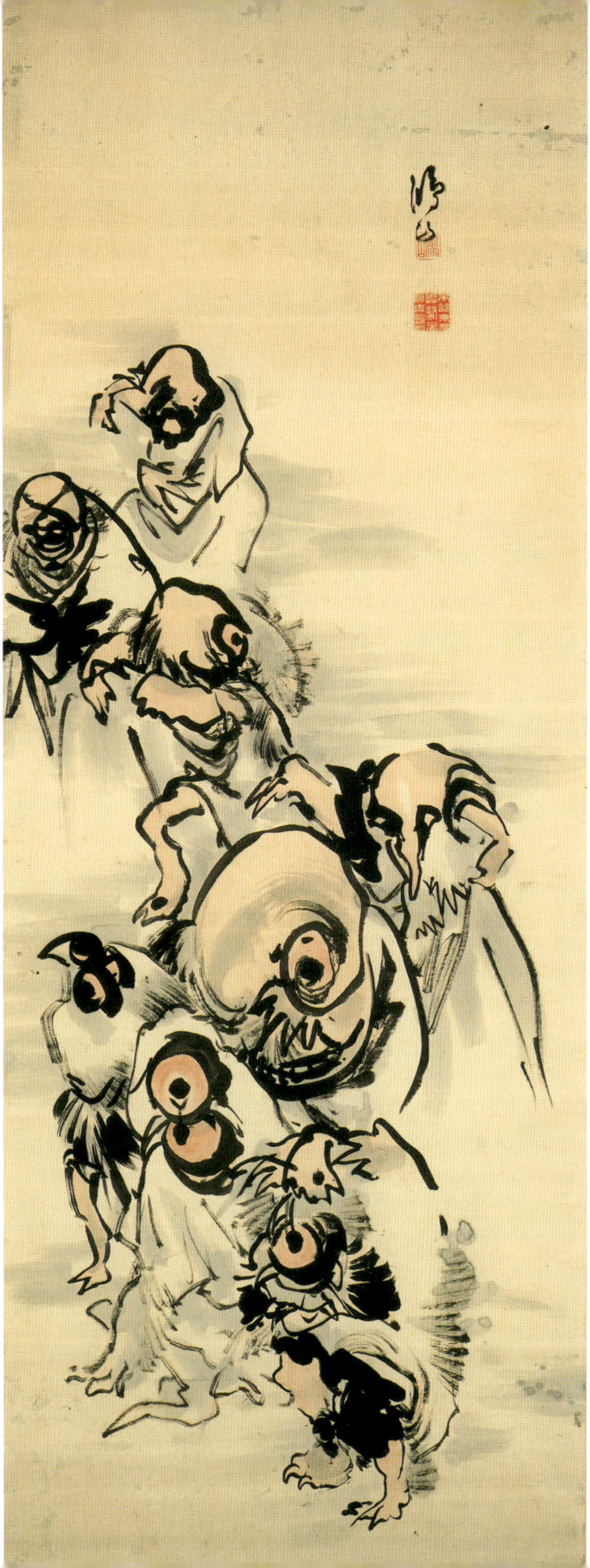

大胆で力強い筆づかいによる妖怪行列。牙の生
えた一つ目、縦並びの二つ目、鼻が長く尖った妖
怪など、どことなく愛らしい妖怪たち。

A cavalcade of *yōkai* in bold, powerful brushwork.
One-eyed and fanged, with two-eyed, long-nosed
and sharp-nosed beasties lining up behind, these
demonic creatures are somehow adorable.

【もののけの図】高井鴻山 江戸時代〜明治時代
信濃国（長野県）小布施の豪商で北斎門下生の鴻山
は、晩年妖怪画の制作に没頭しました。それらの作品は、
幕末維新期に波乱に満ちた人生を送った鴻山自身の
心境を表していると言われています。

Mononoke
by Takai Kōzan (Late 19th century)

A wealthy merchant at Obuse in Shinano, Hokusai's pupil
Kōzan devoted himself to the creation of *yōkai-ga* in his later
years. Kōzan's works are said to reflect his state of mind as
his life was thrown into turbulence during the last days of
the Tokugawa shogunate and the Meiji Restoration.

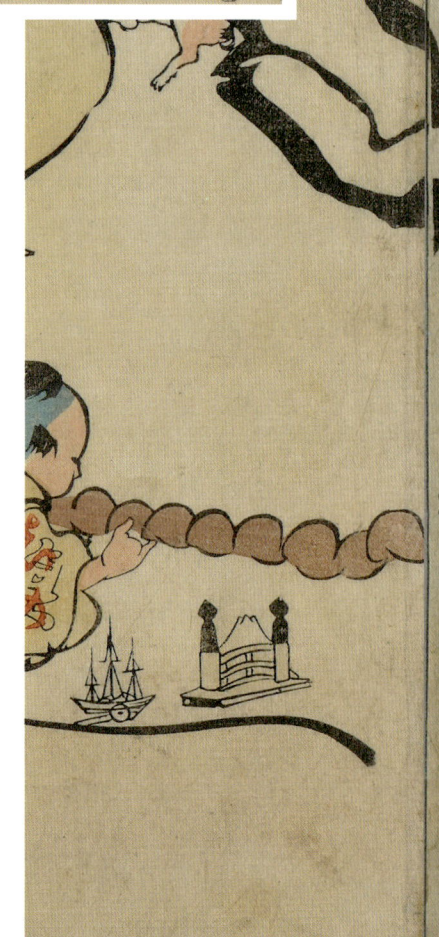

妖
怪

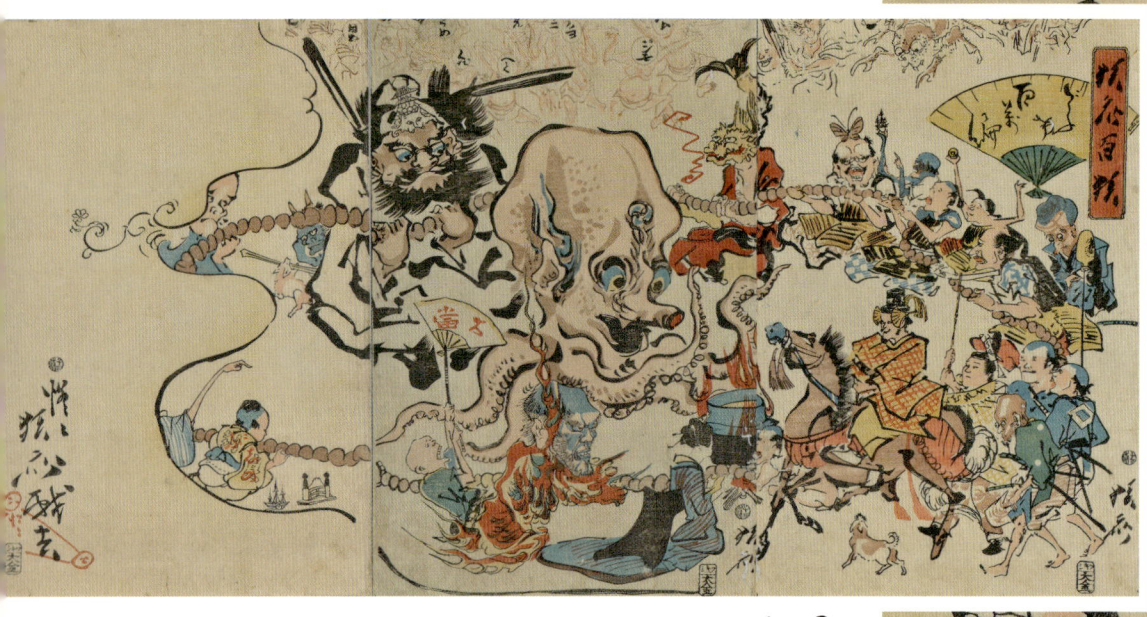

178

A Farcical One Million Prayers
Demonic Creatures (*yōkai*)

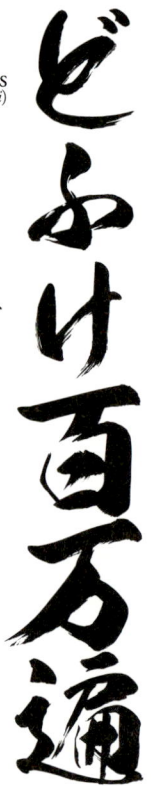

奇妙な姿のものたちが輪になり、念仏を唱えながら一つの大きな数珠を
回す「百万遍念仏」をしています。実は幕末の判じ絵で、攘夷論が高ま
る最中に出版されました。中央の大蛸は骨がないことから、開国により
権威を失った徳川幕府を示しています。鍾馗の水戸藩、鯱の尾張藩、
蝶の長州藩など攘夷派の大名が取り囲み、百万遍念仏のように、なか
なか進まない攘夷を諷刺しています。

Peculiar creatures have formed a circle and are performing the Buddhist ritual
of One Million Prayers (*hyakumanben nenbutsu*); while reciting the name of
Amida Buddha, they rotate a giant set of prayer beads. Actually this is a
pictorial satire of the latter days of the Tokugawa shogunate, published when
the movement to expel foreigners (*jōi ron*) was at its height. The large octopus
in the middle has no backbone, and therefore represents the Tokugawa
shogunate who lost their authority due to the opening of Japan to the outside
world. The octopus is surrounded by anti-foreigner lords, who are satirized for
their inability to make any progress, just like an interminable One Million
Prayers: Mito Domain is symbolized by Shōki (a mythical plague-queller),
Owari Domain by an orca, and Chōshū Domain by a butterfly.

【狂斎百狂 とふけ百万遍】河鍋暁斎 元治元年（1864）

Dofuke Hyakumanben (A Farcical One Million Prayers)
from the series *Kyōsai hyakkyō (Kyōsai's One Hundred Wildnesses)*
by Kawanabe Kyōsai

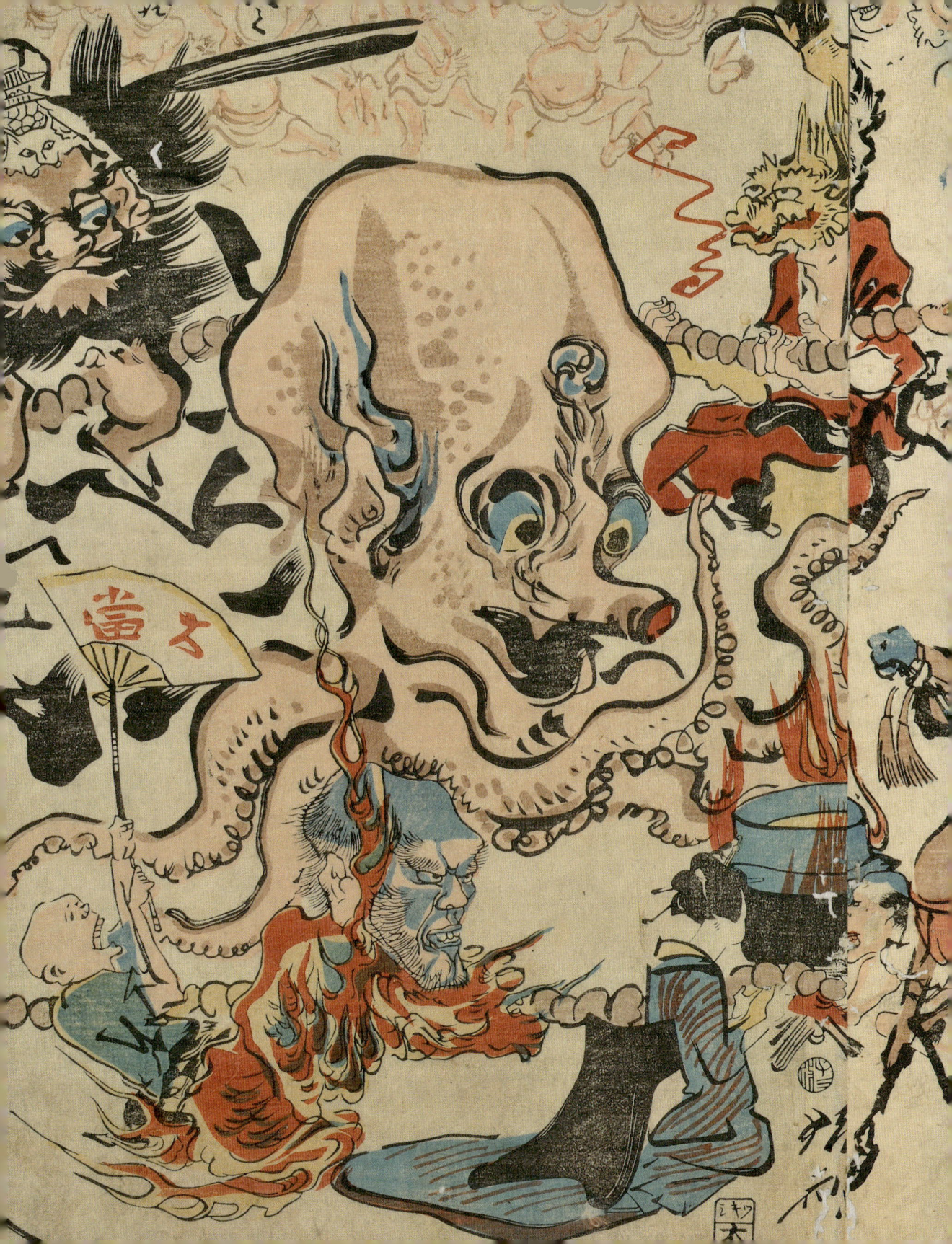

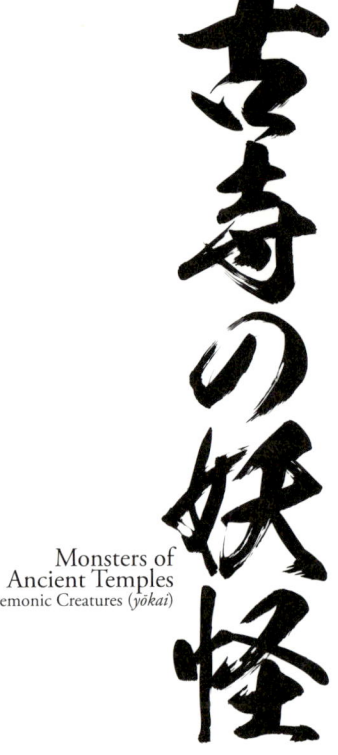

古寺の妖怪

Monsters of
Ancient Temples
Demonic Creatures (*yōkai*)

180

津山藩の森家三勇士の一人、高木午之助は、古寺にすむ妖怪の噂を聞きつけ、他二人とともに訪れます。夜更けに青白い顔をした巨大な化け物が現れますが、午之助は恐れることなく平然としています。

Takagi Umanosuke, one of the three brave samurai of Tsuyama Domain's Mori family, hears rumors of monsters living in an ancient temple, and goes with the other two to investigate. In the middle of the night the blue-white face of a colossal monster appears, but Umanosuke remains unfazed and calm.

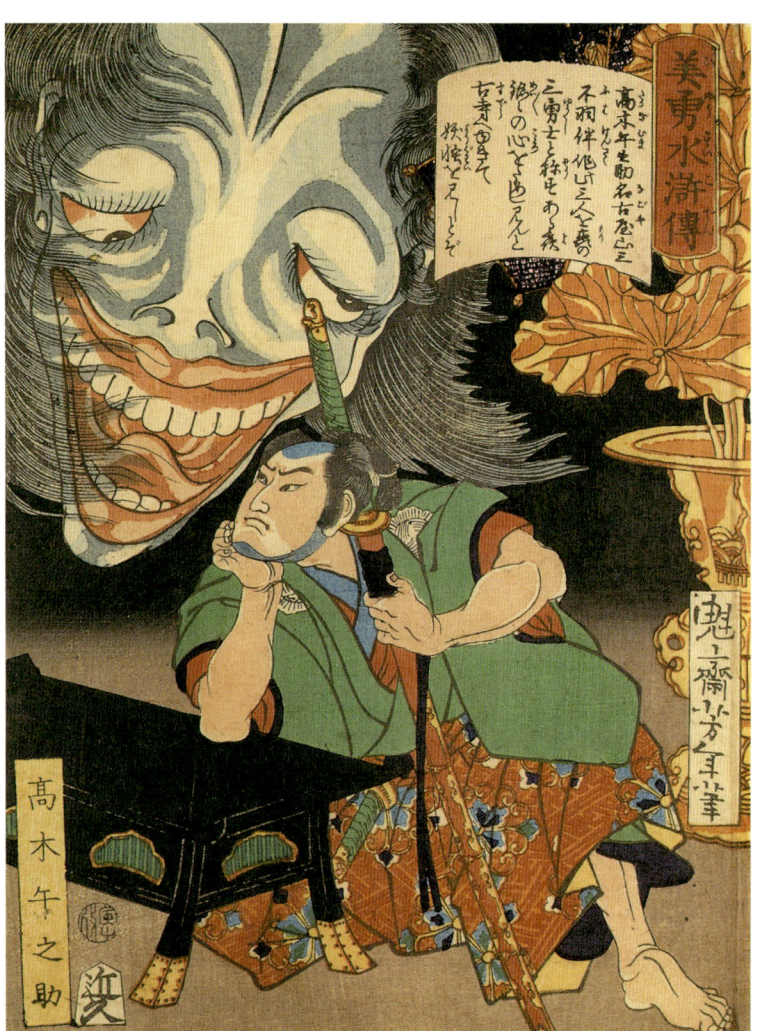

【美勇水滸傳・高木午之助】月岡芳年 慶応2年 (1866)

Takagi Umanosuke from the series Biyū Suikoden (Sagas of Beauty and Bravery) by Tsukioka Yoshitoshi

【古狸】

ろくろ首

Rokurokubi
Demonic Creatures (*yōkai*)

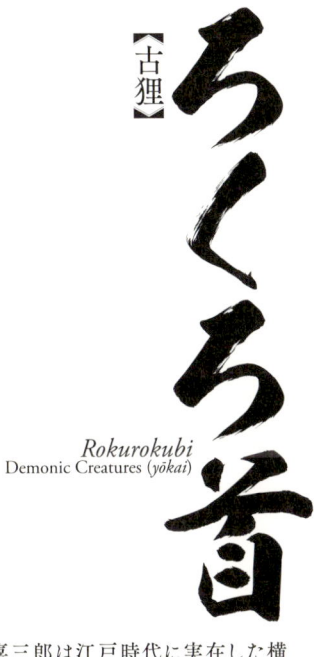

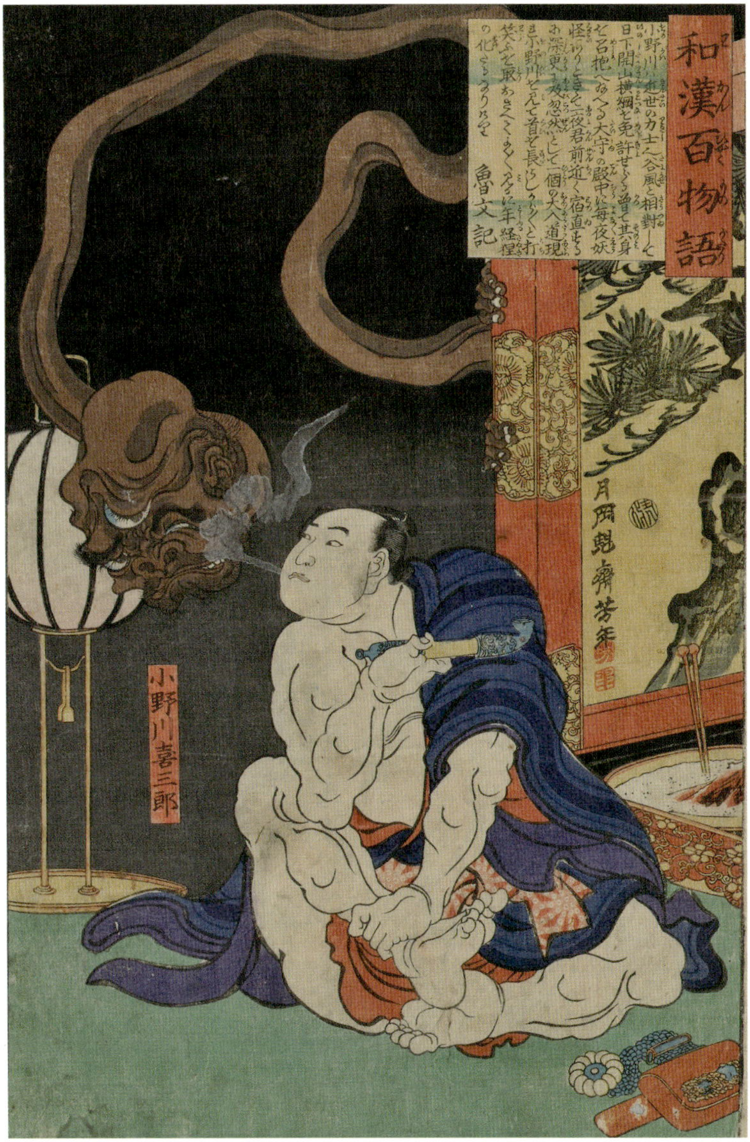

小野川喜三郎は江戸時代に実在した横
綱です。お抱え大名の久留米藩有馬家
の殿中に、夜ごと妖怪が現れると聞き、宿
直をすることになりました。夜更けに大入
道が首を伸ばして現れたので取り押さえる
と、その正体は古狸でした。

Onogawa Kisaburō was a real *yokozuna* (the
highest rank in sumō) of the Edo period. This
is a legend of the noble Arima clan of the
Kurume Domain. Having heard that a
demonic creature was haunting the palace each
night, Kisaburō kept the night watch. In the
middle of the night, a giant priest with an
elongated neck appeared, and he apprehended
it, only to discover that its true form was an
old raccoon dog. Kisaburō is calmly blowing
tobacco smoke at the monster.

【和漢百物語 小野川喜三郎とろくろ首（大入道）】月岡芳年 慶応元年 (1865)

Onogawa Kisaburō and the Rokurokubi (Giant Priest)
from the series *Wakan hyakumonogatari (One Hundred Tales from China and Japan)* by Tsukioka Yoshitoshi

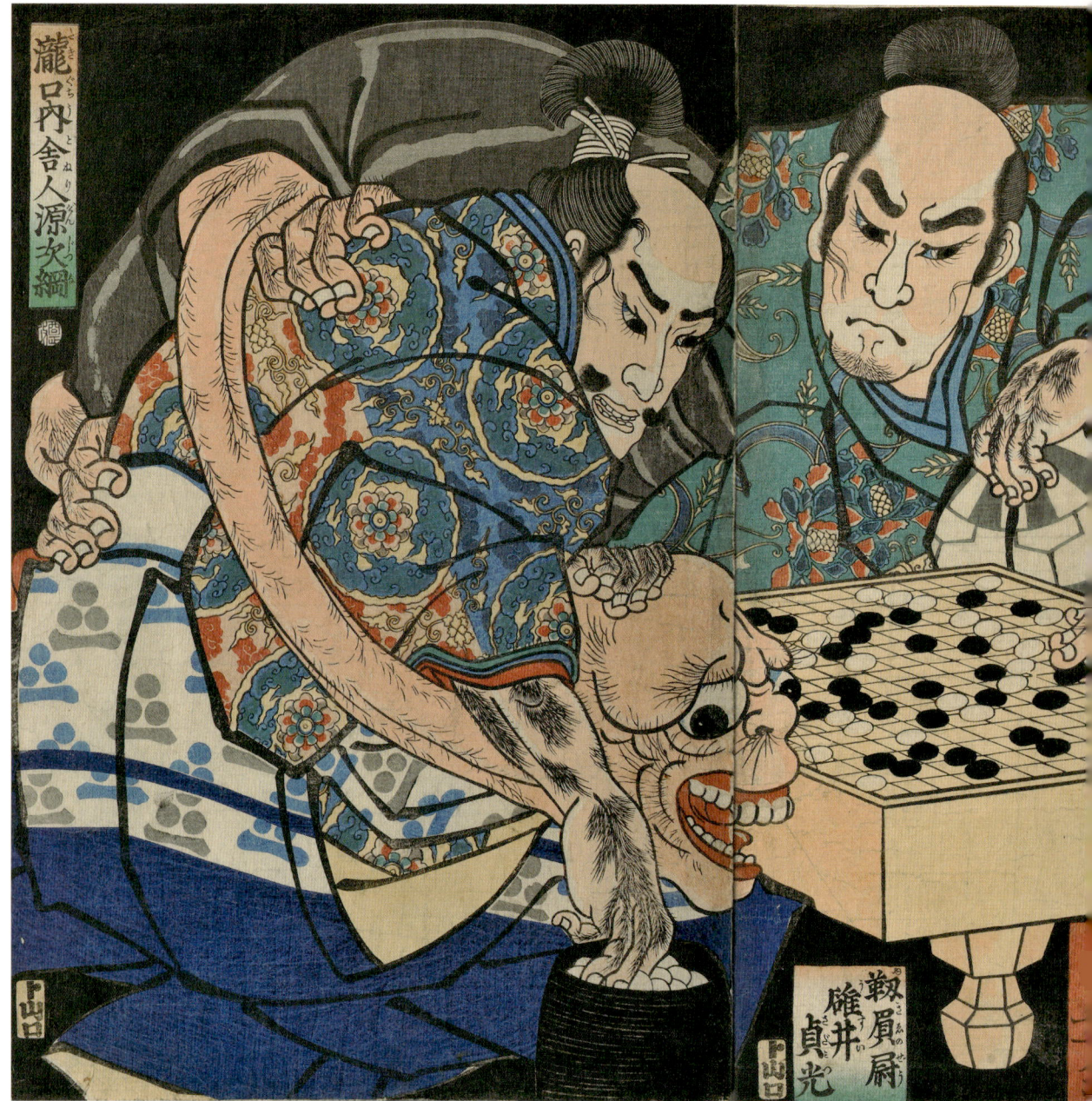

【主馬佐酒田公時 靭負尉碓井貞光 瀧口内舎人源次綱と妖怪】歌川国芳　文久元年（1861）

宿直で碁を打つ頼光四天王のうち、酒田公時（坂田金時とも）と源次綱（渡辺綱）、それを見物する碓井貞光の三人が描かれる。邪魔だと言わんばかりの公時の剛腕に上唇をめくり上げられて慌てふためく茶くみ禿、碁石を取ろうとする綱に伸ばした頭を押し沈められるろくろ首、貞光に見向きもされず握った拳を空しく上げて哀れな表情を見せる一つ目入道など、本来恐ろしいはずの妖怪たちがみじめに描かれておりユーモアを誘う。

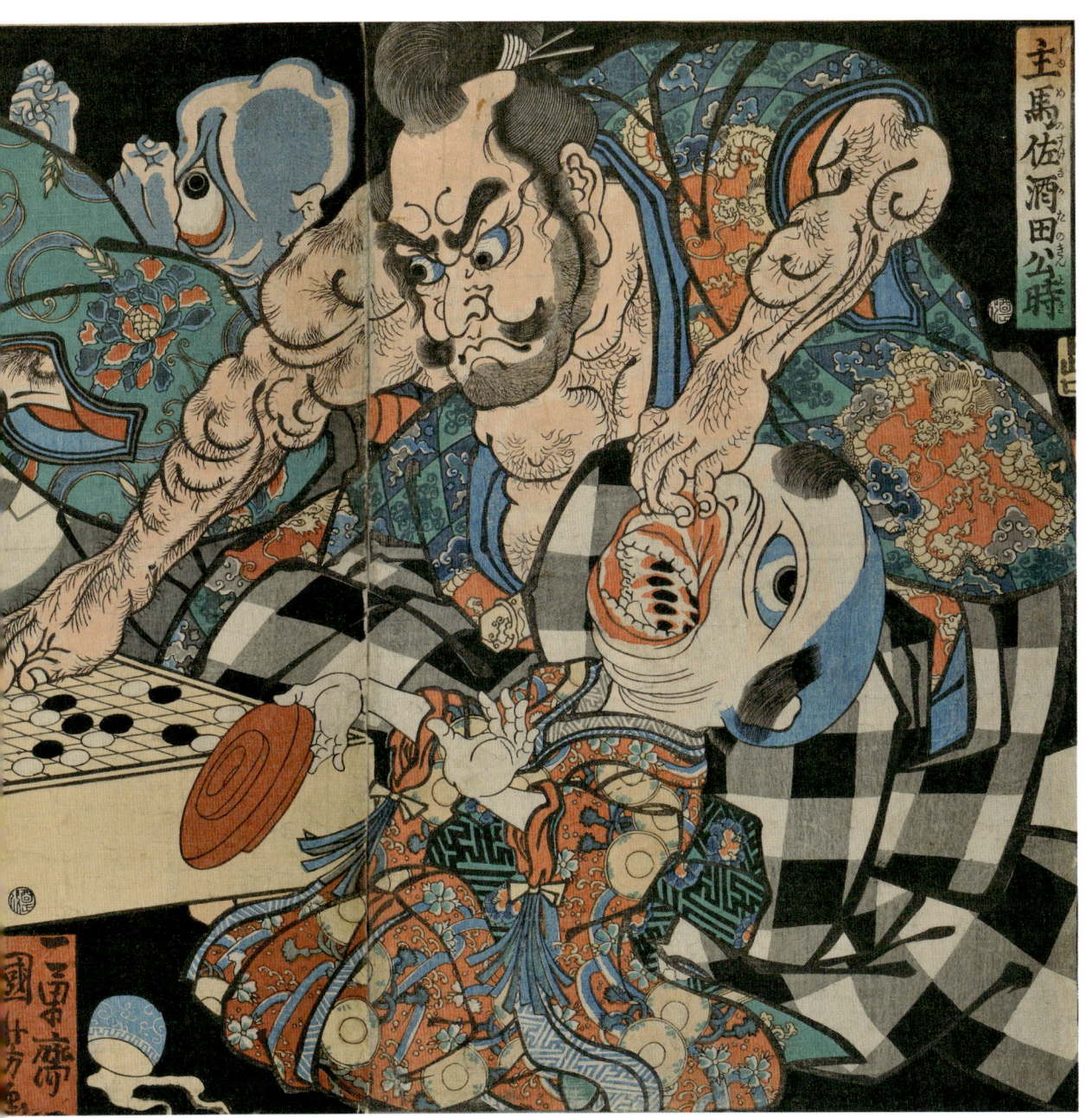

Sakata no Kintoki, Usui Sadamitsu, Genji no Tsuna, and Demonic Creatures by Utagawa Kuniyoshi

Three of the Four Loyal Retainers (Raikō Shitennō) are depicted keeping the night watch; Sakata no Kintoki and Genji (Watanabe) no Tsuna are playing a game of go while Usui no Sadamitsu looks on. The demonic creatures which by rights should be scary, are ridiculous when shown in such a pathetic state; Kintoki is peeling up the top lip of a flustered tea-making kamuro (courtesan's young attendant) with his brawny arm, as if to say "out of my way", the head of a rokurokubi with ropy neck extended to try to steal the go stones is being shoved down by Tsuna, and a one-eyed goblin displaying pitiful frustration and vainly raising a clenched fist is totally ignored by Sadamitsu.

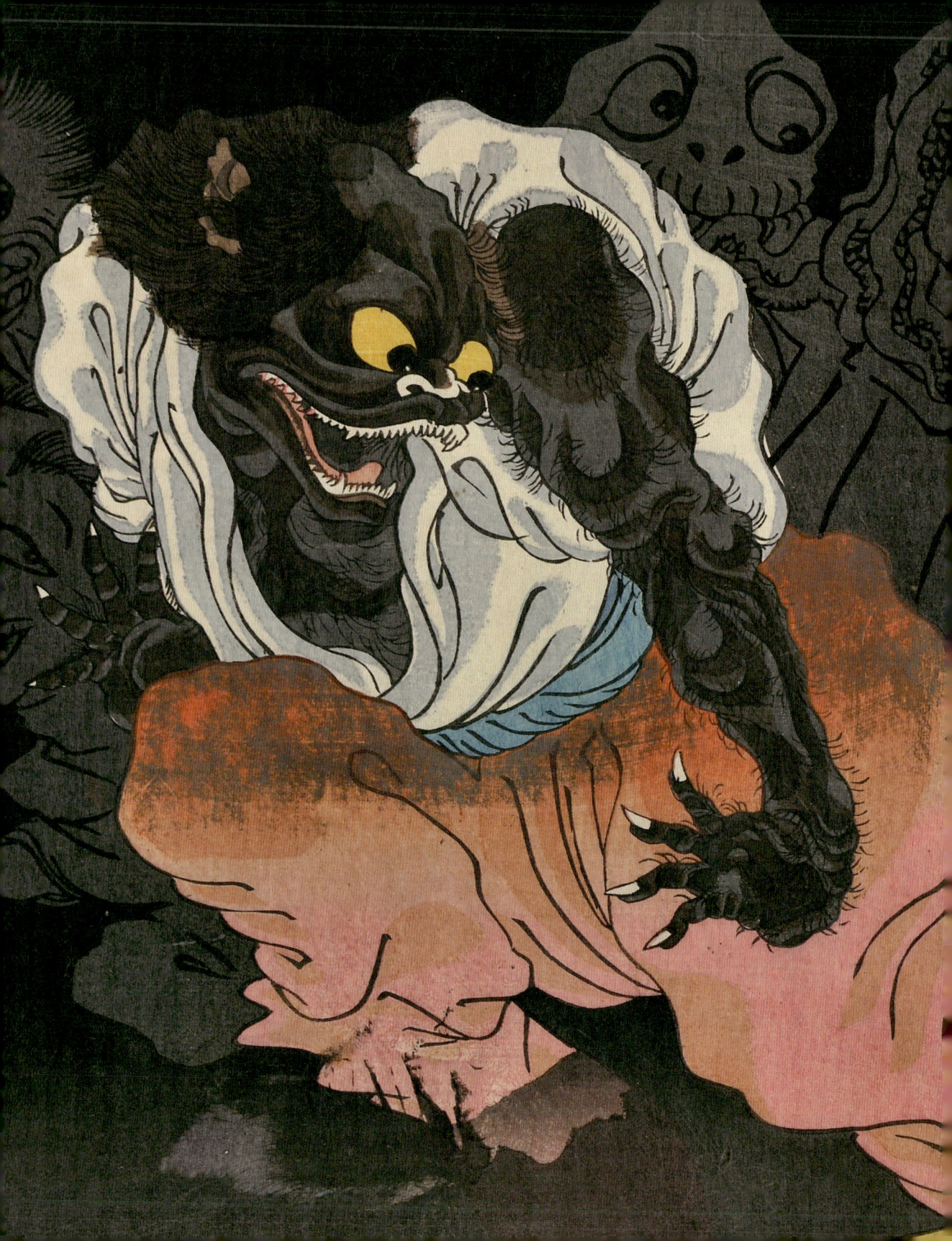

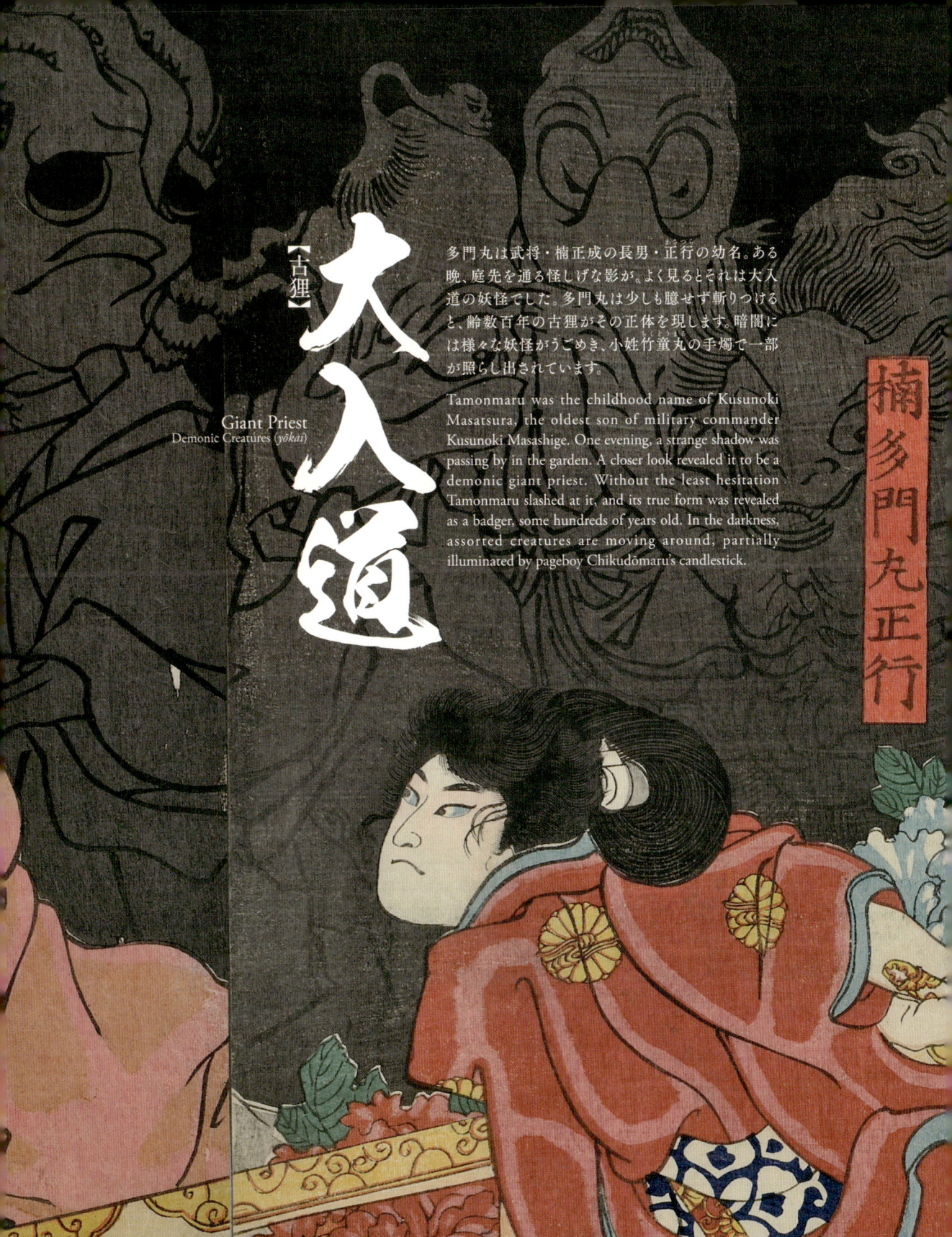

【古狸】

大入道

Giant Priest
Demonic Creatures (*yōkai*)

多門丸は武将・楠正成の長男・正行の幼名。ある晩、庭先を通る怪しげな影が。よく見るとそれは大入道の妖怪でした。多門丸は少しも臆せず斬りつけると、齢数百年の古狸がその正体を現します。暗闇には様々な妖怪がうごめき、小姓竹童丸の手燭で一部が照らし出されています。

Tamonmaru was the childhood name of Kusunoki Masatsura, the oldest son of military commander Kusunoki Masashige. One evening, a strange shadow was passing by in the garden. A closer look revealed it to be a demonic giant priest. Without the least hesitation Tamonmaru slashed at it, and its true form was revealed as a badger, some hundreds of years old. In the darkness, assorted creatures are moving around, partially illuminated by pageboy Chikudōmaru's candlestick.

楠多門丸正行

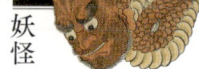

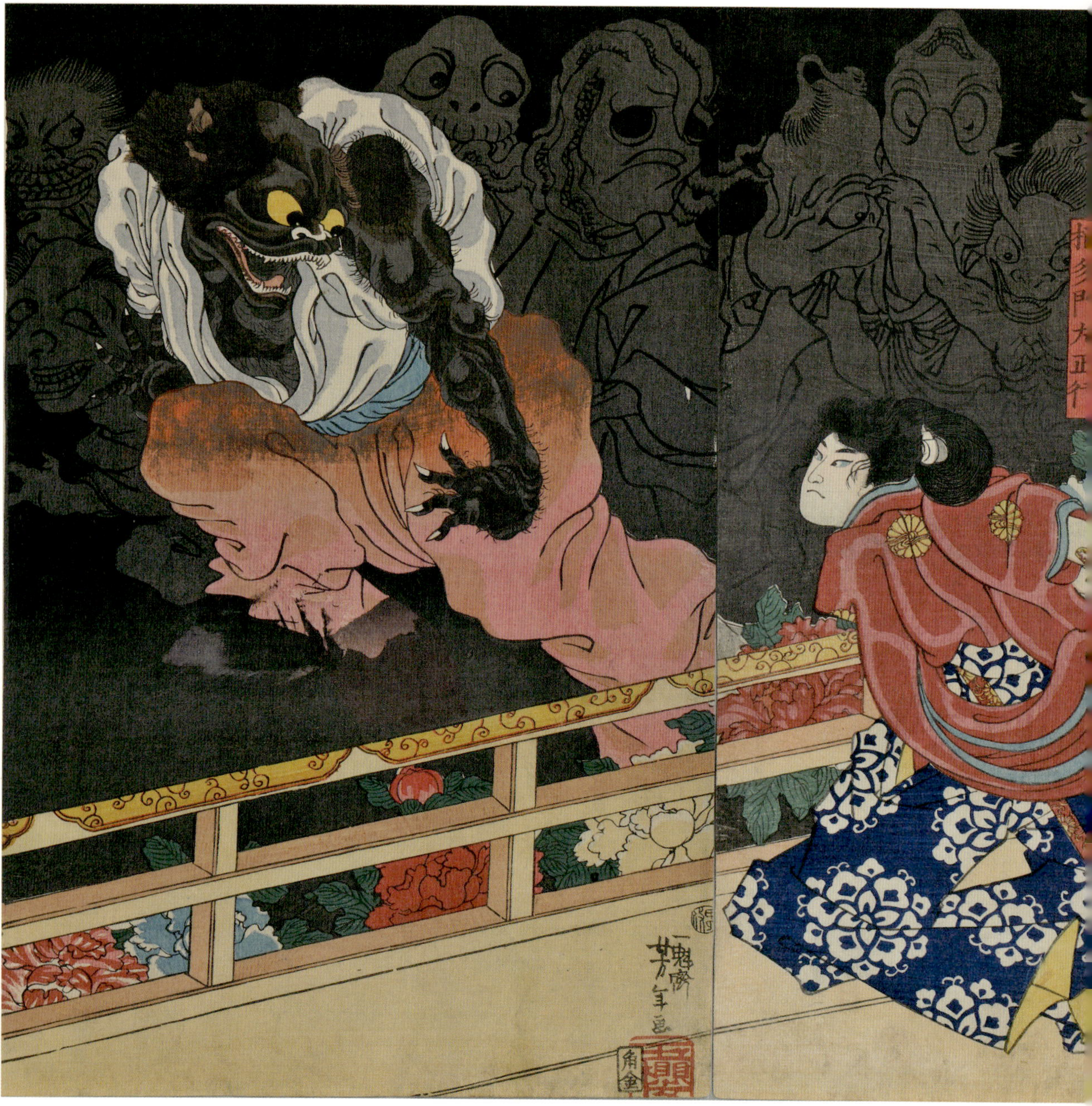

【楠多門丸古狸退治之図】月岡芳年　万延元年（1860）

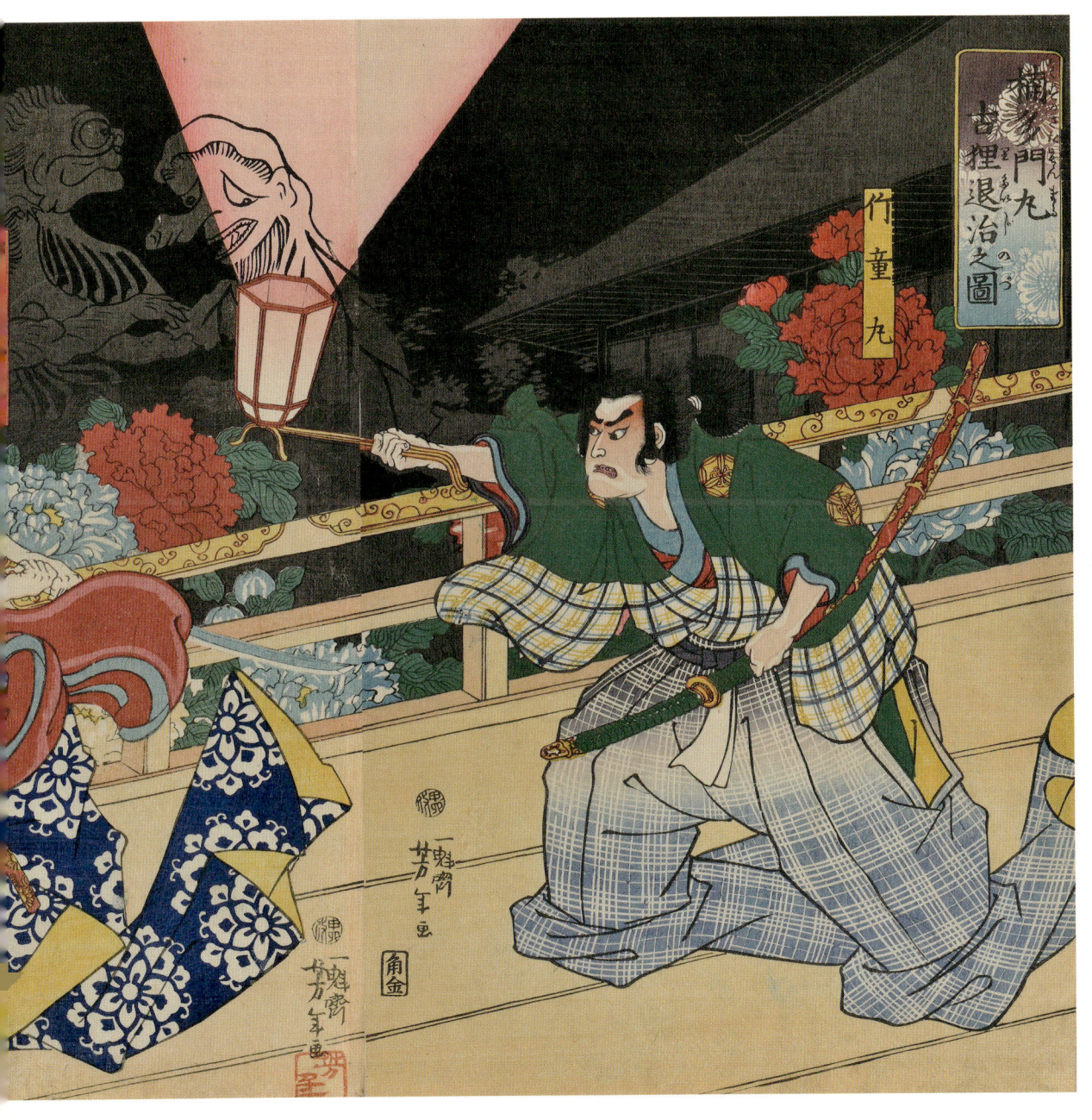

Kusunoki Tamonmaru Conquers the Old Badger by Tsukioka Yoshitoshi

187

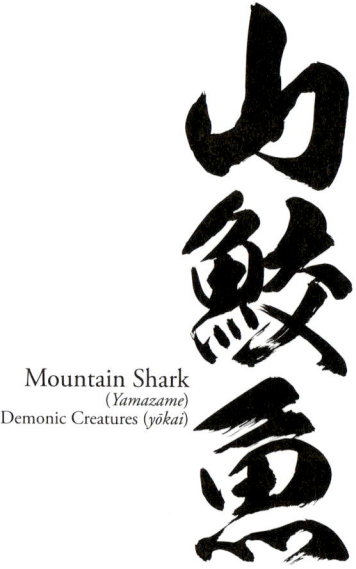

188

Mountain Shark
(*Yamazame*)
Demonic Creatures (*yōkai*)

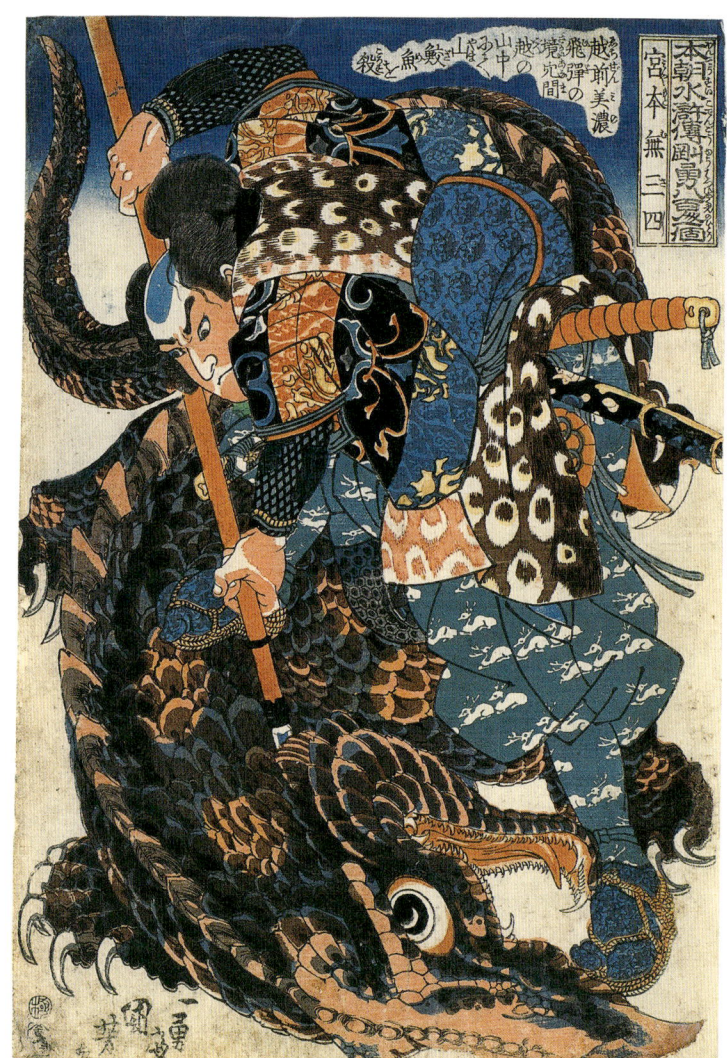

宮本武蔵は諸国修行の際、山中にて武装した
農民たちに出くわします。聞くと、この山にすむ
人喰い山鮫魚を退治しに行くとのこと。これに
助太刀をすることにした武蔵は、ひといきに山
鮫魚を槍で仕留めました。

On his travels across all Japan, Miyamoto Musashi
came across some farmers carrying weapons in the
mountains. When he asked them what they were
doing, they told him they were going to kill the
man-eating mountain shark which lived in those
mountains. Musashi decided to join them, and slew
the mountain shark with a single thrust of his spear.

【本朝水滸伝剛勇八百人一個 宮本無三四】歌川国芳 天保4-6年(1833-45)頃
Miyamoto Musashi, One of the Eight Hundred Heroes of the Japanese Water Margin by Utagawa Kuniyoshi

阿弥陀如来と仁王

Amida Buddha and the Temple Guardians
Demonic Creatures (*yōkai*)

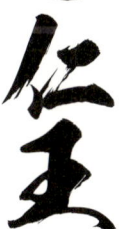

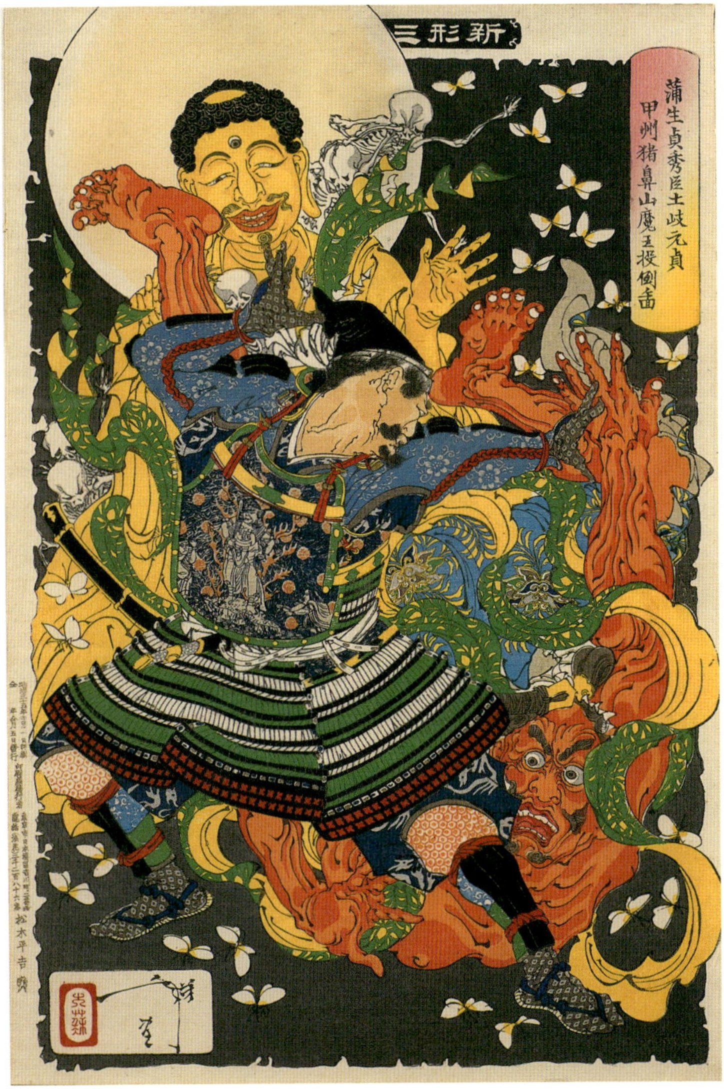

室町時代の武士・土岐元貞は、蒲生貞秀の命を受け、甲州猪鼻山の魔王堂に向かいました。阿弥陀如来（左上）と仁王（右下）に化けた妖怪が相撲を挑んできたので、元貞は投げ飛ばしました。すると、阿弥陀如来の腹から骸骨の軍勢が飛び出し、さらには無数の蝶になってまとわりつきました。

On orders from Gamō Sadahide of the powerful Gamō clan of the Muromachi period, Toki Motosada (center) visited the Hall of the Devil at Mount Inohana in Kai Province. The demonic creatures who took the forms of Amida Buddha (upper left) and a temple guardian (lower right) came to challenge him to a wrestling match, and when Motosada sent them flying, skeleton troops flew out of the Buddha's stomach, turning into countless butterflies which clung to him.

【新形三十六怪撰 蒲生貞秀臣土岐元貞甲州猪鼻山魔王投倒図】月岡芳年 明治23年（1890）

Gamō Sadahide's Servant, Toki Motosada, Hurling a Demon King to the Ground at Mount Inohana in Kai Province from the series *Shinkei sanjūrokkaisen (New Forms of Thirty-Six Ghosts)* by Tsukioka Yoshitoshi

189

Kappa (Water Imp)
Demonic Creatures (*yōkai*)

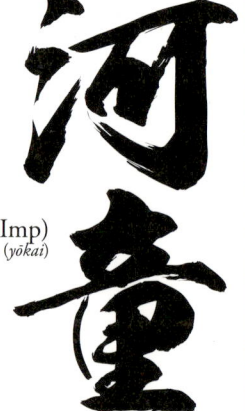

白藤源太は、歌舞伎などに登場する伝説
の力士。ある夏の日、柳の下で涼んでいる
と、河童が相撲を取り始めました。詞書に
よると、河童が力競べを挑んできたので、
投げ飛ばして殺したそうです。

Shirafuji Genta is a legendary sumō wrestler
whose exploits feature in kabuki plays. One
summer's day, as he cooled himself under a
willow, a *kappa* started to wrestle with him.
According to the text, the *kappa* challenges
him to a contest of strength, and he sends it
flying to its death.

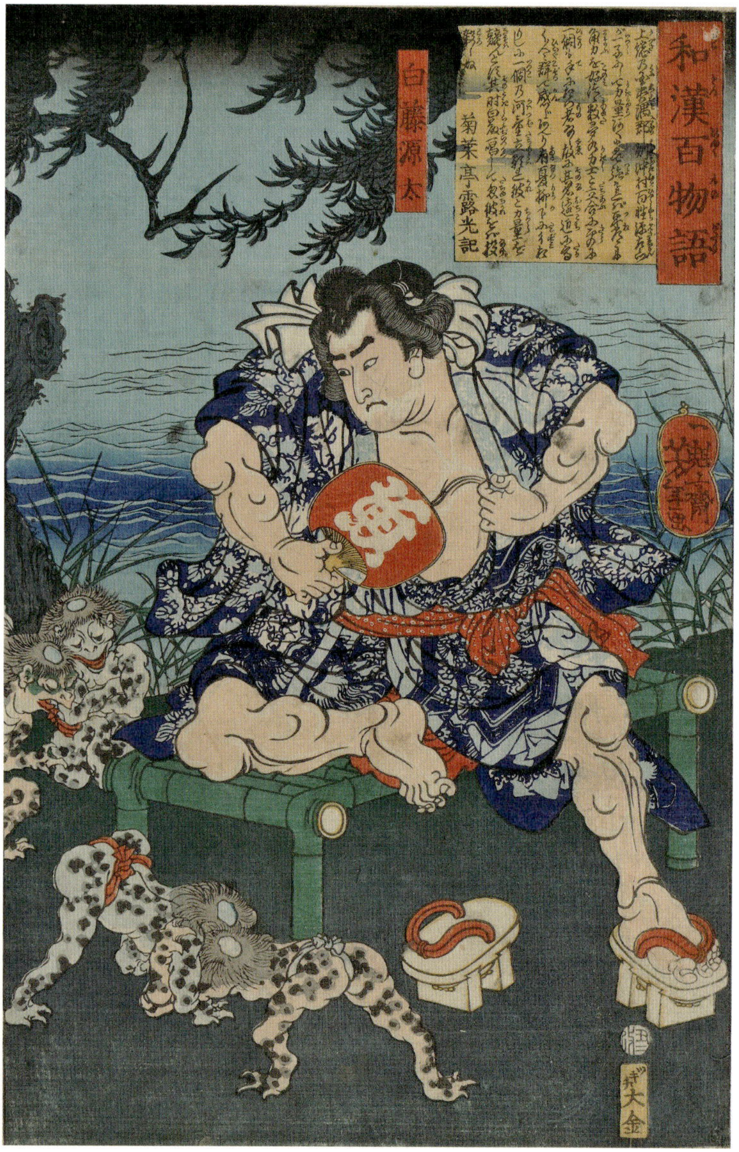

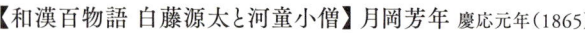

【和漢百物語 白藤源太と河童小僧】月岡芳年 慶応元年（1865）
Shirafuji Genta and the Water Imp from the series *Wakan hyakumonogatari (One Hundred Tales from China and Japan)*
by Tsukioka Yoshitoshi

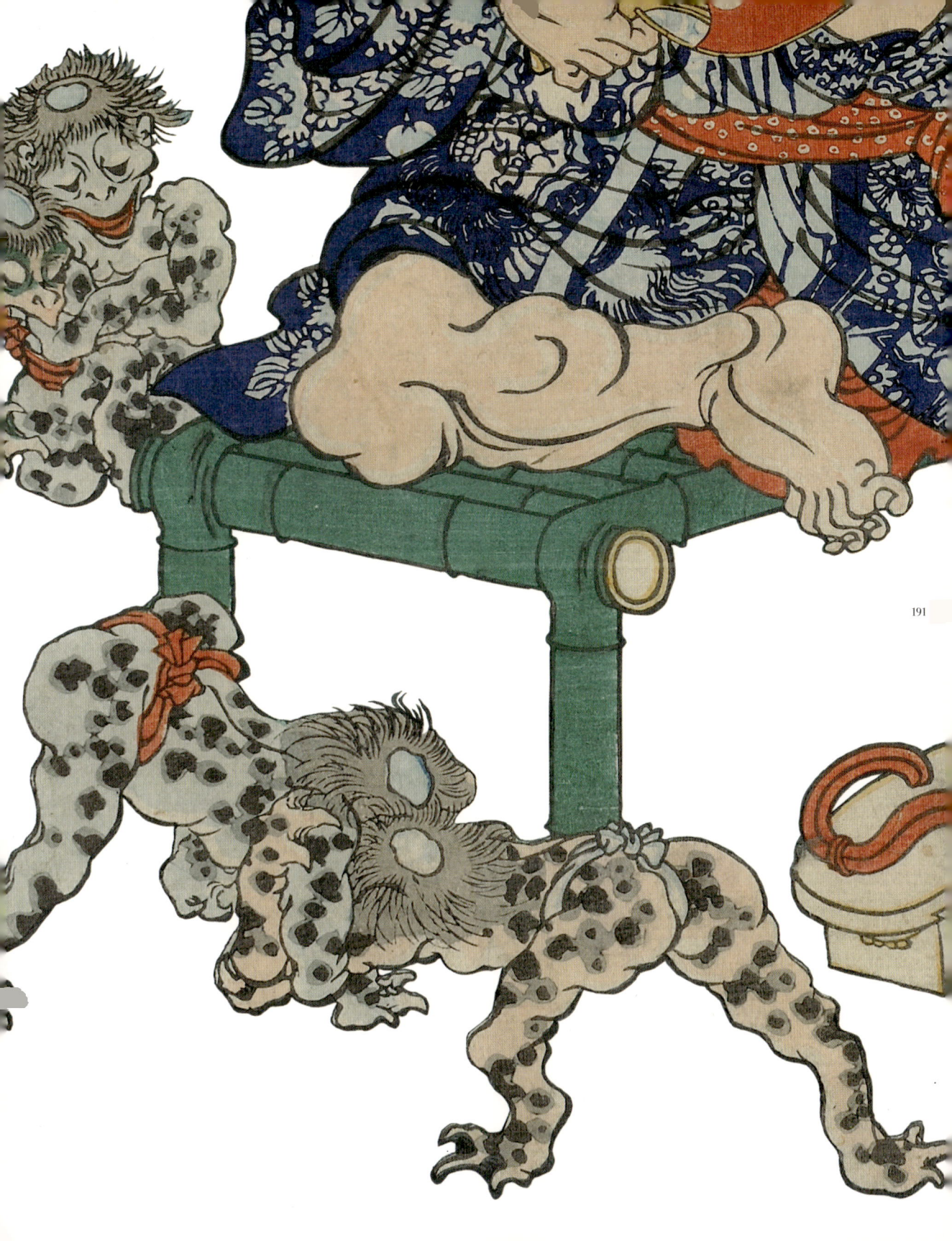

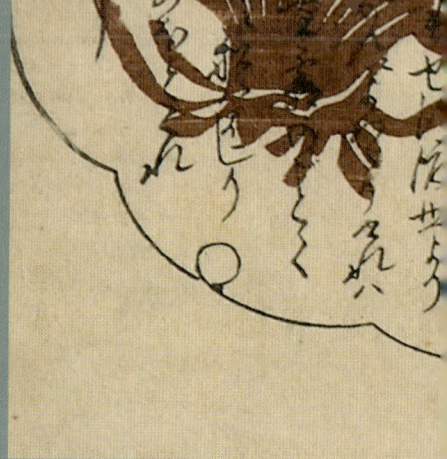

船乗り名人の徳蔵は、禁じられていたにもかかわらず、大晦日に船を出したところ、大嵐が起こり、山のように大きな坊主頭の化け物が現れました。徳蔵は恐れることなく、「渡世より怖いものはない」と大声を張り上げると、化け物は消え失せました。

Master sailor Tokuzō has set sail on New Year's Eve even though it is forbidden to do so, whereupon a violent storm breaks out, and the close-cropped head of a massive monster rises out of the waves like a mountain. Unafraid, Tokuzō calls out, "Nothing is as scary as making one's living!" and the monster vanishes away.

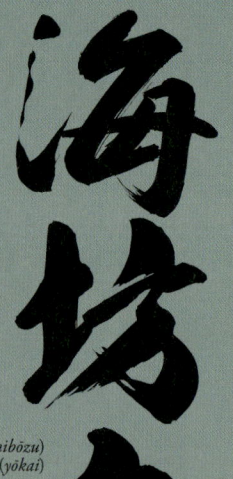

192

Sea Bonze (*Umibōzu*)
Demonic Creatures (*yōkai*)

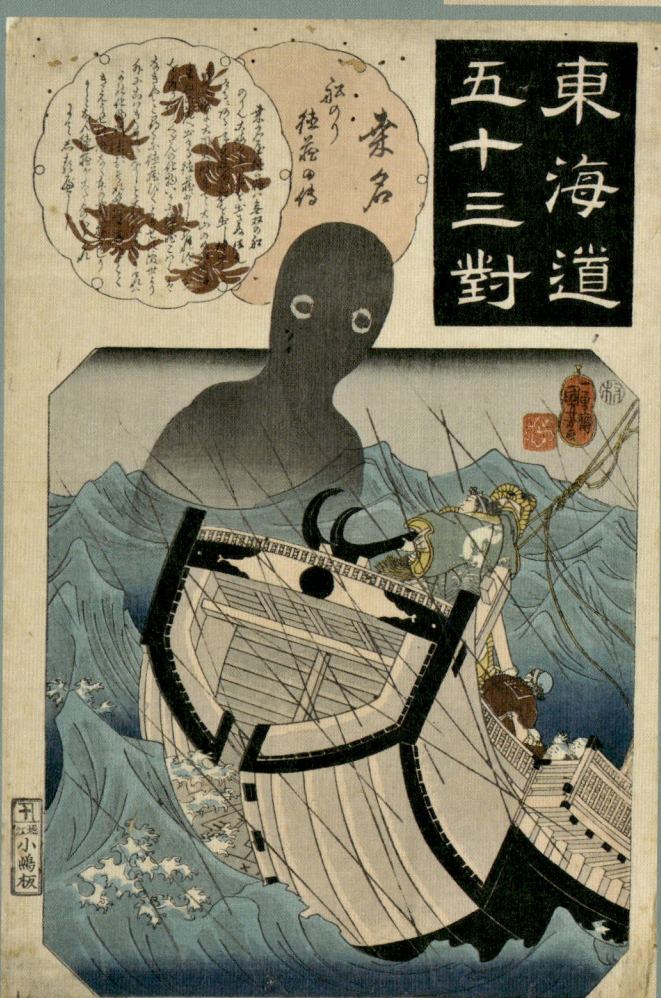

【東海道五十三對 桑名 船のり徳蔵の傳】
歌川国芳 弘化元～3年 (1844-46)
Kuwana: The Tale of Sailor Tokuzō
from the series *The Fifty-Three Stations of the Tōkaidō* by Utagawa Kuniyoshi

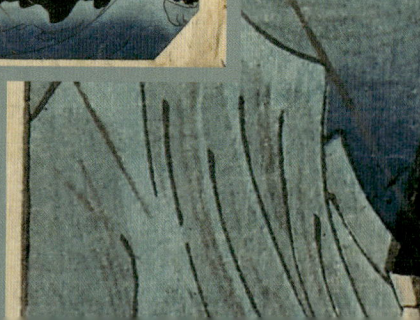

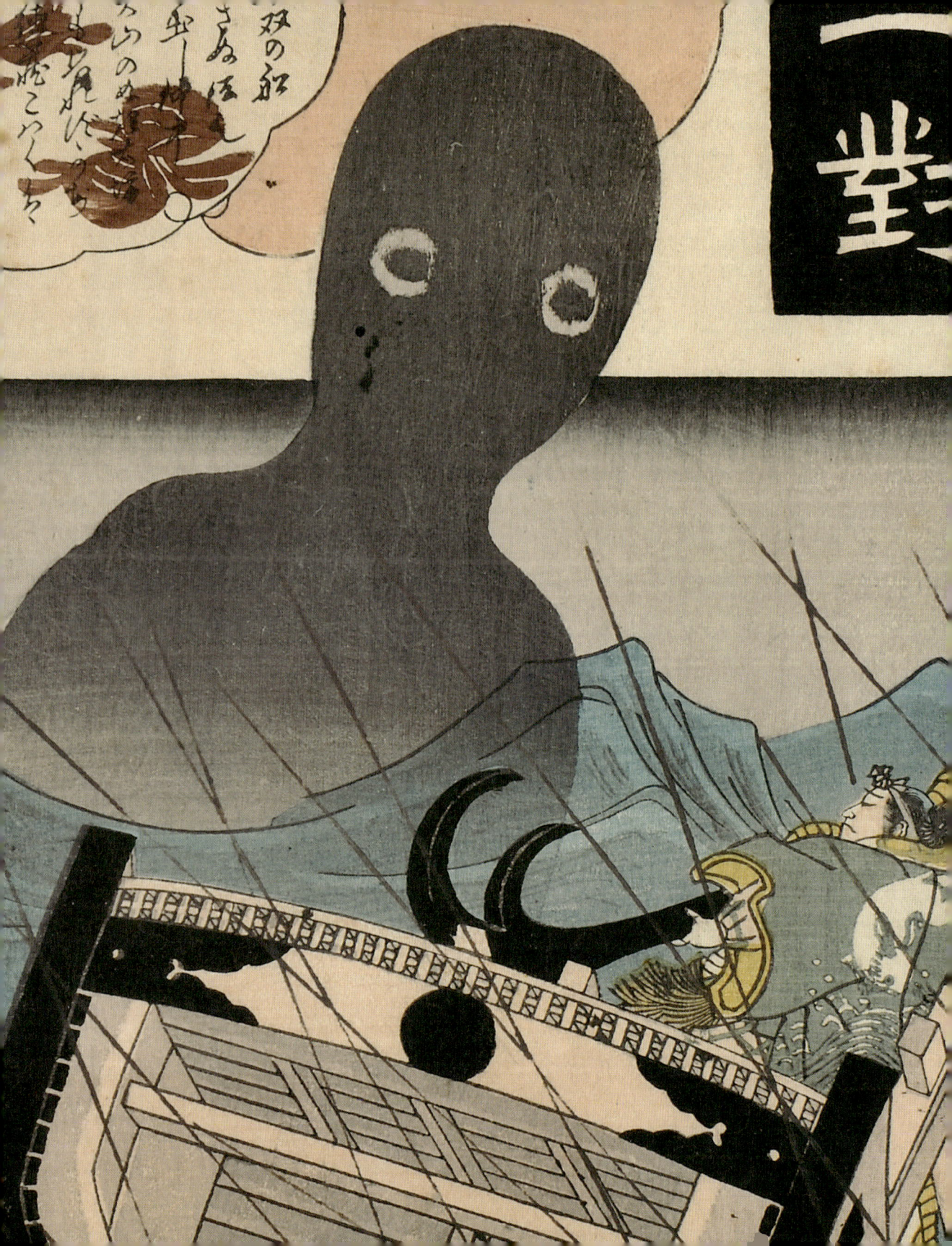

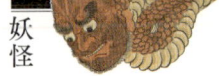

小町桜の精

Spirit of
the Komachi Cherry Tree
Demonic Creatures (*yōkai*)

194

雪積る逢坂山の関に咲く墨染桜。関守
の関兵衛こと、実は天下乗っ取りを企て
る大悪人の大伴黒主が、天下調伏の護
摩木にと、この桜の木を斬ろうとします。と、
その時一人の美女が登場。傾城墨染と
名乗るこの女は実は小町桜の精で、関
兵衛の素性を見破ります。

The Sumizome *sakura* (lit. "cherry blossom
dyed ink-black") flowers by the gate of the
snowy Mount Ōsaka checkpoint.
Gatekeeper Sekibē is actually evil would-be
usurper Ōtomo no Kuronushi, who tries to
cut down the cherry tree to use in a fire
ritual to achieve his dreams of world
domination. As he makes the attempt, a
beautiful woman appears. She introduces
herself as Keisei Sumizome, but she is really
the spirit of the Komachi cherry blossom,
and she discovers Sekibē's true identity and
fights him ferociously.

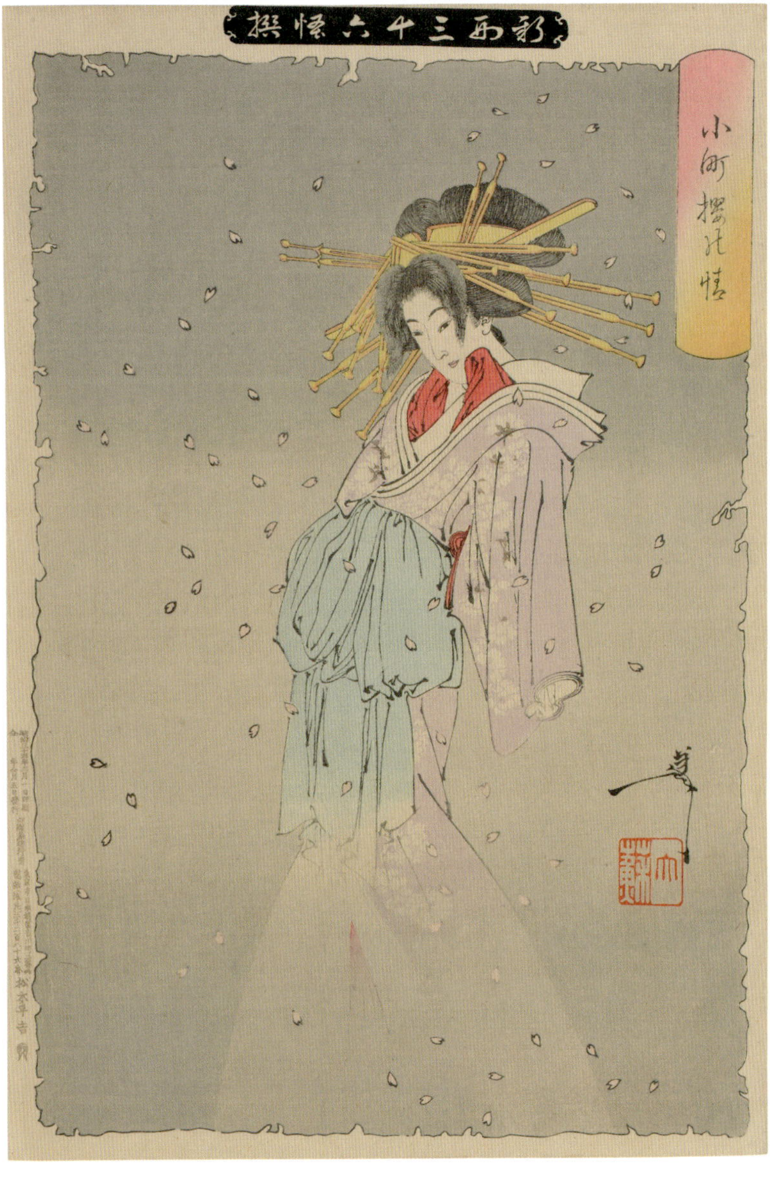

【新形三十六怪撰 小町桜の精】月岡芳年 明治22年（1889）
Spirit of the Komachi Cherry Tree from the series *Shinkei sanjūrokkaisen (New Forms of Thirty-Six Ghosts)*
by Tsukioka Yoshitoshi

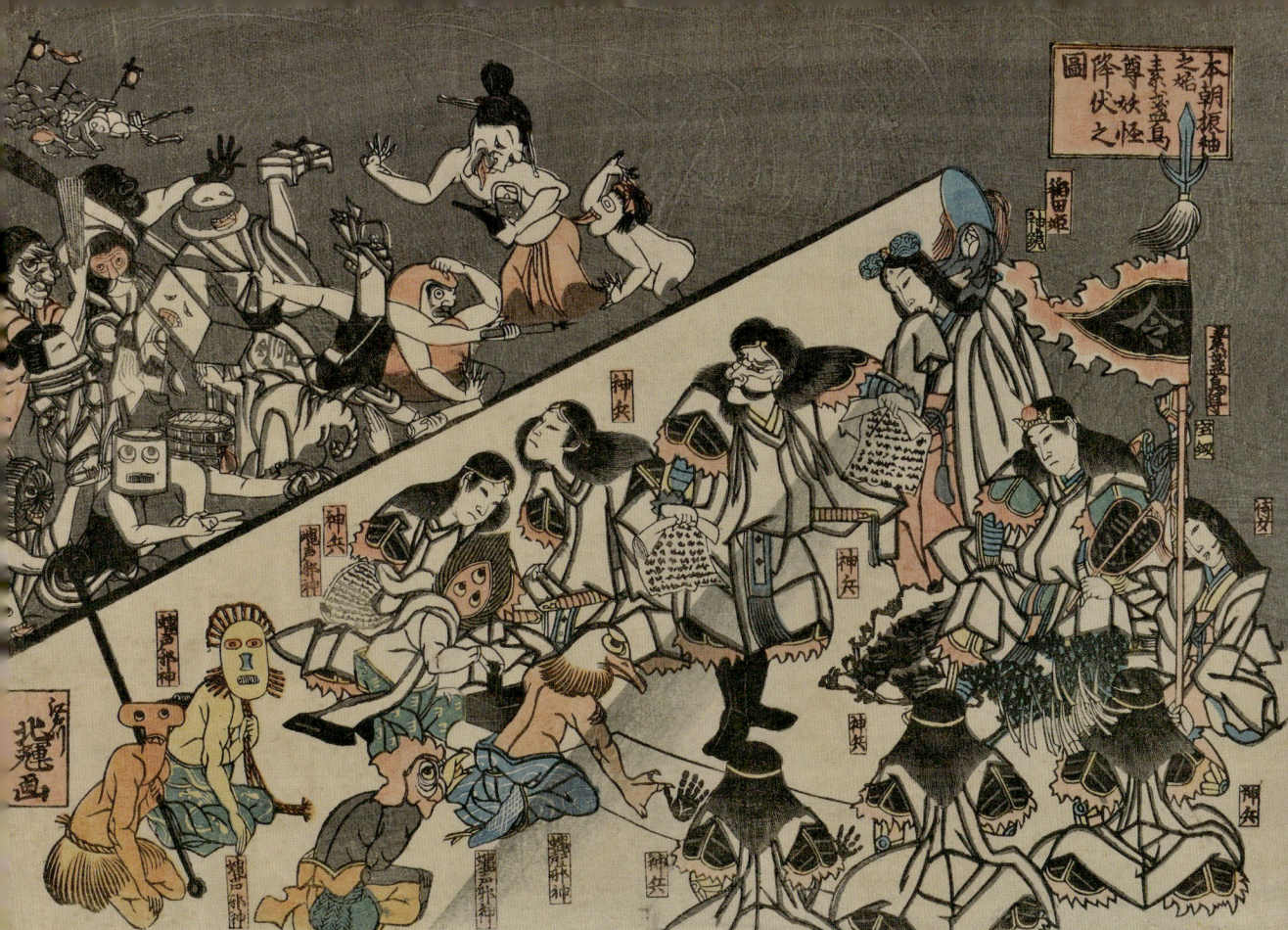

素戔嗚尊の妻、稲田姫が神鏡で照らし出すのは、蠅声邪神たち。この図は、嘉永4年（1851）の問屋仲間再興令を描いた判じ絵となっています。素戔嗚尊と稲田姫は幕府、紙を破く神兵は再興に尽力した遠山景元でしょうか。手判を押す蠅声邪神は両替屋、水鳥屋などで、暗闇の妖怪は売女屋などを示しています。

Princess Inada, wife of Susano'o no Mikoto, illuminates the odd shapes of the false gods with a precious mirror. Actually, this is a visual metaphor for the reinstatement of the merchant guilds in 1851. Susano'o and Princess Inada may represent the *bakufu*, Japan's feudal government, and the emissary of the gods ripping up the paper may be a depiction of Tōyama Kagemoto, who pushed for reinstatement of the guilds. The False Gods with the Voices of Flies making hand prints are currency exchangers, waterfowl sellers and so forth, while the creatures in the dark represent the more disreputable merchants, such as brothel keepers.

蠅声邪神

False Gods with the Voices of Flies
Demonic Creatures (*yōkai*)

【本朝振袖之始 素盞烏尊妖怪降伏之図】江戸川北輝 嘉永4年（1851）

In the Play IIonchō Furisode no Hajime, Susano'o no Mikoto Subdues the Monsters
by Edogawa Hokki

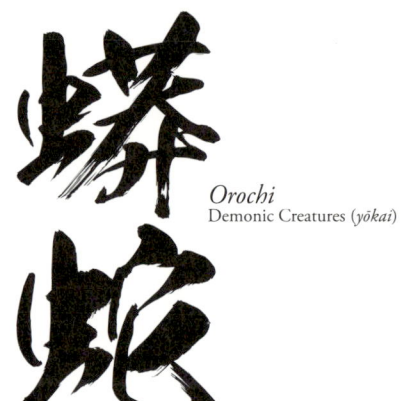

Orochi
Demonic Creatures (*yōkai*)

読本『椿説弓張月』より。源為朝の忠狼・山雄は、主人を狙う蟒蛇に噛みつき、咆え叫んで危険を知らせようとしましたが、為朝の郎党・須藤重季は、山雄が野性を取り戻して為朝を襲おうとしたと勘違いして、山雄を斬り殺してしまいます。

From *yomihon Chinsetsu Yumiharizuki (The Crescent Moon)*. The loyalty of Minamoto no Tametomo's pet wolf Yamao is depicted. To save his master, Yamao sinks his teeth into the *orochi*, snarling to warn his master of danger. Tametomo's retainer Sudō Shigesue incorrectly assumes that Yamao has reverted back to his wild state in the mountains and is attacking Tametomo, and kills him with his sword.

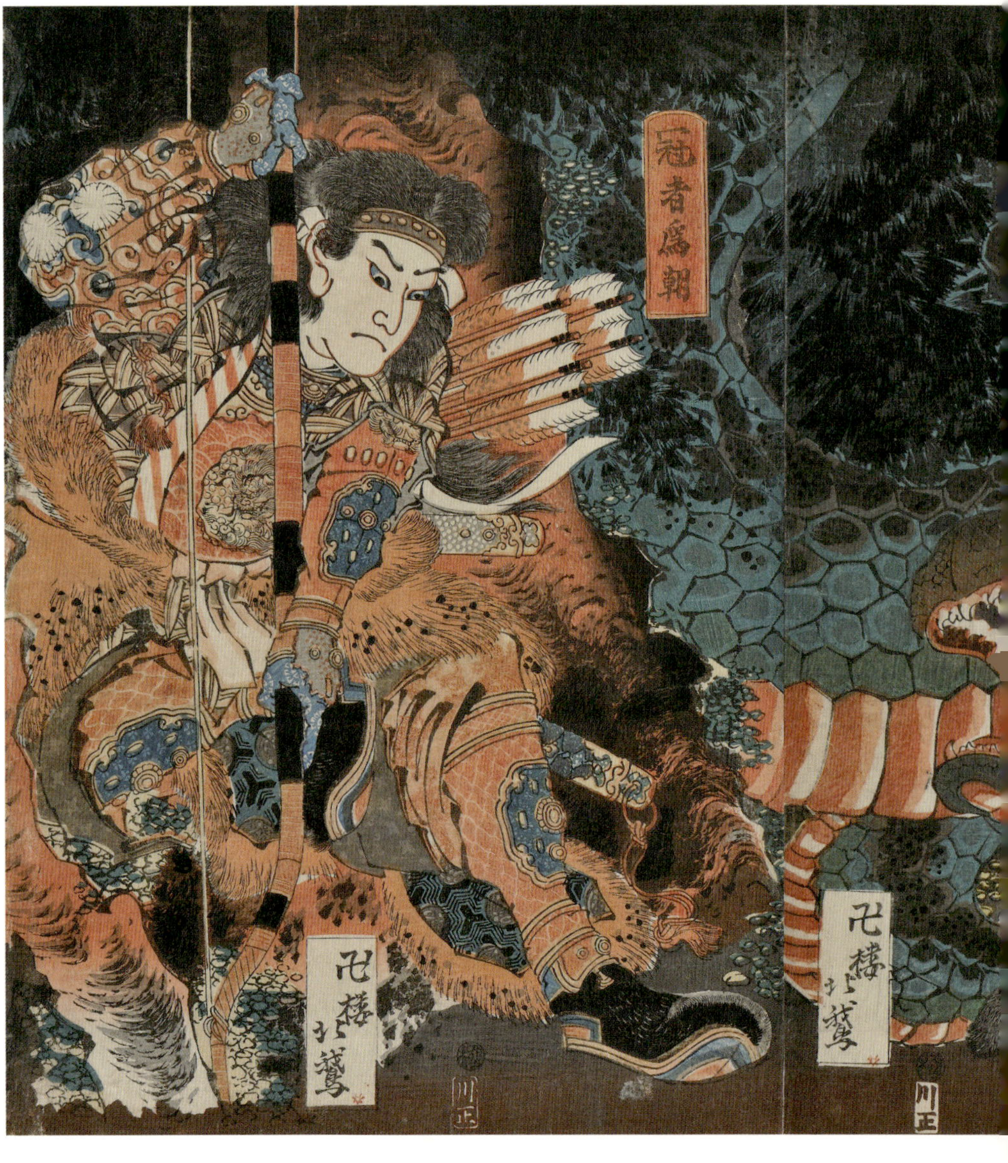

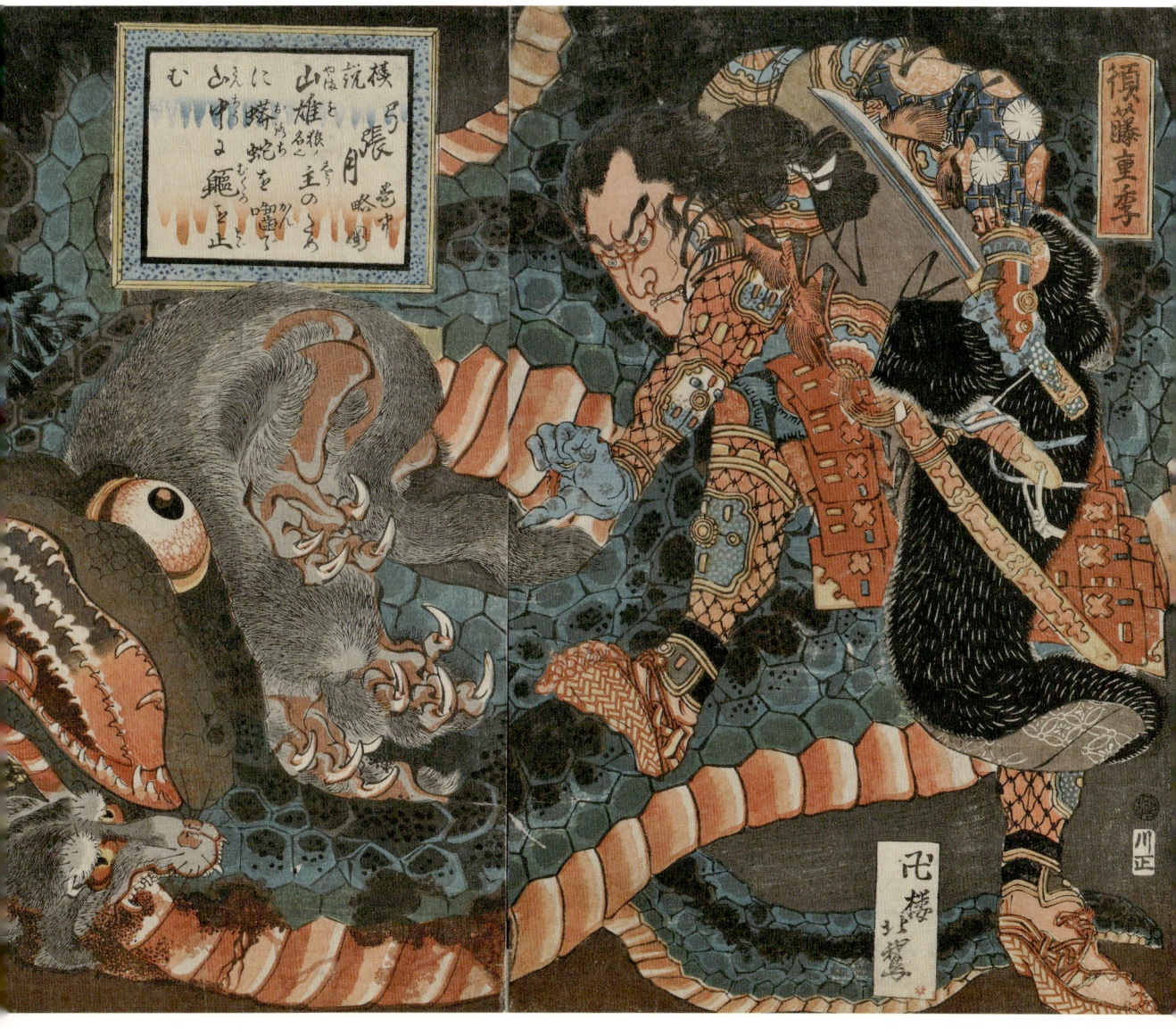

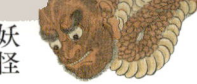

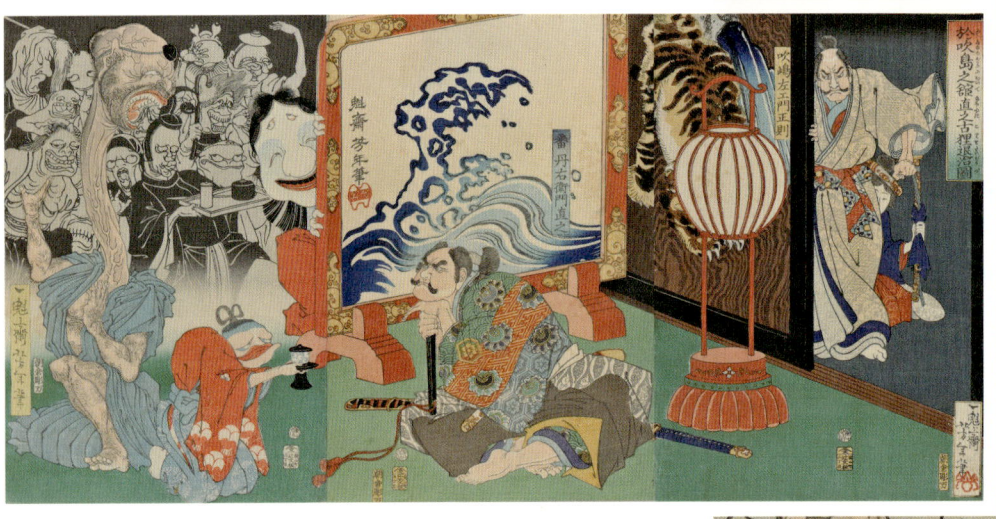

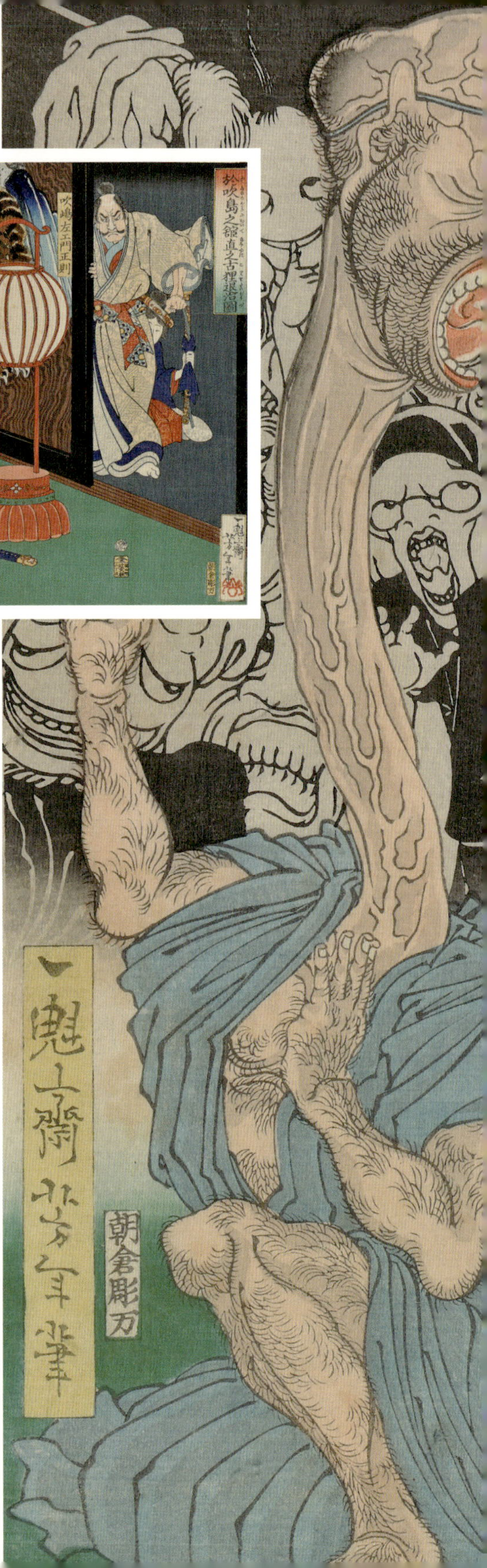

198

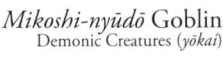

見越し入道【古狸】

Mikoshi-nyūdō Goblin
Demonic Creatures (*yōkai*)

安土桃山時代の武将、塙団右衛門（番丹右衛門直之）が、福島正則（吹嶋左エ門正則）の屋敷で宿直をしていると、古狸が化けた見越し入道が現れました。茶くみ小僧が、団右衛門にお茶を差し出します。

This is a depiction of a legend of the period when Ban Dan'emon (Naoyuki), military commander of the Azuchi-Momoyama period, entered the service of Fukushima Masanori. The *mikoshi-nyūdō* goblin with its long neck extended (left) is a shape-shifting old raccoon dog. Dan'emon glares at them, while a tea-making goblin presents him with a cup of tea.

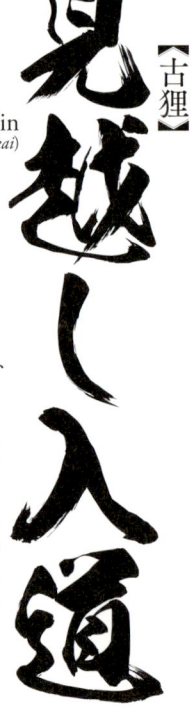

【於吹島之館直之古狸退治図】月岡芳年 慶応2年（1866）
Naoyuki Defeats the Old Raccoon Dog at Fukushima's Mansion by Tsukioka Yoshitoshi

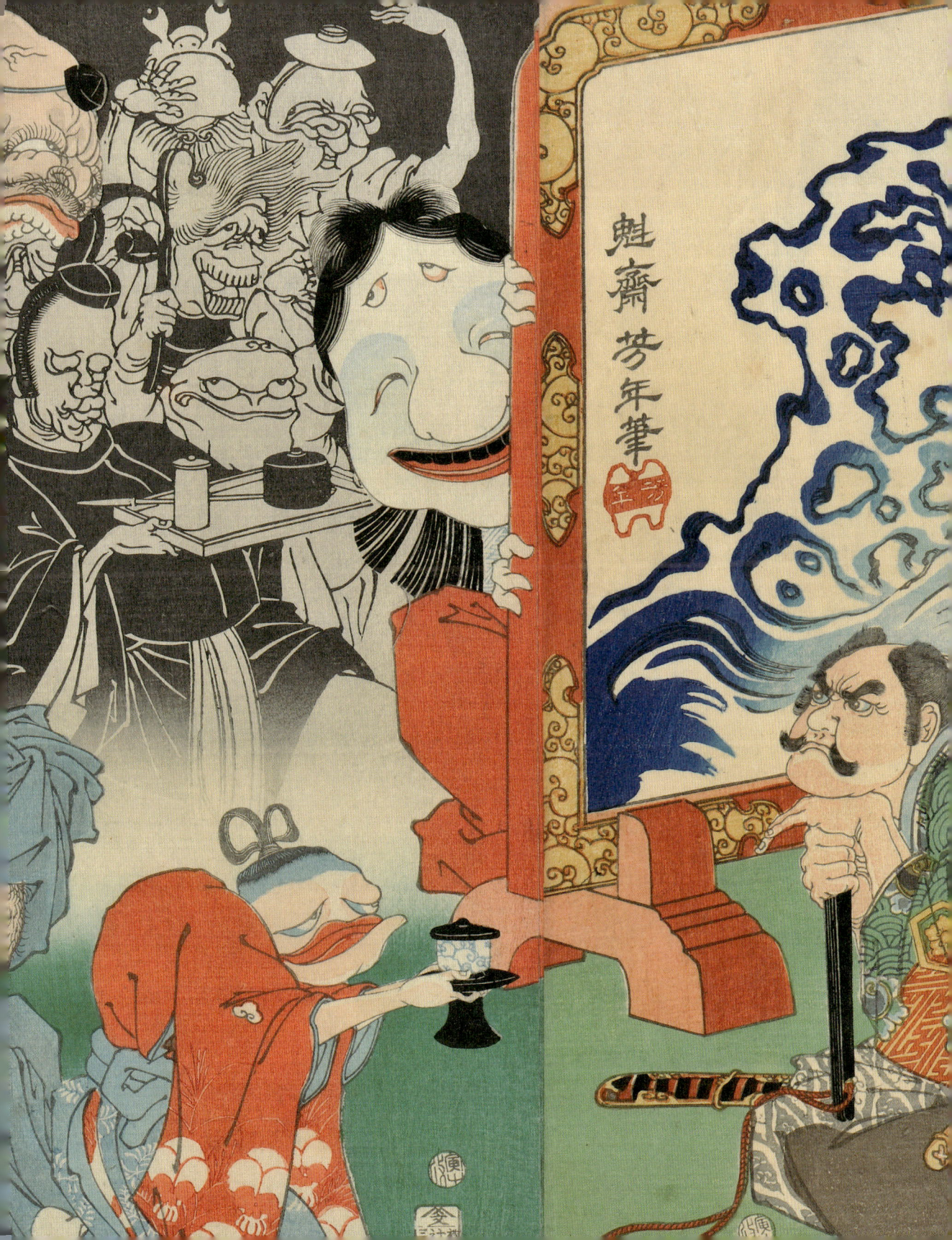

野衾

Nobusuma
Demonic Creatures (*yōkai*)

宮本武蔵が諸国修行をしていた時、山奥で
道に迷ってしまいました。そこで出会ったのは、
野衾というムササビのお化けです。当時、ムサ
サビは何百年も生きた蝙蝠が、妖怪になった
ものと考えられていたそうです。

A legend of the travels of Miyamoto Musashi.
Losing his way, he finds himself deep in the
mountains, where he encounters the giant flying
squirrel monster known as the *Nobusuma*. The
monster pictured resembles a huge bat, but in the
Edo period people believed that *Nobusuma* were
bats who transformed into demonic flying squirrels
after many hundreds or thousands of years.

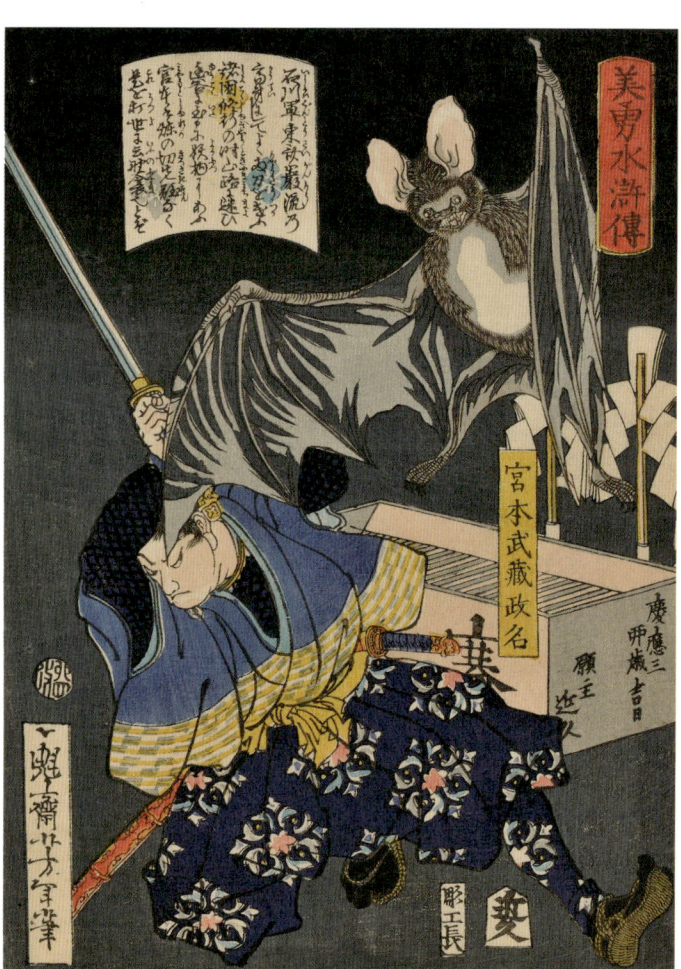

【美勇水滸傳 宮本武蔵政名】月岡芳年 慶応3年(1867)

Miyamoto Musashi Masana from the series *Biyū Suikoden (Sagas of Beauty and Bravery)*
by Tsukioka Yoshitoshi

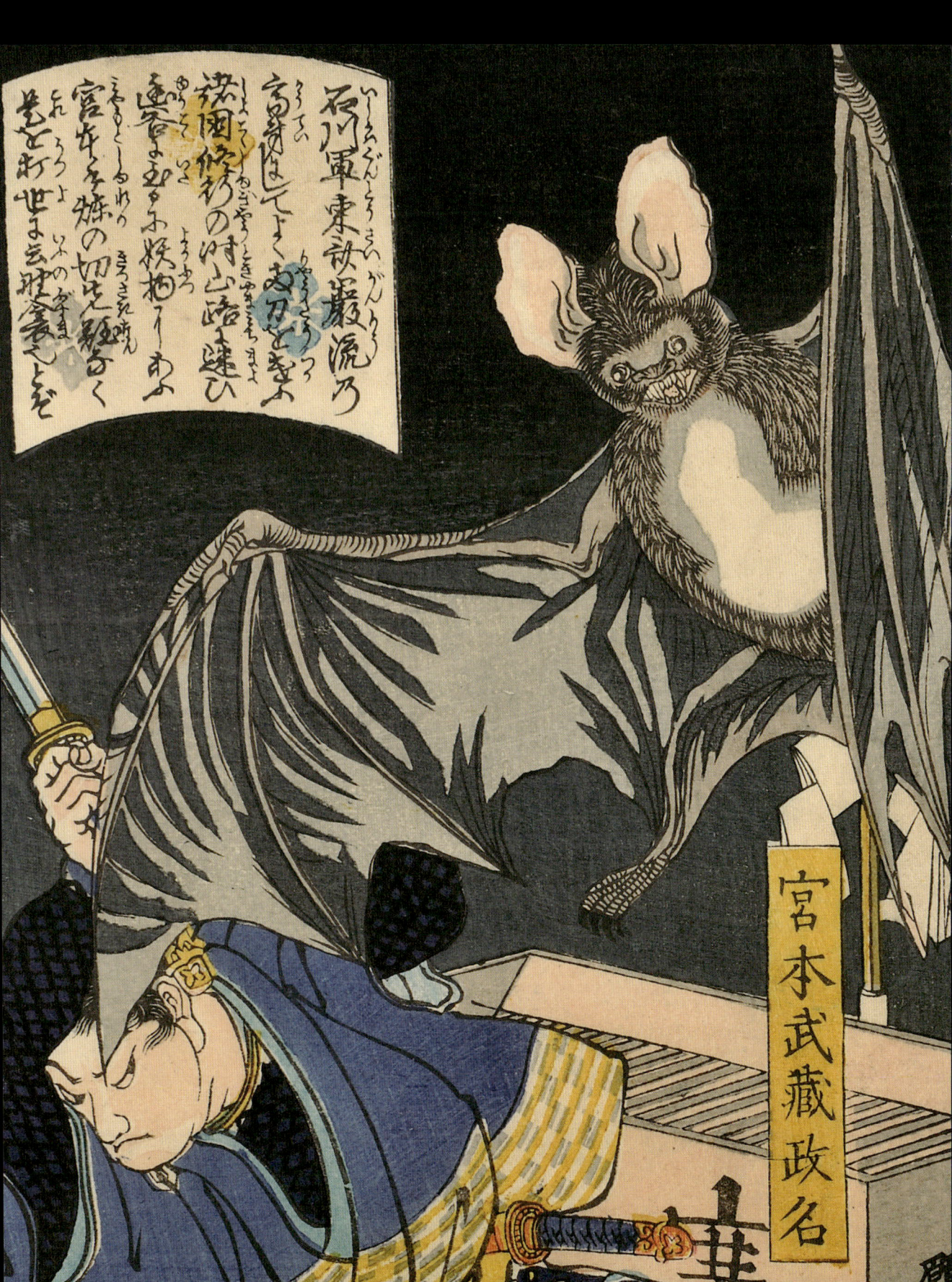

石川軍談巌流ろ
宮本武蔵政名

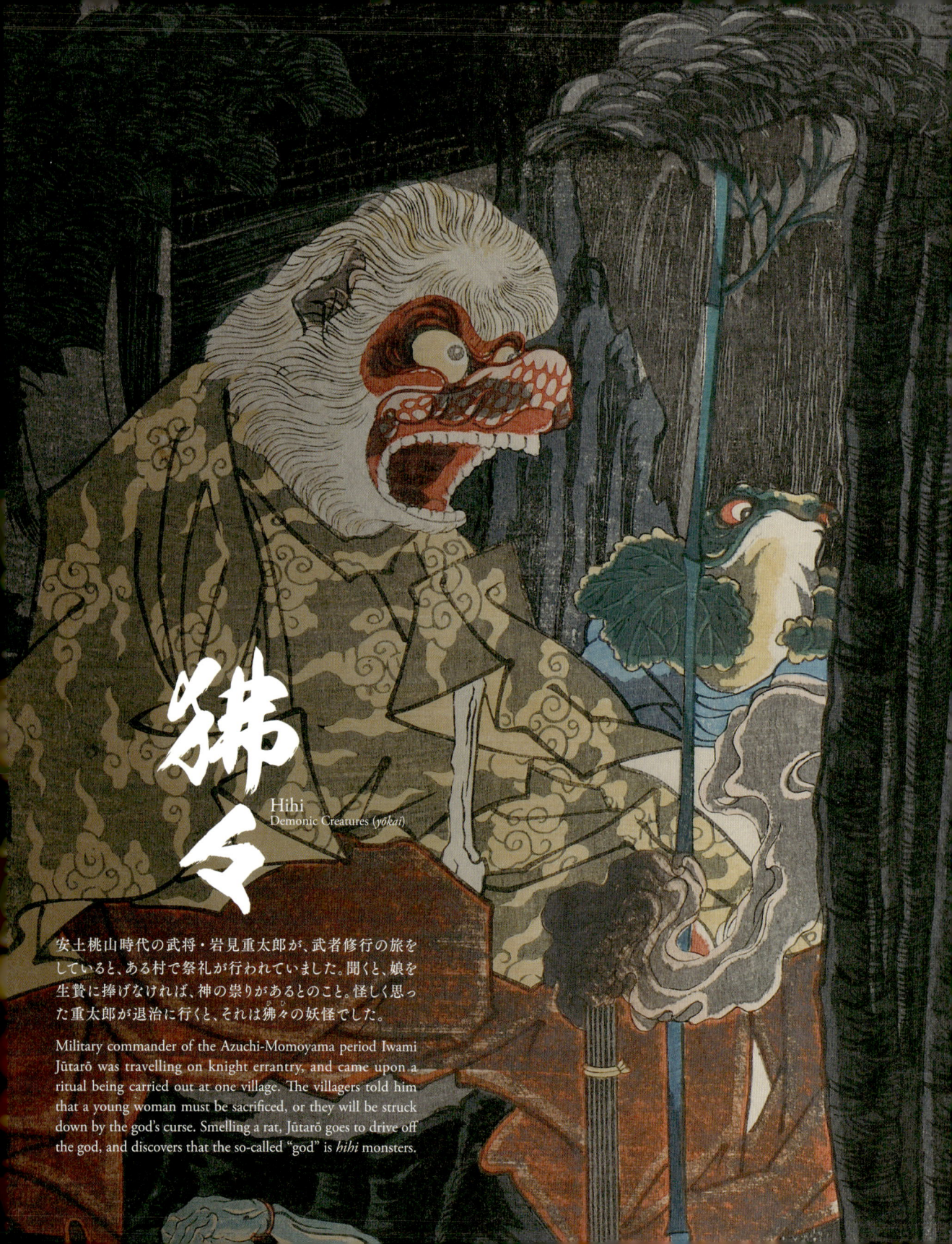

狒々

Hihi
Demonic Creatures (*yōkai*)

安土桃山時代の武将・岩見重太郎が、武者修行の旅を
していると、ある村で祭礼が行われていました。聞くと、娘を
生贄に捧げなければ、神の祟りがあるとのこと。怪しく思っ
た重太郎が退治に行くと、それは狒々の妖怪でした。

Military commander of the Azuchi-Momoyama period Iwami
Jūtarō was travelling on knight errantry, and came upon a
ritual being carried out at one village. The villagers told him
that a young woman must be sacrificed, or they will be struck
down by the god's curse. Smelling a rat, Jūtarō goes to drive off
the god, and discovers that the so-called "god" is *hihi* monsters.

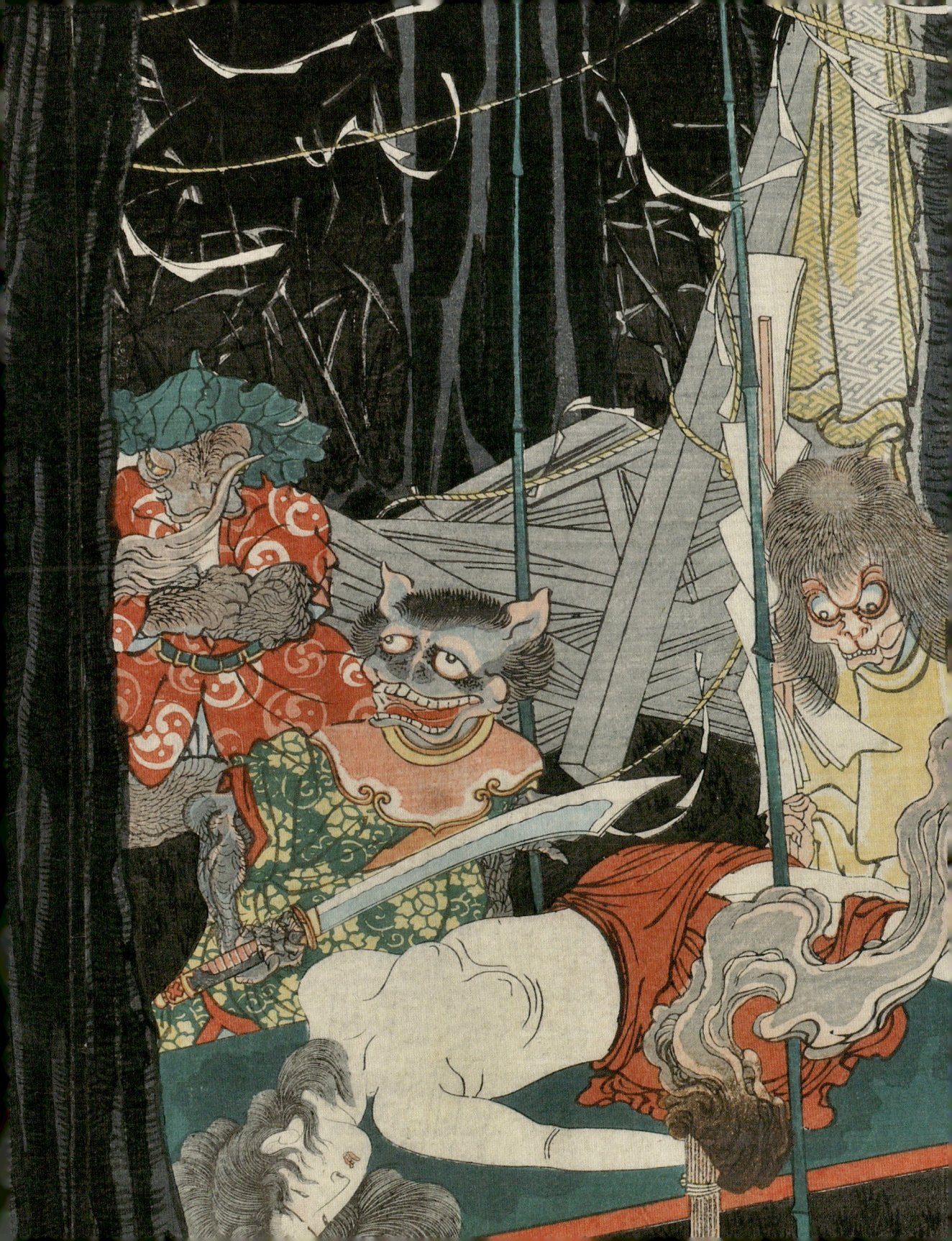

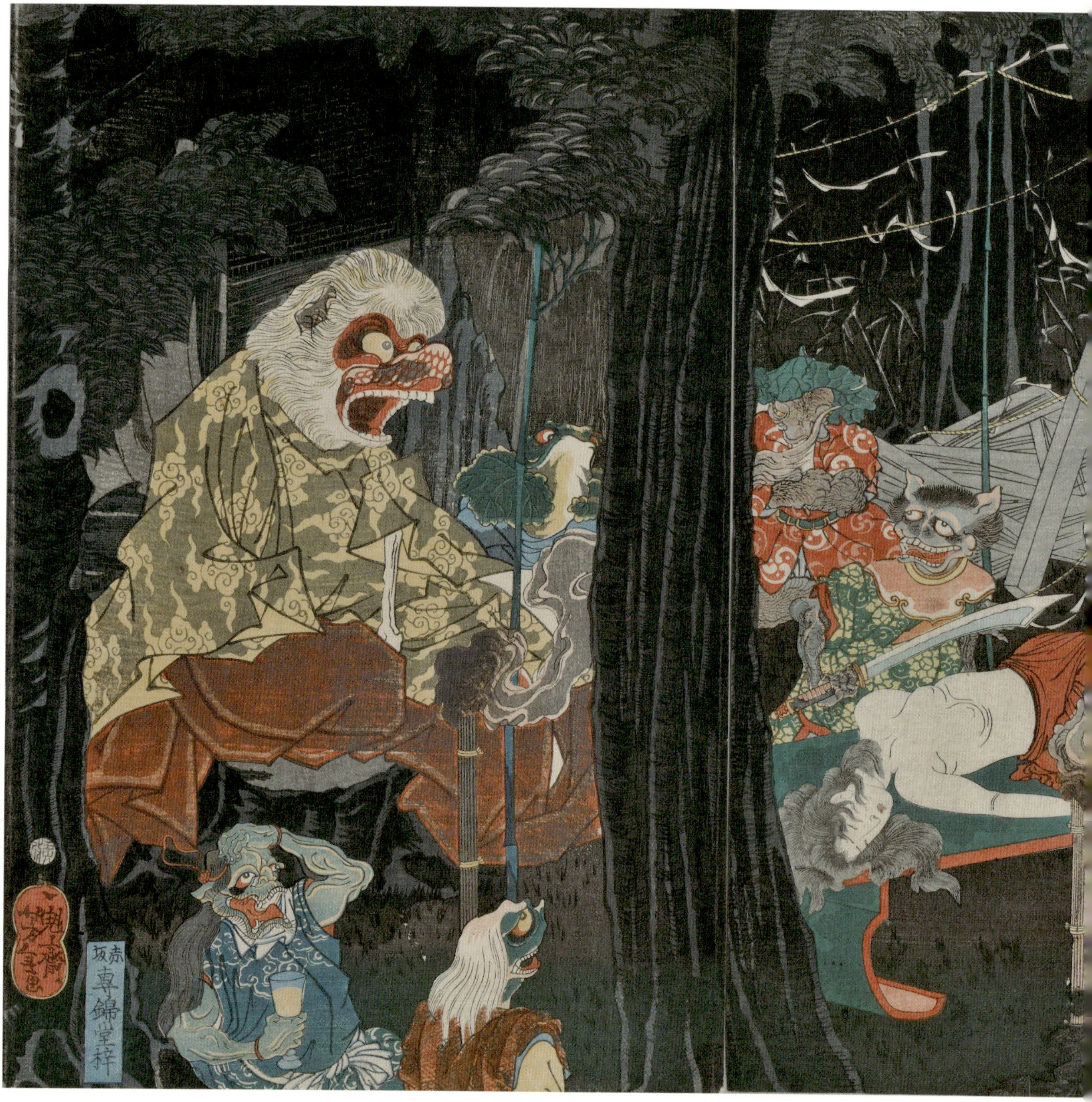

204

【岩見重太郎の狒々退治】月岡芳年　慶応元年（1865）

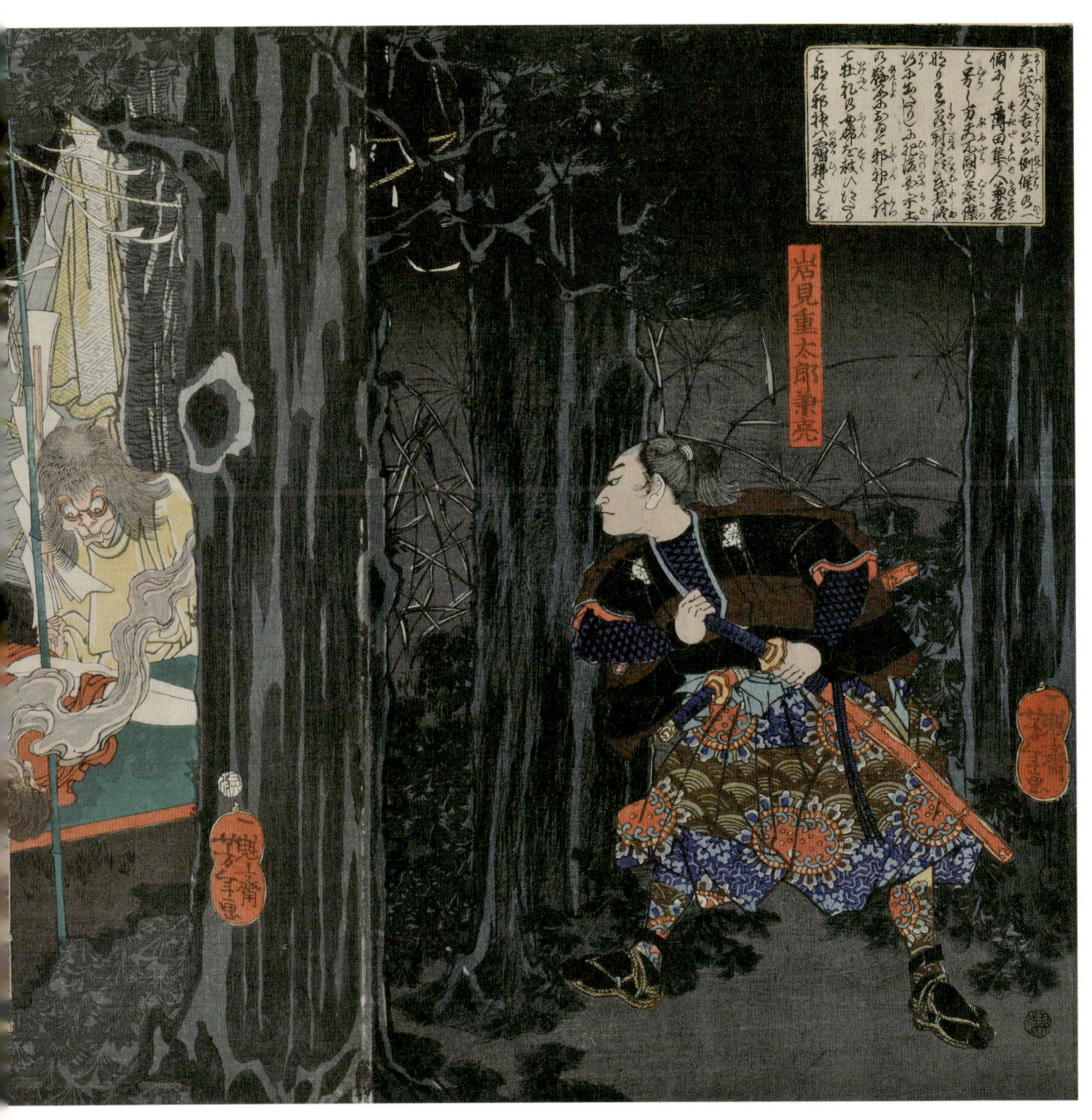

Iwami Jūtarō Routs the Hihi by Tsukioka Yoshitoshi

【怪鼠】

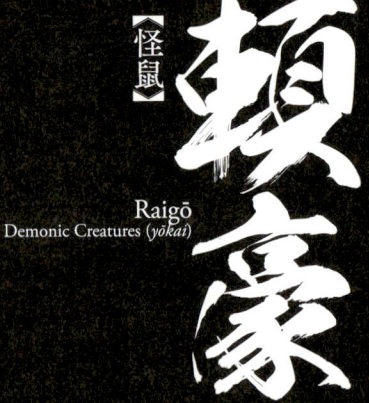

頼豪

Raigō
Demonic Creatures (*yōkai*)

頼豪は平安時代の三井寺の僧。白河天皇の勅命で皇子降誕を祈祷し、恩賞として戒壇造立を請いましたが、敵対する延暦寺に阻止され、怨死します。その怨霊は鼠と化し、数千の鼠を集めて延暦寺の経典を食い破ってしまいました。

Raigō was a priest of Mii Temple in the mid-Heian period. On the orders of Emperor Shirakawa, he prayed successfully for the birth of an imperial prince, and as a reward for this service, pleaded for an ordination platform to be built at his temple, but due to the opposition of Enryaku Temple, his request was denied. Consumed with bitterness, he refused to eat and died with a grudge. There is a legend that his vengeful spirit later changed into a rat, and mustered a thousands-strong swarm of rats to bite and tear the Buddhist scriptures of Enryaku Temple.

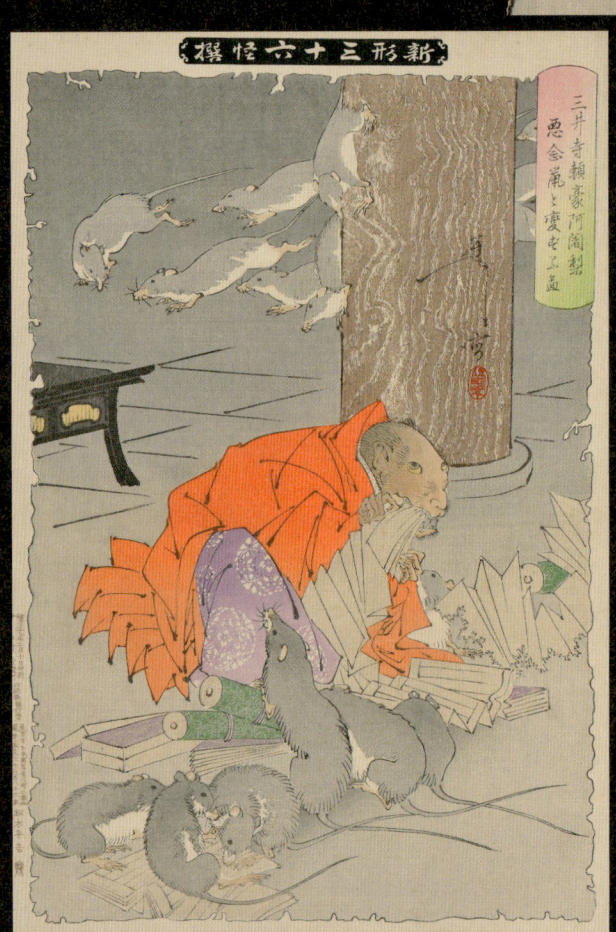

【新形三十六怪撰 三井寺頼豪阿闍梨悪念鼠と変ずる図】月岡芳年 明治24年（1891）

Priest Raigō of Mii Temple Transformed into a Rat by Evil Thoughts
from the series *Shinkei sanjūrokkaisen (New Forms of Thirty-Six Ghosts)* by Tsukioka Yoshitoshi

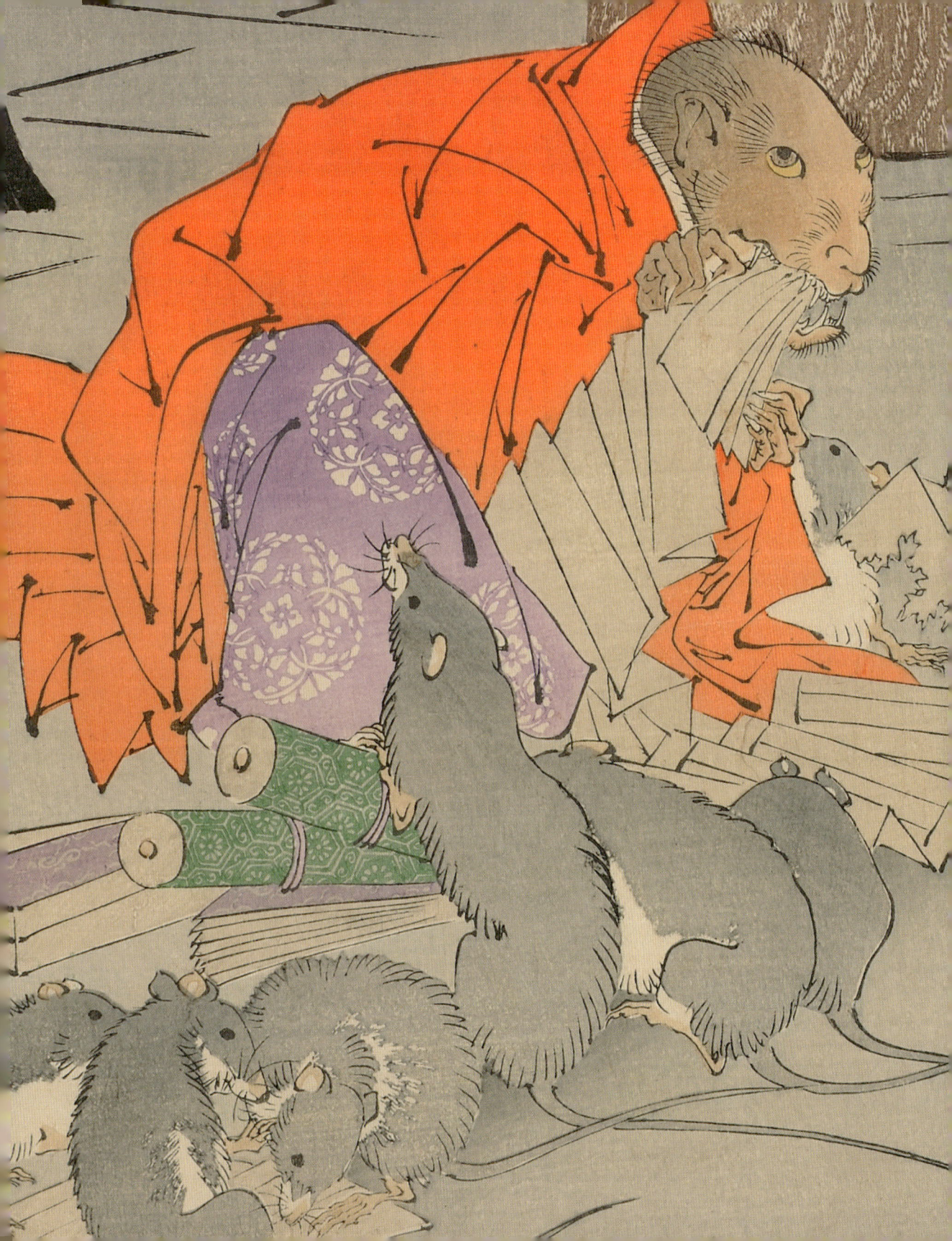

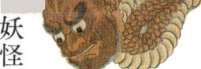

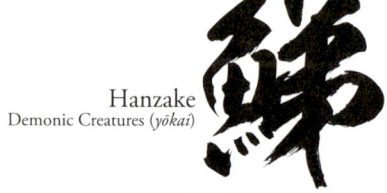

Hanzake
Demonic Creatures (*yōkai*)

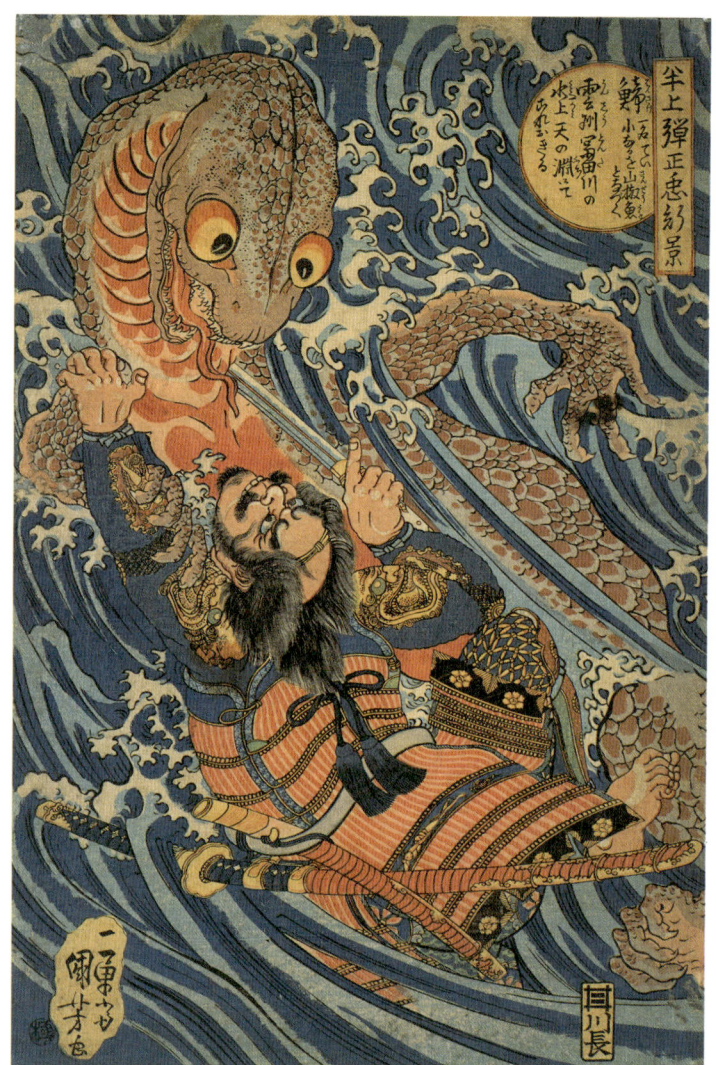

出雲の冨田川に棲む、「鯑」という化け物に、
毛利家忠臣半上氏の末裔、半上弾正ノ忠新
景が、短刀で果敢に斬りつけます。鯑は大山椒
魚の異名で、半分に裂けても死なないとされ、ま
た、見た目の不気味さから恐れられていました。

The monster known as *hanzake*, which dwells in
the Tonda River in Izumo, is boldly stabbed with a
dagger by Hanno'ue Danjō'nojō Arakage, a
descendant of the Hanno'ue family, the loyal
subjects of the Mori clan. *Hanzake* is another name
for large newt; if they are split in half, they will not
die, and they are feared for their bizarre
appearance.

【半上弾正ノ忠新景】歌川国芳　天保4-6年(1833-35)頃
Han-no-ue Danjō-no-jō Arakage by Utagawa Kuniyoshi

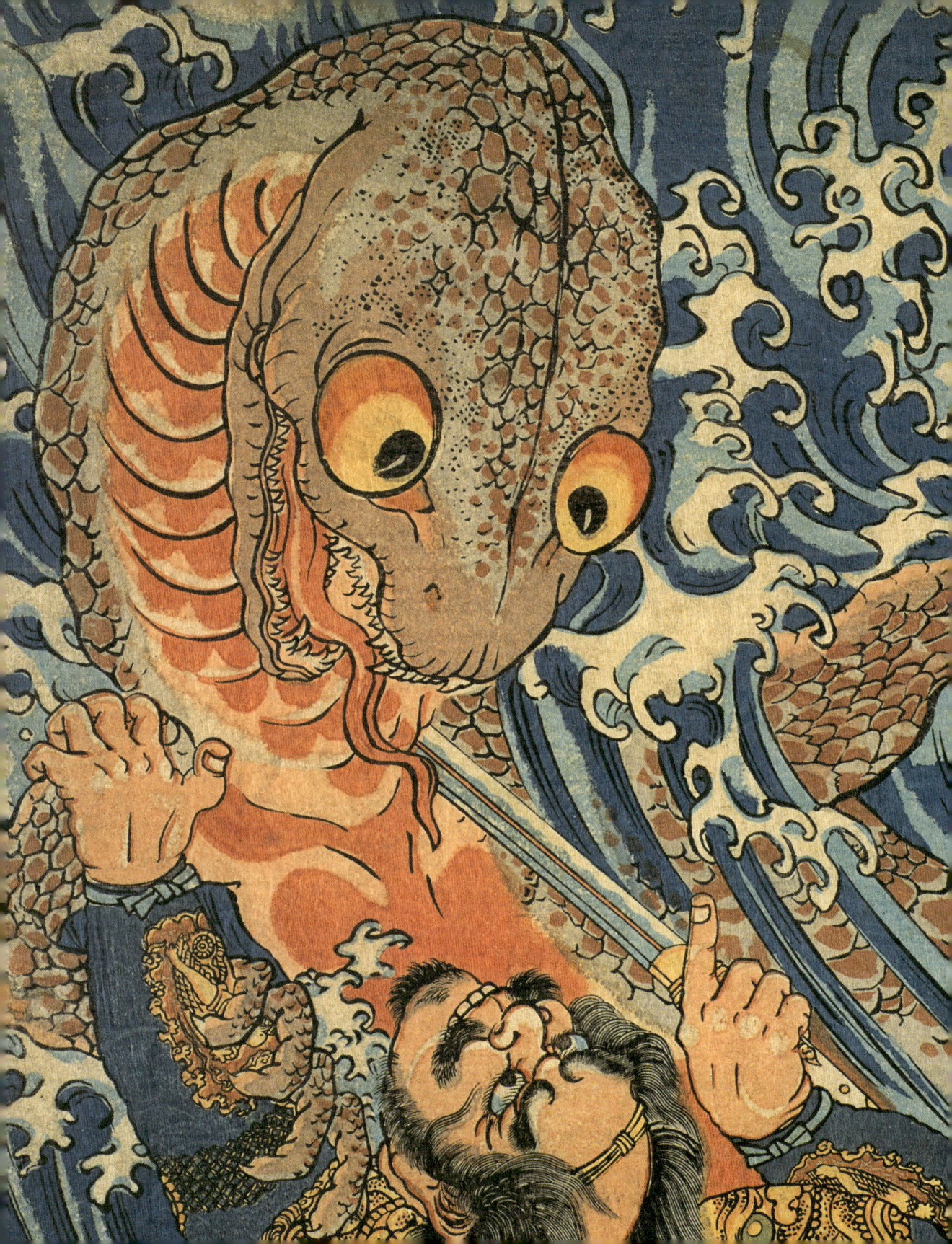

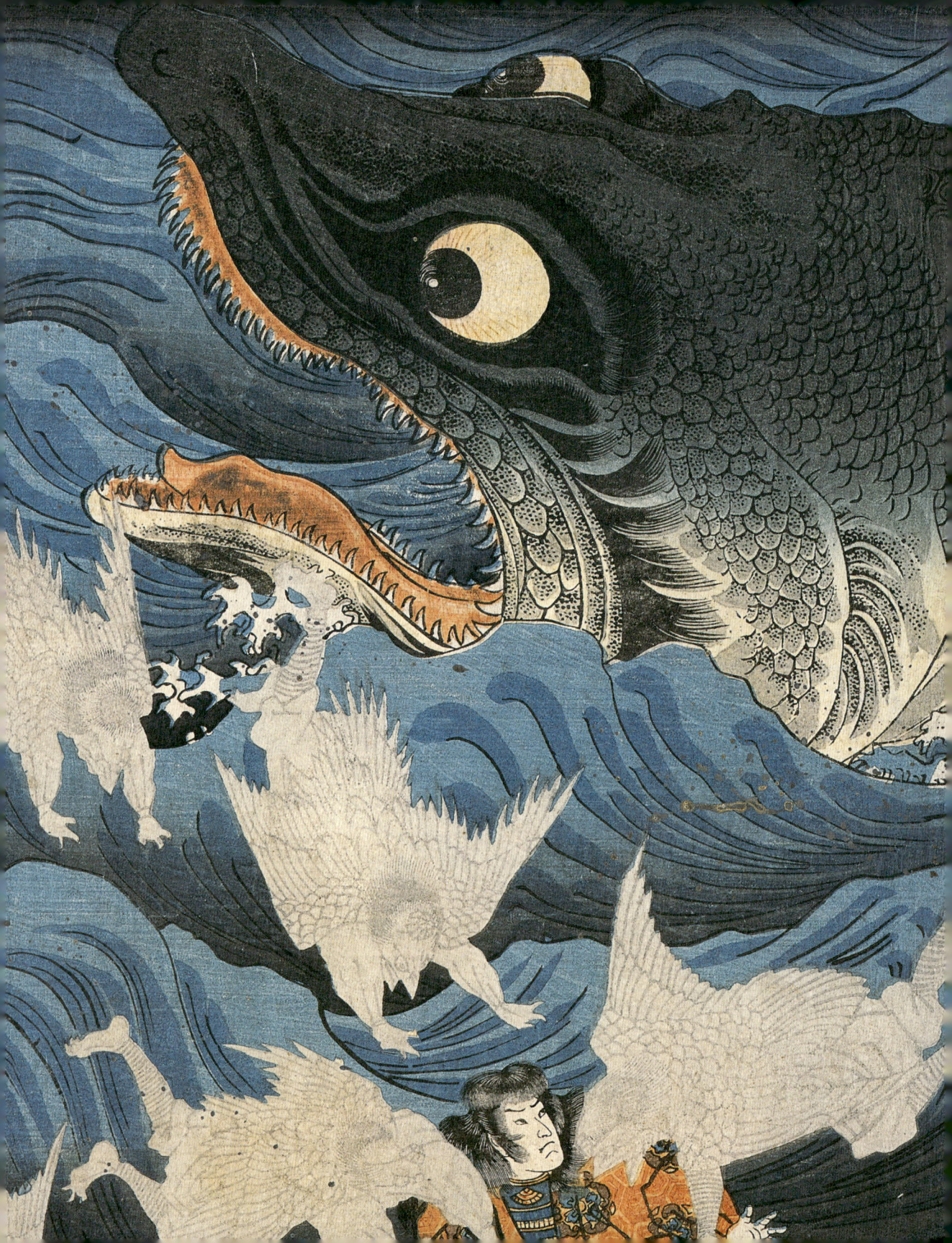

鴉天狗と鰐鮫

Karasu Tengu and Wanizame
(Long-nosed Goblins with Crow Wings and Sea Monster)
Demonic Creatures (yōkai)

読本『椿説弓張月』より。平清盛を討つため船出した源為朝一行は、海で嵐に遭います。妻の白縫姫が自らの命を犠牲にして海に飛び込むと、讃岐院の眷属の鴉天狗が現れ、為朝（左下）を救います。二人の子昇天丸と忠臣喜平治（右上）は、為朝郎党の魂が宿った鰐鮫によって琉球まで運ばれます。

A scene from *yomihon Chinsetsu Yumiharizuki (The Crescent Moon)* which depicts a legend of Minamoto no Tametomo. Setting sail to avenge Taira no Kiyomori, Tametomo's party are caught in a storm on the sea. As his wife Princess Shiranui (right) leaps into the water, *tengu* (long-nosed goblins) who are the flying monkeys of Sanuki-in (formerly known as Emperor Sutoku) come to rescue Tametomo (left). Their son Sutemaru and loyal retainer Kiheiji (upper right) are carried to the Ryukyu Islands (present-day Okinawa) by the sea monster, which is possessed by the spirits of retainer Takama and his wife.

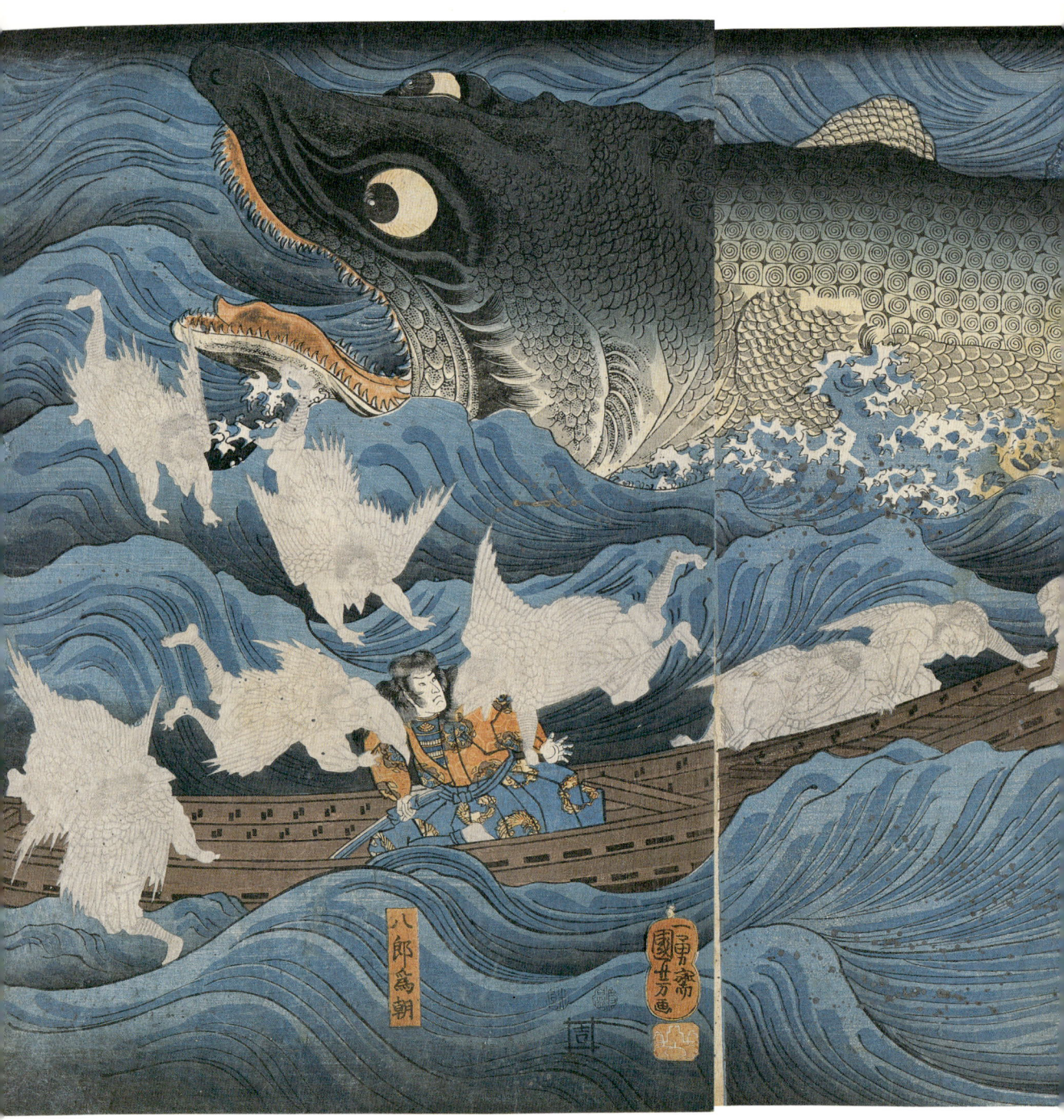

【讃岐院眷属をして為朝をすくふ図】歌川国芳　嘉永4年（1851）

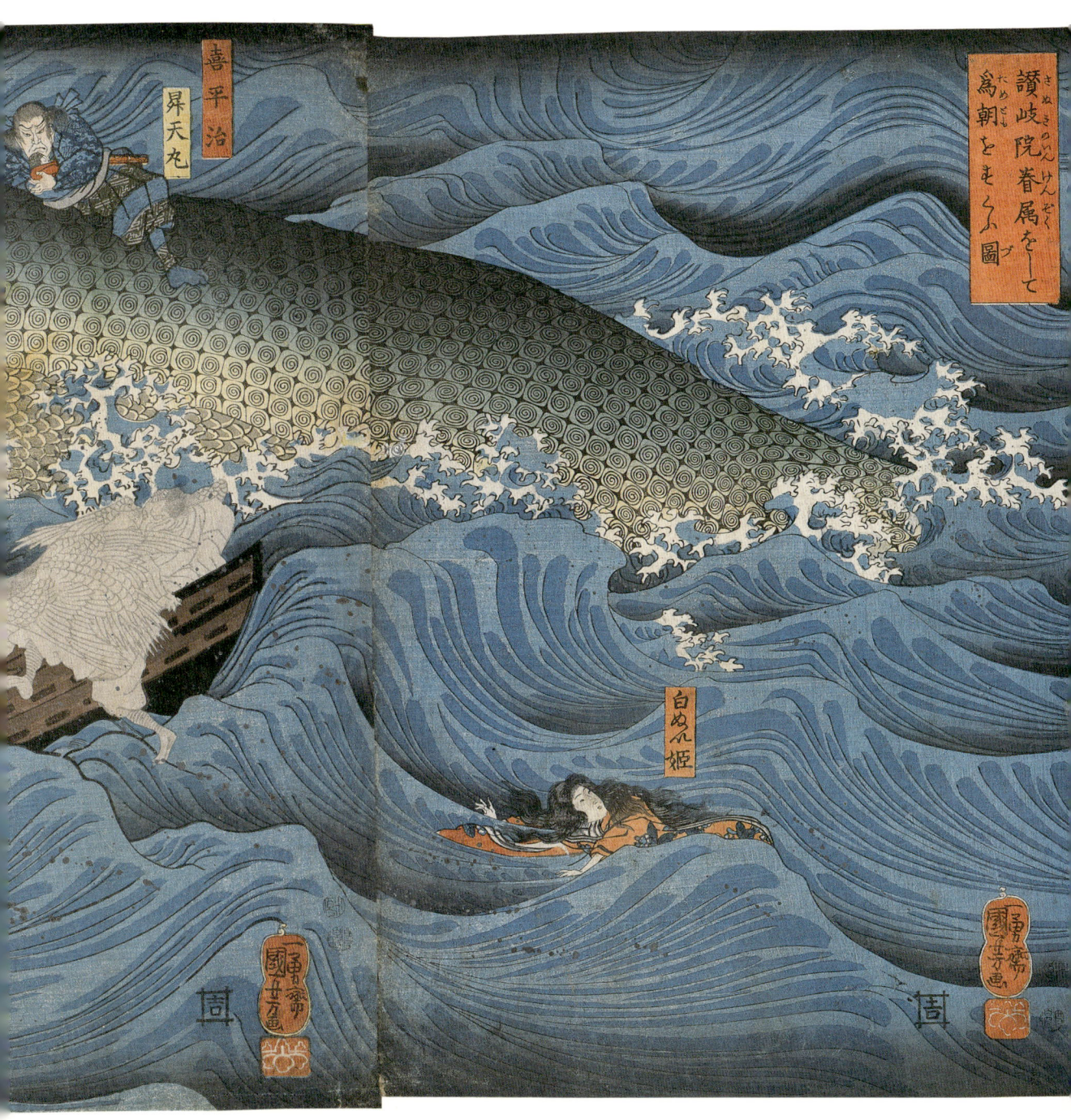

Tametomo Rescued by Tengu by Utagawa Kuniyoshi

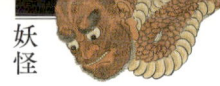

鬼婆

Hags
Demonic Creatures (*yōkai*)

214

逆さ吊りにされた半裸の妊婦。その下で包丁を研ぐ老
婆。胎児の生血を手に入れるため、一晩の宿を貸した
旅人の妻を惨殺します。この話は、鬼女がすんだという
黒塚の伝説をもとに、能や浄瑠璃に脚色されました。

A woman hangs upside down, half-naked and pregnant.
Below her, an old woman sharpens a knife. To get her
hands on the life's blood of an unborn child, the hag plans
to murder this traveller's wife to whom she offered
accommodation for the night. This story is based on the
legend of Kurozuka, where it was said a hag lived, and was
dramatized in Noh and *jōruri*.

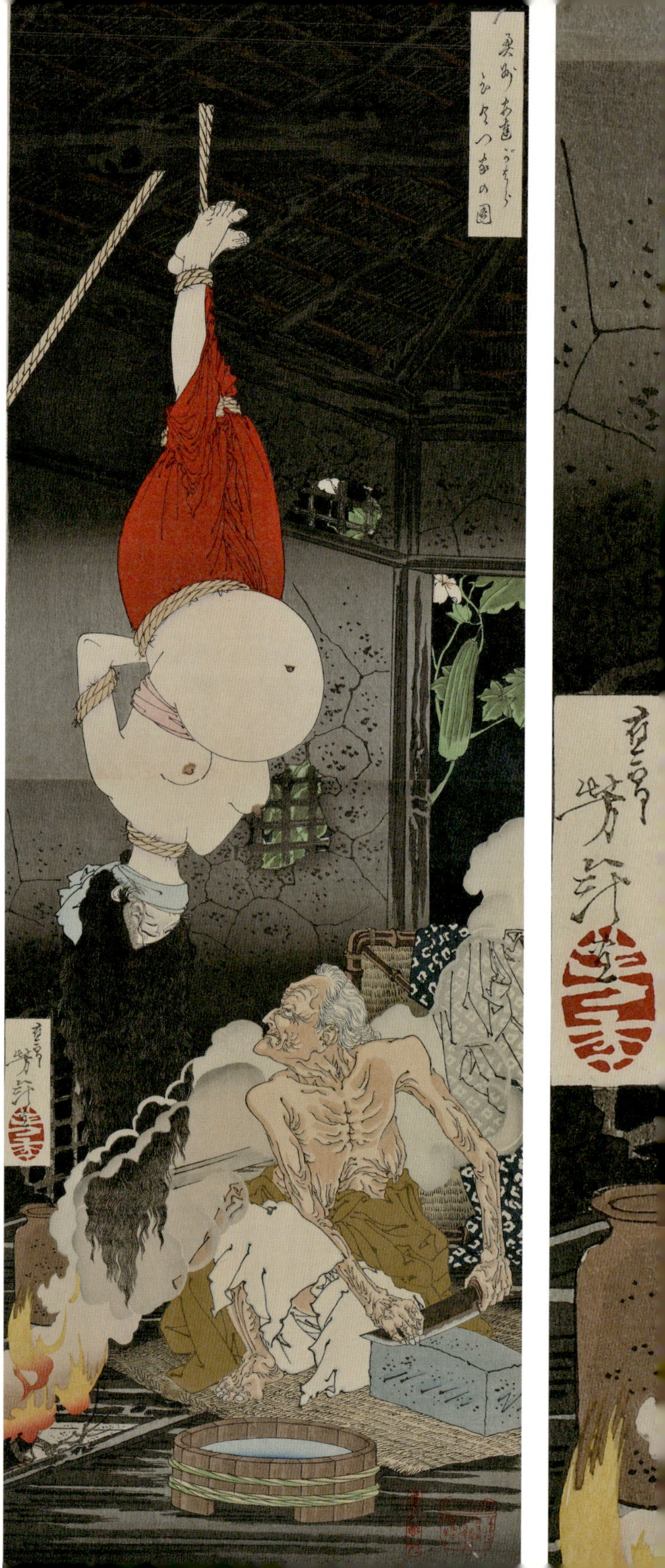

【奥州安達がはらひとつ家の図】
月岡芳年 明治18年 (1885)

The Lonely House at Adachigahara in Ōshū
by Tsukioka Yoshitoshi

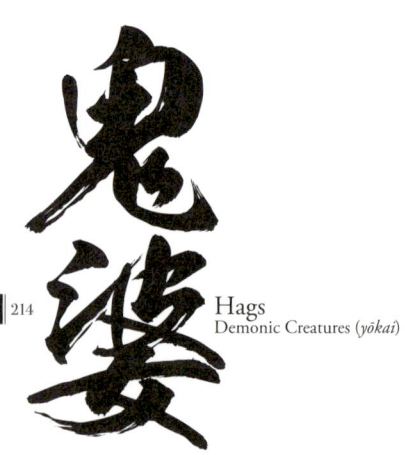

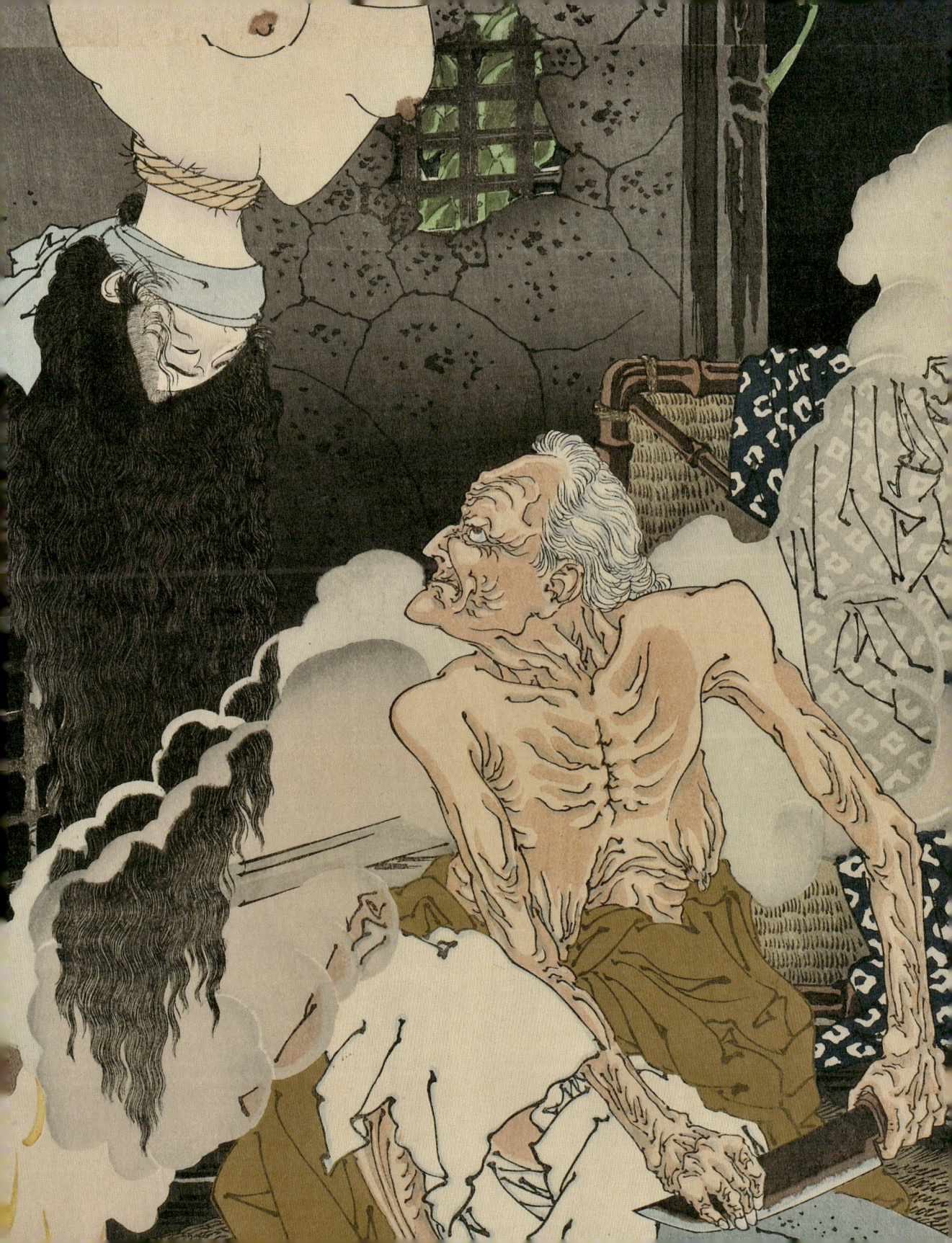

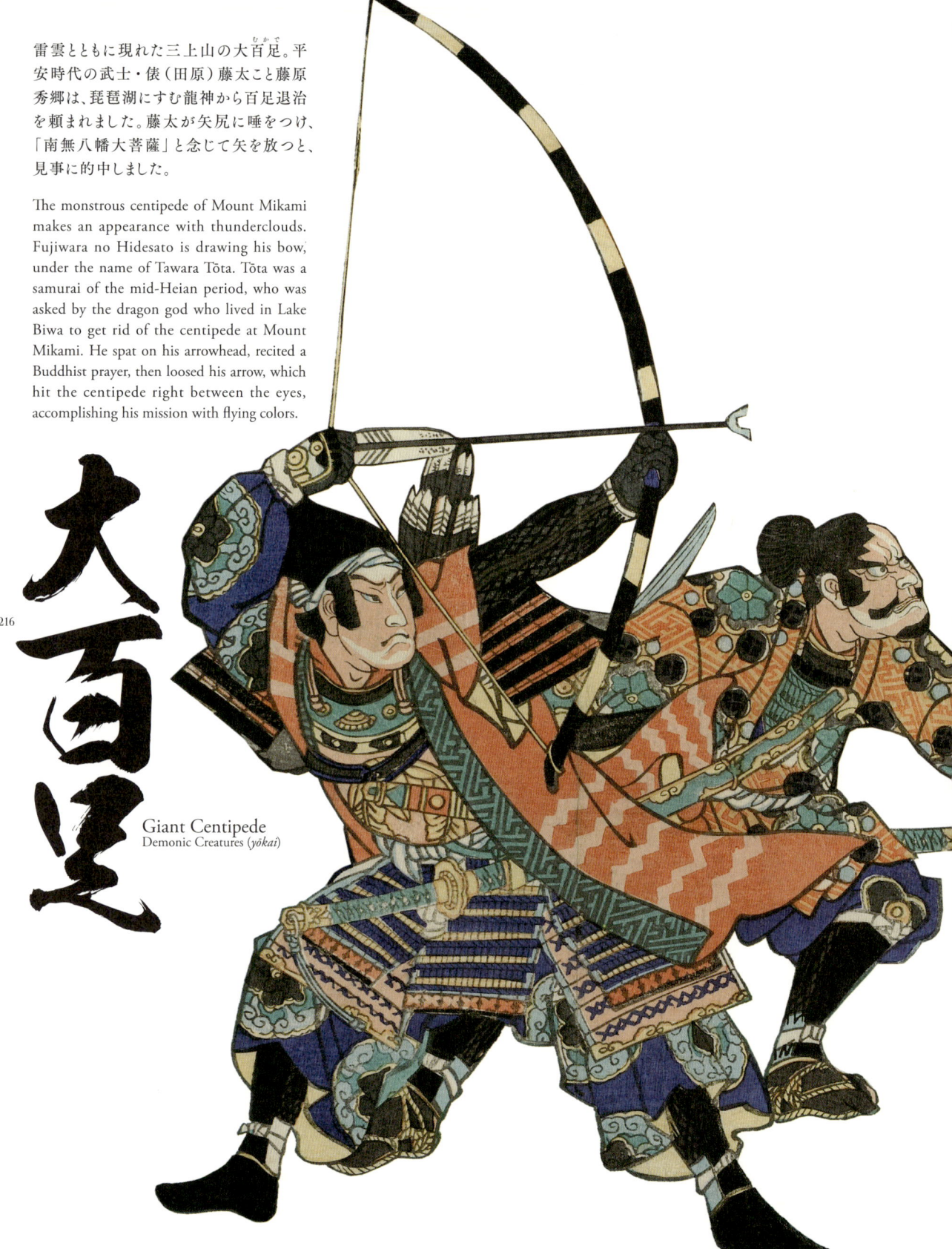

雷雲とともに現れた三上山の大百足。平安時代の武士・俵（田原）藤太こと藤原秀郷は、琵琶湖にすむ龍神から百足退治を頼まれました。藤太が矢尻に唾をつけ、「南無八幡大菩薩」と念じて矢を放つと、見事に的中しました。

The monstrous centipede of Mount Mikami makes an appearance with thunderclouds. Fujiwara no Hidesato is drawing his bow, under the name of Tawara Tōta. Tōta was a samurai of the mid-Heian period, who was asked by the dragon god who lived in Lake Biwa to get rid of the centipede at Mount Mikami. He spat on his arrowhead, recited a Buddhist prayer, then loosed his arrow, which hit the centipede right between the eyes, accomplishing his mission with flying colors.

大百足

Giant Centipede
Demonic Creatures (*yōkai*)

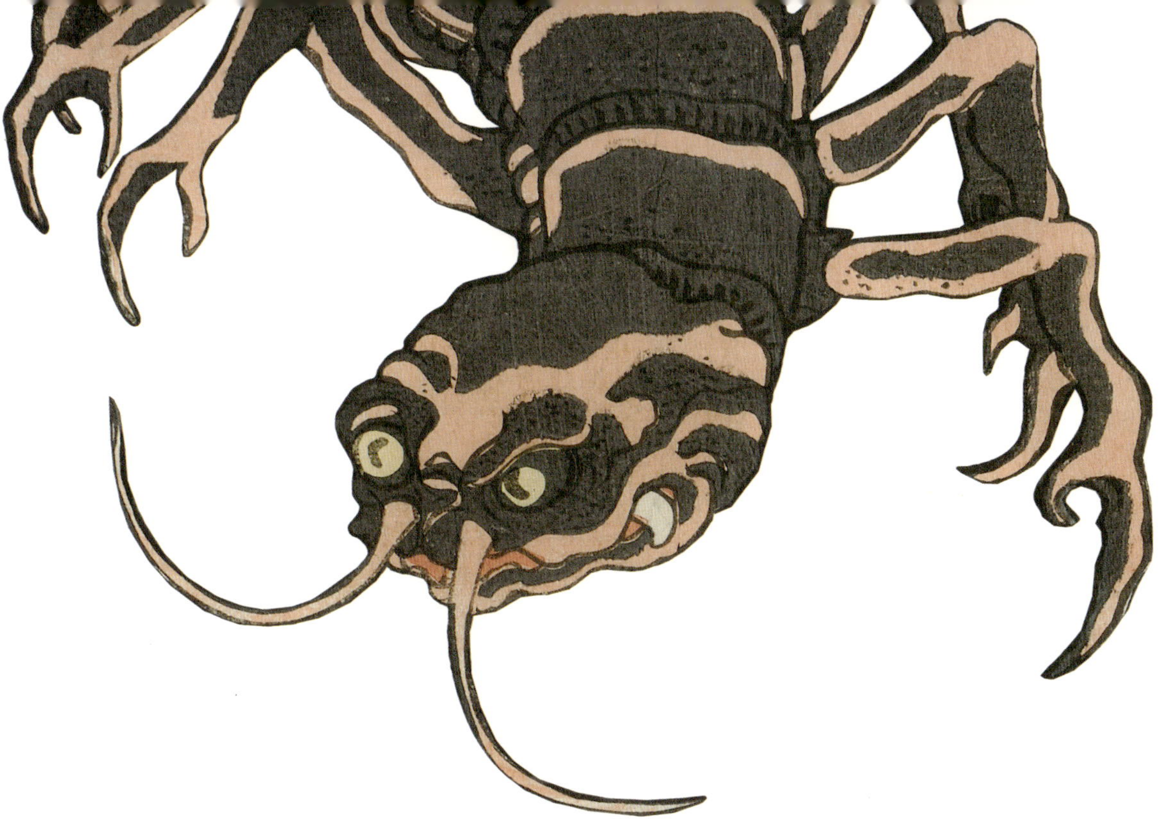

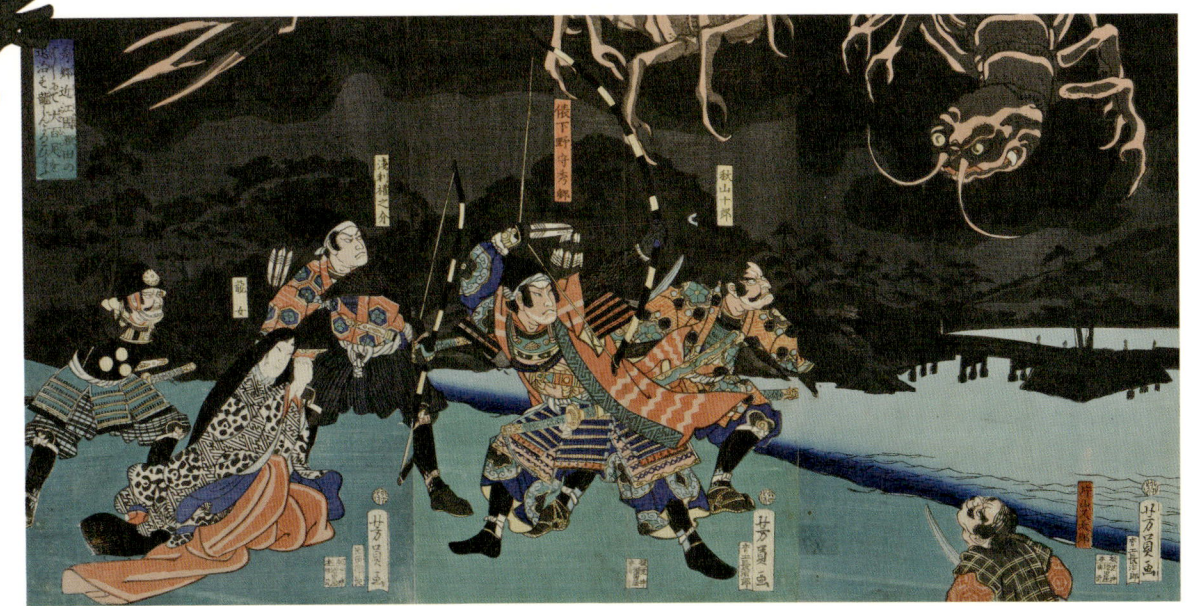

【秀郷近江国瀬田のはしにて大百足を退治す龍じんよろこび給ふ】
歌川芳員 慶応3年（1867）

Hidesato Kills the Giant Centipede at Seta Bridge in Omi Province: The Dragon God is Pleased
by Utagawa Yoshikazu

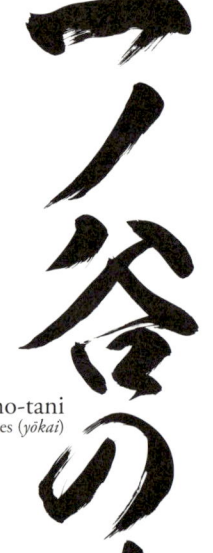

一ノ谷の猪

The Boar of Ichi-no-tani
Demonic Creatures (*yōkai*)

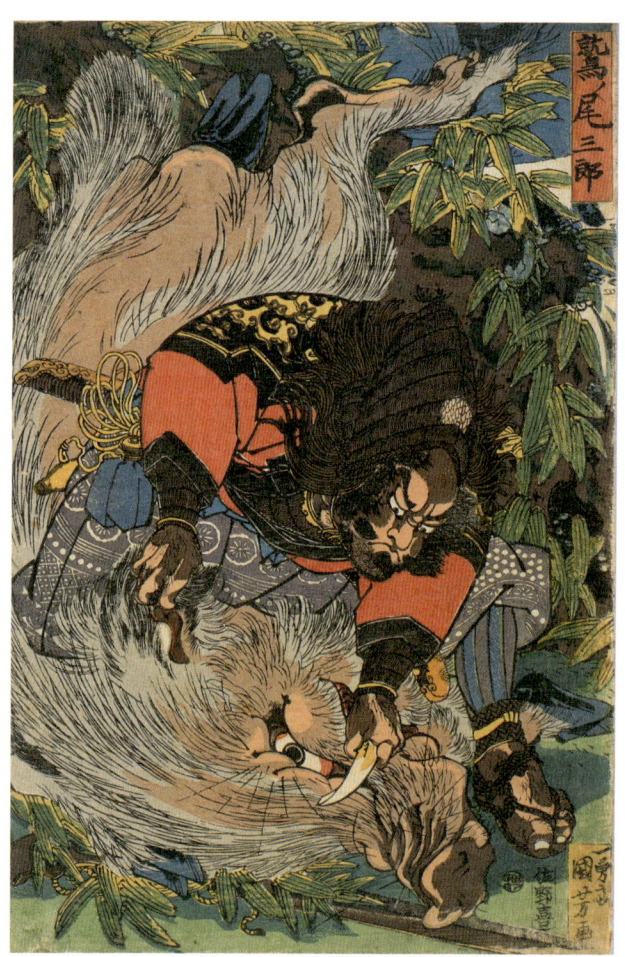

鷲（ノ）尾三郎は、源平合戦の一ノ谷の戦いに登場する猟師の子で、義経の「鵯越の逆落とし」において先頭に立ちました。その際、熊を退治した伝説が残っていますが、図では猪となっています。三郎は、そのまま義経郎党となりました。

The son of a huntsman who featured in the Battle of Ichi-no-tani of the Genpei War, Washi-no-o Saburō took a leading role in Yoshitsune's downhill attack at Hiyodorigoe. Legends from that time tell of the killing of a bear, but a boar is pictured. Saburō became one of Yoshitsune's followers.

【鷲ノ尾三郎】歌川国芳　文政9-10年（1826-1827）頃
Washi-no-o Saburō by Utagawa Kuniyoshi

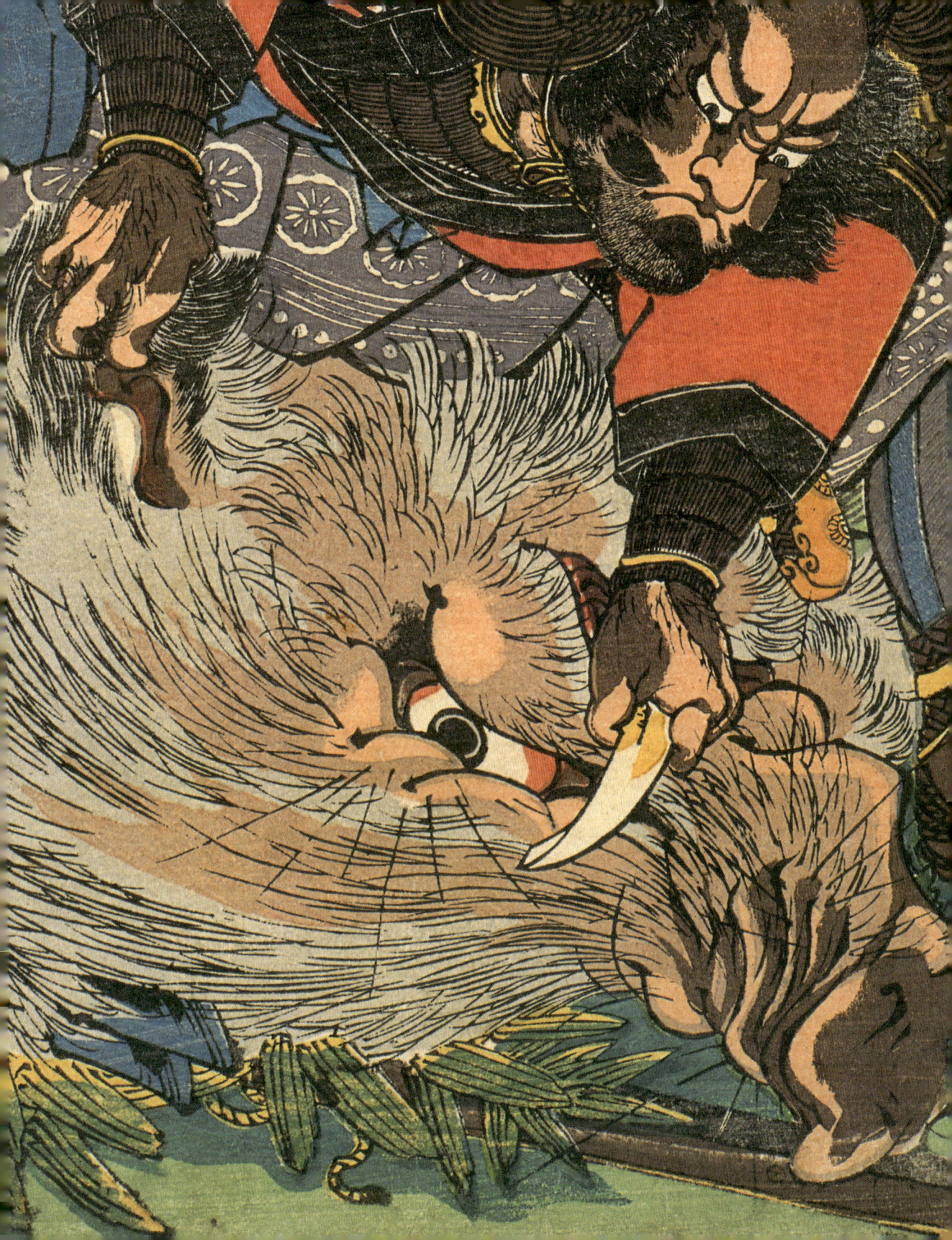

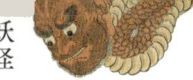

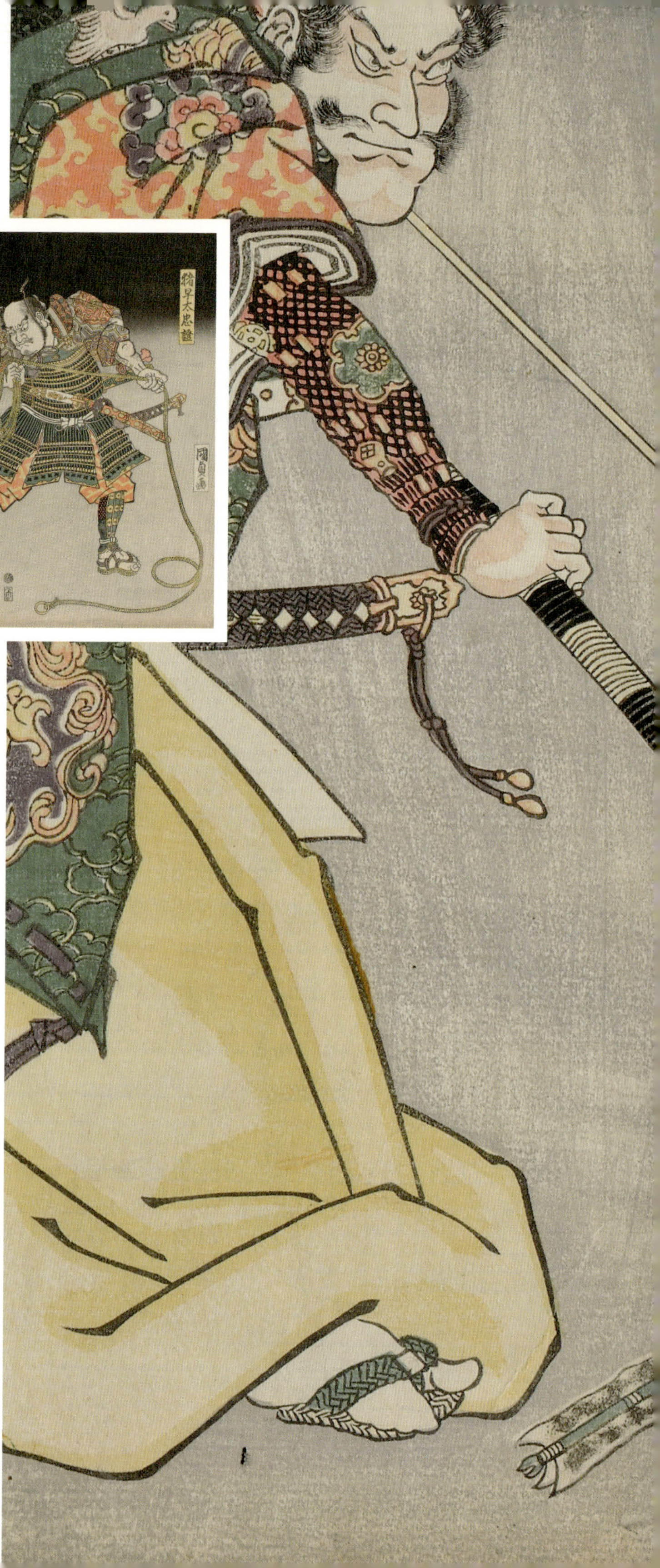

妖怪

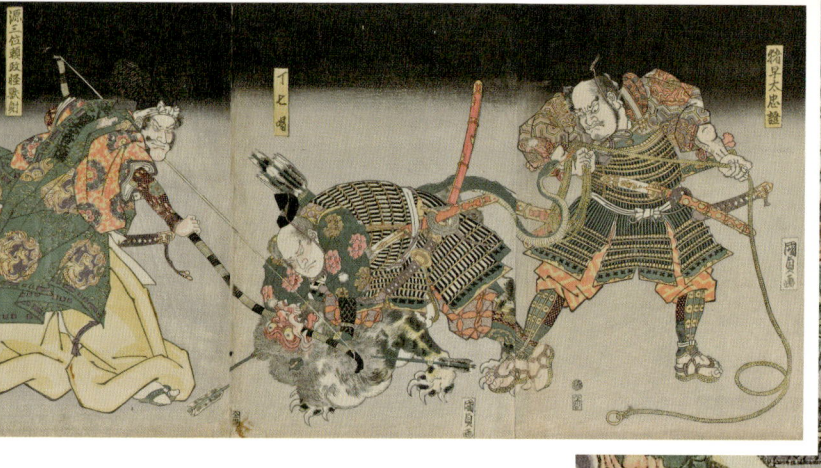

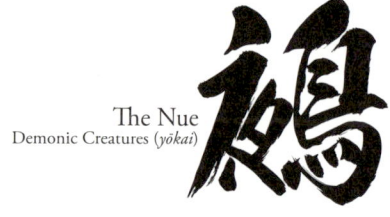

The Nue
Demonic Creatures (*yōkai*)

鵺

平安末期、内裏の紫宸殿上に、鵺という頭は猿、胴は
狸、尾は蛇、手足は虎に似た正体不明の化け物が現れ
ます。夜ごと不気味な声で鳴き、帝を苦しめました。勅命
を受けた源三位入道こと源頼政（左）が鵺を射落とし、
郎党の猪早太（右）と丁七唱（中）が取り押さえます。

In the late Heian period, the obscure monster with the head
of a monkey, the body of a raccoon dog, the tail of a snake,
and the limbs of a tiger, known as the Nue, appeared on
Shishinden Hall in the Imperial Palace. Each night its weird
cries terrorized the Emperor. By Imperial command,
Minamoto no Yorimasa of the Third Rank (left) shoots
down the Nue, and retainers Ino Hayata (right) and
Chōshichi Tonau (center) overpower it.

【源三位頼政怪獣射】
歌川国貞（三代豊国）文化年間（1804-18）末期

*Minamoto no Yorimasa of the Third Rank Shooting
a Monster* by Utagawa Kunisada
(also known as Utagawa Toyokuni III)

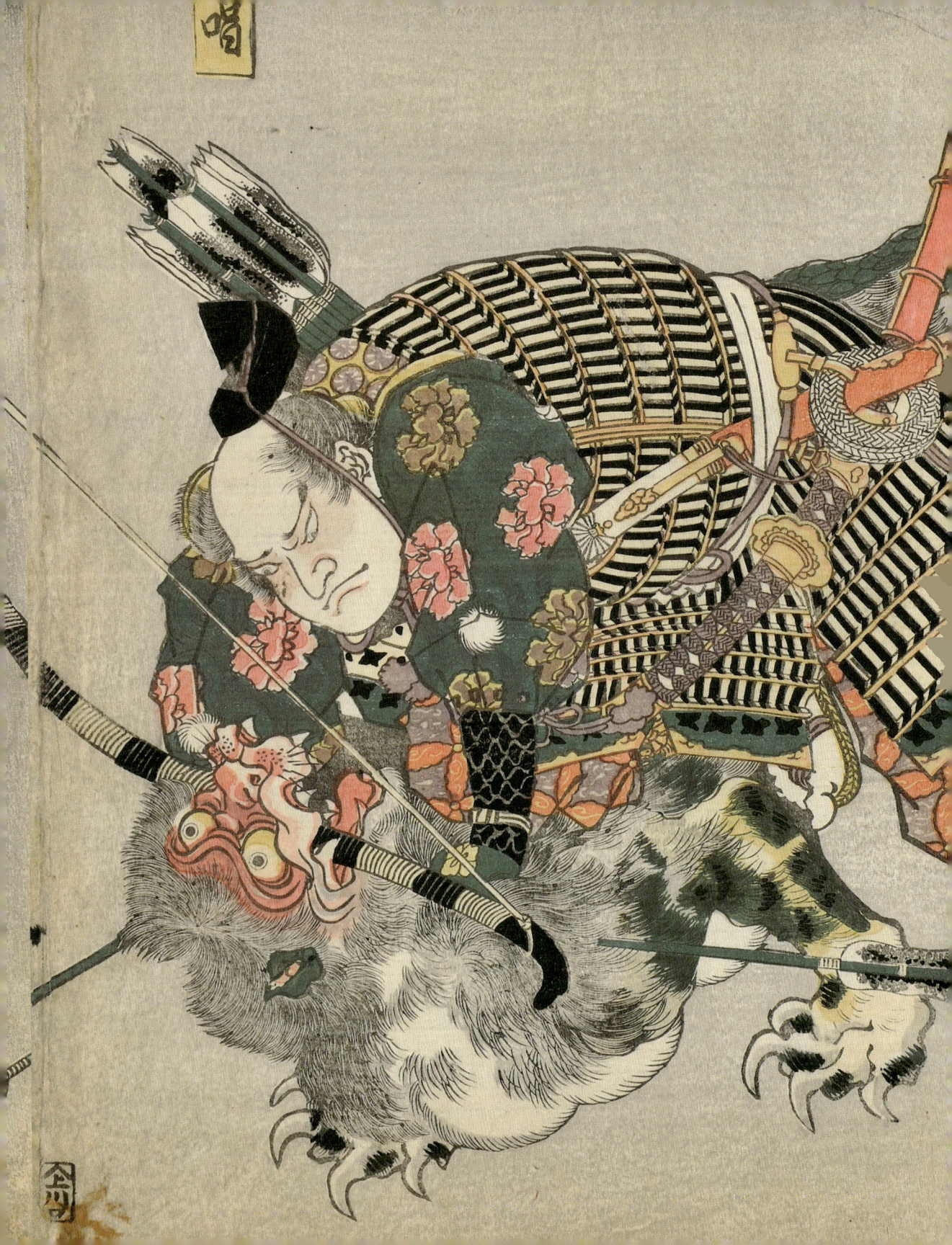

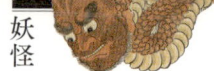

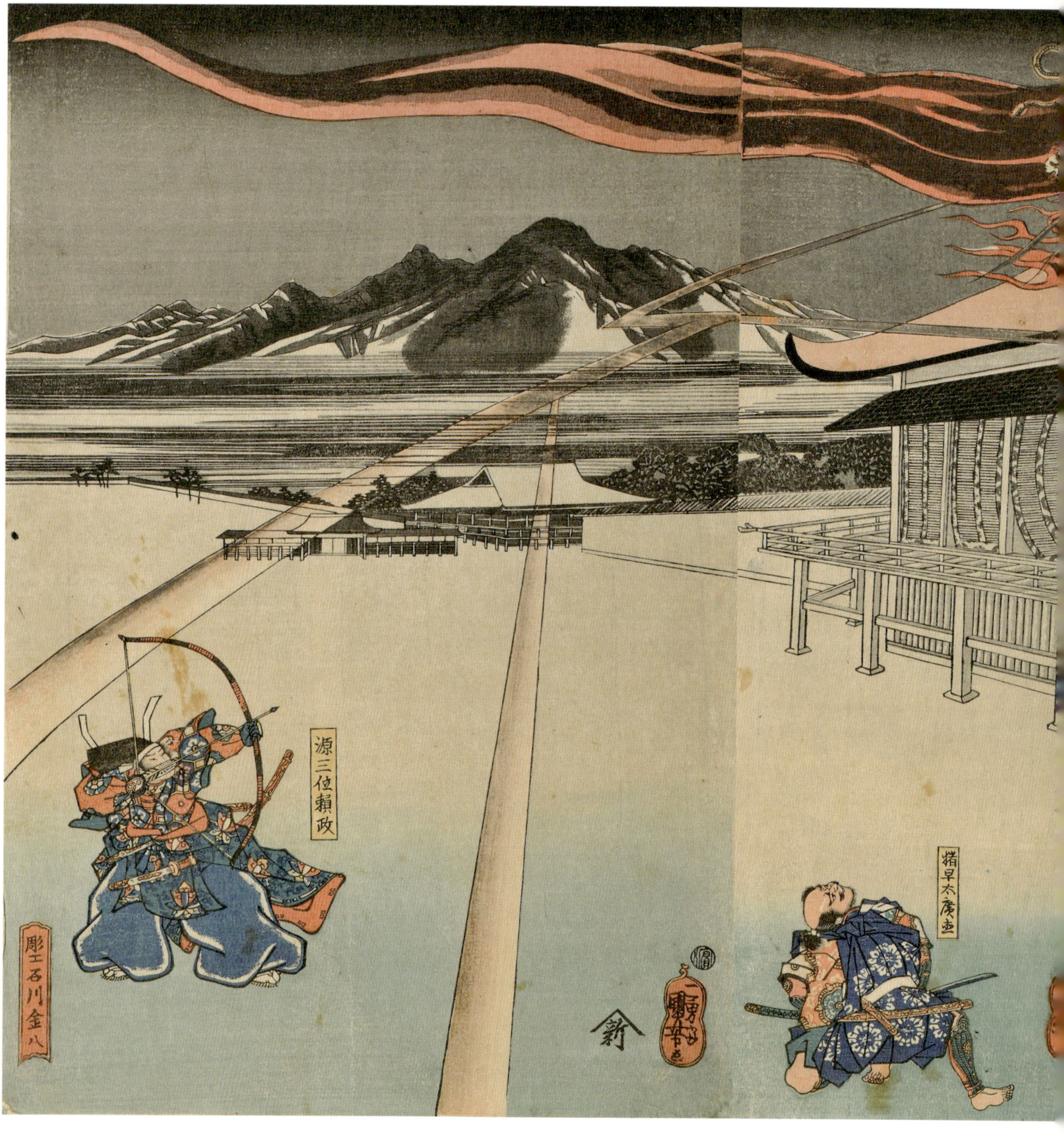

【近衛院の内裏に怪鳥あらわれる】歌川国芳 天保14年（1843）
夜な夜な、東三条の森のほうからやってきて、紫宸殿上を覆う黒雲。そこから発せられる不気味な声に、近衛天皇は怯えます。
勅命を受けた源三位頼政が、黒雲目がけて弓を構えます。

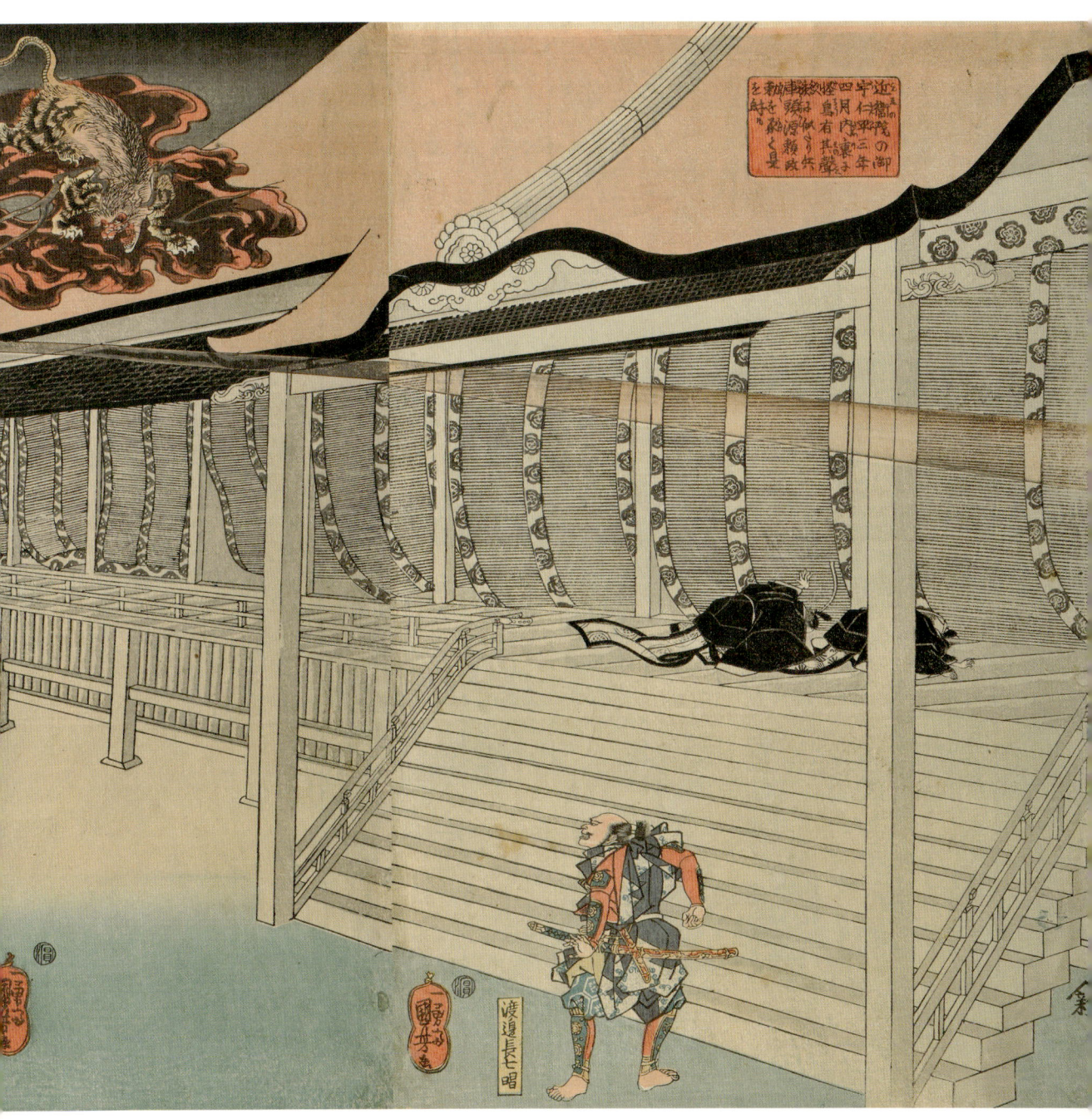

In the Reign of Emperor Konoe, a Monstrous Bird Appears by Utagawa Kuniyoshi

Night after night, from the forest of Higashi-Sanjō, a black cloud came to cover Shishinden Hall. An uncanny cry emanating from within it frightened Emperor Konoe. Yorimasa of the Third Rank (left), by Imperial command, has his bow and arrow at the ready to shoot at the black cloud.

【源三位頼政鵺退治の図】歌川国芳 文政9-10年(1826-27)頃

「南無八幡大菩薩」と念じて頼政が放った矢は、見事、鵺に命中。落ちて来る鵺を斬ろうと、猪早太が待ち構えます。
渡辺丁七唱が両手を大きく広げて駆けつけます。

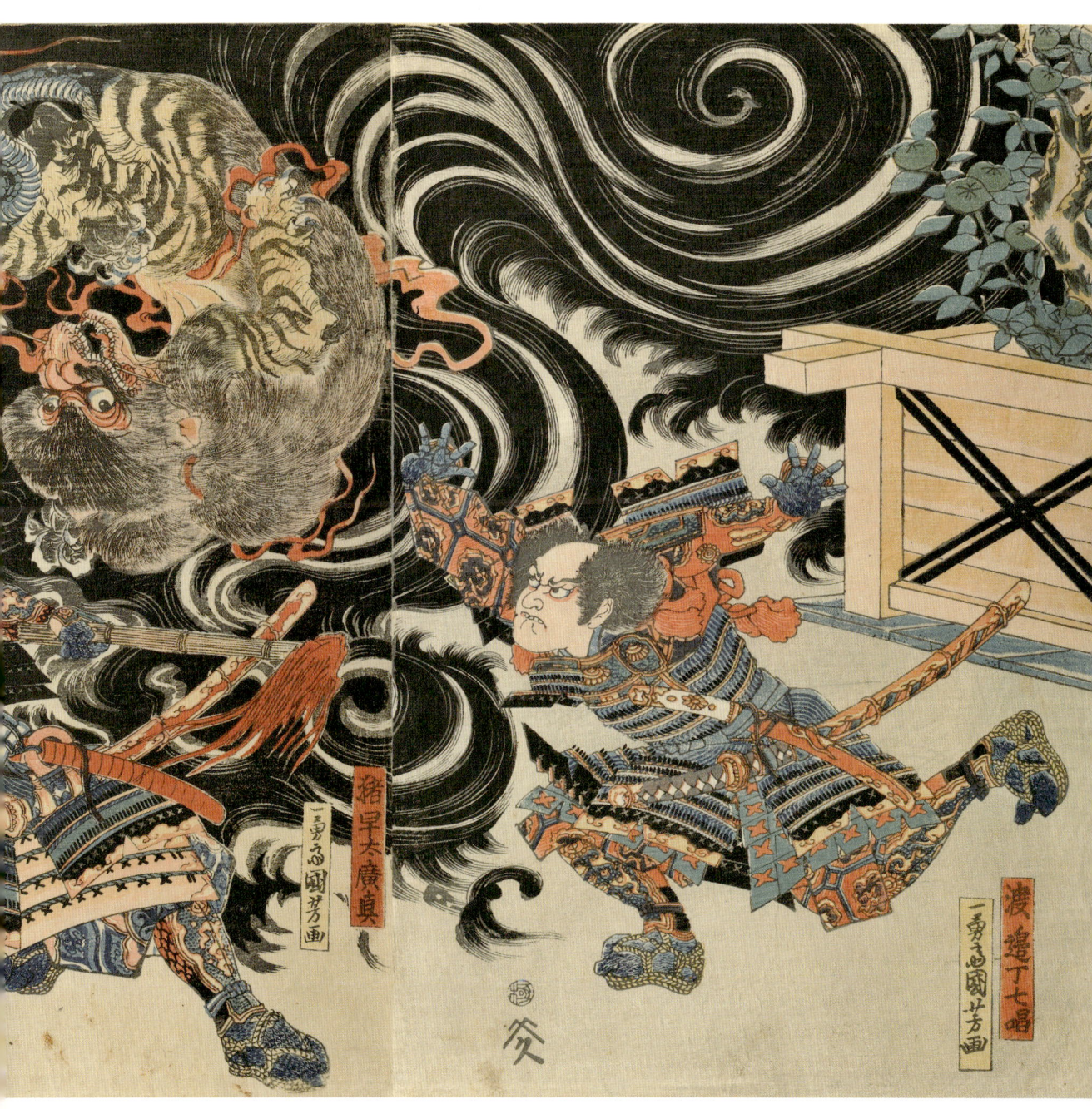

Yorimasa of the Third Rank Slaying the Nue by Utagawa Kuniyoshi

The arrow Yorimasa loosed while praying has scored a direct hit. Ino Hayata is ready and waiting to slash at the falling Nue. Watanabe Chōshichi Tonau is rushing forward with arms wide open.

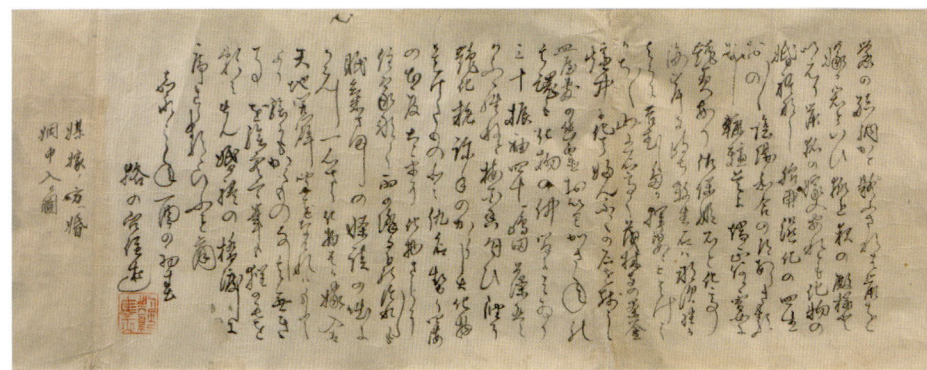

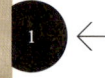

【妖怪嫁入り絵巻】
盤礴居　嘉永6年（1853）
*Scroll Painting of
a Yōkai Marriage*
by Banhakukyo

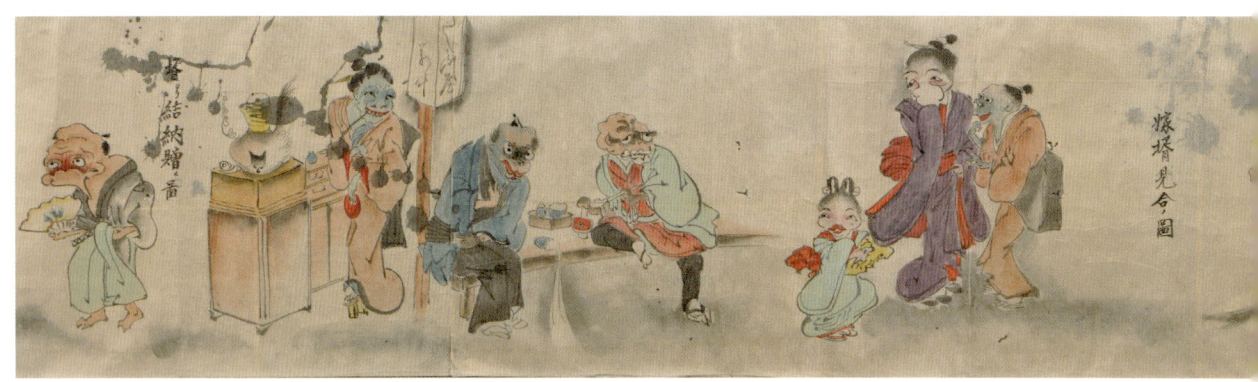

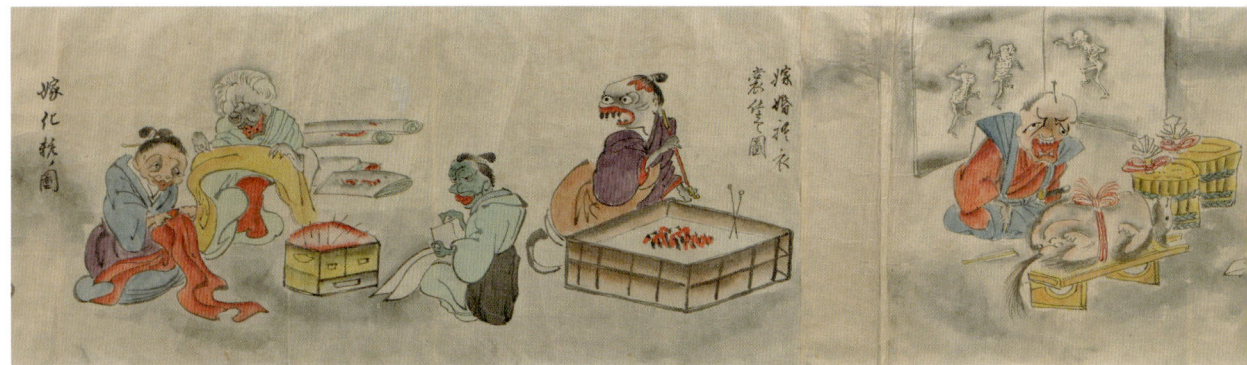

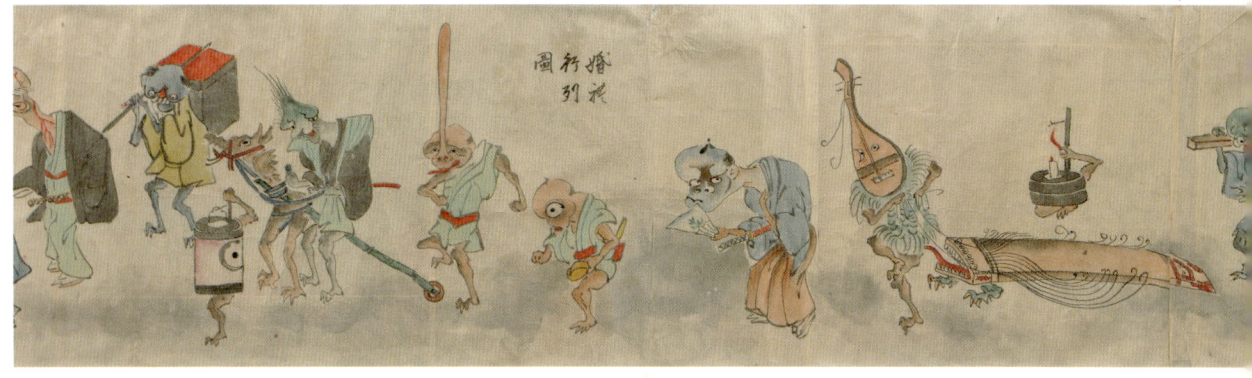

226

妖怪同士の結婚物語を描いた絵巻。仲人の縁組からはじまり、お見合い、結納、嫁入り支度、道具入れ、花嫁行列、祝言、祝い膳、腹帯祝い、出産、出産祝い、お宮参りと物語が進みます。そして、最後は日の出とともに一斉に退散します。長寿の祝詞とともに宝船がやってきて、めでたしめでたし。

A scroll painting (*emaki*) depicting the story of a marriage between *yōkai* (demonic creatures). The story progresses quickly from the engagement of matchmakers, to the introduction of the prospective marriage partners (*o-miai*), the betrothal gifts, the bride's outfit, the presentation of wedding gifts of furniture from the husband's family, the bride's procession, quotes for the occasion, the offering of congratulations, baby shower, birth, gifts for the new baby, and baby's first shrine visit. Finally, everything vanishes with the break of day. Accompanied by Shinto prayers for long life, their treasure ship (*takarabune*) comes in, and they all live happily ever after.

*Scrolls unscroll from right to left.

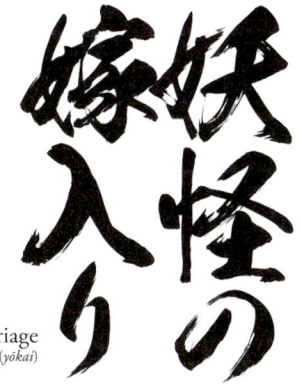

Yōkai Marriage
Demonic Creatures (*yōkai*)

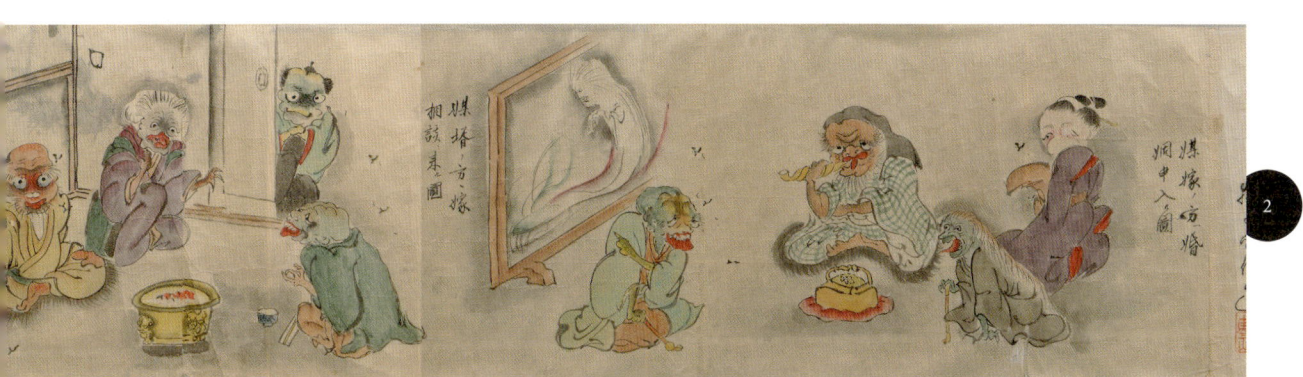

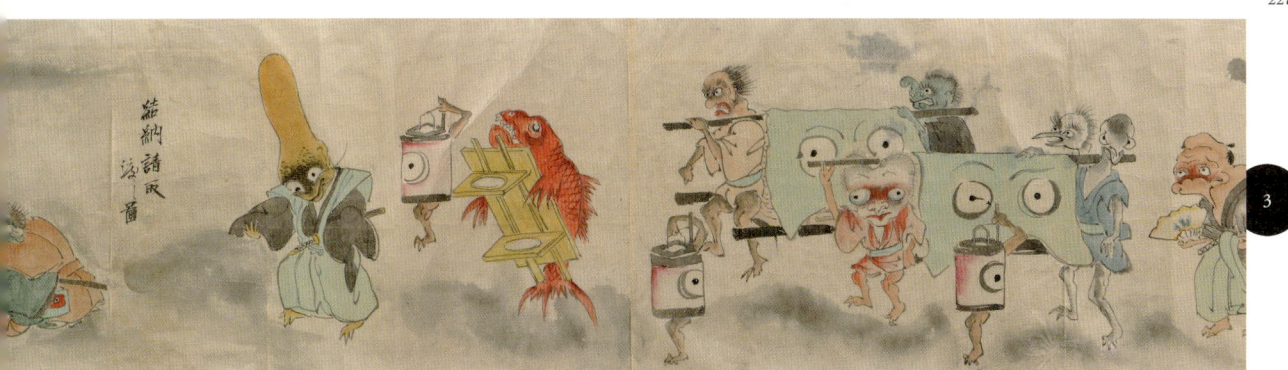

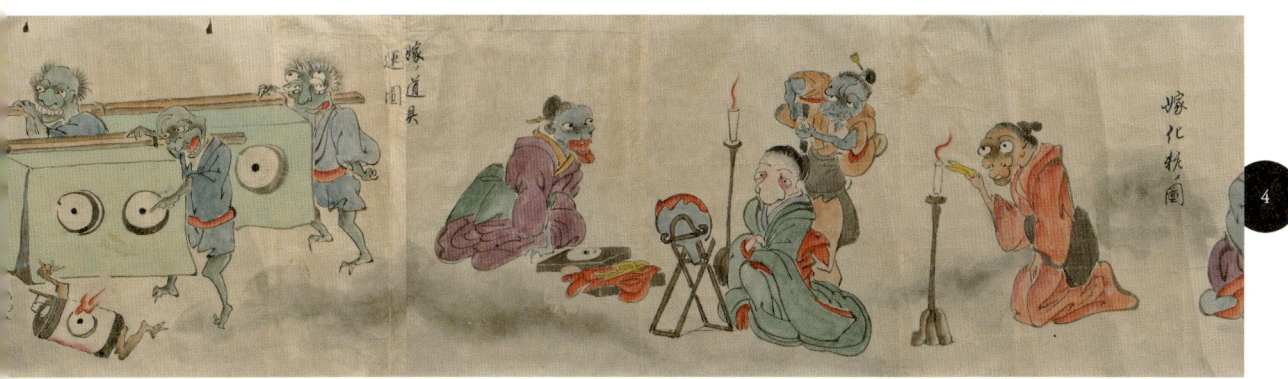

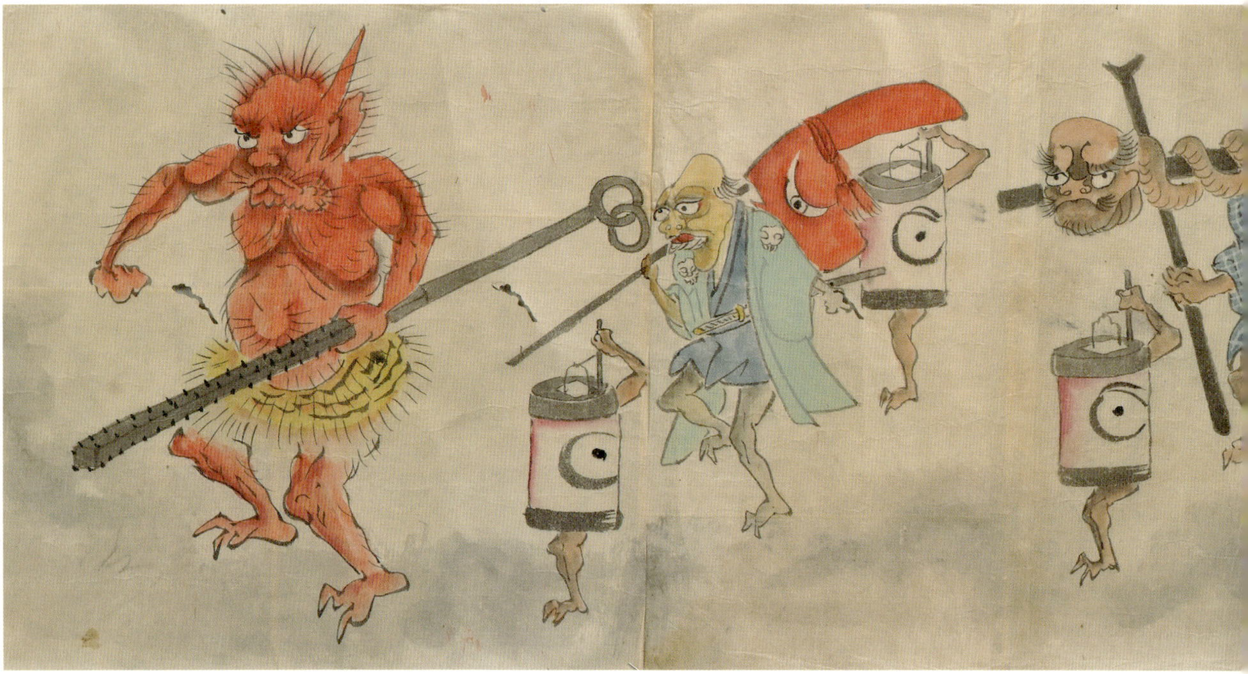

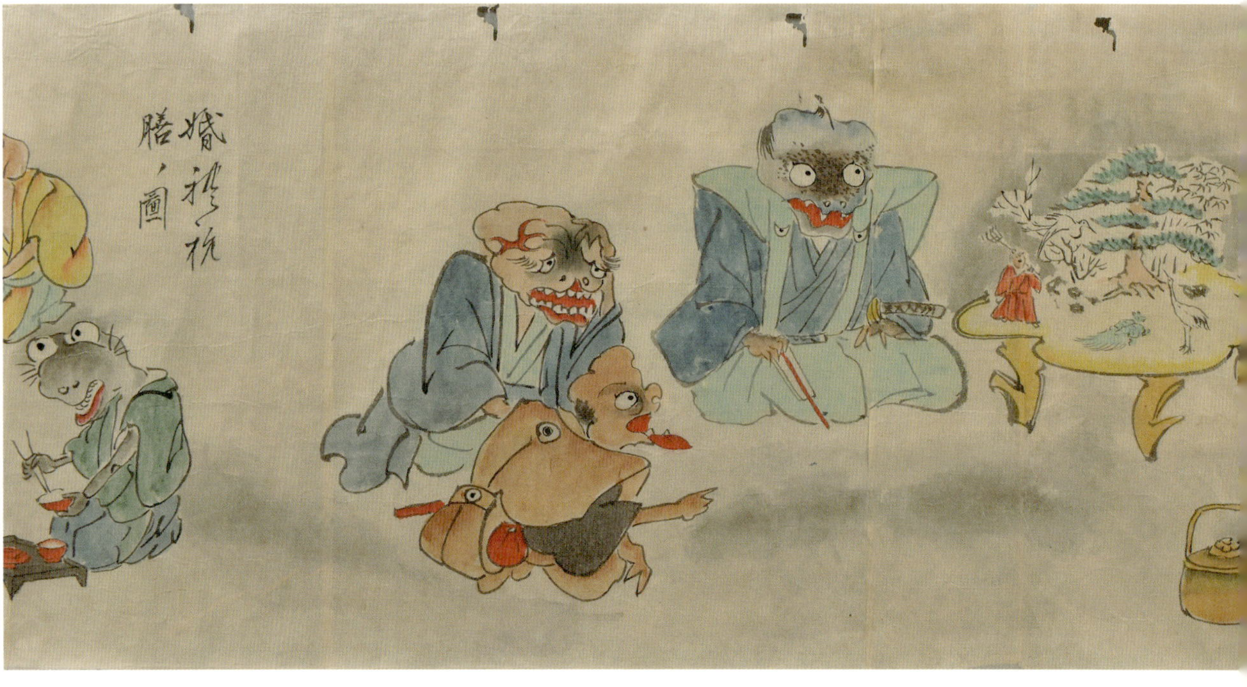

婚礼祝
膳ノ圖

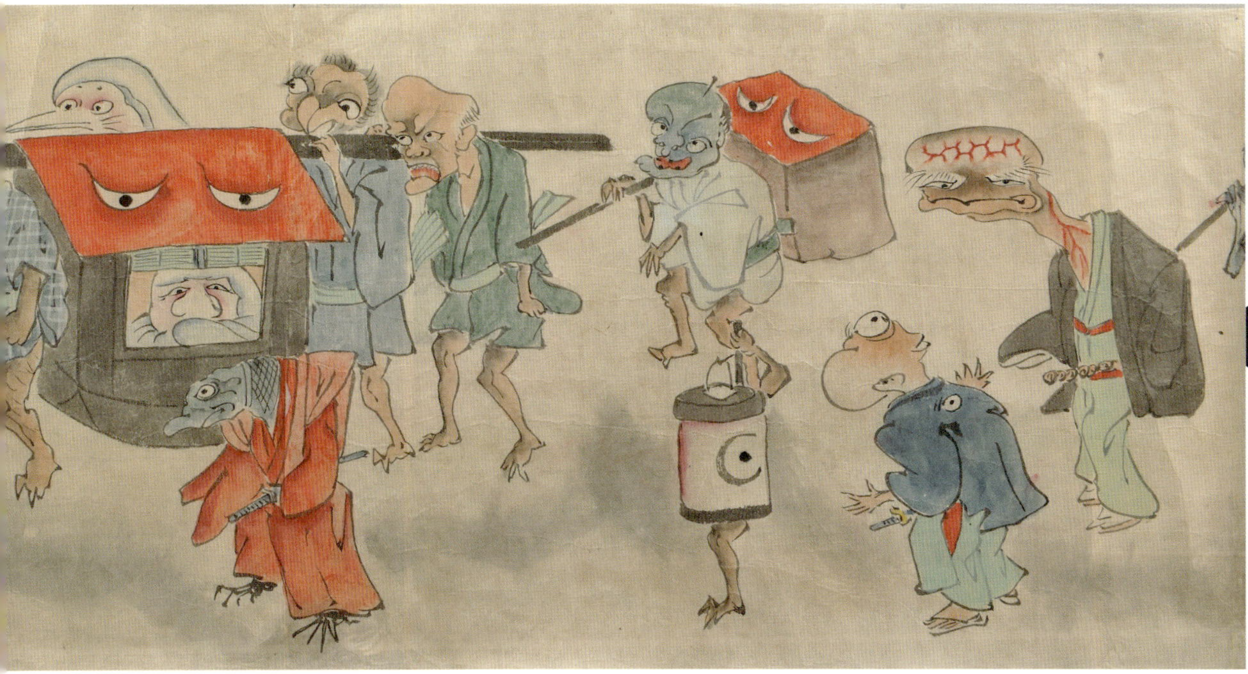

嫁入り行列ノ図 The bride's procession.

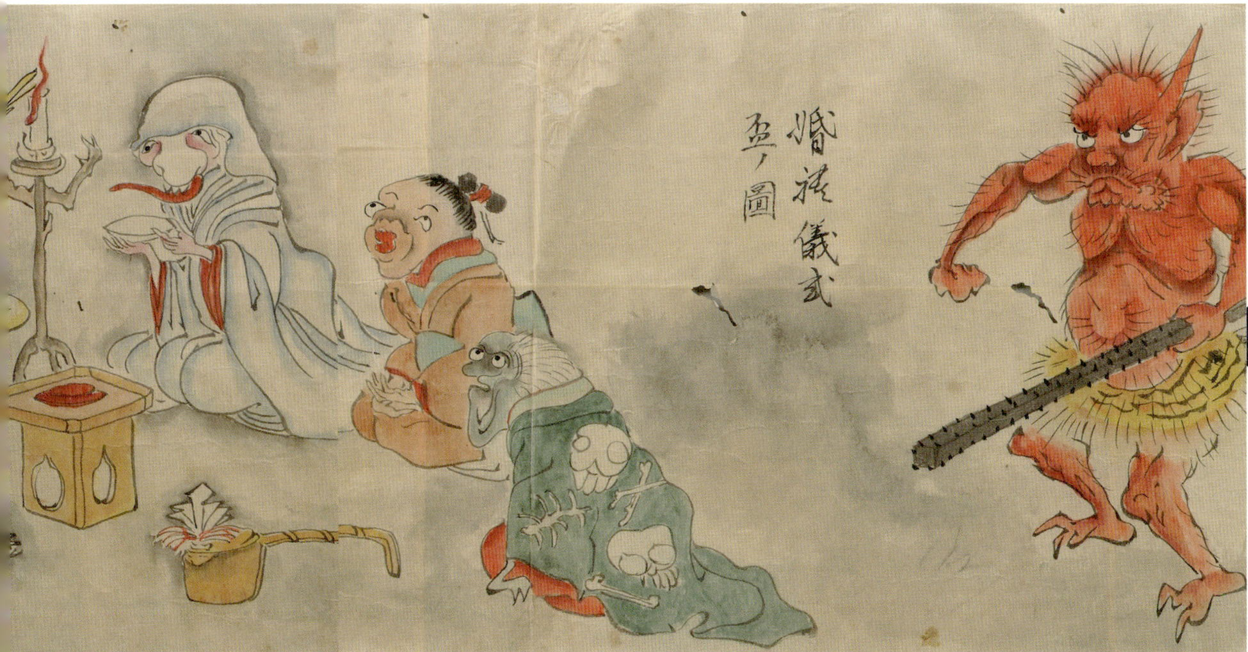

婚礼儀式盃ノ図 The offering of congratulations (toast).

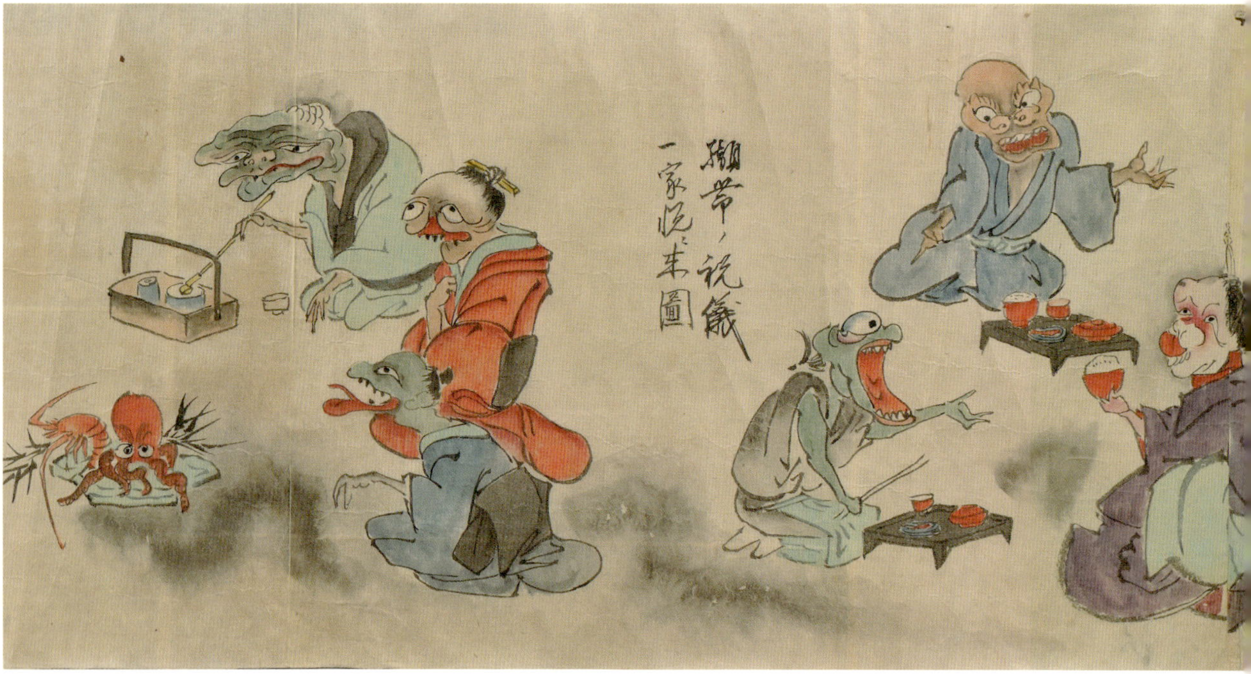

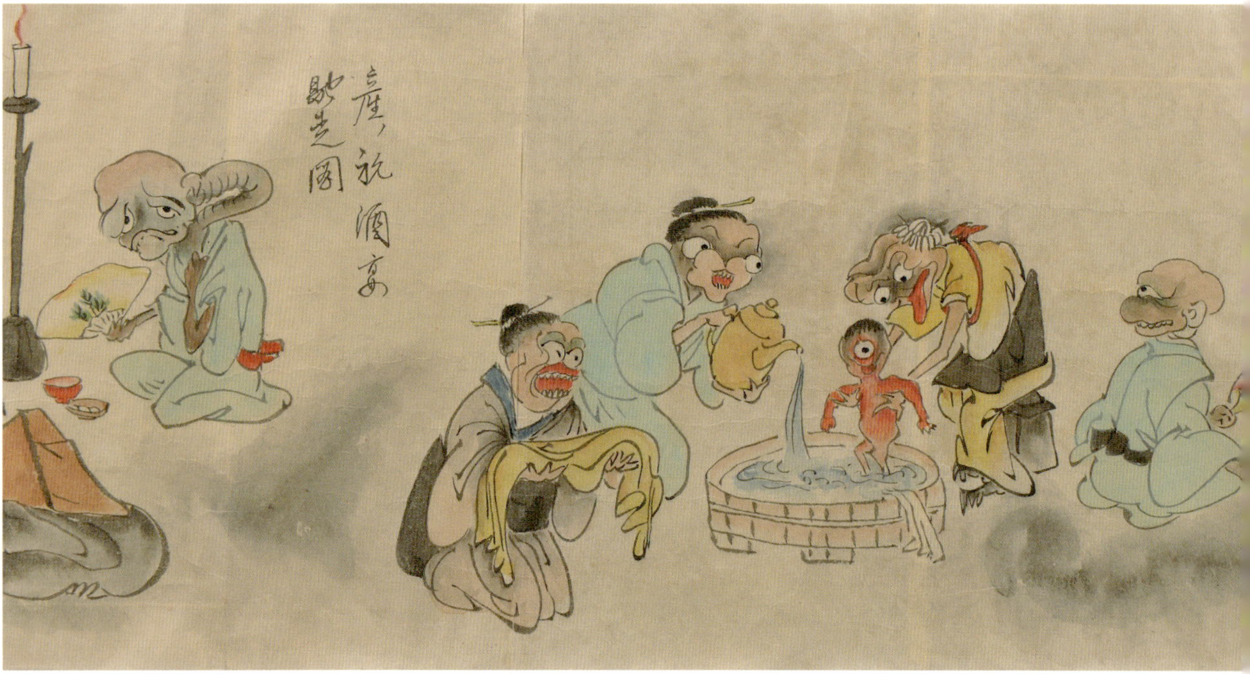

臍帯ノ祝儀 一家呪ヒ来ル圖

産ノ祝酒宴 駄差圖

安産ノ図　The birth.

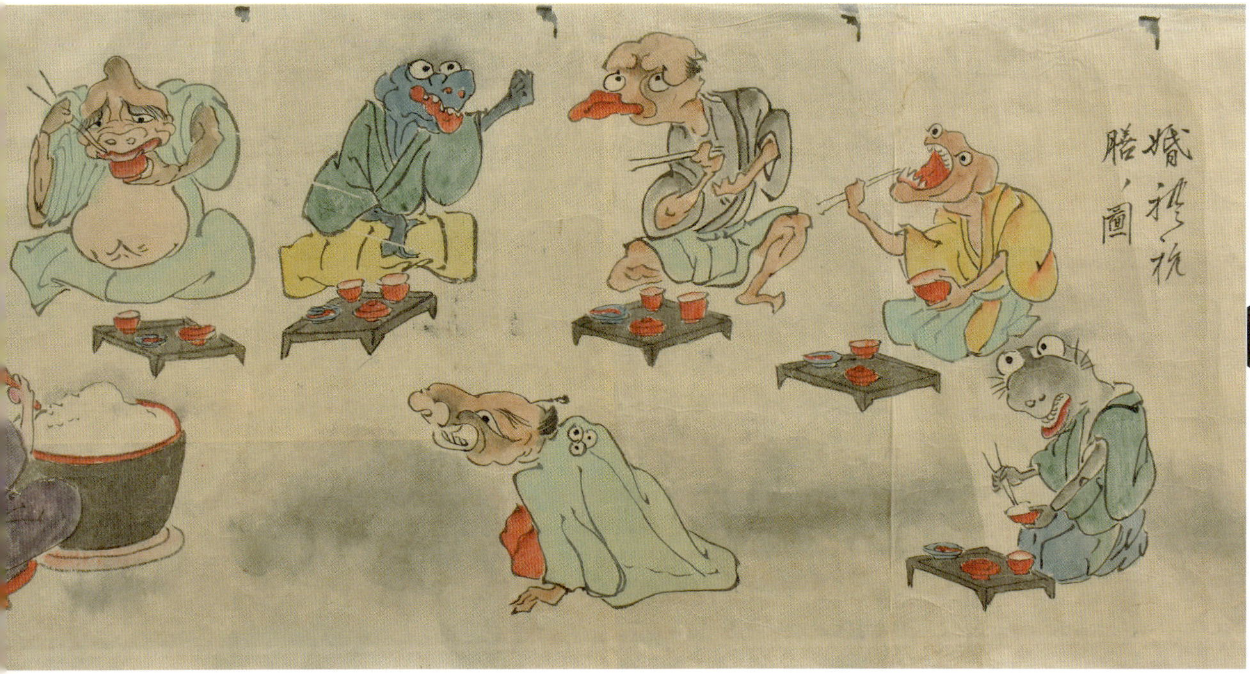

婚礼祝膳ノ図　The offering of congratulations (feast).

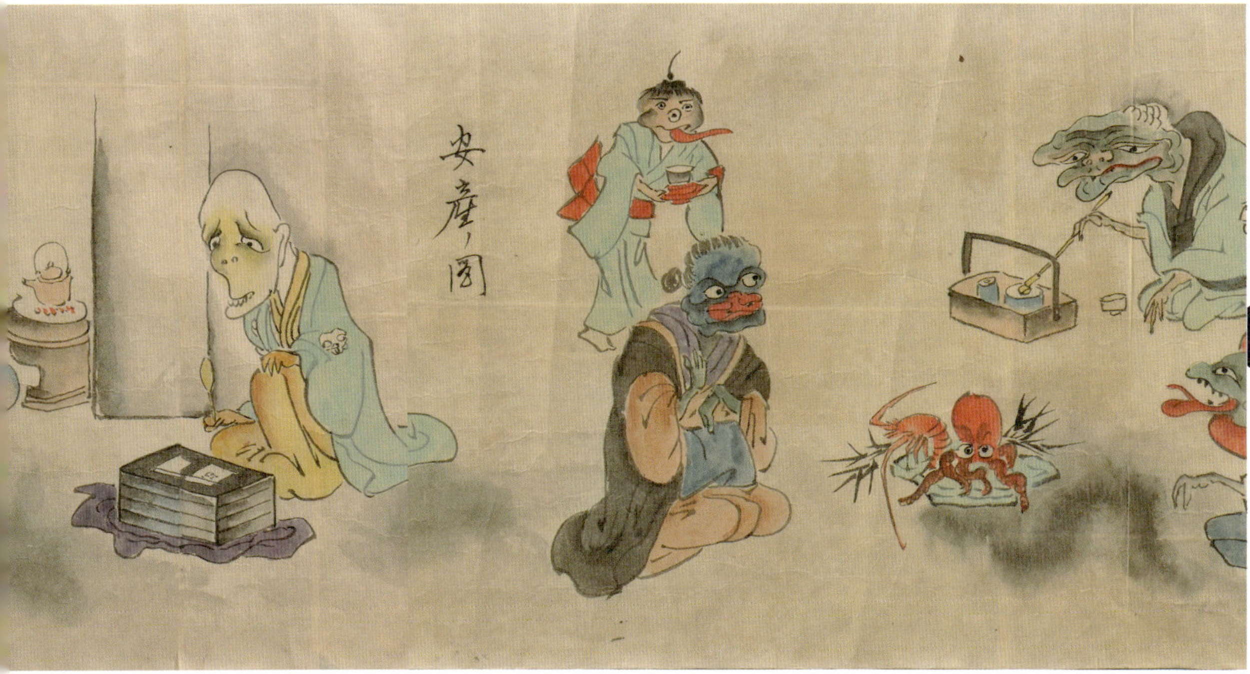

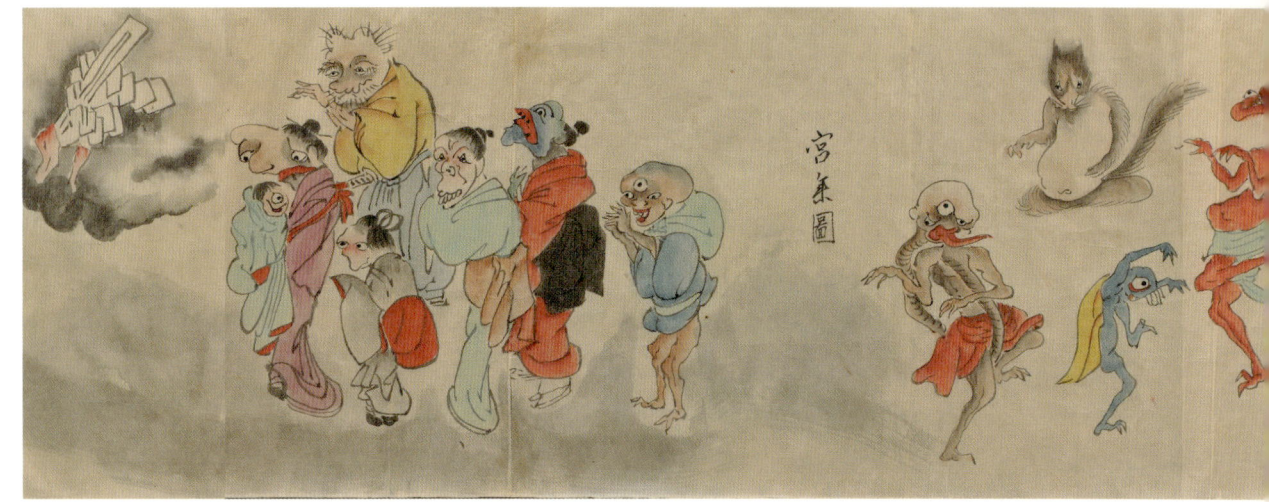

宮参り図 The baby's first visit to shrine.

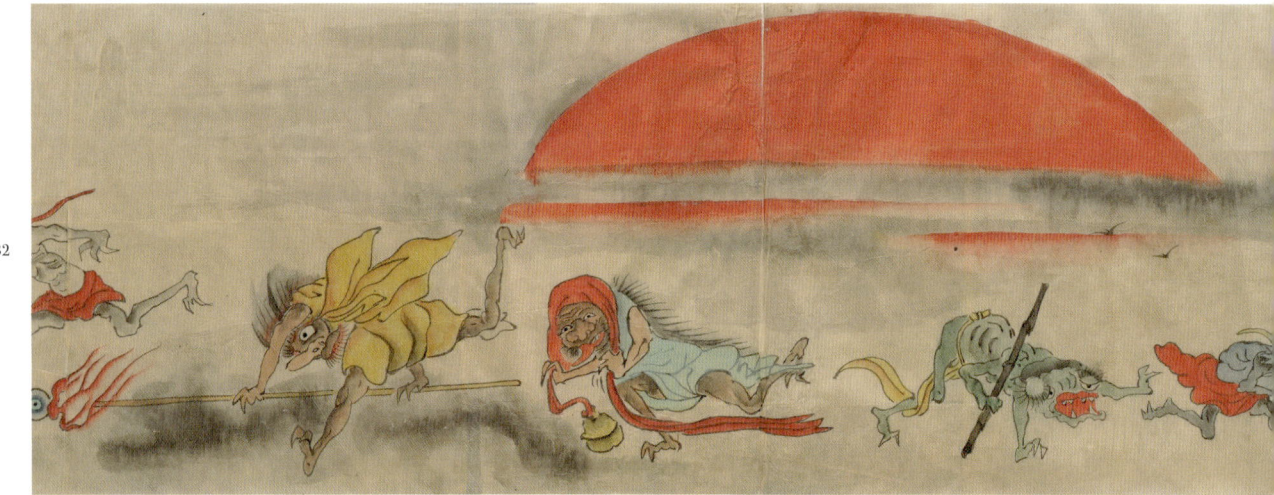

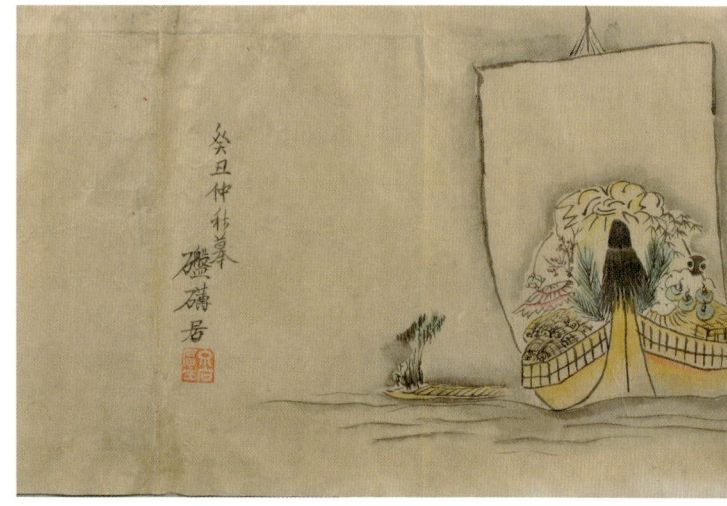

千秋萬歳宝入船 *Takarabune* (lit. treasure ship), a symbol of auspiciousness.

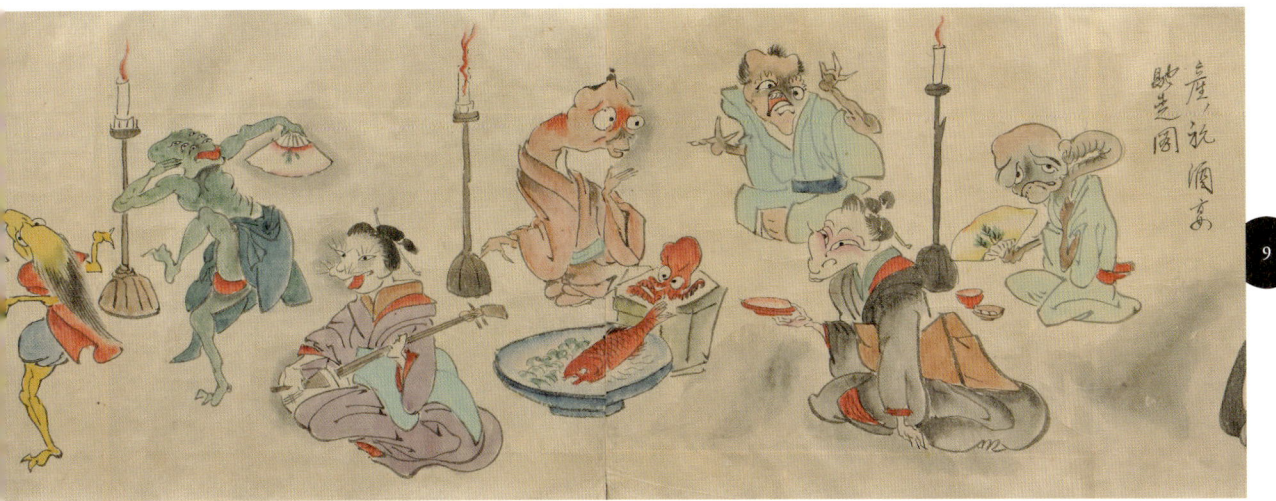

産の祝 酒宴馳走図 Congratulating for birth (feast).

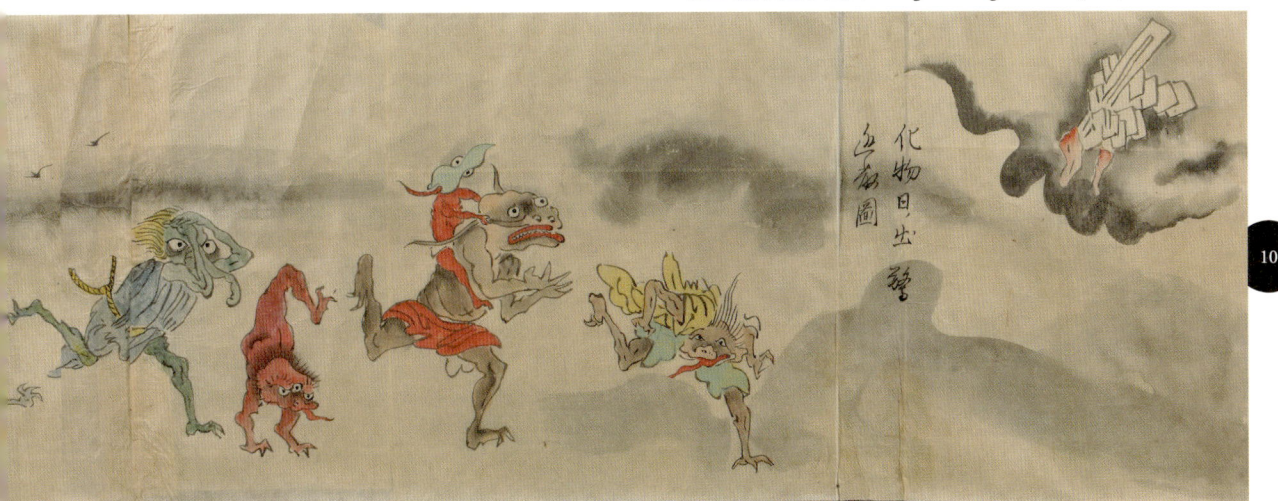

化物日の出撃退放図 Fleeing from the rising sun.

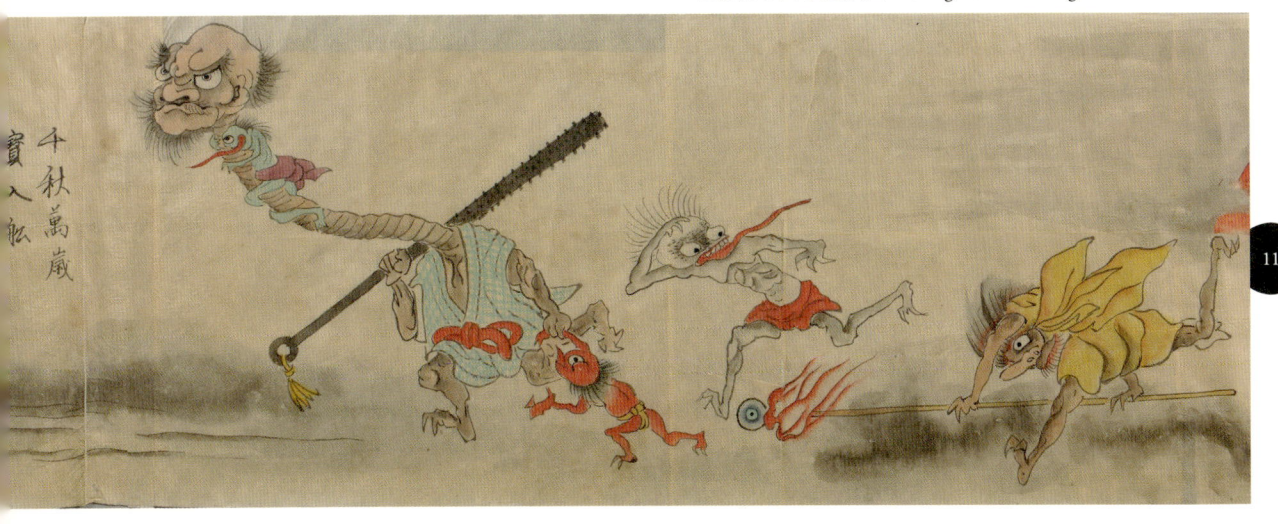

浮世絵とは

今から350年ほど前の江戸時代初期、日本(江戸)で「浮世絵」は誕生しました。浮世絵とは、浮き世(今とき)の生活や風景を描いた絵のことです。多くが木版画で何枚も同じ絵柄を摺ることができ、元の絵を描く絵師と、版を作る彫師と、色を摺り上げる摺師と、それを出版する版元との共同作業で作られました。浮世絵版画は、高級な芸術品と違って、庶民が気軽に買うことができました。絵師(画家)が紙や絹に直接描いたこの世に1点しか存在しない肉筆画の浮世絵もあります。

歌麿、北斎、写楽、豊国、広重、国芳など、今でも人気があり有名な浮世絵師がたくさん登場しました。

彼らは、人気のある歌舞伎役者を描いたり、町の風景を描いたり、庶民の日常生活を描いたり…今で言う人気スターのブロマイド、観光ガイドブック、漫画として、人々に娯楽を提供していたのです。今はテレビやネットで世界中の情報を知ることができますが、当時は浮世絵がその手段として、お芝居や流行の情報を得る、貴重な情報源になっていました。

About *Ukiyo-e*

Three hundred and fifty odd years ago, in the early Edo period the art of *ukiyo-e* was born in Japan (Edo). *Ukiyo-e* referred to pictures (*e*) drawn of *ukiyo* (the "floating world"), or the lifestyle and scenes of the day. Unlike more upmarket works of art, *ukiyo-e* prints were readily available to the general population. *Ukiyo-e* were mostly woodblock prints, so it was possible to print the same picture as many times as desired, and they were a creative collaboration between the artist (*e-shi*) who drew the original picture, the engraver (*hori-shi*) who made the printing plate, the printer (*suri-shi*) who applied colour and rubbed to print, and the publisher who published them. There are also *ukiyo-e* painted by artists directly onto paper or silk, of which there is only one original in existence.

Even today many *ukiyo-e* artists are famous and popular, such as Utamaro, Hokusai, Sharaku, Toyokuni, Hiroshige, Kuniyoshi, and many more.

These artists provided entertainment through drawings of popular kabuki actors, scenes from the town, and the everyday life of ordinary people... what would now be called celebrity Instagrams, tourist guide books, and *manga* (comics). These days, it is easy to find out what is going on in the world through television and the internet, but back in those days, *ukiyo-e* played a major role as an important source of information on entertainment and fashions.

絵師解説

葛飾北斎
宝暦10年(1760)〜嘉永2年(1849)。江戸後期の浮世絵師。号は画狂人など。春章門人。名所絵など様々な分野で活躍。代表作は「富嶽三十六景」。

江戸川北輝
生没年未詳。江戸後期の浮世絵師。北斎門人。

葛飾北洋
生没年未詳。江戸後期の大坂の浮世絵師。号は丹青堂など。北斎門人。役者絵を得意とする。

高井鴻山
文化3年(1806)〜明治16年(1883)。江戸後期〜明治初期の信濃の豪商、文人、志士。北斎門人。肉筆の妖怪画を得意とする。

卍楼北鵞
生年未詳〜安政3年(1856)。江戸後期の浮世絵師。画風は北斎風を継ぐが関係は不明。文化文政期に同名で北斎門人の絵師がいるが関係は未詳。

勝川春亭
生年未詳〜文政7年(1824)。江戸後期の浮世絵師。号は松高斎など。春英門人。武者絵の礎を築く。

初代歌川豊国
明和6年(1769)〜文政8年(1825)。江戸後期の浮世絵師。号は一陽斎。歌川派の開祖豊春門人。役者絵、美人画を得意とする。

歌川国長
寛政2年(1790)頃〜文政12年(1829)頃。江戸後期の浮世絵師。号は一雲斎。初代豊国門人。浮絵を得意とする。

歌川国貞(三代豊国)
天明6年(1786)〜元治元年(1864)。江戸後期の浮世絵師。号は五渡亭など。初代豊国門人。のちに豊国を襲名。役者絵、美人画を得意とする。

Notes on Artists

Katsushika Hokusai　Hōreki 10 - Kaei 2 (1760-1849). *Ukiyo-e* artist of the late Edo period. One of the pseudonyms (*gō*) he used was Gakyōjin, the Madman of Art. Pupil of Shunshō. Active in various genres including landscapes (*meisho-e*). His best-known work is *Thirty-Six Views of Mount Fuji*.

Edogawa Hokki (also known as Katsushika Hokki)　Dates of birth and death unknown. *Ukiyo-e* artist of the late Edo period. Pupil of Hokusai.

Katsushika Hokuyō　Dates of birth and death unknown. *Ukiyo-e* artist of the late Edo period in Osaka. One of the pseudonyms (*gō*) he used was Tanseidō. Pupil of Hokusai. Specialized in kabuki actor prints (*yakusha-e*).

Takai Kōzan　Bunka 3 - Meiji 16 (1806-1883). Wealthy merchant of Shinano Province, *bunjin* (one of the literati), and *shishi* (royalist) of the late Edo to early Meiji period. Pupil of Hokusai. Specialized in paintings of *yōkai* (demonic creatures).

Manjirō Hokuga　Date of birth unknown - Ansei 3 (-1856). *Ukiyo-e* artist of the late Edo period. His style is that of a successor to Hokusai but the exact relationship is unclear. Another pupil of Hokusai's used the same name in the Bunka-Bunsei era, but there is no known relationship.

Katsukawa Shuntei　Date of birth unknown - Bunsei 7 (-1824). *Ukiyo-e* artist of the late Edo period. One of the pseudonym (*gō*) he used was Shōkōsai. Pupil of Shun'ei. Pioneer of the warrior print genre (*musha-e*).

Utagawa Toyokuni I　Meiwa 6 - Bunsei 8 (1769-1825). *Ukiyo-e* artist of the late Edo period. His pseudonym (*gō*) was Ichiyōsai. Pupil of Utagawa Toyoharu, founder of the Utagawa school. Specialized in kabuki actor prints (*yakusha-e*) and depictions of beautiful women (*bijin-ga*).

Utagawa Kuninaga　Kansei 2 - Bunsei 12 (c. 1790-c. 1829). *Ukiyo-e* artist of the late Edo period. His pseudonym (*gō*) was Ichiunsai. Pupil of Toyokuni I. Specialized in *uki-e* (lit. "floating pictures") which use linear perspective.

Utagawa Kunisada (also known as Utagawa Toyokuni III)　Tenmei 6 - Genji 1 (1786-1864). *Ukiyo-e* artist of the late Edo period. One of the pseudonyms (*gō*) he used was Gototei. Pupil of Toyokuni I. He later succeeded to the name Toyokuni. Specialized in kabuki actor prints (*yakusha-e*) and depictions of beautiful women (*bijin-ga*).

歌川貞秀
文化4年（1807）〜明治11、12年（1878、79）頃。
江戸後期〜明治初期の浮世絵師。号は五雲亭など。
鳥瞰図による風景画を得意とする。

豊原国周
天保6年（1835）〜明治33年（1900）。江戸末期〜明治中期の浮世絵師。
号は一鴬斎など。長谷川派豊原周信、国貞（三代豊国）門人。役者絵、美人画を得意とする。

楊洲周延
天保9年（1838）〜大正元年（1912）。江戸末期〜明治末期の浮世絵師。
国貞（三代豊国）、国周門人。美人画、風俗画を得意とする。

竹内柳蛙（五代歌川国政）
生没年未詳。明治後期の浮世絵師。三代歌川国貞（四代国政）の長男。号は梅堂。
五代国政同一人物とされるが、別人説もある。

歌川広重
寛政9年（1797）〜安政5年（1858）。江戸後期の浮世絵師。号は一立斎など。
豊広門人。名所絵の第一人者。代表作は「東海道五十三次之内」。

歌川国芳
寛政9年（1797）〜文久元年（1861）。江戸後期の浮世絵師。号は一勇斎など。
初代豊国門人。武者絵の第一人者。

歌川芳艶
文政5年（1822）〜慶応2年（1866）。江戸後期の浮世絵師。号は一英斎など。
国芳門人。武者絵を得意とする。

歌川芳虎
文政11年（1828）頃〜明治20年（1887）頃。
江戸後期〜明治前期の浮世絵師。号は一猛斎など。国芳門人。
武者絵、横浜絵を得意とする。

歌川芳藤
文政11年（1828）〜明治20年（1887）。江戸後期〜明治前期の浮世絵師。
号は一鵬斎。国芳門人。おもちゃ絵を得意とする。

歌川芳員
生没年未詳。江戸末期〜明治初期の浮世絵師。号は一川斎など。国芳門人。
横浜絵を得意とする。

落合芳幾
天保4年（1833）〜明治37年（1904）。江戸末期〜明治初期の浮世絵師。
号は一恵斎など。国芳門人。無残絵、新聞錦絵を得意とする。

月岡芳年
天保10年（1839）〜明治25年（1892）。江戸末期〜明治前期の浮世絵師。
号は大蘇など。国芳門人。武者絵、歴史画を得意とする。

歌川国梅
慶応2年（1866）〜明治36年（1903）。明治の浮世絵師。号は修斎など。
芳年門人。のちの二代年信。役者絵を得意とする。

駒井源琦
延享4年（1747）〜寛政9年（1797）。江戸中期の京都の絵師。円山応挙門人。
同門の長沢芦雪と並び称される。美人画、花鳥画を得意とする。

梶田半古
明治3年（1870）〜大正6年（1917）。明治後期の絵師。
鍋田玉英、鈴木華邨に学ぶ。風俗画、小説挿絵を得意とした。

伊藤晴雨
明治15年（1882）〜昭和36年（1961）明治から昭和初期の絵師。
野沢堤雨門人。責め絵を得意とする。

桃湖
詳細不明。

盤礴居
詳細不明。

竹信
詳細不明。

静湖
生没年未詳。琵琶湖多景島の絵師。

春江斎北英
生年未詳〜天保7年（1836）。江戸後期に大坂で活躍した浮世絵師。
号は春梅斎など。北洲門人。役者絵を主に描く。

Utagawa Sadahide Bunka 4 - Meiji 11 or 12 (1807-1878 or 1879). *Ukiyo-e* artist of the late Edo to early Meiji period. One of the pseudonyms (*gō*) he used was Gountei. Pupil of Kunisada. Specialized in landscape painting from a bird's eye view.

Toyohara Kunichika Tenpō 6 - Meiji 33 (1835-1900). *Ukiyo-e* artist from the end of the Edo to the mid-Meiji period. One of the pseudonyms (*gō*) he used was Ichiōsai. Pupil of Toyohara Chikanobu of the Hasegawa school, and Toyokuni III (Kunisada). Specialized in kabuki actor prints (*yakusha-e*) and depictions of beautiful women (*bijin-ga*).

Yōshū Chikanobu Tenpō 9 - Taisei 1 (1838-1912). *Ukiyo-e* artist from the end of the Edo period to the end of the Meiji period. Pupil of Toyokuni III and Kunichika. Specialized in *bijin-ga* (depictions of beautiful women) and *fūzoku-ga* (paintings of daily life, manners and customs).

Takeuchi Ryu-a (also known as Utagawa Kunimasa V) Dates of birth and death unknown. *Ukiyo-e* artist of the late Meiji period. Oldest son of Utagawa Kunisada III (Kunimasa IV) His pseudonym (*gō*) was Baidō. He is also known as Kunimasa V, but there is a theory that this may be a different individual.

Utagawa Hiroshige Kansei 9 - Ansei 5 (1797-1859). *Ukiyo-e* artist of the late Edo period. One of the pseudonyms (*gō*) he used was Ichiryūsai. Pupil of Toyohiro. The foremost painter of *meisho-e* (pictures of famous places). His best-known work is the series *The Fifty-Three Stations of the Tōkaidō*.

Utagawa Kuniyoshi Kansei 9 - Bunkyū 1 (1797-1861). *Ukiyo-e* artist of the late Edo period. One of the pseudonyms (*gō*) he used was Ichiyūsai. Pupil of Toyokuni I. The foremost painter of *musha-e* (pictures of warriors).

Utagawa Yoshitsuya Bunsei 5 - Keiō 2 (1822-1866). *Ukiyo-e* artist of the late Edo period. One of the pseudonyms (*gō*) he used was Ichieisai. Pupil of Kuniyoshi. Specialized in *musha-e* (pictures of warriors).

Utagawa Yoshitora Bunsei 11 - Meiji 20 (c. 1828-c. 1887). *Ukiyo-e* artist of the late Edo to early Meiji period. One of the pseudonyms (*gō*) he used was Ichimōsai. Pupil of Kuniyoshi. Specialized in *musha-e* (pictures of warriors) and *Yokohama-e* (pictures of foreigners at the port of Yokohama).

Utagawa Yoshifuji Bunsei 11 - Meiji 20 (1828-1887). *Ukiyo-e* artist of the late Edo to early Meiji period. His pseudonym (*gō*) was Ichihōsai. Pupil of Kuniyoshi. Specialized in *omocha-e* (lit. "toy pictures").

Utagawa Yoshikazu Dates of birth and death unknown. *Ukiyo-e* artist from the end of the Edo period to the beginning of the Meiji period. One of the pseudonyms (*gō*) he used was Issensai. Pupil of Kuniyoshi. Specialized in *Yokohama-e* (pictures of foreigners at the port of Yokohama).

Ochiai Yoshiiku Tenpō 4 - Meiji 37 (1833-1904). *Ukiyo-e* artist from the end of the Edo period to the beginning of the Meiji period. One of the pseudonyms (*gō*) he used was Ikkeisai. Pupil of Kuniyoshi. Specialized in *muzan-e* (pictures depicting violent atrocities) and illustrations for the newspapers.

Tsukioka Yoshitoshi Tenpō 10 - Meiji 25 (1839-1892). *Ukiyo-e* artist of the late Edo to early Meiji period. One of the pseudonyms (*gō*) he used was Taiso. Pupil of Kuniyoshi. Specialized in *musha-e* (warrior prints) and *rekishi-ga* (depictions of famous historical scenes).

Utagawa Kuniume Keiō 2 - Meiji 36 (1866-1903). *Ukiyo-e* artist of the Meiji period. One of the pseudonyms (*gō*) he used was Shūsai. Pupil of Yoshitoshi. Later became Toshinobu II. Specialized in kabuki actor prints (*yakusha-e*).

Komai Genki Enkyō 4 - Kansei 9 (1747-1797). Kyoto artist of the mid-Edo period. Pupil of Maruyama Ōkyo. Ranked alongside fellow pupil Nagasawa Rosetsu. Specialized in *bijin-ga* (depictions of beautiful women) and *kachō-ga* (pictures of birds and flowers).

Kajita Hanko Meiji 3 - Taisei 6 (1870-1917). Artist of the late Meiji period. Studied under Nabeta Gyokuei and Suzuki Gako. Specialized in *fūzoku-ga* (paintings of daily life, manners and customs), and illustrations for novels.

Itō Seiu Meiji 15 - Shōwa 36 (1882-1961). Artist from the Meiji to the beginning of the Shōwa period. Pupil of Nozawa Teiu. Specialized in *seme-e* (pictures of torture).

Tōko Details unknown.

Banhakukyo Details unknown.

Takenobu Details unknown.

Seiko Dates of birth and death unknown. Artist of Takeshima Island on Lake Biwa.

Shunkōsai Hokuei Date of birth unknown - Tenpō 7 (-1836). *Ukiyo-e* artist of the late Edo period based in Osaka. One of the pseudonyms (*gō*) he used was Shunbaisai. Pupil of Hokushū. Mainly produced kabuki actor prints (*yakusha-e*).

作品目録

236

Index

【浮世絵でみる！ お化け図鑑】

2016年7月9日　初版第1刷発行
2023年3月7日　第10刷発行

監修　中右 瑛

テキスト　山本 野理子

翻訳　シャーニ・ウィルソン

資料協力　中右コレクション
　　　　　竹久夢二文学館神戸文庫(有)
　　　　　朝比奈文庫

デザイン　真々田 稔 (rocka graphica)

協力　株式会社アートワン

編集　大場義行
　　　原 瑛莉子

編集協力　田中里奈 (ヒヨコ舎)

発行人　三芳寛要

発行元　株式会社パイインターナショナル
　　　　〒170-0005 東京都豊島区南大塚 2-32-4
　　　　TEL. 03-3944-3981　FAX. 03-5395-4830
　　　　sales@pie.co.jp

印刷・製本　株式会社広済堂ネクスト

著作物の利用に関するお問い合わせはこちらをご覧ください。
https://pie.co.jp/contact/

本書の収録内容の無断転載・複写・複製等を禁じます。
ご注文・乱丁落丁本の交換等に関するお問い合わせは、小社営業部までご連絡ください。

Something Wicked from Japan
Ghosts, Demons & Yōkai in Ukiyo-e Masterpieces

Supervisor:
Ei Nakau

Text:
Noriko Yamamoto

Translation:
Sharni Wilson

Photo credits:
Nakau Collection, Takehisa Yumeji Bungakukan Kobe Bunko Ltd., Asahina Bunko

Editorial Design:
Minoru Mamata (rocka graphica)
In Association with Artone Co., Ltd.

Editors:
Yoshiyuki Oba, Eriko Hara

Editorial Assistant:
Rina Tanaka (Hiyoko-sha)

PIE International Inc.
2-32-4 Minami-Otsuka, Toshima-ku, Tokyo 170-0005 JAPAN
sales@pie.co.jp

©2016 Ei Nakau/PIE International
ISBN978-4-7562-4810-7 C0071
Printed in Japan

扉絵

【五拾三次之内　猫の怪】
歌川芳藤　弘化4年 (1847)

「寄せ絵」と呼ばれる手法で、大小九匹の猫が巨大な化け猫の顔を形づくります。目は飼い猫の首につける鈴で、口は首輪の緒。この年上演の歌舞伎「尾上梅寿一代噺」に登場する、岡崎の化け猫をイメージしています。

The Mystery of the Cat from Traveling the Fifty-Three Stations
by Utagawa Yoshifuji

The technique known as *yose-e* (lit. "assembled picture") has been used to create the face of a huge monster cat out of nine assorted cats. Its eyes are the bells around the necks of pet cats, and its mouth is a collar. This is a depiction of the Monster Cat of Okazaki, who appeared in theaters in kabuki play *Onoe Kikugorō Ichidai Banashi* the same year this print was published.

主要参考文献

【単行書】
鶴屋南北著・郡司正勝ほか編『鶴屋南北全集』全12巻、三一書房、1971-74年
佐藤深雪校訂『山東京伝集』(『叢書江戸文庫』18) 国書刊行会、1987年
中右瑛著『魑魅魍魎の世界 江戸の劇画・妖怪浮世絵』里文出版、2005年
国際浮世絵学会編『浮世絵大事典』東京堂出版、2008年
吉田漱監修・惠俊彦編『月岡芳年の世界』復元ドットコム、2010年

【展覧会図録】
『没後150年 歌川国芳展』日本経済新聞社、2011年
『没後150年記念 破天荒の浮世絵師 歌川国芳』NHKプロモーション、2011年
『没後120年記念 月岡芳年』太田記念美術館、2012年
『歌川国芳 奇想天外 江戸の劇画家 国芳の世界』青幻舎、2014年
『江戸妖怪大図鑑』太田記念美術館、2014年

【欧文文献】
Andreas Marks, *Publishers of Japanese Woodblock Prints: A Compendium*, Leiden, Hotei Publishing, 2011